International Yearbook of Futurism Studies

International Yearbook of Futurism Studies

International Yearbook of Futurism Studies

Volume 13

Special Issue
Neo-Futurism

Edited by
Günter Berghaus, Dalila Colucci and Tim Klähn

With the assistance of Nicola Baird and Sze Wah Lee

DE GRUYTER

ISBN 978-3-11-131829-5
e-ISBN (PDF) 978-3-11-131839-4
ISSN 2192-0281

A CIP catalog record for this book has been applied for at the Library of Congress.

Bibliographic information published by the Deutsche Nationalbibliothek
The Deutsche Nationalbibliothek lists this publication in the Deutsche Nationalbibliografie; detailed bibliographic data are available on the Internet at http://dnb.dnb.de.

Typesetting: 3w+p GmbH, Rimpar
Printing and binding: CPI books GmbH, Leck

www.degruyter.com

Table of Contents

3 Asia and Latin America

4 Music, Sculpture and Architecture

5 Artist Statements

Section 2: **Reports**

Section 3: **Critical responses to new publications**

Section 4: **Bibliography**

Section 5: **Back Matter**

Günter Berghaus

Editorial

Although scholars argue about the exact time frame of the historical avant-garde and which movements belonged to it, few would question the fact that Futurism laid the foundations for our modern concept of the artistic 'avant-garde', that it had an exceptional longevity (35 years) and that its impact extended across continents into nearly all artistic media.[1] F.T. Marinetti was certainly one its most influential and longest-serving leaders. As a young man, he joined the first avant-garde, Symbolism, and when, nearly fifty years later, he died, the last vestiges of the classical avant-garde had vanished in the devastations of the Second World War.

But soon after, a revival set in. Artists across Europe and the United Stages were harking back to ideas developed in the first third of the century. Abstract Expressionism, based on European sources and developed with the help of European émigrés, had shifted the centre of Western art from Paris to New York. Soon after 1945, it made its influence felt in Europe, where it merged with the sensual and gestural qualities of Tachisme and Abstraction Lyrique.

Similarly, Colour Field and Hard-Edge Painting had their roots in the cool and austere forms of abstract art developed in Europe over a timespan of some thirty years. US-American institutions were instrumental in bringing them back to Europe, where they fused with indigenous traditions of geometric abstraction. Much of post-war Modernist aesthetic had thus a revivalist quality, openly acknowledged when subsequent movements such as Happening and Fluxus were characterized as 'Neo-Dada'. Although the Happening and Fluxus movement took inspiration primarily from Tzara and his followers, their attempt to overcome the artistic stagnation of the previous decade was also based on the Futurist conception of fusing art and life (which Tzara himself had been inspired by[2]). When Allen Ginsberg was interviewed by Antonello Branca in a documentary film of 1967, he judged that "the prophecies of Marinetti are coming true; some of them, the wilder, more poetic ones."[3] Many Fluxus artists were familiar with the theoretical writings of the Dada movement, either in their original or via Motherwell's anthology *Dada Painters and Poets* of 1951. But also Russolo's *The Art of Noise* left a significant mark on their music.[4] The whole notion of *Intermedia*, formulated

---

1 The *Handbook of International Futurism* contains entries on 13 artist media and 39 countries. See G. Berghaus: *Handbook of International Futurism.*

2 See Berghaus: "Tristan Tzara: From pre-Dadaism to post-Futurism."

3 Branca: *What's Happening?*

4 See Berghaus: "Tomas Schmit: A Fluxus Farewell to Perfection."

https://doi.org/10.1515/9783111318394-001

by Dick Higgins in 1966,[5] was firmly rooted in Futurist poetics, as American sculptor and Pop Art painter George Segal acknowledged when he remembered that "Marinetti's 'radio broadcasts' were of great interest to us. The combination of words and sound made by noises produced by whatever objects clearly were a rich source for John Cage. It seems it was only the Italian futurists' embrace of Mussolini that gave them a bad reputation. The aesthetic that has to do with living in modern cities, I think, is still worth exploring."[6]

In this volume of the *International Yearbook of Futurism Studies*, Esther Schmitz-Gundlach outlines to what extent the post-war musical avant-garde was operating with models based on Futurism.[7] Ara H. Merjian and Nicola Lucchi, in a more expansive outline of the postwar situation in the United States of America, highlight this influence of Futurism as a spiritual source of the provocative ethos of the neo-avant-garde:

> The Happenings staged during the late 1950s by composer John Cage and later by performance artist Allan Kaprow (1927–2006) had, at least in part, the same ethos as the early twentieth-century *serate futuriste*. The shock value and relational antagonism that characterized the work of American performance and body artists in the 1960s and 1970s, such as Carolee Schneeman (b. 1939) and Vito Acconci (1940–2017), as well as the multisensorial strategies of projects like *Exploding Plastic Inevitable* (1966–1967) by Andy Warhol (1928–1987) find their roots in early avant-garde performance, and particularly in the Futurist programmatic attempts to *épater la bourgeoisie.*[8]

Although Futurism had a bad name after 1945, due to its entanglements with Fascism, its aesthetic principles (pre-dating Fascism by a good ten years) were rediscovered in the late 1940s in the exhibition *Quarante ans d'art italien du futurisme à nos jours* (Forty Years of Italian Art from Futurism to the Present Day), shown in Lausanne and Lucerne in 1947, and *Rassegna nazionale di arti figurative* (National Exhibition of Visual Arts), organized by the Quadriennale di Roma in 1948, with twenty-six works by ten Futurist artists.[9] It was also promoted by ex-Futurists (Giovanni Acquaviva, Enzo Benedetto, Angelo Caviglioni, Tullio Crali, Tullio d'Albisola,

5 Higgins: "Intermedia."

6 Bertozzi: "An Interview with George Segal", pp. 27–28. See also Pasquale Fameli's essay "Futurism in Italian Verbo-Visual Poetry after the Second World War" below, p. 7.

7 "Back to the Future of 'The Art of Noises': The After-Life of Futurism in Twentieth-Century Music."

8 Merjian and Lucchi: "United States of America", p. 889.

9 Piero Girace spoke for many when he wrote in 1948: "Amongst the most interesting aspects of this Quadriennale is the retrospective of the Futurist painters. It has a tremendous importance and will serve as a yardstick to assess the recent experiments in the fine arts". Quoted in Agnese and Sagramora: *I futuristi e le Quadriennali*, p. 105.

Mino Delle Site, Gerardo Dottori, Antonio Marasco, Emilio Pettoruti, Alberto Sartoris and many others) and new disciples such as Serafino Babini and Antonio Fiore (Ufagrà).[10]

The youthful energy and radical drive that had characterized Futurism in its first, 'heroic' phase, was rediscovered within a wider process of re-evaluating the historical avant-garde in universities, museums and exhibition halls. It led the gallery owner Luciano Inga-Pin to launch in 1984 the 'Nuovi Futuristi' group and to stage under this label a large number of exhibitions by Gian Antonio Abate, Innocente, Marco Lodola, the Plumcake trio and various others.[11]

Futurism's elimination of the boundary between art and life and between high and popular culture, its opposition to museological and academic concepts of 'art', its extended art forms (multimedia, collage, montage, text-image combination, etc.), its literary revolution (destruction of syntax, punctuation, the literary 'I', the book as object, new typography, etc.), its discovery of noise as musical material, its elevation of the recipient to a position of producer of art, its abolishment of the fourth-wall convention and fusion of stage and auditorium in the theatre – this and many other achievements of historical Futurism became integral elements of the neo-avant-garde.

Peter Bürger's thesis that the imitation of avant-garde practices and aesthetics was in contradiction to their professed aim of a radical break with tradition did not prevent groups and individual artists to develop an experimental literature indebted to the historical avant-garde, and Futurism in particular. In the field of literature, it gave rise to Concrete Poetry, Visual Poetry, recitations and performances of the Beat Generation, intermedial art practices (conceptual art, art & language, theatre of images, performance art, postdramatic theatre). Also in its political and ideological concerns (feminism, anti-colonialism, ecological concerns) it adopted an engaged stance typical of the historical avant-garde.[12] Contrary to Bürger's condescending view of the neo-avant-garde as an attempt to recycle forms and strategies from the first decades of the twentieth century, Clement Greenberg, amongst others, emphasized the specific qualities of cultural production in the 1950s to 70s.[13] Benjamin Buchloh argued for a dialectical approach towards

---

10 Berghaus: "The Postwar Reception of Futurism: Repression or Recuperation?" and Berghaus: "The Historiography of Italian Futurism." See also Babini's essays, as well as Bossaglia and Di Genova's characterization of Fiore as a "Modern-day Futurists" and Livello: "Dal futurismo all'Agrà."

11 See the catalogues edited by Renato Barilli.

12 See Hopkins and Schaffner: *Neo-Avant-Garde.* Scheunemann: *Avant-garde / Neo- Avant-Garde.* Vervaeck: *Neo-Avant-Gardes.*

13 See, amongst others, Greenberg: *Late Writings.*

these two positions[14] and Hal Foster saw the neo-avant-garde enacting the avant-garde project, in a deferred action, for the first time and thus bringing it to fruition.[15]

In this sense, Neo-Futurism was not just a recycling of its predecessor, but a revitalization of experimental and emancipatory practices under changed circumstances. Within the institutions of High- or Postmodernism, the Neo-Futurists developed alternative, critical or subversive practices within the hegemonic culture of their times. Rather than producing second-hand Futurist works, they investigated aesthetic principles and practices of historical Futurism, interpreted them in novel fashions, voiced a critique of their predecessors' political-ideological orientations and developed from their analyses innovative products of a critical, creative and invigorating quality.

Previous volumes of the *International Yearbook of Futurism Studies* have reiterated, again and again, that the impulses of Italian and Russian Futurism in other countries and on other continents led to something original that went far beyond the precepts of Marinetti's manifestos. In the same sense, the recuperation of historical Futurism in Highmodern or Postmodern times was a dialectic process:

> The Hegelian term 'Aufhebung' [...] in German entails three meanings, all of which can be encountered in the specific reception processes we are concerned with here: to cancel out, to preserve and to raise to a higher level. Thus, the Futurist impulse coming from Marinetti and his Italian followers was simultaneously repealed and preserved in the receiving cultural environments [...and] creatively transformed into a new aesthetics that operated on a different level.[16]

In the twenty-first century, the avant-garde has changed its tone, scope and dynamics, and its geographical horizon has vastly expanded in a genuinely globalized world. In 1924, Marinetti conceived of a 'Futurisme mondial'; but Neo-Futurist tendencies resonate more than ever outside the Western hemisphere, giving rise to terms such as Afrofuturism, Chicanafuturism, Sinofuturism, Islamofuturism etc. So far, the *International Yearbook of Futurism Studies* has not addressed these very recent phenomena as they are more concerned with techno-scientific processes and notions of science fiction that with the literary and artistic traditions of the Futurist movement. Yet, they show that the forward-looking qualities of historical

14 Buchloh: *Neo-Avantgarde and Culture Industry.*

15 Foster: "What's Neo about the Neo-Avant-Garde?" Foster: *The Return of the Real.*

16 Günter Berghaus in his editorial to the special issue on *Iberian Futurisms* of *International Yearbook of Futurism Studies.* Vol. 3 (2013), p. IX.

Futurism[17] are constantly developed further. And some of these tendencies are being investigated in the 12 essays contained in this volume.

Bibliography

Agnese, Gino, and Alessandro Sagramora, eds.: *I futuristi e le Quadriennali*, Milano: Electa, 2008.

Babini, Serafino: "Dopo Il futurismo Il futurismo continua: Il movimento in Romagna." *Idea: Rivista mensile di cultura e politica* 45:7–9 (July-September 1989): 69–72.

Babini, Serafino: "Futurismo – ottant'anni: Il nostro futurismo oggi." *In Rumâgna: Aspetti della storia, della cultura, della tradizione* 14–15 (1990–1991): 96–98.

Babini, Serafino: "Futurismo che continua." *La piê: Rassegna di illustrazione romagnola* 54:1 (January-February 1985): 27–31.

Babini, Serafino: "Il futurismo continua in Romagna: La riscoperta del futurismo." *In Rumâgna: Aspetti della storia, della cultura, della tradizione* 12–13 (1988–89): 15–48.

Barilli, Renato, ed.: *Nuovo Futurismo: Abate, Innocente, Lodola, Plumcake, Postal.* Exhibition catalogue. Rovereto (TN): Museo d'Arte Moderna e Contemporanea, Archivio del '900, 7 luglio – 2 ottobre 1994. San Marino: Galleria Galleria Nazionale d'Arte Moderna, Logge dei Balestrieri, 9 luglio – 4 settembre 1994. Milano: Electa, 1994.

Barilli, Renato, ed.: *Nuovo Futurismo: Gianantonio Abate, Clara Bonfiglio, Innocente, Marco Lodola, Luciano Palmieri, Plumcake (Cella, Pallotta, Ragni), Umberto Postal.* Exhibition catalogue. Groningen: Groninger Museum, 23 februari – 31 maart 1985.

Barilli, Renato: "Le due eredità del futurismo." Eugenio Gazzola, ed.: *Le conseguenze del futurismo.* Piacenza: Scritture, 2009. 106–121.

Berghaus, Günter: "The Historiography of Italian Futurism." G. Berghaus, ed.: *Handbook of International Futurism.* Berlin & Boston/MA: De Gruyter, 2019. 3–27.

Berghaus, Günter: "The Postwar Reception of Futurism: Repression or Recuperation?" Geert Buelens, Harald Hendrix, and Monica Jansen, eds.: *The History of Futurism: The Precursors, Protagonists, and Legacies.* Lanham/MD: Lexington Books, 2012. 377–403

Berghaus, Günter: "Tomas Schmit: A Fluxus Farewell to Perfection." *The Drama Review* 38:1 (T141) (Spring 1994): 79–97.

Berghaus, Günter: "Tristan Tzara: From pre-Dadaism to post-Futurism. Italian Influences in the Cabaret Voltaire." *Les Cahiers Tristan Tzara = Caietele Tristan Tzara* 18:3–4 (2013): 205–216.

Berghaus, Günter, ed.: *Handbook of International Futurism.* Berlin & Boston: De Gruyter, 2019.

Bertozzi, Barbara: "An Interview with George Segal." B. Bertozzi, ed.: *George Segal.* Milano: Charta, 1994. 26–29.

Bossaglia, Rossana, and Giorgio Di Genova, eds.: *Antonio Fiore: Un futurista d'oggi.* Bologna: Bora, 1999.

Branca, Antonello: *What's Happening?* New York, Filmmakers Research Group, 1967. DVD edition Roma: Kiwido, 2010.

Buchloh, Benjamin H. D.: *Neo-avantgarde and Culture Industry.* Cambridge/MA: MIT Press, 2000.

Bürger, Peter: *Theory of the Avant-Garde.* Minneapolis/MN: University of Minnesota Press, 1984.

17 Marinetti's prescient qualities have been discussed in Cigliana: "'Tutto dovete sperare dall'avvenire': Marinetti e il mondo del futuro, tra profezia e fantascienza."

Cigliana, Simona: "'Tutto dovete sperare dall'avvenire': Marinetti e il mondo del futuro, tra profezia e fantascienza." Antonio Saccoccio, and Roberto Guerra, eds.: *Marinetti 70: Sintesi della critica futurista.* Roma: Armando, 2014. 23–32.

Foster, Hal: "What's Neo about the Neo-Avant-Garde?" *October* 70 (Autumn 1994): 5–32.

Foster, Hal: *The Return of the Real: The Avant-Garde at the End of the Century.* Cambridge/MA: MIT Press, 1996,

Greenberg, Clement: *Late Writings.* Minneapolis/MN: University of Minnesota Press, 2007.

Higgins, Dick: "Intermedia." *Something Else Newsletter* 1:1 (1966): 1–6.

Hopkins, David, and Anna Katharina Schaffner, eds.: *Neo-Avant-Garde.* Amsterdam: Rodopi, 2006.

Livello, Renato: "Dal futurismo all'Agrà: Conoscenza dialettica di una eredità." *Idea: Rivista mensile di cultura e politica* 45:7–9 (July-September 1989): 17–22.

Merjian, Ara H., and Nicola Lucchi: "United States of America." Günter Berghaus, ed.: *Handbook of International Futurism.* Berlin & Boston: De Gruyter, 2019. 883–893.

Scheunemann, Dietrich, ed.: *Avant-garde / Neo-Avant-Garde.* Amsterdam: Rodopi, 2005.

Vervaeck, Bart, ed.: *Neo-Avant-Gardes: Post-War Literary Experiments across Borders.* Edinburgh: Edinburgh University Press, 2021.

Günter Berghaus, Dalila Colucci and Tim Klähn

Volume Editors' Preface

This thirteenth volume of the *International Yearbook of Futurism Studies* explores some of the many facets of Neo-Futurism from the second half of the twentieth century to the present day. It looks both at the revival and the continuation of Futurist aesthetics, whether in explicit or palimpsest form, in a variety of media: literature, visual art, design, music, architecture, theatre and photography. We have chosen to focus on the far-reaching legacy of Futurism, far beyond the demise of its initial phases usually denoted with the terms *Primo* and *Secondo Futurismo.* At first sight, this might look like a contradiction to a well-known passage in the *Foundation and Manifesto of Futurism* (1909), where Marinetti predicts the death of the movement after a short and unsettling existence:

> The oldest among us are thirty; so we have at least ten years in which to complete our task. When we reach forty, other, younger, and more courageous men will very likely toss us into the trash can, like useless manuscripts. And that's what we want![1]

Yet this myth of disappearance was entrusted to a younger generation whose "hearts overflow with love and admiration for us".[2] Later in life, Marinetti accepted this continuity because it both devours Futurism and propels it into the Future. Such an assimilated, heterodox and dialectical form of Futurism he discovered in 1944 in Carlo Belloli's *Testi-poemi murali* (Mural Texts-Poems), a form of *poème-affiche* that became the incubator of Concrete Poetry. Admiringly, he wrote an introduction in which he acknowledged the fact that "Belloli as the youngest Futurist is determined to develop the positions already reached [...] in new, essential, lapidary, agile forms, and the generations of tomorrow will be inspired by them. [...] Belloli has intuited the future of Futurism."[3] Marinetti recognized that after his death – which occurred only a few months after having written this preface – a re-fashioned Futurist avant-garde, equipped to face the upcoming challenges, would provide the postwar era with further waves of artistic experimentation.

The essays collected in this volume delve into this broad spectrum of artistic research and offer a good dozen case studies that document, with a transnational

1 Marinetti: "The Foundation and Manifesto of Futurism", p. 16.

2 Ibid.

3 "Belloli è il più giovane futurista deciso a sviluppare in nuove forme agili lapidarie essenziali le posizioni raggiunte [...] e le generazioni di domani vi si ispireranno. [...] belloli ha intuito il futuro del futurismo." Marinetti: "'Testi-poemi murali' di Carlo Belloli", pp. 279–280.

https://doi.org/10.1515/9783111318394-002

and interdisciplinary orientation, the manifold forms of Neo-Futurism in various parts of the world, from the 1940s to the present day. They investigate how historical Futurism's intellectual and artistic perspective was appropriated and developed further in a more or less conscious, faithful and original way, all the while confronting its progenitor's cultural, social and political misconceptions.

The manifold intellectual and artistic movements that placed themselves under the banner of Neo-Futurism evoke 'Futurism' in its Italian and Russian traditions. The prefix 'Neo' suggests a desire to reinvent their techno-optimism, utopianism, formal and linguistic experimentation and to expand them into new epistemologies. A new creative and experimental attitude gave rise to a visual, dynamic and poetic world rooted in, yet at the same time different from, historical Futurism. Thus, the legacy of Futurism around the world seems to cluster around the principle of art as an ever-changing, synaesthetic process capable of resisting (or ignoring) alienating ideologies. Neo-Futurism, in particular, questions the problematic function of art and literature as archival and memorial practices, as well as the concepts of originality, authorship and authority.

In this preface, the three co-editors of this yearbook offer brief outlines of the contributions that compose the present volume and thus help the reader to navigate through the rich and diverse materials assembled here.

Section 1 focusses on Italy and is concerned with Neo-Futurism's numerous declinations in arts, literature and popular culture. In the aftermath of the Second World War, Marinetti's collusion with Fascism determined a critical disapproval of Futurism. **Pasquale Fameli**, in his essay **Futurism in Italian Verbo-Visual Poetry after the Second World War**, reconstructs the political and cultural context that delayed a proper assessment of Marinetti's movement and describes the scholarly debate that took place between the end of the 1960s and the early 1970s, when critics such as Renato Barilli, Luciano De Maria and Luigi Ballerini evaluated the debts of Italy's polymorphic forms of visual poetics – including Concrete Poetry, Visual Poetry, *epistaltismo* – to Futurism. Fameli traces the creative expanses of seven poets and artists – Carlo Belloli, Arrigo Lora Totino, Maurizio Nannucci, Mimmo Rotella, Lamberto Pignotti, Stelio Maria Martini and Paolo Albani – who played a key part in retrieving Futurist theories and practices, with the aim of achieving a visual and material transformation of the poetic act. Their experimental products – artists' books, collages, performative and environmental poems – were squarely rooted in the total aesthetics and intermedia practice of Futurism. For them, the *tavole parolibere* (Free-Words Tables) in particular were a forerunner of the verbo-visual phenomena in the post-war period. Fameli's contribution ultimately offers an insight into an area where much research remains to be done and shows the connections between Italian Neo-Futurist verbo-visual strategies and the transnational network of Dadaism, Surrealism, Lettrism and Conceptual Art.

The productive legacy of Boccioni's dynamism, Balla's chromatism, Depero's playfulness, together with that of Sant'Elia's utopian architecture and the provocative *serate futuriste*, form the core of the 'ninth art',[4] examined here by **Duccio Dogheria** in his essay **Bang Tumb Tuuum! The Influence of Futurism on Italian Avant-Garde Comic Strips.** Drawing on a rich trove of materials presented in the exhibition *Depero New Depero* (held at the Museo di Arte Moderna e Contemporanea di Trento e Rovereto in 2021),[5] Dogheria sheds light on an art form that was rarely used in historical Futurism but was of great interest to a number of Neo-Futurists from the 1960s to 1990s. He analyses several experimental magazines devoted to comic strips – *Frigidaire, Alter Alter* and *Dolce vita*, in particular – and focusses on artists who openly incorporated Futurist topics and themes in their stories. He thus demonstrates how Pablo Echaurren, Massimo Giacon, Massimo Iosa Ghini, Igort and Giorgio Carpinteri employed Futurism as a rich source of inspiration for their Postmodern graphic narratives and media-based arts. Indeed, a large part of Dogheria's thorough investigation into an interdisciplinary reading of the Neo-Futurist world of comic strips reveals a fusion of comics and other media such as advertising, music, fashion, interior and graphic design, establishing the relevance of Futurist imagery for Italian and international design and popular culture.

As **Raffaello Palumbo Mosca** points out in his essay **Even the Great Marinetti Got it Wrong: Giovanni Tuzet's Logical Neo-Futurism,** the panorama of Italian poetry from the 1970s to today was characterized by thematic dispersion, fragmentation and a lyrical retreat. Moving his analysis within this background, Palumbo Mosca offers an account of the literary movements that have pursued, from around 2000 onwards, "a generic call back to the 'original' Futurism", in reaction to the commercial literary market. After a brief discussion of trends as diverse as *Net.Futurismo, transumanesimo* or *pornofuturismo*, he focusses on the Italian thinker and poet Giovanni Tuzet (*1972) and his proposal for a new form of poetry built on the Futurist archetype of "dynamism, energy and the synthesis of art and life" that draws on logical principles, that is, the "articulated structure of clauses" rejected by Marinetti in the *Technical Manifesto of Futurist Literature* (1912). The essay follows Tuzet's engagement and confrontation – through both his poetic and critical production – not only with Marinetti but also with other poets of the original movement (Corrado Govoni above all), to ground his poetics

4 The definition of the comic strip as ninth art was coined first in 1964 by film critic Claude Beylie. The other arts would be, in Beyile's categorization: 1) architecture; 2) sculpture; 3) painting; 4) music; 5) dance; 6) poetry; 7) film; 8) television.

5 See Mancebo Roca: "Depero New Depero: Rovereto Presents the Artist and His Reception after 1960."

in some "less-explored Futurist intuitions", such as the ability to shape the natural in a non-naturalistic manner. His concept of poetry as an architectural act is also indebted to Boccioni's *Manifesto of Futurist Architecture* (c.1913–14). Palumbo Mosca ultimately sees the most relevant aspect of Tuzet's Neo-Futurism in a form of narrative poetry within Futurist poetics, capable of relaunching Futurism's idea of a non-lyrical art without excluding the lyrical 'I', and meant to carry its most authentic, contradictory innovations into the contemporary world.

Section 2 on Russia has a different historical background than the one on Italy. In the Soviet Union, Socialist Realism was imposed as the official style at the First Congress of Soviet Writers in 1934. Any literary and artistic expression that did not conform to the new doctrine was forcefully suppressed, and all traces of the Russian avant-garde – including Futurism – were erased from the official art scene. Works that did not comply with the aesthetics of Socialist Realism were banned, and access to books in libraries and archives was severely restricted. In this context, the tradition of the avant-garde was kept alive only amongst 'unofficial', 'nonconformist' writers and artists, who could distribute their works only clandestinely in self-published *samizdat* publications.

Contrary to the Russian Futurists' demand to throw any previous generations of writers "overboard from the Ship of Modernity", the Russian neo-avant-gardists were eager to preserve the memory of the historical avant-garde and to continue in the tradition of their predecessors (at times literally by developing further ideas found in texts and fragments of the Futurists). While often emphasizing their predecessors' formal experimentation, they tended to reject their utopianism.

Tim Klähn shows in his essay **Gennady Aygi and Russian Futurism** that the Chuvash-Russian poet Aygi was a driving force of Neo-Futurism in the Soviet Union and that he played an important rôle in the attempt to preserve the heritage of the interrupted tradition of the historical avant-garde from the 1960s onwards. Klähn traces Aygi's debts to Futurists such as Vladimir Mayakovsky, Velimir Khlebnikov and Kazimir Malevich as well as his friendships and encounters with surviving members of the historical avant-garde, including Boris Pasternak, Aleksei Kruchenykh, David Burliuk, and Vasilisk Gnedov. A central chapter of the essay is devoted to Aygi's work at the Mayakovsky Museum where he could gain access to otherwise restricted rare materials. At the Mayakovsky Museum, Aygi and Nikolai Khardzhiev organized short-lived but highly influential semi-legal exhibitions of works by artists of the historical avant-garde. Klähn shows how Aygi situated his own poetics within what he called the "poetic territories" that were discovered by the Futurists, how he engaged in a "conversation at a distance" with them through numerous intertextual references, and how he collaborated on artists' books that emulated Futurist publications. Analyses of selected poems by Aygi show the influence of Malevich and demonstrate how Aygi's poetics differs from the experiments of the historical avant-garde by merging the Futurist heritage with influences from Chuvash folk culture and contemporary European literature and by opening his Neo-Futurist poetry to spiritual concerns.

While the Russian Transfurists' appropriation and continuation of Russian Futurism has already received ample scholarly attention, **Valentina Parisi** focusses in her essay **Serge Segay, Rea Nikonova and Italy: Between Futurism and Mail Art** on Segay's and Nikonova's collaborations with Italian artists and visual poets, from Carlo Belloli, whose *Testi-poemi murali* (Mural Texts-Poems 1944) had been praised by Marinetti as showing the "future of Futurism", to younger generations involved in the international Mail Art network. Parisi draws on archival documents to trace Segay's first journey to Italy in 1989. He had been invited there by Marzio Marzaduri to participate in the international conference *Futurismo transmentale e dadaismo nella cultura russa* (Transmental Futurism and Dadaism in Russian Culture) in Venice. On this occasion, he met Mikhail Evzlin who helped him set up in 1989 the ephemeral publishing house Edizioni Serge Sigej in Italia (Editions Serge Segay in Italy) in Trento. Parisi analyses Carlo Belloli's admiration of Segay's work in his preface to Segay's book *Poèmes pour ballerines de Grand Théâtre de l'URSS* (Poems for Ballerinas of the Great Soviet Theatre, 1990) and how Segay discovered in Belloli a direct link to Marinetti and Italian Futurism. Parisi interprets the international Mail Art movement as a continuation of Futurist experiments with *arte postale*; she surveys Segay's and Nikonova's engagement in this network through their collaborations with Anna Boschi Cermasi, Vittore Baroni, Ruggero Maggi, Alberto Vitacchio and Carla Bertola, who shared with Parisi archival documents and personal recollections for this essay.

Mikhail Pavlovets introduces in his essay **Konstantin K. Kuzminsky as a Neo-Futurist** the life and work of a poet, a prose writer, an expert of the Russian historical avant-garde and the editor of the monumental nine-volume *The Blue Lagoon: Anthology of Modern Russian Poetry*, as well as a notorious provocateur and troublemaker who exceeded the Futurists' sense of *épatage* in his own take on the concept of *zhiznetvorchestvo* (life creation) by going beyond all bounds of propriety. Pavlovets analyses Kuzminsky's early poems as inspired by the Cubo-Futurist David Burliuk and traces Kuzminsky's polyglossia back to experiments undertaken by Elena Guro and Vasily Kamensky. Several thematic books are interpreted by Pavlovets as expanding on various Futurist poetic devices, while Kuzminsky's poem *Vavilonskaia bashnia* (The Tower of Babel, 1967–72) is interpreted as a neo-avant-garde 'super-text' in the vein of Khlebnikov's 'super-saga' *Zangezi* (1922), with further references taken from Mayakovsky's *Oblako v shtanakh* (A Cloud in Trousers, 1915) and *Fleita-pozvonochnik* (Backbone Flute, 1915). During the 1970s, Kuzminsky emigrated to the United States, and Pavlovets highlights his publications of texts by Futurists such as Vasilisk Gnedov and David Burliuk, as well as the publication of the *Blue Lagoon* anthology which "almost single-handedly undertook the mission of summing up the 40-year experience of uncensored art (most importantly, poetry) in such a way as to [...] include it in the line of succession of the historical avant-garde of the first third of the twentieth century that was repressed in the Soviet era."

Section 3 concerning Asia and Latin America begins with **Sun-yung Park**'s essay **The Post-utopian Avant-garde Poetics of the Korean 'Futurist' Min-jeong Kim.** The inverted commas in the title suggest that we are not dealing here with a representative of Neo-Futurism as in other countries. Rather, Min-jeong Kim belongs to the generation of poets about whom we already published an essay in Yearbook 2016.[6] Futurism came to be known in Korea at a time when it was under Japanese colonial rule. But whereas in Japan the imported and translated manifestos of both Italian and Russian Futurists led to an upsurge of Modernist and Futurist art, Marinetti's programme was not much discussed in Seoul nor did it lead to the formation of a Futurist group there. In fact, the formation of a Modernist Korean literature only set in after 1930, and there were few representatives who adopted aspects of the Futurist poetics. However, in the early 2000s a new wave of experimentation set in and poets who broke with traditional lyricism were referred to as 'Miraepa' (Futurists). They unleashed a poetic revolution and sought to establish an alternative to established traditions in Korean literature. Yet, as these poets never formed a cohesive group, they tended to reject the label and are therefore distinguished by Sun-yung Park from historical formations of Futurism by the lower-case term 'futurists'.

Min-jeong Kim quickly entered the history of Korean literature and is considered in university courses a major representative of Futurism / 'futurism', although she never published any proclamations and manifestos in which she defined herself with either name. Sun-yung Park focusses in her analysis on four of Kim's poetry anthologies published between 2005 and 2019. She characterizes their stylistic features (lyrical compression, onomatopoeia, graphical typography) and discusses the parallels between Kim's poetics of rupture and the aesthetic credo of historical Futurism, especially Marinetti's desire to 'murder' the literary 'I' and to introduce 'the ugly' into literature. Min-jeong Kim's poetry breaks taboos, parodies the sacred world order and subverts established hierarchies. As such she reflects the anti-traditionalist aesthetics of historical Futurism and offers what the Russian Futurists called "a slap in the face of public taste".[7] She has thus broadened the horizons of

6 See Cho: "Futurism in Korea: From the Historical to the Postmodern Avant-garde."
7 See Burliuk et al.: "Poshchechina obshchestvennomu vkusu."

Korean literary circles and has ushered in a new generation of innovative and avant-garde 'futurist' poets in her country.

Claudio Palomares-Salas and Ángel Díaz Miranda discuss in their essay **The Infrarealist Movement and its Futurist Roots** a group of Latin American writers who, in the mid-1970s, considered themselves to be the inheritors of historical avant-garde groups, in particular of 1920's Stridentism in Mexico. Like Manuel Maples Arce and his colleagues some fifty years earlier, the Infrarealists approached Futurist concepts from a Latin American perspective. They shared with the Futurists a rebellious stance against antiquated mores and traditionalist culture, a desire to convince, shock and disturb, and a notion of heroism similar to Marinetti's *beaux gestes libertaires*. They also wanted to see poets acting as catalysts of change and to use poetry as a means to transform the realms of art, politics and social life. Although Futurism is not explicitly cited in the Infrarealists' manifestos, Palomares-Salas and Díaz Miranda show that the Futurist ethos and incendiary rhetoric inhabit their texts and proclamations. The two scholars investigate the Futurism-Infrarealism relationship by comparing Mario Santiago Papasquiaro and Roberto Bolaño's manifestos with those of the historical Futurists. They also investigate the quasi-Futurist celebration of speed and dynamism in Roberto Bolaño's novel *Los detectives salvajes* (The Savage Detectives, 1998), and the poetic evocation of Futurist aeropainting and aerial theatre in the novel *Estrella distante* (Distant Star, 1996). They thus demonstrate a lasting influence of the Futurist heritage on subsequent generations of Latin American artists and writers.

Odile Cisneros's essay on **Russian Futurism and Brazilian Avant-garde Poetry** examines the adoption of Futurist principles by the brothers Haroldo and Augusto de Campos and their fellow poet Décio Pignatari, founders of the Concrete Poetry movement in Brazil. When, in the 1950s, they rediscovered Mário and Oswald de Andrade and Brazilian Modernism, they also looked at the inspiration these two received from the historical avant-garde. Italy, France and Russia, in particular, contributed to their conception of the materiality of language and the interaction of the verbal and non-verbal in modern poetry. For quite some time, Cisneros has been exploring what the Brazilian representatives of Concrete Poetry knew about historical Futurism, what relationship they established to that tradition and how they assimilated and developed further ideas stemming from the historical avant-garde. She discovered that there were not only influences by Marinetti and his entourage of poets, but also by Vladimir Mayakovsky and other Russian Futurists. This becomes visible in a number of theoretical writings: the manifesto-like essays "Poesia concreta" (Concrete Poetry, 1956), "Aspectos da poesia concreta" (Aspects of Concrete Poetry, 1957), the manifesto *Plano-piloto para poesia concreta* (Pilot Plan for Concrete Poetry, 1958) and other early theoretical writings collected in *Teoria da poesia concreta* (Theory of Concrete Poetry, 1965). These efforts resulted in two collections of translations, *Poemas de Maiakóvski* (Mayakovsky's Poems, 1967) and *Poesia russa moderna* (Modern Russian Poetry, 1968), compiled in collaboration with the scholar of Russian literature, Boris Schnaiderman. The poetics and revolutionary stance of the Russian Futurists injected a breath of fresh air into Brazilian Concrete Poetry. As recently as 2019, Augusto de Campos also published *Esses russos* (Those Russians), a chapbook with his own lavish visual elaborations and transcreations of 'ferroconcrete' poems by Kamensky and Iliazd, among others. As a kind of postscript, Cisneros also looks at the Russian-German touring exhibition *Transfutur* (1990–1992), co-edited by the Brazilian artist and poet André Vallias, which presented examples from both Russian Futurism, the German tradition of Visual or Concrete Poetry and the Russian 'Transfurist' group (Serge Segay, Rea Nikonova and Boris Konstriktor). She thus shows how a tradition that emerged in Russia in the early twentieth century could continue in postwar Brazil and was still alive in the latter part of the twenty-first century.

Section 4 shows that the ideas of early – Italian and Russian – Futurism also resurged in the form of experimental music, sculpture, photography and architecture, both in Italy and abroad. What all these fields seem to have in common is a – more or less elaborate and conscious – retro-futurist,[8] citational attitude. They are united by a desire to retrieve the most diverse creative forms of historical Futurism and to imagine them as a complex aesthetic process of confrontation with problematic paradigms, such as history, modernity and progress.

In this context, **Esther Schmitz-Gundlach** explores the reception of musical Futurism in her essay **Back to the Future of *The Art of Noises:* The After-Life of Futurism in Twentieth-Century Music.** She explains how, in the second half of the twentieth century, composers such as Edgard Varèse, John Cage, Pierre Schaeffer and György Ligeti developed innovative modes of production and reception of music, in parallel with the new technical possibilities of sound generation that became available at the time. They thus continued the Futurists' liberation of sound in Luigi Russolo's 'Art of Noises', achieved by means of mechanical sound generators. While Futurism had missed out on the actual production of new music and never became part of a tradition that could be deemed a musical 'school', these new visionary composers retrieved Russolo's concepts of music as sound structures and applied them in the fields of serial and electronic music.

Edgard Varèse did not treat sound and noise as antithetical units, but as integral components of a musical chord (Klang). John Cage's 'All-Sound Music of the Future' expanded the concept of sound to its very limits. Instead of imitating natural sounds and treating music as an art of expression, he based his music on alea-

8 See, for example, Guffey and Lemay: "Retrofuturism and Steampunk."

toric principles and expanded the world of music by including 'silence'. Pierre Schaeffer's *musique concrète*, instead, detached sounds from their original context and handled them as objects with a musical quality. Finally, György Ligeti examined the technical possibilities offered in an electronic studio and applied them to the compositional process of instrumental music, layering individual sounds of orchestral instruments in a manner similar to sine waves in electronic music. The aesthetic re-evaluation of sound by these composers led to an ever-expanding conception of music, to the point that music could be treated as a mere 'sonic structure'. Declaring sound to be musical material also required a new listening attitude and assigned to the audience a new rôle in the musical communication process. Schmitz-Gundlach concludes that what could be considered Neo-Futurist in these composers is the detachment of noise from its original sonic environment and the adoption of technology as a potential stimulus of musical creativity.

In **Postcolonial Retro-Futurism: Alessandro Ceresoli's *Linea Tagliero* Prototypes**, **Tenley Bick** takes another path, addressing an Italian artist's deeply original exploration of Futurist colonial architecture in East Africa, aero-Futurism and glasswork in Eritrea. In 2009, Ceresoli (*1975) moved to Asmara and produced six items of furniture with a local glassware manufacturer. Bick shows that the *Linea Tagliero* prototypes reflect Giuseppe Pettazzi's aeroplane-shaped Fiat Tagliero service station (1938), a residue of local Futurist architecture from the years of Fascist colonialism. Ceresoli, in particular, mimics and subverts the Futurist (and futuristic) aesthetics of technology and aviation, at once unveiling and problematizing Italy's violent colonial past in the 1930s. Bick theorizes that Ceresoli's *Linea Tagliero* prototypes subvert the colonial dynamics of racial marginalization and embody what she calls a "postcolonial Retro-Futurism" and "retrofuturism". The former term indicates a "critical return to a historical (and in this case, colonialist) version of second-wave Futurism", while the second, with lower-case 'r', refers to the "seemingly analeptic redeployment of an atavistic historical 'futurism' in a general view of or concern with the future". Ceresoli's reflections on 'the future of the past' ultimately suggests a form of post-colonial deconstruction of the future(s) imagined by that Futurism which endorsed the Italian Empire, denouncing and seeking to overcome its political, colonial and Modernist failures by "opening it up and offering new histories and future possibilities yet to come". Demonstrating that the problematic legacy of Italian colonialism still remains to be critically investigated, Bick highlights the fundamental distinction between a Fascist and an anti-Fascist Futurism, a distinction that is often lost in popular accounts of the movement.

The twelve scholarly essays of Part One of this Yearbook are followed in Section 5 by four artists' statements. The first is by **Artur R. Sztukalski and Guillaume Touissant**, a Polish-French duo active in the fields of music, philosophy and avant-garde art, who have been involved with various informal networks since the 1990s. Their artistic beliefs were strongly influenced by Futurism, albeit in a Postmodern incarnation to which they gave the name **'Transfuturism'.** A manifesto outlining their ideas was written in 2015 and published in 2023 in conjunction with a compact disc of noise music issued on the Impulsy Stetoskopu label. The performance artist **Giovanni Fontana** discusses his praxis of Futurist poetry recitation in **From Words-in-Freedom to Epigenetic Poetry: Evolutions in Futurist Recitation and Performance.** In the first part, he focusses on Marinetti's practice of poetry declamations, in particular, that of *parole in libertà* (Words-in-Freedom) and *tavole parolibere* (Free-Word Tables), where the sonority of the text is heightened in a vocal spectacle charged with tension and dynamics that spills over into the audience. Marinetti condemned traditional methods of declamation and sought to replace it with a modern, dynamic acting and a use of voice that went beyond any pre-established timbre, tonal and rhythmic scheme. These poetic compositions were set up as visual spectacles with dynamic forms of gesture and movement and led to synaesthetic artworks that brought to fruition the intersections, contaminations and synaesthetic interrelations between voice, body and environment. This quest for a 'total poetry' was taken up again in the postwar period by various artists. In Italy, Arrigo Lora Totino pursued research into the interrelations between poetry, art and electronic music. He promoted the work undertaken by his predecessors in a historical-critical anthology of sound poetry (*Futura: Poesia sonora*, 1978) with Cramps Records in Milan. From this, he developed 'mimo-declamations' that fostered phono-gestual languages, and 'gymnastic poetry' that asserted the physical aspects of the poet's body.

Similarly, Fontana's work goes beyond the writing of poetic texts and produces polytexts by means of a voice and a body vibrating in sympathy with other arts. The written text is here only a pre-text, which in its graphic form contains many germs capable of metamorphosing beyond the page into time and space. As a performer, he is a polyartist who appropriates electronic and videographic practices, cinema, photography, the universe of sound art, the theatrical medium and the kinetic domain of rhythmic movement. His performances are always acts of *poiesis* which undergoes successive processes of re-organization. This spatio-temporal evolutionary process he calls 'epigenetic poetry'.

The third statement is authored by **Marcella Giulia Lorenzi**, a scientist who also engages in experimental digital photography. Her artistic work has been inspired by Futurist photography, which she has attempted to translate into our contemporary world by taking recourse to new technical means of capturing, processing and distributing images. Her statement concerning **The Future of Futurism in Digital Photography** discusses the Futurists' prediction that there might come a time when the established forms of art will be seen as an anachronism and be replaced with new forms of expression. She shows how the torch has been passed from the Futurists to a new generation of artists in the twenty-first century by focussing on the technology of digital photography, which goes beyond the classic conceptions of time, place and action. Lorenzi lingers, in particular, on some of the technical capabilities of 'light paintings', produced in a Generative Art process that allow movement to be captured in a manner that the Futurists could only dream about.

Finally, **Lindsay Hunter's** artist statement **The Infinite Wrench: An Ensemble Member Reflects on the Theatre Company 'The Neo-Futurists' During and After Greg Allen's Tenure** reflects on Greg Allen's Theatre Companies in the years 1988–2022. While offering an account of the experimental theatre group The Neo--Futurists, founded in Chicago in 1998 as an illusion-free approach to performance, with political and satirical objectives, her personal perspective as a performer in the New York branch of the company retraces the selected yet legible debts of Neo-Futurist performance to historical Futurism, particularly in relation to speed, dynamism, actor-audience contact and abolition of theatrical illusion. She then focusses on the changes to the ensembles' long-running flagship show, *Too Much Light Makes the Baby Go Blind* and its 2017 transformation into *The Infinite Wrench*, as a consequence of Allen's decision to withdraw the performance rights of the original show from the Neo-Futurist ensemble in Chicago. Analysing Allen's authoritarian move – which he justified as an engaged reaction to Trump's election as president of the United States – Hunter examines how his decision to turn Neo-Futurist theatre into "a machine to fight Fascism" (in Allen's words) was ultimately rooted in a misconception of historical Futurism, reduced to an ill-advised association with political authoritarianism. Allen's misunderstanding of historical Futurism became apparent in 2016 in a press release in which he defined his own Neo-Futurism as an "updating of Italian Futurism, a movement which, ironically, was created by artists who later supported Mussolini". Hunter calls into question Allen's attachment to popular perceptions of Futurism in the United States and sheds light on the shifting and intriguing relationship between historical Futurism and Neo-Futurist performance, revealing the dangers of any form of cultural simplification.

The second part of this yearbook contains several **reports**, beginning with the eighth biannual conference of the European Network for Avant-Garde and Modernism Studies. Since its founding in 2007, EAM has dedicated much attention to Futurism (which the *International Yearbook of Futurism Studies* has repeatedly reported on). **Günter Berghaus** informs in **EAM2022 in Lisbon: The Global Expansion of Futurism in the 1910s and 1920s** on the eighth meeting that had *Globalising the Avant-garde* as its general theme. Futurism was discussed in various sections, some of which are highlighted in this report. There were also plans to have four Russian scholars discuss Futurism at the conference, but soon after the Russian invasion of Ukraine on 24 February 2022 it became obvious that these colleagues would not be able to attend. The organizers in Lisbon therefore arranged a special section, entitled *Russian Futures*, where they were provided with remote access via a Skype video link. The largest thematic panel of the 2022 conference, extending over three sessions, was "The Global Expansion of Futurism in the 1910s and 1920s". It featured twelve papers that examined how Futurist ideas and stylistic features entered the artistic languages in many countries around the world. Particular emphasis was laid on how writers and artists used the stimulus of Italian or Russian Futurism to develop their own Modernist ideas and to merge the newly emerging concepts with indigenous traditions. The panel in Lisbon scrutinized this dialectic process of rejection and absorption in a global perspective. Speakers investigated the relations between centre and periphery that determined how new artistic trends in European capitals were responded to in the former colonies. The report also highlights that EAM has finally moved away from its focus on Europe. Researchers from Africa, Asia and Latin America discussed in Lisbon many non-Western forms of Modernism and addressed a wide range of developments on several continents, even including the Arctic region.

Leandro Pasini reports in **Futurism and the Brazilian Week of Modern Art: Some Thoughts Prompted by the Centenário da Semana de 22** on a string of events celebrating and reassessing Brazilian Modernism. The Week of Modern Art held in São Paulo in 1922 was a key event in the cultural history of Latin America and has been the topic of many books and countless essays, which have analysed how the European avant-gardes, their magazines and manifestos impacted on Brazil and stimulated a development, of which the Week of Modern Art was a high point. In the years 1909–1922, Futurism was widely discussed in Brazil, but not always on the basis of the works and theoretical writings of the movement's key protagonists. Marinetti's movement was often misrepresented, satirized, ridiculed and used as a buzzword for characterizing all sorts of modern aberrations. In view of this, it was astonishing to what degree Futurism was sidelined in the centenary celebrations. What should have been an occasion to revisit the contributions Futurism made to the development of a modernist and avant-garde art and literature in Brazil, was strangely absent in the monumental event.

Pasini highlights in his report that this lacuna was rather typical of how, over the past years, Marinetti and his followers have been approached in Brazil. His report is less concerned with the centenary of the Semana de 22 itself, but with the ways in which the European roots of Brazilian Modernism have been reassessed in recent scholarship. Pasini examines how largely forgotten characters such as Afonso Henriques de Lima Barreto, Paulo Menotti del Picchia and José Pereira da Graça Aranha participated in the debates on Futurism one hundred years ago and how this is being resurrected. He also questioned São Paulo's position as a hotbed of

Modernist culture, as has been generally assumed in the past fifty years or so, and he highlights the need to extend our geographical focus when discussing modern culture in Brazil. When bringing the north-east and north of Brazil into our critical horizon, a whole range of rarely considered reactions to Futurism in the years 1910s and 20s can be discovered. Thus, a new image of the relation between Futurism and Modernism in Brazil emerges in his report. It demystifies many false assumptions about Brazilian culture, questions dominant narratives of Brazilian Modernism and shows how Futurism found diverging responses in many major and minor cities in Brazil. Futurism served as a blueprint for the battle between innovators and traditionalists that reached its apogee in the Week of Modern Art in 1922. Pasini therefore asks for this neglected aspect to be recovered and for further research to be undertaken on the connections between the Brazilian and the Italian avant-garde.

Simona Cigliana reports in **Anton Giulio Bragaglia: The Archive of a Visionary** on a major archive recently incorporated into the National Gallery of Modern and Contemporary Art in Rome. The purchase gave rise to the exhibition *Anton Giulio Bragaglia: L'archivio di un visionario*, curated by Claudia Palma in 2022. The papers which the artist left behind after his death in 1960 were only rarely made available to scholars by his daughter Antonella Vigliani Bragaglia. After her death, the heirs decided to offer this immense patrimony of documents to a major museum in Italy, thus preventing its sale at auction and its dispersal amongst many private collectors. Any person who has worked in Bragaglia's old apartment in Via Lombardia can only confirm Cigliana's assessment that the archive is of fundamental importance not only for the reconstruction of Bragaglia's life and œuvre, but also for the study of the avant-garde, of Italian Futurism and of the history of the performing arts in Italy. It is therefore of great significance for Futurism scholars and will soon be available for their research.

Anton Giulio Bragaglia, as many readers will know, was a theorist and essayist, a critic, stage designer, theatre and film director, an impresario, author of numerous publications on the history of dance and theatre, an editor of several periodicals. He had close connections to the early Futurist group but was despised by Umberto Boccioni. Although Bragaglia's artistic ideas should have made him a member of the Futurist group, he never became more than an ally. Anton Giulio Bragaglia, together with his brothers Arturo and Carlo Ludovico, entered the field of photography and set out his creative concepts in the brochure *Fotodinamismo futurista* (Futurist Photodynamism, 1913). Following this brush with the Futurist group of painters, Bragaglia threw himself into a series of new ventures. He began a successful career in journalism, and published the influential *Cronache d'attualità* (Chronicles of Current Affairs). He also founded the Novissima film company and secured the support of Enrico Prampolini as set designer, which gave the few files he produced a distinctly avant-garde feel. Together with his brother Carlo Ludovico he founded the Casa d'Arte Bragaglia, which also exhibited a variety of Futurist artists. In 1922, it moved into the underground premises of Palazzo Tittoni, where it was complemented by an experimental theatre, the Teatro degli Indipendenti, which became one of the most important Italian art theatres. Here, the Compagnia Spettacoli Bragaglia premièred many plays by major Italians, by major European dramatists then unknown in Italy (e.g. Wedekind, Schnitzler, Jarry, Shaw, Strindberg and Brecht), and by F.T. Marinetti. Bragaglia alternated his activity in his own theatre with directing opera. He was also the author of important historical studies of Roman and Italian popular theatre, of dance and music.

This activity is now neatly archived in the GNAM in approximately 172 linear metres of box files, containing correspondences, musical scores, scripts, stage designs, photographs, playbills and programmes. These and his huge library of books and magazines will prove to be an extremely valuable resource for Futurism scholarship.

Edyth von Haynau is better known to Futurism experts by her pseudonym Rosa Rosà, and her complex artistic œuvre has also featured in the *International Yearbook of Futurism Studies.*[9] **Lisa Hanstein** reports in **Rosa Rosà / Edith Arnaldi / Edyth von Haynau (1884–1978): A Woman Photographer and her Futurist Inspiration** on the discovery of more than 232 photographic prints and 10,800 negatives that testify that Von Haynau's occupation with the 'eighth art' went far beyond that of an amateur. Her work in this domain was recently presented to the general public in the exhibition *Fotografe! = Women Photographers*, held in Florence in 2022, including two shots that reflect aspects of Futurist aesthetics. Both were made in 1939 during the Siennese Palio (horse races). Hanstein discusses how Von Haynau's dissolution of solid outlines and decomposition of outer forms, her interpenetration and simultaneity of objects and environments related to ideas promoted in the books and manifestos of the Futurist painters and by Anton Giulio Bragaglia in his booklet *Fotodinamismo futurista* of 1913. She also shows how Von Haynau visualized in her images ideas expressed in the manifesto *La fotografia futurista* (Futurist Photography, 1931), written jointly by Filippo Tommaso Marinetti and Tato. Hanstein's discussion shows that Edyth von Haynau's alter ego Rosa Rosà – most active in the years 1917–18 – had not been entirely buried by the 1930s. Like her colleague Wanda Wulz from Trieste, she deserves to be given more consideration in the chronicles of Futurist photography.

9 Hanstein: "Edyth von Haynau: A Viennese Aristocrat in the Futurist Circles of the 1910s."

In the third part, **Critical responses to publications,** three new books are being discussed, beginning with **Deidre O'Grady**'s critical assessment of Iveta Slavkova's highly ambitious study *Reparer l'homme: La crise de l'humanisme et l'Homme nouveau des avant-gardes autour de la Grande Guerre (1909–1929).* The book provides a multidisciplinary discourse on the 'New Man' in both Futurism and the Bauhaus. Its main focus is on war and its many socio-political and mythical aspects, including its artistic expression, with Futurism seen here principally through the works of F.T. Marinetti and Umberto Boccioni. The 'homme nouveau du futurisme' is portrayed through both literary and painterly works, with a particular focus on the perfectly mechanized (human) being as the protagonist of a new social order. **Lucia Re** discusses Claudia Salaris's new volume on *Donne d'avanguardia*, a survey of the life and art of some thirty avant-garde women artists, who intersected more or less directly with the mainstream of Italian Futurism. Salaris takes a distinctly biographical approach to her subject and presents a series of life stories of unconventional and irreverent women, presented by her as "pioneers in the history of women's liberation". **Adrian R. Duran** appraises Raffaele Bedarida's wide-ranging study *Exhibiting Italian Art in the United States from Futurism to Arte Povera.* Bedarida traces five specific moments in the interactions between Italian and US-American culture, from 1929–69, and demonstrates that the USA were enmeshed in a myriad ways with the international avant-garde. Duran focusses on Bedarida's first two chapters, concerned with Fortunato Depero and Italian Americanism (revisiting Depero's relationship with the city of New York), and the Fascist international outreach in the 1930s and early 1940s, which sought to promote Italian art within a global context by means of exhibitions and sponsorship of galleries. These analyses are not without contemporary relevance, as in recent decades new centres for Italian modern art have been founded in the USA and have thus given Italian art (including Futurism) greater international visibility.

Finally, our **Bibliographic Section: Publications on Futurism**, covering the years 2020–2023, provides information on 21 exhibition catalogues, 5 special periodical issues, 7 edited volumes of conference proceedings, 18 collective volumes, 60 monographic studies, 35 editions, 2 volumes that turn Futurism into fiction. These 148 book publications are supplemented by 2 film recordings which, altogether, show that Futurism Studies continues to be a fertile field of inquiry in many academic quarters around the world.

Bibliography

Burliuk, David, Aleksandr [Aleksei] Kruchenykh, Vladimir Maiakovskii, and Viktor [Velimir] Khlebnikov: "Poshchechina obshchestvennomu vkusu." *Poshchechina obshchestvennomu vkusu: Stikhi, proza, stat'i.* Moskva: Kuz'min, 1912. 5–6.

Cho, Kyoo Yun: "Futurism in Korea: From the Historical to the Postmodern Avant-garde." *International Yearbook of Futurism Studies* 6 (2016): 3–21.

Guffey, Elizabeth, and Kate C. Lemay: "Retrofuturism and Steampunk." Rob Latham, ed.: *The Oxford Handbook to Science Fiction.* Oxford: Oxford University Press, 2014. 434–448.

Hanstein, Lisa: "Edyth von Haynau: A Viennese Aristocrat in the Futurist Circles of the 1910s." *International Yearbook of Futurism Studies* 5 (2015): 333–365.

Mancebo Roca, Juan Agustín: "Depero New Depero: Rovereto Presents the Artist and His Reception after 1960." *International Yearbook of Futurism Studies* 12 (2022): 385–397

Marinetti, Filippo Tommaso: " 'Testi-poemi murali' di Carlo Belloli." F.T. Marinetti: *Collaudi futuristi.* Napoli: Guida, 1977. 279–280.

Marinetti, Filippo Tommaso: "The Foundation and Manifesto of Futurism." F.T. Marinetti: *Critical Writings.* Ed. by Günter Berghaus. New York: Farrar, Straus and Giroux 2006. 11–17.

Section 1: **Futurism Studies**

1 Italy

Pasquale Fameli

Futurism in Italian Verbo-Visual Poetry after the Second World War

Abstract: This essay explores the ever-changing panorama of verbo-visual poetry after the Second World War in Italy, tracing back its manifold, divergent and articulated forms – spanning Concrete, Visual, Symbiotic or Epistaltic Poetry – to Futurist theories and practices. By reconstructing the complicated political and cultural debate that delayed a proper assessment of Marinetti's movement – due to its ambiguous association with Fascism in the 1920s to 40s – and following the few critical voices in Italy during the second half of the twentieth century (Masnata, Barilli, Ballerini) that fostered an essential scholarly change of course, I aim to contextualize the debt of Italian poetic neo-avant-garde(s) to Futurism. Showing how Italy was at the forefront of an international artistic turmoil that sought to affect a visual and material transformation of the poetic experience, the analysis focusses on the creative and theoretical works of a number of poets and artists, who played a significant rôle in the critical revision and practical prosecution of Futurism from the mid-1960s onwards and promoted the rediscovery and further development of *paroliberismo:* namely, Carlo Belloli (1922–2003), Arrigo Lora Totino (1928–2016), Maurizio Nannucci (1939-), Mimmo Rotella (1918–2006), Lamberto Pignotti (1926-), Stelio Maria Martini (1934–2016) and Paolo Albani (1946-). Examining the unique physical and formal characteristics of their outcomes in the framework of the Italian cultural climate of the time, all the while highlighting their instances of continuity with the earlier Italian avant-garde, the ultimate aim of the essay is to re-evaluate a series of little-studied, albeit fundamental experiences for a complete and systematic reclaiming of a (Neo)Futurist aesthetics.

Keywords: Verbo-visual Poetry; Words-in-Freedom and Free-Word Tables; poetry recitation; poetry and fine arts; sound poetry; Italian neo-avant-gardes; Carlo Belloli; Arrigo Lora Totino; Maurizio Nannucci; Mimmo Rotella; Lamberto Pignotti; Stelio Maria Martini; Paolo Albani

https://doi.org/10.1515/9783111318394-003

Introduction: from Futurism to the neo-avant-garde (and back)

In most Western countries, the period after the Second World War was informed by the gradual re-introduction, in a normalizing fashion, of ideas and aesthetic solutions anticipated by the historical avant-gardes in every field of artistic creativity and experimentation. Fostered by the new possibilities of modern technology that exploded in the nineteenth century,[1] the most daring avant-garde experiments, however, frequently eluded any systematic approach. So much so, that their groundbreaking practices in the field of poetry and art have often been misunderstood as naive and childish outcomes of obstinate innovation. The so-called 'neo-avant-garde'[2] emerged during the 1960s and provided a more coherent, meditative and anti-heroic attitude in the world of art and literature, transforming the artistic possibilities of detachment and opposition into more articulated systems also in the field of poetry.[3] While the historical avant-garde had begun a cultural battle that aimed at a total social and political revolution, the neo-avant-garde focussed mainly on the *formal* aspect of expressive media.[4] Its revival, however, never consisted of slavish repetitions or sterile mannerisms. The activity of neo-avant-garde artists was fuelled by a critical rehabilitation of those original operating logics within a new material framework, marked by the introduction of mass-market strategies into cultural processes, as had been foreseen by their predecessors.[5] It is no coincidence that one of the first and most important scholars of mass culture, Marshall McLuhan, declared, in the mid-1960s, that avant-garde art is "precise advance knowledge of how to cope with the psychic and social consequences of the next technology" and that "in experimental art, men are given the exact specifications of coming violence to their own psyches from their own counter-irritants or technology."[6]

---

1 Still helpful to understand the scope of this revolution is Kern: *The Culture of Time and Space.*

2 In this essay, I am distinguishing between the 'neo-avant-garde' as a generic term for a variety of art movements (Pop Art, Nouveau Réalisme, Conceptual Art, Visual Poetry, Fluxus, Happenings, Minimalism, Body Art, etc.) and the Italian *neoavanguardia,* a literary movement which coincides with the Gruppo 63, formed in Italy in 1963 and oriented towards radical experimentations with language. For further information on the Gruppo 63, see Barilli and Guglielmi: *Gruppo 63: Critica e teoria.*

3 As pointed out by Barilli: "Marinetti e il nuovo sperimentalismo", p. 89.

4 See Sanguineti: "Avanguardia e sperimentalismo", p. 67.

5 Calvesi's *Avanguardia di massa* is still fundamental to understanding these processes.

6 McLuhan: *Understanding Media: The Extensions of Man,* p. 66.

More than any other avant-garde movement, Italian Futurism demonstrated awareness of these issues. On various occasions, critics have highlighted the affinities between Marinetti and McLuhan's visions,[7] both based on the formative rôle that technological inventions exert on perception, constantly reconfiguring our experience and our patterns of behaviour. The Futurist aesthetic revolution was built on the use of multiple means and languages to achieve simultaneity of sensory stimulations. As such, the notion of 'intermedia' as formulated by Dick Higgins in 1966, in agreement with McLuhan's theories,[8] can find its very roots in Futurist poetics. American Pop-Art painter and sculptor George Segal pointed out the international scope of this legacy as follows:

> In 1958–59, Kaprow and I stayed up until two or three in the morning arguing aesthetics. Kaprow was brilliant in conveying the Avant-garde ideas of Dadaism, Surrealism and Futurism, especially Futurism. For example, Marinetti's "radio broadcasts" were of great interest to us. The combination of words and sound made by noises produced by whatever objects clearly were a rich source for John Cage. It seems it was only the Italian futurists' embrace of Mussolini that gave them a bad reputation. The aesthetic that has to do with living in modern cities, I think, is still worth exploring.[9]

These words demonstrate the utmost attention paid by the new international avant-garde to radical Futurist inventions, in a period in which Italian culture looked at them with suspicion.

Once again a 'Conquest of the Stars': A slow rehabilitation

The association of some leading members of Futurism with Fascism burdened the movement for a very long time. As suggested by Segal, the ideological stigma which resulted from this limited the reception of Futurism's most daring inventions in the post-war period. Although it is possible to trace numerous signs of its critical rediscovery in Italy well before the 1960s,[10] its full reaffirmation has been long and

---

7 See Calvesi: *Il futurismo*, p. 2; De Maria: "Marinetti poeta e ideologo", p. XXIII; Barilli: "Marinetti e il nuovo sperimentalismo", p. 94 and Agnese: "Prima Marinetti, poi McLuhan."

8 See Emerson: *Reading Writing Interfaces*, pp. 88–89.

9 Bertozzi: "An Interview with George Segal", pp. 27–28.

10 See, in this regard, Berghaus: "The Postwar Reception of Futurism: Repression or Recuperation?" and "The Historiography of Italian Futurism".

complex, not only amongst conservative intellectuals, but also among the members of the most prominent neo-avant-garde literary group in Italy, known as the Gruppo 63. Indeed, one of the harshest condemnations came from one of its key members, the left-wing poet, writer and critic Edoardo Sanguineti. In an essay of 1966, he traced back Marinetti's aesthetics to the despotic and egocentric theories of Mario Morasso, rooting his "aesthetic apology of the machine, speed, industry [...] in an attitude of violent undemocratic hatred."[11] Two years later, Sanguineti wrote a review of Luciano De Maria's pivotal book *Teoria e invenzione futurista* (Futurist Theory and Invention, 1968), arguing that industrial war was for Marinetti the "the truth of the world" and its aesthetic defence "the central node" of his "thought and of the entire cultural politics of fascism (or fascisms)."[12] Sanguineti's views on Futurism are largely outdated today, but they had significant impact in Italy at the time. He rejected De Maria's polemological interpretation of Marinetti's idea of war,[13] and his ideological arguments had serious repercussions on its reception of the movement. As many other ex-Futurists, Pino Masnata[14] openly complained about this kind of misunderstanding, carried out by the Italian *neoavanguardia:*

11 "[...] l'apologia estetica della macchina, della velocità, dell'industria [...] in un atteggiamento di violento odio antidemocratico". Sanguineti: "L'estetica della velocità", p. 143. This and all subsequent translations from Italian in this essay are mine, unless otherwise noted.

12 "[...] la verità del mondo [...] il nodo centrale di Marinetti e di tutta la politica culturale del fascismo (o dei 'fascismi')." Sanguineti: "La guerra futurista", p. 43.

13 Drawing on the influences of Nietzsche's philosophy and the Darwinian *struggle for life*, De Maria uses a neologism that literally refers to the "study of war" (from the ancient Greek *polemos* = "war" and *logos* = "study"): "Il pensiero di Marinetti è intimamente, profondamente polemologico: la guerra si identifica con una legge fondamentale della vita. Umanità e necessità di lottare divengono sinonimi. [...] Per Marinetti la guerra, se da una parte è legge profonda della vita, dall'altra nella sua manifestazione concreta, è festa, nel senso etnologico lumeggiato da Roger Callois, esuberanza vitale, dispendio giocondo di energie, igiene non in senso preventivo, ma attivo e liberatorio. Assistiamo, nella visione futurista della guerra, a un'imponente estetizzazione del fenomeno bellico. Di più, diremmo che nell'ideologia futurista la guerra assume una coloritura erotico-estetica." De Maria: "Marinetti poeta e ideologo", pp. XLIV-XLV. For more up-to-date reflections on the topic, see also Berghaus: "Violence, War, Revolution: Marinetti's Concept of a Futurist Cleanser for the World" and Di Stefano: "The Futurists and the Aesthetics of War". Sanguineti's own positions, however, evolved in time, as can be seen in "La parola futurista" (1998), which contains much more temperate judgements than his essays from the 1960s.

14 Masnata was an exponent of the second phase of Futurism and co-authored with Marinetti the manifesto *La radia* (The Radio, 1933). For more information on Masnata, see Modena: *Pino Masnata: Vita di un futurista* and Margaret Fisher's Introduction to *Radia: Pino Masnata's Gloss of the 1933 Futurist Radio Manifesto.*

> Young people who refer to themselves as the Italian *neoavanguardia* or *Gruppo* 63 begin with a flood of words and commonplaces. They regularly talk about the superficial nature of Futurism, clearly demonstrating that they know nothing about it. [...] Maybe it's not their fault. They are young and books about Futurism are hard to come by. [...] I am pleased that they are still asking what the language of poetry is. New explorers and scouts are emerging from the Italian poets who have strengthened their force by climbing the lower slopes. [...] What I am saying is: "Be aware that you will find in Futurism all the launching pads for your flights. You will find Giuseppe Guglielmi's expressive audacities. You will find (in the poetry of technicalities[15]) the language of Elio Pagliarani's physics lessons [...]. You will find in the Free-Word Tables and in the lines to be read synchronically the premises for Renato Pedio's multiple pattern poetry [...], whose experimentation is undoubtedly still alive and interesting." [16]

The publication, in 1970, of an issue of *Il Verri* entirely dedicated to Futurism was critical for a reconsideration of Marinetti's movement, at least in Italy. The publication had been called for by Luciano Anceschi – founder and director of the journal – as an attempt to re-evaluate the Italian avant-garde beyond the old and reductive schemes. In his essay for *Il Verri*, Renato Barilli lamented the lack of recognition for Marinetti's contribution to literary experimentalism, but also noted the limits imposed by an inner disjunction in Marinetti's activity: on the one hand a theoretical audacity and on the other a literary production still marked by dishevelled rebelliousness and expressionistic resentments typical of the Scapigliatura movement.[17] Marinetti's poetic production still remained attached to traditional genres even in the most advanced moments of literary production. Barilli therefore advocated the need to rethink his lesson from the perspective of the visual arts, giving him credit for having initiated a "sensorial revolution" aimed at the

15 Marinetti published in 1940 a *Poema non umano dei tecnicismi* (The Nonhuman Poem of Technicalities).

16 "I giovani che si autodefiniscono la 'neo-avanguardia' italiana o il 'gruppo 63' partono con un fiume di parole e di luoghi comuni. Il solito è quello della superficialità del futurismo di cui dimostrano chiaramente di non conoscere nulla. [...] Forse non è colpa loro. Sono giovani e i libri del futurismo sono introvabili. [...] Sono lieto che rimettano ancora in discussione ciò che è il linguaggio della poesia. Nuove pattuglie esploranti sorgono dai poeti italiani che si erano fortificati su le prime alture. [...] E dico: 'Guardate che nel futurismo troverete predisposte tutte le piste di lancio per i vostri voli. Troverete le audacie espressive di Giuseppe Guglielmi. Troverete (nella poesia dei tecnicismi) il linguaggio della lezione di fisica di Elio Pagliarani [...]. Troverete nelle tavole parolibere e nelle righe da leggere sincronicamente le premesse per la poesia a schema multiplo di Renato Pedio [...] il cui esperimento è indubbiamente vivo e interessante'". Masnata: *Poesia visiva: Storia e teoria*, p. 211.

17 Scapigliatura refers to an artistic movement that developed in Italy after the Risorgimento (1815–71) and included poets, writers, musicians, painters and sculptors. The term 'scapigliato' literally means 'unkempt' or 'dishevelled'.

convergence between different arts, and at the achievement of a dynamic conception of space that would support creative exchanges between art and life.

Indeed, it was only with the Futurist exploration of synaesthesia – which had gained a central rôle as early as Romanticism and had been extensively explored by the Symbolists – that a concrete interaction between different sensorial stimuli can be observed. The Futurist revolution, in particular, was built on a novel anthropological concept that identified other intermediate areas of sensitivity and thus went beyond the conventional division of the perceptive apparatus into five sensory spheres. Marinetti believed that only the continuous interplay between tactile, acoustic and olfactory stimuli, caused by the use of manifold technological means, could dismantle the instituted boundaries of genres. This, he felt, would finally tear down Gotthold Ephraim Lessing's separation between the arts of space (painting and sculpture) and the arts of time (poetry and music),[18] and reveal new forms of engagement between word, sound, image and form.[19]

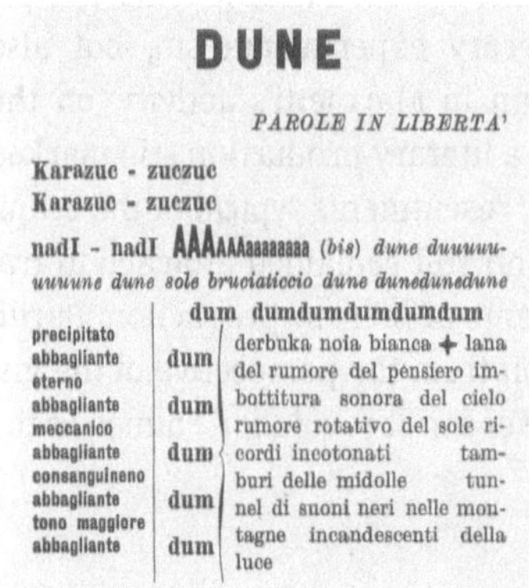
DUNE

PAROLE IN LIBERTA'

Karazuc - zuczuc
Karazuc - zuczuc
nadI - nadI AAAAAAaaaaaaaa *(bis) dune duuuuu-uuuune dune sole bruciaticcio dune dunedunedune*

dum dumdumdumdumdum

precipitato abbagliante eterno abbagliante meccanico abbagliante consanguineno abbagliante tono maggiore abbagliante | dum dum dum dum dum | derbuka noia bianca + lana del rumore del pensiero imbottitura sonora del cielo rumore rotativo del sole ricordi incotonati tamburi delle midolle tunnel di suoni neri nelle montagne incandescenti della luce

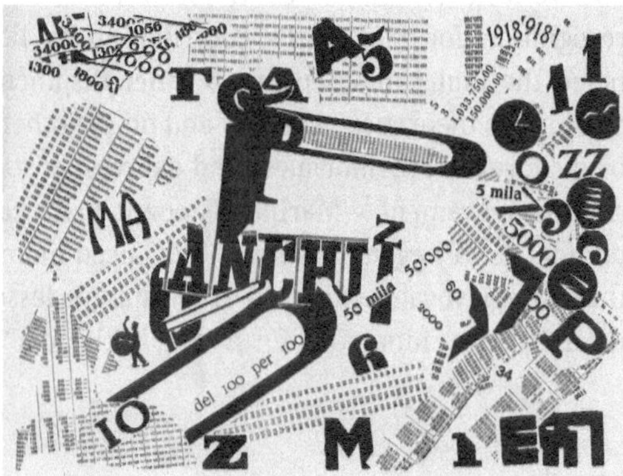

Fig. 1a: An example of a poem in *parole in libertà* style: the beginning of Marinetti's *Dune* from *Lacerba* 2:4 (15 February 1914), p. 51. **Fig. 1b:** An example of a *tavola parolibera: Une assemblée tumultueuse: Sensibilité numérique* (A Tumultuous Assembly: Numerical Sensibility) published in F. T. Marinetti: *Les Mots en liberté futuristes* (1919).

The most significant contributions to this sensorial revolution were undoubtedly Marinetti's *parole in libertà* (Words-in-Freedom, see Fig. 1a) and, even more, the *tavole parolibere* (Free-Word Tables, see Fig. 1b), which animate the word with

18 See Barilli: "Marinetti e il nuovo sperimentalismo", pp. 93–94.

19 Ever since Horace stated in his *Ars poetica* that "ut pictura poesis" (Let the poem be like a picture), the 'paragone debate' has been a central element in European aesthetics. On this 'rivalry of the arts' see Hecht: "The 'paragone' Debate: Ten Illustrations and a Comment."

new material and gestural dynamics: linguistic signs are subjected to forces of compression, dilation or dis-aggregation that overturn their symbolic function, converting them into iconic projections or physical phenomena, according to what Fausto Curi has defined as "a stylistic of matter".[20] This is also the source of the sound-performative character of the Free-Word Tables, which is not limited to the presence of onomatopoeias or noise evocations, but is based on the "phonic relevance" produced by the typographic processing.[21] This dynamic is triggered by the transformative capacity that the space of the Free-Word Tables exercises on its constituent elements; but there is also a gestural quality that induces a 'geometric' or 'topographical' form of recitation that draws on cones, spirals or ellipses projected into space. The determining character of Marinetti's tables ultimately lies in the coexistence of different codes of communication:[22] they offer a unique opportunity to highlight the word as sound or gesture, not only through the dissolution of syntactic bonds, but also thanks to the physical arrangement of graphemes, capable of evoking the movements of the body and the animation of matter.

While Futurist typographic solutions circulated across Europe and had great international influence,[23] the recognition of *paroliberismo* as a great literary achievement was hampered in Italy by a series of deprecating judgement. The first and most naïve attacks came from writers contemporary to Marinetti's movement, for example Gian Pietro Lucini, who complained of a radical disconnection between language and reality;[24] or Giovanni Papini, who compared Words-in-Freedom with "formal strangeness".[25] In the following years, *paroliberismo* suffered from a low public profile that can be attributed to Marinetti himself. The two anthologies of Futurist poetry, *I poeti futuristi* (The Futurist Poets, 1912) and *I nuovi poeti futuristi* (New Futurist Poets, 1925), for instance, contained only poems in traditional verse-form, with many of them still rooted in Late-Symbolist and Crepuscular aesthetics. Technical difficulties in the reproduction of daring graphic and typographical works also had a negative effect on Words-in-Freedom. Although Marinetti declared his desire to reserve his publishing house Edizioni futuriste di "Poesia" only for "purely Futurist works that, due to their forcefulness and radicalism of thought and their typographical difficulties, cannot be published else-

20 Curi: "Una stilistica della materia."

21 See Polacci: "Guardare, declamare, leggere."

22 See Pignotti and Stefanelli: *Scrittura verbovisiva e sinestetica*, p. 35.

23 On the success story of Futurist typography, see Toschi: "Futurism and the Birth of a Modern European Typography."

24 See Lucini: "Come ho sorpassato il futurismo", p. 273.

25 Papini: "Futurismo e Marinettismo", p. 285.

where,"[26] his editorial activity was much more conservative than expected and limited to what could be easily assembled and typeset.[27] In the decades that followed, conservative critics declared the Futurist Words-in-Freedom to be a sterile and marginal phenomenon, thus limiting its appreciation even further.[28] Sanguineti's critique in the mid-1960s ultimately condemned *paroliberismo* and Futurist recitation in Italy because, in his view, both were reflections of Marinetti's imperialist warmongering, totally incompatible with the ideological stance of the *neoavanguardia.*

The rehabilitation of Futurism only set in with scholars such as Maurizio Calvesi, Enrico Crispolti, Mario Verdone and others who, in the 1970s, made it possible to gradually re-evaluate the movement's contribution to modern art and literature. The first signs of this change of direction, however, emerged in the United States where, since the late 1940s, several exhibitions encouraged audiences to have a fresh look at the contribution which Futurism made to the historical avant-garde.[29] An important show in the field of poetry was *Italian Visual Poetry 1912–1972*, organized by Luigi Ballerini at the Finch College Museum (25–28 April 1973). Its fascinating catalogue was distributed by George Wittenborn, an influential publisher and book dealer who was also responsible for the revival of Dada poetry and painting at the time and whose bookshop on Madison Avenue served as an unofficial yet crucial platform for the transatlantic reception of the European historical avant-garde in the USA. Ballerini's efforts succeeded in reviving interest in Futurism (and Futurist poetry, in particular), in Italy too. His exhibition in New York was brought over to the Galleria Civica d'Arte Moderna in Turin in the autumn of 1973, with the slightly different title *Scrittura visuale in Italia 1912–1972.* It presented a new critical approach that benefited from two major

26 "[…] a quelle opere assolutamente futuriste che per la violenza e l'estremismo del pensiero e per le difficoltà tipografiche non possono essere pubblicate dagli altri editori." Marinetti: "'Firmamento' di Armando Mazza", p. 31.

27 See, in this regard, Van den Bossche: "Mots en liberté? Testualità e formati editoriali nel libro futurista."

28 See Flora: *Dal romanticismo al futurismo*; Falqui: *Il futurismo. Il novecentismo*; and Jacobbi: *Poesia futurista italiana.*

29 Amongst these exhibitions, one needs to mention *Twentieth-Century Italian Art*, organized by James Thrall Soby and Alfred Barr at the Museum of Modern Art in New York in 1949 (featuring many Futurist paintings); *Futurism and Later Italian Art* at Palm Beach: The Society of the Four Arts, 9 February – 4 March 1951; *Futurism: Balla, Boccioni, Carrà, Russolo, Severini* in New York: Sidney Janis Gallery, 22 March – 1 May 1954; *The Futurists: Balla. Severini, 1912–1918* in New York: Rose Fried Gallery, 25 January – 26 February 1954; *Futurism* in New York: The Museum of Modern Art, 31 May – 5 September 1961; Detroit: Institute of Arts, 18 October – 19 December 1961; Los Angeles: County Museum, 14 January – 19 February 1962.

changes in Italian neo-avant-garde poetry: on the one hand, the blossoming of diverse verbal-visual approaches, and on the other, the evolution of printing technologies capable of overcoming the practical difficulties that Marinetti's typesetters had to contend with. In the introductory text to the New York exhibition catalogue, Ballerini identified Futurism as the progenitor of all forms of Visual Writing developed after World War II. Analysing the first three tables of Marinetti's *Les Mots en liberté* (1919), he highlighted in particular the placement of verbal symbols into "a wider circulation of typographical signs", surpassing altogether "the idea of a privileged verbal language."[30] The pivotal difference of these Tables, with respect to the initial poetic experimentations of 1912, lies precisely in the use of graphemes as objects and in the autonomy of the typographic elaboration, which is no longer limited to illustrating or graphically emphasizing meanings, but rather establishes a meta-verbal discourse based on the material function of the sign in the "simultaneity of perception".[31]

Luciano Caruso and Stelio Maria Martini's more systematic work moved a stage beyond Ballerini's exhibition. Both of them visual poets themselves, they published in 1975–77 an impressive two-volume anthology entitled *Tavole parolibere futuriste, 1912–1944* (Futurist Free-Word Tables, 1912–1944); organized exhibitions in Florence (*Scrittura visuale e poesia sonora futurista* [Futurist Visual Writing and Sound Poetry], 1977) and Venice (*Tavole parolibere e tipografia futurista* [Free-Word Tables and Futurist Typography], 1977), and issued anastatic reprints of many Futurist texts, thus recovering the main corpus of experimental Futurist poetry. More importantly, they offered a historical reassessment of the relationship between Futurism and Fascism. Caruso and Martini demonstrated the "totale inutilizzazione" (absolute lack of usefulness)[32] of Futurism to the régime, highlighting Marinetti's attempt to heal the Platonic wall that separated words and things by reintroducing the expansive forces of matter into the circuit of language:

> "Their [i.e., the Futurists'] lyricism was based on 'the lyrical obsession for matter' which [...] destroyed the illusory centrality of the self in literature and banned its psychology, in favour of the introduction of subjectivity directly into matter and not projecting it onto a Platonic screen."[33]

30 Ballerini: *Italian Visual Poetry 1912–1972*, p. 6.

31 Ibid., p. 6.

32 Caruso and Martini: "La 'fuga in avanti' del futurismo", p. 6.

33 "Il loro lirismo era 'l'ossessione lirica della materia' che [...] distruggeva l'illusoria centralità dell'io nella letteratura e ne bandiva la psicologia, a vantaggio dell'immissione della soggettività direttamente nella materia e non su di un platonico schermo." Caruso and Martini: "Le tavole parolibere, ovvero La 'rivoluzione culturale' dei futuristi" pp. 49–50.

Indeed, the Free-Word Tables abolish the symbolic function of writing, condensing all the cosmic forces that stimulate our perception.[34] By recognizing the *tavole parolibere* as the first audacious attempt to mend the wound generated between words and matter, Caruso and Martini hence absolved them from the accusations first advanced by Lucini.

Passing on the torch: From Carlo Belloli to Arrigo Lora Totino

The critical rehabilitation of Italian Futurism began in the early 1970s and consolidated over time through exhibitions, publications and specialized studies. This reassessment made it possible to reposition Futurist *paroliberismo* at the origins of some of the most significant verbal-visual phenomena of the post-war period. However, it is yet to be ascertained in which ways and to what extent we can trace any direct connection between historical Futurist poetry and neo-avant-garde poetry in the years preceding this re-evaluation. The limited knowledge of Futurist literature available to Italian writers in the 1950s led to irregular developments, mostly attributable to the creative inclinations of specific authors. Although sporadic and embryonic, the ways in which the Futurist lesson impacted onto Italian verbal-visual works of the second half of the twentieth century was nevertheless more articulated than one might think. Marinetti's Words-in-Freedom initiated a "typographical revolution"[35] aimed at the total deconstruction of all structural and material conventions of the printed page and the book. This revolution soon triggered an interest amongst many designers, publishers and printers, who subsequently laid the foundations for today's forms of visual communication.[36] As Giovanni Lista emphasized, *paroliberismo* was a project open to continuous elaboration and provoked new working methods based on two premises: the interaction between verbal and visual codes, and the implosion of the factual elements of writing.[37] This redefinition not only of poetry, but of the entire system of communication developed into a variety of directions, sometimes even in contradiction to the initial interest in Futurist dynamism and onomatopoeic *rumorismo*. When comparing the inner developments of the Futurist movement with the contributions of those who embraced its heritage in their own autonomous and particular ways,

34 For further explorations on this topic, see Fameli: "L'avanguardia presa in parola."
35 Marinetti: "Destruction of Syntax – Untrammeled Imagination – Words-in-Freedom", p. 128.
36 See Salaris: *La rivoluzione tipografica*, pp. 5–12.
37 Lista: "Dal paroliberismo al libro-oggetto", p. 293.

we find solutions that at times radicalized single graphic, phonic or gestural components or enhanced their circulation by means of up-to-date technological strategies.

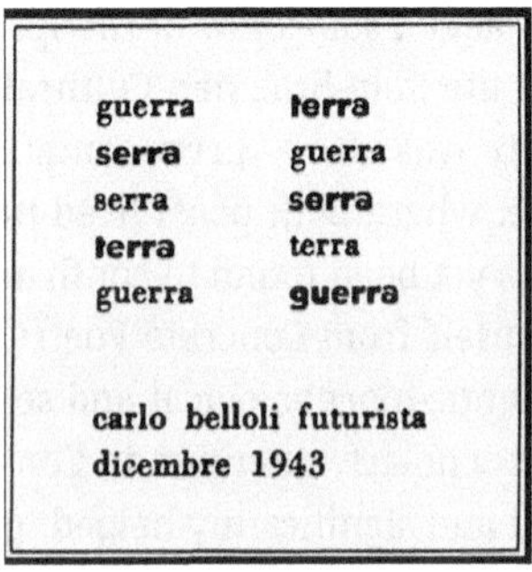

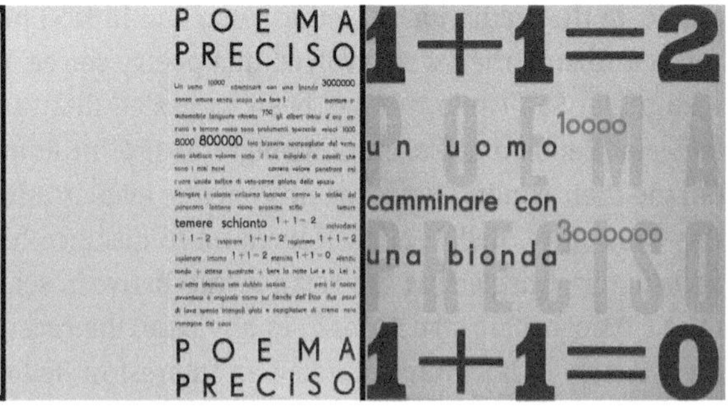

Fig. 2a: Carlo Belloli: *Guerra Terra* (War Earth), from *Parole per la guerra* (Words for the War). Milano: Edizioni di Futuristi in Armi, 1944, p. 9. **Fig. 2b:** F.T. Marinetti: *Poema preciso* (An Accurate Poem), from Tullio D'Albisola and F.T. Marinetti: *Parole in libertà futuriste olfattive tattili* (Words-in-Freedom: Futurist, Olfactory, Tactile and Thermic). Roma: Edizioni futuriste di "Poesia"; Savona: Litolatta, 1932. pp. 12r and 12v.

An important figure in this transition was Carlo Belloli (1922–2003), an exponent of the last generation of Futurist poets, whose Visual Poetry was based on modular relationships between poetry and space. This can already be seen in one of his earliest works, *Guerra Terra* (War Earth), dated December 1943 (see Fig. 2a). This composition is made of two columns of nouns chosen for their assonance: the permutation of the initial consonant generates a multiplicity of spatial connections that allow the text to be read in multiple directions. Matteo D'Ambrosio relates Belloli's model to the *Poema preciso* (An Accurate Poem), conceived by Marinetti in 1932 (see Fig. 2b) and based on diagrammatic or contrasting oppositions created from a severely reduced lexical range.[38] Belloli hence updated the style of poetic-visual research in the light of the principles of a 'mechanical' aesthetics that had been taken up by the Futurist movement during the 1920s.

While it was Marinetti himself who called Belloli's poetry "the future of Futurism",[39] numerous critics also maintain that Belloli was a precursor of the phenomenon of Concrete Poetry, which emerged in the early 1950s in Switzerland and Bra-

38 See D'Ambrosio: "Di come Carlo Belloli, partendo dal 'poema preciso' marinettiano, divenne un precursore della poesia concreta."
39 "Belloli ha intuito il futuro del futurismo." Marinetti: "Testi-poemi murali di Carlo Belloli", p. 280.

zil as a combination of linguistic elements in which the typographical effect is more important than verbal significance. Recent speculation even suggests that he had a direct influence on the Noigandres group.[40] In 1951, Belloli exhibited some of his *Corpi di poesia* (Bodies of Poetry,) at the Circulo Cultural Paulista thanks to the mediation of Emilio Villa, and in 1953 he held a solo show at the Ipiranga Club and then was involved in a poetry soirée at the Italo-Brazilian Cultural Institute of São Paulo.[41] It has been suggested that there was also a direct contact between Belloli and Eugen Gomringer in 1945 in Rome, where both poets lived to pursue their studies; however, no concrete evidence has yet been found to confirm this conjecture. Belloli himself went on to distance himself from Concrete Poetry, accusing it of neglecting the relationship between semantic-morphological and semiotic-typographic structures.[42] In any case, the recent scholarly attention to Concrete Poetry in Italy has rekindled an interest in Belloli and significantly helped to revive the debate on the legacy of Futurist poetry in post-war Italian poetry.

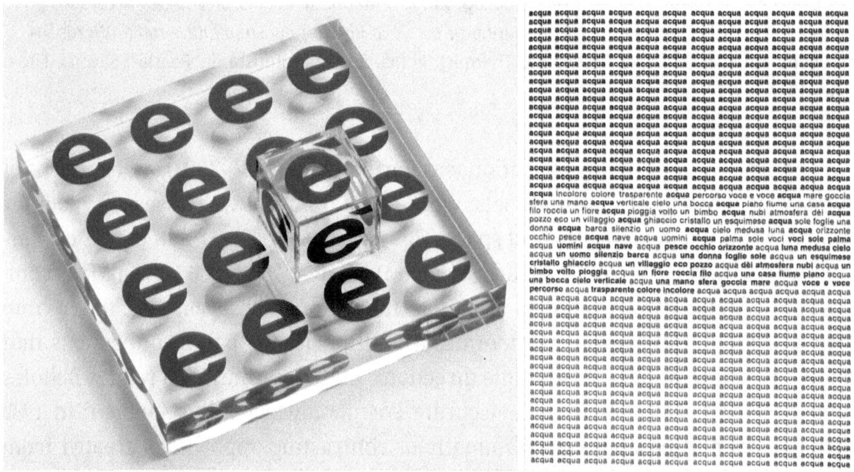

Fig. 3a: Arrigo Lora Totino: *eé – fonema plastico* (EÉ: Sculpted Phoneme, 1967). **Fig. 3b:** Carlo Belloli: *Texte poème poème texte* (Text Poem Poem Text, 1961).

40 On the Noigandres group and Brazilean Concrete Poetry, see Odile Cisneros' essay in this volume of the Yearbook: "Russian Futurism and Brazilian Avant-garde Poetry: Incorporation, Translation, Convergence."
41 See Vinci: "Carlo Belloli in Brasile: Un geniale precursore della poesia concreta."
42 Belloli: "Poesia audiovisuale", pp. 206–207.

It was the Turinese poet Arrigo Lora Totino (1928–2016) who first introduced Belloli into this debate and included him in his anthology of Concrete Poetry, *Modulo* (1966). His personal relationship with the slightly older poet had a significant influence on the direction of his research, as can be seen in his *Verbotetture: Architetture di parole nello spazio della pagina* (Verbotectures: Word Architectures in the Space of a Page), begun in the second half of the 1960s,[43] as well as in his *Corpi di poesia* (Bodies of Poetry), made of Plexiglas from 1967 onward (see Fig. 3a). The latter series recall a homonymous cycle of works created by Belloli in 1951 using the very same material.[44] In 1959, Belloli's theorization of Audiovisual Poetry – intended as a "unified relationship of word, sound and visuality"[45] – inspired a particular interest in the relationship between sign and sound in Lora Totino.

This was already apparent in his early writings on the notion of concretism in poetry. In a text that appeared in *Modulo*, "Ragioni di una scelta per un'antologia della poesia concreta" (Selection Criteria for an Anthology of Concrete Poetry), the author dwells on the "optophonetic" values of Concrete texts and identifies a series of "legitimate precedents", including Marinetti's Words-in Freedom, Velimir Khlebnikov's *zaum'* (transrational) poetry and Luigi Russolo's *rumorismo.* The text concludes with a reference to Belloli's *Texte poème poème texte* (1961) (see Fig. 3b), stating that it offers "an indication to act [...] in an attempt to rationalize a chosen matter in its state of shapeless freedom."[46] It is thanks to this polarization between freedom and rationality that Lora Totino was able to freely associate modular solutions with more dynamic and deconstructed approaches, accepting Mike Weaver's thesis about the oscillation of Concrete Poetry between Constructivism and Expressionism.[47]

Lora Totino's interest in the sonic dimension of poetry became more intense as his theoretical and historical investigation of Concretism expanded. In 1969, he curated, together with Dietrich Mahlow, *Poesia concreta: Indirizzi visuali e fonetici* (Concrete Poetry: Visual and Phonetic Directions), at the Venice Biennale. In an essay written for the catalogue, Lora Totino focusses on two Futurist manifestos

---

43 Regarding Lora Totino's verbal-visual production in this period, see Spignoli: "Arrigo Lora Totino 'architetto di parole': Dalle verbotetture ai cromofonemi."

44 See Lora Totino: "Nuovi corpi di poesia." Belloli's influence on Lora Totino can also be seen in an untitled text prepared for the catalogue of the exhibition *Omaggio a Carlo Belloli* (Homage to Carlo Belloli), organized by the Turinese artist at Studio Santandrea in Milan in 1977.

45 Solt: *Concrete Poetry. A World View*, p. 38.

46 "[...] un'indicazione ad agire [...] nello sforzo di razionalizzare una materia scelta nel suo stato di informe libertà". Lora Totino: "Ragioni di una scelta per un'antologia della poesia concreta", p. 23.

47 See Weaver: "Concrete Poetry." Lora Totino mentions this essay at the beginning of one of his last and most mature critical contributions on Concrete Poetry, "Poesia concreta."

of 1916: Marinetti's *La declamazione dinamica e sinottica* (Dynamic, Multichanneled Recitation) and Fortunato Depero's *L'onomalingua* (Onomalanguage), highlighting that "the poetic function is a system of listening where the poet lives permanently as one of the most perfect biological resonators. [...] The syllable, when stripped of all meaning, can give rise to a new poetic projection, due to its nature as a timbral noise."[48]

The influence of Marinetti's ideas came to the fore with particular strength in the *Poesia liquida* (Liquid Poetry, 1968), a form of sound poetry that involves the modulation of verses and words through a horn full of water built by Pietro Fogliati and named *Idromegafono* (Hydromegaphone). This was a concretization of Marinetti's call to "liquefy" the voice in the manifesto *Dynamic, Multichanneled Recitation,*[49] as the resistance of the water to the phonic vibrations emitted by the poet dilutes the lexical articulations into shapeless gurgles. The *Testi da tuffare* (Lyrics to Dive Into, 1968), written by Lora Totino for these liquid recitations, alternate Words-in Freedom with ironic and playful verbalizations similar to those in Depero's experimental *Onomalingua:*

vverbo liquido	lliquid verb
testo pesce	text fish
pesc pesc	fis fis
pesco parole d'acqua	I fish words of water
parole d'olio petrolio aglio	words of oil petroleum garlic
grasso grosso	fat big
gorgoglio...	gurgling...

Lora Totino's interest in Futurism was not just determined by his relationship with Belloli, but also by the artistic environment of Turin in the early 1960s. A metropolitan and industrial city, Turin looked to Futurism as a model for the design of a positive urban utopia that could overcome the contradictions of subjectivity that had characterized the immediate post-war period.[50] Besides the influence of Pinot Gallizio – a friend of the Futurist artist Farfa, who drew a great deal of inspiration from Futurism's theories, passing them along to Asger Jorn[51] – the Futurist exhibitions held in the city were of great importance in shaping Lora Totino's

48 "La funzione poetica è un sistema di ascolto ove il poeta vive in permanenza come un risuonatore biologico dei più perfezionati. [...] la sillaba, se spogliata d'ogni significazione, può dare origine a una nuova proiezione poetica, per la sua natura di rumore timbrico". Lora Totino: "Poesia da ascoltare", s.p.

49 Marinetti: "Dynamic, Multichanneled Recitation", p. 195.

50 Pola: "Dialoghi tra spazio e tempo: Il sistema dell'avanguardia", pp. 132–133.

51 Lista: "L'eredità futurista", p. 717.

milieu. The Municipal Gallery, for instance, showed *Aspetti del secondo futurismo torinese* (Aspects of Second-Wave Futurism in Turin, 1962) and a retrospective on Giacomo Balla (1963); these were followed by numerous exhibitions dedicated to individual Futurist artists organized by the galleries La Bussola, Martano, Narciso, Notizie and Il Punto, all of which also promoted extra-pictorial researches. These stimuli re-emerge in many of Lora Totino's subsequent works, such as the *Cromofonemi iridescenti* (Iridescent Chromophonemes, 1967), *Poesia ginnica* (Gymnastic Poetry, 1974), *Fotodinamiche simultanee* (Simultaneous Photodynamics, 1976) and *Pappapoemi* (Eat Poetry 1981). At the same time, the artist continued his revaluation of the historical avant-garde, which led him, amongst other things, to performing texts by Marinetti and Depero in numerous venues and on the anthology of sound poetry *Futura*, published by Cramps Records in 1978.

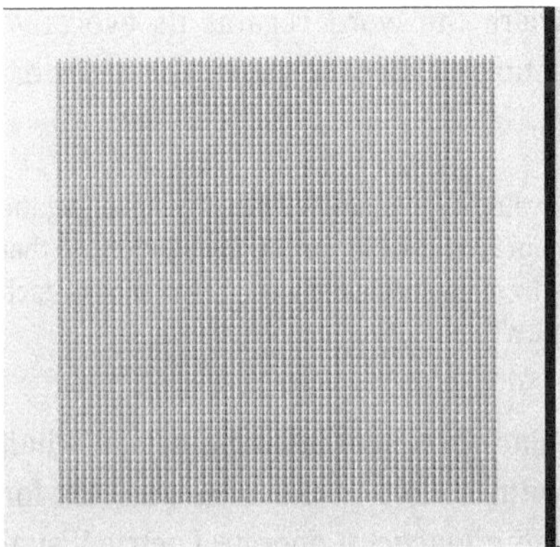

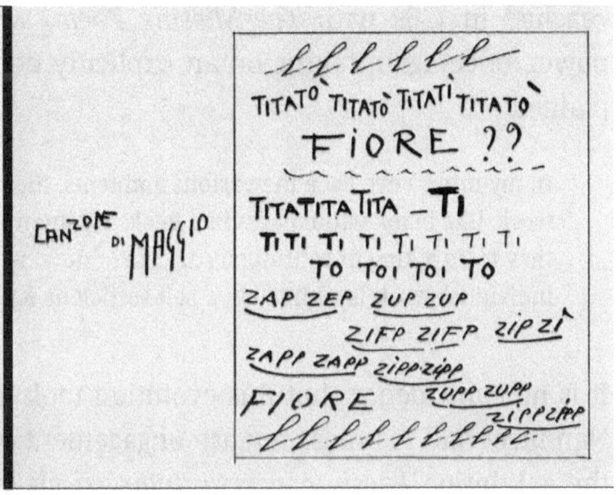

Fig. 4a: Maurizio Nannucci: *Dattilogramma* (Typescript, 1965). **Fig. 4b:** Giacomo Balla: *Canzone di maggio* (May Song, 1915).

'Visual' permeations in Maurizio Nannucci's poetic research

The artistic debut of the Florentine artist Maurizio Nannucci (1939-) was also connected to Concretism: the scholarship he won at the Ulm School thanks to Pio Manzù and his attending the Kunsthochschule Berlin-Weißensee for two semesters between 1960 and 1961, brought him into contact with the work of Gomringer and other members of the Concrete Poetry movement. His first *Dattilogrammi* (Typescripts; see Fig. 4a) date back to 1964: these are linear and minimal graphemic textures created with an Olivetti Lettera 22 typewriter, which had been designed by Marcello Nizzoli, who was once a member of the Futurist group

Nuove Tendenze (New Tendencies). In July 1967, Nannucci met Belloli at the Trieste group exhibition *Segni nello spazio* (Signs in Space), which saw the participation of the former as an artist and the latter as the author of one of the critical essays included in the catalogue. Two other opportunities for collaboration followed: in February 1968, the Centro Ricerche Estetiche F-Uno group, featuring Lanfranco Baldi, Auro Lecci, Paolo Masi and Nannucci, showed their works at Studio 2B in Bergamo, with a catalogue introduced by Belloli; in 1969, he again presented Nannucci's *Dattilogrammi*, this time in a book issued by Exempla, a publishing house founded in Florence by the artist himself. In 1967, Nannucci created his first 'writings' by means of neon tubes hung up in gallery spaces. These first environmental writings derived from the experience of Concretism,[52] but had the indexical and tautological character of coeval Conceptual Art. Works such as *Red Line* or *Corner* (1968) reduced phrases to purely deictic and assertive utterances. A turning point was reached in 1969 with *The Missing Poem*, where the word regains its evocative power, once again taking on an explicitly poetic and literary value. The artist explained:

> In my mind's eye I see the various ambients, the walls of the room in which I'm installing the work, like blank white pages in a book. My intention is to link the various installations so that they form a kind of continuous discourse flowing from one page to another, even though each individual work is ultimately a self-sufficient entity.[53]

It is no coincidence that this evolution took place precisely during a period when Nannucci had his most intense engagement with Belloli. In the catalogue text for the exhibition *Poesia concreta: Indirizzi visuali e fonetici* (Concrete Poetry: Visual and Phonetic Directions; Biennale di Venezia, 25 September – 10 October 1969), where Nannucci also exhibited his work, Belloli insisted on the environmental potential of his Visual Poetry, stating that "the visual poem suitable to be hung on a wall [...] extends the library through an immediate and continuous use of a different degree of readability. It requires a fully optical-psychological participation and

---

52 "For me, neon was above all writing [...] it made it possible to bring light to words and texts that I had made in the early 1960s with the typewriter in the *dattilogrammi* and other linear texts where I used colour." [Per me il neon è soprattutto scrivere [...] è la possibilità di dare luce a parole e testi che nei primi anni Sessanta avevo steso con la macchina da scrivere nelle pagine dei dattilogrammi e di altri testi lineari in cui facevo uso del colore]. Nannucci quoted in Grazioli: "Maurizio Nannucci", p. 58.

53 Friedel: "A Conversation with Maurizio Nannucci", p. 197.

leads to a differentiated visual perception."[54] With the creation of *Poemi stradali* (Street Poems), based on the use of advertising techniques, Visual Poetry then moves "from the internal to the external space, from the home to the street."[55] It should also be noted that, for Belloli, "the street poem participates in the external space of architecture and creates an unusual, yet characteristic animation of anonymous urban spaces."[56] This tendency of poetry exhibited in conventional outdoor locations to modify communal spaces[57] is exactly what interested Nannucci from 1969 onwards. He continuously increased the size of his neon constructions, both indoors and outdoors, clearly inspired by his Futurist predecessors:

> If we want to look for a historical antecedent for Nannucci's mindset, we must go back to the Futurist approach inspired by inventors such as Marconi, brimming with waves and energies, following the entire path that extends from Antonio Sant'Elia's *Propaganda luminosa* to the final sparks when still, in the middle of the Second World War, the unlimited possibilities of expanding the signification of writing in space were reaffirmed, and when a final manifesto predicted "futuristic conurbations where luminous notice boards march over our heads and drive the reader towards other squares-pages".[58]

Although Marinetti was amongst the most convinced supporters of the aesthetic potential of the "avvisi luminosi",[59] Nannucci rather seems to apply here one of

54 "Il poema visuale a situabilità parietale [...] estende la biblioteca al ricorso immediato e continuo di un diverso grado di leggibilità a partecipazione più compiutamente ottico-psicologica e a percezione visiva differenziata." Belloli: "Poesia visuale: Affermazione di una tendenza", p. 24.

55 "[...] dallo spazio interno a quello esterno, dalla casa alla strada." Belloli: "Poesia visuale: Affermazione di una tendenza", p. 24.

56 "Il poema stradale partecipa dello spazio esterno dell'architettura e determina una inconsueta animazione, caratterizzante, dell'anonimato urbano." Belloli: "Poesia visuale: Affermazione di una tendenza", p. 24.

57 See Spignoli: *La parola si fa spazio*, p. 81.

58 "Se vogliamo cercare un antecedente storico all'impostazione mentale di Nannucci bisogna risalire piuttosto al clima di quel futurismo "marconiano", tutto pervaso da onde ed energie, lungo tutta la parabola che va dalla Propaganda Luminosa di Antonio Sant'Elia fino alle ultime scintille, quando ancora, in piena Seconda Guerra Mondiale, si ribadivano le possibilità illimitate di espansione e significazione della scrittura nello spazio, vaticinando, nell'ultimo manifesto, 'urbanismi futuristici [*sic.*] i cui avvisi luminosi marcianti in alto sospingono il lettore verso altre piazze-pagine'". Mugnaini: "Maurizio Nannucci." The quote within the quote is a slightly imperfect reference to the 1942 manifesto *L'arte tipografica di guerra e dopoguerra* (The Art of Typography During and After the War), written by Marinetti together with Alfredo Trimarco, Luigi Scrivo and Piero Bellanova, and published in the journal *Graphicus* 32:5 (May 1942), a special issue on Futurism where they talk about "urbanismi futuristi i cui avvisi luminosi marcianti in alto spingono il lettore verso altre piazze-pagine altri libri altre azioni altri voli sopramarini e stratosferici."

59 Marinetti: "Gli avvisi luminosi" e "Contro gli spegnitori di Milano".

the solutions suggested by the Futurist Escodamè (Michele Leskovic), who suggested in *Immensificare la poesia* (Intensify Poetry, 1933) to "hand over to poets the facades of our houses, our new architectures, so that they replace typefaces with letters of light bulbs and neon tubes."[60] Nannucci relies precisely upon a process of poetic magnification and intensification, given that imaginative phrases arouse a "sense of incommensurability"[61] by interconnecting the experience of reading and viewing.

New abstract verbalizations: Mimmo Rotella's *Epistaltismo*

In the years when Belloli was planning "the future of Futurism" in physical-visual terms, the Calabrian artist Mimmo Rotella (1918–2006) was re-elaborating its phonic-performative aspects in the form of *Epistaltismo*, a type of sound poetry that focussed on the condensation of onomatopoeias and abstract verbalizations, influenced by jazz. The term 'epistaltic' is a neologism coined by the artist for its evocative power. The origin of the term remains unclear, but Enzo Minarelli speculates that it derived from the adjective 'diastaltic', used by the Greek philosopher Aristoxenus to describe exhortative music that propels the listener into action.[62] If we then consider that *épos* means 'word', the term 'epistaltic' could indicate an incitement to treat verbs as action, which is precisely what Rotella sought to achieve with this kind of performative poetry.

The *Manifesto dell'epistaltismo*, written in Paris in 1949, was in line with the ideas of Lettrism, a French poetic movement that aimed at breaking down words into letters and reassembling them into meaningless sound structures. Created by Isidore Isou in 1946, it also had distinct Futurist roots.[63] Rotella probably received his first Futurist inspirations in Naples, where he met Emilio Notte and Eugenio Viti,[64] both close to Cangiullo, and later in Rome, where Prampolini was energetically engaged in promoting avant-garde culture through the Art Club, an association of artists he had founded with Pericle Fazzini, Luigi Montanarini

60 "[...] bisogna dare loro [= ai poeti] le facciate delle nostre case, delle nostre nuove architetture; sostituendo ai caratteri tipografici le lettere di lampadine e tubi neon." Escodamè: "Immensificare la poesia", p. 490.

61 Tazzi: "Maurizio Nannucci", p. 104.

62 Minarelli: *La voce regina: Poesia sonora in pubblico*, p. 70.

63 See Ferrua: "Sur quelques analogies entre le futurisme et le lettrisme" and Gerber: "Futurismo und Lettrisme: Grenzüberschreitende Stadttexte der Avant-garde."

64 Rotella: *L'ora della lucertola*, p. 18.

and others, and where Rotella exhibited in March 1949.[65] We shall also consider the influence of the – by then elderly – Giacomo Balla, who had created phonetic texts with a structure similar to that of Epistaltic poems in the 'heroic' phase of Futurism.

It was Rotella himself who identified Futurism as part of the historical precedents for Epistaltism, leaving handwritten notes on a 1956 typescript of the manifesto, now held in the Archives of the Mimmo Rotella Foundation in Milan. The Dadaists Hugo Ball and Kurt Schwitters are the first to be named here, with a partially erroneous reference to the soirée of 30 March 1916 at the Cabaret Voltaire in Zurich.[66] Futurism is acknowledged immediately after, alongside the date of 1914 and a mention of Marinetti, completed by a reference to the *zaum'* poetry of Aleksei Kruchenykh. This mention of the Russian Futurist appears to be a later addition to the list, as it is inserted in blue pencil in the space between two lines written in pen. Presumably this means that Rotella only at a later stage became aware of the Russian Futurists. The document is furthermore of interest because of its allusions to artists connected to the musical world, such as Edgar Varèse, Pierre Boulez, Pierre Schaeffer and his *musique concrète.* It also contains some information on the earliest channels of circulation for Rotella's invention. His notes mention a recording of Epistaltic poems at the request of the American poet Archibald MacLeish for Harvard University in 1952; an interview with the radio station WDAF in Kansas City and footage for the Italian RAI television programmes *Arrivi e partenze* (Arrivals and Departures, 1954), *Permette una domanda?* (May I Ask a Question?, 1956), as well as for *La settimana INCOM* (The Weekly Newsreel) of 4 March 1955.

Some other archival documents are useful for retracing the relationship between Epistalticism and Futurism, for example *Appunti per un breve documentario* (Notes for a Short Documentary, 1955), a page filled with notes for the INCOM newsreel, where we can read: "Today we live in the middle of noises so [...] we must be taught how to listen to them. The language of art today must be inspired by sounds and noises."[67] The tone and content of this statement recall similar con-

65 Celant: *Mimmo Rotella*, p. 34. The Futurist legacy of the Art Club has been discussed by Gabriele Simongini in "La nuova Italia dell'Art Club 1945–1964" and "La 'scomoda' libertà dell'Art Club".
66 Schwitters was not actually present at that evening and only began to devote himself to phonetic poetry in 1919. On 30 March 1916, the simultaneous poem *L'Amiral cherche une maison à louer* (The Admiral is Looking for a House to Rent) and *Chant nègre I & II* (Negro Song I & II) were performed for the first time by Huelsenbeck, Tzara, Janco and Ball.
67 "Oggi noi viviamo in mezzo ai rumori perciò [...] dobbiamo essere educati a saperli ascoltare – il linguaggio d'arte oggi deve ispirarsi a suoni e rumori". Reproduced in Celant: *Mimmo Rotella*, p. 285. INCOM (Industria Corti Metraggi) was founded in 1938 by Sandro Pallavicini to produce

siderations by Luigi Russolo in his brochure *L'arte dei rumori* (The Art of Noises, 1916): "Every manifestation of life is accompanied by noise. Noise is therefore familiar to our ears and has the power of immediately recalling life itself. [...] We are therefore convinced that by selecting, coordinating and controlling all noises we shall enrich humankind with new and unexpected pleasure."[68] And in the last chapter he explains: "The ear does not understand the confused and fragmentary noises of life. Therefore, the ear must feel them dominated, enslaved, completely mastered, defeated and forced to become an element of art."[69]

In an interview with the American ABC radio show *New Sounds for You* on 15 March 1956, Rotella declared that the musical technique adopted for his compositions involves alternating opaque and vibrating sounds to achieve at the same time contrast and harmony. Here, too, the influence of Russolo's poetics is evident: "We want to tune these extraordinarily diverse sounds, regulating them harmonically and rhythmically. Tuning noises does not mean removing from them all irregularities of tempo and intensity, which characterize their movements and vibrations, but rather giving gradation or pitch to the vibrations that are strongest and most predominant."[70]

Amongst the musical score-poems held at the Rotella Foundation there is an incomplete, undated transcript of two Dada compositions: Ball's *Gadji beri bimba* (1916) and Schwitters's *Ursonate* (1923–32). It is not possible to identify Rotella's sources in detail, but his performance of Christian Morgenstern's *Fisches Nachtgesang* (Night Song of a Fish, 1905) during the filming of *La settimana INCOM* in 1955 is indicative of his reasonably accurate knowledge of German experimental works. The score for the undated poem *Ventimila anni avanti Cristo* (Twenty Thousand Years Before Christ), on the other hand, contains a couple of childish pictograms and some symbols of the Greek alphabet alongside onomatopoeias and abstract verbalizations. This gives us the possibility to juxtapose Epistalticism and Lettrism.

propaganda documentaries and later continued to be one of the most popular sources of information and current affairs in Italy.

68 "Ogni manifestazione della nostra vita è accompagnata dal rumore. Il rumore è quindi famigliare al nostro orecchio, ed ha il potere di richiamarci immediatamente alla vita stessa. [...] Siamo certi dunque che scegliendo, coordinando e dominando tutti i rumori, noi arricchiremo gli uomini di una nuova voluttà insospettata." Russolo: *L'arte dei rumori*, pp. 14–15.

69 "L'orecchio non si raccapezza fra i rumori confusi e frammentari della vita. Bisogna dunque che l'orecchio li senta dominati, asserviti, padroneggiati completamente, vinti e costretti a divenire elementi d'arte". Russolo: *L'arte dei rumori*, p. 91.

70 "Noi vogliamo intonare e regolare armonicamente e ritmicamente questi svariatissimi rumori. Intonare i rumori non vuol dire togliere ad essi tutti i movimenti e le vibrazioni irregolari di tempo e d'intensità, ma bensì dare un grado o tono, alla più forte e predominante di queste vibrazioni." Russolo: *L'arte dei rumori*, p. 14.

In a chart created in 1947, Isou had assigned nineteen noises commonly produced by the phonatory system – aspirations, wheezing, glottal stops and so on – to an equal number of letters from the Greek alphabet, so as to be able to insert them into his scores and make their declamation possible.[71]

Still, there are many reasons for identifying Futurism as the primary precedent for Epistalticism. Rotella's decision to draw up a systematic manifesto set out in a series of points, together with the detailed list of instructions to be followed in the creative processes, provides a clear connection with the early Italian avant-garde. Many of the ideas expressed in the manifesto are then reconnected to those of Futurist poetry: the identification of the word with sound; the urgent need to break down the 'dividing wall' between music and poetry; the escape from the articulations of a codified language; or the conception of voice as an "inexhaustible source of natural musical instruments."[72] These elements were all already present in both Marinetti's *Dynamic, Multichannelled Recitation* and Depero's *Onomalingua*, as well as entailed in the most advanced Dada evenings at the Cabaret Voltaire.[73] However, point 4 of the manifesto offers the clearest confirmation of the hypothesis of a privileged relationship with Futurism. Here, the author affirms that Epistaltic poetry frees words from their ordinary function "to turn them into tracer rockets hurled against the decrepit buildings of syntax and vocabulary."[74] This is a sentence that in all respects takes up the rhetoric of Marinetti's founding manifesto: for the explosive image of words as rockets, the derogatory image of syntax as a dilapidated building, the Promethean value attributed to

71 See Curtay: *La Poésie lettriste*, pp. 42–43.

72 "fonte inesauribile di strumenti musicali naturali". Rotella: *Manifesto dell'epistaltismo.*

73 Opened on 5 February 1916, the Cabaret Voltaire soon relinquished its originally conventional programme – featuring traditional recitation of old-fashioned poetry and folk songs – in favour of truly avant-garde performances, strongly indebted to Futurism. It was Huelsenbeck who first overturned the original trend, reciting poems supposedly derived from Africa (one of which was significantly entitled *Mafarka*) at the end of February. Soon after, Tzara developed his own *chants nègres* and, on 29 March 1916, he performed the simultaneous poem *L'Amiral cherche une maison a louer* (The Admiral is Looking for a House to Rent) together with Janco and Huelsenbeck. A "truly Futurist style of declamation", however, "was only introduced to the Cabaret by Alberto Spaini. We know that on 12 May 1917 he recited Meriano's *Gemma* and on 14 April 1917 he performed Marinetti's *Bombardamento di Adrianopoli*, which he had seen Marinetti declaim on several occasions." Berghaus: "Futurism, Dada, and Surrealism: Some Cross-Fertilizations Among the Historical Avant-garde", p. 289. On the Futurist influence on Dada, see also Berghaus: "Futurism and the Genesis of Dada: Contacts, Contrasts and Continuities"; Lista: "La scena futurista e l'avanguardia storica", pp. XIX-XX; and Bozzi: *Dada da capo*, pp. 88–90. Francesco Cangiullo's contribution "Addiooo" to the single issue of the magazine *Cabaret Voltaire* (May 1916) should also be recalled.

74 "[...] per farne dei razzi traccianti contro gli edifici decrepiti della sintassi e del vocabolario". Rotella: *Manifesto dell'epistaltismo.*

the poetic enterprise, and the emphatic and combative tone of the statement as a whole.

There is a consistent recurrence of onomatopoeias and abstract verbalizations in Epistaltic poems, which are organized according to interruptions, syncopation and diversions of tone, confirming the direct return to the ideas of Marinetti. The structure of Rotella's declamation tables, however, moves away from *paroliberismo* and reverts to the handwritten scores of Giacomo Balla's simultaneous compositions such as *Macchina tipografica – Onomatopea rumorista* (The Printing Machine: Noise-Making Onomatopoeia Typewriter, 1914), *Paesaggio + temporale* (Landscape + Storm, 1915) or *Canzone di maggio* (May Song, 1915; see Fig. 4b). These verbal arrangements are linear, sometimes with elastic dilations caused by the act of writing itself. Not subjected to the same technological limitations as his predecessors, Rotella could record his recitations on magnetic tape and publish them in the magazine *OU*, founded and directed by Henri Chopin in 1964 as a continuation of *Cinquième Saison.*

In his performances, the artist alternated onomatopoeias and abstract verbalizations with jingles, laughter and blowing raspberries that reinforce the comic effect of the recitation, similar to *Piedigrotta*, performed by Cangiullo at the Sprovieri Gallery in Rome in 1914.[75] In Rotella's performances, in any case, phonetic rhythms combine with portmanteau words and haplological compounds produced according to a process of disassembly and reassembly of terms taken from the dictionary, a technique that recalls the additions and stratifications found in the artistic practice of *décollage.*[76] These verbal inventions show evident morphological affinities with various terms of the Italian language, so much so that they could be compared to the practice of grammelot. And yet, a logical precedent of this solution could be found, once again, in one of Balla's works, namely *Discussione di due critici sudanesi intorno al futurismo* (Discussion between Two Sudanese Critics on Futurism, 1914), which relied on the imitation of phonic and morphological values commonly found in pseudo-African languages. A similar approach was also

75 As noted by Marinetti in "Dynamic, Multichanneled Recitation."

76 The art of *décollage* was invented by Wolf Vostell in his Happenings in Paris in 1954. These first "dé-coll/age" paintings made up of layers of unstuck and decomposed posters were the *result* of an action, from which he later developed *The Theatre Takes Place on the Street.* This Happening on Rue de Tour de Vanves instructed the performers to read the texts on the posters, tear down layers of them to create new texts and to interpret through their gestures the elements that could be recognized on the posters. Thereby, the participants were able to go beyond the level of contemplating a work of art (e.g. a décollage) and to reflect critically on themselves and their relationship to reality by participating in a change of their environment. See Sandford: *Happenings and Other Acts*, pp. 310–388.

taken by Ball two years later, but Rotella's experiments remain closer to Futurist ideas for the more pressing rhythm of the declamation and the clearer interruptions between the sections, whose sudden variations of tone aim at the simultaneous expression of contrasting emotional states.

The influence of Words-in-Freedom on Lamberto Pignotti's collages

In a 1974 article, Pietro Favari noted a parallel between two periods of social, economic and political evolution in Italy that impacted on the visual interest of Italian poets. The first was the Giolittian era, when Futurists adapted artistic expression to the emerging industrial civilization;[77] the second corresponds to the 'economic miracle' of the early 1960s, when poets, "drawing on the experiences of Futurism, reintroduced a kind of poetry that takes account of the iconic value of communication."[78] The connection suggested by Favari is fully confirmed by Lamberto Pignotti (1926-), founder of the Gruppo 70 in Florence,[79] who remarked, in the early 1980s, that his *Poesia visiva* resembled Futurist Free-Word Tables.[80] His encounter with Futurism dates back to 1944, the year of Marinetti's death, when Pignotti was looking through magazines at the National Library in Florence. Apart from Futurist poetry and manifestos, he discovered Prampolini's *Arte polimaterica: Verso un'arte collettiva?* (Polymaterial Art: A Step Towards Collective Art?), published that very year. This resulted in his first experiments with graphic collages for a series of self-produced magazines.[81] Pignotti's interest continued for decades and was reinforced by his curiosity for synaesthesia,[82] which may explain his numerous tributes to Balla, Boccioni, Depero, Marinetti and Prampolini in works such as *Francobolli* (Stamps, 1973–75).

Collage largo (Large Collage) is the name that Pignotti gave to his technique of fusing words and images, almost as reflection of Marinetti's warning: "Words freed from punctuation will radiate out toward one another, their diverse magnetisms

77 Favari: "Strumenti verbali e iconici nella scrittura poetica italiana", p. 7.

78 "Ricollegandosi alle esperienze del futurismo, si ripropone una poesia che tenga conto del valore iconico della comunicazione." Favari: "Strumenti verbali e iconici nella scrittura poetica italiana", p. 11.

79 For further information on Gruppo 70, see Spignoli: *La poesia in immagine / L'immagine in poesia: Gruppo 70. Firenze 1963–2013.*

80 Pignotti: "Paroliberismo. Modelli di scrittura verbo-visiva futurista negli anni Dieci", p. 17.

81 See Cerritelli: "Lamberto Pignotti: Omaggio al futurismo", p. 7.

82 See Pignotti: *I sensi delle arti.*

will intersect, in proportion to the continuing dynamism of thought."[83] The Futurist influence also emerged in the early stages of his theoretical elaboration of *Poesia visiva*, for example in an essay on literature and industry published in *Il menabò* in 1962. There, Pignotti wrote a phrase that is highly revealing of the neo-avant-garde cooling down the Promethean momentum of the historical avant-garde. Regarding the need to update poetry and bring it in line with technological developments, he declared: "We don't need to make the stars retire so that we can embrace spaceships. We need to preserve the ability to talk about the moon even when we have regular transport service to take us to our planets."[84] The statement seems to placate the Futurist desire to kill off the moonlight,[85] and instead re-admits the stars and moon to the list of possible subjects for contemporary poetry, as long as the style of poetry – a technological or technologically updated one – makes something new out of an old theme. At the same time, Pignotti was fully aware of the normalizing rôle of the neo-avant-gardes in contemporary culture. At the *Convegno internazionale di artisti, critici e studiosi d'arte* (International Conference of Artists, Critics and Art Scholars) held in Rimini in September 1964, he declared that "the great turning point of the avant-garde comes when it moves from a concept of art for initiates alone to a concept of art for the masses."[86]

The Futurists already saw a need to adapt art and poetry to the technological developments in everyday life.[87] Pignotti's speech at a conference on *Arte e tecnologia* (Art and Technology) in Florence, organized by the Gruppo 70 in June 1964, drew on Marinetti's rhetoric when he distinguished technological art from avant-garde art: "We prefer the living to the dead, we prefer brothers to fathers. To the yellowed pages of the early twentieth-century avant-garde, we prefer the smell of the printer's ink on the pages that convey the morning news."[88] Old and new is not a contradiction but rather a 'homoeopathic' process in which the radicalism of the avant-garde is diluted in the media of mass communication.

---

83 Marinetti: "Answers to Objections", p. 117.

84 "Non si tratterà di mandare in pensione le stelle per assumere le astronavi. Bisognerà saper parlare della luna anche quando sarà istituito col nostro satellite un regolare servizio di linea." Pignotti: "L'industria che non si vede", p. 60.

85 See Marinetti: *Uccidiamo il chiaro di luna! / Tuons le clair de lune* (Let's Kill Off the Moonlight, 1909) and *Noi rinneghiamo i nostri maestri simbolisti, ultimi amanti della luna* (We Renounce our Symbolist Masters, the Last of All Lovers of the Moonlight, 1911).

86 "La grande svolta dell'avanguardia è quella che da una concezione per soli iniziati porta a una concezione di massa dell'arte." Pignotti: "Tecnica e ideologia", p. 78.

87 As described by Spignoli: *La parola si fa spazio*, pp. 148–149.

88 "Ai morti preferiamo i vivi, ai padri preferiamo i fratelli. Alle pagine ingiallite dell'avanguardia primonovecentesca preferiamo le pagine ancora odorose d'inchiostro tipografico con le notizie del mattino." Pignotti: "La suggestione di Gordon Flash", p. 107.

> Since technological art tackles the problems and ways of mass society, it is natural that it is conscious of the limited means of diffusion of art until now. [...] This is why we emphatically suggest that poetry should be transmitted by the loudspeakers in stadia at half-time during championship matches or that paintings should be exhibited on billboards along the highways.[89]

Pignotti's utopian proposal seems to resonate with Marinetti's idea of a poem that moves from the page to the wall and from the wall "towards the town-squares of tomorrow",[90] and with the theory of 'urban poetry' formulated by Belloli.[91] While the techniques and methods may change, the need to understand poetry as a means of social development remains the same for Pignotti. This is demonstrated by the numerous poetic actions organized by Gruppo 70 in Italian streets and squares, designed once again to achieve the all-encompassing integration of poetry into everyday life, as promoted by the Futurists.

The (paroliberist) *Schemi* by Stelio Maria Martini

The Futurist origins of Pignotti's *Collage largo* suggest a re-reading in this light of *Schemi* (Schemes, 1962), a visual masterpiece of the Neapolitan poet Stelio Maria Martini (1934–2016), who has already been mentioned as one of the main proponents of the critical rehabilitation of Futurist Visual Poetry. This peculiar *livre d'artiste* – characterized by the montage of linguistic and photographic fragments taken from gossip magazines, old writings, photographic scraps and religious icons – aims at recovering existential and sentimental values buried in the debris of the collective imagination. Compared to the bipartition of art and mass culture outlined by Favari, Martini's work occupies an intermediate position, as it uses material taken from advertising and magazines not in order to decode (or simply decompose) mass media languages, but to broaden the semantic potential of writing through the combination of irregular materials. Martini notes that it was the painter Mario Persico who initiated him into the practice of verbal-visual collage.[92] Persico was a pupil of Emilio Notte, a Futurist close to Cangiullo, and this is prob-

89 "Essendo quella tecnologica un'arte che assume i problemi e i modi della società di massa, è naturale che essa avverta la limitatezza dei veicoli di diffusione fin qui impiegati dall'arte. [...] Per questo proponiamo emblematicamente che la poesia venga trasmessa dagli altoparlanti degli stadi nell'intervallo delle partite di campionato o che le mostre di pittura vengano trasferite lungo le autostrade." Pignotti: "La suggestione di Gordon Flash", pp. 107–108.

90 "verso le piazze di domani." Marinetti: "Testi-poemi murali di Carlo Belloli", p. 280.

91 Spignoli: *La parola si fa spazio*, p. 145.

92 Giugliano: *Ciò che mostra il tempo*, p. 39.

ably how Martini first came to take an unprejudiced look at Futurist poetry. The ideas he received from Words-in Freedom and Free-Word Tables, in particular, helped him visualize the perceptual experience of polysemic spaces rich with multisensory values. As Dalila Colucci observes in a study entirely dedicated to the work:

> Martini's material semantics draws plenty from Futurist total aesthetics [...]. His collages capitalize on the model of the Free-Word Tables, exceeding their experimental juxtaposition of signifiers by way of the incorporation of other elements than the typographical ones, but also due to the philosophical implications of his idea of visuality, key to unprecedented poetic and intellectual faculties to be performed within the metamorphic modern world, increasingly bound to synesthetic exchanges.[93]

In his preface to *Schemi*, Martini informs us that, apart from printing words on paper, he also considered incorporating other media, both temporal and spatial: "If I had been able to do it in an equally practical way, I would have not hesitated to add auditory elements such as the sounds of instruments, accidental noises or human voices, etc., or elements in relief, mobile, olfactory, etc."[94] Martini's approach to visual writing reflects various aspects of Marinetti's thinking, starting from the idea that any "increase in the pace of life" requires a "balancing act between the physical, intellectual, and emotional upon the tightrope of speed, stretched between two opposite magnetic poles."[95] Indeed, Martini's collage-poem is based on a circular logic that accepts contradictions as elements of life itself.[96] Marinetti maintained that supporting "the absolute freedom of images or analogies" allows the poet to penetrate "into the essence of matter,"[97] just as for Martini the use of images as words demonstrates "the unpredictable power of reception and assimilation (and the adjustability) of sensibility itself and an enrichment of the poetic faculties in their own right."[98]

93 Colucci: "Stelio Maria Martini, 'Schemi', and the Po(i)etics of Collage", pp. 27–28.

94 "[...] se appena l'avessi potuto in maniera altrettanto pratica, non avrei esitato ad aggiungere elementi uditivi quali suoni di strumenti, accidentali o voci umane, ecc., elementi in rilievo, mobili, olfattivi, ecc." Martini: *Schemi*, s.p..

95 Marinetti: "Destruction of Syntax – Untrammeled Imagination – Words-in-Freedom", p. 122.

96 Colucci: "Stelio Maria Martini", p. 28.

97 Marinetti: "Destruction of Syntax – Untrammeled Imagination – Words-in-Freedom", p. 125.

98 "[...] l'imprevedibile potere di ricezione ed assimilazione (e l'orientabilità) della sensibilità stessa e un arricchimento delle stesse facoltà poetiche." Martini: *Schemi*, s.p.

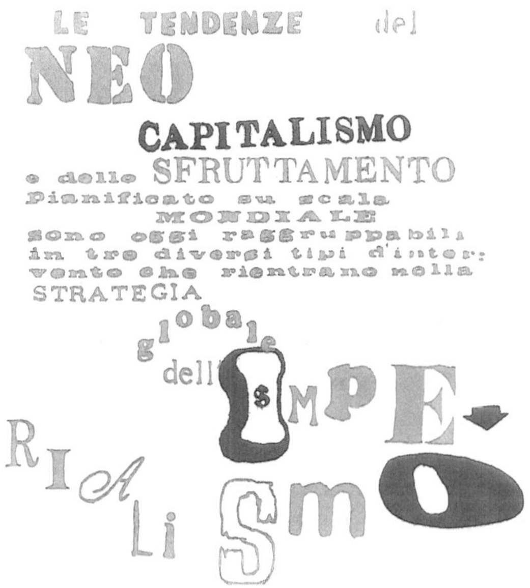

Fig. 5: A page from Paolo Albani: *Manifesto del Neo-Futurismo* (1967).

Note per il Manifesto del Neo-Futurismo by Paolo Albani

Any study of the legacy of Futurism in Italian verbal-visual poetry in the post-war period must consider the *Note per il Manifesto del Neo-Futurismo* (Notes for the Manifesto of Neo-Futurism) compiled by Paolo Albani (1946-), with drawings by Paolo della Bella (1944-). It is a small, square-format, twenty-page volume, printed in one hundred and fifty copies by Berlinghiero Buonarroti of the Gruppo Stanza in Compiobbi (near Fiesole) and published by the Feltrinelli Bookshop in Florence in 1967 (see Fig. 5). Albani's approach to Futurism dates back to the period he was a university student in Florence and met Eugenio Miccini, Lamberto Pignotti and Luciano Caruso. In the opening of his *Notes for the Manifesto* we read that "NEO Futurism was born to BURN DOWN the haystacks of the habit of BOREDOM of absorption in the SYSTEM" and "to tear out the backbone of ADVERTISING",[99] a

99 "IL NEO futurismo è nato per INCENDIARE i pagliai della consuetudine della NOIA dell'assorbimento nel SISTEMA [...] per squarciare l'ossatura della PUBBLICITÀ." "IL NEO futurismo è nato

theme dear to Gruppo 70. Albani also declared that he wanted to detach both from the "new surrogates for protest that amuse the ruling class" and from the "NEW avant-gardes, SICK with aestheticism".[100]

Albani's statement is symptomatic of the disagreements that could be found in the Italian neo-avant-garde. According Caruso, there existed three main currents: an 'official' or 'worldly' part, compromised by its ties with the publishing market and the academic world; a 'clandestine' part that separated aesthetic action from political commitment; and a 'genuinely alternative' (Caruso actually uses the term 'off') part, which included Caruso himself.[101] Albani also fits into this third part as he combines the incendiary quality of Aldo Palazzeschi's poetry with the revolutionary dynamics typical of the 1968 rebellion. Alongside the powerful drawings by Paolo della Bella, Albani's manifesto features reproductions of a number of sketches by Vladimir Mayakovsky concerning the Bolshevik revolution. This serves to underline Albani's ideological position regarding the need to align the artistic to the political revolution.[102] The fact that the publication of the *Notes* took place only five days after the killing of Che Guevara is indicative of this, too. Compared to the generally detached attitude of the neo-avant-garde, Albani's Neo-Futurism rekindled the Promethean fervour of the historical avant-garde, but with a re-defined ideological orientation.

Albani rejected the institutionalization of the neo-avant-garde. To underline this fact, he used a manual screen-printing technique, closer to old artisanal techniques than industrial production methods. In this esoeditorial (that is, independent) approach, he combined the typographic experimentation of Italian Futurism with the use of lithography, probably the most advanced technology of the 1910s, widely used in Russian Futurism.[103] His work – which can be seen as an intermediate form between the genre of the programmatic manifesto typical of Futurism and Visual Poetry – thus fits into a long tradition and tries to resolve the separation between theory and practice in the early avant-garde. Indeed, Albani applied some of the compositional principles of Words-in Freedom to the manifesto form,

---

per INCENDIARE i pagliai della consuetudine della NOIA dell'assorbimento nel SISTEMA […] per squarciare l'ossatura della PUBBLICITÀ." Paolo Albani: *Manifesto del Neo-Futurismo.*

100 "[…] nuovi surrogati della protesta che divertono la classe dominante […] NUOVE avanguardie MALATE di estetismo" "[…] nuovi surrogati della protesta che divertono la classe dominante […] NUOVE avanguardie MALATE di estetismo." Paolo Albani: *Manifesto del Neo-Futurismo.*

101 Caruso: "Contributi per una storia dei gruppi culturali a Napoli (1958–70)", p. 162.

102 See Echaurren & Salaris: *Controcultura in Italia 1967–1977: Viaggio nell'underground*, pp. 65–66.

103 See, for instance, the six lithographed poetry books authored by Aleksei Kruchenykh in collaboration with Larionov, Goncharova and others, produced between October 1912 and February 1913. Janecek: "Kruchenykh contra Gutenberg."

where we can observe the abolition of punctuation and the alternation of different fonts and characters, although the use of capital letters is limited to the highlighting of verbs and keywords. Also recurrent is the alternation of upper- and lowercase letters or of different graphic styles, in order to intensify the rhythmic nature of the text.

Reinterpreting the genre of the manifesto allowed Albani to reduce subjectivity and to reconsider the poetic operation in programmatic terms. The information provided to readers is arranged on each page like verses from a de-structured linear poem (e.g. Mallarmé's *Un coup de dés*); while some short Words-in-Freedom brighten up the reading, and geometric figures and other iconic fragments multiply the levels of interpretation. Consequently, there is an interplay of attractions between words and images. Freed from diacritical constraints, the message expands into the space of the page by means of graphic and chromatic magnetisms, still following Marinetti's "continuing dynamism of thought."[104]

Conclusions

As we have seen, the innovations of Futurist paroliberism entered the imagination of Italian artists and poets after 1945, despite the movement's fluctuating critical fortunes and initially problematic relationship with the neo-avant-garde. Carlo Belloli was an important intermediary who reconnected Futurist poetic experimentalism with the innovations in Concrete Poetry. His lesson was taken up by Arrigo Lora Totino who, beginning with Concretism, extended the verbo-visual and poetic-performative possibilities of Futurism by means of new inventions. It was again a relationship with Belloli that suggested to Maurizio Nannucci the possibility of expanding poetry on an environmental scale through the use of neon. In other ways, Mimmo Rotella took up both paroliberism and Futurist noise art to approach and overcome the solutions of French Lettrism. Through the study of Futurist theory, Lamberto Pignotti then elaborated forms of Visual Poetry capable of spreading into social spaces. If Stelio Maria Martini re-modelled the Futurist Free-Word Tables to obtain synaesthetic images, Paolo Albani ultimately re-invented the form of the manifesto as suggested by Futurism. Italian verbo-visual poetry of the second half of the twentieth century thus showed itself to be firmly rooted in Futurist theory and practice. It finally fulfilled the long-ignored need for a complete and systematic reclaiming of a historical heritage and gave rise to a Neo-Futurist aesthetics.

---

104 Marinetti: "Answers to Objections", p. 117.

Bibliography

Agnese, Gino, "Prima Marinetti, poi McLuhan." Walter Pedullà, ed.: *Il futurismo nelle avanguardie.* Milano: Ponte alle Grazie, 2010. 413–416.

Albani, Paolo: *Note per il Manifesto del Neo-Futurismo.* Firenze: Libreria Feltrinelli, 1967.

Ballerini, Luigi, ed.: *Italian Visual Poetry 1912–1972.* Exhibition catalogue. New York: Finch College Museum, in Conjunction with the 8th Triennial Congress of the Associazione Internazionale per gli Studi di Lingua e Letteratura Italiana, New York, 25–28 April 1973. New York: Istituto Italiano di Cultura. Distributed by Wittenborn, 1973.

Barilli, Renato: "Marinetti e il nuovo sperimentalismo." *Il Verri* 33 (1970): 89–102.

Barilli, Renato, and Angelo Guglielmi, eds.: *Gruppo 63: Critica e teoria.* Torino: Teso & Immagine, 2003.

Belloli, Carlo: "Poesia audiovisuale." Pino Masnata: *Poesia visiva: Storia e teoria.* Roma: Bulzoni, 1984. 204–208.

Belloli, Carlo: "Poesia visuale: Affermazione di una tendenza." Dietrich Mahlow, and Arrigo Lora-Totino, eds.: *Poesia concreta: Indirizzi visuali e fonetici.* Venezia: La Biennale, 1969. 13–18.

Berghaus, Günter: "Futurism, Dada, and Surrealism: Some Cross-Fertilizations Among the Historical Avant-garde." G. Berghaus, ed.: *International Futurism in Arts and Literature.* Berlin: De Gruyter, 2000. 271–304

Berghaus, Günter: "Futurism and the Genesis of Dada: Contacts, Contrasts and Continuities." Walter Pedullà, ed.: *Il futurismo nelle avanguardie.* Roma: Ponte Sisto, 2010. 137–156.

Berghaus, Günter: "Violence, War, Revolution: Marinetti's Concept of a Futurist Cleanser for the World." *Annali d'italianistica* 27 (2009): 23–71.

Berghaus, Günter: "The Historiography of Italian Futurism." G. Berghaus, ed.: *Handbook of International Futurism.* Berlin & Boston: De Gruyter, 2019. 3–27.

Berghaus, Günter: "The Postwar Reception of Futurism: Repression or Recuperation?" Geert Buelens, Harald Hendrix, and Monica Jansen, eds.: *The History of Futurism: The Precursors, Protagonists, and Legacies.* Lanham/MD: Lexington Books, 2012. 377–403.

Bertozzi, Barbara: "An Interview with George Segal." B. Bertozzi, ed.: *George Segal.* Milano: Charta, 1994. 26–29.

Bozzi, Paola: *Dada da capo: Protesta e poesia nel segno del Cabaret Voltaire.* Milano: Mimesis, 2018.

Calvesi, Maurizio: *Il futurismo.* Milano: Fabbri, 1967.

Calvesi, Maurizio: *Avanguardia di massa.* Milano: Feltrinelli, 1978.

Cangiullo, Francesco: "Addiooo." *Cabaret Voltaire* 1 (1916): 30.

Caramel, Luciano: "Prampolini e Burri e la materia attiva." L. Caramel, ed.: *Prampolini e Burri e la materia attiva.* Milano: Fonte d'Abisso, 1990: 9–15.

Caruso, Luciano: "Contributi per una storia dei gruppi culturali a Napoli (1958–70)." *Logos* 1 (1973): 162–176.

Caruso, Luciano, and Stelio Maria Martini: "La 'fuga in avanti' del futurismo." L. Caruso, and S.M. Martini, eds.: *Tavole parolibere futuriste 1912–1944.* Vol. 1. Napoli: Liguori, 1975. 1–7.

Caruso, Luciano, and Stelio Maria Martini: "Le tavole parolibere, ovvero La 'rivoluzione culturale' dei futuristi." L. Caruso, and S. M. Martini, eds.: *Tavole parolibere futuriste, 1912–1944: Antologia.* Vol. 2. Napoli: Liguori, 1977. 13–56.

Celant, Germano: *Mimmo Rotella: Catalogo ragionato.* Vol. 1. Pt. 1. *1944–1961.* Milano: Skira, 2016.

Cerritelli, Claudio: "Lamberto Pignotti: Omaggio al futurismo." Lamberto Pignotti: *Ricostruzione dell'universo futurista.* Firenze: Vallecchi, 2013. 7–13.

Colucci, Dalila: "Stelio Maria Martini, 'Schemi', and the Po(i)etics of Collage." *Piano b* 5 (2020): 23–50.

Curi, Fausto: "Una stilistica della materia." F. Curi: *Perdita d'aureola.* Torino: Einaudi, 1977. 135–169.

Curtay, Jean-Paul: *La Poésie lettriste.* Paris: Seghers, 1974.

D'Ambrosio: Matteo: "Di come Carlo Belloli, partendo dal 'Poema preciso' marinettiano, divenne un precursore della Poesia concreta." *ZRAlt!: Rivista multimediale della Zona Rossa* 6:23–24 (Winter 2018 – Spring 2019): 1–19.

De Maria, Luciano: "Marinetti poeta e ideologo." Filippo Tommaso Marinetti: *Teoria e invenzione futurista.* Milano: Mondadori, 1968. XIX-LXXVII.

Di Stefano, Eva: "I futuristi e l'estetica della guerra." Laura Auteri, Matteo Di Gesù, and Salvatore Tedesco, eds.: *La cultura in guerra: Dibattiti, protagonisti, nazionalismi (1870–1922).* Roma: Carocci, 2015. 243–252.

Drucker, Johanna: "Experimental, Visual, and Concrete: A Note on Historical Context and Basic Concepts." Eric Vos, K. David Jackson, and Johanna Drucker, eds.: *Experimental, Visual, Concrete: Avant-garde Poetry since the 1960s.* Amsterdam: Rodopi, 1996. 39–64.

Echaurren, Pablo, Salaris, Claudia: *Controcultura in Italia 1967–1977: Viaggio nell'underground.* Torino: Bollati Boringhieri, 1999.

Emerson, Lori: *Reading Writing Interfaces: From the Digital to the Bookbound.* Minneapolis/MN: Minnesota University Press, 2014.

Escodamè: "Immensificare la poesia." Luciano Caruso, and Stelio Maria Martini, eds.: *Tavole parolibere futuriste 1912–1944.* Vol. 2. Napoli: Liguori, 1977. 488–491.

Falqui, Enrico: *Il futurismo. Il novecentismo.* Roma: ERI, 1953.

Fameli, Pasquale: "L'avanguardia presa in parola: Caruso, Martini e il riscatto futurista della materia." *Piano b 5* (2020): 85–107.

Favari, Pietro: "Strumenti verbali e iconici nella scrittura poetica italiana." *D'ars* 70 (1974): 5–28.

Ferrua, Pietro: "Sur quelques analogies entre le futurisme et le lettrisme." Béla Köpeczi, and György M. Vadja, eds.: *Actes du VIIIe Congrès de l'Association Internationale de Littérature Comparée, Budapest, 12–17 août 1976 = Proceedings of the 8th Congress* of the International Comparative Literature Association, Budapest, 12–17 August 1976. Stuttgart: Kunst und Wissen / Bieber, 1980. 699–706. Reprinted in *Cahiers roumains d'études littéraires* 6:1 (1978): 79–84.

Fisher, Margaret: "Introduction." M. Fisher, ed.: *Radia: Pino Masnata's Gloss of the 1933 Futurist Radio Manifesto.* Emeryville/CA: Second Evening Art, 2012. 5–68.

Flora, Francesco: *Dal romanticismo al futurismo.* Milano: Mondadori, 1921.

Friedel, Helmut: "A Conversation with Maurizio Nannucci." *Maurizio Nannucci: Another Notion of Possibility.* Wien: Wiener Secession, 1995. 193–197.

Gerber, Andri: "Futurismo und Lettrisme: Grenzüberschreitende Stadttexte der Avant-garde." Vittorio Magnago Lampugnani, and Matthias Noell, eds.: *Stadtformen: Die Architektur der Stadt zwischen Imagination und Konstruktion.* Zürich: GTA, 2005. 40–55.

Giugliano, Dario: *Ciò che mostra il tempo. Stelio Maria Martini e la visualizzazione della scrittura poetica.* Roma: Meltemi, 2020.

Grazioli, Elio: "Maurizio Nannucci." *Flash Art* 123 (1984): 58–59.

Hecht, Peter: "The 'paragone' Debate: Ten Illustrations and a Comment." *Simiolus: Netherlands Quarterly for the History of Art* 14:2 (1984): 125–136.

Jacobbi, Ruggero, ed.: *Poesia futurista italiana.* Parma: Guanda, 1968.

Janecek, Gerald: "Kruchenykh contra Gutenberg." Margit Rowell, and Deborah Wye, eds.: *The Russian Avant-Garde, 1910–1934.* New York: Museum of Modern Art, 2002. 41–49.

Kern, Stephen: *The Culture of Time and Space.* Cambridge/MA: Harvard University Press, 1983.
Lista, Giovanni: “Dal paroliberismo al libro-oggetto.” G. Lista, and Ada Masoero, eds.: *Futurismo 1909–2009.* Milano: Skira, 2009. 293–313.
Lista, Giovanni: “L’eredità futurista.” G. Lista: *Futurismo: La rivolta dell’avanguardia.* Cinisello Balsamo (MI): Silvana, 2008. 716–728.
Lista, Giovanni: “La scena futurista e l’avanguardia storica.” Henri Béhar: *Il teatro dada e surrealista.* Torino: Einaudi, 1976. VII-XL.
Lora Totino, Arrigo: “Nuovi corpi di poesia.” Mirella Bandini, ed.: *Arrigo Lora-Totino: Il teatro della parola.* Torino: Lindau, 1996. 35–36.
Lora Totino, Arrigo: “Poesia concreta.” Claudio Parmiggiani, ed.: *Alfabeto in sogno: Dal carme figurato alla poesia concreta.* Milano: Mazzotta, 2003. 405–418.
Lora Totino, Arrigo: “Poesia da ascoltare.” Dietrich Mahlow, and Arrigo Lora-Totino, eds.: *Poesia concreta: Indirizzi visuali e fonetici.* Venezia: La Biennale, 1969. 19–49.
Lora Totino, Arrigo: “Ragioni di una scelta per un’antologia della poesia concreta.” *Modulo* 1 (1965): 18–23.
Lucini, Gian Pietro: “Come ho sorpassato il futurismo.” Luciano De Maria, ed.: *Filippo Tommaso Marinetti e il futurismo.* Milano: Mondadori, 2000. 270–276.
Masnata, Pino: *Il nome radia e altri scritti futuristi.* A cura di Margaret Fisher. Bologna: Pendragon, 2021.
Marinetti, Filippo Tommaso: “Answers to Objections.” F.T. Marinetti: *Critical Writings.* Ed. by Günter Berghaus. New York: Farrar, Straus & Giroux, 2006. 114–119.
Marinetti, Filippo Tommaso: “Gli avvisi luminosi: Lettera aperta a S.E. Mussolini.” *L’impero* 5:37 (1927): 1.
Marinetti, Filippo Tommaso: “Contro gli spegnitori di Milano.” *Futurismo* 2:1 (1 January 1933): 1.
Marinetti, Filippo Tommaso: “Destruction of Syntax – Untrammeled Imagination – Words-in-Freedom.” F.T. Marinetti: *Critical Writings.* Ed. by Günter Berghaus. New York: Farrar, Straus & Giroux, 2006. 120–131.
Marinetti, Filippo Tommaso: “Dynamic, Multichanneled Recitation.” F.T. Marinetti: *Critical Writings.* Ed. by Günter Berghaus. New York: Farrar, Straus & Giroux, 2006. 193–199.
Marinetti, Filippo Tommaso: “‘Firmamento’ di Armando Mazza.” F.T. Marinetti. *Collaudi futuristi.* Napoli: Guida, 1977. 27–32.
Marinetti, Filippo Tommaso: “Technical Manifesto of Futurist Literature.” F.T. Marinetti: Critical Writings. Trans. Doug Thompson. Ed. by Günter Berghaus. New York: Farrar, Straus & Giroux, 2006. 107–114.
Marinetti, Filippo Tommaso: “Testi-poemi murali di Carlo Belloli.” F.T. Marinetti. *Collaudi futuristi.* Napoli: Guida, 1977. 279–280.
Marinetti, Filippo Tommaso, Lugi Scrivo, and Piero Bellanova: “L’arte tipografica di guerra e dopoguerra.” *Graphicus* 32:5 (May 1942): 1–8.
Martini, Stelio Maria: *Schemi.* Napoli: Documento Sud, 1962.
Masnata, Pino: *Poesia visiva: Storia e teoria.* Roma: Bulzoni, 1984.
McLuhan, Marshall: *Understanding Media: The Extensions of Man.* New York: McGraw-Hill, 1964.
Minarelli, Enzo: *La voce regina: Poesia sonora in pubblico.* Lecce: Manni, 2006.
Modena, Anna: *Pino Masnata: Vita di un futurista. Una biografia attraverso i diari.* Varzi: Guardamagna, 2001.
Papini, Giovanni: “Futurismo e Marinettismo.” Luciano De Maria, ed.: *Filippo Tommaso Marinetti e il futurismo.* Milano: Mondadori, 2000. 283–286.

Pignotti, Lamberto: "L'industria che non si vede." *Questo e altro* 1 (1962): 59–61.
Pignotti, Lamberto: "La suggestione di Gordon Flash." *Marcatrè* 11–13 (1965): 107–109.
Pignotti, Lamberto: "Paroliberismo: Modelli di scrittura verbo-visiva futurista negli anni Dieci." L. Pignotti: *Figure scritture: Su certi segni delle arti e dei mass media.* Udine: Campanotto, 1987. 17–34.
Pignotti, Lamberto: "Tecnica e ideologia." *Letteratura* 73 (1965): 77–78.
Pignotti, Lamberto: *I sensi delle arti: Sinestesie e interazioni estetiche.* Bari: Dedalo, 1993.
Pignotti, Lamberto, and Stefania Stefanelli: *Scrittura verbovisiva e sinestetica.* Udine: Campanotto, 2011.
Pola, Francesca: "Dialoghi tra spazio e tempo: Il sistema dell'avanguardia." Luca Massimo Barbero, ed.: *Torino sperimentale 1959–1969: Una storia della cronaca. Il sistema delle arti come avanguardia.* Torino: Allemandi, 2010. 131–159.
Polacci, Francesca: "Guardare, declamare, leggere: Performatività delle tavole parolibere futuriste." *Mantichora* 1 (2011): 567–583.
Rotella, Mimmo: *L'ora della lucertola.* Milano: Spirali/Vel, 2003.
Russolo, Luigi: *L'arte dei rumori.* Milano: Edizioni futuriste di "Poesia", 1916.
Salaris, Claudia: *La rivoluzione tipografica.* Milano: Sylvestre Bonnard, 2001.
Sandford, Mariellen R., ed.: *Happenings and Other Acts.* New York: Routledge, 1995.
Sanguineti, Edoardo: "Avanguardia e sperimentalismo." Mauro Ponzi, and Aldo Mastropasqua, eds.: *L'Europa futurista: Simultaneità, costruttivismo, montaggio.* Milano: Mimesis, 2015. 67–75.
Sanguineti, Edoardo: "L'estetica della velocità." E. Sanguineti: *La missione del critico.* Genova: Marietti, 1987. 127–149.
Sanguineti, Edoardo: "La guerra futurista." E. Sanguineti: *Ideologia e linguaggio.* Milano: Feltrinelli, 1970. 38–43.
Sanguineti, Edoardo: "La parola futurista." Enrico Crispolti, and Franco Sborgi, eds.: *Futurismo: I grandi temi 1909–1944.* Milano: Mazzotta, 1998. 37–41.
Simongini, Gabriele: "La nuova Italia dell'Art Club 1945–1964 = The New Italy for the Art Club 1945–1964." G. Simongini, ed.: *Art Club 1945–1964.* Pietrasanta: Franche Tirature, 2013. 15–21. 23–27.
Simongini, Gabriele: "La 'scomoda' libertà dell'Art Club = The 'bothersome' Freedom of the Art Club." G. Simongini, ed.: *Art Club 1945–1964: La linea astratta.* Verona: Grafiche Aurora, 1998. 17–25. 26–35.
Solt, Mary Ellen Solt: *Concrete Poetry: A World View.* Bloomington/IN: Indiana University Press, 1970.
Spatola, Adriano: *Verso la poesia totale.* Torino: Paravia, 1978. English translation *Toward Total Poetry.* Trans. by B.W. Hennessey and G. Bennett. Los Angeles/CA: Otis Books; Seismicity, 2008.
Spignoli, Teresa: "No Man's Land: From Free-Word Tables to Verbal-Visual Poetry." Geert Buelens, Harald Hendrix, and Monica Jansen, eds.: *The History of Futurism: The Precursors, Protagonists, and Legacies.* Lanham, MD.: Lexington Books, 2012. 353–376.
Spignoli, Teresa: "Arrigo Lora Totino 'architetto di parole': Dalle verbotetture ai cromofonemi." *Lingue e letterature d'Oriente e d'Occidente* 7 (2018): 83–97.
Spignoli, Teresa: *La parola si fa spazio: Poesia concreta e Poesia visiva.* Bologna: Pàtron, 2020.
Spignoli, Teresa, ed.: *La poesia in immagine / L'immagine in poesia: Gruppo 70. Firenze 1963–2013.* Udine: Campanotto, 2014.
Tazzi, Pier Luigi: "Maurizio Nannucci." Katalin Mollek Burmeister, ed.: *Maurizio Nannucci: Something Happened.* Pistoia: Gli Ori, 2009. 104.
Toschi, Caterina: "Futurism and the Birth of a Modern European Typography." *International Yearbook of Futurism Studies* 10 (2020): 200–215.

Van den Bossche, Bart: “Mots en liberté? Testualità e formati editoriali nel libro futurista.” B. Van den Bossche, Giuseppe Manica, and Carmen Van den Bergh, eds.: *Azione / Reazione: Il futurismo in Belgio e in Europa.* Firenze: Cesati, 2012. 233–248.

Vinci, Maria Gloria: “Carlo Belloli in Brasile: Un geniale precursore della poesia concreta.” *Mutatis mutandis* 9 (2016): 53–67.

Weaver, Mike. “Concrete Poetry.” *The Lugano Review* 5–6 (1966): 100–125.

Internet Resources

Colucci, Dalila: “Twentieth-century Italian Visual Poetry.” Carla Bregman, and Jo Ann Cavallo, eds.: *The Literary Encyclopedia.* Vol. 1. Pt. 6.1: *Italian Writing and Culture.* https://www.litencyc.com/php/stopics.php?rec=true&UID=19534.

Mugnaini, Alberto: “Maurizio Nannucci.” https://flash—art.it/article/maurizio-nannucci-2/.

Duccio Dogheria

Bang Tumb Tuuum! The Influence of Futurism on Italian Avant-garde Comic Strips

Abstract: Futurism had a revolutionizing influence on a great number of artistic media, but one that Marinetti & Co. never addressed was the comic strip, possibly because at the time it was considered part of children's literature or belonging to the genre of satirical illustration (which Futurists were more victims than creators of). The relationship between Futurism and comics only became fruitful in the second half of the twentieth century, especially during the 1980s, when some of the protagonists of Italian avant-garde comic production developed an interest in Futurism and began to incorporate it into their stories. In some cases, these were mere quotations, as in the graphic novels of Pablo Echaurren. In others, they can be considered Postmodern references, for instance, to Boccioni's dynamism, Balla's chromatism, Depero's playfulness, Sant'Elia's utopian architecture, or to the provocative *serate futuriste.* Starting from a first investigation undertaken on the occasion of the exhibition *Depero new Depero* (2021–22), this essay examines the main comics from the 1960s to 2020s, the experimental magazines in which they appeared (*Frigidaire, Alter Alter* and *Dolce vita*, amongst others), as well as their reception by critics. It also highlights the hybridization of genres between avant-garde comics and advertising, video clips, fashion and graphic design.

Keywords: Nuovo Fumetto Italiano; Italian avant-garde comic strips; experimental magazines in the 1980s; *Frigidaire* (1980–present), *Alter Alter* (1977–85); Valvoline group (founded 1983); comics and music; comics and video; comics and fashion; comics and interior design

Futurism and the Comic Strip

This essay aims at delineating the influence of Futurism on Italian avant-garde comic strips from the 1960s to 2020s, resuming and amplifying an earlier study prompted by the exhibition *Depero new Depero* (Rovereto: MART, 21 October 2021–5 June 2022).[1] Both the exhibition and my investigations were possible thanks

1 Dogheria: "Remix futuristi formato fumetto." For a discussion of this exhibition see Mancebo Roca: "Depero New Depero: Rovereto Presents the Artist and His Reception after 1960."

https://doi.org/10.1515/9783111318394-004

to the documents preserved in the research centre of the MART Museum in Rovereto, the Archivio del '900, which contains a large part of the magazines and books analysed in the following sections of this essay.

Although some traces of Futurism in Postmodern culture have already been pointed out by critics working in the fields of design, fashion and figurative arts,[2] other spaces of expression remain overlooked; amongst these the 'ninth art', namely, the comic strip. Futurism had a modernizing effect on the expressive and communicative forms of the 1910s and 20s, including the most innovative arts, such as photography and radio, but it ignored the world of comics. A rare exception is the *tavola a fumetti* (a one-panel comic) on the title page of *Roma futurista* no. 83, dated 9 May 1920. It was drawn by Giacomo Soldi and featured a multi-levelled urban scene animated by numerous figures, in which speech bubbles appear with comical and even blasphemous exclamations. It is not yet a strip *per se* – as it stands out as a cartoon with simultaneous scenes in a single image – but certainly an interesting example that foreshadows later developments (see Fig. 1).

Futurism, however, was usually the butt of satirical cartoons rather than the creator of comical narratives[3] such as the comic strip, sardonic illustrations and caricatures. A good example are the vignettes that Umberto Onorato dedicated to Marinetti in *Il travaso delle idee* (The Decanter of Ideas), one of the most longest-lasting satirical periodicals in Italy (it ran from 1900 to 1966);[4] or, even better, the two monographic numbers that the magazine specifically devoted to Futurism: *Il travaso della pastasciutta* (The Decanter of Pasta, issued on 11 January 1931) and *Il travaso delle idee futuriste* (The Decanter of Futurist Ideas, of 24 September 1933). Another interesting case may be found in the issue of *L'Assiette au beurre* (no. 591, 1 September 1912), dedicated to the Italo-Turkish War and illustrated in its entirety by Georges d'Ostoya, with an introduction entitled *Une guerre ultramoderne et futuriste*, a parody of bellicose statements ascribed to F.T. Marinetti but in reality thought up by the French writer Raoul Pellissier.[5]

2 For a general introduction to the topic, see Salaris: *Futurismo*, in particular the chapter *Alle sorgenti del moderno*, pp. 214–231.

3 A rare exception were Luciano Folgore's satirical short stories collected in *Poeti controluce: Parodie*. Foligno: Campitelli, 1922, *Poeti allo specchio: Parodie*. Foligno: Campitelli, 1926 and *Novellieri allo specchio: Parodie*. Milano: Ceschina, 1935.

4 See Rigo: "Caricatures of Futurism in 'Il travaso delle idee'." Many more examples can be found in the Section "Caricatures and Satires of Futurism in the Contemporary Press" in the *International Yearbook of Futurism Studies*, volumes 2014, 2015, 2016, 2017, 2019, 2020.

5 In this case, the illustrations by D'Ostoya did not relate to Futurism, but the literary parody of *Guerra sola igiene del mondo*.

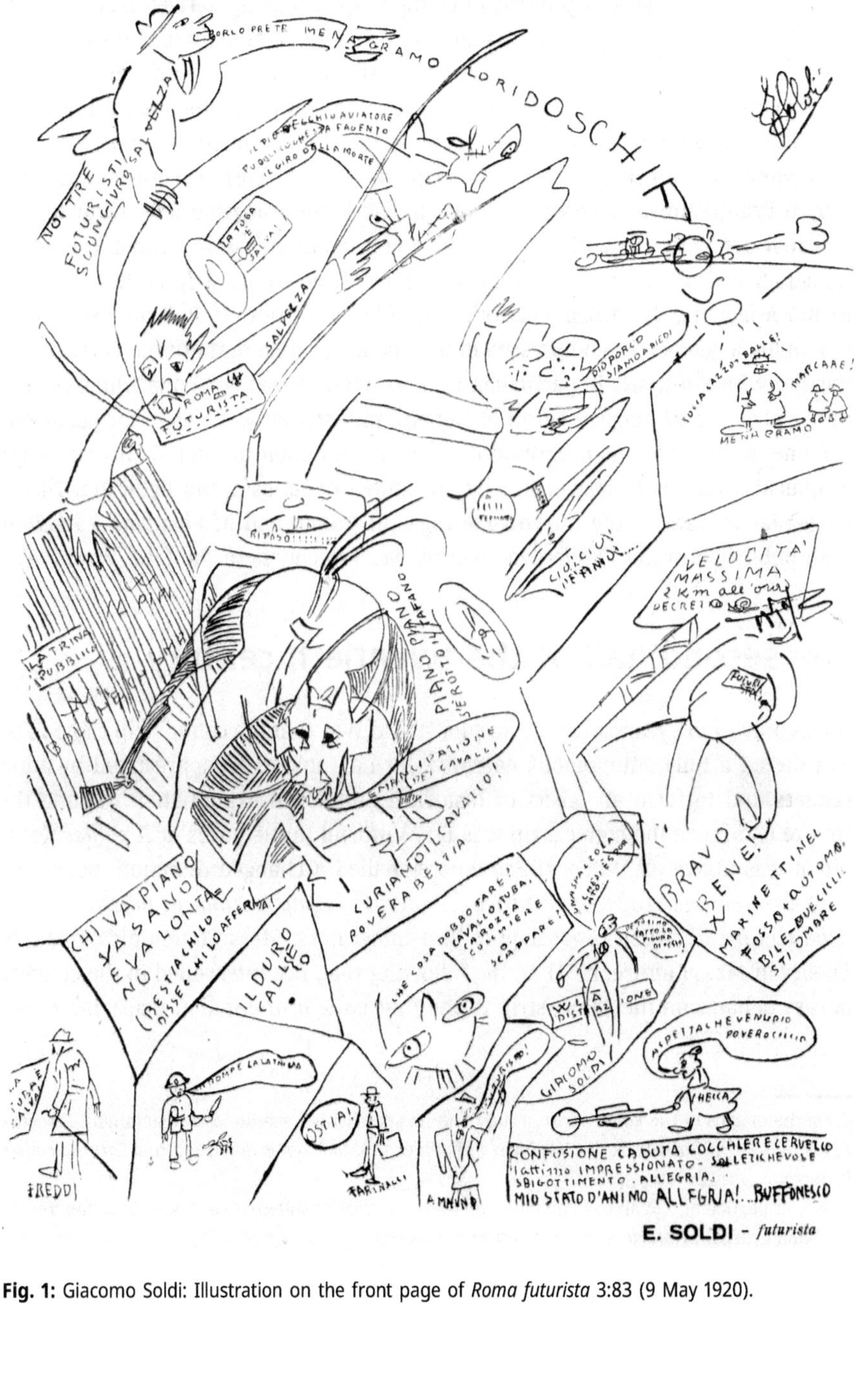

Fig. 1: Giacomo Soldi: Illustration on the front page of *Roma futurista* 3:83 (9 May 1920).

The Futurists' lack of interest in comic strips probably derived from the fact that this verbal-visual medium was largely considered a domain of children's literature,[6] even though it had already been extensively tested in the field of propaganda, especially in the pages of the *Corriere dei piccoli*, directed towards young readers.[7] It is precisely in the weekly supplement to the daily newspaper *Corriere della sera* where we can find some comic strips by authors close to Futurism, notably Enrico Prampolini and Fortunato Depero. The latter was especially wont to mix his own art with elements taken from mass communication, transforming his imaginative writings into visual compositions. Proto-comic strip authors such as Bruno Angoletta, Carlo Bisi, Sergio Tofano (Sto) and Antonio Rubino also tended to employ a geometric, compressed and mechanical style that offered certain similarities with Futurism. In particular, Rubino stands out as someone who was akin to the playful and magical world of Depero, to his vitality, his taste for geometric ornamentation[8] and his pronounced interest – common to many Futurists[9] – for graphical solutions characterized by an ignited dynamism and bellicism. This is particular evident in the improbable sagas of *Italino* and of *Piombino e Abetino*, both published in the *Corriere dei piccoli* over the course of the First World War.

The second half of the twentieth century

It was only in the years after the Second World War that the comic strip came to be considered a fully autonomous narrative format, able to be appreciated by adult readers and to form an object of historical and social examination. Among the first to legitimize the comic strip was Elio Vittorini in the pages of *Il politecnico*;[10] but it was above all Umberto Eco who signalled a changed direction, beginning with the seminal study *Apocalittici e integrati: Comunicazioni di massa e teoria della cultura di massa* (Apocalyptics and Integrators: Mass Communications and Theory of Mass Culture, 1964). In the following year, Eco intervened in the contemporary debates on the comic strip in the first issue of the Italian magazine *Linus*,

6 On the origins of the comic strip in Italy and its specificities, see Bono and Stefanelli: *Fumetto! 150 anni di storie italiane*, Tosti: *Graphic Novel* and *Gaspa: Dal signor Bonaventura a Saturno contro la Terra.*

7 See, in particular, Loparco: *I bambini e la guerra*, Curreri: "Sulle tracce di un Pinocchio 'futurista'" and Scarpa: *Le storie nere del Corriere dei Piccoli.*

8 See, for instance, Bonito Oliva, et al.: *Depero e Rubino.*

9 On the affinities between Antonio Rubino and Futurism, see Pizzi: "Antonio Rubino in odor di futurismo."

10 See Stancanelli: *Vittorini e i balloons.*

together with Elio Vittorini and Oreste Del Buono. In 1966, he published with the artist Eugenio Carmi the multi-media volume *Stripsody*, dedicated to the simultaneously sonorous and verbal-visual universe of the comic strips, interpreted vocally in the attached vinyl by the mezzo-soprano Cathy Berberian.

In the course of the 1960s, the first experimental comic strips which geared towards an adult readership appeared, in many cases promoted by artists. Of prime importance were the editions of the Bolognese publisher Sampietro,[11] including the comics of Achille Perilli and Gastone Novelli published in the magazine *Grammatica* as early as 1964. These included Novelli's *I viaggi di Brek* (Brek's Travels, 1967),[12] Dino Buzzati's *Poema a fumetti* (Comic-Strip Poem, 1969) and the first 'incunable' of drawn literature inspired by Futurism, Paolo Albani's *Note per il manifesto del neo-futurismo* (Notes for a Neofuturist Manifesto, 1967). The latter is a strongly political pamphlet that simultaneously pays homage to Marx and Mayakovsky, Marinetti and Fidel Castro, with drawings by Paolo della Bella.[13]

After 1965, the comic strip entered the artistic world of one of the great protagonists of *poesia visiva*, Lamberto Pignotti (born 1926). In the series entitled *Francobolli* (Stamps, 1965–68), some speech bubbles cropped from various comics were affixed to the mechanism of the artwork next to common Italian stamps, with unsettling results.[14] This series continued for many years, often touching upon Futurist topics.[15] In 1977, Pignotti, who had participated two years earlier in a conference in Bologna on the relationship between art and the comic strip, *Fumetto fra arte e impegno* (Comics between Art and Commitment), extended his use of comics in his artists' book *Biblia pauperum* (Paupers' Bible, 1977). This volume, featuring introductions by Eugenio Battisti and Umberto Eco amongst others, presented a series of biblical prints from the 1800s, satirically metamorphosed by means of speech bubbles.[16]

---

11 That is, *Il caso limite 1* by Carlo Santachiara (1966), *Il fabbro armonioso* by Giovanni Morelli (1966) and *Palomares* by Antonio Faeti (1967), all of which were published in the "Piccola collana '70", amongst the first comics to be sold in bookstores.

12 See Perna: *Gastone Novelli e le bandes dessinées.*

13 The work, hand printed in Compiobbi by the Gruppo Stanza in 150 silkscreen copies, constitutes a true hybrid of comics and artists' books. For more on this manifesto, see pp. 31–33 of this volume of the Yearbook.

14 See, in particular, Pignotti and Stefanelli: *La scrittura verbo-visiva*, pp. 189–190 and pp. 27–29 in this volume of the Yearbook.

15 Exemplary in this respect is Pignotti: *Ricostruzione dell'universo futurista.*

16 The subversion of popular prints with biblical themes in a verbal-visual key without the use of speech bubbles had already been undertaken a few years earlier by François Cavanna in the French satirical magazine *Hara Kiri* and in the volume *Les Aventures de Dieu* (Paris: Editions

This work, irreverent and strongly provocative, brought Pignotti close to the creative wing of the so-called 'indiani metropolitani' (Urban Red-Indians)[17], a protest movement within the Italian far left. Numerous analogies between these groupings and Futurism have already been traced by scholars such as Maurizio Calvesi in his *Avanguardia di massa* (Avant-garde of the Masses, 1978), Umberto Eco in his columns for *L'espresso* (1977–78), later re-issued under the title *Sette anni di desiderio* (Seven Years of Desire, 1983), and Claudia Salaris in *Il movimento del Settantasette: Linguaggi e scritture dell'ala creativa* (The Movement of '77: Languages and Writings of the Creative Wing, 1997).

In this context, it is necessary to highlight how Futurist echoes can be found in some of the comic strips of the so-called 'counterculture movement',[18] promoted by independent publishers. Sometimes, these similarities involved a common taste for violence, mixed with an iconoclastic – and at times hallucinatory – playfulness, which recalls Futurist provocation and illogicality, albeit indirectly. This is the case, for example, with *Le avventure della boccia Ernesta* (The Adventures of the Boule Ball Ernesta) by Trash (pseud. of Marco D'Alessandro), published in June 1977 in the first issue of the fanzine *Cannibale.* Its surreal protagonists are a Molotov cocktail thrown by members of the Autonomia Operaia (Workers' Autonomy, an Italian leftist movement active from 1976 to 1978) and tear gas shells of the police.[19] In other cases, references to Futurism become more direct and explicit: on the back cover of the third issue of *Cannibale* (June 1978; see Fig. 2a), Andrea Pazienza, an author who, amongst other things, shared with many Futurists a taste for syncopated writing, re-created the iconic photo of Marinetti & Co. taken in Paris in 1912 (see Fig. 2b). In the illustration, which has the air of a manifesto,

du Square, 1971; Italian edition: *Le avventure di Dio.* Rome: Savelli, 1974, with a preface by Oreste del Buono).

17 This protest movement wore face-paint like the war-paint of Native Americans and supported the urban guerrilla activity and occupations of universities during the *anni di piombo*, a period of social and political turmoil in Italy.

18 The counterculture movement of the 1960s was characterized by Beat music, hippie culture, the civil rights movement and the protests against the Vietnam War. Out of this grew in France the 1968 rebellion and in Italy the 1977 *Indiani metropolitani* movement. About the Italian counterculture movement see, amongst others, Ballesi, et al.: *L'edicola che non c'è*; Ciaponi: *Underground*; De Donno and Martegani: *Yes Yes Yes Revolutionary Press in Italy 1966–1977*; Echaurren and Salaris: *Controcultura in Italia 1966–1977*; Gallino: *1965–1985 20 anni di Controcultura*; Gazzotti: *Vietato vietare*. The *Movimento del '77* culminated in the occupation of several Italian universities in March 1977. On 11 March, during clashes between demonstrators and police forces in Bologna, Francesco Lorusso, a student and militant member of Lotta Continua, was killed. See, amongst others, Galfré and Neri Serneri: *Il movimento del '77* and Mariscalco: *Dai laboratori alle masse.*

19 See the anthology by Mordente and Rizzardi: *Nuvole sotterranee.*

the five members of the Futurist group are replaced by the proponents of *Cannibale,* in the same attire and assuming the same poses: Tanino Liberatore in the clothes of Luigi Russolo, Stefano Tamburini in those of Carlo Carrà, Massimo Mattioli in those of Umberto Boccioni (the illustration, however, is by Liberatore), Filippo Scozzari in those of Gino Severini, and Pazienza himself in those of F.T. Marinetti.

Pablo Echaurren's pop-historical approach to Futurism

One of the 'Urban Red-Indians' was the Roman artist Pablo Echaurren, who re-imagined the panels of *Tex,* a comic strip created in 1948 by screenwriter Gian Luigi Bonelli and cartoonist Aurelio Galleppini in a manner similar to that of the Situationists, substituting the original texts in the speech bubbles with Maoist-Dadaist slogans typical of the '77 movement. In 1978, Echaurren discovered Futurism and, thanks also to his direct contact with some still-living protagonists of Marinetti's movement, launched a number of futuristic publications together with his wife, the Futurism scholar Claudia Salaris. This encounter with Futurism deeply influenced his artistic production and publishing activities, noticeable in two artists' books of 1979, which reveal the influence of Corrado Govoni's *Rarefazioni e parole in libertà* (Defusions and Words-in-Freedom, 1915) and anticipate his subsequent production of comic strips. *Evaporazioni* (Disappearances) and, above all, *Hurrà!*[20] present a strong interaction between word and image, with explicit references to Futurist Words-in-Freedom.[21]

Echaurren's first comic-strip stories[22] were marked by a style that took inspiration from Fortunato Depero.[23] They were published in 1984 in *Frigidaire,* a periodical founded in 1980 by Vincenzo Sparagna together with Stefano Tamburini and Filippo Scozzari.[24] Amongst the many strips drawn for this magazine and collected

20 This large-format work was dedicated to Marinetti.

21 "The typographic innovations splash, jump, dance [...] volcanoes found the literature that form the words, finally freed." (Le innovazioni tipografiche schizzano saltellano ballano [...] i vulcani fondono le lettere che formeranno le parole, finalmente libere). Echaurren: *Hurra,* p. 25.

22 For a reconstruction of the relationship between Futurism and comics in Echaurren's work, see Dogheria: *Marinetti, Majakovskij & Co.*; on Echaurren's comics, see Lo Monaco: "Il graphic novel secondo Pablo Echaurren" and Vacchelli: *Pablo Echaurren.*

23 On the influence of Depero on Echaurren, see Bonito Oliva: *Pablo Echaurren.*

24 See, in particular, Sparagna: *Frigidaire* and Sparagna: *L'avventura maivista di "Frigidaire" 1980–2020.* In May 1987, the exhibition *Znort! La prima linea del fumetto* in Colle di Val d'Elsa pre-

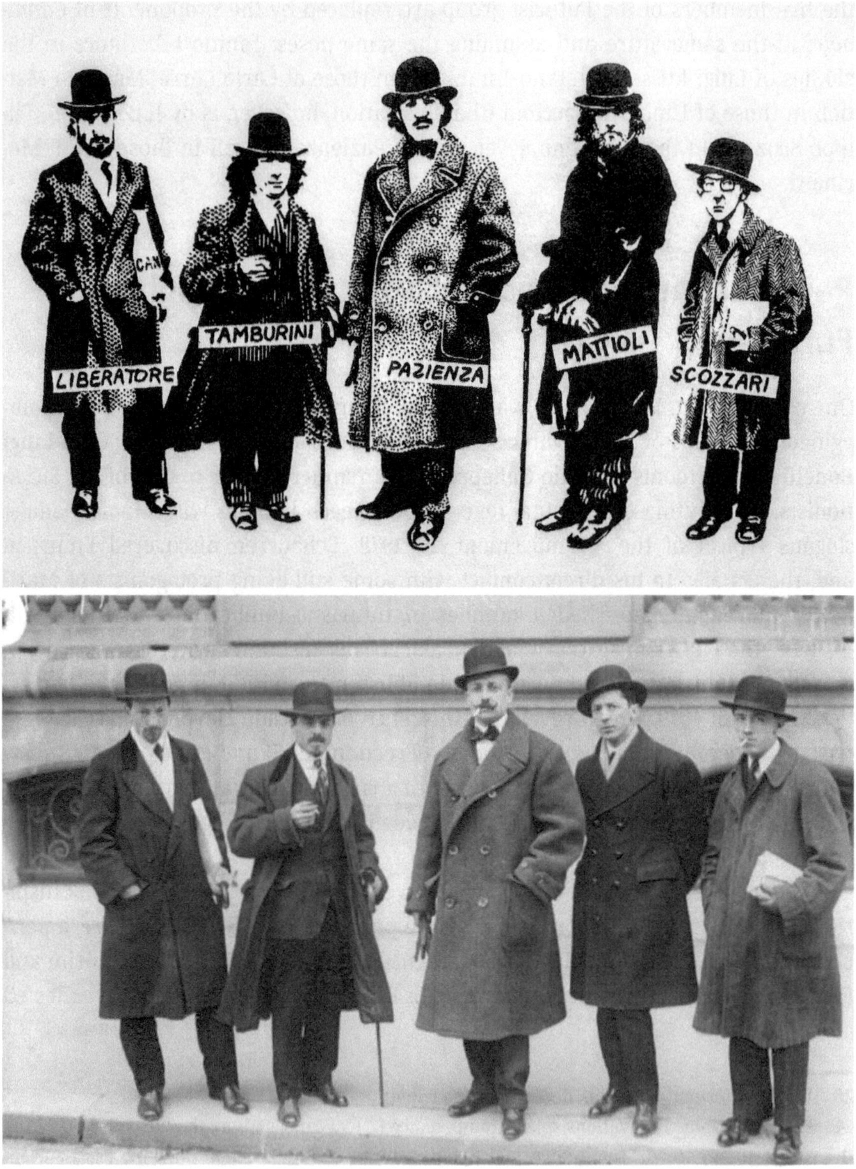

Fig. 2a: Andrea Pazienza: Back cover of *Cannibale* no. 3, June 1978. **Fig. 2b:** The Futurist group in Paris 1912. From Left to right: Luigi Russolo, Carlo Carrà, Filippo Tommaso Marinetti, Umberto Boccioni and Gino Severini.

in the album *Saette* (Thunderbolt, 1985), we find some dedicated to Fortunato Depero, F.T. Marinetti, Carlo Carrà, to the genre of *aeropittura* as well as to Marinetti and Fillìa's *Manifesto dell'arte sacra futurista* (Manifesto of Futurist Sacred Art, 1931). Others strips appeared in comic magazines such as *Linus*, *Alter Alter*, *Comic Art*, *Zut* and *Il grifo*, but also in political periodicals such as *Rinascita*, and design magazines such as *Ollo: Rivista senza messaggio* (Ollo: Magazine without a Message), directed by Alessandro Mendini. In the first number of *Ollo* (1988), the artist dedicated a short comic-strip story to the Futurist Volt (pseud. of Vincenzo Fani). In 1986, Echaurren also launched a series of comics that resembled the graphic novel, although the term was not in common use at the time. These works – portions of which were sometimes printed in magazines – reveal his creative and historicist approach, dense with both visual and textual references to figures and events of the historical avant-garde.

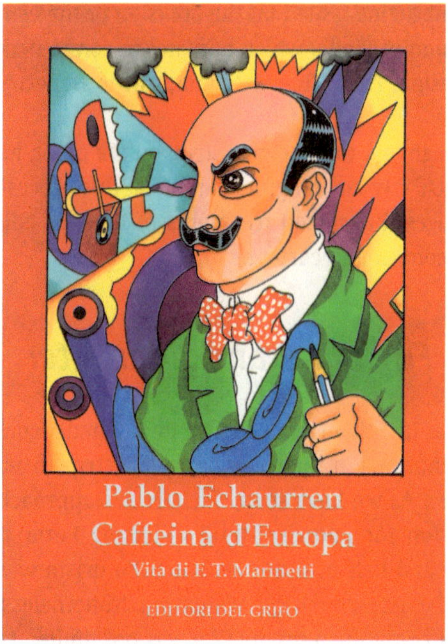

Fig. 3: Pablo Echaurren: *Caffeina d'Europa: Vita di* F.T. Marinetti. Montepulciano (SI): Editori del Grifo, 1988. Some of the illustrations were first published in *Linus* in 1986.

sented 300 works from the authors of *Frigidaire*, such as Brolli, Echaurren, Giacon, Igort, Liberatore, Mattioli, Pazienza and Scozzari.

First in chronological order came the large-format album *Majakovskij: Pitture parlanti* (Mayakovsky: Talking Pictures, 1986), with a presentation by Vincenzo Mollica. Following on from this, in 1988, was *Caffeina d'Europa: Vita di* F.T. Marinetti (The Caffeine of Europe: The Life of F.T. Marinetti, 1988), with an introduction in which Hugo Pratt emphasizes Echaurren's synthesis of Futurism and Walt Disney (see Fig. 3). The subsequent *Nivola vola: Storia disegnata di Tazio Nuvolari* (Nivola Flys: Graphic Story of Tazio Nuvolari, 1992) narrates in an oblong format the life of a protagonist on four-wheels, a theme so dear to the Futurists. Later appeared *Vita di Pound* (Life of Pound, 1993), *Evola in Dada* (1994), *Vita disegnata di Dino Campana* (Life of Dino Campana, Drawn in Pictures, 1994), *Futurismo contro* (Futurism Contra, 1995) – a work with metallic binding and paper of varying weights, with obvious echoes of Depero's *libro imbullonato* (the 'bolted book' *Depero futurista 1913–1927*), *Dada con le zecche* (Dada with Ticks, 1997) and *Terremoto Picasso* (Earthquake Picasso, 2006). Finishing the series was *Vestire il futuro* (Dressing the Future, 2009), an album-magazine issued on the occasion of the centenary of Futurism by the Industrial Union in Biella, which narrates in comic-strip form the history of Futurist fashion design, from Thayaht's jumpsuit to Depero's waistcoats.

If, on the one hand, Echaurren brought art to the comic strip, on the other, he grafted the comic strip onto art. A particularly meaningful example of this process is *Iconoclasta*, a series created by collages that mixed fragments of Futurist editions with celebrated characters from comics and cartoons.[25]

Postmodern magazines: *Frigidaire* and *Alter Alter*

The pop-historical approach to Futurism in Echaurren's comics undoubtedly constitutes a unique position within the panorama of international comic strips from the second half of the twentieth century. As we have seen, Eucharren's approach resulted from his own particular passion for Futurism (and collecting Futurist publications) that dated back to the second half of the 1970s when Futurism was only beginning to become the subject of a serious critical evaluation. Nonetheless, the influence of Futurism on the Italian comic strip production was not limited to one artist, but encompassed a great number of proponents of experimental comic strips published since the beginning of the 1980s in magazines such as *Linus*, *Pin-*

25 See, in particular, Echaurren: *Iconoclasta!* and Parmiggiani: *Pablo Echaurren, iconoclast!*

guino, *TIC*, *Fuego*, *Dolce vita* and, above all, in *Alter Alter* and the aforementioned *Frigidaire.*[26]

It was in *Frigidaire* (1980 – present) and *Alter Alter* (1977–85) that the so-called *Nuovo fumetto italiano* (New Italian Comic) took form. Here, the suggestions of the historical avant-gardes, and of Futurism in particular, intermingled with other sources, derived from the most disparate fields of contemporary creative communication, ranging from music to graphic design, from fashion to architecture, from advertisements to alternative cultures, from the harbingers of computer graphics to music video clips, from postal communication[27] to visual arts and television. The editorial of *Frigidaire*'s first issue (November 1980), entitled "Viaggiare tra le merci" (Travelling Amongst Goods), with photos by the Italian pop artist Mario Schifano, explained the heterogeneous mix of approaches taken by the magazine. It was meant to be 'cool' (i. e. fashionable, topical, trendy), as the magazine's title literally suggested, and to offer a complex mixture of hybrid elements: "Finding a thread to bind and make sense of this aggregate appropriately placed *in frigidaire* is a questionable, if not impossible, undertaking".[28]

The analogies between comic strips and Futurism became progressively more pronounced and relevant in the 1980s, a period of technological innovation and industrial progress. It was iconically represented by Pier Vittorio Tondelli in *Un weekend postmoderno: Cronache dagli anni Ottanta* (A Postmodern Weekend: Chronicles from the Eighties, 1990), a long novel based on the most innovative and experimental trends in fashions, music and literature, and accords prominent space to contemporary comic strips.[29] These publications demonstrate a number of parallels to Futurism in the 1920s and 30s, synthesized in magazines such as *Stile futurista* (1934–35), a promoter of a decorative style that mixed genres from every aesthetic and cultural field. It was precisely this multifaceted flow of stimuli that drove the interest of the makers of *Frigidaire.* They were not so much oriented towards Futurist art itself, but to its reinterpretation in a kaleidoscopic, Postmodern key. The pages of *Frigidaire* in its first years offered novel forms of comic strips

---

26 *Figidaire* also published the supplementary magazines *Tempi supplementari* and *Frizzer.* See Boschi: *Frigo valvole e balloons.*

27 The field of Mail Art was one of the most vibrant reinventions of the historical avant-gardes. See Baroni: *Arte postale*, Belloli: "Armando Mazza", Giannì: *La Mail Art tra Futurismo e Inismo* and, with regard to artists' postcards, Sturani: *Nuove cartoline*, and pp. 135–165 of this Yearbook.

28 "Trovare un filo che leghi e renda razionale questo aggregato opportunamente messo in frigidaire è impresa discutibile, se non impossibile." Sparagna: "Viaggiare tra le merci", p. 5.

29 The volume, which mostly collected texts that had previously been published in magazines, such as *Linus* and *Alter Alter,* dedicates some chapters to avant-garde comics. In particular: *Nuovo fumetto italiano* (pp. 204–208), *Andrea Pazienza* (pp. 209–212), *Giovanotti Mondani Meccanici* (pp. 246–248).

that aimed at interacting with the European avant-garde,[30] together with remarkable pieces of investigative journalism as well as articles on novel fields of exploration in the world of art, music, theatre and cinema.

Some of these experiments were in part indebted to Futurism, for example the *neo-rumorismo* of Post-Punk and No-Wave groups, or of the creation of the Nuovi Futuristi group, Studio Alchimia (1976–1992) and Memphis Design (1980–1988). The Nuovi Futuristi group was a post-conceptual art group launched in 1983 by the gallery owner Luciano Inga-Pin; the latter two were collectives run by Alessandro Mendini and Ettore Sottsass Jr., who sought to revitalize the idea of the *case d'arte futuriste* (a combination of artists' workshops, exhibition galleries and sale rooms). Explicit reminders of Futurism can be found in some issues of the magazine, for example no. 71 (October 1986), which contained an interview with Enzo Benedetto, founder of the *Futurismo oggi* group; or no. 25 (December 1982), featuring a calendar entitled *La cucina futurista*, which included a text by Paolo Brogi and culinary compositions by Alan Denis, drawing on recipes of Fillìa, Farfa, Prampolini, Caviglioni and others previously published in *La cucina futurista* (The Futurist Cookbook, 1932).[31]

The Postmodernism of *Frigidaire* and its reception of the historical avant-garde can be found in its comic strips and other design features of the magazine. The latter was entrusted, in its first years, to the versatile Stefano Tamburini, who came from the magazines *Cannibale* (1977–79) and *Combinazioni* (1974–76).[32] In *Frigidaire*, Tamburini also handled music (under the pseudonym Red Vinyle) as well as fashion, a field in which many Futurist references can be found, particularly in his collages printed on multi-coloured paper. For instance, the front cover of issue 26 (January 1983) shows many allusions to Depero, while the creations of the fashion label Vudu Moda (Spring-Summer collection of 1984), published in *Frigidaire* no. 29 (April 1983), contains clear references to Volt's *Manifesto della moda femminile futurista* (Futurist Manifesto of Women's Fashion, 1920).[33]

---

30 European magazines in contact with *Frigidaire* were *Actuel* in France, *El vibora* in Spain, *Etc* in Sweden, *Mais* in Portugal, *Oor* in Holland, *The Face* in England, *Tip* in Germany and *Wiener* in Austria. See the *Speciale Europa* of *Frigidaire* 35–36 (October 1983), made in collaboration with all of these magazines.

31 See Sparagna: *Frigidaire*, in particular the sub-chapter *Frigidaire e il futurismo*, p. 79. Futurist cuisine had also inspired a series of strips by Nicola Corona, which appeared in issue 3 (January 1981) of the periodical under the title *Lunghi tempi di cottura: Artificial food!*

32 The work of Stefano Tamburini has been investigated by Mordente: *Stefano Tamburini: Muscoli e forbici*, and Mordente: *Tutto Tamburo.*

33 Tamburini: "Roma Vudu Moda", pp. 34–35 presents indeed items "in single-use plastic" (in plastica da buttare dopo l'uso), an "evening robe in sculpted yellow foam-rubber" (accappatoio da sera in gommapiuma gialla scolpita) and a black suit with asymmetrical sleeves accompanied by a "boa

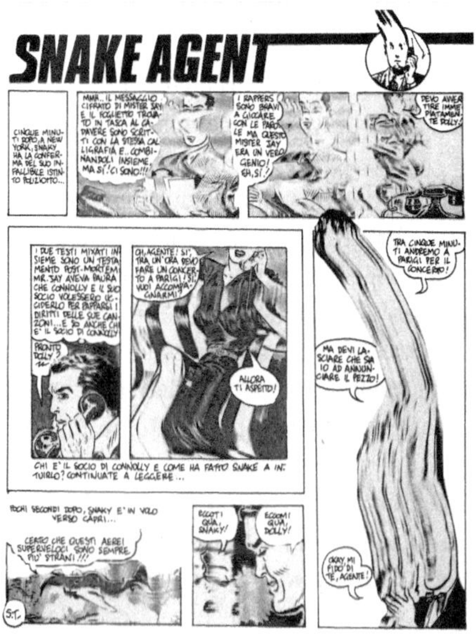

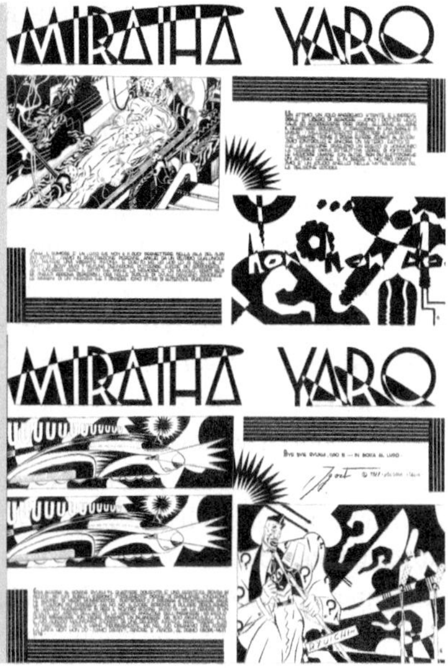

Fig. 4a: Stefano Tamburini: *Snake Agent* (from *Frigidaire* no. 43, June 1984). **Fig. 4b.** Igort and Ryuichi Sakamoto: *Miraiha Yaro* (from *Frigidaire* no. 86, April 1986).

Tamburini's comic strips for *Frigidaire* were steeped in the Futurist myth of the machine. His most celebrated character in the graphic novel series *RanXerox* (1978), introduced in *Cannibale* and drawn by Tanino Liberatore in *Frigidaire*, was a violent android created on a Rank Xerox photocopying machine. And the electrostatic duplication machine was precisely the medium that brought to life another of Tamburini's comic strips, *Snake Agent* (see Fig. 4a), published in *Frigidaire* between 1980 and 1984 and then collected in the comic book *Muscles* (1984). It harked back to Anton Giulio Bragaglia's Photo-dynamism by accentuating dynamism and simultaneity of compositions, created by moving the strips during the duplication process on a photocopy machine. This idea of a 'machine-made'

in contrasting colours made of foam-padded rubber" (da boa in colori contrastanti di raso imbottito in gommapiuma): clothes that seem to be inspired by Volt's urge to "open wide the doors of the ateliers of fashion to paper, cardboard, glass, tinfoil, aluminium, majolica, rubber, fish skin" (Noi spalancheremo le porte degli ateliers di moda alla carta al cartone al vetro, alla stagnola, all'alluminio, alle maioliche, al caucciù, alla pelle di pesce). See Volt: "Manifesto della moda femminile futurista".

comic strip looked at the same time at the creative use of xerography practiced by the ex-Futurist Bruno Munari.[34]

Technology and electricity, so dear to Marinetti that he predicted the advent of the computer era,[35] characterized the production of two other multimedia authors active in *Frigidaire* between 1984 and 1987: Antonio Glessi (who designed the images) and Andrea Zingoni (screenwriter, who wrote the texts), known as Giovanotti Mondani Meccanici (GMM). From issue 42, featuring an introductory report by Carmen Bertolazzi,[36] the duo began a series of 3-bit computer-generated comic strips, which mainly recount[37] the night-time shenanigans of three youngsters, who with their irreverence and shamelessness evoke the quarrelsome Futurist *serate*. The Postmodern style of these stories marked the advent of electronic culture and introduced various temporal dimensions, ranging from the Rome of Julius Caesar to the modernity of dance clubs.

The comic strips by GMM, which also featured on the front cover of *Frigidaire* no. 46 (September 1984), were designed on a graphic tablet attached to an Apple II computer. This digital phase of creation was then followed by an analogue one, in which various photo-lithographic processes were used to transpose digital designs onto paper. Apart from techno-juvenile stories created with pixel-based computer programmes,[38] GMM also converted one of their music videos, *Tamburo*, created in 1985 for the singer Teresa De Sio, into a computer comic published in *Linus* no. 255 (June 1986). The computer videos ultimately represent the evolution of GMM's technological experiments within the medium of comics. Amongst these, the animated series *Le avventure di Marionetti*, produced by RAI Radiotelevisione Italiana in 1986, recalls in the name of its protagonist both Marinetti and marionettes.

The Postmodern flair typical of *Frigidaire* can also be found, especially in the years 1983–1985, in *Alter Alter* (1977–85), originally begun as a supplement to *Linus* (1965 – present). *Alter Alter*'s experimental attitude was initially limited to the comic strip alone, with the creation of an insert entitled *Valvoline Motorcomics*, which first appeared in issue 1 (January 1983) and was promoted by the nascent group Valvoline, formed by Igort (pseud. of Igor Tuveri), Giorgio Carpinteri, Marcello Jori, Lorenzo Mattotti, Daniele Brolli and Jerry Kramsky (pseud. of Fabrizio

34 See Munari: *Xerografie originali*, notably the examples of vertical and horizontal slippage in the images.

35 "Quegli uomini possono scrivere in libri di nickel, il cui spessore non supera i tre centimetri, non costa che otto franchi e contiene, nondimeno, centomila pagine." Marinetti: *Guerra sola igiene del mondo*, p. 128.

36 Bertolazzi: "Il primo fumetto al computer."

37 Among the exceptions to this is "Il colore delle tenebre" in *Frigidaire* 49 (December 1984).

38 They were recently republished in volume form in Spampinato: *Giovanotti Mondani Meccanici.*

Ostani). Many of their comics, particularly those created by Carpinteri and Igort, drew explicitly on the Futurist and Cubo-Futurist imaginary. Echoes of the historical avant-garde and the fairy-tale worlds of Depero are also evident in Lorenzo Mattotti's *Il Signor Spartaco* (Mr. Spartacus, 1982), in which some industrial architectures evoke Mario Sironi, *Fuochi* (Fires, 1984) and *Doctor Nefasto* (1983, with texts by Jerry Kramsky), all of which were successfully re-published after their episode-by-episode appearance in *Alter Alter* as comic books.

Between 1984 and 1985, *Alter Alter* multiplied its activities and dedicated space to other sectors such as music, cinema and fashion, often combining them with comic strips. In this manner, apart from some reports on contemporary interior design,[39] memorable monographic issues appeared on music videos in no. 6 (1984), where Mattotti and Kramsky interpreted *I Don't Remember* by Peter Gabriel, and in no. 11 (1984) on the *cravatta-fumetto* (tie-comic), in which we also find an article by Claudia Salaris on the *Manifesto futurista della cravatta italiana* (The Futurist Manifesto of the Italian Tie) written by Renato Di Bosso and Ignazio Scurto in 1933, illustrated with designs by Massimo Giacon in a Neo-Futurist style.

Valvoline Futurism: Igort and Carpinteri

Frigidaire and *Alter Alter*, the two comics magazines most attentive to Futurism and to a recovery of the historical avant-gardes in Postmodern times, did not exist in competition to each other; on the contrary, many of the protagonists of the so-called 'New Italian Comic Strip' were active in both periodicals. In November 1984, *Frigidaire* hosted a tribute to the *Valvoline* group born the previous year within *Alter Alter*, in a special issue called *Valvorama*, in which even Massimo Mattioli participated as an outsider.

In Bologna, Valvoline acted as a full-fledged factory[40] after three of its leading authors – Igort, Carpinteri and Mattotti – had tested different approaches to the comic strip genre in single-issue magazines such as *Pinguino Studios* (also produced by them) and *Nemo in blue*, promoted by Storiestrisce. In the course of the 1980s, Igort, animator of the Valvoline group as well as of innumerable edito-

39 See, for example, the report by Lucilla Saccà on the Memphis design company in issue 3 of March 1984.

40 For more information on Valvoline, see Barbieri: *Valvoforme Valvocolori*, and Igort, et al.: *Valvoline Story*. In the latter catalogue, a photo of Marinetti and Depero appears at the beginning of the chapter *Valvoline racconta* (p. 15), along with one of the 1920 *Dada Messe* from Berlin and a collage by Max Ernst.

rial initiatives in the domain of comic strips,[41] looked especially to Russian Futurism of the post-Revolutionary period, as well as to Boccionian dynamism, certain inventions by Depero[42] and to the Futurist myth of velocity. In *Frigidaire*, he used stories with a strong chromatic impact to create worlds simultaneously Modernist and *futurable*, characterized by a utopian architecture that is reminiscent of Sant'Elia. Soviet iconographies were fused with a hyper-decorative style, particularly in stories such as *Phantomas* (no. 60/61, 1985) or *Balalaiche innamorate* (Balalaikas in Love; no. 39, 1984), both with texts by Brolli, where the hammer and sickle became an abstract pattern that runs along the border of all the strips. Soviet imagery can also be found on the cover of *Melódico moscovita* (Muscovite Melody), the first vinyl of Igort's band *Slava Trudu* (Glory to Labour), defined by him as being the result "of romantic-futurist inspiration"[43] and reviewed by Mariuccia Casadio in *Frigidaire* no. 54 (1985). In other stories, instead, the decomposition of the panels borders on abstraction, as in *L'antiquario di Norimberga* (The Antique Dealer in Nuremberg; no. 48, 1984).

The last of Igort's works in *Frigidaire* which is connected to Futurism was *Miraiha Yaro* (The Futurist Scoundrel, 1986), a story resembling Depero's graphic decorativism with its black-and-white figures in abstract-geometric style (see Fig. 4b).[44] The narration, published in issue 65 (1986) of the magazine,[45] develops in a vertical orientation and is grounded on texts from the Japanese composer and musician Ryuichi Sakamoto, who in that same year recorded the LP *Futurista*, illustrated with some strips by Igort and by the logo of Depero's magazine *Dinamo futurista*.

East Asian and, in particular, Japanese Modernist architecture provided the scenery for many of Igort's meta-temporal stories depicting 'possible worlds', published in *Alter Alter* in the course of the 1980s. Examples of this include *Goodbye Baobab* (1982, republished in 1985 in the Valvoline collection by Milano Libri) and a

---

41 Amongst the magazines, apart from Pinguino, see Dolce vita (1987–1989), Fuego (1990) and the unique large-format issue L'eco di Papassinas (2017). Furthermore, Igort gave life to the publishing houses Coconino and Oblomov, for whom he published some of his most famous graphic novels, such as *5 è il numero perfetto* (5 Is the Perfect Number, 2002) and the series of the *Quaderni giapponesi* (Japanese Notebooks, since 2015). To learn more about the author, see Igort: That's All, Folks! and Igort: Inchiostro su carta.

42 See Igort: *Inchiostro su carta*, p. 145, in relation to a 1983 strip for *Alter Alter*.

43 Igort, et al.: *Valvoline story*, p. 84.

44 Although the drawings of *Miraiha Yaro* are reminiscent of graphics by Japanese Futurists such as Tomoyoshi Murayama, Shuichiro Kinoshita or Yabashi Kimimaro, disseminated by the magazine *Mavo*, the primary inspiration of the story was, according to Igort himself (who confirmed this with me in a personal communication of 2022), the work by Fortunato Depero. Black and white stylizations recur in many of his works from the 1980s.

45 This was recently republished as Igort: *Kokoro*.

masterpiece of Futurist elegance, *Parador Style* (begun in *Alter Alter* in 1982 and continued in *Frigidaire* in 1986). Then followed *Sinfonia a Bombay* (1983, but to be appreciated at its best in a colour version edited by Coconino Press in 2013) and *Ishiki no Kashi* = *Il letargo dei sentimenti* (The Lethargy of Feelings, 1984), a story set in an ultra-modernist Tokyo, dominated by figures dedicated to the cult of beauty and monumental architectures that take inspiration from Sant'Elia, Adalberto Libera, Walter Gropius and Erich Mendelsohn. Igort characterized his comic strips from the mid-1980s as follows: "From Marinetti and company, I borrowed the idea of a 'Futurist refashioning of the universe', hence in paraphrasing and utilizing instruments of design, I wanted to create a universe in which everything was reinvented, from the shape of the vehicles to the buildings, furniture, even clothes that the characters wore."[46]

Echoes of Futurism, and more explicitly of Depero, characterize many of the comic strips of another central figure to the Valvoline group, Giorgio Carpinteri,[47] who borrowed the black-and-white geometric compositions based on stark chiaroscuro contrasts in the illustrations to Gilbert Clavel's *Un istituto per suicidi* (An Institute for Suicides, 1917). These influences can already be seen in *L'uomo non visibile* (The Non-Visible Man), a story published in the single-issue *Nemo in blue* (1980), and became more abstract and geometric in the following year, in *Frigidaire: Incrocio magico* (Magic Crossroads; no. 5, 1981). Still based on a stark contrast between black and white, the latter comics recounts the adventures of a puppet-like killer who wears the clothes of *Signor Bonaventura* by Sto (pseud. of Sergio Tofano)[48] and who, from one crime to the next, lovingly cultivates geometrical polyhedron-shaped figures by watering them.[49] These strong chromatic contrasts were reinforced in other cases by a Constructivist use of colour, often without chiaroscuro. This is clearly noticeable in the (often surreal) stories that Carpinteri created for *Frigidaire*, for example *Parigi precoce* (Early Paris; no. 13, 1981, with Brolli), *Mumble rumble* (no. 17, 1982, together with Jori) and *Sotto la cintura* (Below the Belt; no. 20, 1982).

46 "Da Marinetti e soci avevo mutuato l'idea di 'ricostruzione futurista dell'universo', dunque parafrasando e utilizzando gli strumenti del disegno volevo creare un universo in cui tutto era reinventato, dalla forma dei veicoli agli edifici, agli arredi, sino agli abiti indossati dei personaggi." Igort: *Inchiostro su carta*, p. 164.

47 See, among the other collections of Carpinteri's stories, *Incrocio magico* (1999), *Pop eye* (2018), and the comic book *Aquatlantic* (2018).

48 The character of Signor Bonaventura, created by Sergio Tofano (Sto), appeared for the first time in the *Corriere dei piccoli* (no. 43, October 1917); in each issue, his adventures were structured in eight colour vignettes, displayed on a single page, with text in verse.

49 Geometric settings similar to those of *Incrocio magico* were used by Carpinteri in 1982 to illustrate the cover of the album *Loving Machinery* by the group Central Unit.

Besides these stories – collected in 1983 in the comic book *Flirt*, with an artist's preface by Art Spiegelman and Françoise Mouly (authors, from 1980 to 1991, of the celebrated American magazine *Raw*) – echoes of Depero's style[50] can be also be seen in some of Carpinteri's works for *Alter Alter*, notably in *Polsi sottili* (Thin Wrists), begun in January 1983 and included in 1985 in the aforementioned Valvoline collection by Milano Libri. This comic strip again contains plenty of evocations of Depero's style. His use of black and white, dominated by a stark juxtaposition of light and shadow, would also mark Carpinteri's later creations, both in comic strips – as, for example, in *I diritti del jazz* (The Rights of Jazz), published in the fourth issue of *Fuego* (1990) – and illustrations, as those he conceived in the course of the 1990s for the Communist newspaper *Il manifesto* and its food and wine supplement *Gambero rosso* (Red Prawn).

Massimo Giacon and Massimo Iosa Ghini

Connected to the Valvoline group and active simultaneously in *Frigidaire* and *Alter Alter* were two other exceptional authors who sought Futurist solutions, but from contrasting positions and different starting points: Massimo Giacon and Massimo Iosa Ghini. After having debuted in the pages of *Il mago* (The Magician; 1972–80), just as Carpinteri did, Massimo Giacon began producing comic strips populated by puppet-like figures with sharp and jagged profiles, built with rigid lines and acute angles, which in many respects evoke the playful iconographies of Depero, albeit distorted and altered by an aesthetic that was both post-punk and sensationalist in nature. These stories with vibrant colour schemes first turned up in *Linus* in 1982 with the adventures of *Beppe Starnazza e i vortici* (Beppe Starnazza and the Vortices), written by Giacon together with Roberto "Freak" Antoni (Beppe Starnazza was one of his nicknames), leader of the 'comedy punk' band Skiantos, formed in Bologna in 1975.

The performances of Skiantos had much in common with the irreverence and the provocation of the Futurist *serate*. In *Largo all'avanguardia* (Make Way for the Avant-garde, 1978), they mocked the audience with verses such as: "The alternative avant-garde / doesn't give group discounts / The avant-garde is very rough / That's why it is scary / Make way for the avant-garde / You're a shitty audience / You ap-

50 On the re-use of Depero's style in the work of Carpinteri, see Castaldi: *Drawn and Dangerous*, pp. 125–128.

plaud by inertia / But the avant-garde is very serious").[51] On various occasions, members of the band threw all sorts of vegetables into the audience, taking a page from the book of the Futurist soirées of the 1910. A playful, and at the same time wiry hyper-decorativism also characterized Giacon's *Fuzzi Bugsi è un uomo brutto* (Fuzzi Bugsi Is an Ugly Man), published in *Alter Alter* between 1984 and 1985, a frenzied story with a Neo-Futurist taste, also graphically connected to the cover of the 1984 album *Fuzzi Bugsi tumpa il bongo!* (a play with words, referring to the main character playing the bongo drum), released by Giacon's band at the time, the Spirocheta Pergoli (1984–85).

From January 1983 onwards, Giacon provided comics with texts by Mimì Colucci in *Frigidaire* and its appendices, *Tempi supplementari* and *Frizzer*; stories which were later collected in the comic book *Mecanostorie* (Mechanical Stories, 1985). Amongst the many comic strips by Giacon that recall stylistic features of Futurism, I should like to mention at least two examples. The first is *Photo de rêves (aerei in picchiata)* (Photo of Dreams: Nosediving Aeroplanes) from *Frigidaire* no. 51–52 (1984), an homage to Futurist *aeropittura*. The second is *Snaporazz Restaurant*, created in conjunction with Ettore Sottsass, featured in issue 64 (1986) and focussed on a project which unfortunately only remained on paper: a restaurant that evoked Futurist cabarets such as Balla's *Bal Tic Tac* (1921) and Depero's *Cabaret Diavolo* (1922). Giacon's relationship with Sottsass – a celebrated architect and Postmodern designer who showed great admiration of Depero's playful creativity – did not come by chance. Giacon had collaborated with the Sottsass Studio in 1985, an experience he recounted in several comic strips: first, in *Fuochi d'artificio* (Fireworks), published in episodes in the magazine *TIC*, starting from its very first issue (1989); and later in the comic book *Ettore: Mr. Sottsass Jr. e il mistero degli oggetti* (Ettore: Mr. Sottsass Jr. and the Mystery of Objects, 2015).

Another icon of Italian comics concerned with aspects of interior design and architecture was Massimo Iosa Ghini, who worked for some years with Valvoline (although he was never an official member of the group). His activity in the world of comics was short but intense. He began with some short stories in *Frigidaire*, in which he experimented with a fusion of comics and photography. One of these was *Ornamento e delitto* (Ornament and Crime) in no. 19, 1982, which recalled Adolf Loos' eponymous essay of 1908, *Ornament und Verbrechen*, and featured Mies van der Rohe and Walter Gropius as characters. Another one was *Estate 1971* (Summer 1971, 1983), which tells a summer love adventure through earthy colours

---

51 "L'avanguardia alternativa / Non fa sconti comitiva / L'avanguardia è molto dura / E per questo fa paura / Fate largo all'avanguardia / Siete un pubblico di merda / Applaudite per inerzia / Ma l'avanguardia è molto seria."

and abstract images. Iosa Ghini's most mature comic strips, developed in the pages of *Alter Alter*, where between 1983 and 1984 he published *Sillavengo* in five episodes (see Fig. 5a). This long story, with texts by Maurizio Corrado, recounts the vicissitudes of Edoardo Antonio Sillavengo, an Italian captain in colonial Africa during the 1930s, inspired by the memories of a relative of the architect Luigi Caccia Dominioni (1913–2016). The aviator is masterfully evoked in a style that fuses comics with architecture and design, drawing on Futurism and *Valori plastici* (a magazine published in Rome between 1918 and 1922), Boccioni's dynamism and *aeropittura*. The Modernist architectures in these stories also recall Frank Gehry, Erich Mendelsohn and Antonio Sant'Elia. The *bas-de-page* make use of sketches of architectures and of design objects from the 1900s, including works by Adalberto Libera, Luciano Baldessari, Sottsass and Iosa Ghini himself, as well as references to Sottsass Jr.'s Memphis Studio. In its complexity, *Sillavengo* was an all-encompassing and experimental work, later reissued in the magazines *Heavy Metal* (USA, 1977 – present) and *Ryūkō tsūshin* (Japan, 1979–2007).

Iosa Ghini's experience in the field of experimental comics related to Futurism was short-lived, but significantly influenced his later aesthetic research, notably that which was connected to Bolidismo.[52] Bolidism as a word was related to fireballs or rockets, referring to a cardinal theme of Futurism – velocity. He had co-founded this movement in 1986 and contributed to it by means of his fluid and dynamic designs, bordering on the immaterial and focussing on curved lines, as in the Bolidò, a discotheque with furniture of a Neo-Futurist taste, projected by the architect in New York in 1988.[53]

Futurism and the comics today

Up to this point, I have discussed some protagonists of the so-called 'Italian avant-garde comics', who received aesthetic lessons from Futurism in a certain phase of their professional careers. Many more took inspiration from the historical avant-gardes in a more spontaneous manner. From amongst these, I should like to mention Daniele Scandola, who created comics in an abstract-geometric style in *Alter Alter*, for example *La retta e il labirinto* (The Straight Line and the Labyrinth), with Guido Beltramini, in issue 5 of May 1984; or Gianluca Lerici, alias Professor Bad Trip, who was active both in *Frigidaire* and in various other fanzines, in which

52 The Bolidist Movement was founded in 1986 in Bologna by sixteen architects and interior designers. Their accentuated dynamism of forms cited Futurism and the Memphis and Alchimia groups.

53 See Giacomoni: "Ha portato il futurismo anche in discoteca."

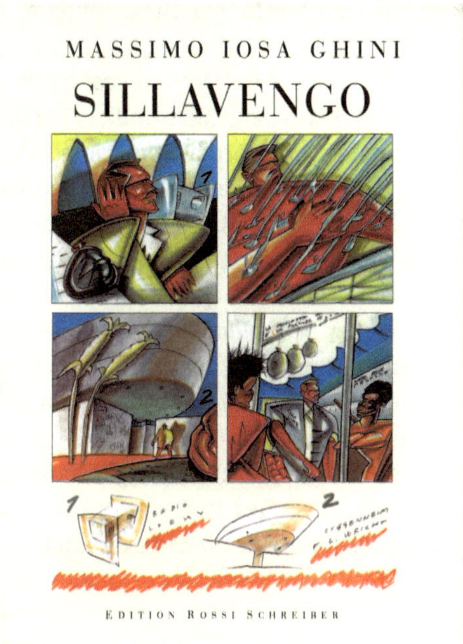

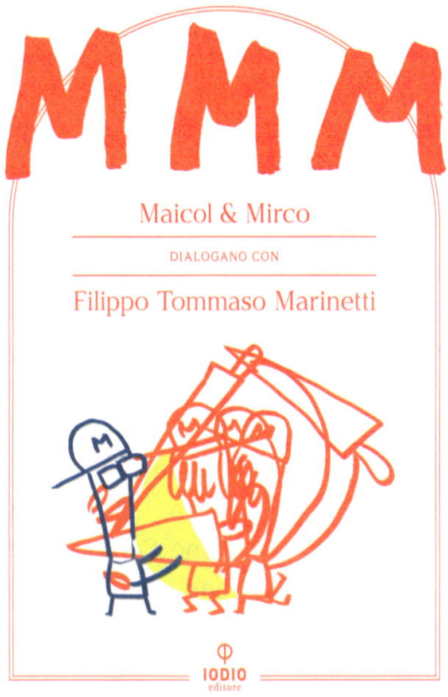

Fig. 5a: Massimo Iosa Ghini (texts by Maurizio Corrado): *Sillavengo*. Munich: Rossi Schreiber, 1991, previously published in instalments, between 1983 and 1984, in *Alter Alter*. **Fig. 5b:** Maicol & Mirco: *MMM: Maicol & Mirco dialogano con Filippo Tommaso Marinetti*. San Benedetto del Tronto (AP): Iodio, 2020. Artist's edition in 300 copies.

he created vignettes dedicated to Luigi Russolo, for example in issue 4 (June 1992) of the musical magazine *Rumore*.

References to Futurism and its protagonists are also present in the complex panorama of contemporary Italian comics, despite being occasional and often issued outside the normal publishing world. For instance, Marinetti's movement is evoked in *La dottrina* (The Docrine, 2002–10) by Carmine di Giandomenico with texts by Alessandro Bilotta. The comic uses a retro and at the same time futuristic setting, as well as quotations at the beginning of each chapter from Marinetti, Aldo Palazzeschi, Enrico Cavacchioli, Tullio D'Albisola, Luciano Folgore and Ardengo Soffici.

Intonarumori (Noise-Intoners, 2018) by Andrea De Franco, by contrast, is a dreamlike story in comic form, in which the sonorous harmony of Russolo's instruments is graphically transposed into images verging on Art Brut and pure abstraction. Another work, *Colore inferno: Artisti spezzati dalla Grande Guerra 1914–1918* (Colour of Hell: Artists Broken by the Great War, 2018) by Cecilia Valagussa and Ariel Macchi recounts in intense images the tragic disappearance of nine artists

– including Boccioni and Sant'Elia – during the First World War. Here, Futurism is evoked on the front cover by a design that emulates Marinetti's *Zang Tumb Tuuum* (1914). Another example that is relevant in this context is *MMM: Maicol e Mirco dialogano con Filippo Tommaso Marinetti* (MMM: Maicol and Mirco Talk to Filippo Tommaso Marinetti, 2020; see Fig. 5b). This book, in large format and printed only in 300 numbered copies, presents the caustic scribbles of the comic star Maicol & Mirco (pseud. of Michael Rocchetti) and evokes several of Marinetti's manifestos, reproduced in their entirety. Furthermore, I need to mention *Il magico mondo dei Muffi!* (The Magical World of the Muffi, 2021) by Hurricane (pseud. of Ivan Manuppelli). This is a parody of the comic series *Les Schtroumpfs* (The Smurfs) by the Belgian artist Peyo (pseud. of Pierre Culliford) and includes a recreation of the poster *Nuovo teatro futurista* (New Futurist Theatre, 1924) by Fortunato Depero. And finally, the graphic novel *Dynamic Depero, 1928–30: Avventure a New York* (Dynamic Depero, 1928–30: Adventures in New York) by Sergio Varbella with texts by Gaetano Cappa and Marco Drago, dedicated to Depero's first trip to New York and published on the occasion of the aforementioned exhibition *Depero new Depero* at MART Rovereto in 2021–22.

Trespassing the genre boundaries: Music, video, fashion, design

After highlighting the great diversity of comic strips in Italy and their debts to Futurism, I shall finally turn to the issue of Postmodern hybridization, i.e. the fusion of comics and other media in the 1980s, in particular those designed for musicians and bands of the time. It is important to underline that some of these authors engaged intensively in musical activities, notably Giacon, who in 1994 composed a mechanical march entitled *Ascoltando Depero* (Listening to Depero). Amongst the works of Igort, we should take note of his onomalingua poetry[54] and noise compositions inspired by Russolo and performed with his band Slava Trudu. Mention should also be made of the singular case of Igort's comic *Parador Style*, transformed by the band Surprize on a soundtrack of their album *In movimento* (1984). A curious blend of music and Happening could be observed on 10 April 1983 at the Teatro La Soffitta in Bologna during a *Valvoline Party* sponsored by *Alter Alter*. The whole Valvoline group participated, with Massimo Giacon dressed

54 Onomalingua was an abstract form of verbalization developed by Depero in the 1910s, mixing onomatopoeia and vocal noise into a 'universal language' that can be intuitively understood by everybody.

in musician's garb, Massimo Iosa Ghini creating design objects for the occasion[55] and Beppe Starnazza (Roberto 'Freak' Antoni) acting as host. A year later, in August 1984, the discotheque Aleph Club in Gabicce Mare near Rimini – a celebrated hub of the Italian New Wave scene – hosted a week-long *Frigidaire Party*, animated by Tamburini, Scozzari and the Giovanotti Mondani Meccanici.

The correlations between comics and interior design were also significant. An exemplary case is that of the Memphis group, founded by Ettore Sottsass Jr. and acting as a Postmodern heir to the Futurist *case d'arte* of Balla, Depero and Rizzo.[56] In 1987, the exhibition *Architectural Strip* was held in their Milanese premises, with works by Baldazzini, Brolli, Carpinteri, Giacon, Giandelli, Iosa Ghini, Igort, Mattotti and Scandola, accompanied by a catalogue edited by Barbara Radice. The Studio Alchimia also engaged with the Valvoline group in an event called *Valvotappeti volanti* (Flying Carpet Cleaners, 1989), featuring Igort, Carpinteri, Mattotti Jori and Brolli. Another case was the Swiss Swatch Group, which outsourced some of their watch designs to Italian artists such as Echaurren, Igort and Giacon. That the company's creative laboratory that had developed the Swatch brand took cues from Futurism is demonstrated by a Pop-Swatch model called *The Woodleaker*, produced in 1993 on the basis of an image from Depero's imaginary zoo.

In addition to the fields of music videos and television reels, created by authors such as Iosa Ghini, Echaurren, Igort, Mattotti, the GMM and Carpinteri, another sector in which the hybridization of Postmodern genres could be observed during the 1980s is fashion design. Besides the aforementioned Vudu line presented by Tamburini in *Frigidaire*, and the comic album *Vestire il futuro* (Dressing the Future) by Echaurren issued on the occasion of the centenary of Futurism, the advertisements made by Iosa Ghini for W.P. Lavori in Corso, Ferré and Krizia need to be mentioned here, as well as the neckties made by Giacon and Iosa Ghini for Memphis; the advertisements by Scozzari for Barbour and Vans; and, above all, the numerous comic strips by authors from the Valvoline group for Condé Nast's *Vanity* magazine. Eventually, in 1985, a fashion show connected to the textile producer Picchi in Prato brought to the catwalk some Modernist outfits inspired by Igort's comics *Ishiki no Kashi = Il letargo dei sentimenti.* Fashion was also at the centre of some articles published in *Frigidaire* and *Alter Alter* by prominent stylists such as Elio Fiorucci[57] who, in 1984, transposed his pop imagination into a well-known collection of promotional figurines commercialized by Panini.[58]

55 See Tondelli: "Valvoline Party."

56 About one dozen of these *case d'arte* are portrayed in Ruta: "Interior Design, Furniture, and Decorative Arts." On Sottsass' debts to them see Ruta: *Arredi futuristi*, p. 24.

57 See, for example, Fiorucci: "Vestirsi."

Critical reception

Italian avant-garde comics had a vast echo abroad during the 1980s and were reported on in the most prestigious international comic magazines, such as *L'Écho des savanes* in France, *El vibora* in Spain and *Raw* in the United States. Furthermore, in France, *Editions Artefacts* published in 1984 an anthology in the form of an LP, *Musicomix (Made in Italy)*, which was introduced with a text by Daniele Brolli and featured several authors from *Frigidaire* and Valvoline. This collection of stories centred on music and was presented in a performative soirée at the discotheque Les Bains Douches in Paris.

One of the most peculiar aspects of this vibrant period of Italian comics was that it anticipated the rediscovery and popularization of Futurism in the wake of the path-breaking *Futurismo & Futurismi* exhibition at Palazzo Grassi in Venice in 1986. Many of the above-mentioned artists in fact participated in important exhibitions dedicated to the fusion of art and comics, for example *Registrazione di frequenze* (Frequency Recording, 1982) in Bologna, in a special section curated by Francesca Alinovi,[59] or the travelling show *Anniottanta* (The Nineteen-Eighties, 1985), organized by Roberto Daolio,[60] or *Zark! Le tavole narranti* (Zark! Narrative Panels, 1985) in Jesi, promoted by Mariella Mastri.[61] In the catalogue of the latter exhibition, several essays investigated the new Italian comic authors' debts to Futurism. Giovanni Anceschi, for example, compared certain figures of Boccioni to the stories of *Pentothal* by Pazienza, while simultaneously highlighting the Futurist traces in the works of Echaurren and Igort;[62] Daniele Barbieri likened Marinetti's movement to the irreverent actions and the spirit of the *Cannibal* group of authors who, by no accident, adopted certain Futurist features in Pazienza's aforementioned strip.[63] Finally, Lucia Corrain traced various connections between these authors and historical Futurism, from the concepts of simultaneity and dynamism to fashion design, citing Igort, Iosa Ghini and Mattotti.[64]

Also in 1985, Pablo Echaurren reflected on the relationship between comics and the avant-garde in *Alter Alter.* He reclaimed for the contemporary art comics

58 Panini is synonymous worldwide with stickers and albums. It is the brand name of an Italian company based in Modena and named after the Panini brothers, who founded it in 1961.

59 Alinovi: "Frontiere di immagini". On the occasion of this exhibition, the scholar coined the term 'Nuovo fumetto italiano' (New Italian Comic).

60 Daolio: "L'immagine 'strisciante': Il nuovo fumetto italiano."

61 Mastri: *Zark! Le tavole narranti.*

62 Anceschi: "Introduzione all'arcadia teppistica", p. 9.

63 Barbieri: "Antropofagi e gigolo", pp. 13–16.

64 Corrain: "Effetto avanguardia", pp. 21–22.

a radical attitude that was similar to the innovative drive of the historical avant-garde in all artistic fields.[65] The fusion of Futurism and comics also emerged in the critical discourse from the exhibition *Futurismo & Futurismi* in 1986. Echaurren was once again the first to emphasize, in a special issue of *Alfabeta* dedicated to the event in Venice, the analogies between the Futurist avant-garde and the authors of the Postmodern comics.[66] A few months later, in another special issue of the magazine, this time on comics, Omar Calabrese highlighted the fact that the new Italian comics were greatly indebted to the historical avant-garde.[67] At the same time, Lorenzo Miglioli, on the pages of *Frigidaire*, attacked the exhibition at Palazzo Grassi because its curator, Pontus Hultén, had not invited any post-WWII successors of Futurism, such as Carpinteri, Igort, Echaurren, Iosa Ghini, Mattotti or Giacon.[68]

In 1989, the exhibition *Artoon*, curated in Rome by Achille Bonito Oliva, offered a different point of view, namely that of the influence of comics on twentieth-century art. Amongst the featured artists, there were both Futurist 'influencers' such as Depero, and the 'followers' such as Pablo Echaurren.[69] In 1991, the theme was further explored in the exhibition *Nuovo fumetto italiano: Frigidaire, Valvoline, Dolce Vita e dintorni*, curated by Carlo Branzaglia and Roberto Daolio in Reggio Emilia,[70] which definitively enshrined the peculiarity and the avant-garde spirit of these innovators in the medium of comic strips.

A final stage in the critical exploration of the links between Futurism and the comic strip was Claudia Salaris' *Futurismo: L'avanguardia delle avanguardie*,[71] which had a chapter entitled "Alle sorgenti del moderno" (At the Source of Modernity), in which the influence of Futurism on fashion, design, typography, music and comics is analysed, with detailed references to Echaurren, Giacon, Iosa Ghini, Mattotti, Pazienza and Tamburini.

In conclusion, it seems that the relationship between Futurism and comics deserves a more careful and interdisciplinary critical investigation, one that avoids those prejudices that were typical in earlier studies, now long superseded. This

---

65 "The typical seeds of the 1900s artistic avant-gardes have been introduced into comics [...], the need for novelty, for the demolition of ossified rules so as to allow itself full liberty." Echaurren: "Fumetto d'avanguardia", p. 71.

66 "[Postmodern comics] demonstrate clear references to the dynamism of Balla and Boccioni, to the architecture of Sant'Elia and the aero-architecture of the 1930s, to the pre-pop robotization of Depero, to the aviation myths of *aeropittura*." Echaurren: "Il futurismo di attualità", p. 155

67 Calabrese: "Il fumetto può essere arte?"

68 Miglioli: "Futur-ismo / stupidità."

69 Bonito Oliva: *Artoon*.

70 Branzaglia and Daolio: *Nuovo fumetto italiano*.

71 Salaris: *Futurismo*, pp. 214–231.

essay is intended to be a first step in this direction, which at a later stage will be expanded to include the production in other countries as well.

Bibliography

Studies

Alinovi, Francesca: "Frontiere di immagini." Francesca Alinovi et al., eds.: *Registrazione di frequenze.* Exhibition catalogue. Bologna: Galleria d'Arte Moderna, from 20 March 1982. Casalecchio di Reno: Grafis, 1982. 2–9.

Anceschi, Giovanni: "Introduzione all'arcadia teppistica." Mariella Mastri, ed.: *Zark!: Le tavole narranti.* Montepulciano (SI): Editori del Grifo, 1985. 9.

Ballesi, Chiara, et al., eds.: *L'edicola che non c'è: La stampa underground a Milano.* Milano: Agenzia X, 2020.

Barbieri, Daniele: "Antropofagi e gigolo." Mariella Mastri, ed.: *Zark!: Le tavole narranti.* Montepulciano (SI): Editori del Grifo, 1985. 13–16.

Barbieri, Daniele: *Valvoforme Valvocolori.* Milano: Idea Books, 1990.

Baroni, Vittore: *Arte postale: Guida al network della corrispondenza creativa.* Bertiolo: AAA edizioni, 1997.

Belloli, Carlo: "Armando Mazza: Precursore 'mail art' futurista d'assalto." *Futurismo-oggi* 16:11–12 (November-December 1984): 15–20.

Bertolazzi, Carmen: "Il primo fumetto al computer." *Frigidaire* 42 (May 1984): 21.

Bonito Oliva, Achille, ed.: *Pablo Echaurren: "Pitture."* Exhibition catalogue. Roma: Galleria Giulia, dal 20 January 1989.

Bonito Oliva, Achille, et al., eds.: *Artoon: L'influenza del fumetto nelle arti visive del 20. secolo.* Exhibition catalogue. Roma: Palazzo della Civiltà del Lavoro, novembre 1989 – gennaio 1990. Napoli: Electa, 1989.

Bonito Oliva, Achille, et al., eds.: *Depero e Rubino: Ovvero il futurismo spiegato ai bambini ed il bambino spiegato ai futuristi.* Exhibition catalogue. Parma: Palazzo Pigorini, 17 ottobre 1999–30 gennaio 2000. Milano: Mazzotta, 1999.

Bono, Gianni, and Matteo Stefanelli, eds.: *Fumetto! 150 anni di storie italiane.* Milano: Rizzoli, 2012, 2nd edn 2016.

Boschi, Luca: *Frigo valvole e balloons: Viaggio in vent'anni di fumetto italiano d'autore.* Roma: Theoria, 1997.

Branzaglia, Carlo, and Roberto Daolio, eds.: *Nuovo fumetto italiano: Frigidaire, Valvoline, Dolce vita e dintorni.* Exhibition catalogue. Reggio Emilia: Ex Stalloni, 29 giugno – 18 agosto 1991. Milano: Fabbri, 1991.

Calabrese, Omar: "Il fumetto può essere arte?" *L'arte del fumetto.* Supplement to *Alfabeta* 91 (December 1986): 1.

Calvesi, Maurizio: *Avanguardia di massa.* Milano: Feltrinelli, 1978.

Castaldi, Simone: *Drawn and Dangerous: Italian Comics of the 1970s and 1980s.* Jackson/MI: University Press of Mississippi, 2010.

Ciaponi, Francesco: *Underground: Ascesa e declino di un'altra editoria.* Milano: Costa & Nolan, 2007.

Corrain, Lucia: “Effetto avanguardia.” Mariella Mastri, ed.: *Zark!: Le tavole narranti.* Montepulciano (SI): Editori del Grifo, 1985. 21–22.
Curreri, Luciano: “Sulle tracce di un Pinocchio ‘futurista’: La variante Pinocchietto alla guerra europea.” Bart Van den Bosche, Giuseppe Manica, and Carmen Van den Bergh, eds.: *Azione/Reazione: Il futurismo in Belgio e in Europa.* Firenze: Cesati, 2012. 305–314.
Daolio, Roberto: “L’immagine ‘strisciante’: Il nuovo fumetto italiano.” Carlo Gentili, ed.: *Anniottanta.* Milano: Mazzotta, 1985. 398–399.
De Donno, Emanuele, and Amedeo Martegani, eds.: *Yes Yes Yes Revolutionary Press in Italy 1966–1977: From Mondo Beat tu Zut.* Milano: a+m bookstore, 2018.
Dogheria, Duccio: “Marinetti, Majakovskij & Co: L’avanguardia a fumetti di Pablo Echaurren.” Claudio Gallo, Nicola Spagnolli, Andrea Tenca, and Ingrid Zenari, eds: *Il cocktail gradevole e levigato dei linguaggi nel fumetto contemporaneo.* Rovereto (TN): Accademia degli Agiati, 2023. 61–71.
Dogheria, Duccio: “Remix futuristi formato fumetto.” Nicoletta Boschiero, ed.: *Depero new Depero.* Cinisello Balsamo (MI): Silvana, 2021. 110–117.
Echaurren, Pablo: “Fumetto d’avanguardia.” *Alter Alter* 12:5 (May 1985): 71–72.
Echaurren, Pablo: “Le futurisme d’actualité = Il futurismo d’attualità.” *Alfabeta / La Quinzaine littéraire* 8:84 (May 1986): 154–155.
Echaurren, Pablo, and Claudia Salaris: *Controcultura in Italia 1966–1977: Viaggio nell’underground.* Torino: Bollati Boringhieri, 1999.
Eco, Umberto: *Apocalittici e integrati.* Milano: Bompiani, 1964.
Eco, Umberto: *Sette anni di desiderio.* Milano: Bompiani, 1983.
Fiorucci, Elio: “Vestirsi.” *Alter Alter* 12:7 (July 1985): 57–58.
Galfré, Monica, and Simone Neri Serneri: *Il movimento del ‘77: Tadici, snodi, luoghi.* Roma: Viella, 2018.
Gallino, Ignazio Maria, ed.: *1965–1985: 20 anni di controcultura in Italia: Frammenti storici dell’underground italiana. Memorie, opuscoli, periodici, volantini, manifesti, ciclostilati, fogli di controinformazione dei movimenti underground alternativi e giovanili italiani.* Milano, Gallino, 2017.
Gaspa, Pier Luigi: *Dal Signor Bonaventura a Saturno contro la terra: Agli albori del fumetto in Italia (1908–1945).* Roma: Carocci, 2020.
Gazzotti, Melania, ed.: *Vietato vietare: Controcultura in Italia, 1968–1977.* Mantova: Corraini, 2019.
Giacomoni, Silvia: “Ha portato il futurismo anche in discoteca.” *Arte: Rivista mensile di arte, cultura, informazione* 20:207 (May 1990): 100–103.
Giannì, Eugenio: *La Mail Art tra futurismo e inismo.* Valencia: El Doctor Sax, 2011.
Igort [pseud. of Igor Tuveri]: *Inchiostro su carta: Artbook.* Quartu Sant’Elena (CA): Oblomov, 2021.
Igort, ed.: *That’s All, Folks!* Exhibition catalogue. Reggio Emilia: San Domenico, 3 luglio – 15 agosto 1993. Bologna: Granata, 1993.
Igort, et al., eds.: *Valvoline Story.* Exhibition catalogue. Bologna: Fondazione del Monte, 2–30 marzo 2014.
Iosa Ghini, Massimo: *Sillavengo.* München: Edition Rossi Schreinber, 1991.
Lo Monaco, Giovanna: “Il graphic novel secondo Pablo Echaurren” Elisabetta Bacchereti, Federico Fastelli, and Diego Salvadori, eds., *Il graphic novel: Un crossover per la modernità.* Firenze: Florence University Press, 2020, 207–222.
Loparco, Fabiana: *I bambini e la guerra. Il “Corriere dei piccoli” e il primo conflitto mondiale (1915–1918).* Firenze: Nerbini, 2011.
Mancebo Roca, Juan Agustín: “Depero New Depero: Rovereto Presents the Artist and His Reception after 1960.” *International Yearbook of Futurism Studies* 12 (2022): 385–397.

Marinetti, Filippo Tommaso: *Guerra sola igiene del mondo.* Milano: Edizioni futuriste di "Poesia", 1915.
Mariscalco, Danilo: *Dai laboratori alle masse: Pratiche artistiche e comunicazione nel movimento del '77.* Verona: Ombre Corte, 2014.
Mastri, Mariella, ed.: *Zark!: Le tavole narranti.* Exhibiton catalogue. Jesi: Palazzo dei Convegni, 20 luglio – 4 agosto 1985. Montepulciano (SI): Editori del Grifo, 1985.
Miglioli, Lorenzo: "Futur-ismo / stupid-ità." *Frigidaire* 71 (October 1986): 64–65.
Mordente, Michele, and Gianmario Rizzardi, eds.: *Nuvole sotterranee: Il fumetto underground italiano degli anni Settanta.* Agropoli: Muscles Edizioni Uderground, 2015.
Mordente, Michele, ed.: *Stefano Tamburini: Muscoli e forbici. Un'antologia grafica definitiva.* Roma: Coconino Press, 2017.
Mordente, Michele, ed.: *Tutto Tamburo.* Vols. 1–7. Agropoli: Muscles Edizioni Uderground, 2018–2022.
Munari, Bruno, ed.: *Xerografie originali.* Bologna: Zanichelli, 1977.
Parmiggiani, Sergio, ed.: *Pablo Echaurren, iconoclast!* Exhibition catalogue. London: Estorick Collection of Modern Art, 20 January – 19 April 2014. Cinisello Balsamo (MI): Silvana, 2014.
Perna, Raffaella: "Gastone Novelli e le bandes dessinées: Alle origini dei Viaggi di Brek." Gastone Novelli: *I viaggi di Brek.* Milano: Postmediabooks, 2020. 31–63.
Perna, Raffaella: *Pablo Echaurren: Il movimento del '77 e gli indiani metropolitani.* Milano: Postmediabooks, 2016.
Pignotti, Lamberto: *Ricostruzione dell'universo futurista.* Firenze: Vallecchi, 2009. 2nd edn 2013.
Pignotti, Lamberto, and Stefania Stefanelli: *La scrittura verbo-visiva.* Roma: L'Espresso, 1980.
Pizzi, Katia: "Antonio Rubino in odor di futurismo." Claudio Bertieri, ed.: *Mondo fanciullo: Antonio Rubino narratore per i ragazzi.* Sanremo: Comune di Sanremo, 2005. 67–80.
Rigo, Paolo: "Caricatures of Futurism in 'Il travaso delle idee'." *International Yearbook of Futurism Studies* 10 (2020): 324–327.
Ruta, Anna Maria: "Interior Design, Furniture, and Decorative Arts." Günter Berghaus, ed.: *Handbook of International Futurism.* Berlin & Boston: De Gruyter, 2019. 175–192.
Ruta, Anna Maria: *Arredi futuristi: Episodi delle case d'arte futuriste italiane.* Palermo: Novecento, 1985.
Salaris, Claudia: *Futurismo: L'avanguardia delle avanguardie.* Firenze: Giunti, 2009.
Salaris, Claudia: *Il movimento del Settantasette: Linguaggi e scritture dell'ala creativa.* Bertiolo: AAA, 1997.
Scarpa, Laura, ed.: *Le storie nere del "Corriere dei piccoli": Il colonialismo italiano del primo 900 a fumetti.* Roma: ComicOut, 2019.
Spampinato, Francesco, ed.: *Giovanotti Mondani Meccanici: Computer Comics 1984–1987.* Roma: Nero, 2021.
Sparagna, Vincenzo: "Viaggiare tra le merci." *Frigidaire* 1 (November 1980): 5.
Sparagna, Vincenzo: *Frigidaire: L'incredibile storia e le sorprendenti avventure della più rivoluzionaria rivista d'arte del mondo.* Milano: BUR, 2008.
Sparagna, Vincenzo, ed.: *L'avventura maivista di "Frigidaire" 1980–2020.* Giano dell'Umbria (PG): Frigidaire, 2020.
Stancanelli, Annalisa: *Vittorini e i balloons: I fumetti del "Politecnico".* Acireale (CA): Bonanno, 2008.
Sturani, Enrico: *Nuove cartoline: Cartoline postali di ieri e di oggi in un'ottica d'avanguardia.* Roma: Savelli, 1981.
Tamburini, Stefano: "Roma Vudu Moda." *Frigidaire* 29 (April 1983): 30–35.
Tondelli, Pier Vittorio: *Un weekend postmoderno: Cronache dagli anni Ottanta.* Milano: Bompiani, 1990.
Tondelli, Pier Vittorio: "Valvoline Party." *Alter Alter* 7 (July 1983): 52–53.

Tosti, Andrea: *Graphic novel: Storia e teoria del romanzo a fumetti e del rapporto fra parola e immagine.* Latina: Tunué, 2016.
Vacchelli, Carlotta: *Pablo Echaurren: Controfumetto.* Exhibition catalogue. Cremona: PQV Fine Art, 9 giugno – 10 luglio 2022. Cremona: Centro fumetto "Andrea Pazienza", 2022.
Volt [pseud. of Vincenzo Fani Ciotti]: "Manifesto della moda femminile futurista." *Roma futurista* 2:72 (29 February 1920): 1. Reprinted in Guido Andrea Pautasso, ed.: *Moda futurista.* Milano: Abscondita, 2016. 65–68. English translation "Futurist Manifesto of Women's Fashion." Lawrence Rainey, Christine Poggi, and Laura Wittman, eds.: *Futurism: An Anthology.* New Haven/CT: Yale University Press, 2009. 253–254.

Comics

Albani, Paolo, and Paolo della Bella: *Note per il manifesto del neo-futurismo.* Firenze: Edizioni Libreria Feltrinelli, 1967.
Buzzati, Dino: *Poema a fumetti.* Milano: Mondadori, 1969.
Carpinteri, Giorgio: *Flirt.* Milano: Primo Carnera, 1983.
Carpinteri, Giorgio: *Polsi sottili.* Milano: Milano Libri, 1985.
De Franco, Andrea: *Intonarumori.* Francavilla Fontana (BO): De Press, 2018.
Di Giandomenico, Carmine, and Alessandro Bilotta: *La dottrina.* Vols. 1–3. Ariccia (RM): Magic Press; Reggio Emilia: Gruppo Saldatori, 2002–2010. Reprinted Milano: Feltrinelli, 2019.
Drago, Marco, Sergio Varbella, and Gaetano Cappa: *Dynamic Depero, 1928–30: Avventure a New York.* Rovereto (TN): MART Museo di Arte Moderna e Contemporanea di Trento e Rovereto, 2021.
Echaurren, Pablo: *Caffeina d'Europa: Vita di* F.T. Marinetti. Montepulciano (SI): Editori del Grifo, 1998.
Echaurren, Pablo: *Dada con le zecche.* Mantua: Corraini, 1997.
Echaurren, Pablo: *Evaporazioni.* Poggibonsi: Lalli, 1979.
Echaurren, Pablo: *Evola in Dada.* Roma: Settimo Sigillo, 1994.
Echaurren, Pablo: *Futurismo contro.* Mantova: Corraini, 1995.
Echaurren, Pablo: *Hurrà!* Roma: Cascella, 1979.
Echaurren, Pablo: *Iconoclasta!* Faenza: Circolo degli Artisti, 1994.
Echaurren, Pablo: *Majakovskij: Pitture parlanti.* Roma: Edizioni del Serraglio, 1986.
Echaurren, Pablo: *Nivola Vola: Storia disegnata di Tazio Nuvolari.* Mantua: Corraini, 1992.
Echaurren, Pablo: *Saette.* Milano: Primo Carnera, 1985.
Echaurren, Pablo: *Terremoto Picasso*. Bagheria: Drago, 2006.
Echaurren, Pablo: *Vestire il futuro.* Biella: Gruppo Istituto Editoriale Biellese, 2009.
Echaurren, Pablo: *Vita di Pound.* Rimini: Guaraldi, 1993.
Echaurren, Pablo: *Vita disegnata di Dino Campana.* Montepulciano (SI): Editori del Grifo, 1994.
Eco, Umberto, and Eugenio Carmi: *Stripsody.* Roma: Arco d'Alimbert; Houston/TX: Kiko Galleries, 1966.
Giacon, Massimo, and Mimì Colucci: *Mecanostorie.* Milano: Primo Carnera, 1985.
Giacon, Massimo: *Ettore: Mr. Sottsass Jr. e il mistero degli oggetti.* Milano: 24 Ore Cultura, 2015.
Igort [pseud. of Igor Tuveri]: *Goodbye Baobab.* Milano: Milano Libri, 1985.
Igort [pseud. of Igor Tuveri]: *Kokoro.* Quartu Sant' Elena (CA): Oblomov, 2019.
Hurricane [pseud. of Ivan Manuppelli]: *Il magico mondo dei Muffi!* Milano: Self-edition, 2021.
Iosa Ghini, Massimo, and Maurizio Corrado: *Sillavengo.* München: Schreiber & Leser, 1991.

Maicol & Mirco [pseud. of Michael Rocchetti]: *MMM: Maicol & Mirco dialogano con Filippo Tommaso Marinetti.* San Benedetto del Tronto (AP): Iodio, 2020.
Mattotti, Lorenzo: *Il Signor Spartaco: Viaggi di un epicentrico.* Milano: Milano Libri, 1985.
Novelli, Gastone: *I viaggi di Brek.* Venezia: Alfieri, 1967. Reprint. Milano: Postmedia Books, 2021.
Pignotti, Lamberto: *Biblia pauperum.* Roma: Elle Ci, 1977.
Tamburini, Stefano: *Muscles.* Milano: Primo Carnera, 1984.
Tamburini, Stefano, and Tanino Liberatore: *RanXerox.* Milano: Primo Carnera, 1987.
Valagussa, Cecilia, and Ariel Macchi: *Colore inferno: Artisti spezzati dalla Grande Guerra 1914–1918.* Roma: Ifix, 2018.

Raffaello Palumbo Mosca

Even the Great Marinetti Got It Wrong: Giovanni Tuzet's Logical Neo-Futurism

Abstract: In his influential book *La poesia verso la prosa* (Poetry Towards Prose, 1994), Italian critic Alfonso Berardinelli claimed that even the most advanced and "iconoclast" twentieth-century literary avant-gardes, such as Futurism, ended up in the riverbed of "pure poetry". Denouncing Marinetti's crucial mistake in his *Technical Manifesto of Futurist Literature* (1912) to reject the articulated structure of clauses, contemporary Italian thinker and poet Giovanni Tuzet (*1972) advocates for a more narrative poetry, but still moves within Futurist poetics. He aims at recuperating and renewing some key principles of Futurism – dynamism, energy and the synthesis of art and life – through what he calls 'logical' or 'architectural' poetry. By investigating Tuzet's prose, poetry and criticism, this essay offers a comprehensive examination of his poetics and shows how it draws on some less-explored Futurist conceptions, but also proposes something radically new. My analysis of Tuzet's engagement with Marinetti's theoretical works, as well as with the creative solutions of other Futurist poets (Corrado Govoni and Luciano Folgore, in particular), locates his Neo-Futurism within a dynamic, architectural relationship of both continuity and rupture with past aesthetics, all the while measuring his distance from historical Futurism (esp. Marinetti's literary manifestos and Boccioni's *Manifesto of Futurist Architecture*) and from various contemporary strains of Neo-Futurism.

Keywords: Logical Neo-Futurism, Logical Poetry, Architectural Poetry, technology and Nature, the natural and the artificial, the lyrical 'I' and dehumanized poetry

Introduction: Italian poetry, fragmentation and Neo-Futurism

The complex development of Italian poetry from the 1970s onwards was captured by critic Alfonso Berardinelli a few decades ago in the metaphor of an "exploded star" (*un astro esploso*).[1] By this he meant a form of poetry that is permanently

1 Berardinelli, quoted in Anceschi: "Variazione su alcuni equilibri della poesia che san di essere precari", p. 5. This and all translations from the Italian in this essay are mine, unless otherwise noted.

https://doi.org/10.1515/9783111318394-005

adrift, detached from an established tradition and formal unity, and above all characterized by the work of poets operating in isolation from each other. This perceptive definition, subsequently used by a great number of scholars such as Luciano Anceschi, Paolo Giovannetti, Gianluigi Simonetti,[2] describes a postmodern Italy where a general 'end of poetics' was caused by the sudden exhaustion of Hermeticism (which had dominated the first half of the century, thanks to poets like Giuseppe Ungaretti, Eugenio Montale and Salvatore Quasimodo), as well as of the neo-avant-garde experimentations of the Gruppo 63. Consequently, literary genres and the poetic canon became increasingly more elastic, variable and subject to hybridization. Major philosophical, linguistic and social changes – e. g., the crisis of the subject, technological progress, the merger of literary and everyday language, as well as of those between prose and poetry – produced an uneasy and apprehensive relationship with modernity, perceived at the same time as unavoidable, cumbersome and useless. The two opposing reactions to this situation were 'affective spontaneism' (a celebration of poetry as an emotional act, typical of the 1980s) and 'neurotic mannerism' (a formalistic and affected style typical of the following decades).[3] To arrange the radically different, and increasingly numerous, Italian poetic experiences of the last fifty years in a cohesive framework would be as difficult as to find the elements that could tie them to tradition. According to Giorgio Ficara, this continuity seems irredeemably lost also in contemporary prose.[4] Therefore, as Andrea Afribo has rightly concluded, "the new poetry, from the 1970s to today, appears, and essentially continues to appear, as an object that is not, or only very poorly, defined."[5]

Neo-Futurist poetry in Italy has not escaped this process of disintegration and fragmentation. Indeed, since the beginning of the 2000s, no clearly defined group has appeared on the scene, while there are manifold, more or less discernible and coherent trends that are fleetingly following a generic call back to the 'original' Futurists. Three that can be named here include *Net.Futurismo*, an internet-based, quasi-anarchic movement founded in 2005 by Antonio Saccoccio (*1974), which draws on Futurism as much as on Situationism and relies on "the communicative channels offered by the Internet [...] to promote the idea of breaking down barri-

2 Anceschi: "Variazione su alcuni equilibri della poesia che san di essere precari"; Giovannetti: *Modi della poesia contemporanea: Forme e tecniche dal 1950 a oggi*; Simonetti: "Mito delle origini, nevrosi della fine."

3 See Simonetti: "Mito delle origini, nevrosi della fine", pp. 139–226.

4 See Ficara: *Lettere non italiane.*

5 "La nuova poesia, dagli anni settanta a oggi, appare e continua sostanzialmente ad apparire come un oggetto non, o poco, identificato." Afribo: "Poesia", p. 193. See also the presentation of Net.-Futurism in International Yearbook of Futurism Studies 1 (2011), pp. 32–34.

ers, like those between artists and non-artists".[6] By contrast, *transumanesimo futurista* (Futurist Transhumanism), founded by the Ferrarese poets Riccardo Campa (*1967) and Roberto Guerra (*1960), is an interdisciplinary, cybernetic futurology interested in the enhancement of the human being through technology. *Pornofuturismo* is the brainchild of Vitaldo Conte (*1949), who was already a protagonist of the revival of Futurism in the 1960s under the aegis of Enzo Benedetto and his magazine *Futurismo-oggi* (Futurism Today, 1969–93) and seeks a renewal of the eccentric impulses of Futurist eroticism.

Carlo Bo rightfully emphasized that, on the one hand, Futurism in Italy was an altogether vague configuration (being more of an "encounter of different men, tied for a moment to a common inspiration"[7] than a unitary movement or school) and, on the other, that its programme of renewal was putting more emphasis on demolition (its *pars destruens*) than construction (its *pars construens*). The same could be said of these recent Neo-Futurist experiences. As Roberto Guerra pointed out, "the end of Neo-Futurism" as an organized movement, at least in Italy and in the literary field, is the result of a fragmentation and decomposition of structured networks.[8] Seen from this perspective, the case of Giovanni Tuzet seems even more interesting. It is true that he never formally adhered to any Neo-Futurist groupings and signed none of their manifestos, but he participated in some of the activities of the Neo-Futurists in Ferrara.[9] Tuzet also searched, notably in his critical and theoretical work, for a direct link not only to Marinetti, but also to other Futurist poets such as Corrado Govoni (1884–1965), Luciano Folgore (1888–1966) and Aldo Palazzeschi (1885–1974), as well poets in other countries, Paul Valéry (1871–1945) above all.

Tuzet was born in Ferrara in 1972 and in 2007 became Professor of Philosophy of Law at the Bocconi University in Milan. He published many scholarly works, for example on C.S. Pierce (*Dover decidere: Diritto, incertezza e ragionamento,* 2010), or on the differences between knowledge and legal proof (*Filosofia della forma giur-*

---

6 Regnani: "Futurism and Photography: Between Scientific Inquiry and Aesthetic Imagination", p. 193. See also the presentation of Net.Futurism in *International Yearbook of Futurism Studies* 1 (2011), pp. 32–34.

7 "Incontro di uomini diversi, legati per un momento a una ispirazione comune." Bo: "La nuova poesia", p. 13. Almost twenty years later, Antonio Saccone also begins his analysis by reiterating the combative and polemical stance (*trama polemologica*) of the Futurists at the beginning of the twentieth century. *"Secolo che ci squarti... secolo che ci incanti": Studi sulla tradizione del moderno*, p. 52.

8 "In questo epocale anno 2020 [...], dopo alcuni anni di esaurimento del cosiddetto Neofuturismo come Rete, anche organizzata, è tempo di decretarne la fine, almeno in questo senso." Guerra: *Futurismo Duemila*, p. 11.

9 See Guerra: *Futurismo Duemila*, p. 7.

idica, 2013). His theory of *poesia logica* (logical poetry) seeks to trace a line of continuity – methodological and thematic – between his activity as a scholar and that as a poet. And it is precisely his concept of 'logical poetry' that is particularly relevant here, since it represents a concrete attempt at approaching Futurism as an 'archetype', beyond its technical and thematic suggestions. Tuzet not only wants to update and renew Futurism from its foundations, but also to 'correct' it, above all in what he perceives as a lack of critical discipline and creative achievement. Just as Bo,[10] Tuzet confines his vision of Futurism – and its alleged failures – to the strictly poetic sphere, disregarding the thousands of works of art generated by Futurists in other fields (painting, sculpture, and prose, for that matter). And yet, it is from this specific perspective, as we shall see, that an archetypically Futurist form of creativity that embodies a most innovative poetic proposal emerges.

The archetype of Futurism and poetry as construction

The connection between Tuzet's Logical Poetry and Futurism is first attested in two short programmatic writings, *Sia la poesia logica!* (Let There be Logical Poetry!) and *Dieci cartucce per rinascere* (Ten Cartridges for Being Reborn), both of which are contained in the volume *A regola d'arte* (By the Book, 2007).[11] Even though the essays were written four years apart from each other – one in 2003, and the other in 2007 – they are to be read together: the first, with its more discursive and reasoned development, provides the foundation for the schematic quality of the second, which imitates or rather refashions the Futurist most popular genre, the manifesto. It is therefore in the latter that the example of the past is related to the present and the future: "Enough with nostalgia. Let us look at the archetype of Futurism. The challenge, the experiment. The ruthless joy of the inventor!"[12] Hoping for a new poetry that might be born from the Futurist spirit – and, thus, not from its texts and precepts – Tuzet relates himself to a tradition to be partially rejected and in many respects to be overhauled. The point of departure, however, is

10 "Tutti i movimenti possono essere riconosciuti nelle loro opere, il futurismo no: ancora oggi è soprattutto proposta e, più ancora, una protesta." Bo: "La nuova poesia", p. 16.

11 *Sia la poesia logica!* was originally published in *Il domenicale: Settimanale di cultura* 2:20 (17 May 2003).

12 "Bando alla nostalgia. Guardiamo all'*archetipo* del futurismo. La sfida, l'esperimento. La gioia spregiudicata dell'inventore!" Tuzet: *A regola d'arte*, p. 54.

the same, namely the necessity to renew a national (Italian) culture that is perceived, now exactly as then, as literally 'exhausted':

> The *Manifesto of the Futurist Painters* (1910) condemned the sad clichés of its time: the Portraitists, the Genre Painters, the Lake Painters, the Mountain Painters ... We can't take any more of the *Montalisti*, the *Ossi-seppisti*, the *Scoglieristi*... Nor of the postmodernist brew in which the sirens of the New Age find their place alongside the excretions of the *Cannibalisti, Paroliberisti, Pluri-neo-avanguardisti* and poetic disorders of all sorts.[13]

Tuzet's rejection is total: not only of tradition – here exemplified by Eugenio Montale, perhaps the most canonized Italian poet of the twentieth century and his most celebrated volume, *Ossi di seppia* (Cuttlefish Bones, 1925) – but also of the Italian neo-avant-garde. The latter is represented, above all, by the Gruppo 63, whose alienating linguistic experiments had dismantled that very tradition to the point of quashing all discursive coherence. Refusing all "pure poetry" (*poesia pura*) – which not even the "seemingly wildest enemies of aesthetic purity in the twentieth-century avant-gardes"[14] could escape – Tuzet follows Berardinelli move "toward prose"[15] and declares: "We no longer want those tired marine subjects, but instead poems about navigators, about the manoeuvres of vessels in straits, or dialogues between fish."[16] The intent is clear: to reclaim and re-propose energy and dynamism – that sense of the New that is somehow the most important residue of Futurism – and to purify them from all militaristic nationalism. Indeed, Marinetti's bellicose chauvinism was nothing but the corollary of a more important philosophical theme, the contrast between the natural and the artificial which, for Tuzet, was an instrument of "overcoming that natural and static order which the advances of technology undermine and denounce."[17]

Ever since *The Founding and Manifesto of Futurism* (1909), the concept of dynamism was central to Futurism. Tuzet seeks both to recover and go beyond it by

---

13 "Nel *Manifesto dei pittori futuristi* (1910) si condannavano i tristi cliché dell'epoca: i pittori *Ritrattisti, Internisti, Laghettisti, Montagnisti*... Noi non ne possiamo più di Montalisti, Ossi-seppisti, Scoglieristi... Ma anche del brodo post-moderno in cui trovano posto le sirene della *new age* assieme alle incontinenze di Cannibalisti, Paroliberisti, Pluri-neo-avanguardisti e disordini verbali d'ogni sorta." Tuzet: *A regola d'arte*, p. 52.

14 "Anche le avanguardie novecentesche più audaci e iconoclaste, più sfrenatamente nemiche in apparenza della purezza estetica, come il futurismo e il surrealismo, sono finite in realtà nello stesso alveo della 'poesia pura', magari per altre vie." Berardinelli: *La poesia verso la prosa*, p. 13.

15 Berardinelli: *La poesia verso la prosa*, p. 13.

16 "Non vorremmo più quegli stanchi soggetti marini, ma poesie sui navigatori, sulle manovre degli scafi negli stretti, o dialoghi tra pesci." Tuzet: *A regola d'arte*, p. 52.

17 "Superamento di quell'ordine naturale e statico che l'avanzare delle macchine scardina e condanna." Tuzet: *A regola d'arte*, p. 49.

turning the celebratory function of poetry into a gnoseological means. Then, it would no longer be a matter of exalting "aggressive action, a restive wakefulness, life at the double, the slap and the punching fist",[18] but rather of understanding and reproducing the mechanisms of physical movement, artistic creativity and Nature. This would then, by necessity, lead to "a poetry of ploughed land, of embankments and perfectly maintained pastoral sanctuaries, of gestures, movements, stories."[19]

This tendency toward prose, however, does not involve a hypertrophy of the poetic ego (the lyrical 'I' which Marinetti wanted to "destroy", along with the "moonlight"[20]). What is at play here is the capacity of poetic texts to articulate movement, to scan it and make it visible, and in so doing, understandable. Such an attempt is evident right from the titles of Tuzet's first poetry collections – *365 / primo* (365 / first), *365 / secondo* (365 / second) and *365 / terzo* (365 / third) – which do not allude to the overall length of a year, but to the "happening of days, the elapsing of time."[21] The progression expressed by the titles foreshadows a syntactical and emotive articulation, which requires a very rich use of punctuation, in direct opposition to what Marinetti had proposed in his *Technical Manifesto of Futurist Literature:*

> The great Marinetti did not always see it right. Contrary to what he said in the *Technical Manifesto of Futurist Literature* (1912), it is precisely the *lack of articulations* which impedes dynamism. Already the brilliant Russian Futurist [Benedikt] Livshits sensed this when he complained to the founder of Futurism, saying that an abyss separated the written text of *Zang Tumb Tumb* (1914) and its author's recitation of it. Why is there such a great difference between the Words-in-Freedom on paper and the words articulated in the recitation? [...] All respect to Marinetti, but what an error and what a mess it is to condemn the traditional sentence and its logic, only to implicitly reinstate it with the suggestive means of gesture, intonation, volume and vocal rhythm! Colons, exclamation marks, parenthesis, structures and scansions of every type, form and content provide *rhythm.* Logical poetry is dynamic because it exploits all kinds of articulations.[22]

---

18 Marinetti: "The Foundation and Manifesto of Futurism", p. 13.

19 "[...] una poesia di terra arata, di argini e santuari campagnoli perfettamente tenuti, di gesti, passi, storie." Tuzet: *A regola d'arte*, p. 52.

20 "We are systematically destroying the literary 'I', so that it is dispersed throughout the universal flux, and we are coming to the expression of the infinitesimally small and molecular agitation." Marinetti: "Geometrical and Mechanical Splendor and Sensitivity Toward Numbers", p. 136.

21 "succedersi dei giorni, lo scorrere del tempo." Tuzet: *365 / terzo*, p. 81.

22 "Il grande Marinetti non sempre vide giusto. Contrariamente a quanto disse nel *Manifesto tecnico della letteratura futurista* (1912), è proprio la *mancanza di articolazioni* ad impedire il dinamismo. Già l'acuto Livsic, futurista russo, lo intuì e lo obbiettò al fondatore del Futurismo: fra il testo scritto di *Zang Tumb Tumb* (1914) e la sua declamazione dalla voce dell'autore correva un abisso. Perché tanta differenza tra le parole in libertà sulla carta e le parole organizzate nella re-

The key points of Tuzet's argument are the antithetical 'mess' (*pasticcio*) and 'logic' (*logica*); for him, there is no vision without order. His point of departure is the acknowledgement that the correlations between literature, philosophy and architecture enable the latter to "construct beauty simultaneously as a visual and abstract work."[23] In other words, Tuzet wants to seize the constant tension and dynamism in Nature and to organize an often-incandescent matter into a series of phrases that have the tone, the formal rigour and often the lexicon used in analytical philosophy. Tuzet's relationship with the avant-garde is thus, as Gian Mario Villalta has argued, both positive and surprising: "[Tuzet] wants a systematic approach but, at every stage, he reinvents images and sounds; he wants a comprehensive reform of the poetic language, but he constantly draws on the tones, phrasal juxtapositions and the lexicon of poetic tradition."[24] Let us look at two examples from *365 / terzo:*

sillogismo dell'unico	syllogism of the unique
dice mio padre di essere un cane vecchio: ogni giorno un dolore nuovo, qui o là – e non ha diversi figli ma solo me, che penso e scrivo cose	my father says that he is an old dog: every day a new pain, here or there – and he does not have many [children, only me, who thinks and writes things
irripetibili. a questa prima evidenza si somma un accidente: ho un occhio che mi scappa, quando [inghiotto o sono nervoso. ad ogni modo:	unrepeatable. to this first fact an accident can be summed: I have an eye that slips out, when I swallow or I am nervous. anyway:
se cado io, resta solo lui; se cade lui, resto solo io. conclusione: ancora non so dire quanto costata è la morte di lei	if I fall, only he remains; if he falls, only I remain. conclusion: I can't tell yet how much her death has cost

citazione? [...] Onore a Marinetti, ma che errore e che pasticcio condannare la proposizione tradizionale e la sua logica, per poi riabilitarla implicitamente con i mezzi suggestivi del gesto, dell'intonazione, del volume e del ritmo della voce! Due punti, punti esclamativi, parentesi, strutture e scansioni di ogni tipo, forma e contenuto danno il *ritmo.* La poesia logica è dinamica poiché sfrutta ogni tipo di articolazione." Tuzet: *A regola d'arte,* pp. 52–53; emphasis in the original.

23 "L'architettura è costruzione della bellezza, sua opera visibile e al contempo astratta." Tuzet: *A regola d'arte*, p. 30.

24 "[Tuzet] vuole la sistematicità, ma reinventa a ogni passo immagini e suoni, vuole la riforma totale della lingua poetica, ma pesca continuamente nei toni, nella disposizione frastica e nel lessico della tradizione poetica." Villalta: "Conoscenza per errore, tentativi per conoscenza", p. 6.

sillogismo della fontana	syllogism of the fountain
sta una femmina fontana dove	there is a female fountain where
un argomento va, scorre e rinasce	an argument goes, flows and is reborn
in premesse a limpide conclusioni	in introductions to clear conclusions
come in arabo giardino a Granada	as in an Arabian garden in Granada
ma fra gli uomini non sono che due	but amongst men there are but two
le stagioni: o logica, o guerra	seasons: either logic, or war
e qui si sente acre e rincalzato	and here is felt, acrid and tucked-in,
il marciare dell'ultima. Così	the marching of the latter. In this way,
femmina fontana, parlaci ancora	female fountain, speak to us again
non finire di scorrere e cullare	do not cease to flow and to cradle
la ragione, anche se qui e se	reason, even if, here and
sempre nelle teste fermenta il sangue[25]	forever, blood ferments in our heads

Reading these verses, one could think of Marinetti's demand to "bring the 'ugly' into literature and kill off its ritual pomp wherever we find it".[26] However, Tuzet belongs to his time and is thus conscious of how, at least from the neo-avant-gardes onwards, the 'poetic sublime' has become intolerable.[27] Yet the lowering strategy adopted here is original: Tuzet not only welcomes everyday language (or, to use Antonelli's expression, the *hyperaverage* language),[28] but also mimics, in his verses, the structure of an Aristotelian syllogism: two initial thoughts are posited as premises, from which, in a third step, a conclusion is deduced. This is further reinforced, on the one hand, by the use of a corresponding technical and philosophical jargon ("accident", "introductions"), and on the other, by repeated markers of time, space and cause that punctuate and order the stanzas, immediately placing the reader in the centre of the picture, as the Futurist painters had demanded in their technical manifesto[29] and Boccioni had combined, in his manifesto of Futurist Architecture (1914), with an enveloping "spiral of architectonic forces":[30]

---

25 Tuzet: *365 / terzo*, p. 68 and 69.

26 Marinetti: "Technical Manifesto of Futurist Literature", p. 113.

27 See Simonetti: "Mito delle origini, nevrosi della fine", p. 143.

28 Antonelli: *Lingua ipermedia: la parola di scrittore oggi in Italia.*

29 "Noi porremo lo spettatore nel centro del quadro." Boccioni, et al.: "La pittura futurista: Manifesto tecnico", p. 9.

30 "Abbiamo detto che in pittura porremo lo spettatore al centro del quadro facendolo cioè centro dell'emozione invece che semplice spettatore. Anche l'ambiente architettonico delle città si trasforma in senso avvolgente. Noi viviamo in una spirale di forze architettoniche." Boccioni: "Architettura futurista: Manifesto", p. 40.

Velluto	Velvet
Dove: vineria a Torino Cosa: l'oste con un sorriso di bosco ci dice che il tipo si impiccò	Where: winery in Turin What: the host with a forest-smile tells us that the guy hanged himself
Chi: quello che d'inverno, gelata la sera, volle offrirmi questo vino di velluto	Who: him who, in the winter, the night frozen, wanted to offer me this velvety wine
Perché: un'oscura vicenda di figli, mogli e una goccia ad imbuto, così, perlata (succede così, no?)[31]	Why: an obscure episode with children, wives and a funnel-shaped drop, as such, pearled (this is how it happens, isn't it?)

If the relationship with philosophy seems immediately clear in Tuzet's poetry, that with architecture operates in a more hidden form. In *A regola d'arte*, Tuzet approaches it from four different angles: 1. architecture in poetry; 2. architecture as poetry; 3. poetry in architecture (meant not as the study of "references to poetry in architectural works" but rather as the "study of the influence of certain poetics on architecture"[32]); and 4. poetry *as* architecture. Tuzet employs a notion that is equally common in architecture and poetry: that of 'construction'. This is used, first and foremost, to deny what he considers to be a "neo-romantic conception" of poetry based on "feeling, inspiration, momentum". Instead, he argues for a *norm* that can function as a "fundamental presupposition" in the act of poetic writing.[33] Through this, another point of contact between the two arts can be established: both gravitate towards a synthesis between thought and deed, between abstract project and concrete realization. In Paul Valéry's dialogue *Eupalinos, ou L'architecte* (Eupalinos, or The Architect, 1921), Socrates notes how music and architecture are unlike and nobler than figurative art because they, "by means of numbers and relations of numbers, engender in us not a fable, but the hidden power which makes all fables".[34] Similarly, Tuzet emphasizes the formal element of poetry, raising it to the same level of abstraction. He therefore values poetry as a closed form in its own right: its structural rules determine the power of lan-

---

31 Tuzet: *Logiche e mancine*, p. 10.

32 "riferimenti alla poesia in opere architettoniche"; "studio dell'influenza di certe poetiche sull'architettura." Tuzet: *A regola d'arte*, p. 26. It is not insignificant that Tuzet establishes a relationship here between Marinetti's *Foundation and Manifesto of Futurism* (1909) and Antonio Sant'Elia's *Manifesto of Futurist Architecture* (1914).

33 Tuzet: *A regola d'arte*, p. 32.

34 Valéry: *Eupalinos, or The Architect*, p. 97. The sentence is quoted, in Italian, in Tuzet: *A regola d'arte*, p. 30.

guage, its ability to say – and understand – the “whirlwind of the world”. Tuzet concludes that it is thanks to the study and use of the norm that Valéry – and Baudelaire before him – managed to “give order to chaos”.[35] By following Valéry’s search for an equilibrium between inspiration from classical models and desire for innovation, he opts for a poetry that is, first and foremost, form, meant here as a state of equilibrium between project and realization, order and disorder, the process of understanding and the persistence of the unknown.

What pervades Tuzet’s poetry is, then, a persistent *esprit de géométrie*, the desire to put some order into the chaos of the world, considered an ‘evil’ state of being. However, the order that is thus created is often unexpectedly shattered in the concluding verses. The magma of the real – the blood which ferments in the head, the pain of losing a mother and a wife, the absurdity of suicide – cannot be eradicated through reasoning and form. They remain poetically unexplained and crystallize into highly symbolic images: “an eye that slips out”, a “funnel-shaped drop”. In truth, Tuzet’s poetic movement, his dynamism, is not thematic but inscribed in the process of composing poetry, in the struggle against limits, in the continual conflict between a method (logic, norm, structure) and that which inexorably escapes it. It is not without reason that death is perhaps the most relentlessly explored theme in Tuzet’s poetry. It may be the death of a man in *Velluto*, or of a “young rodent” (*un piccino roditore*) in *Una canzone* (A Song), or of “two hundred sheep” (*duecento pecore*) in *Meraviglie* (Wonders), or of some believers gathering at a papal mass. However, the persistent presence of death is always devoid of rhyme: “Now, in the sailing clouds, high and dark, / you can really see the ship of the dead, / its immaculate sails are full and / the mouse, the woman and the brother are there / on the prow, singing a song / rhymeless.”[36] It is a death which neither intellect nor religion can make sense of: “Natural law does not offer / justice nor causes. / Somebody is finishing. / I don’t know why but I know who. / Do you see the law that regulates the evil? / Black, piercing / it strikes randomly”.[37] The challenge in architectural construction, justice (legal philosophy) and poetry alike is to find that point of equilibrium “between project and execution”, between a form that orders and the complexity of life. And Tuzet does not neglect to note that equilibrium does not mean stasis:

35 “dare ordine al caos.” Tuzet: *A regola d’arte*, p. 31.

36 “Ora, nelle nuvole salpate, alte e buie, / la vedi eccome la barca dei morti, / ha piene le vele immacolate e / il topo, la donna e il fratello sono là / sulla prua, a cantare una canzone / senza rime.” Tuzet: *Logiche e mancine*, p. 11.

37 “Il diritto naturale non offre / giustizia né cause. / Qualcuno sta finendo. / Perché non so ma so chi. / Vedi la legge che regola il male? / Nero, perforante / colpisce a caso.” Tuzet: *Logiche e mancine*, p. 80.

> To construct is to find forms of equilibrium. Just as there is equilibrium in justice, so there is equilibrium in beauty: to calibrate the full and the empty, to put verses in order, to arrange words and stanzas, to ponder the elements and their possible meanings, and to do so in a dialectic process of project and execution. But bear in mind: equilibrium is not stasis. It is the – often precarious – point at which elements that were not previously connected or arranged reach a form of harmony [...] To build an equilibrium is to establish a dynamic relationship between the parts and the whole.[38]

In this sense, Tuzet's poetic conception seems, once again, indebted to Boccioni's dynamic vision of architecture, "the liberal art *par excellence*, the vastest in the aspiration toward the absolute" which is also "the most enslaved and tied to life's contingencies" and is for this very reason constantly evolving.[39] There is, however, still a further sense in which equilibrium implicates dynamism, and this is also entangled with the internal struggle of poetry between entropy and norm. As Tuzet himself affirms, it is precisely from the difficulty – and the precariousness – of this often aspired to yet only rarely reached equilibrium that poetry draws its capacity to "provoke new attempts and further questions, of which we do not yet know the criteria for response, but only the desire for them".[40] In this kind of poetry, the reader is not only projected into the story, but also reaches dynamically *beyond* it, toward a new adventure of understanding.

The natural and the artificial: Govoni, Folgore, Rimbaud

The distinction between the natural and the artificial is one of the most notable themes in Futurism, boldly proclaimed in Marinetti's *Technical Manifesto of Futurist Literature:*

---

38 "Costruire è trovare forme di equilibrio. Come c'è un equilibrio nella giustizia, c'è un equilibrio nella bellezza: calibrare il pieno e il vuoto, mettere in ordine i versi, disporre le parole, le strofe, soppesare gli elementi e i significati possibili, in una dialettica fra progetto ed esecuzione. Si noti: equilibrio non è stasi. È il punto, spesso precario, in cui elementi non prima collegati o disposti raggiungono una forma d'armonia [...] Costruire un equilibrio è realizzare un rapporto dinamico fra parti e tutto." Tuzet: *A regola d'arte*, p. 32.

39 "L'architettura, l'arte libera per eccellenza, la più vasta nell'aspirazione all'assoluto è purtroppo e la più schiava e la più legata alle contingenze della vita." Boccioni: "Architettura futurista: Manifesto", p. 36.

40 "[...] provocare nuovi tentativi e suscitare domande ulteriori, di cui spesso, ancora, non si conoscono i criteri di risposta, ma solo l'esigenza." Boccioni: "Architettura futurista: Manifesto", p. 33.

> After the animal kingdom, behold the beginning of the mechanical kingdom. With the knowledge and friendship of matter, of which the scientists can know only the physiochemical reactions, we are preparing the creation of the mechanical man, one who will have parts that can be changed.[41]

Yet, it also remains amongst the most problematic issues in Futurism that needs to be overhauled and replaced with new forms of innovation. Tuzet expresses his complex relationship with this Futurist tangle as follows:

> Sono un futurista archeologo
> che cerca il latte appena munto
> e vuole il salame del popolo
> che ci scampi dall'OGM
>
> Amo le cose polverose
> vecchie, dispettose e bacucche,
> tutte sposo le novità
> che il passato s'inventa e sbriglia[42]

> I am an archaeological Futurist
> who seeks freshly-gathered milk
> and wants the simple folk food
> that can save us from GMOs
>
> I love things dusty,
> old, spiteful and decrepit,
> I marry all the novelties
> which the past invents and unbridles

Although in Futurism there is a notable distinction between the 'natural' – considered passéist – and the 'artificial' – considered modern – Tuzet finds the meaning of the two terms unclear and therefore asks: "What does the naturalness of a human being consist of? If we substitute in a man limbs and organs with artificial parts, is he then no longer a man but, for example, a machine or a computer?"[43] Tuzet's intention is, once again, to depart from Futurist theorization in order to move beyond it. This 'beyond', however, does not prevent him from tying to recover solutions and novelties of the past which he still deems relevant to today's civilization.

Of the four parts that compose the short essay *Prima e seconda natura* (First and Second Nature), also contained in the book *A regola d'arte*, the most interesting in this sense are the last two sections: *Il naturale come metodo poetico* (The Natural as a Poetic Method) and, above all, *Il naturale come tema poetico* (The Natural as a Poetic Theme).[44] In the former, Tuzet analyses some reflections on poetry carried out by Mario Luzi (1914–2005) in his essay collection *Discorso naturale*

---

41 Marinetti: "Technical Manifesto of Futurist Literature", pp. 113–114.

42 Tuzet: In *Logiche e mancine*, p. 46.

43 "[…] in che cosa consiste la naturalezza di un essere umano? Quando un uomo non è più un uomo ed è ad esempio una macchina o un computer, se ad arti e organi sostituiamo parti artificiali?" Tuzet: *A regola d'arte*, p. 41.

44 The first two parts are entitled, respectively, *Il naturale in filosofia* (The Natural in Philosophy) and *Il naturale in poesia* (The Natural in Poetry).

(Natural Discourse, 1980). He notes how Luzi does not treat the natural just as poetical matter, but rather as something much more complex that is fundamental for the equilibrium between natural and artificial (something which also Tuzet tends towards). Indeed, the natural is treated here as a *modality* and, in parallel with religious experiences, as *the modality of being human.* The poet, according to Luzi, writes naturally, "allowing his or her own voice and internal needs to flow out".[45] However, as Tuzet emphasizes, such a subjective perspective does not imply a gushing forth of feelings. Rather, it signals a 'natural' capacity to freely voice that which human beings have in common: "The poet must follow his own voice and vocation, but where his doing is authentic, he will turn to that which, as a man, unites him to other men. [...] Thus one may speak of a 'natural light' in poetry, that is, of an instinctive capacity to grasp the 'common nature', to strike the cords that vibrate in each of us."[46]

The final section of the essay contrasts Marinetti's position against that of Giuseppe Ungaretti (1888–1970) and Andrea Zanzotto (1921–2011). Both of these two Italian poets possessed, as Tuzet emphasizes, "Futurist roots", yet both distanced themselves from Futurism in two crucial ways: one concerns the representation of the natural and the artificial; the other that of war. Indeed, whereas Futurism chose to celebrate the artificial and war as a means of purification, Ungaretti and Zanzotto opted with great clarity for the representation of the natural and the pursuit of a peace (violated by the First and Second World War, respectively). Tuzet, seeks a 'third way', an *equilibrium* of natural and artificial terms:

> The option in favour of the natural and the one in favour of the artificial are flanked by two other options, which are at least as difficult as they are fascinating: (i) depicting the natural in a non-naturalistic manner (for example: a sun lamp), and vice versa (ii) depicting the non-natural in a naturalistic manner (such as: the backbone of a motor, a bundle of electric cables).[47]

The second option, widely practiced by the Futurists and by Marinetti, above all, seems to Tuzet to be the least modern, and the least philosophically justified

---

45 "lasciando scorrere la propria voce e la propria interiore necessità." Tuzet: *A regola d'arte*, p. 46.
46 "Il poeta deve seguire la propria voce e vocazione, ma il suo fare sia autentico si rivolgerà a ciò che in quanto uomo lo unisce agli altri uomini. [...] così si potrebbe parlare di *lume naturale* in poesia, ossia di una capacità istintiva di cogliere la 'natura comune', di toccare le corde che vibrano in ognuno." Tuzet: *A regola d'arte*, pp. 46–47.
47 "All'opzione in favore del naturale e quella a favore dell'artificiale si affiancano due altre opzioni, almeno, tanto più difficili quanto affascinanti: (i) raffigurare in modo non naturalistico il naturale (ad esempio: la lampada del sole), e viceversa (ii) raffigurare in modo naturalistico il non-naturale (come: la schiena del motore, un fiume di fibre elettriche)." Tuzet: *A regola d'arte*, p. 49

choice. He prefers, instead, to look at the natural "with artificial eyes from our own time".[48] Some excerpts from *365 / terzo* may demonstrate the coherence between Tuzet's theoretical and poetic works. The first example is a description of birds, in which the natural and the artificial are placed side-by-side, not by making a comparison or using a simple metaphor, but by fusing the two into a unified whole:

come vecchio che il passo non comanda rimiro da una panca sbigottito spirituali e prodigiosi uccelli:	as an old man unable to control his walk I look from a bench, stunned, at spiritual and prodigious birds:
1) della rondine il micro-motore 2) la punta del merlo scattante 3) l'elica dell'upupa 4) la cabina dei mini-pettirossi 5) la carlinga delle gazze 6) il carrello dei colombi 7) l'arsenale dei piccioni 8) dei passeri la flotta festante ... così li guardo in angoscia meravigliosa e chiedo di vegliare la notte liscia ed avvertire come il pilota i fari scuri della civetta e il canto misterioso delle anime[49]	1) of the swallow, the micro-motor 2) the point of the whippy blackbird 3) the propeller of the hoopoe 4) the cabin of mini-robins 5) the cargo compartment of the magpies 6) the cart of the doves 7) the arsenal of the pigeons 8) of the sparrows, the festive fleet ... so I watch them in marvelled anguish and I ask to wake the smooth night and to follow like a pilot the dark lighthouses of the owl and the mysterious chant of souls

Tuzet's ability to shape the natural in a non-naturalistic manner ultimately draws on Futurist models, above all on Corrado Govoni's *Poesie elettriche* (Electrical Poems, 1911) and, even more so, *Rarefazioni e parole in libertà* (Defusions and Words-in-Freedom, 1915). In the essay *Govoni dentro il paesaggio* (Govoni within the Landscape, 2003), Tuzet examines Govoni's representations of the Po Valley (that is, the Pianura Padana), underlying that the lists of objects, which characterize early collections such as *Armonia in grigio et silenzio* (Harmony in Grey and Silence, 1903), are used to signify a lack of causal connections between events. Such lists then mirror and enhance the idea of the plain itself as a "place of absence" (*luogo dell'assenza*):[50] a tranquil place, which emerges indirectly "from the depiction of interiors, balconies, courtyards, convents".[51] Even though they

48 "ma con gli occhi artificiali del nostro tempo." Tuzet: *A regola d'arte*, p. 51.

49 Tuzet: *365 / terzo*, p. 33.

50 Tuzet: *A regola d'arte*, p. 5.

51 "Il paesaggio si evince dalle raffigurazioni di interni, balconi, corti, conventi." Tuzet: *A regola d'arte*, p. 6.

may be fascinating, such representations of the natural are, according to Tuzet, not truly experimental. It is, in fact, with *Poesie elettriche*, and thanks to his Futurist sensibility, that Govoni found a new way to depict – and interpret – the plain of the River Po. The natural is here, for the first time, represented "through non-natural elements", and the "aesthetic appeal" of both the natural and the artificial is augmented.[52]

This approach becomes even more evident in the very first lines of *Campana di chiaro di luna* (Moonlight Bell; see Fig. 1), the second *suite* of *Parole in libertà*, which is mentioned in Tuzet's essay on Govoni, together with *Autoritratto* (Self-Portrait) and *Il palombaro* (The Diver). Here, we can find the analogy, printed in larger characters than the rest, between the landscape and a "green theatre of the forest" (*teatro verde del bosco*).[53] Further on, a garden is compared to "a suburb of flowers with the car lights of the dandelions in their labile haloes" (*sobborgo di fiori coi fanali dei soffioni nei loro labili aloni*),[54] where the natural element (the flowers) is associated with technological inventions (the car lights). Still in the same composition, we then find "the prompter cricket as a typewriter" (*il grillo suggeritore dal cri cri di macchina dattilografica*), the fireflies described as "phosphor dancers" (*ballerine di fosforo*) and an "orchestra of flowers" (*orchestra di fiori*).[55] This plurality of analogies, in which the comparative function is assumed by the technological object, ultimately sanctions a dynamic, almost competitive and yet harmonious movement between natural and artificial beauty, which overcomes any static representation.

Tuzet echoes Govoni's poetry and recovers its listing format, now diverted to mimic scientific taxonomies, to embody a desire for order and gnoseology that forms the base of his new poetic style. Tuzet also explores a similar entanglement between the natural and the non-natural in *Il naturale come tema poetico*, through the example of another Futurist poet, Luciano Folgore. He focusses in particular on *Mondo sotto lucernario verde* (World Under Green Skylight, 1919) and *Limiti fatti di foglie* (Boundaries Made of Leaves, 1919), in which the intertwining of natural and artificial elements, of landscape and human being, form a single scenario "where the rhythm of spring and the works of men seem to merge into a richness 'of mel-

52 "La rappresentazione della pianura, luogo dell'assenza, si nutre di elementi nuovi, artificiali. Il loro fascino estetico aumenta se possono prestarsi alla rappresentazione del naturale." Tuzet: *A regola d'arte*, p. 7.

53 Govoni: *Rarefazioni e parole in libertà*, p. 27.

54 Ibid., p. 29.

55 Ibid., p. 27.

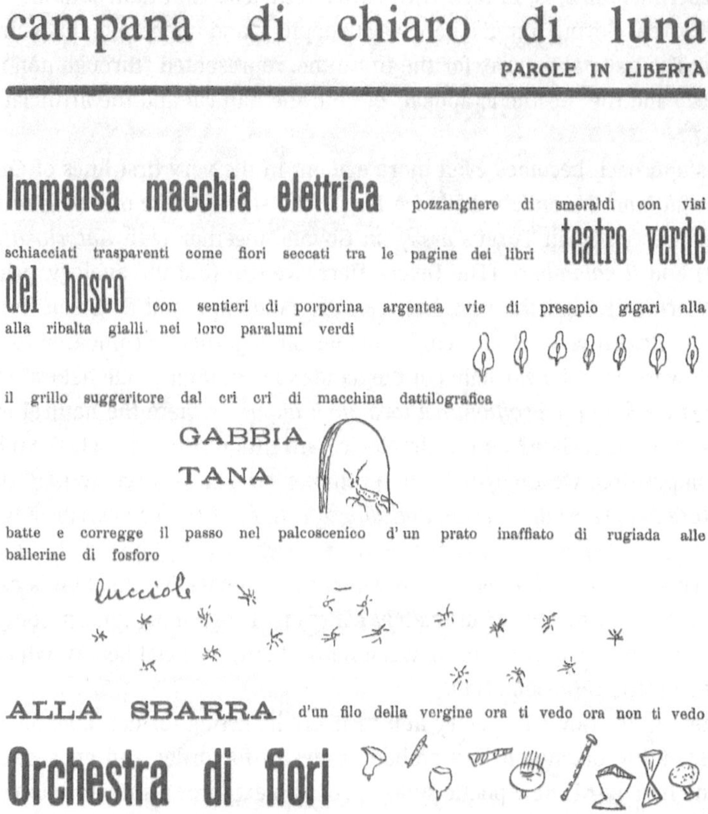
campana di chiaro di luna
PAROLE IN LIBERTÀ

Immensa macchia elettrica pozzanghere di smeraldi con visi schiacciati trasparenti come fiori seccati tra le pagine dei libri teatro verde del bosco con sentieri di porporina argentea vie di presepio gigari alla alla ribalta gialli nei loro paralumi verdi

il grillo suggeritore dal cri cri di macchina dattilografica

GABBIA
TANA

batte e corregge il passo nel palcoscenico d'un prato inaffiato di rugiada alle ballerine di fosforo

lucciole

ALLA SBARRA d'un filo della vergine ora ti vedo ora non ti vedo

Orchestra di fiori

Fig. 1: First page of Corrado Govoni's *Campana di chiaro di luna* (Moonlight Bell) in *Rarefazioni e parole in libertà* (Defusions and Words-in-Freedom, 1915).

ancholy and miraculous / curiosity'."[56] Tuzet points out that such representation is indebted to Arthur Rimbaud's *Illuminations* (1886), which is therefore recognized as a primary intertext for Folgore. It is then through the threefold poetic line – Govoni and Folgore, mediated by Rimbaud – that Tuzet places himself soundly within

56 "[...] la cadenza della primavera e le opere degli uomini sembrano fondersi in una ricchezza 'di melanconie e di curiosità / miracolose.'" *Ibidem*, p. 50. Tuzet here quotes Folgore's verses from *Limiti fatti di foglie.*

Futurism (or, rather, within its archetype), finding at once that synthesis of the natural and the artificial which seems to him to be the most philosophically and poetically well-founded.

Veglie (Wakes): A Neo-Futurist experiment

Eccoli in dodici qui, i colpi netti a fissare la veglia a punta, ogni apostolo rigoroso	Here are the twelve, with hammering blows awaiting the appointed vigil, each of the unbending apostles
conoscibile dai denti e dal passo che ti spinge a capire, inchiodare	recognizable by his teeth and gait that pushes you to understand, to nail down
vedere chiaramente, anche le [cose oscure.[57]	to see clearly, even obscure things.

In *La Préparation du roman* (Preparation of the Novel, 1978–80, publ. 2003), Roland Barthes suggests that the middle of a journey does not indicate a mathematical division, but that moment in which time irreparably splits into a before and an after.[58] It is the wound-event that signals "the pain's asset", the new cognizance that "death is real".[59] For Tuzet, it is the moment in which evil becomes an active and unavoidable force that condemns us to suffer:

Dicono che sia assenza di bene. Ma qui c'è qualcosa che batte davvero. Come potremmo essere battuti da un'assenza? Dev'essere, il male, qualcosa di più spesso e solido. Come una casa in mano ad un esercito.[60]	They say that it is absence of good. But here there is something that really beats. How could we be beaten by an absence? The evil should be something thicker and more solid. Like a house in the hand of an army.

Veglie (Wakes), the third and final part of the collection entitled *Logiche e mancine* (Logical and Left-Handed, 2017), is also the most intense and most private one: it is a chronicle of the personal experience of being catapulted into the centre of pain (the path towards the middle of the journey is not, and cannot be, gradual). The

57 Tuzet: *Veglie*, p. 80.
58 Barthes: *The Preparation of the Novel*, pp. 3–5.
59 Ibid., p. 5.
60 Tuzet: *Logiche e mancine*, p. 80.

section is a difficult, albeit necessary commemoration of the loss of his mother, in which the everyday quality of memory reveals the poet's desire to leave his own voice free, by intuitively tying memory and personal pain to common experience. After all, as Marcel Proust wrote on 19 July 1919 in a letter to Daniel Halévy, "it is the apogee of the particular that begets the general".[61]

Dire la verità: sui dubbi sugli errori sulle crepe, che si sappia la loro magnitudine che le pigne si sentano cadere.	To speak the truth: about doubts errors crevices, let their magnitude be known let the pines feel like falling.
Tutta la verità: andare all'incontro, fissare gli occhi, togliere il tono spogliandosi in piedi dare il fianco per essere battuti.	All the truth: to go to the meeting, to stare into eyes, to shed the tone, undressing while standing to offer a vulnerable flank to be wounded.
Solo la verità: tutta la verità nient'altro che - ammettere e gioire, che si veda la nostra intera, nuda umanità.[62]	Only the truth: all the truth nothing but – admitting and rejoicing, so that our whole, naked humanity may be seen.

Veglie is thus a story of a sepia world that has vanished forever: "Aquileia, the family home / white Moorish muzzle at the entrance. / A time / martyrdom of Byzantine attitudes, / patriarchs / [...] Grandfather in the black and white photo, / dressed severely, grease / [...] / What remains is for us to be a snippet."[63] But *Veglie* is also, most importantly and in coherence with Tuzet's previously explained poetic search, an *experiment*. It is an attempt to put into practice all the theoretical principles hitherto pursued by Tuzet, achieving a non-lyric and narrative poetry or, better yet, retrieving a new lyricism *within* the narrative impulses of a poetry that is founded on the perpetual strive for equilibrium and draws from and yet surpasses Futurism in the name of logic. The latter is applied in *Veglie* to the theme of evil, its incontestable presence and possible remedies. It almost resembles the diary of a scientist who, at the end of the day, compiles impressions and observations on the absurdity of life while examining the nature of justice and judgement. If the poem entitled *Il male* (The Evil) sets the problem out and examines its nature, in *Sapere* (Knowledge) we witness the bitter claim of the ir-

61 Quoted in Barthes: *The Preparation of the Novel*, p. 43.

62 Tuzet: *Logiche e mancine*, p. 93.

63 "Aquileia, la casa di famiglia / bianco muso di moro sull'entrata. / Un tempo / martirio di movenze bizantine, / patriarchi / [...] Nonno nella foto in bianco e nero, / severo vestito, brillantina / [...] / Ci resta d'essere un ritaglio." Tuzet: *Logiche e mancine*, pp. 78, 79.

reversibility of trauma: "The restoration of an original state / is futile. / If mum dies / we shall have a hole in our face".[64] There is still an effort to "elicit praises and laments"[65] – that is, to protest against the evil – but the silence of God, his absence, is ultimately deafening:

Intanto pregano altri malati impalano pupille al muro in alto (come se Dio potesse uscire dal soffitto, sforzandosi fra i mattoni).[66]	Meanwhile other invalids pray impale pupils on the higher wall (as if God could exit from the ceiling and force himself through the bricks).

The author's lyrical 'I' is unable to decide between an escape from evil and an attempt at understanding it: "Without knowing / if it would suffice to get out of it, or if we should seek to *know*". Thus, the act of understanding is called into question and "turns itself into a nihilistic sort":[67]

Getteremo i frutti nelle fosse per produrre tale cifra di male necessaria a sopportare il resto[68]	We will throw the fruits into the graves to produce such an amount of evil necessary to handle the rest

This is the moment in which reason seems to surrender. The verse turns into a lullaby for children, while language descends into dialect and ends up in a disjointed babble:

64 "La riduzione in pristino / è vana. / Se la mamma muore / avremo un buco in faccia." Tuzet: *Logiche e mancine*, p. 84. Note the use of judicial jargon here, as an extreme attempt to domesticate the evil, to reduce it to a norm: *restitutio in pristinum* is a Latin term used in legal language to refer to a restoration of a damaged property to the state that existed prior to a damage caused. In the Italian Civil Code, *riduzione in pristino* refers the minimum distances between buildings that have to be re-established in case something has been erected in violation of the building laws.

65 "innalzeremo lodi e lamentazioni." Tuzet: *Logiche e mancine*, p. 84

66 Tuzet: *Logiche e mancine*, p. 86

67 "senza sapere / se basti uscirne, o si cerchi sapere"; "si volge in spezia nichilista". Tuzet: *Logiche e mancine*, p. 85. Emphasis in the original.

68 Tuzet: *Logiche e mancine*, p. 85.

Cherubini, cavalini, angioleti	Cherubim, ponies, little angels
gli scherzi balerini	the dancing jokes
i ga portado via i cavei	have taken away the horses
e i caveleti -	and the ponies –
in fondo, i cavai xe lì per esser liberao	in the end, the horses are here to be liberated
da chi li porta via da l'alto.	by those who take them away from above.
Non rimane che aspettare il colpo duro	All that remains is to await the hard strike
(gavemo de spetar il colpo duro).	(we have to await the hard strike).
[...]	[...]
e allora dondolare are are	and so rocking ing ing
allora scomparire ire ire	so disappearing ing ing
quasi musiche	almost musicals
cantilene	lullabies
cavallini	ponies
mentre Notte quatto quatto	while Night slowly slowly
copre tutta la città.[69]	covers the whole city.

The effect of this sudden descent into nonsense – obtained by way of a procedure that might recall, at least in its onomatopoetic and musical associations, the Futurist Words-in-Freedom – is potentiated by the proximity of these verses to others filled with technical (often juridical) jargon, where a logically structured chronology seems to contain, demarcate and break down pain as an intellectual problem. *E l'alba* (And the Dawn), the poem that concludes the book, finally represents the conquest of some essential yet fragile truths, perhaps already known but now reappropriated by way of the painful journey that has been completed. First of all, the irrevocability of what has been experienced together is alluded to: "The fact that I wrote this *Wake* and that you read it / will be true forever as it is now / just as it is true that one is born on one day / and disappears another."[70] This holds the revelation of a possible sense that reverberates in the future: "Therefore we advance the exploration / there are numerous natural provinces / of the kingdom, / science is the path of knowledge toward / it and this is with the amplest measure."[71] And if this knowledge, so strongly affirmed, seems impotent in the face of the pain undergone, this poverty coincides also with the discovery of a new liberty:

---

69 Ibid., p. 90.

70 "[...] che abbia scritto questa Veglia e che tu legga / sarà vero per sempre come ora / come è vero che si nasce un giorno / e in un altro si sparisce." Tuzet: *Logiche e mancine*, p. 91.

71 "Pertanto avanziamo l'esplorazione / vi sono numerose province naturali / del regno, / la scienza è il passo del sapere verso / esso e ciò nella più ampia misura." Tuzet: *Logiche e mancine*, p. 92.

Ora la libertà di chi non ha	Now the liberty of those who do not have
niente più, nemmeno una briciola	anything else, not even a crumb
mi appare come il modo	seems to me to be the way
di parlare finalmente ai miei fratelli.[72]	to finally speak to my brothers.

L'avversario (The Enemy): Beyond Futurism

The poetic programme advanced with *Veglie* was continued in the following poetry collection, *L'avversario* (The Enemy, 2021), which contains four sections: *In natura* (In Nature); *In famiglia* (Within Family); *In società* (In Society); *Atti e passioni dei martiri* (Acts and Passions of the Martyrs). They testify to Tuzet's definitive overcoming of Futurism by means of the logical deconstruction of two of its cornerstones (at least in Marinetti's view): the unlimited potency of the poetic subject and the exaltation of violence. In particular, Tuzet strengthens the philosophical vocation of his poetry by seeking more than most other contemporary poets to "re-establish the first person [...] by transforming it into a 'non-poetic', philosophical, 'person'."[73] It is not surprising, then, that the entire first section of *L'avversario* is an exploration of that which had already been defined in *A regola d'arte* as the most ancient philosophical theme: Nature, its mechanisms and principles. Is this, then – as in Ortega y Gasset's *La deshumanización del arte* (The Dehumanization of Art, 1925) – a 'dehumanized poetry'? Yes and no, since if it is true that the human figure seems marginalized here, the various texts of the section are laid out dialectically, showing the relationship between Nature and culture, and between the rôle of violence in Nature and in human society. The first often appears necessary, even beautiful, luminous (or numinous):

Le uova deposte si schiudono	The laid eggs hatch
e le piccole larve invadono il bruco	and the small larvae invade the caterpillar
nel corpo	in its body
ne divorano le parti grasse, però	they devour its fatty parts, but
– guidate da un istinto meraviglioso	– driven by a marvellous instinct
non intaccano gli organi vitali.[74]	they do not damage its vital organs.

72 Ibid., pp. 92–93.

73 "rifondare la prima persona [...] trasformandola in 'persona non poetica, ma filosofica." Simonetti: "Mito delle origini, nevrosi della fine", p. 196. On this concept, see also Testa: *Per interposta persona: Lingua e poesia nel secondo Novecento.*

74 Tuzet: *L'avversario*, p. 21.

Human violence, on the other hand, reveals itself in its brutality (culture, or in the definition borrowed by Pascal, the "second nature", can be, apparently paradoxically, more savage than nature itself):

Cammina un'ape sull'ocra pavimento indotta forse dallo scirocco ubriaco a penetrare un altro mondo verso il nocciola della lisca a piastrelle intorpidita. Sarò veloce, efficace più di te ape tardiva perché natura me lo impone	A bee walks on the ochre ground perhaps brought in by the drunken south wind to penetrate another world towards the nut of the tiled backbone, numbed. I shall be quicker, more efficient than you, tardy bee, because Nature imposes it on me[75]

In the second and third sections of the volume, Tuzet's verse, which previously seemed so gaunt and objective, becomes more narrative to the point of dissolving itself, perhaps, into chanting, with some hints of biography. There, indeed, we can find the re-evocation of the travels of an ancestor who sold silk (in the poem called *Il signore degli eserciti* [The Lord of the Armies]); memories of love (in the poem *Souvenir*); and even a theme which is both biographical and existential, and once again eminently historical and philosophical, namely that of the home:

Queste case abitano un confine. [...] È la casa dei miei ad Aquileia lunga e stretta come la gente in Friuli [...] Questa casa a Milano sovrasta le mura spagnole [...] ma i versi indifesi mi legano qui felicemente a cantare e ridere solo come un raro felino che sulle mura ci piscia e gode e a volte lacrima.[76]	These houses inhabit a border. [...] It is my folks' house in Aquileia long and narrow like the people in Friuli [...] This house in Milan overlooks the Spanish walls [...] but the undefended verses bind me here happily to sing and laugh alone like a rare feline that pisses at the walls and enchants and at times weeps.

Nature and violence, the house as a refuge, love and evil: these are the themes, adapted and traced in Tuzet's poetry as objects of examination in his inexhaustible reasoning through verse. Even more significant, in this sense, is the final section of

75 Tuzet: *L'avversario*, p. 20.
76 Ibid., p. 45.

the book, *Atti e passioni dei martiri.* At a superficial glance, it looks dissimilar to the others but, in actual fact, it constitutes a logical conclusion to the dialectical structure of the volume. If the first sections – dedicated to natural and human violence – denounced an absence of sense (that is, the gratuity of violence), relegating beauty and meaning to the private sphere that only exists outside history, in the following ones, Tuzet gradually recovers a possibility of the sublime. This culminates in *Atti e passioni di martiri*, a section that should be read, in my opinion, like the consecutive panels of a church fresco. Such a form of the sublime does not rest in the lyrical 'I', but points towards the universality of the symbol as an alternative to shallow subjectivism in both its lyrical and aggressive forms. Tuzet sets religious truth and transcendence in opposition to the void of history and rediscovers the necessity of pain because it belongs to the natural world at a higher level. Tuzet's journey is finally completed: his poetry has progressed from an entomologist's report to a transfigured world, from multiplicity to its unique cause (God as the Aristotelian prime mover).

Conclusions

Viewed as a whole, Tuzet's poetic journey resembles that of an apprenticeship. Each stage is closely linked to the previous ones until they form a path which – despite its meandering character – appears continuous and homogenous. Futurist principles are always adopted in a critical manner, as props or simple cues for further reflection, in order to achieve a poetry which Tuzet does not only want to be in tune with the contemporary world, but to overcome the current state of existence and to move forward into the future. His starting point – the need for a radical renewal of poetry – is similar to the beginning of Futurism, but the outcomes are different, sometimes even the opposite. Even in his critical-theoretical writings, where Tuzet's reflections on Futurism are more stringent and Marinetti's example is more cogent, the introduction of logic – Tuzet's true *pensée obsédante* and an element of fundamental originality in his poetic thought – establishes an essential difference to historical Futurism. Tuzet's verses are at their best when they express the failure of every programme, because every ordering will is shattered by a magmatic and irredeemable Real. Tuzet accepts that it is ultimately impossible to reconcile the pursuit of knowledge with the enduring mysteries of Life: although the "restoration of an original state / is futile", it is still desirable to do so. Tuzet's Neo-Futurist poetry illuminates this fundamental tension and its impossible dissolution.

Bibliography

Afribo, Andrea: "Poesia." Andrea Afribo, and Emanuele Zinato, eds.: *Modernità italiana: Cultura, lingua e letteratura dagli anni Settanta a oggi.* Roma: Carocci, 2011. 181–260.
Anceschi, Luciano: "Variazione su alcuni equilibri della poesia che san di essere precari." *Il Verri* 1 (1976): 5–20.
Antonelli, Giuseppe: *Lingua ipermedia: La parola di scrittore oggi in Italia.* Lecce: Manni, 2006.
Barthes, Roland: *The Preparation of the Novel: Lecture Courses and Seminars at the College de France (1978–1979 and 1979–1980).* Trans. Kate Briggs. New York: Columbia University Press, 2011.
Berardinelli, Alfonso: *La poesia verso la prosa: Controversie sulla lirica moderna.* Torino: Bollati Boringhieri, 1994.
Bo, Carlo: "La nuova poesia." Emilio Checchi, and Natalino Sapegno, eds.: *Storia della letteratura italiana.* Vol. 5.2. Milano: Garzanti, 1987. 9–208.
Boccioni, Umberto: "Architettura futurista: Manifesto." U. Boccioni: *Altri inediti e apparati critici.* A cura di Zeno Birolli. Milano: Feltrinelli, 1972. 36–40.
Boccioni, Umberto, Carlo Carrà, Luigi Russolo, Gino Severini, and Giacomo Balla: "La pittura futurista: Manifesto tecnico." U. Boccioni: *Gli scritti editi e inediti.* A cura di Z. Birolli. Milano: Feltrinelli, 1971. 7–11.
Ficara, Giorgio: *Lettere non italiane.* Firenze: Giunti, 2016.
Folgore, Luciano: "Limiti fatti di figlie." Edoardo Sanguineti, ed.: *Poesia italiana del Novecento.* Vol. 2. Torino: Einaudi, 1971. 615–618.
Giovannetti, Paolo: *Modi della poesia contemporanea: Forme e tecniche dal 1950 a oggi.* Roma: Carocci, 2005.
Govoni, Corrado: *Lettere a* F. T. Marinetti *(1909–1915). Rarefazioni e parole in libertà (1915).* A cura di Matilde Dillon Wanke. Milano: Scheiwiller, 1990.
Guerra, Roberto: *Futurismo Duemila: Breve storia del neofuturismo.* Ferrara: Tiemme Edizioni Digitali, 2021.
Luzi, Mario: *Discorso naturale.* Milano: Garzanti, 1984.
Marinetti, Filippo Tommaso: "Technical Manifesto of Futurist Literature." F. T. Marinetti: *Critical Writings.* Trans. Doug Thompson. Ed. by Günter Berghaus. New York: Farrar, Straus & Giroux, 2006. 107–119.
Marinetti, Filippo Tommaso: "Geometrical and Mechanical Splendor and Sensitivity Toward Numbers." F. T. Marinetti: *Critical Writings.* Trans. Doug Thompson. Ed. by Günter Berghaus. New York: Farrar, Straus & Giroux, 2006. 135–142.
Ortega y Gasset, José: *The Dehumanization of Art and Other Essays on Art, Culture, and Literature.* Princeton/NJ: Princeton University Press, 1984.
Regnani, Gerardo: "Futurism and Photography: Between Scientific Inquiry and Aesthetic Imagination." Günter Berghaus, ed.: *Futurism and the Technological Imagination.* Amsterdam: Rodopi, 2009. 177–200.
Saccone, Antonio: . *"Secolo che ci squarti… secolo che ci incanti": Studi sulla tradizione del moderno.* Roma: Salerno, 2019.
Simonetti, Gianluigi: "Mito delle origini, nevrosi della fine." G. Simonetti: *La letteratura circostante.* Bologna: Il Mulino, 2018. 139–226.
Testa, Enrico: *Per interposta persona: Lingua e poesia nel secondo Novecento.* Roma: Bulzoni, 1999.
Tuzet, Giovanni: *A regola d'arte.* Ferrara: Este, 2007.
Tuzet, Giovanni: *365 / terzo.* Rimini: Raffaelli, 2010.

Tuzet, Giovanni: *Logiche e mancine.* Borgomanero (NO): Ladolfi, 2017.

Tuzet, Giovanni: *L'avversario.* Montecassiano (MC): Vydia, 2021.

Valéry, Paul: "Eupalinos, or the Architect." P. Valéry: *The Collected Works of Paul Valery.* Vol. 4. Ed. by Jackson Mathew. Princeton/NJ: Princeton University Press, 1989. 65–152.

Villalta, Gian Marco: "Conoscenza per errore, tentativi per conoscenza." G. Tuzet: *365 / Terzo.* Rimini: Raffaelli, 2010. 5–9.

2 Russia

Tim Klähn

Gennady Aygi and Russian Futurism

Abstract: This essay explores the work of the Chuvash-Russian poet Gennady Aygi (1934–2006), his dialogue with Russian Futurism and his attempts to reactivate the interrupted tradition of the historical avant-garde in the Soviet Union (with particular reference to Mayakovsky, Khlebnikov and Malevich). Working at the Mayakovsky Museum in Moscow during the 1960s granted Aygi access to otherwise restricted rare materials and allowed him to organize semi-legal exhibitions of works by Malevich, Tatlin, Filonov, Larionov, Goncharova, Chagall, Matyushin, Ender, Chekrygin, Guro and others, which were visited by artists and writers such as Ilya Kabakov, Lev Nusberg, Francisco Infante, Mikhail Shvartsman and Mikhail Grobman. This essay focusses on how these and other connections with members of the historical avant-garde – including Kruchenykh, Burliuk and Gnedov – allowed Aygi to establish a counter-memory, disseminating avant-garde materials in samizdat publications and unofficial networks, all the while attempting to circulate them also via official publications. In this essay, I examine Aygi's publications – featuring anthologies, translations and essays on Russian Futurist poetry – and trace the influence of Futurist experiments in his own poems. My analysis aims to demonstrate how, during the era of *glasnost* and *perestroika* in the late 1980s/early 1990s, Aygi was a driving force of Neo-Futurism, emulating the historical avant-garde's penchant for collaborative intermediality and the production of artists' books.

Keywords: Russian Neo-Futurism, rediscovery of historical Futurism during the *glasnost* and *perestroika* years (1980s-90s), Samizdat publications, artists' books, unofficial and semi-official avant-garde exhibitions in late-Soviet Moscow, Kazimir Malevich, Velimir Khlebnikov, Aleksei Kruchenykh, Vladimir Mayakovsky

Introduction

Gennady Aygi (1934–2006)[1] was a Chuvash[2]-Russian poet and translator characterized as an "extraordinary poet of today's Russian avant-garde" by the linguist and

1 Bibliographical references preserve the Library of Congress transliteration of names (e.g., Aigi or Maiakovskii), while common anglicized spellings are used throughout the essay (e.g., Aygi or Mayakovsky). Incidentally, Aygi changed his surname from the Russified name Lisin, which had been adopted by his father during the Soviet Russification of native populations, to the Chuvash

https://doi.org/10.1515/9783111318394-006

literary theorist Roman Jakobson.[3] While Aygi's poetry merged a variety of influences, from Chuvash folk culture to Baudelaire, Celan, Char, Kafka, Kierkegaard, Nietzsche, Norwid or Tranströmer, Aygi demonstratively inscribed himself into the tradition of the historical Russian avant-garde, disseminating numerous references to Russian Futurists in his poetry, essays and interviews. In 1974, for example, he told Zbigniew Podgórzec about his admiration for Velimir Khlebnikov and Kazimir Malevich:

> I am much indebted to the heritage of the Russian 'avant-gardists', especially [...] Khlebnikov, Malevich... As I said, I consider the achievements of the Russian 'avant-garde' to be the heritage of all Russian poetics, all Russian literature. This is a classical heritage, and I am convinced that today it is impossible to engage with literature and visual art without going through the school of Khlebnikov and Malevich.[4]

Likening the historical avant-garde to a "classical heritage"[5] in Soviet times meant a deliberate affirmation of a literary and artistic past that had been erased from the official discourse since the early 1930s. Indeed, books and artworks that did not conform to the aesthetics of Socialist Realism were banned,[6] access to materials in libraries and archives was restricted,[7] and the mere possession of forbidden texts

---

family name Aygi (Chuvash for "that one"; spelled Айги with a 'g' in Russian and Айхи with a 'kh' in Chuvash). For biographical information on Aygi, see France: "Gennadii Aigi (21 August 1934–12 February 2006)" and Robel: *Aiguï.*

2 The Chuvash Republic, or Chuvashia, is an autonomous republic within the Russian Federation, approximately 600 kilometres east of Moscow in the Volga Upland south of the Mari El Republic and west of the Republic of Tatarstan. For a comprehensive introduction to the history and culture of the Chuvash people, see, for example, Kappeler: *Die Tschuwaschen: Ein Volk im Schatten der Geschichte.*

3 "J'aimerais nommer un poète extraordinaire de l'avant-garde russe d'aujourd'hui, Gennadij Aïgui: il disait récemment que pour lui Malévitch est 'le premier parmi les artistes, le plus aimé, non seulement le premier parmi les peintres, mais le premier artiste'." Jakobson: "Message sur Malévitch", p. 293.

4 "[...] я многим обязан наследию русских 'авангардистов', особенно [...] Хлебникову, Малевичу... Как я уже сказал, достижения русского 'авангарда' я считаю достоянием всей русской поэтики, всей русской словесности. Это – классическое наследие, и я убежден, что нельзя сегодня заниматься словесным и изобразительным искусством, не пройдя 'хлебниковскую', 'малевичианскую' школу." Aigi: *Razgovor na rasstoianii: Stat'i, esse, besedy, stikhi* [Conversation at a Distance: Articles, Essays, Conversations, Poems], p. 23.

5 Aigi: *Razgovor na rasstoianii*, p. 23.

6 At times, the erasure happened literally by retroactively enforcing the removal of paragraphs, pages, chapters or complete books from libraries and bookstores. See, for example, Blium: "Iskalechennye knigi" [Crippled Books].

7 See Aygi's recollections in an interview with Irina Vrubel'-Golubkina, in which he stated that it was impossible to get anything by writers such as Nietzsche, Akhmatova or Gumilev at the Lenin

could lead to severe repercussions, despite a temporary relaxation of repression and censorship during the first decade after Stalin's death in 1953. Within this context and contrary to the slogan of the Russian Futurists to throw previous generations of writers "overboard from the Ship of Modernity",[8] Aygi strove to enter into a dialogue with Futurism and to re-establish and continue a long-interrupted literary tradition that had been suppressed by the cultural politics in the Soviet Union. Due to his work in the Mayakovsky Museum in Moscow and his personal contacts with Aleksei Kruchenykh, David Burliuk, Vasilisk Gnedov and others, he was able to develop a thorough knowledge of the historical Russian[9] avant-garde, organize several semi-legal exhibitions and, as a well-connected figure within the network of the unofficial culture in the Soviet Union, promote and disseminate avant-garde materials in Russian samizdat and tamizdat publications,[10] as well as in Chuvash translations.

State Library of the USSR (now Russian State Library) in Moscow; Vrubel'-Golubkina: *Razgovory v zerkale* [Conversations in the Mirror], p. 171.

8 "A Slap in the Face of Public Taste." Lawton and Eagle: *Russian Futurism Through Its Manifestoes, 1912–1928*, pp. 51–52.

9 The term 'Russian' needs some qualification here: Malevich was born to a Polish family in Kyiv and self-identified as Ukrainian in autobiographical notes and on official documents (see, for example, Vakar and Mikhienko, eds.: *Malevich o sebe, sovremenniki o Maleviche* [Malevich on Himself, Contemporaries on Malevich], vol. 1, pp. 26 and 549); he published his theoretical texts in Russian, Ukrainian, Polish and German (see, for example, the second volume of Malevich: *Sobranie sochinenii v piati tomakh* [Collected Works in Five Volumes]). Larionov and Kruchenykh were born in the Kherson Governorate; Burliuk was born in a village near Lebedyn to an ethnic Belarusian mother and a father who descended from Ukrainian Cossacks; and the first Cubo-Futurist group Hylaea (Russian spelling: Гилея (Gileia)) was named after the region around the Burliuk estate near Chernianka in the Kherson Oblast, which Herodotus in his *Histories* (c. 430 BC) had referred to as the Scythian region Hylaea (Υλαια).

10 Samizdat is a Russian term ('sam' for 'self, by oneself', and 'izdat', an abbreviation for 'izdatel'stvo', 'publishing house') for clandestine, self-published literature, usually passed from hand to hand. Tamizdat refers to literature that is published abroad ('tam' is Russian for 'there') and clandestinely brought back to the Soviet Union. On samizdat and tamizdat, see, for example, Komaromi: "The Material Existence of Soviet Samizdat", Steiner: "On Samizdat, Tamizdat, Magnitizdat and Other Words that Are Difficult to Pronounce", Kind-Kovács and Labov: *Samizdat, Tamizdat and Beyond: Transnational Media During and After Socialism* and Komaromi: *Soviet Samizdat: Imagining a New Society.*

Early influences

Gennady Aygi first encountered the works of the Russian Futurist Vladimir Mayakovsky when he and his teenage friends from a neighbouring village found "a large volume" of Mayakovsky's works in one of their houses in Chuvashia, in 1948. Aygi later remembered that, at the time, Mayakovsky made "an incredible impression"[11] on him and that he began to imitate him in his own poetry. With the support of the Chuvash National Poet Peter Khuzankai (Russian spelling: Peder Khuzangai), Aygi was sent to study at the Gorky Literary Institute in Moscow in 1953. The institute's student residence was located in the writers' colony Peredelkino, in the outskirts of Moscow, where Aygi met Boris Pasternak, a former member of the Futurist group Tsentrifuga (Centrifuge), and became a close friend of his. In his memoir of his time with Boris Pasternak, Aygi explained the lasting importance of Mayakovsky for him:

> I came to the capital knowing only Mayakovsky amongst the Russian poets of the twentieth century. I adored him; for a long time I imitated him, distorting my own way of writing, my own 'lyric voice', over many years. Boris Leonidovich [Pasternak] sensed very clearly this 'presence of Mayakovsky' in me.[12]

Initially, Aygi had written in Chuvash, producing Russian interlinear translations of his poems for his teachers, but Pasternak and Nâzım Hikmet urged him to gradually switch to Russian. Aygi recalled Pasternak's reaction to his Russian interlinear translation of the poem *Zaviaz'* (Beginning, 1954) as follows:

> Boris Leonidovich [Pasternak] summed up his opinion in one sentence: 'Half of it I like very much; half I don't like at all.' […] I could clearly see which 'half' he didn't like – everything with traces of 'Mayakovskyism' in the 'anatomization' and 'physiologization' of the images.[13]

---

11 "А в сорок восьмом мальчишки из соседней деревни […] нашли у одного из них в доме большой том Маяковского. Вот он произвел на меня невероятное впечатление. Я начал подражать Маяковскому."; Vrubel'-Golubkina: *Razgovory v zerkale*, p. 170.

12 Aigi [Aygi]: *Time of Gratitude*, p. 16. "В столицу я приехал, зная из русских поэтов XX века только Маяковского. Я обожал его, долго писал 'под него', исковеркав на многие годы свою манеру письма, собственный 'лиризм'. Б. Л. прекрасно чувствовал это 'присутствие Маяковского' во мне." Aigi: *Razgovor na rasstoianii*, p. 102.

13 Aigi [Aygi]: *Time of Gratitude*, pp. 35 f. "О ней Б. Л. отозвался одной фразой: – Половина мне очень понравилась, половина очень не понравилась. […] Мне было ясно, какая 'половина' не понравилась Б. Л., – все то, где были остаточные следы 'маяковизма' – в 'анатомизации' и 'физиологизации' образов." Aigi: *Razgovor na rasstoianii*, p. 112.

Aygi's teachers at the Gorky Literary Institute, the poet Mikhail Svetlov and the Formalist critic and poet Viktor Shklovsky, also noticed that the images in this poem were indebted to the Futurist poet.[14] The title of one of Mayakovsky's best-known long poems, *Vo ves' golos* (At the Top of My Voice, 1929/30), is directly alluded to in the verses "Let me be in your midst / a dusty coin turning up / among rustling banknotes / in a slippery silk purse: / it would ring at the top of its voice / but there's nothing hard to ring on".[15]

In 1958, during a committee meeting of the Komosomol[16] at the Gorky Literary Institute, one of Aygi's poems was denounced as resembling pre-revolutionary poems by Pasternak,[17] who had fallen out of favour with the Soviet authorities and had been forced to decline the Nobel Prize for Literature the same year. Aygi's membership in the association was subsequently rescinded and he was expelled from the Literary Institute "for writing a hostile book of poems that undermines the foundations of the method of Socialist Realism".[18] Nonetheless, in the following year, Aygi managed to obtain his diploma from the Literary Institute by submitting his Chuvash translation of Tvardovsky's war poem *Vasily Terkin*,[19] which was subsequently published without any mention of the translator's name. A few of Aygi's early Chuvash poems appeared in Russian translations undertaken by poets such as Bella Akhmadulina and David Samoilov in 'official' Soviet journals and sporadically also in Chuvash journals;[20] other than that, Aygi had

14 See Vrubel'-Golubkina: *Razgovory v zerkale*, p. 172.

15 English translation by Peter France; Aigi [Aygi]: *Selected Poems, 1954–94*, p. 31; "[...] пускай я буду среди вас / как пыльная монета оказавшаяся / среди шуршащих ассигнаций / в шелковом скользком кармане: / звенеть бы ей во весь голос / да не с чем сталкиваться чтобы звенеть"; Aigi: *Sobranie sochinenii.* Vol. 2. *Stikhi* [Collected Works. Vol. 2. Poems], p. 22.

16 Komsomol, short of Коммунистический Союз Молодёжи (Kommunisticheskii Soiuz Molodezhi; Communist Youth League), was the youth division of the Communist Party in the Soviet Union.

17 "Стихотворение 'Вдруг' – это Пастернак, который служился до революции." Ibid., p. 143.

18 "[...] исключить Г. Лисина из рядов ВЛКСМ за написание враждебной книги стихов, подрывающих основы метода социалистического реализма". Orlitskii, Azarova and Derpa: *Aigi: Materialy, issledovaniia, esse v dvukh tomakh* [Aygi: Materials, Research, Essays in two volumes], vol. 1, pp. 141. For a redacted transcript of the meeting that led to Aygi's expulsion from the Komsomol on 12 March 1958, see ibid., pp. 141–150.

19 For more context, see Frank: "Literaturnyi Institut (i Vysshie literaturnye kursy): Interfeis andergraunda? Sluchai Gennadiia Aigi" [The Literature Institute (and Advanced Literary Courses): Interface of the Underground? The Case of Gennady Aygi], pp. 308–319.

20 See Kuborskaia-Aigi, et al.: *Gennadii Aigi: Nauchno-vspomogatel'nyi ukazatel'*. Vol. 1 [Gennady Aygi: Research Reference Index. Vol. 1], p. 132.

to rely on samizdat and tamizdat publications until the *perestroika* years.[21] Notable early tamizdat publications in the West were *Stikhi 1954–1971* (Poems 1954–1971), published in Germany in 1975, and *Otmechennaia zima* (Noted Winter), which was issued in Paris in 1982. The cover of the latter was designed by Igor' Makarevich, with a drawing by Aygi that seems to have been inspired by Kazimir Malevich's Suprematism (see Fig. 1).

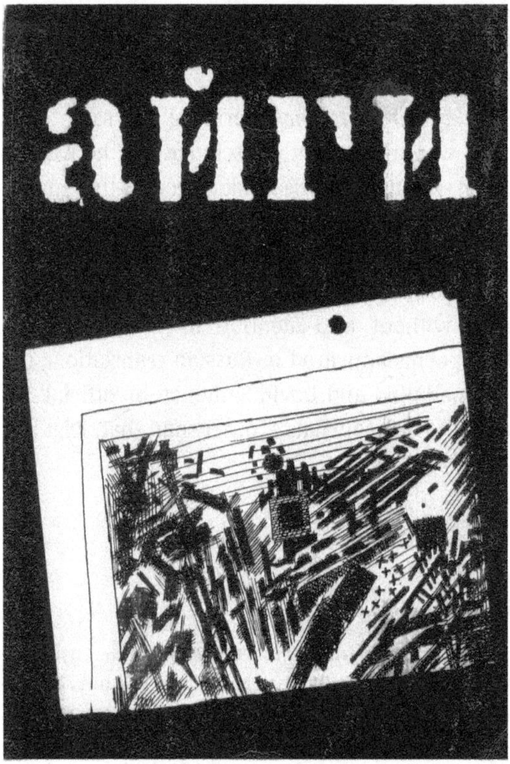

Fig. 1: Gennadii Aigi: *Otmechennaia zima: Sobranie stikhotvorenii v dvukh chastiakh* (Noted Winter: Collected Poems in Two Parts). Paris: Sintaksis, 1982. Cover design by Igor' Makarevich, with a drawing by Gennady Aygi in Suprematist style.

Aygi used the royalties from his Chuvash translation of Tvardovsky's poem to buy a little house on the outskirts of Moscow, which became a venue of the 'under-

21 Aygi's Russian poetry was no longer published after 1964 in the Soviet Union and could only be clandestinely distributed as samizdat or tamizdat editions. His Chuvash poetry, however, was still being published, even in book form.

ground' culture which Aygi began to associate with. In an interview with Galina Gordeyeva in 1990, Aygi stressed the rôle of the composer and musician Andrei Volkonsky[22] as a "catalyst"[23] who maintained connections with foreign friends[24] and organized art exhibitions, concerts and poetry readings in his apartment during the late 1950s and 1960s. Volkonsky introduced Aygi to music, art and literature otherwise not easily accessible in the Soviet Union, including works by Schoenberg and Webern, foreign art publications, contemporary French literature, as well as many other unofficial and nonconformist Russian composers, artists and writers.[25] During this time, Aygi also attended gatherings at Oskar Rabin's place in Lianozovo[26]) and befriended the artist Igor' Vulokh as well as writers such as the Neo-Futurist Valentin Khromov, Stanislav (Stas) Krasovitski and Leonid Chertkov.[27] Aygi was most closely associated at the time with the group around Aleksandr Vasil'ev, Vladimir Yakovlev and Igor' Voroshilov. In an interview with Zbigniew Podgórzec in 1974, Aygi characterized the late 1950s as "our 'budetlianin' youth"[28] and "our own brief *Slap in the Face of Public Taste* epoch".[29] He recalled that "for us, the

22 For Aygi's recollections of Volkonsky and Volkonsky's rôle in unofficial Soviet music, see Schmelz: *Such Freedom, If Only Musical: Unofficial Soviet Music During the Thaw.*

23 See Aigi: *Razgovor na rasstoianii*, p. 271.

24 Volkonsky's family had returned to the Soviet Union from France after the war.

25 See Talochkin and Alpatova: *"Drugoe iskusstvo": Moskva, 1956–76: K khronike khudozhestvennoi zhizni.* Vol. 1 ["The Other Art": Moscow 1956–76: Towards a Chronology of Artistic Life. Vol. 1], p. 49. In 1968, Aygi managed to publish a substantial anthology of his translations of French poetry in Chuvash. It included modernist and contemporary poetry that was otherwise inaccessible in the Soviet Union. The translations have recently been reprinted in Aigi: *Sobranie sochinenii.* Vol. 1. *Stikhi, poemy, perevody na chuvashskom iazyke* [Collected Works. Vol. 1. Poems, Longer Poems, Translations. In Chuvash], pp. 349–528.

26 This suburb of Moscow was the centre of the Lianozovo group, which included amongst its members Yevgeny and Lev Kropivnitsky, Genrikh Sapgir, Igor' Kholin and Vsevolod Nekrasov.

27 For more on Krasovitski's, Chertkov's and especially Khromov's Neo-Futurist aesthetics, see Maurizio: "Neofuturizm v moskovskom samizdate stalinskogo i poslestalinskogo (ottepel'nogo) perioda na primere poezii N. Glazkova, V. Khromova i L. Gubanova" [Neo-Futurism in the Moscow Samizdat of the Stalin and Post-Stalin (Thaw) Period as Exemplified by N. Glazkov, V. Khromov and L. Gubanov], pp. 153–156.

28 "[...] наша 'будетлянская' юность". Aigi: *Razgovor na rasstoianii*, p. 22. The neologism 'budetlianin' was Khlebnikov's preferred Russian term for 'Futurist' ('budet' is the future tense of the verb 'to be').

29 Aygi alludes to the Futurist publication *Poshchechina obshchestvennomu vkusu* (Slap in the Face of Public Taste; 1912); "своя краткая эпоха *Пощечины общественному вкусу*"; Aigi: *Razgovor na rasstoianii*, p. 22.

main poet was Khlebnikov"[30] who served as a model for "our unwritten manifestos".[31]

As the tradition of the Russian avant-garde had been interrupted since the 1930s and replaced with the official discourse of Socialist Realism, the underground community served as a counter-cultural *milieu de mémoire*,[32] in which the older generation's recollections of the forbidden past became part of a daily experience. Aygi mentioned, in particular, the poets Nikolai Glazkov, Ian Satunovsky and Yevgeny Kropivnitsky, who were telling younger poets "about Guro, about the Cubists and Kazimir Malevich".[33] In the introduction to his anthology of avant-garde poetry, which he had been working on since the 1960s[34] and which was finally published between 1989 and 1990, he called to mind that Aleksei Kruchenykh "still haunts Moscow [...] like a Hoffmannesque spectre".[35]

Aygi at the Mayakovsky Museum

Concerned about Aygi's precarious situation at the time, Andrei Volkonsky managed to secure a position for him at the State Mayakovsky Library-Museum in 1961. Aygi continued to work there for ten years, first as a senior bibliographer, later as head of the museum's visual-art section. At the time, the Mayakovsky Museum was located in a building on Gendrikov Lane (now Mayakovsky Lane), where Mayakovsky had lived in a *ménage à trois* with his lover and muse Lilya Brik and her husband Osip Brik. The apartment was the meeting point of the group associ-

---

30 "Главным поэтом для нас был Хлебников"; Kulle and Aigi: "'Poet – eto nesostaiavshiisia sviatoi...': Beseda Viktora Kulle s Gennadiem Aigi, Moskva, 25 sentiabria 1998 g." [A Poet – That's a Saint Manqué: Conversation of Viktor Kulle with Gennady Aygi, Moscow, 25 September 1998], p. 16. Vasil'ev, in fact, was notorious for having typed the "most complete" samizdat collection of works by Khlebnikov, as Aygi's biographer Leon Robel asserts. See Robel: *Aigi*, p. 38.

31 "У нас был[и] [...] свои неписаные манифесты." Aigi: *Razgovor na rasstoianii*, p. 22.

32 Nora: "Between Memory and History: 'Les lieux de mémoire'", p. 7.

33 "In the village of Lianozovo near Moscow, a strange old man (born in the same year as Mayakovsky) – Yevgeny Kropivnitsky – tells a couple of youngsters about Guro, about the Cubists and Kazimir Malevich" ("В подмосковном поселке Лианозово нескольким юношам рассказывает о Гуро, о кубистах и Казимире Малевиче странный старик (родившийся в один год с Маяковским) – Евгений Кропивницкий".) Aigi: *Razgovor na rasstoianii*, p. 198.

34 See, for example, Ivanova: "Mir Gennadiia Aigi – tishina" [The World of Gennady Aygi – Silence], pp. 166 f.

35 "And, like a Hoffmannesque spectre, the fidget Kruchenykh who became a collector of literary autographs and rare editions still haunts Moscow." ("И бродит еще по Москве, как гофмановский призрак, непоседа Крученых, ставший собирателем литераторских автографов и редких изданий.") Aigi: *Razgovor na rasstoianii*, p. 198.

ated with *LEF* (Levyi front iskusstv: Left Front of the Arts) and continued to serve as the editorial office of the journal *Novy LEF* (New LEF), which had quickly become the centre of cultural life in Moscow. The Mayakovsky Museum, as a building and an archive, had later become a problematic container of memories invested with a "symbolic aura".[36] It represented the State-sanctioned aspects of Mayakovsky's work and acted as a landmark for the posthumously canonized Mayakovsky. It thus played the dual rôle of a memorial of official culture canonized by Stalin and, often precariously, of a site of unofficial narratives related to the suppressed Futurist past.

When Aygi worked at the Mayakovsky Library-Museum, it held a substantial collection containing Mayakovsky's manuscripts and around 165,000 books, journals and other materials by and about Mayakovsky and Russian Futurism. Here, Aygi had unrestricted access to an abundance of materials on the Russian avant-garde, which were otherwise unattainable in Soviet repositories at the time. Amongst these, he found Kazimir Malevich's theoretical works, which were to become central to his poetics.[37] Aygi used his privileged position to excerpt by hand many documents from the museum's collection; he also arranged for friends to smuggle rare books and documents across the border, thus providing, for example, Wiktor Woroszylski (who was not permitted to leave Poland at the time) with material for his biography on Mayakovsky.[38]

Working at the Mayakovsky Museum also provided Aygi with opportunities to meet proponents of the historical avant-garde, including the Futurists David Burliuk,[39] Vasilisk Gnedov[40] and, most significantly, Aleksei Kruchenykh, with whom he became friends and whom he frequently met from 1963 to 1968 (the year of

---

36 Nora: "Between Memory and History: 'Les lieux de mémoire'", p. 19.

37 "Then, since 1961, I began working at the Mayakovsky Museum, began to read Malevich." ("Потом, с 1961-го, я начал работать в Музее Маяковского, стал читать Малевича."); Kulle and Aigi: "'Poet – eto nesostaiavshiisia sviatoi…': Beseda Viktora Kulle s Gennadiem Aigi, Moskva, 25 sentiabria 1998 g.", p. 16.

38 Woroszylski: *Życie Majakowskiego* [The Life of Mayakovsky]. See Woroszylska [Voroshil'skaia]: "Vstrechi s Aigi" [Encounters with Aygi].

39 Aygi met Burliuk in August 1965. See his poem "For David Burliuk" ("Davidu Burliuku") which is dated "August 1965 / Moscow, Mayakovsky Museum" ("Август 1965 / Москва, Музей Маяковского"; Byrkina and Mordvinova: *Mir etikh glaz.* Vol. 2, p. 39) and his poem "D.D. and M.N. Burliuk: Farewell" ("D.D. i M.N. Burliukam: Na proshchan'e"; Aigi: *Sobranie sochinenii.* Vol. 2. *Stikhi*, p. 149), dated 27 August 1965. David Burliuk lived in exile and had petitioned the Soviet government in 1940 to be given permission to visit his homeland; he could only visit the Soviet Union in 1956 and 1965.

40 See Aigi: *Razgovor na rasstoianii*, p. 198 f.

death of this key figure in historical Futurism).[41] They regularly discussed the history of the avant-garde, and Kruchenykh introduced Aygi to rare materials from his own substantial collection.[42] Several Futurist publications with autograph dedications by Kruchenykh to Aygi have been preserved.[43] Over the years, Aygi also recorded Kruchenykh reciting unpublished poems,[44] which he then transcribed and prepared for an authorized anthology that was meant to appear in the journal *Literaturnaia Gruziia* (Literary Georgia), to coincide with Kruchenykh's eightieth birthday in 1966. Unfortunately, this publication, which would have been the first 'official' publication of Kruchenykh's works since 1934, did not materialize.[45]

Furthermore, Aygi organized soirées in which Kruchenykh recited his poetry. Tomas Venclova remembered "one such reading at Andrei Volkonsky's apartment: it was a Happening that bordered on the incredible. Kruchenykh was not just a poet who broke all the rules of grammar and common sense, but was a talented actor as well."[46] Curiously, despite his close friendship with and admiration for Kruchenykh,[47] Aygi insisted in an interview with Sergey Biryukov in 1990 that Kruchenykh did not have any influence on his own poetry; he rather recognized Kru-

---

41 "G.A. [=Gennadii Aigi]: […] When he was still alive, Kruchenykh called me every day." ("Г.А.: […] Крученых, пока был жив, каждый день звонил мне.") Vrubel'-Golubkina: *Razgovory v zerkale*, p. 180 f.

42 For Anna Lavrova's recollections of her meetings with Aygi and Kruchenykh, see Lavrova: *Klassik Krucha: Vospominaniia* [The Classic Krucha: Recollections]. Other writers who became acquainted with Kruchenykh during those years were Ian Satunovskii, Viktor Sosnora and Vladimir Kazakov.

43 Kruchenykh's 1963 dedication to Aygi in *Zapisnaia knizhka Velimira Khlebnikova* (Velimir Khlebnikov's Notebook, 1925) is reproduced in Aigi: *Razgovor na rasstoianii*, p. 210 and in Byrkina and Mordvinova: *Mir etikh glaz.* Vol. 2, p. 38. For reproductions of Kruchenykh's dedications to Aygi in *Zudesnik* (*Itchician*) and *Pobeda nad solntsem* (Victory over the Sun), see ibid., p. 37 f. Aygi later remarked that those books as well as Kruchenykh's *15 let russkogo futurizma* (15 Years of Russian Futurism, 1928), *Ironiada* (1930) and a copy of Malevich's *Bog ne skinut* (God is not Cast Down, 1922) were the only valuables left when he was trying to raise money to publish his own poetry in Paris. See Dronnikov: *Iz dnevnika poeta.* Vol. 1 [From the Poet's Diary: Book 1] [s.p. (entry from 9 March 1979)].

44 See, for example, Ivanova: "Mir Gennadiia Aigi – tishina", p. 167. A manuscript page of Aygi's transcription of one of the poems read by Kruchenykh is reproduced in Aygi: *Razgovor na rasstoianii*, p. 209.

45 See Sukhoparov: *Aleksei Kruchenykh: Sud'ba budetlianina* [Aleksei Kruchenykh: The Fate of a Futurist], p. 135 and Sukhoparov: *Aleksei Kruchenykh v svidetel'stvakh sovremennikov* [Aleksei Kruchenykh in Testimonies of Contemporaries], p. 296. In 1976, Aygi wrote a preface to a collection of unpublished poems by Kruchenykh (archive of the Forschungsstelle Osteuropa, FSO 01–218).

46 Hinsey and Venclova: *Magnetic North: Conversations with Tomas Venclova*, p. 176.

47 "Kruchenykh is a real poet, not a minor, but a great poet." ("Крученых – настоящий поэт, не малый, а большой поэт.") Aigi: *Razgovor na rasstoianii*, p. 288.

chenykh's importance for him "as a brilliant critic, an excellent linguist. [...] I do not find that his poetry has in any way affected me. Except for maybe some small things, where I used an aspect of his playfulness."[48]

At the Mayakovsky Museum, Aygi also met Nikolai Khardzhiev, a writer, art critic, erudite collector and archivist of the Russian avant-garde, who had been acquainted with Mayakovsky, Khlebnikov, Kruchenykh, Malevich, Kharms, Vvedensky, Oleinikov, Mandelshtam, Akhmatova and many other important figures of the Russian Silver Age. Aygi considered Khardzhiev a living memory of the avant-garde[49] as well as a "teacher".[50] Together, they organized several semi-legal exhibitions of works by Malevich, Tatlin, Filonov, Larionov, Goncharova, Chagall, Matyushin, Ender, Chekrygin, Guro and others, as well as an exhibition celebrating Velimir Khlebnikov's eightieth birthday (see Fig. 2), testing the limits of what was tolerated by the authorities. Most of the materials exhibited came from Khardzhiev's own collection, from other private ones, or from relatives and descendants of the artists. According to Ann Komaromi, these exhibitions at the Mayakovsky Museum, most of which had a short time span of one to three days, "helped acquaint many dissident artists and writers with the Russian avant-garde heritage".[51] Aygi described the exhibitions as "large-scale events with a pan-European resonance; for Moscow's cultural life, they were phenomena that had no equivalents at that time."[52] The artist and poet Mikhail Grobman remembered, for instance, that the vernissage for the Khlebnikov exhibition on 12 November 1965 was attended by the Futurist Aleksei Kruchenykh, as well as by contemporary artists such as Francisco Infante, Lev Nusberg, Mikhail Shvartsman

48 "Он на меня имел влияние, безусловно, не как поэт, а как блистательный критик, превосходный лингвист. [...] Я не нахожу, чтобы на мне его поэзия как-то сказалась. Кроме, может быть некоторых небольших вещей, где я использовал игровой момент." Aigi: *Razgovor na rasstoianii*, p. 281.

49 See, for example, Mikhail Grobman's recollection of meeting Khardzhiev and Aygi at the Mayakovsky Museum: "We talked with Nik. Iv. Khardzhiev, he told us about the Burliuks and about that time." ("Мы беседовали с Ник. Ив. Харджиевым, он рассказывал о Бурлюках и о том времени.") Grobman: *Leviafan: Dnevniki 1963–1971 godov* [Leviathan: Diaries 1963–1971], p. 80.

50 "Николай Иванович Харджиев, наш крупнейший искусствовед, которого я смею назвать своим учителем."; Aigi: *Razgovor na rasstoianii*, p. 276.

51 Komaromi: *Uncensored: Samizdat Novels and the Quest for Autonomy in Soviet Dissidence*, p. 9.

52 "Мы с ним в тяжелейшие хрущевско-брежневские времена делали в течение десяти лет выставки Малевича, Татлина, Ларионова, Филонова, Гончаровой, Чекрыгина, Елены Гуро [...] а ведь это были события крупного масштаба, они имели общеевропейский резонанс, а для московской культурной жизни это явления, не имевшие аналогов в то время." Aigi: *Razgovor na rasstoianii*, p. 276. See also, for example, Mikhail Chernyshev's assessment of the exhibition with works by Malevich and Tatlin in Talochkin and Alpatova: *"Drugoe iskusstvo": Moskva, 1956–76: K khronike khudozhestvennoi zhizni.* Vol. 1, pp. 131–133.

and Ilya Kabakov,[53] whose studio was located right across the street. Kabakov recalled:

> There, in that museum, worked Gena Aygi at the time. [...] There they organized 'progressive' exhibitions, I remember, in '64 or '65, there was a small Malevich exhibition. Our studio across the street would be enlivened by such proximity, particularly during the exhibitions and the soirées organized by the museum.[54]

Grobman further noted that he saw Eduard Steinberg at the exhibition of Vasily Chekrygin in 1964; Boris Ender's widow attended the vernissages of the Guro and Ender show and the Larionov and Goncharova exhibition in 1965, as also did, for example, Yefim Royak, a student of Chagall and Malevich. Employees of foreign embassies also showed up at these events.[55] In his essay "Listki – v veter prazdnika: K stoletiiu Velimira Khlebnikova" (Leaves – Into a Festive Wind: For the Centenary of Velimir Khlebnikov, 1985), Aygi remembered that the Futurist Vasilisk Gnedov delivered a speech at the Khlebnikov exhibition in 1965.[56] He also stressed that the "Museum itself did not organize any of these exhibitions or retrospectives"; rather, they were initiated by Khardzhiev, who "did not work for the Museum" but was merely acting as a "consultant".[57] Khardzhiev "came up with a simple, but very clever, move. He called his series of exhibitions 'Illustrators of the Works of V. V. Mayakovsky'. Neither the official censors nor the Museum administration could object,"[58] although the links to illustrations of Mayakovsky's works were at times rather far-fetched, as for example in the case of Chagall who had not been very prolific in this respect.

The first two exhibitions in this series took place before Aygi worked at the Mayakovsky Museum. However, beginning with the third exhibition in April 1961, Aygi "was responsible for putting Khardzhiev's ideas and concepts for the

53 See Grobman: *Leviafan: Dnevniki 1963–1971 godov*, p. 109.

54 "Там, в этом музее, в то время работал Гена Айги. [...] там устраивались 'прогрессивные' выставки, помню, в 64 или 65 была небольшая выставка Малевича. Наша мастерская напротив стала оживленнее из-за такого соседства, особенно во время выставок и вечеров, которые устраивал музей."; Kabakov: *60-e – 70-e...: Zapiski o neofitsial'noi zhizni v Moskve* [60s–70s...: Notes on the Unofficial Life in Moscow], p. 20.

55 See Grobman: *Leviafan: Dnevniki 1963–1971 godov*, pp. 43, 81 and 100.

56 "I was lucky enough to see Gnedov in 1965 at the Mayakovsky Museum in Moscow, at a celebration of the eightieth anniversary of Velimir Khlebnikov's birth." Aigi [Aygi]: *Time of Gratitude*, p. 44. ("Мне удалось увидеть Гнедова в 1965 году в Государственном Музее В. В. Маяковского на вечере, посвященном 80-летию со дня рождения В. Хлебникова." Aigi: *Razgovor na rasstoianii*, pp. 198 f.)

57 Aigi: "Nikolai Khardzhiev and the Maiakovsky Museum, Moscow", p. 43.

58 Ibid., p. 44.

Museum into practice and later on, as head of the visual section [...], supervised all exhibitions".[59] Based on Georgii Kizeval'ter's list of official and unofficial exhibitions from 1950 to 1970, it is possible to reconstruct the following timeline of the shows organized by Khardzhiev and Aygi at the Mayakovsky Museum:[60]

No. 1 (April 1957): Vasily Chekrygin
No. 2 (18–19 November 1960): El Lissitzky
No. 3 (21 April 1961): Gustav Klutsis
No. 4 (28–30 December 1961): Mikhail Matyushin, Pavel Filonov
No. 5 (19–21 April 1962): Vladimir Tatlin, Kazmir Malevich[61]
No. 6 (24–26 December 1964): Vasily Chekrygin
Hors-série (18–20 March 1965): Varvara Stepanova
No. 7 (10–12 June 1965): Elena Guro, Boris Ender
No. 8 (23–30 September 1965): Mikhail Larionov, Natalia Goncharova[62]
Hors-série (12 November 1965): *Khlebnikov's 80th anniversary:* Pavel Filonov, Olga Rozanova, Kazimir Malevich, Vladimir Mayakovsky, David Burliuk, Vladimir Tatlin, Marc Chagall, Alexander Rodchenko and others
No. 9 27–31 January 1967 [shut down by the authorities]: Georgy Yakulov, Vladimir Tatlin, Olga Rozanova, Marc Chagall, Alexander Rodchenko

According to Aygi, Nina Gorodetskaya, the director of the Museum at the time, "had the power to forbid us to do this or that, but her resistance was very weak".[63] Aygi recounted the anecdote that for exhibition no. 5, with works by Malevich and

59 Ibid., p. 44.
60 See Kizeval'ter: *Vremia nadezhd, vremia illiuzii: Problemy istorii sovetskogo neofitsial'nogo iskusstva 1950–1960 gody. Stat'i i materialy* [Time of Hope, Time of Illusions: Problems of a History of the Soviet Unofficial Art of the 1950s and 1960s. Essays and Materials], pp. 399–441. The numbers refer to those indicated on the printed invitations of the series "Khudozhniki – oformiteli proizvedenii V. V. Maiakovskogo" ("Illustrators of the Works of V. V. Mayakovsky"); the Stepanova and Khlebnikov exhibitions were not part of this series.
61 The printed invitation for this exhibition is reproduced in Byrkina and Mordvinova: *Mir etikh glaz*. Vol. 2, p. 35. In his speech at the finissage of the Malevich exhibition at the Tretyakov Gallery in 1989, Aygi recounted that the 1962 exhibition lasted three days but was extended by two days. See Aigi: *Sobranie sochinenii.* Vol. 4. *Stat'ia, retsenzii, interv'iu, esse, vospominaniia* [Collected Works. Vol. 4. Articles, Reviews, Interviews, Essays, Recollections], p. 136.
62 Khardzhiev recalls that the Larionov and Goncharova exhibition lasted longer than planned, because the director of the Mayakovsky Museum was on vacation during those days. See Khardzhiev: *Stat'i ob avangarde v dvukh tomakh.* Vol. 1 [Essays about the Avant-Garde in Two Volumes. Vol. 1], p. 374.
63 Aigi: "Nikolai Khardzhiev and the Maiakovsky Museum, Moscow", p. 45.

Tatlin, he "arranged it so that she signed off on the invitation – mixed in with other documents. I went to the censor's office with her signature. And then, once the invitations were printed, you had to see her face, for she was under the impression that she hadn't given her permission. Nonetheless, the exhibition took place."[64]

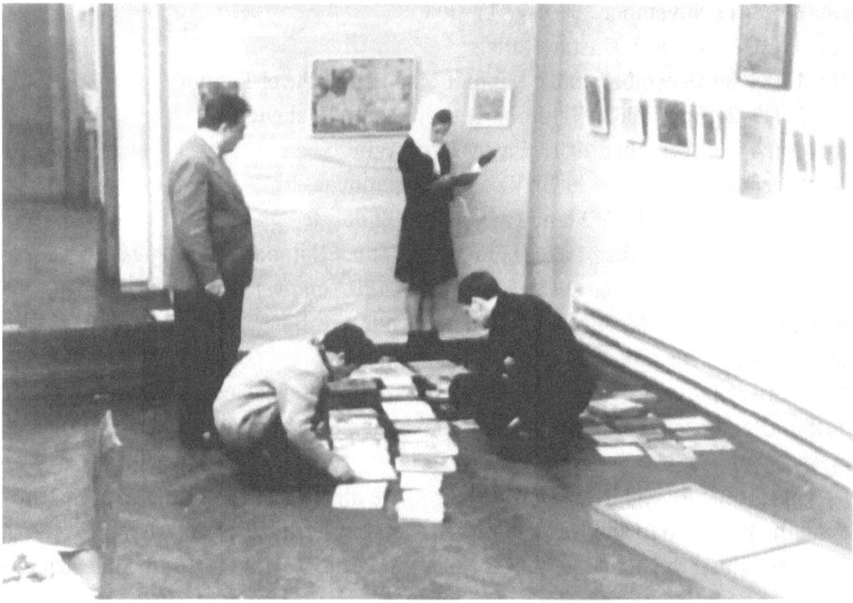

Fig. 2: Nikolai Khardzhiev, Gennady Aygi, Nataliia Aleshina and Rudolf Duganov installing the Khlebnikov exhibition at the Mayakovsky Museum in 1965.

Khardzhiev was aware that this art was banned at the time and that they were running a considerable risk of getting officially censored or penalized.[65] He recalls that the Larionov and Goncharova exhibition was dismantled just in time before government inspectors showed up at the museum. The last exhibition, with works by Chagall and others, already hung, was shut down by the authorities before it could open. Khardzhiev recalled that he "almost got arrested"[66] and that this

64 Ibid., p. 45.

65 "Тогда это искусство было под запретом, и это было риск." Khardzhiev: *Stat'i ob avangarde v dvukh tomakh.* Vol. 1, p. 373.

66 "[...] меня чуть не арестовали." Khardzhiev: *Stat'i ob avangarde v dvukh tomakh.* Vol. 1, p. 374.

incident was seen as a “provocation by the director”.[67] Aygi described the incident as follows:

> For three days, we were in a state of siege. (The museum was cordoned off by the police.) [...] I was not allowed to go upstairs. But, out of curiosity, one policeman went to see [the exhibition] and met Nikolai Ivanovich Khardzhiev who explained to him the peculiarities of Chagall’s paintings. The policeman turned out to be so interested and fascinated that he could be asked to secretly guide our friends to the exhibition hall.[68]

After this incident, no further exhibitions were mounted and relations with the museum administration deteriorated.[69] In 1971, when a new director was appointed and Aygi was asked to highlight the nationalist tendencies in Mayakovsky’s works in an upcoming event, he resigned.[70]

Dissemination of avant-garde materials

The catalogue of the Mayakovsky Museum exhibition *Vladimir Vladimirovich Maiakovskii, 1893–1930: Vystavka. Zhivopis, grafika, risunki* (Vladimir Vladimirovich Mayakovsky, 1893–1930: Exhibition. Painting, Graphic Art, Drawings, 1963)[71] remained Aygi’s only official Russian publication on the historical avant-garde until the end of the 1980s. Other than this, he managed to publish Chuvash translations of Futurist works, including his translations of Mayakovsky’s long poem *Oblako v shtanakh* (A Cloud in Trousers, 1914/15), which appeared in the literary journal *Tăvan Atăl* (Native Volga) in 1973,[72] and Mayakovsky’s play *Klop* (The Bed-

---

67 “Это была провокация директорши”. Khardzhiev: *Stat’i ob avangarde v dvukh tomakh.* Vol. 1, p. 374.

68 “В течение трех дней мы были на осадном положении. (Музей оцепила милиция.) [...] Меня наверх не пускали. Но один милиционер из любопытства пошел посмотреть и встретился с Николаем Ивановичем Харджиевым, который растолковал ему особенности живописи Шагала. Милиционер оказался настолько заинтересованным и увлекшимся человеком, что его можно было попросить, и он тайком проводил наших друзей в зал с экспозицией.” Talochkin and Alpatova: *“Drugoe iskusstvo”: Moskva, 1956–76: K khronike khudozhestvennoi zhizni.* Vol. 1, p. 160; reprinted in Byrkina and Mordvinova: *Mir etikh glaz.* Vol. 2, p. 36.

69 In 1969, for instance, when Aygi had received an invitiation from the French Ministry of Culture, the director Nina Gorodetskaya provided a negative reference to the Soviet authorities that prevented him from being granted permission to leave the Soviet Union.

70 See Aigi: *Razgovor na rasstoianii*, p. 273.

71 Lisin [=Aigi]: *Vladimir Vladimirovich Maiakovskii, 1893–1930.* For the cover design, Aygi recruited the nonconformist artist (and his close friend) Igor’ Vulokh; the cover is reprinted in Aigi: *Razgovor na rasstoianii*, p. 195.

72 Aigi: *Stikhi, poemy, perevody na chuvashskom iazyke*, pp. 323–344.

bug, 1928/29),[73] which was performed in Cheboksary in 1974 and published as a book, with an afterword by Aygi, in 1979. Chuvash translations of a poem by Pasternak and ten poems by Khlebnikov followed in the book *Khalal* (Testament) in 1988.[74]

In 1989, during the *perestroika* years, Aygi was finally able to publish, in several instalments, an anthology of Russian avant-garde poetry in the journal *V mire knig* (In the World of Books). It carried the title "Chernyi kvadrat: Russkii poeticheskii avangard" (Black Square: The Russian Poetic Avant-garde; see Fig. 3a) and was accompanied by an introduction and essays, memoirs and poetic reflections on the Futurist poets Elena Guro, Bozhidar (pseud. of Bogdan Petrovich Gordeev), Vasilisk Gnedov, Pavel Filonov and Aleksei Kruchenykh, as well as the lesser-known Vasily Mazurin.[75]

In the introduction, Aygi provided a brief overview of various Russian Futurist groups (Cubo-Futurists, Ego-Futurists, Tsentrifuga and others).[76] His stated aim was to (re-)introduce to a wider audience in the Soviet Union texts of forgotten avant-garde poets. For example, the anthology opened with works by Elena Guro that had last been printed in Russia in 1914,[77] it included poetic works by Filonov, who was at the time better known for his paintings than his poetry,[78] and it republished many of Kruchenykh's Futurist poems, including his well-known *zaum'* poem *Dyr bul shchyl* (1913). In the same anthology, Aygi also reprinted the entire book *Smert' iskusstvu* (Death to Art, 1913) by Gnedov, whose works had been championed by Serge Segay in the samizdat journal *Transponans* during the first half of the 1980s.[79] The inclusion of Bozhidar and Mazurin in the anthology drew attention to two almost entirely forgotten poets. After the fourth instalment of Aygi's anthology, the journal *V mire knig* underwent editorial changes, was

73 Aigi: *Perevody na chuvashskom iazyke*, pp. 310–355.

74 Aigi: *Stikhi, poemy, perevody na chuvashskom iazyke*, pp. 344–347.

75 See Aigi: "Russkii poeticheskii avangard", "Elena Guro", "Bozhidar. Vasilisk Gnedov", "Pavel Filonov. V.P. Mazurin" and "Aleksei Kruchenykh". Subsequently, the essays were reprinted in Aigi: *Razgovor na rasstoianii*, pp. 190 ff. and the essays and poems in Aigi: *'Tvortsy budushchikh znakov': Russkii poeticheskii avangard* ['Creators of Future Signs': The Russian Poetic Avant-Garde].

76 Aygi: "Russkii poeticheskii avangard" [The Russian Poetic Avant-garde].

77 On similarities between Guro's and Aygi's poetry, see Grauz: "'My chitaem ne slova, a postranstvo mezhdu slovami': Elena Guro – Gennadii Aigi. Opyt sopostavleniia" ['We are not reading words, but the space between the words': Elena Guro – Gennady Aygi: Attempt at a Comparison].

78 On Aygi and Filonov, see Makarevskii and Makarevskii: "G. N. Aigi o P. Filonove – krupneishem predstavitele khudozhestvenno-poeticheskogo avangarda" [G. N. Aygi on P. Filonov, the Most Important Representative of the Artistic and Poetic Avant-Garde].

79 Works by Gnedov had been published in *Transponans* Nos. 9, 11, 13, 16, 21. See Klähn: "Rea Nikonova and the Legacy of Russian Futurism", p. 407.

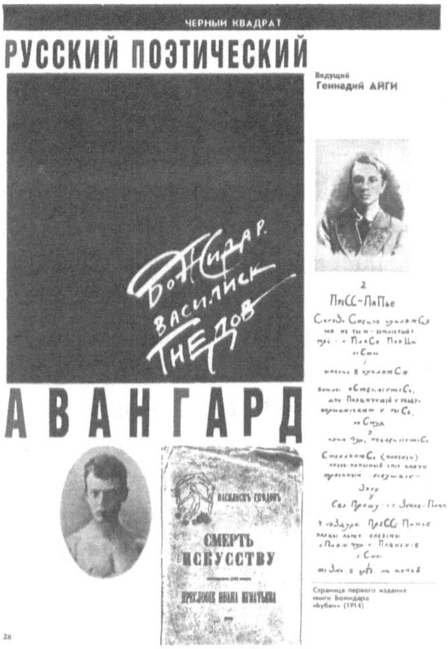

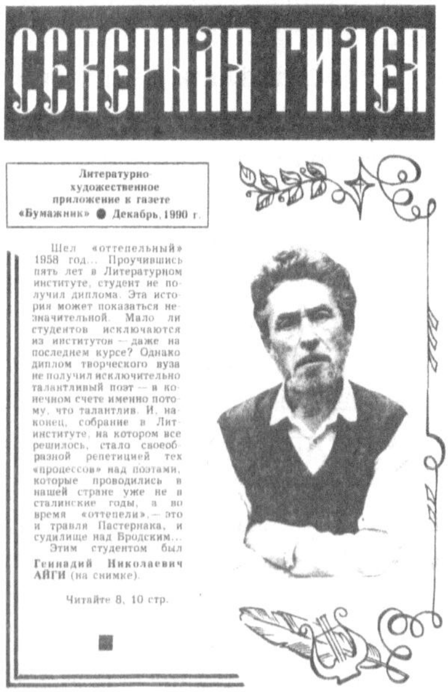

Fig. 3a: First page of the second instalment of Gennady Aygi's anthology *Chernyi kvadrat: Russkii poeticheskii avangard* (Black Square: The Russian Poetic Avant-garde), published in the journal *V mire knig* (In the World of Books) no. 2 (1989). It shows portraits of Vasilisk Gnedov and Bozhidar, reproductions of the cover of Gnedov's book *Smert' iskusstvu* (Death to Art, 1913) and of a page from Bozhidar's book *Buben* (Tambourine, 1914). **Fig. 3b:** Cover of the December 1990 issue of *Severnaia Gileia* (Northern Hylaea) with a photograph of Aygi.

renamed *Slovo* (Word) and halted the publication of the anthology. The next instalment, which included a selection of poems by Larionov and Aygi's essay on him, was hence printed in a special issue of the samizdat journal *Sumerki* (Twilight) in 1990. Issue 10+1 carried the title *Teoriia i praktika Igry v adu: K 80-letiiu russkogo avangarda* (Theory and Practice of the Game in Hell: On the 80th Anniversary of the Russian Avant-garde) and was entirely devoted to the historical avant-garde. Aygi contributed an essay on Larionov as well as several poems that were dedicated to or alluded to poets of the historical avant-garde.[80]

---

80 Aigi: "Mikhail Larionov." For a discussion of the samizdat journal *Sumerki*, see Mirzaev: "Sumerki: 30 let spustia" [Twilight: 30 Years Afterwards]; for Mirzaev's recollections of Aygi's involvement in the special issue, see Mirzaev: "Gennadii Aigi i Nikolai Dronnikov" [Gennady Aygi and Nikolai Dronnikov], p. 195; for a discussion of *Sumerki* and the tradition of artists' books, see Bezrodnyi: "Listaia 'Sumerki': Samizdat i 'iskusstvo knigi'" [Leafing through the Pages of 'Sumerki': Samizdat and the 'Art of the Book']. The design of the special issue on the avant-garde re-enacts the

Furthermore, Aygi collaborated with the editors of *Severnaia Gileia* (Northern Hylaea; see Fig. 3b),[81] a monthly literary supplement to the newspaper *Bumazhnik* (Wallet) in Novodvinsk that ran from 1990 to 1991 and included poems by Kruchenykh[82] and a poetic text on Kazimir Malevich, entitled *V chest' Mastera – neskol'ko absatsev* (In Honour of the Master – Several Paragraphs),[83] which introduced a selection of poems by Malevich. Aygi's text and Malevich's poems were also published in book form in 1991 by Gileia,[84] which became a major independent publishing house, still active today. Incidentally, the book of poems by Malevich was Gileia's first publication, or, rather, publication number 'zero', before its official first publication in 1992.[85] Aygi's text on Kruchenykh, "Da, tot samyi Kruchenykh, ili Neizvestneishii iz znameniteishikh" ("Yes, Kruchenykh Himself, or The Least Known of the Most Famous"),[86] which had previously been published in his avant-garde anthology, served as introduction to the Kruchenykh reprint of 1992 and set out to "rehabilitate" him and "to place his name alongside those of leading figures of twentieth-century European art such as Khlebnikov and Malevich, Mayakovsky and Apollinaire, Breton and Picasso."[87] Aygi is also credited with having inspired Gileia's publication of Malevich's *Sobranie sochinenii v piati tomakh* (Collected Works in Five Volumes, 1995–2004).[88]

playfulness of Futurist publications by incorporating handwritten words and crude drawings and by placing the title page in the centre of the book and page numbers ascending and descending from there.

81 For a more thorough description of this journal, see Nikitaev: "Severnaia Gileia" [Northern Hylaea], pp. 65–67.

82 Aigi: "[Aleksei Kruchenykh: Stikhi]." [Aleksei Kruchenykh: Poems], pp. 4–5.

83 Aigi: "V chest' Mastera: Neskol'ko absatsev" [In Honour of the Master: Several Paragraphs], p. 10.

84 Malevich: *Po lestnitse poznaniia: Iz neopublikovannykh stikhotvorenii* [On the Stairway of Knowledge: From Unpublished Poems].

85 It contained reprints of Kruchenykh's *Faktura slova* (Moskva 1923); *Sdvigologia russkogo stikha* (Moskva, 1922); *Apokalipsis v russkoï literature* (Moskva, 1923)

86 Kruchenykh: *Kukish proshliakam* [A Fig to the Dated], pp. 3–8.

87 "[...] поставить его имя в ряд выдающихся имен европейского искусства XX века – Хлебникова и Малевича, Маяковского и Аполлинера, Бретона и Пикассо." Kruchenykh: *Kukish proshliakam*, p. 8.

88 See the acknowledgements in vol. 5, p. 620 and his speech at the closing of the Malevich exhibition at the Tretyakov Gallery in Moscow in February 1989 in Aigi: *Sobranie sochinenii.* Vol. 4. *Stat'ia, retsenzii, interv'iu, esse, vospominaniia*, pp. 135–139.

Poetic territories

Aygi did not only write the introductions to avant-garde anthologies, but also composed essays about members of the Russian avant-garde, including "O Vladimire Maiakovskom: Otvety na anketu 'Literaturnoi gazety'" (On Vladimir Mayakovsky: Answers to a Questionnaire in the Literary Newspaper, 1993)[89] and "Obydennost' chuda: Vstrechi s Borisom Pasternakom, 1956–1958" (Everyday Miracle: Meetings with Boris Pasternak, 1956–1958; 1990).[90] Furthermore, he gave numerous interviews in which he promoted the historical avant-garde and long-forgotten poets, situating his own poetry in that tradition.[91] In conversations with Vitaly Amursky in 1989 and 1990, for instance, Aygi declared that Khlebnikov was for him the second-greatest Russian poet, after Pushkin.[92] In an interview with Sergey Biryukov in 1990, instead, he mentioned that he once "confessed" to Roman Jakobson that "it was not Khlebnikov who had such an influence on me, but your [i. e., Roman Jakobson's] book on Khlebnikov from 1921".[93] He argued that this was so because "everything that is new, all of Khlebnikov's magnificent innovations are concentrated in this book in an admirable, very thorough analysis."[94] He further confessed: "This book, indeed, together with Malevich, pushed me most strongly in the newest direction of what might be called the avant-garde."[95]

What this meant for Aygi's own poetry is most concisely laid out in his essay "Listki – v veter prazdnika: K stoletiiu Velimira Khlebnikova" (Leaves – Into a Fes-

---

89 Aigi: *Razgovor na rasstoianii*, pp. 96–98.

90 Ibid., pp. 99–114.

91 For Aygi's interviews, see, for example, Aigi [Ajgi]: *Ausgewählte Werke.* Vol. 2. *Blätter in den Wind: Gespräche, Reden, Essays*, Aigi: *Razgovor na rasstoianii* and Aigi: *Sobranie sochinenii.* Vol. 4. *Stat'ia, retsenzii, interv'iu, esse, vospominaniia.*

92 "Therefore, I consider Khlebnikov the second greatest, most comprehensive poet of the nation." ("Хлебникова, таким образом, я считаю вторым по величине, всеобъемлющим поэтом нации.") Amurskii: "V poiske samotsennogo slova: Beseda s Gennadiem Aigi" [In Search of the Self-Sufficient Word: Interview with Gennady Aygi], p. 211.

93 "Я ему признался однажды: 'Вы знаете, Роман Осипович, на меня больше повлиял не Хлебников, а ваша книга о Хлебникове 21-ого года'." Aigi: *Razgovor na rasstoianii*, p. 281. Aygi refers to Jakobson's book *Noveishaia russkaia poeziia: Nabrosok pervyi: Podstupy k Khlebnikovu* [The Newest Russian Poetry: First Sketch: Approaches to Khlebnikov].

94 "Потому что все новаторское, все великие нововведения Хлебникова в этой книге сконцентрированы в совершенно замечательном, глубочайшем анализе." Aigi: *Razgovor na rasstoianii*, p. 281.

95 "И действительно, эта книга была для меня (наравне с Малевичем) сильнейшим толчком в ту новейшую сторону, назовем ее пусть авангардной." Aigi: *Razgovor na rasstoianii*, p. 281.

tive Wind: On the Centenary of Velimir Khlebnikov, 1985).[96] Regarding the importance of Khlebnikov's method of *slovotvorchestvo* (word-creation) for his own poetics, he declared:

> The most important of all these 'beginnings' was Khlebnikov's *word-creation.* How the poet sometimes desires not to *speak* with the definitive *logos*-word, but to *ring out!* – to resonate with a kind of absolute beauty of the beautiful! – as in music. Khlebnikov's 'word-creation' was the first breakthrough toward this 'absolute beauty', which continues to demand almost superhuman efforts from the poet; the 'absolute' remains unattainable, but it is precisely this ever more evident unattainability that gives poetry its incandescent quality.[97]

Aygi also referred in this context to Marinetti, pointing out that Khlebnikov's prose text *Iskushenie greshnika* (A Sinner's Temptation), which contained elements of *slovotvorchestvo*, was published in October 1908, that is, slightly before Marinetti's *Foundation and Manifesto of Futurism* (20 February 1909).[98] Instead of attempting to imitate Khlebnikov or other Futurists, Aygi argued that their poetic discoveries were landmarks on otherwise unexplored poetic territories, which still waited to be inhabited and developed:

> The Tatar raids of the 'avant-garde' on unknown 'poetic territories,' even in a single year (1913), were enough to last a century. One 'landmark' after another was erected, one poetic 'discovery' followed another, each one more daringly projected into some kind of distance, some 'future.' These 'landmarks' remained on the great map of Poetics, but the territory itself remained 'unexploited', unfortified – it simply remained empty, and in many ways is still empty today. Now it is we who have to work on these 'lands' [...] We have to inhabit [...] the territories over which the troops of the avant-garde marched victoriously with no old-fashioned, hard-working, spiritual concern for their 'earthly' condition. To inhabit them, to fill them with a spiritual content, one cannot live by 'landmarks' alone, one must live and work the earth, whether it brings forth fruit in our time or not.[99]

---

96 Aigi: *Razgovor na rasstoianii*, pp. 86–95. For a more thorough discussion of this text, see Weststeijn: "Ajgi and Chlebnikov".

97 Aigi [Aygi]: *Time of Gratitude*, pp. 44f. "Было важнейшее начало всех начал – хлебниковское словотворчество. Как, иногда, хочется поэту не говорить неотменимым словом-логосом, а зазвучать! – зазвучать некоею 'самою' красотою прекрасного! – как в музыке. Хлебниковское 'словотворчество' – первый прорыв в сторону того 'абсолюта красоты', который не перестает требовать от поэта почти сверхчеловеческих усилий, 'абсолют' остается недостижимым, но поэзия накаляется именно в силу этой – все более явной – недостижимости." Aigi: *Razgovor na rasstoianii*, p. 88.

98 Aigi: *Razgovor na rasstoianii*, p. 88.

99 Aigi [Aygi]: *Time of Gratitude*, p. 46. "Татарские набеги 'авангарда' на неизведанные 'поэтические земли' даже за один 1913 год были совершены – на сто лет 'вперед'. Ставились 'вехи' за 'вехами', одно 'открытие' в поэтике следовало за другим, – все более дерзостное, все резче закинутое в некую даль – некоего 'будущего'. 'Вехи' оставались отмеченными

The art of the book: Aygi's collaboration with Dronnikov

Emulating the avant-garde's penchant for collaborative intermediality, Aygi seized every opportunity to follow this line in his artists' books. Amongst others, he worked with Igor' Vulokh,[100] Günther Uecker,[101] the publisher and printer Rainer Pretzell[102] or the Paris-based Russian émigré artist Nikolai Dronnikov, who since 1989 devoted dozens of books to Aygi, who, in turn, dedicated several poems to him.[103] Dronnikov's books are reminiscent of the "lithographic [...] editions at the beginning of the century" and of "the typographic and writing experiments of the Futurists",[104] as Arsen Mirzaev stated in a review of Dronnikov and Aygi's book *Ditia-i-roza* (Child-and-Rose, 1990). Indeed, this book contains an abundance of typographic experiments, abstract forms including a black square on the title page, paper in various colours and thickness and striking portraits of Aygi by Dronnikov. Other books jointly produced by the artists contain letterpress texts in

---

на огромной карте Поэтики, а само пространство оставалось 'необработанным', неукрепленным, – оно просто пустовало, во многом пустует – и доныне. Теперь с этими 'землями' имеем дело мы [...]. Это – заполнять [...] территории, пройденные "авангардистами" воинственным маршем, без старо-душевной трудовой заботы об их "земном" состоянии. Заполнять – духовным содержанием (не жить же одними 'вехами', – надо жить – самой землей, плодоносит ли она сегодня или нет)." Aigi: *Razgovor na rasstoianii*, p. 89.

100 Aigi: *Svechi vo mgle i neskol'ko pesenok* [Candles in the Dark and a Few Songs].

101 Aigi [Ajgi]: *Chishche chem smysl' / Reiner als Sinn.*

102 See, for example, Aigi [Ajgi]: *Sneg v sadu / Im Garten Schnee* (1993). Rainer Pretzell worked with artists such as Dieter Roth, A. R. Penck, Emmett Williams, Marcel Broodthaers and Damien Hirst.

103 Dronnikov published books with texts by Larionov, Goncharova, Lifar, Bobrov, Poplavsky, Aygi, Brener, Mirzaev, Biriukov, Lebedev and others. Incidentally, Dronnikov was one of the printers who worked on the 1982 tamizdat edition of Aygi's poems *Otmechennaia zima* (Noted Winter). See Dronnikov: *Vospominaniia, razmyshleniia, risunki* [Recollections, Reflections, Drawings], p. [47]. In 2012, the Moscow-based publisher Gileia collaborated with Dronnikov, jointly producing limited editions of works by Iliazd and Poplavsky under the imprint Gileia v Parizhe (Gileia in Paris). About Dronnikov's artists' books, see Khuzangai: *Sem' deskriptsii k obrazu russkogo mastera v Parizhe* [Seven Descriptions towards the Image of the Russian Master in Paris], Mirzaev: "Slovo kak zrenie" [The Word as Sight], Mirzaev: "Gennadii Aigi i Nikolai Dronnikov" [Gennady Aygi and Nikolai Dronnikov] and Mirzaev: "Gennadii Aigi v krugu druzei-khudozhnikov: Vladimir Iakovlev, Igor' Vulokh i Nikolai Dronnikov".

104 "невольно вспоминаются литографические и стеклографические издания начала столетия; типографические и шрифтовые эксперименты футуристов; книги современных поэтов-трансфуристов"; Mirzaev: "Slovo kak zrenie".

various sizes, stamped and blind embossed texts, linocuts, photocopies of varying quality and digital prints next to handwritten texts and original drawings, gouaches, postcards and photographs of people and artworks. They also sport various kinds of crude cloth or wallpaper bindings, in an apparent homage to Futurist books.[105]

Several of Aygi's poems were reprinted in various constellations in several of Dronnikov's books, evoking Kruchenykh's habit during the late 1910s and early 1920s of re-arranging and re-using his texts in later publications. According to Felix Philipp Ingold, this corresponds to a central aspect of Aygi's poetics, who did not assign his texts a fixed place in specific books. Rather, they re-emerge in ever-changing combinations with other texts, like a moveable body of texts that can re-appear in different contexts.[106]

There are also inconsistencies across copies of a book that carry the same title, similar to what Janecek has described for Kruchenykh's handwritten or hectographed books. From *Mirskontsa* (Worldbackwards, 1912) to the works produced in Tbilisi between 1917 and 1920, his books could have "variations in page order".[107] Sometimes, pages (and book sections) could reappear in other books. Books with the same title could have variations of contents, thus reintroducing "the concept that each copy of a book will be unique".[108] Similarly, Aygi and Dronnikov's book *Tri stichotvoreniia Malevichu* (Three Poems for Malevich, 1994) appeared in an edition of 33 numbered and signed copies, which vary in their use of colours of paper and paperboard. The cover pages were illustrated by hand, using slightly different brushstrokes; printed elements are scattered throughout the copies; the portrait of Aygi (signed by Dronnikov and Aygi) at the end of the

105 See, for example, Aigi: [*Nikolaiiu Dronnikovu: Pri poluchenii ocherednoi "nashei" (s nim) knizhki]* [For Nikolai Dronnikov: Upon Receipt of the Next of "Our" (with Him) Books] or Dronnikov: *Serzh Lifar', Mikhail Larionov, Nataliia Goncharova*, which contains Aygi's poem "N. Kh. sredi kartin: K vystavke M. Larionova i N. Goncharova v Muzee Maiakovskogo" ("N. Kh. Among the Paintings: At an Exhibition of M. Larionov and N. Goncharova at the Mayakovsky Museum, 1965).

106 "Für Ajgis Schaffensweise ist es charakteristisch, daß die einzelnen Gedichttexte nicht, wie sonst üblich, zu Büchern komponiert werden und somit einen festen Ort innerhalb des gedruckten Werks zugeordnet bekommen: daß sie vielmehr in ständig wechselnden Textkonstellationen eingehen und deshalb auch aus der einen in die andere Konstellation übernommen werden können. Sämtliche von Ajgi bisher veröffentlichten Lyriksammlungen sind als bewegliche Textkörper konzipiert." Aigi [Ajgi]: *Mit Gesang: Zur Vollendung*, p. 285.

107 Janecek: "Kruchenykh contra Gutenberg", p. 43. Several of Dronnikov's books are collections of loose leaves as well, which do not prescribe any specific page order, for example Aigi: *Monmartr (deistvo): Poeziia. Muzyka. Zhivopis'* [Montmartre (Action): Poetry. Music. Painting] and Aigi: *Listki v Sen-Lui: Piat' stikhotvornykh poslanii* [Leaves in St. Louis: Five Poetic Messages].

108 Janecek: "Kruchenykh contra Gutenberg", p. 44.

book differs from copy to copy, as do the textual contents. The main part of the book, Aygi's poems about Malevich, is reproduced in Aygi's handwriting, as if in honour of Kruchenykh and Khlebnikov's manifesto *Bukva kak takovaia* (The Letter as Such, 1913).[109]

Conversation at a distance

Aygi's poems abound with dedications and allusions to friends and like-minded writers, artists, composers and musicians, as the author acknowledged in his preface to the French edition of his poetry collection *Zimnie kutezhi* (Winter Revels, 1977): "I consciously tried to put myself in 'dialogical' situations: 'poetically' responding, for example, to friendships, to the 'stories' of friendships".[110] This dialogue extended beyond Aygi's immediate circle of friends and embraced writers and artists from abroad and from the past, such as Paul Celan, Franz Kafka and the Russian Futurists, thus linking his own poetry and the unofficial counter-culture in the Soviet Union with world literature and with the avant-garde. In an interview published under the title "Razgovor na rasstoianiia" (Conversation at a Distance, 1985), Aygi reflected on his 'conversation' with writers from the past:

> It was as if I was addressing the writers themselves rather than their ideas, whether literary or otherwise. […] In this way, the still continuing influence of genuinely *living images* of certain teachers constituted for me their 'legacy', their lifelong support, and the strength of this kind of 'contact' was more powerful than any literary considerations.[111]

109 See Khlebnikov: *Sobranie sochinenii v shesti tomakh.* Vol. 6.1, pp. 339–342. In the English translation, Kruchenykh and Khlebnikov write: "It is not mandatory that the wordwright be also the copyist of a handwritten book: indeed, it would be better if the wordwright entrusted this job to an artist. But there haven't been any such books until recently. They were issued by the Futurians for the first time. Namely: *Old-Fashioned Love* was rewritten in longhand for printing by M. Larionov, *Explodity* by N. Kulbin et al., *Duck's Nest* by O. Rozanova. […] A piece may be rewritten in longhand by someone else or by the creator himself, but if he does not relive the original experience, the piece will lose all the charm acquired by means of free handwriting during 'the wild snowstorm of inspiration'." Kruchenykh and Khlebnikov: "The Letter as Such", p. 64. Other books by Aygi that rely on reproductions of handwritten text include *Svechi vo mgle i neskol'ko pesenok* [Candles in the Dark and a Few Songs] and *Mir Sil' vii* [Silvia's World].

110 "[…] я сознательно старался ставить себя в 'диалогические' ситуации: 'стихотворно' реагировать, например, на дружбу, на 'истории' дружб". Aigi: *Razgovor na rasstoianii*, p. 129.

111 Aigi [Aygi]: *Field-Russia*, p. 7. "я […] обращался как будто к ним самим, – больше, чем к их литературным и иным 'концепциям'. […] Итак, доныне действующие, поистине живые образы нескольких учителей и являются для меня – их 'наследием', их пожизненной под-

Accordingly, many of Aygi's poems contain overt or hidden intertextual references to Futurist and avant-garde texts, or they are dedicated to avant-gardists, or they evoke their names. Most often, Aygi referred to Velimir Khlebnikov,[112] Aleksei Kruchenykh[113] and Kazimir Malevich,[114] but also to David Burliuk,[115] Benedikt Livshits,[116] Boris Pasternak,[117] Bozhidar,[118] Mikhail Larionov, Natalia Goncharova, Marc Chagall,[119] El Lissitzky and Daniil Kharms.[120]

Examples of direct intertextual references can, for instance, be found in his poem *Davidu Burliuka* (For David Burliuk, 1965),[121] in which quotation marks clearly indicate which segments of the text have been borrowed. However, the

---

держкой, сила такого 'контакта' – превыше всяких литературных рассуждений." Aigi: *Razgovor na rasstoianii*, p. 156.

112 Aigi: *Sobranie sochinenii.* Vol. 1. *Stikhi, poemy, perevody na chuvashskom iazyke*, p. 174; Vol. 2. *Stikhi*, pp. 70, 149, 161, 473 f.; Aigi: *Teper' vsegda snega: Stikhi raznikh let 1955–1989* [Now Always Snow: Poems of Various Years 1955–1989], p. 130 f. On Aygi and Khlebnikov see, for example, Weststeijn: "Ajgi and Chlebnikov", Sokolova: *Ot avangarda k neoavangardu: Iazyk, sub'ektivnost', kul'turnye perenosy* [From the Avant-Garde to the Neo-Avant-Garde: Language, Subjectivity, Cultural Transfers], pp. 118 ff., Orlitskii and Pavlovets: "Nasledniki Khlebnikova: Genrikh Sapgir, Gennadii Aigi, Aleksandr Kondratov, Sergei Biriukov" [Khlebnikov's Heirs: Genrikh Sapgir, Gennady Aygi, Aleksandr Kondratov, Sergey Biryukov], Pashkin: "Obraz Velimira Khlebnikova v poezii Gennadiia Aigi" [The Image of Velimir Khlebnikov in Gennady Aygi's Poetry] and Janecek: "Tri Kuznechika: Khlebnikov, Kammings, Aigi" [Three Grasshoppers: Khlebnikov, Cummings, Aygi].

113 Aigi: *Sobranie sochinenii.* Vol. 2. *Stikhi*, pp. 117, 154; Aigi: *Raspolozhenie schast'ia* [The Location of Happiness], p. 39; Byrkina and Mordvinova: *Mir etikh glaz.* Vol. 2, p. 38. See Sokolova: *Ot avangarda k neoavangardu*, pp. 42 ff.

114 Aigi: *Sobranie sochinenii.* Vol. 2. *Stikhi*, pp. 136, 70, 185; Aigi: *Teper' vsegda snega: Stikhi raznikh let 1955–1989*, p. 130 f.; Aigi: *Razgovor na rasstoianii*, p. 170. On Aygi and Malevich see also Sokolova: *Ot avangarda k neoavangardu*, pp. 25 ff., Khuzangai: "Aigi v zerkale chernogo kvadrata" [Aygi in the Mirror of the Black Square], Khuzangai: *Malevich / Aigi*, Ichin: "Bespredmetnoe slovo G. Aigi: Dialog s K. Malevichem" [The Non-Objective Word of G. Aygi: Dialogue with K. Malevich], and Belozorovitch: "Ajgi e Malevič: Dialogo a distanza", Belozorovitch: "Gennadij Ajgi e Kazimir Malevič: Artista della visione, artista della conoscenza" and Belozorovitch: "Malevič e Ajgi: bianco su bianco".

115 Byrkina and Mordvinova: *Mir etikh glaz.* Vol. 2, p. 39 and Aigi: *Sobranie sochinenii.* Vol. 2. *Stikhi*, p. 149.

116 Aigi: *Sobranie sochinenii.* Vol. 2. *Stikhi*, p. 159.

117 Aigi: *Razgovor na rasstoianii*, pp. 116–124. See Sokolova: *Ot avangarda k neoavangardu*, pp. 138 ff.

118 Aigi: *Sobranie sochinenii.* Vol. 2. *Stikhi*, p. 150.

119 Ibid. pp. 105, 166; Byrkina and Mordvinova: *Mir etikh glaz.* Vol. 2, p. 36.

120 Aigi: *Sobranie sochinenii.* Vol. 2. *Stikhi*, p. 70.

121 Byrkina and Mordvinova: *Mir etikh glaz.* Vol. 2, p. 39.

sources – in this case, poems by Khlebnikov – are not identified.[122] Unmarked quotations can, for example, be found in Aygi's poem *Na temu Bozhidara* (On a Theme by Bozhidar, 1965).[123]

Malevich's influences

Aygi's emphasis on white spaces, pauses and silence[124] and his use of abstract graphic elements in his poetry seem to have taken Malevich's paintings, drawings and theoretical treatises as a starting point. The poem *Obraz – v prazdnik (V den' 100-letiia K.S. Malevicha)* (Image – On the Occasion of the Feast: On K.S. Malevich's 100th Anniversary, 1978),[125] for instance, seems to figuratively enact one of Malevich's *White on White* paintings: linking abstract images with very concrete ones of snow-covered fields in the Chuvash countryside, Aygi imagines "with the knowledge of the whiteness / a man in the distance / on the white snow / as if carrying an invisible banner".[126]

122 The line "to decorate the Andes with the head of Burliuk" ("украсить Анды – головой Бурлюка"; ibid.), for instance, is a partial quote from Velimir Khlebnikov's "Predlozheniia" (Proposals, 1915–1918): "Украсить […] Анды – головой Бурлюка."; Khlebnikov: *Sobranie sochinenii v shesti tomakh* [Collected Works in Six Volumes], vol. 6, book 1, p. 242.), while the line "they are seven they are seven they are a hundred" ("их семеро их семеро их сто"; Byrkina and Mordvinova: *Mir etikh glaz.* Vol. 2, p. 39.) is a quote from an untitled poem by Khlebnikov (1916, first published in 1924): "Их семеро, их семеро, их сто!" Khlebnikov: *Sobranie sochinenii v shesti tomakh*, vol. 1, p. 363.

123 The 'theme' comes from Bozhidar's poem "Press-pap'e" (Paper-Weight; see Bozhidar: *Buben: stikhi* [Tambourine: Poems], p. 39.) Aigi: *Sobranie sochinenii.* Vol. 2. *Stikhi*, p. 150.

124 On Aygi's poetry of silence, see for example Janecek: "Poeziia molchaniia u Gennadiia Aigi" [The Poetry of Silence in Gennady Aygi], Valentine: "Music, Silence, and Spirituality in the Poetry of Gennady Aigi", Sem'ian: "Visual'noe prostranstvo tekstov Gennadiia Aigi" [The Visual Space of Gennady Aygi's Texts], Skoropanova: "'Vakuumnye' teksty Gennadiia Aigi" [Gennady Aygi's 'Vacuum' Texts] or Skoropanova: "'Vakuumnye' teksty russkikh neoavangardistov" ['Vacuum' Texts of Russian Neo-Avant-Gardists].

125 Aigi: *Tri stichotvoreniia Malevichu* [Three Poems for Malevich], p. 7; Aigi: *Sobranie sochinenii.* Vol. 2. *Stikhi*, p. 185.

126 "со знанием белого / вдали человек / по белому снегу / будто с невидимым знаменем"; Aigi: *Sobranie sochinenii.* Vol. 2. *Stikhi*, p. 185.

Abstract graphic elements are also introduced in the poem *Pervaia travka* (First Grass, 1976), which depicts a red cross above the words "pervaia travka" in green handwriting, repeated on the following page in black (see Fig. 4).[127]

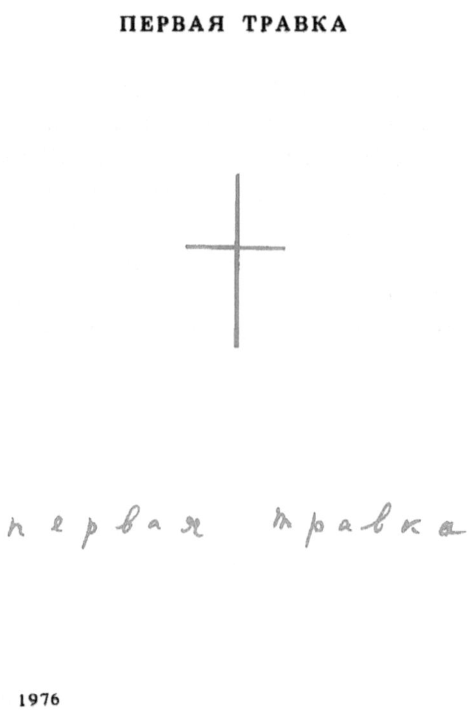

Fig. 4: Gennadii Aigi: "Pervaia travka" (First Grass, 1976), in G. Aigi: *Otmechennaia zima: Sobranie stikhotvorenii v dvukh chastiakh* (Noted Winter: Collected Poems in Two Parts). Paris: Sintaksis, 1982, p. 470.

The poem *Bez nazvaniia* (Untitled, 1964; see Fig. 5a)[128] begins with a red square, a single verse, a smaller red square, and the conjunction "i:" (and:), followed by white space and another verse in parentheses. It is accompanied by instructions how to read this poem – *O chtenii vslukh stikhotvoreniia 'Bez nazvaniia'* (On Reading

127 Aigi: *Otmechennaia zima: Sobranie stikhotvorenii v dvukh chastiakh* [Noted Winter: Collected Poems in Two Parts], p. 470f. Regarding the symbol of the cross in Aygi's poetry, see Nikolaeva: "Znak kresta v poetike G. Aigi" [The Symbol of the Cross in G. Aygi's Poetics].

128 Aigi: *Sobranie sochinenii.* Vol. 2. *Stikhi*, p. 107.

the Poem 'Untitled', 1965; see Fig. 5b)[129] – which include notes akin to stage directions as well as musical notations. According to Ilma Rakusa, Aygi resorts in these poems to graphic symbols and musical notation because he seeks to include "spheres of expression that lie outside the realm of words, but are able to complement it in a meaningful way".[130] Similarly, Doris Boden argues that the unspeakable elements in Aygi's poetry produce a "poetry without reference that aims at approaching the true being *ex negativo*",[131] leading to a "quasi-sacral" or "ontological"[132] poetry, likening the page, as Vladimir Novikov asserts, "to an icon".[133]

On the one hand, the reader is tempted to assign meaning to the seemingly meaningless abstract red squares, which seem to recall Malevich's Suprematist *Krasnyi kvadrat* (Red Square, 1915) and which, in turn, connotes Orthodox icons.[134] On the other hand, the accompanying poem *O chtenii vslukh stikhotvoreniia 'Bez nazvaniia'* (On Reading the Poem 'Untitled', 1965),[135] with its apparent 'translation' of the squares into musical notation, seems to suggest that the visual elements can (or should be) translated from one semiotic system into another, to be 'read' as music. This translation, however, remains at the level of the signifier – both the visual and the musical one – which is not recognizably linked to any signified object, although the possibility is implied by the insistence that a translation *is* necessary. According to Doris Boden, the text of this explanatory poem is similarly hermetic:[136] in the communicative act, the denied signified is replaced by a signified of a different order,[137] which can be interpreted in a religious or spiritual

129 Ibid., pp. 107 f.

130 "In einigen Fällen greift Ajgi auch zu graphischen Symbolen (Quadrat, Kreuz) und zur musikalischen Notation, zwecks Einbeziehung von Ausdruckssphären, die außerhalb des Wortbereichs liegen, diesen jedoch sinnvoll zu ergänzen vermögen." Rakusa: "Gennadij Ajgis lyrischer Suprematismus", p. 171.

131 "[E]ine Dichtung ohne Referenz, die auf eine Annäherung an das wahre Sein *ex negativo* ziele"; Boden: "Das 'Lesen' von Quadraten: Intermedialität und extrapolierte Medialität bei Gennadij Ajgi", p. 139.

132 Ibid.

133 "Айги придает большое значение поэтической графике: оформление текстовой страницы входит в художественную структуру: страницу можно уподобить иконе"; Novikov: "O poezii Gennadiia Aigi" [About Gennady Aygi's Poetry], p. 13.

134 Malevich called his Black Square (1915) "a naked icon of my time, without a frame" ("голая, без рамы, икона моего времени"; Malevich: *Sobranie sochinenii v piati tomakh*, vol. 1, p. 82) and placed it in the corner of the room reserved for an Orthodox icon at the exhibition 0,10 (see photo ibid., p. 28).

135 Aigi: *Sobranie sochinenii.* Vol. 2. *Stikhi*, p. 107 f.

136 Boden: "Das 'Lesen' von Quadraten: Intermedialität und extrapolierte Medialität bei Gennadij Ajgi", p. 142 f.

137 Ibid., p. 145 f.

way. At the same time, these poems go well beyond the experiments of the historical avant-garde, by exhibiting a metatextuality and an absolute state of polysemy that is unsettling in its unresolvedness.

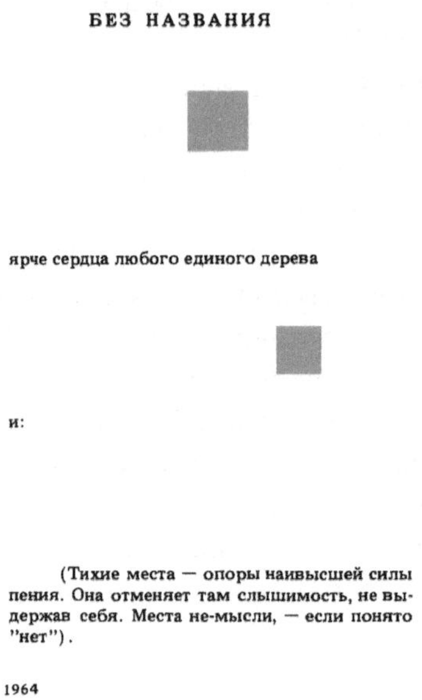

БЕЗ НАЗВАНИЯ

ярче сердца любого единого дерева

и:

(Тихие места — опоры наивысшей силы пения. Она отменяет там слышимость, не выдержав себя. Места не-мысли, — если понято "нет").

1964

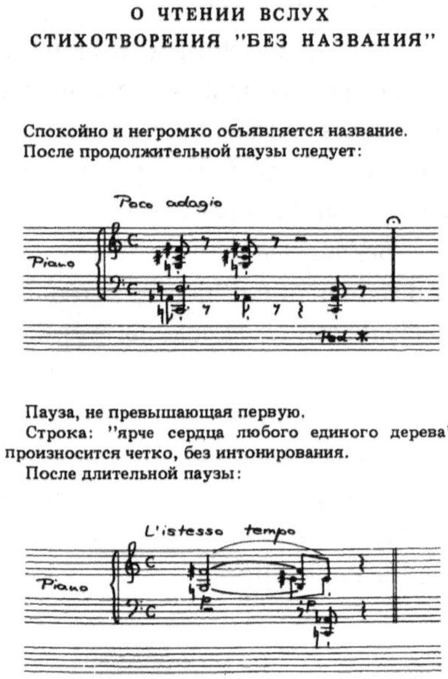

О ЧТЕНИИ ВСЛУХ СТИХОТВОРЕНИЯ "БЕЗ НАЗВАНИЯ"

Спокойно и негромко объявляется название.
После продолжительной паузы следует:

Пауза, не превышающая первую.
Строка: "ярче сердца любого единого дерева" произносится четко, без интонирования.
После длительной паузы:

Fig. 5a: Gennadii Aigi: "Bez nazvaniia" (Untitled, 1964), in G. Aigi: *Otmechennaia zima: Sobranie stikhotvorenii v dvukh chastiakh* (Noted Winter: Collected Poems in Two Parts). Paris: Sintaksis, 1982, p. 102. Translation: "Untitled / [red square] / brighter than the heart of any single tree / [smaller red square] / and: // (Quiet places – supports of the highest strength of singing. It takes away hearing there, unable to hold back. Places of non-thoughts – if you understand 'non')."[138]] Fig. 5b: Gennadii Aigi: "O chtenii vslukh stikhotvoreniia 'Bez nazvaniia'" (On Reading the Poem 'Untitled', 1965); in G. Aigi: *Otmechennaia zima: Sobranie stikhotvorenii v dvukh chastiakh* (Noted Winter: Collected Poems in Two Parts). Paris: Sintaksis, 1982, pp. 103 f. Translation: "On reading aloud the poem 'Untitled' / The title is stated calmly and softly. / After a long pause, there follows: / [sheet music] / A pause, not longer than the first. / The line: 'brighter than the heart of any single tree' / is pronounced distinctly, without intonation. / After a long pause: / [sheet music] / Another extended pause. / The line: 'and:' should be pronounced with a noticeable intensifying of the voice. / After a pause twice as long as the previous one, the prose section is read: slowly, with as little expressiveness as possible."[139]]

138 Translation by Sarah Valentine in Valentine: *Witness and Transformation: The Poetics of Gennady Aygi*, pp. 68 f.
139 Ibid., pp. 73 f.

Conclusion

Categorized by Naum Leiderman and Mark Lipovetskii as a "Neo-Futurist"[140] alongside Vladimir Kazakov and Viktor Sosnora,[141] Aygi was one of several non-conformist writers[142] who explicitly began to refer back to Russian Futurism. Aygi played an important rôle in the attempt by the Russian neo-avant-garde to establish a counter-memory that preserved the heritage of an interrupted tradition by organizing semi-legal avant-garde exhibitions, distributing and publishing texts from the historical avant-garde, writing about its authors, promoting them in countless interviews, and incorporating references and allusions to their works in his own poetry. Yet, while Aygi acknowledged his debt to Mayakovsky, Khlebnikov and Malevich, he also called himself an "Anti-Futurist".[143] He neither subscribed to the historical avant-garde's socio-political utopianism,[144] nor was he obsessed with the formal devices of the Russian Futurists. Instead of imitating their transrational language and word-creation, he opened his poetry up to "spiritual concerns"[145] and merged the Russian heritage with influences from Chuvash folk culture and contemporary European literature. The result was a genuinely new poetry in a Neo-Futurist key.

Bibliography

Aigi, Gennadii: "Aleksei Kruchenykh." *V mire knig* [In the World of Books] 4 (1989): 50–56.
Aigi, Gennadii: "Bozhidar. Vasilisk Gnedov." *V mire knig* [In the World of Books] 2 (1989): 28–31.

140 See, for example, Leiderman and Lipovetskii: *Sovremennaia russkaia literature 1950–1990-kh godov.* Vol. 1. *1950–1968* [Contemporary Russian Literature 1950s–1990s. Vol. 1. 1950–1968], pp. 379–391.

141 On Aygi and Sosnora see Sokolova: *Neoavangardnaia poeziia G. Aigi i V. Sosnory* [G. Aygi's and V. Sosnora's Neo-Avant-Garde Poetry] and Iakovleva and Petrova: "Nekotorye zametki po tvorchestvu G. Aigi and V. Sosnory" [A Few Remarks on the Work of G. Aigi and V. Sosnora].

142 He joined a row of writers such as Nikolai Glazkov, Eduard Kondratov, Aleksandr Kondratov, Mikhail Krasil'nikov, Yuri Mikhailov, Leonid Gubanov, Elizaveta Mnatsakanova, Serge Segay, Rea Nikonova, Boris Vantalov/Konstriktor, Vladimir Erl', A. Nik, Vadim Kozovoy, Anna Al'chuk, Aleksei Khvostenko, Anri Volkonsky, Kari Unksova, Konstantin Kuzminsky, Aleksandr Ocheretiansky, Konstantin Kedrov or Sergey Biryukov, to name but a few.

143 Aigi: *Razgovor na rasstoianii*, p. 23.

144 See Korchagin: "The Neo-Futurists".

145 Aigi [Aygi]: *Time of Gratitude*, p. 46. "Заполнять – духовным содержанием (не житьже одними 'вехами', – надо жить – самой землей, плодоносит ли она сегодня или нет)." Aigi: *Razgovor na rasstoianii*, p. 89.

Aigi, Gennadii: "Elena Guro." *V mire knig* [In the World of Books] 1 (1989): 14–19.

Aigi, Gennadii: "I: O Maleviche." [And: About Malevich] *LIK: Literatura. Iskusstvo. Kul'tura* 4 (2015): 157–160.

Aigi, Gennadii: "Mikhail Larionov." *Sumerki* 10+1 (1990): 21–22.

Aigi, Gennadii: "Nikolai Khardzhiev and the Maiakovsky Museum, Moscow." John E. Bowlt, and Mark Konecny, eds.: *A Legacy Regained: Nikolai Khardzhiev and the Russian Avant-Garde.* St. Petersburg: Palace Editions, 2002. 43–49.

Aigi, Gennadii: "Pavel Filonov. V.P. Mazurin." *V mire knig* [In the World of Books] 3 (1989): 14–18.

Aigi, Gennadii: "Russkii poeticheskii avangard." [The Russian Poetic Avant-garde] *V mire knig* [In the World of Books] 1 (1989): 14–17.

Aigi, Gennadii: "Tri stichotvoreniia Malevichu." [Three Poems for Malevich] *Chernovik* (New York) 2 (1989): 84–87.

Aigi, Gennadii: "V chest' Mastera – neskol'ko absatsev." [In Honour of the Master – Several Paragraphs]. *Severnaia Gileia* 2:6 (#8) (1991): 10.

Aigi, Gennadii: "V chest' Mastera – neskol'ko absatsev." [In Honour of the Master – Several Paragraphs]. Kazimir Malevich: *Po lestnitse poznaniia: Iz neopublikovannykh stikhotvorenii* [On the Stairway of Knowledge: From Unpublished Poems]. Moskva: Gileia, 1991. 2.

Aigi, Gennadii: *Aigi – Dronnikovu* [Aigi – for Dronnikov]. [Parizh]: Dronnikov, 1994.

Aigi, Gennadii [Gennadij Ajgi]: *Blätter in den Wind: Gespräche, Reden, Essays. Ausgewählte Werke.* Band 2. Herausgegeben von Felix Philipp Ingold. Wien: Per Procura, 1998.

Aigi, Gennadii [Gennadij Ajgi]: *Chishche chem smysl' / Reiner als Sinn.* St. Gallen: Erker, 1997.

Aigi, Gennadii: *Ditia-i-roza* [Child-and-Rose]. Parizh: Dronnikov, 1990.

Aigi, Gennadii [Gennady Aygi]: *Field-Russia.* Translated from the Russian by Peter France. New York: New Directions, 2007.

Aigi, Gennadii: *Listki – v veter prazdnika (k stoletiiu Velimira Khlebnikova); Sneg v polden'* [Leaves – Into a Festive Wind: For the Centenary of Velimir Khlebnikov; Snow at Noon]. Parizh: Dronnikov, [1991].

Aigi, Gennadii: *Listki v Sen-Lui: Piat' stikhotvornykh poslanii* [Leaves in St. Louis: Five Poetic Messages]. Parizh: Dronnikov-Konovalov, 2001.

Aigi, Gennadii: *Mir Sil' vii* [Silvia's World]. Moskva: Izdatel'stvo a i b, 2001.

Aigi, Gennadii: *Monmartr (deistvo): Poeziia. Muzyka. Zhivopis'.* Vols. 1–2 [Montmartre (Action): Poetry. Music. Painting]. Parizh: Dronnikov, 2001.

Aigi, Gennadii: [*Nikolaiiu Dronnikovu: Pri poluchenii ocherednoi "nashei" (s nim) knizhki*] [For Nikolai Dronnikov: Upon Receipt of the Next of "Our" (with Him) Books]. Parizh: Dronnikov-Konovalov, 1998.

Aigi, Gennadii: *Otmechennaia zima: Sobranie stikhotvorenii v dvukh chastiakh* [Noted Winter: Collected Poems in Two Parts]. Paris: Sintaksis, 1982.

Aigi, Gennadii: *Poklon – Peniiu: Kniga tret'ia. Dvadtsat' vosem' variatsii na temy chuvashskikh i udmurtskikh narodnykh pesen 1999–2000* [Salute – to Singing: Twenty-Eight Variations on Chuvash and Udmurt Folk Songs 1999–2000]. Parizh: Dronnikov-Konovalov, 2000.

Aigi, Gennadii: *Raspolozhenie schast'ia: Rekonstruktsiia Natalii Azarovoi i Tat'iany Grauz* [The Location of Happiness: Reconstruction by Nataliia Azarova and Tat'iana Grauz]. Moskva: Knizhnoe obozrenie / ARGO-RISK, 2014.

Aigi, Gennadii: *Razgovor na rasstoianii: Stat'i, esse, besedy, stikhi* [Conversation at a Distance: Articles, Essays, Conversations, Poems]. Sankt-Peterburg: Limbus Press, 2001.

Aigi, Gennadii [Gennady Aygi]: *Selected Poems, 1954–94.* Edited with Translations by Peter France. Bilingual Edition. Evanston/IL: Northwestern University Press, 1997.

Aigi, Gennadii [Gennadij Ajgi]: *Sneg v sadu / Im Garten Schnee.* Berlin: Rainer, 1993.

Aigi, Gennadii: *Sobranie sochinenii v semi tomakh* [Collected Works in Seven Volumes]. Moskva: Gileiia, 2009.

Aigi, Gennadii: *Sobranie sochinenii.* Vol. 1. *Stikhi, poemy, perevody na chuvashskom iazyke* [Collected Works. Vol. 1. Poems, Longer Poems, Translations. In Chuvash]. Cheboksary: Chuvashskoe knizhnoe izdatel'stvo, 2008.

Aigi, Gennadii: *Sobranie sochinenii.* Vol. 2. *Stikhi* [Collected Works. Vol. 2. Poems]. Cheboksary: Chuvashskoe knizhnoe izdatel'stvo, 2009.

Aigi, Gennadii: *Sobranie sochinenii.* Vol. 3. *Perevody. Na chuvashskom iazyke* [Collected Works. Vol. 3. Translations. In Chuvash]. Cheboksary: Chuvashskoe knizhnoe izdatel'stvo, 2014.

Aigi, Gennadii: *Sobranie sochinenii.* Vol. 4. *Stat'ia, retsenzii, interv'iu, esse, vospominaniia* [Collected Works. Vol. 4. Articles, Reviews, Interviews, Essays, Recollections]. Cheboksary: Chuvashskoe knizhnoe izdatel'stvo, 2019.

Aigi, Gennadii: *Stikhi 1954–1971.* Redaktsiia i vstupitel'naia stat'ia V. Kazaka [Poems 1954–1971. Ed. and introduction by W. Kasack]. München: Sagner, 1975.

Aigi, Gennadii: *Svechi vo mgle i neskol'ko pesenok* [Candles in the Dark and a Few Songs]. [Moskva:] Izdatel' S.A. Nitochkin / Raritet-537, 1992.

Aigi, Gennadii: *Teper' vsegda snega: Stikhi raznikh let 1955–1989* [Now Always Snow: Poems of Various Years 1955–1989]. Moskva: Sovetskii pisatel', 1992.

Aigi, Gennadii [Gennady Aygi]: *Time of Gratitude.* Translated from the Russian by Peter France. New York: New Directions, 2017.

Aigi, Gennadii: *Tri stichotvoreniia Malevichu* [Three Poems for Malevich]. Moskva: Tret'iakovskaia galereia, 1989.

Aigi, Gennadii: *Tri stichotvoreniia Malevichu* [Three Poems for Malevich]. Parizh: Dronnikov-Konovalov, 1994.

Aigi, Gennadii: *Tri stikhotvoreniia.* Graviury N. Dronnikova [Three Poems. Etchings by N. Dronnikov]. Parizh: Dronnikov, 1991.

Aigi, Gennadii: *'Tvortsy budushchikh znakov': Russkii poeticheskii avangard* ['Creators of Future Signs': The Russian Poetic Avant-garde]. [Moskva]: Salamandra P. V. V., 2011.

Aigi, Gennadii [Gennadij Ajgi]: *Und: Für Malewitsch.* Zürich: Howeg, 1992.

Aigi, Gennadii: *Zdes': Izbrannye stikhotvoreniia 1954/1988* [Here: Selected Poems 1954/1988]. Moskva: Sovremennik, 1991.

Aigi, Gennadii, ed.: "[Aleksei Kruchenykh: Stikhi]." [Aleksei Kruchenykh: Poems]. *Severnaia Gileia* [Northern Hylaea] 2:11 (#13) (1991): 4–5.

Aigi, Gennadii [Gennadii Lisin], ed.: *Vladimir Vladimirovich Maiakovskii, 1893–1930: Vystavka. Zhivopis, grafika, risunki* [Vladimir Vladimirovich Maiakovskii, 1893–1930: Exhibition. Painting, Graphic Art, Drawings]. Moskva: Gosudarstvennaia biblioteka-muzei V. V. Maiakovskogo, 1963.

Amurskii, Vitalii: "V poiske samotsennogo slova: Beseda s Gennadiem Aigi." [In Search of the Self-Sufficient Word: Interview with Gennady Aygi] Vitalii Amurskii: *Ten' maiatnika i drugie teni: Svidetel'stva k istorii russkoi mysli kontsa XX – nachala XXI veka* [The Shadow of the Pendulum and Other Shadows: Testimonies of the History of Russian Thought at the End of the 20th Century and the Beginning of the 21st Century]. Sankt-Peterburg: Izdatel'stvo Ivana Limbakha, 2011. 209–221.

Belozorovitch, Anna: "Ajgi e Malevič: Dialogo a distanza." *Comparatismi: Rivista della consulta di critica letteraria e letterature comparate* 4 (2019): 82–93.

Belozorovitch, Anna: "Gennadij Ajgi e Kazimir Malevič: Artista della visione, artista della conoscenza." *AGON: Rivista internazionale di studi culturali, linguistici e letterari* 23 (2019): 143–164.

Belozorovitch, Anna: "Malevič e Ajgi: Bianco su bianco." *AGON: Rivista internazionale di studi culturali, linguistici e letterari* 24 (2020): 121–146.

Bezrodnyi, Mikhail: "Listaia 'Sumerki': Samizdat i 'iskusstvo knigi'." [Leafing through the Pages of 'Sumerki': Samizdat and the 'Art of the Book'] *Russkii tekst* [Russian Text] 2 (1994): 140–149.

Biriukov, Sergei: "Gennadii Aigi pered litsom russkogo avangarda: Kommentarii k odno besede." [Gennady Aygi in the Face of the Russian Avant-garde: Remarks on a Conversation] *Literaturnoe obozrenie* [Literary Review] 5–6 (1998): 53–54.

Biriukov, Sergei: "Gennadii Aigi pered litsom russkogo avangarda." [Gennady Aygi in the Face of the Russian Avant-garde] Atner Khuzangai, ed.: *Tvorchestvo Gennadiia Aigi: Literaturno-khudozhestvennaia traditsiia i neoavangard. Materialy mezhdunarodnoi nauchno-prakticheskoi konferentsii, posviashchennoi LXXV-letiiu so dnia rozhdeniia Narodnogo poeta Chuvashii Gennadiia Aigi, Shupashkar/Cheboksary 17–18 sentiabria 2009 g* [Gennady Aygi's Œuvre: Literary and Artistic Tradition and Neo-Avant-garde (Conference Proceedings)]. Cheboksary: Chuvashskii gosudarstvennyi institut gumanitarnykh nauk, 2009. 6–7.

Biriukov, Sergei: *Vstrecha na aveniu Aigi* [Meeting on Avenue Aigi]. [Parizh]: Dronnikov, 2009.

Blium, Arlen Viktorovich: "Iskalechennye knigi: Po sekretnym dokumentam Glavlita SSSR)." [Crippled Books: On Secret Documents of the Soviet Censorship Office)] Mikhail Karasik, ed.: *BUKHKAMERA ili Kniga i stikhii* [BOOKCAMERA or The Book and The Elements]. Sankt-Peterburg: M.K., 1997. 27–32.

Boden, Doris: "Das 'Lesen' von Quadraten: Intermedialität und extrapolierte Medialität bei Gennadij Ajgi." Alfrun Kliems, Ute Raßloff, and Peter Zajac, eds.: *Intermedialität: Lyrik des 20. Jahrhunderts in Ost-Mittel-Europa.* Vol. 3. Berlin: Frank & Timme, 2007.

Bozhidar: *Buben* [Tambourine]. Moskva: Liren', 1914.

Burliuk, David, et al.: *Poshchechina obshchestvennomu vkusu* [A Slap in the Face of Public Taste]. Moskva: Kuz'min i Dolinskii, [1913].

Byrkina, Alina, and Antonina I. Mordvinova, eds.: *Mir etikh glaz.* Vol. 2. *Aigi i ego khudozhestvennoe okruzhenie: Al'bom-katalog* [The World of These Eyes. Vol. 2. Aigi and His Artistic Surrounding: Album-Catalogue]. Cheboksary: Chuvashskii gosudarstvennyi khudozhestvennyi muzei, 1997.

Dronnikov, Nikolai: *Iz dnevnika poeta* [From the Poet's Diary]. [Parizh]: DK [Dronnikov-Konovalov], 2007.

Dronnikov, Nikolai: *Iz dnevnika poeta: Tetrad' vtoraia* [From the Poet's Diary: Second Notebook]. [Parizh]: DK [Dronnikov-Konovalov], 2008.

Dronnikov, Nikolai: *Vospominaniia, razmyshleniia, risunki* [Recollections, Reflections, Drawings]. Cheboksary: Free Poetry, 2009.

France, Peter: "Gennadii Aigi (21 August 1934 – 12 February 2006)." Karen Rosneck, ed.: *Dictionary of Literary Biography.* Vol. 359. *Russian Poets of the Soviet Era.* Detroit/IL: Gale, 2011. 3–20.

Frank, Susi K. [Siuzanna Frank]: "Literaturnyi Institut (i Vysshie literaturnye kursy); Interfeis andergraunda? Sluchai Gennadiia Aigi." [The Literature Institute (and Advanced Literary Courses): Interface of the Underground? The Case of Gennady Aygi] *Toronto Slavic Quarterly* 61 (2017): 308–319. http://sites.utoronto.ca/tsq/61/Frank61.pdf (consulted 01/06/2022).

Grauz, Tat'iana: "'My chitaem ne slova, a postranstvo mezhdu slovami': Elena Guro – Gennadii Aigi: Opyt sopostavleniia." ['We are not reading words, but the space between the words': Elena

Guro – Gennady Aygi: Attempt at a Comparison] Atner Khuzangai, ed.: *Tvorchestvo Gennadiia Aigi: Literaturno-khudozhestvennaia traditsiia i neoavangard. Materialy mezhdunarodnoi nauchno-prakticheskoi konferentsii, posviashchennoi LXXV-letiiu so dnia rozhdeniia Narodnogo poeta Chuvashii Gennadiia Aigi, Shupashkar/Cheboksary 17–18 sentiabria 2009 g* [Gennady Aygi's Œuvre: Literary and Artistic Tradition and Neo-Avant-garde (Conference Proceedings)]. Cheboksary: Chuvashskii gosudarstvennyi institut gumanitarnykh nauk, 2009. 74–79.

Grobman, Mikhail: *Leviafan: Dnevniki 1963–1971 godov* [Leviathan: Diaries 1963–1971]. Moskva: Novoe literaturnoe obozrenie, 2002.

Hinsey, Ellen, and Tomas Venclova: *Magnetic North: Conversations with Tomas Venclova.* Rochester/NY: University of Rochester Press, 2017.

Ichin, Korneliia: "Bespredmetnoe slovo G. Aigi: Dialog s K. Malevichem." [The Non-Objective Word of G. Aigi: Dialogue with K. Malevich] Ivan Kalinin and K. Ichin, eds.: *Energiia krizisa: Sbornik v chest' Igoria Pavlovicha Smirnova* [Energy of Crisis: Collection in Honour of Igor' Pavlovich Smirnov]. Moskva: Novoe literaturnoe obozrenie, 2019. 364–373.

Ivanova, D.: "Mir Gennadiia Aigi – tishina." [The World of Gennady Aygi – Silence] *Grani* [Facets] 70 (1970): 165–171.

Jakobson, Roman: *Noveishaia russkaia poeziia: Nabrosok pervyi. Podstupy k Khlebnikovu* [The Newest Russian Poetry: First Sketch: Approaches to Khlebnikov]. Praha: Tipografija Politika, 1921.

Jakobson, Roman: "Message sur Malévitch." *Change* 26–27 (1976): 293–294.

Janecek, Gerald: "Tri Kuznechika: Khlebnikov, Kammings, Aigi." [Three Grasshoppers: Khlebnikov, Cummings, Aigi] *Przegląd rusycystyczny* 22:1 (#89) (2000): 22–33.

Janecek, Gerald: "Poeziia molchaniia u Gennadiia Aigi." [The Poetry of Silence in Gennady Aygi] Mirjam Goller, and Georg Witte, eds.: *Minimalismus zwischen Leere und Exzess. Wiener slawistischer Almanach. Sonderband.* Vol. 51. Wien: Gesellschaft zur Förderung slawistischer Studien, 2001. 433–446.

Janecek, Gerald: "Kruchenykh contra Gutenberg." Margit Rowell, and Deborah Wye, eds.: *The Russian Avant-Garde Book 1910–1934.* New York: The Museum of Modern Art, 2002. 41–49.

Kabakov, Il'ia: *60-e – 70-e...: Zapiski o neofitsial'noi zhizni v Moskve* [60s–70s...: Notes on the Unofficial Life in Moscow]. *Wiener Slawistischer Almanach. Sonderband.* Vol. 47. Wien: Gesellschaft zur Förderung Slawistischer Studien, 1999.

Kappeler, Andreas: *Die Tschuwaschen: Ein Volk im Schatten der Geschichte.* Köln: Böhlau, 2016.

Khardzhiev, Nikolai: *Stat'i ob avangarde v dvukh tomakh.* Vol. 1 [Essays about the Avant-garde in Two Volumes. Vol. 1]. Moskva: RA, 1997.

Khlebnikov, Velimir: *Sobranie sochinenii v shesti tomakh* [Collected Works in Six Volumes]. Moskva: Institut mirovoi literatury imeni A.M. Gor'kogo, Rossiiskaia akademiia nauk, 2000–2006.

Khuzangai, Atner: *Sem' deskriptsii k obrazu russkogo mastera v Parizhe* [Seven Descriptions towards the Image of the Russian Master in Paris]. Parizh: Dronnikov, 2000.

Khuzangai, Atner, ed.: *Tvorchestvo Gennadiia Aigi: Literaturno-khudozhestvennaia traditsiia i neoavangard. Materialy mezhdunarodnoi nauchno-prakticheskoi konferentsii, posviashchennoi LXXV-letiiu so dnia rozhdeniia Narodnogo poeta Chuvashii Gennadiia Aigi, Shupashkar/Cheboksary 17–18 sentiabria 2009 g* [Gennady Aygi's Œuvre: Literary and Artistic Tradition and Neo-Avant-garde (Conference Proceedings)]. Cheboksary: Chuvashskii gosudarstvennyi institut gumanitarnykh nauk, 2009.

Khuzangai, Atner, ed.: *Malevich / Aigi.* Cheboksary: Free Poetry, 2015.

Khuzangai, Atner: "Aigi v zerkale chernogo kvadrata." [Aigi in the Mirror of the Black Square] *LIK: Literatura. Iskusstvo. Kul'tura* 4 (2015): 152–157.

Kind-Kovács, Friederike, and Jessie Labov, eds. *Samizdat, Tamizdat and Beyond: Transnational Media During and After Socialism.* New York: Berghahn Books, 2013.

Kizeval'ter, Georgii: *Vremia nadezhd, vremia illiuzii: Problemy istorii sovetskogo neofitsial'nogo iskusstva 1950–1960 gody. Stat'i i materialy* [Time of Hope, Time of Illusions: Problems of a History of the Soviet Unofficial Art of the 1950s and 1960s. Essays and Materials]. Moskva: Novoe literaturnoe obozrenie, 2018.

Klähn, Tim: "Rea Nikonova and the Legacy of Russian Futurism." *International Yearbook of Futurism Studies* 5 (2015): 395–424.

Komaromi, Ann: "The Material Existence of Soviet Samizdat." *Slavic Review* 63:3 (2004): 597–618.

Komaromi, Ann: *Uncensored: Samizdat Novels and the Quest for Autonomy in Soviet Dissidence.* Evanston/IL: Northwestern University Press, 2015.

Komaromi, Ann: *Soviet Samizdat: Imagining a New Society.* Ithaca/NY: Northern Illinois University Press, 2022.

Korchagin, Kirill: "The Neo-Futurists." Mark Lipovetsky, Ilja Kukuj, Tomáš Glanc, Maria Engström, and Klavdia Smola, eds.: *The Oxford Handbook of Soviet Underground Culture.* Oxford: Oxford University Press, 2021. [1–20].

Kruchenykh, Aleksei: *Golodniak* [Hunger]. Moskva: Tipografiia TsIT, 1922.

Kruchenykh, Aleksei: *Kukish proshliakam* [A Fig to the Dated]. Moskva: Gileia, 1992.

Kruchenykh, Alexei, and Velimir Khlebnikov: "The Letter as Such." Anna Lawton, and Herbert Eagle, eds.: *Russian Futurism Through its Manifestoes, 1912–1928.* Ithaca/NY: Cornell University Press, 1988. 63–64.

Kuborskaia-Aigi, Galina, et al., eds.: *Gennadii Aigi: Nauchno-vspomogatel'nyi ukazatel'.* Vols. 1–2 [Gennady Aygi: Research Reference Index. Part I and II.]. Cheboksary: Natsional'naia biblioteka Chuvashskoi Respubliki, 2004.

Kulle, Viktor, and Gennadii Aigi: "'Poet – eto nesostaiavshiisia sviatoi…': Beseda Viktora Kulle s Gennadiem Aigi, Moskva, 25 sentiabria 1998 g." [A Poet – That's a Saint Manqué: Conversation of Viktor Kulle with Gennady Aygi, Moscow, 25 September 1998] *Literaturnoe obozrenie* [Literary Review] 5–6 (#271/272) (1998): 14–19.

Lavrova, Anna: *Klassik Krucha: Vospominaniia.* S prilozheniem tsikla Gennadiia Aigi "Piat' stikhotvorenii" [The Classic Krucha: Recollections. Supplemented with Gennady Aygi's cycle "Five Poems"]. Kherson: Pilotnye shkoly, 1997.

Lawton, Anna, and Herbert Eagle, eds.: *Russian Futurism through Its Manifestoes, 1912–1928.* Ithaca/NY: Cornell University Press, 1988.

Leiderman, Naum L., and Mark N. Lipovetskii: *Sovremennaia russkaia literature 1950–1990-kh godov: Posobie dlia vuzov v dvukh tomakh.* Vol. 1. *1950–1968* [Contemporary Russian Literature 1950s–1990s. University Textbook in Two Volumes. Vol. 1. 1950–1968]. Moskva: Akademiia, 2003. 379–391.

Makarevskii, Valerii Ivanovich, and Vladislav Valer'evich Makarevskii: "G.N. Aigi o P. Filonove – krupneishem predstavitele khudozhestvenno-poeticheskogo avangarda." [G.N. Aigi on P. Filonov, the Most Important Representative of the Artistic and Poetic Avant-garde] Atner Khuzangai, ed.: *Tvorchestvo Gennadiia Aigi: Literaturno-khudozhestvennaia traditsiia i neoavangard. Materialy mezhdunarodnoi nauchno-prakticheskoi konferentsii, posviashchennoi LXXV-letiiu so dnia rozhdeniia Narodnogo poeta Chuvashii Gennadiia Aigi, Shupashkar/Cheboksary 17–18 sentiabria 2009 g* [Gennady Aygi's Œuvre: Literary and Artistic Tradition and Neo-Avant-garde (Conference Proceedings)]. Cheboksary: Chuvashskii gosudarstvennyi institut gumanitarnykh nauk, 2009. 82–87.

Malevich, Kazimir: *Po lestnitse poznaniia: Iz neopublikovannykh stikhotvorenii* [On the Stairway of Knowledge: From Unpublished Poems]. Moskva: Gileia, 1991.
Malevich, Kazimir: *Sobranie sochinenii v piati tomakh* [Collected Works in Five Volumes]. Moskva: Gileia, 1995–2004.
Maurizio, Massimo [Massimo Mauritsio]: "Neofuturizm v moskovskom samizdate stalinskogo i poslestalinskogo (ottepel'nogo) perioda na primere poezii N. Glazkova, V. Khromova i L. Gubanova." [Neo-Futurism in the Moscow Samizdat of the Stalin and Post-Stalin (Thaw) Period as Exemplified by N. Glazkov, V. Khromov and L. Gubanov] Kornelia Ichin, ed.: *I posle avangarda – avangard: Sbornik statei* [And after the Avant-garde – the Avant-garde: Collection of Essays]. Belgrad: Izdatel'stvo filologicheskogo fakul'teta v Belgrade, 2017. 147–159.
Mirzaev, Arsen: "Gennadii Aigi i Nikolai Dronnikov." [Gennady Aygi and Nikolai Dronnikov] Iurii B. Orlitskii, Nataliia Azarova, and Dmitrii Derpa, eds.: *Aigi: Materialy, issledovaniia, esse. V dvukh tomakh.* Vol. 1 [Aigi: Materials, Research, Essays. In two volumes. Vol. 1]. Moskva: Vest-Konsalting, 2006. 193–202.
Mirzaev, Arsen: "Slovo kak zrenie." [The Word as Sight] *Russkaia mysl'* [Russian Thought] (Paris), 27 March 1992. 13.
Mirzaev, Arsen: "Sumerki: 30 let spustia." [Twilight: 30 Years Afterwards] *Toronto Slavic Quarterly* 61 (2017): 193–215.
Mirzaev, Arsen: "Gennadii Aigi v krugu druzei-khudozhnikov: Vladimir Iakovlev, Igor' Vulokh i Nikolai Dronnikov." [Gennady Aygi in the Circle of Friends and Artists: Vladimir Iakovlev, Igor' Vulokh and Nikolai Dronnikov] Korneliia Ichin, Shinichi Murata, and Irina Shatova, eds.: *Intermedial'naia poetika avangarda: Sbornik statei* [Intermedial Poetics of the Avant-garde: Collection of Essays]. Belgrad: Filologicheskii fakul'tet, 2018. 157–174.
Mordvinova, A. I.: "Gennadii Aigi i ego khudozhestvennoe okruzhenie: Chuvashskie khudozhniki na vystavke 'Mir etikh glaz–2'." [Gennady Aygi and His Artistic Surrounding: Chuvash Artists at the Exhibition 'The World of These Eyes–2'] *Chuvashskoe iskusstvo: Voprosy teorii i istorii. Sbornik statei.* Vol. 4 [Chuvash Art: Questions of Theory and History. Collection of Essays. Vol. 4]. Cheboksary: Chuvashskii gosudarstvennyi institut gumanitarnykh nauk, 2001. 87–104.
Nikitaev, A. T.: "Severnaia Gileia." [Northern Hylaea] *De visu* 2 (1993): 65–67.
Nikolaeva (Chekhmi), Alevtina Nikolaevna: "Znak kresta v poetike G. Aigi." [The Symbol of the Cross in G. Aigi's Poetics] Atner Khuzangai, ed.: *Tvorchestvo Gennadiia Aigi: Literaturno-khudozhestvennaia traditsiia i neoavangard. Materialy mezhdunarodnoi nauchno-prakticheskoi konferentsii, posviashchennoi LXXV-letiiu so dnia rozhdeniia Narodnogo poeta Chuvashii Gennadiia Aigi, Shupashkar/Cheboksary 17–18 sentiabria 2009 g* [Gennady Aygi's Œuvre: Literary and Artistic Tradition and Neo-Avant-garde (Conference Proceedings)]. Cheboksary: Chuvashskii gosudarstvennyi institut gumanitarnykh nauk, 2009. 105–107.
Nikolaevskaia, Tat'iana, ed.: *Gennadii Aigi – Vladimir Iakovlev: Druzhba, tvorchestvo, sotvorchestvo* [Gennady Aygi – Vladimir Iakovlev: Friendship, Creation, Collaboration]. Moskva: Virtual'naia galereia, 2004.
Nora, Pierre: "Between Memory and History: 'Les lieux de mémoire'." *Representations* 26 (1989): 7–25.
Novikov, Vladimir: "O poezii Gennadiia Aigi." [About Gennady Aygi's Poetry] Tat'iana Nikolaevskaia, ed.: *Gennadii Aigi – Vladimir Iakovlev: Druzhba, tvorchestvo, sotvorchestvo* [Gennady Aygi – *Vladimir Iakovlev: Friendship, Creation, Collaboration*]. Moskva: Virtual'naia galereia, 2004. 13.
Orlitskii, Iurii B., Nataliia Azarova, and Dmitrii Derpa, eds.: *Aigi: Materialy, issledovaniia, esse.* Vols. 1–2 [Aigi: Materials, Research, Essays. Vols. 1–2]. Moskva: Vest-Konsalting, 2006.

Orlitskii, Iurii B., and Mikhail G. Pavlovets: "Nasledniki Khlebnikova: Genrikh Sapgir, Gennadii Aigi, Aleksandr Kondratov, Sergei Biriukov." [Khlebnikov's Heirs: Genrikh Sapgir, Gennady Aygi, Aleksandr Kondratov, Sergei Biriukov] *Vestnik Sankt-Peterburgskogo universiteta. Iazyk i literatura* 15:1 (2018): 94–110.

Pashkin, Dmitrii Aleksandrovich: "Obraz Velimira Khlebnikova v poezii Gennadiia Aigi." [The Image of Velimir Khlebnikov in Gennady Aygi's Poetry] http://avantgarde.narod.ru/beitraege/bu/dp_ajgi.htm (consulted 01/06/2022).

Rakusa, Ilma: "Gennadij Ajgis lyrischer Suprematismus." Peter Brang, Georges Nivat, and Robert Zett, eds.: *Schweizerische Beiträge zum IX. Internationalen Slavistenkongress in Kiev, September 1983.* Bern: Lang, 1983. 149–171.

Robel, Leon: *Aiguï.* Paris: Seghers, 1993. Russian edn *Aigi.* Moskva: Agraf, 2003.

Schmelz, Peter J.: *Such Freedom, If Only Musical: Unofficial Soviet Music During the Thaw.* New York: Oxford University Press, 2009.

Sem'ian, Tat'iana: "Visual'noe prostranstvo tekstov Gennadiia Aigi." [The Visual Space of Gennady Aigi's Texts] Iurii B. Orlitskii, Nataliia Azarova, and Dmitrii Derpa, eds.: *Aigi: Materialy, issledovaniia, esse.* Vol. 1 [Aigi: Materials, Research, Essays. Vol. 1]. Moskva: Vest-Konsalting, 2006. 84–90.

Skoropanova, Irina Stepanovna: "'Vakuumnye' teksty Gennadiia Aigi." [Gennady Aygi's 'Vacuum' Texts] Aleksandr I. Golovnia, ed.: *IV chteniia, posviashchennye 70-letiiu so dnia rozhdeniia professora V. A. Karpova. Minsk, 19–20 marta 2010.* Vol. 2, pt. 1. Minsk: Respublikanskii institut vysshei shkoly, 2010. 86–92.

Skoropanova, Irina Stepanovna: "'Vakuumnye' teksty russkikh neoavangardistov." ['Vacuum' Texts of Russian Neo-Avant-Gardists] Danila M. Davydov, and Ol'ga V. Sokolova, eds.: *Stikh. Proza. Poetika: Sbornik statei v chest' 60-letiia Iu. B. Orlitskogo.* [Verse. Prose. Poetics. Collection of Articles in Honor of the 60th anniversary of Yury Orlitsky] New York: Ailoros, 2012. 369–378.

Sokolova, Ol'ga: *Neoavangardnaia poeziia G. Aigi i V. Sosnory* [G. Aigi's and V. Sosnora's Neo-Avant-garde Poetry]. Ph.D. Dissertation. Tomsk: Tomskii gosudarstvennyi universitet, 2007.

Sokolova, Ol'ga: "'Bespredmetnaia zhivopis': K. Malevicha i 'bespredmetnaia poeziia' G. Aigi." ['Non-objective Painting': K Malevich's 'Non-Objective Art' and G. Aigi's 'Non-Objective Poetry'] *Vestnik Tomskogo gosudarstvennogo universiteta. Filologiia* 1:2 (2008): 67–79.

Sokolova, Ol'ga: "Vital'nyi potentsial mortal'nogo: Kontseptsiia 'vtorogo rozhdeniia' B. Pasternaka i printsip 'pervozdannosti' G. Aigi." [The Vital Potential of the Mortal: B. Pasternak's Concept of 'Second Birth' and G. Aigi's Principle of 'Primordiality'] Atner Khuzangai, ed.: *Tvorchestvo Gennadiia Aigi: Literaturno-khudozhestvennaia traditsiia i neoavangard. Materialy mezhdunarodnoi nauchno-prakticheskoi konferentsii, posviashchennoi LXXV-letiiu so dnia rozhdeniia Narodnogo poeta Chuvashii Gennadiia Aigi, Shupashkar/Cheboksary 17–18 sentiabria 2009 g* [Gennady Aygi's Œuvre: Literary and Artistic Tradition and Neo-Avant-garde (Conference Proceedings)]. Cheboksary: Chuvashskii gosudarstvennyi institut gumanitarnykh nauk, 2009. 92–95.

Sokolova, Ol'ga: *Ot avangarda k neoavangardu: Iazyk, sub'ektivnost', kul'turnye perenosy* [From the Avant-garde to the Neo-Avant-garde: Language, Subjectivity, Cultural Transfers]. Moskva: Kul'turnaia revoliutsiia, 2019.

Sukhoparov, Sergei: *Aleksei Kruchenykh: Sud'ba budetlianina* [Aleksei Kruchenykh: The Fate of a Futurist]. München: Sagner, 1992.

Sukhoparov, Sergei, ed.: *Aleksei Kruchenykh v svidetel'stvakh sovremennikov* [Aleksei Kruchenykh in Testimonies of Contemporaries]. München: Sagner, 1994.

Steiner, Peter: "On Samizdat, Tamizdat, Magnitizdat and Other Words that Are Difficult to Pronounce." *Poetics Today* 29:4 (2008): 613–628.

Talochkin, Leonid, and Irina Alpatova, eds.: *"Drugoe iskusstvo", Moskva, 1956–76: K khronike khudozhestvennoi zhizni.* Vol. 1 ["The Other Art", Moscow 1956–76: Towards a Chronology of Artistic Life. Vol. 1]. Moskva: Khudozhestvennaia galereia Moskovskaia kollektsiia / SP Interbuk, 1991.

Vakar, Irina A., and Tat'iana N. Mikhienko, eds.: *Malevich o sebe, sovremenniki o Maleviche.* Vol. 1 [Malevich on Himself, Contemporaries on Malevich. Vol. 1]. Moskva: RA, 2004.

Valentine, Sarah: "Music, Silence, and Spirituality in the Poetry of Gennady Aigi." *Slavic and East European Journal* 51:4 (2007): 675–691.

Valentine, Sarah: *Witness and Transformation: The Poetics of Gennady Aygi.* Brighton: Academic Studies Press, 2015.

Vrubel'-Golubkina, Irina: *Razgovory v zerkale* [Conversations in the Mirror]. Moskva: Novoe literaturnoe obozrenie, 2014.

Weststeijn, Willem G.: "Ajgi and Chlebnikov." *Russian Literature* 79–80 (2016): 5–12.

Woroszylska, Natalia [Natal'ia Voroshil'skaia]: "Vstrechi s Aigi." [Encounters with Aigi] *Novaia Pol'sha* [New Poland] 4 (2006): 49–50.

Woroszylski, Wiktor: *Życie Majakowskiego* [The Life of Mayakovsky]. Warszawa: Państwowy Instytut Wydawniczy, 1965.

Valentina Parisi

Serge Segay, Rea Nikonova and Italy: Between Futurism and Mail Art

Abstract: This essay examines the contacts between the Russian artists Rea Nikonova and Serge Segay and Italian authors of Visual Poetry, with a special focus on the international Mail Art network in the second half of the 1980s. While Nikonova and Segay's literary works and their rôle in the formation of the Transfurist group have already been well researched, their relationship with Italian artists interested in the Futurist tradition has not yet received much scholarly attention. Drawing on a rich spectrum of archival materials, this essay shows how this creative exchange was instrumental in the re-positioning of the Russian couple in the 1990s, focussing in particular on the case of Segay, who characterized his trip to Italy in November 1989 as "going back" to the roots of Futurism and as a means of "moving forwards". While Carlo Belloli's preface for Segay's *Poèmes pour ballerines de grand théâtre de l'URSS* (Poems for Ballerinas of the Great Soviet Theatre, 1990) situated his Russian colleague within the 'family' of Futurism, Segay's interest in Italian art was indeed more broadly oriented. He undertook a number of collaborations with Italian authors of Visual Poetry and mail artists inspired not only by Futurist, but also Dadaist and Surrealist strategies. In this essay, particular attention will be devoted to two books authored by Segay and Nikonova with Vittore Baroni, using the technique of the *cadavre exquisite*, as well as to their sound improvisation with the Turinese artists Alberto Vitacchio and Carla Bertola, *Zvukovoi kvadrat* (Sound Square), released as a record in 2007. Lastly, my analysis will refer to Nikonova and Segay's collaboration with the Milan-based artist Ruggero Maggi, which led to a series of exhibitions oscillating between the idea of "a museum without walls" (pursued at that time within the Mail Art network) and the interaction with local communities in Yeysk and Milan.

Keywords: Transfurism, Visual Poetry, Mail Art, Concept Art, collaborative art, *samizdat* literature, sound art, *zaum'*, Carlo Belloli, Ruggero Maggi, Vittore Baroni, Alberto Vitacchio, Carla Bertola

https://doi.org/10.1515/9783111318394-007

"If you move forwards, you will go backwards": Segay's path to Marinetti, via Belloli

In a letter dated 10 December 1982, the Russian artist Serge Segay (pseud. of Sergei Vsevolodovich Sigov, 1947–2014) wrote to the conceptualist poet Dmitry Aleksandrovich Prigov:

> In culture, the concept of 'time' […] is created by the poet. Therefore, you worry in vain about the incompatibility of the 'Futurist experience with our time'. Yes, the poet […] must 'move forwards', rejecting the past and creating the New. But the Japanese have come to another conclusion: *If you move forwards, you will go backwards.* Therefore, better to go backwards and swear allegiance to Futurism, so as to move forwards![1]

In his own attempt at going backwards to move forwards, Segay entered into a dialogue not only with the legacy of Russian Futurism, which was still largely ignored in the Soviet Union at that time, but also (and inevitably) with its Italian counterpart. Both Russian and Italian Futurists provided the poet with great inspiration to comply with his demand that "every word must be supplemented"[2] by the reciter's body movements and voice, as he had first formulated in his declaration "Dopolneniia ko Khlebnikovu" (Additions to Khlebnikov) in 1969.

Striving to preserve the tradition of Russian Futurism – as Segay did by making their texts by avant-garde poets available in his samizdat journal *Transponans*[3] between 1979 and 1987 – was for him inseparable from developing historical Futurism further and building on old texts in order to create new ones. This method be-

---

1 "В культуре понятие 'время' […] – творится поэтом. Поэтому – Вы совершенно напрасно так много беспокойтесь о несоответствии 'футуристического опыта нашему времени'. Да, поэт […] объязан 'идти вперед', отвергая бывшее и творя новое. Но – были японцы, давшие второе установление: идя вперед – придешь назад. Так что – лучше идти назад и клясться футуризмом, чтобы в результате прийти вперед!". Sigei: "Kommentarii k pis'mam N.I. Khardzhieva", p. 228. Here and elsewhere, translations from the original Russian are mine, unless otherwise noted. Bibliographical references preserve the Library of Congress transliteration of proper names and place names (e.g., Sigei or Eisk), while common anglicized spellings are used throughout the essay (e.g., Segay or Yeysk).

2 "Каждое слово должно быть дополнено." Sigei: "Dopolneniia ko Khlebnikovu" [Additions to Khlebnikov], p. 5.

3 *Samizdat* is a Russian term for self-published literature, distributed clandestinely during Soviet times. On the samizdat journal *Transponans* (1979–1987), see, for instance, Kukui: "Laboratoriia avangarda: Zhurnal 'Transponans'" (Laboratory of the Avant-Garde: The Journal *Transponans*); Klähn: "Rea Nikonova and the Legacy of Russian Futurism"; Hildebrand-Schat: "Anarcho-Futurism Revisited: The Magazine 'Transponans'."

came the main tenet of the Transfurist movement, which he had founded in 1983 in Yeysk, together with his wife Rea Nikonova (pseud. of Anna Aleksandrovna Tarshis, 1942–2014). The prefix 'trans' refers here to the Russian word *transponirovanie* (transposition) and describes a process in which historical source material is transformed into a new, contemporary context. Remarkable, in this respect, was Segay's appropriation of the many books and booklets created at the beginning of the twentieth century by the Russian Cubo-Futurist and *zaum'* (transrational) poets Velimir Khlebnikov, Vasilisk Gnedov, Ilya Zdanevich, Aleksandr Tufanov, Aleksei Kruchenykh and Aleksei Chicherin,[4] all of whom Segay revered. Over the course of several decades, acting as both a copyist and an interpreter, he re-elaborated and 'transposed' parts of these texts, creating an impressive number of highly original, handmade "book works"[5] based on the combination of pictorial and verbal elements.[6]

Whereas Segay's commitment to reconnect with Russian Futurism has already attracted ample scholarly attention, his interest in Italian visual poets who continued in the line of Filippo Tommaso Marinetti and his followers is less known. Yet, the couple's 'debt' to Italian Futurists in the early part of the twentieth century[7] resulted in numerous collaborations with authors of Visual Poetry, carried out mainly through the channels of Mail Art. In this respect, it is interesting what Segay wrote about Filippo Tommaso Marinetti, while commenting on Rea Nikonova's theatre:

> After all, the avant-garde theatre owes everything to Marinetti. Despite all efforts made by the Russian Futurists (with the exception of Zdanevich) to distance themselves from this ingen-

4 See Compton: *Russian Avant-Garde Books, 1917–1934* and *The Russian Avant-Garde Book, 1910–1934.*

5 Many of these books are accessible at the LS Collection in the Van Abbemuseum, Eindhoven; scans of selected pages have been reproduced in Stommels and Lemmens: *Bookwork: Rea Nikonova & Serge Segay*, and online at https://ls.vanabbemuseum.nl/S/segay/text/bookwork.htm. See, for instance (with LS Collection reference numbers in parentheses): Iliazd (Ilya Zdanevich), *Lidantiu faaram* (Le-Dantiu as a Beacon; 1979–09); Gnedov, *Stichi dlia verbliudov* (Poems for Camels; 1984–02); Tufanov, *Ushkuiniki* (Ushkuiniks; 1984–15); Kruchenych, *Arabeski iz Gogolia* (Arabesques from Gogol; 1986–09); and Iliazd (Ilya Zdanevich), *Ostraf Paskhi* (Easter Island; 1994–09).

6 On this aspect, see Zvenigorodskaia: "Rukopisnye knigi i kollazhi Sergeia Sigeia kak sposob issledovaniia poezii russkogo futurizma" [Handmade Books and Collages by Serge Segay: A Way to Study Russian Futurist Poetry].

7 "Театр авангарда всем обязан всё-таки Маринетти. Как бы не открещивались от гениального энергатора русские футуристы (кроме Зданевича), а даже 'Победа над солнцем' вызвала 'столкновение и споры', выкрики из зала и тэ пэ, которых страстно жаждал на театре первый футурист." Sigei: "Kvintessentsiia stsenizma" [The Quintessence of the Scenic], p. 70.

> ious energizer, even *Victory over the Sun* provoked all those 'clashes and quarrels', shouts from the audience, etc., that the first Futurist craved for in the theatre"[8]

This essay will thus focus on this little-studied aspect of their œuvre, by reconstructing the connections which the couple established in the second half of the 1980s with the poets Carlo Belloli, Ruggero Maggi, Alberto Vitacchio, Carla Bertola and Vittore Baroni who, as representatives of different generations, approached the legacy of Italian Futurism in a variety of manners. This exchange proved particularly fruitful, given the rôle that Segay played in the rediscovery of Russian Futurism in Italy. For instance, the *Sobranie stikhotvorenii* (Collected Poems) by the Ego-Futurist Vasilisk Gnedov were published for the first time in Trento in 1992, thanks to the efforts of the philologist Marzio Marzaduri and the collector Nikolai Khardzhiev, with introductions and notes by Segay:

> In June 1989, in Moscow, I handed Professor Marzio Marzaduri (1930–1990) the book by Gnedov that I had compiled, and I received assurances from him that it would be immediately published. Unfortunately, he could not deal with it before the "Zaum Symposium" since he was devoting all his energies to organizing this unique event.[9]

The "Zaum Symposium" referred to above was the international conference *Futurismo transmentale e dadaismo nella cultura russa* (Transmental Futurism and Dadaism in Russian Culture), held in Rovereto and Venice on 8–11 November 1989. Here, Segay became acquainted with Mikhail Evzlin (1952–2020), who taught Russian literature at the University of Trento with Marzaduri and who later founded the Ediciones del Hebreo Errante in Madrid which, among other things, re-pub-

8 Mail Art developed in the 1940s and 50s out of Ray Johnson's New York Correspondence School of Art and, during the 1960s, became a global movement related to Fluxus and other forms of Visual Poetry. It allowed artists to establish a world-wide distribution and communication channel outside the restrictions of commercial art galleries and publishing houses. Collages of words, signs, texts etc. were sent out to colleagues and friends, usually in multiple copies, by means of postcards, letters or parcels. Some of these receptacles also included objects, rubber stamped images, records, audio tapes, or anything that could be mailed via the postal service.

9 "…в июне 1989 в Москве я вручил профессору Марцио Марцадури (1930–1990) составленную мной книгу Гнедова, получил от него заверения в том, что она будет незамедлительно издана. К сожалению, до заумного симпозиума он не мог ею заниматься, поскольку тратил все силы на организацию этого уникального мероприятия", Sigei: "Kommentarii k pis'mam N.I. Khardzhieva" [Comments on N.I. Khardzhiev's Letters], p. 291. Incidentally, Segay was quite disappointed by the *Collected Works* when the book was finally published, largely because the publication, which was delayed for two years due to Marzaduri's death, contained many typos. See Sigei: "Kommentarii k pis'mam N.I. Khardzhieva", p. 292

lished texts by Russian Futurists and by Segay, Nikonova and other contemporary avant-gardists.

The materials Segay appropriated and incorporated in his Visual Poetry in line with the Transfurist principle of *transponirovanie* allow us to trace his 1989 journey through Italy. An official letter signed by Marzaduri, stating that "the Soviet citizen Serge Segay" had participated in the conference with a paper on Ilya Zdanevich and had remunerated him with the sum of 750.000 lire, was, for example, xeroxed and reworked as a palimpsest, with the inclusion of a visual poem by Kurt Schwitters, to which Segay added the Old Cyrillic letter Yat (Ѣ).[10] Similarly, Segay added to one of his visual compositions a letter by the mail artist John Held Jr., whom he had apparently asked for Evzlin's telephone number: "Dear Serge, I was surprised to receive communications from you from Italy! I tryied [sic] to find the telephon [sic] number of Mr. M. Evzlin but I did'nt [sic] find it –".[11] (See Fig. 1)

Eventually, Segay met Evzlin again, and in his text "Fragmenty polnoi formy" (Fragments of a Full Form, 2006) he mentioned the Italian edition of Paul Éluard's poems that Evzlin had given to him as a present, describing how he had almost immediately begun to transform it by cutting triangles and letters out of it.[12] More importantly, Segay's meetings with Evzlin led to the creation of the ephemeral Edizioni Serge Sigej in Italia (Serge Segay Publication House in Italy), which released only two books, Nikonova's *Protsess nad Shotlandtsem* (The Scotsman's Trial, 1989) and the authology *Transpoety* (1989). Nikonova's first typographical publication, written between 1966 and 1967, featured on its front and back covers Segay's above-mentioned composition that incorporates the letter exchanged with John Held Jr; *Transpoety*, instead, was a collection of works by several Transfurist poets including, alongside Segay and Nikonova, A. Nik (pseudonym of Nikolai Aksel'rod) and Boris Konstriktor. The *impromptu* character of this publication can be gleaned from the inclusion of the playful poem that Konstriktor had written for Segay, before his departure to Italy: "Mama mia ital'iano / Mama mia dva stakana / Mama Roma / Mama vodka / Mama rzhavaia selëdka" (Mama mia italiano / Mama mia two glasses / Mama Roma / Mama vodka / Mama rusty herring).[13] Despite the short lifespan of the Edizioni Serge Sigej in Italia, the collaboration with Evzlin continued in the following years, with Segay and Nikonova contributing to many

10 On Segay's predilection for this particular letter, see Greve: *Writing and the "Subject"*, p. 276.
11 John Held papers relating to Mail Art in the Archives of American Art, Smithsonian Institution, Washington, DC. Box 4, Folder 4. https://edan.si.edu/slideshow/viewer/?damspath=/CollectionsOnline/heldjohn/Box_0004/Folder_004.
12 Sigei: "Fragmenty polnoi formy" [Fragments of a Full Form], p. 307.
13 Sigei: *Transpoets*, p. 7.

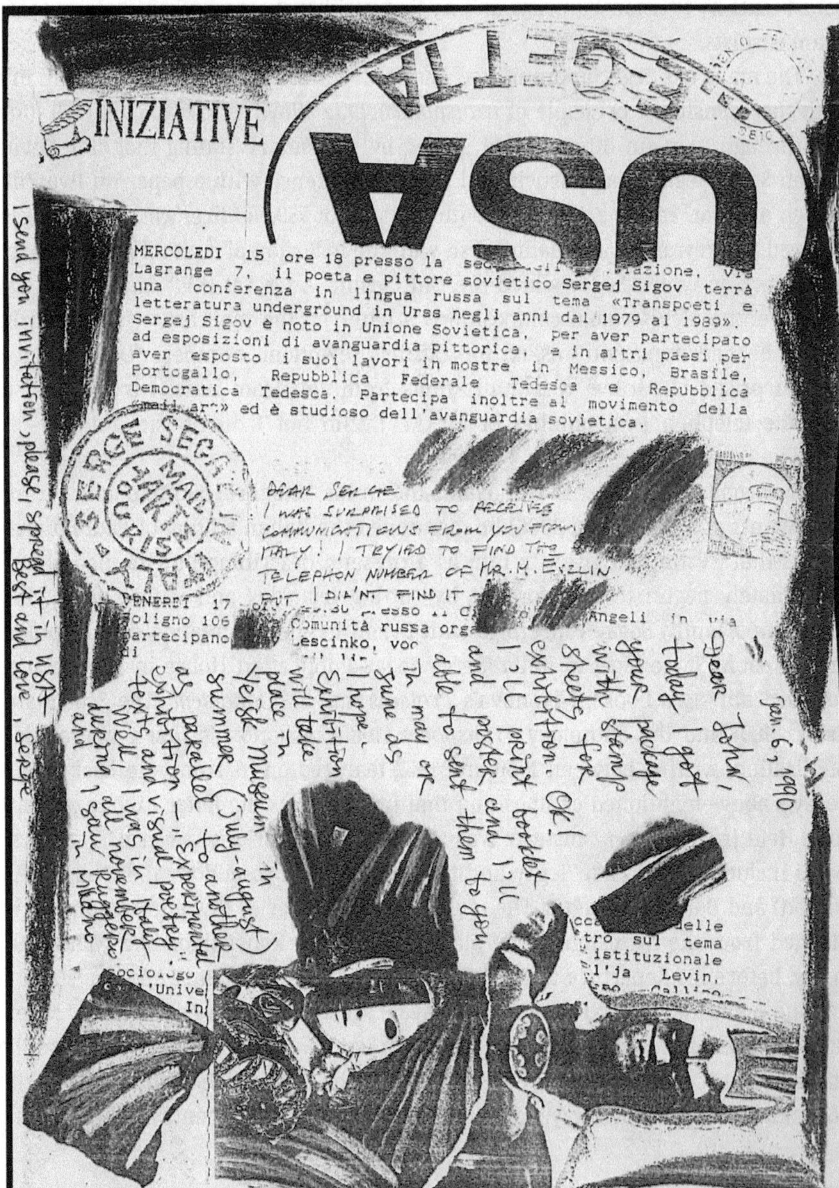

Fig. 1: Serge Segay: Visual composition sent to John Held Jr. in 1990.

of the beautifully designed editions of rare and often forgotten Russian avant-garde authors published by Evzlin's Ediciones del Hebreo Errante, during the 2000s and early 2010s. In memory of Marzio Marzaduri, moreover, Evzlin named his Russian book series "Marz" (as Khardzhiev used to call Marzaduri, who died in 1990).

At that time, Segay was also in contact with Carlo Belloli (1922–2003), who had joined the Futurist movement in 1943 and whose verbo-visual *Testi-poemi murali* (Mural Texts-Poems) were welcomed in 1944 by Marinetti as "the future of Futurism".[14] In March 1944, Marinetti published ten free-word texts by Belloli under the title *Parole per la guerra* (Words for the War) in his publishing house Edizioni di Futuristi in Armi. Several poets and critics, including Mary Ellen Solt and Arrigo Lora Totino, have interpreted as an anticipation of the Concrete Poetry experiments carried out by Eugen Gomringer and the Noigandres group almost ten years later.[15] During the 1950s, Belloli played a major rôle in gathering Futurists from the old guard and organizing a number of Futurist group exhibitions. In 1959, he distanced himself from Concretism, criticizing the lack of a clear visual-typographical organization of the page and opposing "our [i. e. the Futurists'] mathematics of semantic-morphological structures, correlated to typographical structures" to the "verbal calembours"[16] created by concrete poets. This position was shared by Segay, who repeatedly maintained that Visual Poetry has more to do with graphic art than with poetry.[17]

It is worth mentioning that Belloli was surprisingly knowledgeable of the Russian avant-garde, at a time when information on this subject was still comparably scarce. In the introduction to the catalogue of the exhibition *Il contributo russo alle avanguardie plastiche* (The Russian Contribution to Plastic Arts), which he curated in 1964 at the Galleria del Levante in Milan and Rome, Belloli sketched out an overview of the Russian avant-garde that was unusually rich, albeit quite partial – if not downright biased – as he tried to demonstrate Marinetti's influence on Russian Cubo-Futurism and Rayism. Belloli's promptness in acknowledging the contribution which Russian artists made to modern art ultimately helped the development

14 See the essay "Futurism in Italian Verbo-Visual Poetry after the Second World War" by Pasquale Fameli in this volume of the Yearbook, pp. 5–38.

15 For further information on the Noigandres group, see the essay "Russian Futurism and Brazilian Avant-garde Poetry: Incorporation, Translation, Convergence" by Odile Cisneros in this Yearbook, pp. 253–282.

16 Belloli: *Poesia audiovisuale: Note per un'estetica dell'audiovisualismo,* p. 206. On Belloli and his influence on the postwar avant-garde, see D'Ambrosio: "Di come Carlo Belloli, partendo dal 'Poema preciso' marinettiano, divenne un precursore della poesia concreta."

17 See, for instance, the conversation with Mikhail Ryklin in October 1988, printed in "O prirode vizual'noi poezii" [On the Nature of Visual Poetry].

of an international neo-avant-garde movement and facilitated his cooperation with Segay.

In his commentary on Khardzhiev's *Pis'ma v Sigeisk* (Letters to Sigeisk), Segay recalled that he made the Russian collector laugh when he explained how he had succeeded in writing to Belloli in French, a language he had no command of: "Well, I took inspiration from the letters Valery Bryusov sent to Émile Verhaeren: 'Dear and respected maître, etc.'"[18] Segay contacted Belloli asking him to write a preface for his artist's book *Poèmes pour ballerines de grand théâtre de l'URSS* (Poems for Ballerinas of the Great Soviet Theatre). In October 1987, Belloli sent him a text, which eventually served as an introduction to the book, published in Canada in 1990. When Khardzhiev asked him why he had chosen Belloli and not another poet, Segay confessed that since his childhood he had had an admiration for Marinetti, whose disciple Belloli was: "Marinetti once wrote a preface for a book by this then still young poet... I wanted continuity."[19]

Segay included one of Belloli's letters, dated 29 October 1990, in the essay *Fragments of a Full Form*. In this message, Belloli thanked Segay ("cher poète et ami") for sending a copy of the book. Moreover, he asked for an additional five to six copies to distribute amongst art and literary critics in Italy and Switzerland, as well as to public libraries. In the letter, Belloli also expressed his admiration for Segay's work: "It is a remarkable collection that represents the trajectories of your favourite visual universe by establishing a dynamic constellation, which at the same time is explosive and exciting."[20] In his preface to *Poèmes pour ballerines de grand théâtre de l'URSS*, Belloli characterized Serge Segay as "a brother from Khlebnikov's land who inaugurated the universal Zaumist poetics"[21] and situated his poems

18 "Ну да, я списывал мои письма у Валерия Брюсова, который когда-то переписывался с Верхарном: 'Дорогой и многоуважаемый Мэтр и тэ дэ'." Sigei: "Kommentarii k pis'mam N.I. Khardzhieva", p. 294.

19 "Мне пришло признаться в моем еще с детства преклонении перед Маринетти, учеником которого был Беллоли: – Маринетти написал однажды предисловие к книжке этого тогда еще юного поэта...мне хотелось преемственности..." Sigei: "Kommentarii k pis'mam N.I. Khardzhieva", p. 294. Marinetti's preface to *Testi-poemi murali* is discussed in Pasquale Fameli's essay in this Yearbook, "Futurism in Italian Verbo-Visual Poetry after the Second World War", pp. 5–38

20 "Il s'agit d'une admirable plaquette que suggere les itineraires de l'univers visuel qui vous est congenial, etablissant une constellation dinamique, explosive et exaltante." Sigei: "Fragmenty polnoi formy", p. 155. The slightly incorrect spelling follows the publication in the journal *Russian Literature.*

21 "[...] confrère du pays de Klebnikoff qui inaugura la poétique universelle zaumiste". Belloli: "Préface", p. 5.

within “the great adventure of international Visual Poetry”.[22] Flattered by this tribute, Segay reproduced in the book the manuscript of Belloli’s original letter to him, to which he added (here and twice elsewhere in the book) the note that it contained a “préface de Carlo Belloli”. Thus, he paid homage to Belloli, presenting him as a kind of spokesperson for the latter-day Futurists seeking to establish a line of continuity with the “ingenious energizer Marinetti”[23] while, at the same time, inserting his own name into this very genealogy.

“…the only salvation”: Mail Art as an open-ended, collective process

The homage to Belloli, however, was not the only strategy adopted by Segay in *Poèmes pour ballerines* to place himself into a group of well-established authors (see Fig. 2). Indeed, at the end of the book, he provided a re-elaboration of the famous ‘cow sticker’ originally made by the artist Carlo Battisti in 1978 (with names of artists replacing those of cuts of beef) and then altered and disseminated by the visual artist and collector Guglielmo Achille Cavellini. Segay appropriated Cavellini’s sticker, turned the cow into a bat, and included his own surname in a list of international mail artists: (Vittore) Baroni, (Lamberto) Caravita, (Arturo G.) Fallico, (Ryosuke) Cohen, (Shozo) Shimamoto, (John) Held, and others.[24]

At that point, Segay and Nikonova were already involved in the Mail Art network. Instrumental for their admittance into this global, fluid community was the Experimental Art Exhibition, organized in 1985 at the Fiatal Művészek Klubja (Young Artist’s Club), “Budapest’s legendary hang-out for underground artists and oppositional intelligentsia”,[25] as Beáta Hock described it. Segay and Nikonova

---

22 “[…] la grande aventure de la poésie visuelle internationale”. Belloli: “Préface”, p. 5.

23 Sigei: “Kvintessentsiia stsenizma”, p. 70.

24 In an attempt of ‘self-historization’, which is reminiscent of Cavellini’s conceptual self-promotion, Segay showcased Belloli’s preface in the exhibition of Visual Poetry that he curated together with Rea Nikonova in Yeysk in 1990. See Sigei, ed.: *Mezhdunarodnaia vystavka vizual’noi poezii* [International Exhibition of Visual Poetry], p. 10. Unfortunately, Belloli’s papers at the Istituto Internazionale di Studi sul Futurismo, Milan, were not available to me and, therefore, I was unable to investigate further the intriguing subject of his exchange with Segay.

25 Hock: “‘162 Artists from over 50 Countries’: Artistic Networking in the Mainstream and on the Margins”, p. 127. Contrarily to Soviet artists, Hungarians were much earlier involved in Mail Art circuits. The neutrally titled *Experimental Art Exhibition* followed the more politically provocative exhibition *Hungary Can Be Yours! International Hungary* organized the previous year, in the same venue, by György Galántai. On the basis of the materials solicited for the “Hungary” issue of the international Mail Art magazine *Commonpress*, the exhibition provided an alternative image of

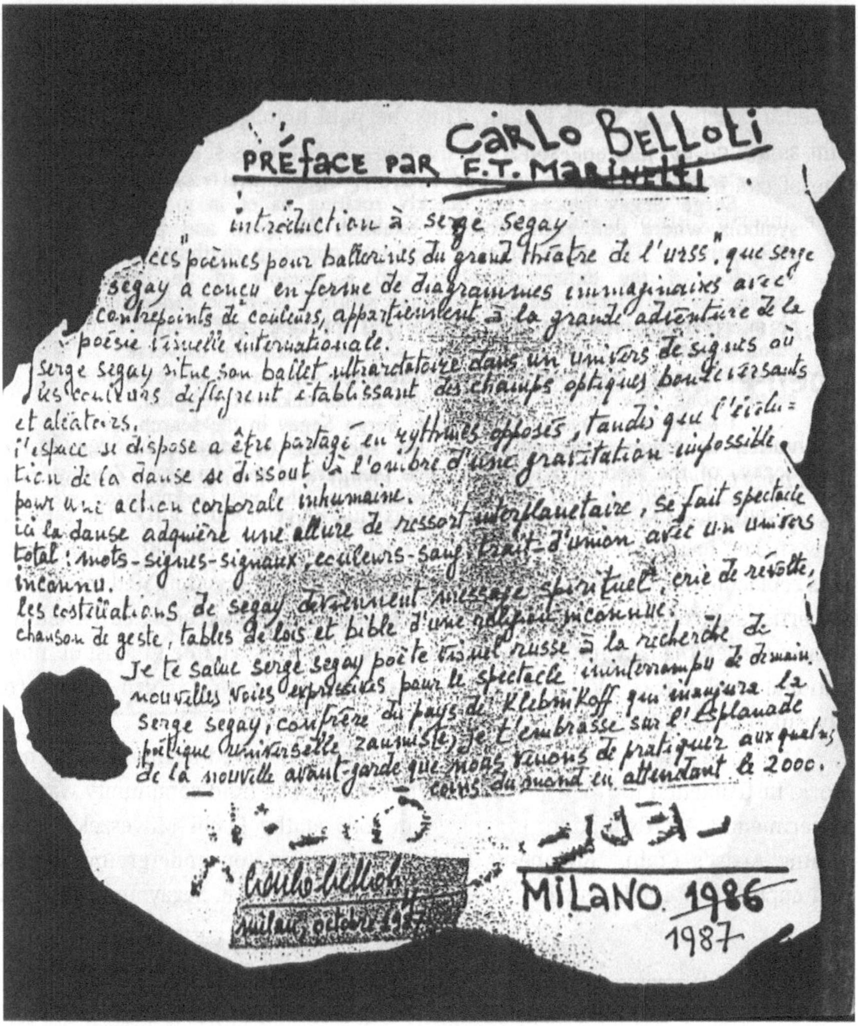
CARLO BELLOLI
PRÉFACE PAR ~~F.T. MARINETTI~~

introduction à serge segay

ces "poèmes pour ballerines du grand théâtre de l'URSS" que serge segay a conçu en forme de diagrammes imaginaires avec contrepoints de couleurs, appartiennent à la grande aventure de la poésie visuelle internationale. serge segay situe son ballet ultraradiotoire dans un univers de signes où les couleurs déflagrent établissant des champs optiques bouleversants et aléatoires, en rythmes opposés, tandis que l'évolution de la danse se dissout à l'ombre d'une gravitation impossible. l'espace se dispose à être partagé pour une action corporale inhumaine. ici la danse adquière une allure de ressort interplanétaire, se fait spectacle total: mots-signes-signaux, couleurs-sang, trait-d'union avec un univers inconnu. les costruations de segay deviennent message spirituel, crie de révolte, chanson de geste, tables de lois et bible d'une religion inconnue.

Je te salue serge segay poète visuel russe à la recherche de nouvelles voies expressives pour le spectacle ininterrompu de demain. serge segay, confrère du pays de Klebnikoff qui inaugura la poétique universelle zaumiste, je t'embrasse sur l'Esplanade de la nouvelle avant-garde que nous venons de pratiquer auxquels coins du monde en attendant le 2000.

carlo belloli
milan, octobre 1987

MILANO ~~1986~~
1987

Fig. 2.: Carlo Belloli: Preface to Serge Segay's *Poèmes pour ballerines de grand théâtre de l'URSS* (Poems for Ballerinas of the Great Soviet Theatre, 1990).

took part in the exhibition and began to send letters to artists whose addresses were published in the catalogue. Joining this alternative network was for Segay

---

the country through responses to Galántai's call sent by 46 Hungarians and 58 artists from 18 other countries,.

and Nikonova a sort of 'going back to move forwards', given that they were fully aware of the experiments undertaken by Italian Futurists in the 1910s and 1920s within the realm of mail communication. Marinetti's adherents can be seen as precursors of Mail Art;[26] and, as Enrico Crispolti has argued, "the Futurist creative involvement in the domain of mail communication represents a by no means marginal aspect of their intention to refashion futuristically the whole universe, which characterizes all the creative endeavour of the movement."[27]

Futurist experiments with the mail service produced a heterogeneous array of aesthetic solutions, ranging from the series of promotional postcards released by Tato (pseud. of Guglielmo Sansoni, 1896–1974) in collaboration with the Florentine publishing house Ballerini e Fratini in order to advertise the participation of aero-painters in the XIV Venice Biennale (1924) and in the Third Rome Biennale (1925), to the unique postcards which Giacomo Balla used to send to his relatives and friends, reworking his own sketches and drawings. As Giovanni Lista pointed out in his pioneering volume devoted to Futurist 'postal art', the creation of highly original postcards was a constant praxis for Balla between 1912 (when he sent postcards realized in the style of *Compenetrazioni iridescenti* (Iridescent Interpenetrations, 1912–14) from Düsseldorf to his relatives and to his student Gino Galli) and the early 1930s. Such a tenacious rejection of standardized mail production resulted in the dissemination of "ephemeral artistic creations, constantly adapted to their addressees and contents"[28] amongst many members of the Futurist network, including Růžena Zátková, Primo Conti, Mario Broglio, Fortunato Depero and Tullio Crali. According to Lista, this strategy was consistent with the Futurist aspiration to desacralize art and to turn it into a feature of everyday life.

A similar commitment to adapting the principles of Futurism to postal communication can be seen in Francesco Cangiullo's mail experiments. In 1915, with his letters and postcards "tipo Cangiullo" (in Cangiullo's style), the artist invented a new kind of postal communication, which was shaped according to the rules expressed in Marinetti's *Technical Manifesto of Futurist Literature:* suppression of syntax, punctuation, adverbs and adjectives. In line with the simplification of mail communication required by war, the 'synthetic' postcards 'tipo Cangiullo' in-

26 See also Britsch, et al.: *Le avanguardie artistiche e la cartolina postale* and Salaris: *Futurismo postale = Futurist Mail.*

27 "[...] l'intervento nel dominio della comunicazione postale rappresenta un aspetto, e tutt'altro che marginale, di quell'intenzione di ricostruzione futurista dell'universo che caratterizza tutta la tensione creativa del movimento." Crispolti: "La creatività 'postale' futurista", p. 13.

28 "[...] cartes postales envoyées à ses amis, comme des supports éphémères d'une création artistique toujours exécutée à la mesure du message et de son destinataire." Lista: *L'Art postal futuriste*, p. 23. Translation from the original French is mine.

cluded a pre-determined set of topics (Futurism, war, news and businesses, entertainment, women, travels and appointments, greetings or insults). The answers given by the sender provided a compressed indication of his or her state of mind. Even more radical were the mail collages that Ivo Pannaggi sporadically sent to his friends from 1925 onwards, often re-using his own personal correspondence as a support for abstract compositions, with spaces left free for stamps, tags, labels, etc. to be added by the postal service. Here, "the postal and artistic event coincides perfectly",[29] because the artist was not the only creator of the work, but the instigator of a collective creative experiment that involved the post office and its employees.

The Futurist aestheticization of mail communication anticipated strategies elaborated by American artist Ray Johnson (1927–1995) and the New York Correspondence School of Art; interestingly, in a series of articles, Carlo Belloli described the Italian Futurists as the true precursors of Mail Art and mentioned, in particular, the almost forgotten name of Armando Mazza, who published a set of letters from the front in *Cartoline postali di guerra* (Wartime Postcards, 1917) and ten postcards under the title *10 liriche d'amore* (10 Love Lyrics, 1919).[30] Belloli formed part of this genealogy as, during the 1940s, he had also sent postal poems called 'messaggi ludopoetici' (playful poetic messages) by military mail, as Mazza had done during the First World War.[31] Nevertheless, as Crispolti convincingly argued,[32] in the eyes of the Italian Futurists mail communication represented an *additional* way of expression, not the only, privileged one, as was the case of mail artists in the 1960s when they attempted to find a substitute for commodified art objects. The postcards sent by Futurists often performed a promotional function, as they frequently contained typographical reproductions of easel paintings or sculptures. That was the case, for instance, with the *Futuristische Postkarten* (Futurist Postcards), which Ruggero Vasari, editor of the journal *Der Futurismus* and owner of the homonymous art gallery, published in Berlin in 1923. This series was particularly important, not only because it placed Italian Futurism in the context of the international avant-garde alongside groups such as *Der Sturm*, but also because it documented otherwise lost works, such as the 1911 painting *La Danse du "Pan Pan" à Monico* (The Pan-Pan Dance at the "Monico", 1909–11) by Gino Severini.

29 "En laissant à la poste le soin de compléter son œuvre par les étiquettes, les timbres, les tampons et les cachets [...] evènement postal et évènement artistique coïncident ainsi parfaitement." Lista: *L'Art postal futuriste*, p.. 37.

30 See Salaris: *Futurismo postale*, pp. 136–138.

31 See Belloli: "Mail-Art: Origini, posizioni, sviluppi"; and Belloli: "Armando Mazza: Precursore 'mail art' futurista d'assalto."

32 Crispolti: "La creatività 'postale' futurista", p. 14.

In contrast to the Futurist artists of the early twentieth century, Serge Segay and Rea Nikonova as the very first Soviet mail artists were confronted with considerable financial expense, as they confessed to Hans Ruedi Fricker in 1989: "Sending letters by registered mail is a very costly undertaking, and an artist who lives in the USSR can hardly afford it."[33] Nonetheless, Mail Art was for them "the only salvation", as indicated in the very title of this account, and Segay regretted that his Soviet colleagues did not sufficiently participate in this venture, despite the fact that this art allowed them to avoid "censorship, borders, state patronage".[34] Thus, when Rea Nikonova began to assemble *Double: International Mail Art & Visual Poetry Review* in 1991, the journal featured almost no Russian authors, with the exception of an old friend of the couple, the Sverdlovsk poet Evgeny Arbenyev, and a few other ephemeral contacts, such as German Iordanskii, Igor' Il'ichev, Andrei Rubtsov and Vladimir Babushkin. Many Italian authors, however, contributed to *Double*. During the first half of the 1990s, Segay and Nikonova networked not only with Baroni, Maggi, Vitacchio and Bertola, but also with Giovanni Broi, Enrico Marani, Umberto Stagnaro, Bruno Pollacci, Giovanni Donaudi, Bruno Cassaglia, Ametista Arnaldi, Olga Maggiora, Massimo Pattaro, Beatrice Forte, Luigi Zecchini and Piermario Ciani.

While Rea Nikonova assembled the submissions for the journal *Double*, she and her husband experienced difficulties sending their own works abroad, not only because of the expense involved, but also because of postal censorship. Whereas the Italian artist Marcello Diotallevi exposed the mechanisms ruling the postal exchange in his *Lettere al mittente* (Letters Returned to the Sender) in 1981, by intentionally making the addresses unintelligible or writing in imaginary alphabets, Segay followed Boris Konstriktor's suggestion to rework the red postcards that the Soviet mail service had returned to him, thus creating from the poof of non-delivering a visual composition. In both Diotallevi's and Segay's case, the mail service became a co-author of the work (similar to Pannaggi's collag-

33 "Briefe mit eingeschriebener Post zu verschicken, ist ein sehr teures Vergnügen, und kaum ein Künstler aus der UdSSR kann sich das einfach ohne weiteres leisten." Segay: "Mail-Art ist die einzige Rettung", p. 92.

34 Segay: "Mail-Art ist die einzige Rettung", p. 92. Segay and Nikonova contributed to *Total* no. 13 (which came out in January 1987) a remake of a page from a book by Stephen Ullmann. See Greve: "Zaumland", p. 456. When Segay showed the issue – edited by Nenad Bogdanović in the Serbian town Odžaci – to Andrei Monastyrsky in April 1987, they both discussed at length who in Moscow could be willing to contribute to the magazine, but struggled to come up with any names.

es), with Segay emphasizing the 'miracle' of a successful delivery, as attested by stamps and/or the recipient's signature.[35]

A successful exchange of letters could be observed in the correspondence that Segay and Nikonova initiated at the beginning of the 1990s with Anna Boschi Cermasi (*1944), a visual and mail artist from Bologna, who invited them to take part in her long-running thematic Mail Art projects. A result of this exchange was the re-elaboration of a reproduction of Leonardo's *Mona Lisa* from her personal archive. Rea Nikonova sent to Boschi Cermasi in 1992 a collage created from Leonardo's painting and ironical admixtures taken from Soviet political posters portraying revolutionary and party leaders (see Fig. 3a). Another interesting example is a text composition that paid homage to Ray Johnson. Here, the names "Ray Johnson" and "Rea Nikonova" are intertwined by letting the letters of their names share two columns, thus inscribing Nikonova's name into that of the legendary founder of Mail Art (see Fig. 3b).

Despite the problems that they had to face (including the lack of any means to copy or reproduce their works), Segay and Nikonova were not only very active in the Mail Art network, but also engaged in several attempts to introduce Soviet citizens to this new art form. In June 1988, Rea Nikonova delivered a lecture on Mail Art, but it is difficult to ascertain what kind of impact it had on the Society for Experimental Art in Leningrad. Segay's theoretical introduction to Mail Art printed just before his trip to Italy deeply impressed his correspondent John Held Jr., who summarized it in English:

> Mail Art has been written about many times, but mostly in general interest, rather than specialized art magazines. A notable exception was the appearance of the article, "Where the Secret is Hidden", by Soviet mail artist Serge Segay in the October 1989 issue of *Iskusstvo* (Art), the official publication of the USSR Ministry of Culture.[36]

Segay's knowledge of avant-garde styles and techniques not only facilitated the integration of the Transfurist couple into the international Mail Art network, as Charlotte Greve maintains,[37] but also helped members of this community to reflect on their own practice and to go beyond their usually spontaneous approach. From

35 "Our victory is the joy of discovering that our letters have reached the addressee. All of this would be humorous were it not so sad!" Nikonova: "Mail Art in the U.S.S.R.", p. 99. Diotallevi took part in the *International Zaum* project, initiated by Rea Nikonova and Segay; see Sigei: *Mezhdunarodnaia vystavka vizual'noi poezii*, pp. 26 and 33.

36 Held: *Archiving Advanced Art*, pp. 77–78.

37 "Especially their knowledge of Russian Avant-garde art (Chlebnikov and Malevič) and their active reworking of Zaum and Russian Avant-garde imagery, techniques, and poetry gave them a name within the network community." Greve: "Zaumland", pp. 460–461.

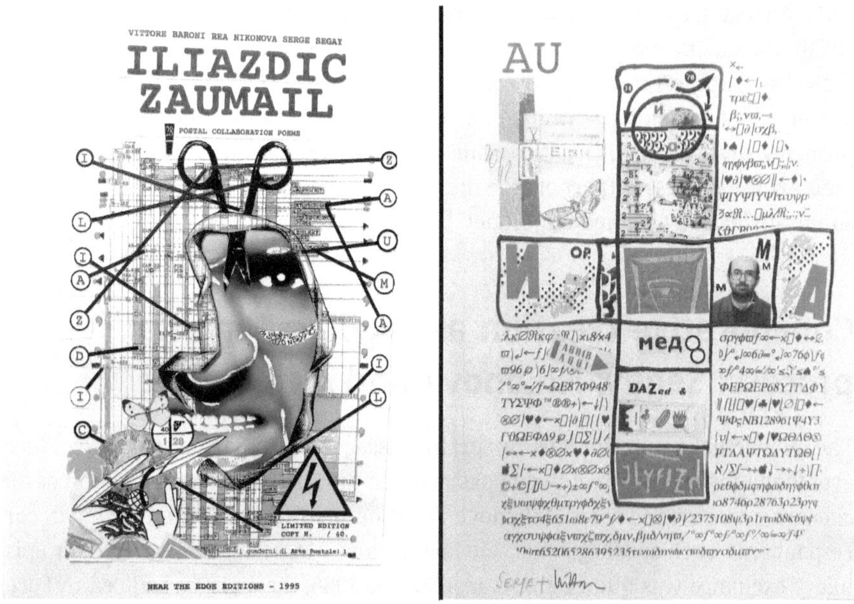

Fig. 3a: Cover of *Iliazdic Zaumail*, 1995. **Fig. 3b:** Serge Segay and Vittore Baroni: A page from *Iliazdic Zaumail*, 1995.

the mid-1980s onwards, there was a rush to commodify and commercialize unofficial Soviet art, which Segay and Nikonova fiercely objected to. They appreciated Mail Art for being a "decentralized expansive open gallery" or "an alternative gallery space outside the official art institution."[38] However, describing their engagement in Mail Art in these terms would be reductive. More essentially, they were attracted by the collaborative, anti-individualistic nature of Mail Art, which allowed them to carry out collective projects with other artists in an open-ended, horizontal, unpredictable manner. "The Belgian mail artist Guy Bleus maintains that the essence of Mail Art is collective creation resulting from communication and exchange",[39] Segay wrote in the introduction to the catalogue of the Mail Art Exhibition he curated at the State Historical and Regional Museum in Yeysk

38 Greve: "Zaumland", pp. 460–461.

39 "Бельгический мэйл-художник Гюи Блеюс считает сутью мэйл-арта именно коллективное творчество, являющееся результатом коммуникации и обмена". Sigei: *Meil-art: K vystavke v Eiskom muzee* [Mail Art: On the Exhibition at the Yeysk Museum), p. 14. A few months earlier, in January 1989, Rea Nikonova had curated the first exhibition of Mail Art in the Soviet Union, *International Mail Art Exhibition: Artists from 25 Countries*, at the Art School in Yeysk, where she taught.

(July–August 1989). Such a position resounds with the words of Vittore Baroni (1956), an Italian mail artist who at that time had already been corresponding with the couple: "From day one of my involvement in the Mail Art circles [...] I see no point in taking advantage of alternative communication systems just to push my own work (like a surrogate to the traditional art gallery circuits): in Mail Art the process is (part of) the message and the (brain) *massage* is something so unsatisfactorily carried out alone!"[40]

Collaborative creation as "egoless" mental process: Segay, Nikonova and *Arte postale!*

The intellectual group stimulus, or "brain massage" which Baroni sought to induce, eventually took the form of two books made in the Surrealist-Dada tradition of the *cadavre exquisite.* Segay and Nikonova never net Baroni – unlike other Italian correspondents, such as Maggi, Vitacchio and Bertola – in person. However, their epistolary exchange was quite intense. In 1987 and 1988, the artist, who lived in Forte dei Marmi and later in Viareggio, published a few of their visual compositions in three consecutive issues (nos. 56–58) of *Arte postale!*, the magazine devoted to Mail Art published in English from August 1979 to 2009. The works that Segay sent to Baroni in spring and August 1987, published as a special issue, *Connections mia*, consisted of stencils, rubber stamps and rubbings in coloured pencils, all fully handmade.

Interestingly, while introducing Segay to his readers as "my first correspondent from Russia", Baroni warned them that some of Segay's visual poems may not be in their copy. He consoled them: "Don't cry, you may find in its place one of the 25 fake 100$ bills printed by Arturo Fallico [...] or one of 20 'give up art' stickers by Tony Lowes."[41] Indeed, given the difficulties to gain access to suitable reproduction equipment in Yeysk, Segay could not fulfil Baroni's request for a certain number of copies to be included in issue no. 56 of *Arte postale!*. It is no accident that the composition published in no. 58 was produced by means of the *frottage* technique, which Segay intentionally revitalized to reproduce his own works without taking recourse to a Xerox machine.[42] Elements such as typescript, stencil

40 Baroni: "Iliazdic Zaumail Explained", p. I.
41 *Arte postale!* 56 (January–June 1987), p. 21.
42 See Segay: "Mail-Art ist die einzige Rettung", p. 93. The *frottage* technique (from the French *frotter*, 'to rub') involves a textured surface, on which a sheet of paper is placed. By rubbing a graphite-containing object (e.g. a pencil or crayon) over it, the raised portions of the surface below can be

prints, lettering done with solvents on photograph negatives, conferred to the Transfurists' contributions – according to Baroni – an old-fashioned, exotic allure, which contrasted with the visual experiments that he received from Western correspondents, who at that point could already rely on computers or professional Letraset.[43] At the same time, such an outdated appearance looked entirely appropriate for those "Eastern gifts" (as he called them) because they overtly referred to the history of Futurism and Dada.

In his turn, Segay gave wide publicity to *Arte postale!* in Russia. In a letter to Held, dated 30 April 1990 and focussed on the English summary of his *Iskusstvo* article on Mail Art, he regretted that he could not find in it any trace of what he wrote "about this edition and its history."[44] At the same time, in his booklet accompanying the 1989 collective exhibition in Yeysk, he defined Baroni as "the leader of contemporary Italian Mail Art."[45] Interestingly, in the catalogue, Segay provided a wrong translation of Baroni's provocative statement, an English phrase taken from one of his visual compositions, "In the age of brainless art the mail artist is king", and turning it into its very opposite: "В пространстве мозгового искусства мэйл-художник – король." (In the realm of cerebral art, the mail artist is king). This *lapsus linguae* probably originated from another quote from Baroni that Segay referred to on the same page: "Mail Art is mostly a mental process."[46]

Mail Art as a mental and creative process was at the core of the collaboration between Baroni, Segay and Nikonova. Eventually, it resulted in two books by the Tuscan artist: *Iliazdic Zaumail: Postal Collaboration Poems* (1995; see Fig. 4) and *Alphanumeric Scherzo: A Score of Visual Poetry for Trio* (2007). Both were realized by means of the *cadavre exquisite* technique, all the while taking advantage of Mail

transmitted to the sheet above. The method can be used to reproduce an existing image or text. Xerox duplication machines were invented in 1938 and made commercially available in 1959. While photocopiers revolutionized Western offices, the Soviet leaders worried about their ability to reproduce uncensored literature and they restricted access to them. *Samizdat* publishers therefore tended to use the slow carbon copiers (hectographs) or even more primitive methods of duplication.

43 Letraset was a company that manufactured sheets of typefaces, where letters could be rubbed-down onto surfaces. This dry transfer lettering system was popular amongst graphic designers and artists in the 1960s to 1980s.

44 John Held papers relating to Mail Art in the Archives of American Art, Smithsonian Institution, Washington, DC. Box 4, Folder 4, https://edan.si.edu/slideshow/viewer/?damspath=/CollectionsOnline/heldjohn/Box_0004/Folder_004.

45 Sigei: *Meil-art: K vystavke v Eiskom muzee*, p. 8.

46 "Мэйл арт – это прежде всего ментальный процесс." Sigei: *Meil-art: K vystavke v Eiskom muzee*, p. 3.

Art's new creative potential (especially in terms of unpredictability and aleatoric procedures).

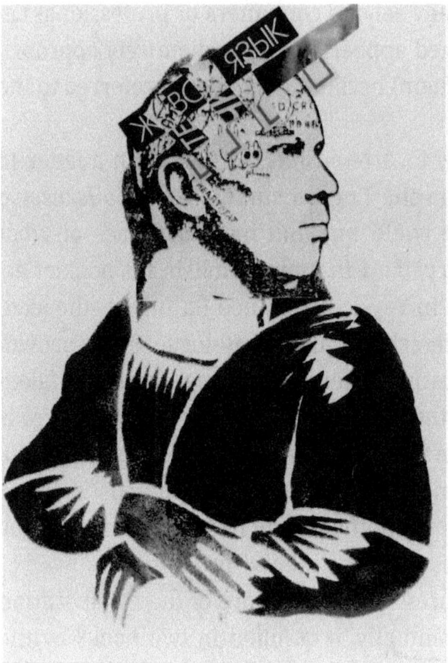

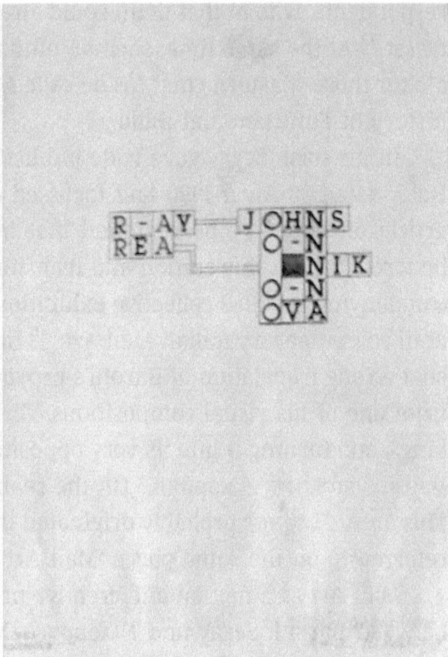

Fig. 4a. Rea Nikonova: Composition from Anna Boschi's personal archive, 1992. **Fig. 4b:** Rea Nikonova paying tribute to Ray Johnson. Composition from Anna Boschi's personal archive, 1992.

Interestingly, Baroni conceived the making of *Iliazdic Zaumail* as a trip back to his artistic roots in networks that belonged to the traditional mailing system,[47] while at that time (in the 1990s) he had already equipped himself with a computer for operating on the World-Wide-Web. This chronological / technological gap between Baroni and his Russian correspondents was fully compensated by their common attachment to values promoted by Mail Art, which Baroni summarized as "a generous spirit of community and cooperation, the freedom to break or disregard all rules (including the separation between 'high' and 'low' culture), a tendency to mix the most different media of expression and some wild utopian aspirations."[48]

47 Baroni: "Iliazdic Zaumail Explained", p. II.
48 Ibid.

As Baroni explained, *Iliazdic Zaumail* was the first of a series of handmade booklets which reflected both his "fondness for the good old scissors-work"[49] and his love for one-to-one "small publishing cooper-actions [*sic*]".[50] An aggressive, colourful aesthetics characterizes the whole book, which arose from previous collaborations with Nikonova. In 1992, Baroni and Piermario Ciani had sent stickers to Nikonova which she incorporated into her cover designs for *Double* nos. 3 and 4. In December 1993, Serge Segay organized a personal exhibition for Baroni at the Yeysk Museum, as he had already previously done for John Held Jr. (1990). In January 1994, Baroni sent a series of fourteen works to Segay, which were mostly made up of used international postage stamps and turned into collages. "In a few weeks", he explained, "Serge and his companion Rea sent me back my transformed works [...] introducing the underlying theme of an homage to Iliazd."[51] At that point, Baroni had never heard of Ilya Zdanevich, alias Iliazd (1894–1975),[52] although an exhibition of his books had taken place at the National Library in Florence and in other venues just three years earlier.[53] Meanwhile, the term *zaum'* had become Segay's trademark in the global Mail Art community, having been incorporated into the circular rubberstamp he used for his correspondence as a sort of visual signature.[54] While unintelligible to most of his fellow artists, the Russian abbreviation for *zaumnyi iazyk* (transrational language) succeeded in providing inspiration for a number of linguistic games. For instance, Segay's letters were sent from "Zaumland" by means of "Zaum mail", and his correspondents Angela Pähler, Peter Küstermann and Kimmo Framelius created a series of "Zaum post" stamps for *Double* no. 4, as an homage to Nikonova. In the booklet made in collab-

49 Ibid, p. I.

50 Ibid., p. II. The image of the scissors is programmatically replicated on the cover and re-appears inside the book in Nikonova's "architectural treatment" (i. e. graphic re-elaboration) of a letter written by Baroni, this time re-shaped in the form of a penis.

51 Baroni: "Iliazdic Zaumail Explained", p. II. Again, the quote is in his imperfect English.

52 Acknowledged as one of the poets who introduced Marinetti's theories in Russia long before the October Revolution, Iliazd issued in Tbilisi books such as *Ostraf pAschi* (Easter Island, 1919) and later in Paris *lidantIU fAram* (Le-Dantiu as a Beacon, 1923) under the imprint 41°. These books are considered masterpieces of typographic art and were later both appropriated and 're-made' by Segay. After Iliazd moved to Paris, he became a revered publisher of the *livre d'artiste*, working with Pablo Picasso, Alberto Giacometti, Max Ernst and Joan Mirò. For a short survey on him see Thomas J. Kitson's introduction to his translation of Iliazd's novel *Voskhishchenie* [Rapture] and Berghaus: "Ilya Zdanevich (Iliazd): Ambassador of Georgian Futurism."

53 See Calcagni Abrami: *I libri di Iliazd: Dall'avanguardia russa alla scuola di Parigi.*

54 Thanks to Segay, *Zaum* was included in the "Overview of words used in mail art & networking Part 2", released by TAM-publication (a publication of I.U.O.M.A. – the unofficial 'union' of mail artists – edited by Ruud Janssen). Here, *Zaum* is defined as a "system of poetics including creative languages". Greve: "Zaumland", p. 458.

oration with Baroni, "Zaumail" became a channel of truly transrational / transnational cooperation. In an article published by Hans Rudi Fricker, Rea Nikonova expressed her appreciation for such a possibility: "The back and forth from one artist to the other artist of works that gradually find completion is particularly valuable."[55]

As far as stylistics is concerned, in the pages made by Segay and Baroni, a thick black marker separates verbal fragments of *zaum'* texts from colourful collage inserts or stencils. By contrast, the visual compositions co-authored by Rea Nikonova and Baroni are easily recognizable for their chaotic, entangled appearance, with the individual interventions by the two artists hardly discernible. John M. Bennett, another of the couple's collaborators, wrote about their transrationalist, translinguistic approach that it usually results in "an 'egoless' literature, if we define 'ego' as the superconscious self that is constructed and observed in the everyday rational parts of the mind, that is our social being."[56] In its turn, the concept of "egoless literature" is, of course, reminiscent of the *Technical Manifesto of Futurist Literature*, where Marinetti demanded: "In literature, eradicate the 'I,' which means all psychology."[57]

The same 'wild' aesthetics of *Iliazdic Zaumail* also inspired *Accumulator of Networking Spirit*, a series of postage stamps created jointly by Baroni and Segay and then released by the Italian artist in 2001. While being perforated and 'issued' by Baroni according to a well-established practice in Mail Art, these stamps offered inspiration for a performative action. Namely, the authors urged their correspondents to join the "purifying mail action" promoted by Guy Bleus in the "Ethereal Open Network":[58] "a) hold one stamp in your hand thinking about a deceased Mail Art friend; b) burn the stamp; c) send the ashes to a living Mail Art friend".[59] Here a reference can be seen, perhaps, to the concept of the "eternal network" coined by the artist-sociologist Robert Filliou, who saw in Mail Art a method for forming fluid, ongoing global communities, "comprised of

55 "Das Hin und Her von Künstler zu Künstler allmählich sich vollendender Arbeiten ist besonders wertvoll." Nikonova: "Meine Idee ist die Überschreitung der Grenzen", p. 97.

56 Bennett: "The Translinguistic Collaborative Poetry of Serge Segay, Rea Nikonova and John M. Bennett", p. 364.

57 Marinetti: "Technical Manifesto of Futurist Literature", p. 110.

58 'Ethereal Open Network' or 'E.O.N.' was a term coined around 1985 for the international Mail-Art community and is also the name Baroni gave to his Mail-Art archive in Viareggio.

59 *Accumulator of Networking Spirit*, series of postage stamps, copy provided by the author Vittore Baroni.

people who may never meet each other in person"[60] yet exist and work together in dialogue.[61]

Alphanumeric Scherzo: A Score of Visual Poetry for Trio (published in 2007) followed the same procedure as "add to and return to", established by Ray Johnson, the founder of the New York Correspondence School or Art. The first 'movement' of this poetic trio consisted of one coloured table and three in black and white, started by Baroni and completed by Segay. The second one consisted of one coloured table and three in black and white, started by Baroni and completed by Segay. The mixing of interventions and the creation of a superindividual whole are reflected in the re-elaboration of the names of the participants,[62] listed on the cover as follows: Rea Baroni, Serge Nikonova, Vittore Segay. Furthermore, according to the idea of the 'opera aperta' (open work),[63] *Alphanumeric Scherzo* was open-ended: on the last page, the authors ask their readers to "play" the score and to send them a documentation of their performances. Baroni admits that no reactions were received, most likely because the book was released in an edition of only thirty copies. According to his idea of an 'eternal remaking', Segay reworked *Alphanumeric Scherzo* in 2012 as one of his very last editions. Here, he combined xeroxed pages on coloured paper and irregular, smaller-sized pages with collages in a fashion that resembles the artist book *Od'R*, which he made the following year for the portable library of the Metamorphosis project initiated by Albert Lemmens and Serge-Aljosja Stommels (LS publishers) in Nijmegen.[64]

---

60 Friedman: "Foreword: The Eternal Network", p. XV.

61 Again, this idea was anticipated by Marinetti in his manifesto *Le Futurisme mondial* (Paris, 1924), which contained a list of 68 supposed members of an "international Futurist movement" and, even earlier, by the *Directorio de vanguardia* (Avant-Garde Directory), published by the Mexican poet Manuel Maples Arce in the first issue of the leaflet *Actual* (December 1921). On the *Directorio* see the essay "The Infrarealist Movement and its Futurist Roots" by Claudio Palomares-Salas and Ángel Díaz Miranda in this issue of the Yearbook, pp. 227–252.

62 See Marinetti's experiments with collective writing (e. g., with I Dieci; Associazione letteraria Il Gruppo dei Dieci), which was very unusual at the time, and his contributions to *Il novissimo segretario galante* (1928) and *Lo Zar non è morto* (1929). For more info on Marinetti's concept of "scrittura a più mani" in a "Gruppo d'azione" see Comberiati: "I romanzi collettivi de 'I Dieci' negli anni Venti", and Medaglia: " 'Lo Zar non è morto': La scrittura a più mani nel futurismo."

63 See Eco: *Opera aperta: Forma e indeterminazione nelle poetiche contemporanee.*

64 See *De Metamorfose: 25 jaar Russische kunstenaarsboeken uit de LS collectie*, https://vanabbemuseum.nl/en/programme/programme/the-metamorphosis/index.html .

Transnational / transrational gifts

While Rea Nikonova and Segay explored Mail Art's creative potential as a co-operative procedure in their exchanges with Baroni, the collaboration with the visual poets Carla Bertola (1935–2023) and Alberto Vitacchio (1942) had a more traditional character. It mainly consisted of finished works which were included by Vitacchio and Bertola in the periodicals *Offerta speciale: Ricettario di poesia internazionale* and *Busta sorpresa*, which they edited in Turin from 1984 onwards, respectively. Close friends of Arrigo Lora Totino (1928–2016).[65] Bertola and Vitacchio saw works by Nikonova and Segay at the Mail Art Exhibition that Ruggero Maggi (1950) organized at his Milan Art Center in January 1990, a few weeks after Segay's trip to Italy. Impressed by Segay's and Nikonova's visual compositions, Bertola and Vitacchio wrote a letter to them a few days later, as they explained in essays devoted to their Transfurist friends.[66] Soon, Nikonova and Segay began to contribute to *Offerta speciale* and *Busta sorpresa*. The two compositions Rea Nikonova published in the May 1990 issue of *Offerta speciale* marked the beginning of a prolific collaboration inspired by the main principles that informed Transfurist experiments, namely, appropriation and transposition. This is evident from Rea Nikonova's graphic re-elaboration of letters she received from other authors, including Bertola and the 'environmental artist' Paolo Barrile,[67] or from *Sound Impressions*, Segay's re-elaboration of a poem written by Lora Totino in November 1995. This latter example is particularly interesting because he erased Lora Totino's text with his typical black marker strokes and then added little circles and drops with a ballpoint pen to create an alternation of rhythms. He appropriated an already existing text according to his principle of writing "the new directly into the old, over it, or chopping it off by taking away everything unnecessary bit by bit."[68] As a result, in the words of Charlotte Greve, Segay's intervention "overturns the status of previous

65 Similarly to Belloli, Lora Totino took the Futurist *paroliberismo* (poetry written in the style of Words-in-Freedom) as his point of departure, especially in the new genre of the *verbotetture* (verbtectures), then evolved towards intermediality and sound poetry ("poesia sonora"). It is very likely that Segay admired this shift toward performativity, since in the conversation with Ryklin he distinguished the "visualization of poetry" from "visual poetry" in the true sense of the word, which always contains an element of manipulation. See Segay and Ryklin: "O prirode vizual'noi poezii", p. 10.

66 See Vitacchio and Bertola: "Rea Nikonova & Serge Segay: Notes on a Journey Through Art", p. 488, and Bertola and Vitacchio: "For Rea and Serge", p. 344.

67 See *Offerta speciale*, May 1992 and May 1993. The contributions did not carry any individual titles.

68 Serge Segay, as quoted in Zhumati and Galeeva: "The Uktuss School: Coding Changes", p. 31.

texts as complete and untouchable works and of the author as the incontestable originator of this or that work of art."[69]

Furthermore, Segay established a peculiar, geographical triangulation while contributing to a review published in Turin (*Offerta speciale*) with his 'transposition' of a poet living in Turin (Lora Totino) who, in his turn, had a keen interest in experimental Russian literature and especially in *zaum'* poetry, as testified by his critical-historical anthology of sound poetry, *Futura* (1978), which included recordings of poems by Khlebnikov and Kruchenykh. Indeed, in Bertola and Vitacchio's art collection there is an interesting work by Lora Totino, *Dar Kruchenomu* (A Present for Kruchenykh), where lexical occurrences related to the poem's title and the verb *krutit'* (to turn around) are self-referentially assembled as an image of a vortex (see Fig. 5).

The title of this work resounds with *Dar Khlebnikovu* (A Present for Khlebnikov), yet another work by Lora Totino, significantly centred on the idea of a 'gift'. Such a concept was crucial in the Concrete Poetry / Mail Art network. Suffice it to mention the intentional ambiguity of Ray Johnson's statement "The New York School has no history, only a present", with the word 'present' signifying not only 'current time', but also 'gift'. In the catalogue of *Mezhdunarodnaia vystavka vizual'noi poezii* (International Exhibition of Visual Poetry], held in Yeysk in 1990, Segay defined Lora Totino's poem, specially written for the exhibition, "an original homage to the Russian poet and to the Russian viewers".[70] However, the catalogue did not contain any reproduction of it.[71]

Although Mail Art always remained at the periphery of Vitacchio and Bertola's œuvre, they took part in almost all issues of *Double*, as well as in the booklet that

69 Greve: "Zaumland", p. 456. The same critique of the Modernist principle of uniqueness and intangibility was rooted in Mail Art from its very beginning. In his theoretical introduction to the catalogue of the Mail Art exhibition in Yeysk, Segay observed that Ray Johnson's New York Correspondence School of Art was a parody of the New York School of American Abstract Expressionism, at that time already perceived as too 'serious' and thus destined for the museum. See Sigei: *Meil-art: K vystavke v Eiskom muzee*, p. 2.

70 "[...] своеобразный знак уважения к русскому поэту и русским зрителям", Sigei: *Mezhdunarodnaia vystavka vizual'noi poezii*, p. 10.

71 Apparently, Segay visited Turin on his Italian trip. The previously mentioned composition consisting of works by Maggi and letters from and to John Held Jr. includes a clipping related to a conference presentation that he seems to have delivered on 15 November 1989 in Via Lagrange 7 on the topic of "Transpoets and Underground Literature in the USSR between 1979 and 1989." The name of the venue is illegible; however, it is common knowledge that the Turin branch of the Associazione Internazionale "Amicizia" Italia-Russia (International Italy-Russia Friendship Association) was located at that address at that time. Interestingly, when he reworked the clipping, Segay overlaid the name of the association, "Italia-URSS", with a sticker by Maggi that had "USA" written on it.

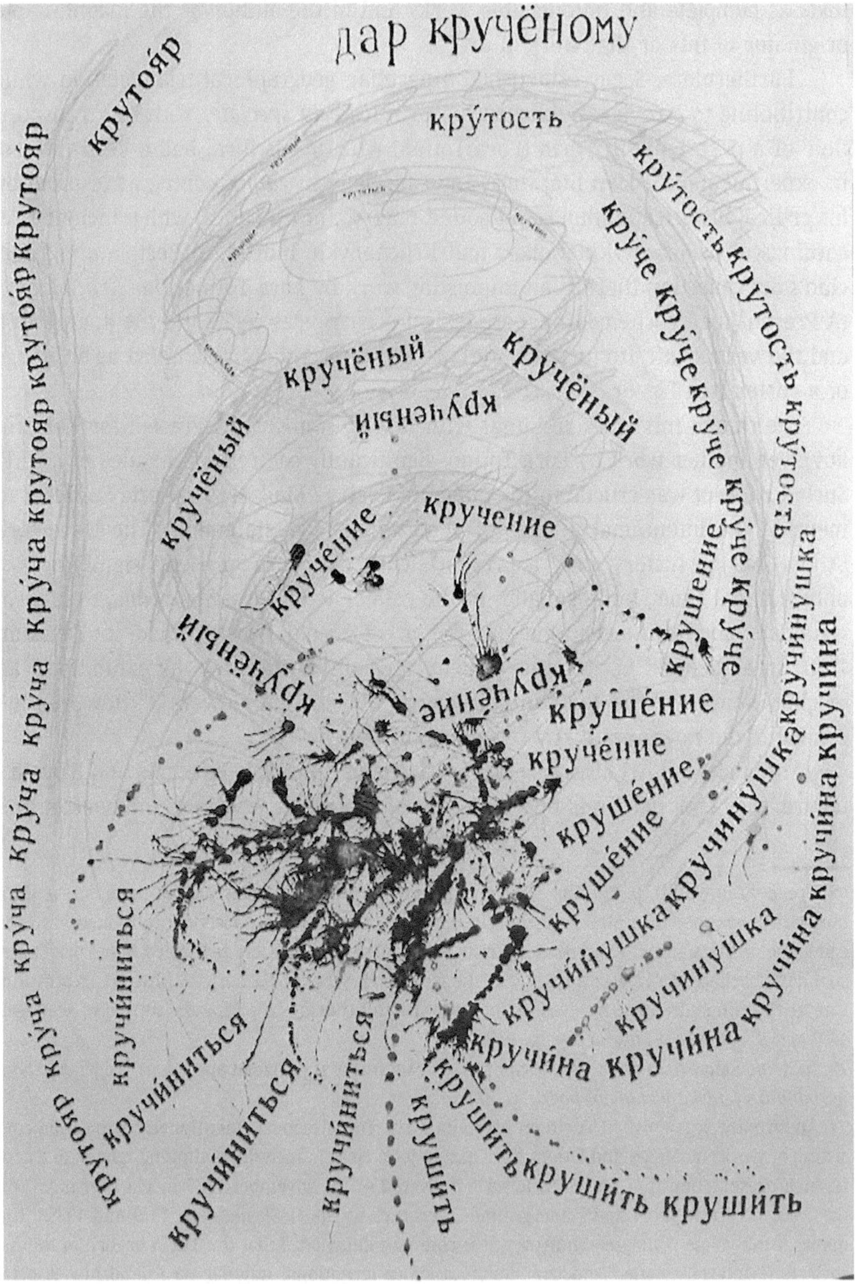

Fig. 5: Arrigo Lora Totino: *Dar Kruchenomu* (A Present for Kruchenykh, s.d.).

Rea Nikonova made when she curated the exhibition *Mezhdunarodnaia vakkumnaiia poeziia* (International Vacuum Poetry) at the Yeysk Museum in 1994. Whereas Nikonova and Segay's contributions to *Offerta speciale* and *Busta sorpresa* have already been described by Vitacchio and Bertola,[72] no analysis has been devoted yet to the visual compositions that Vitacchio and Bertola sent to Yeysk in the first half of the 1990s. For issue no. 4 of *Double*, for instance, Vitacchio provided a collage on translucent paper, while Bertola contributed a minimalist but refined assemblage of a small piece of yellow crepe paper with a wool thread – an element often present in her works – based on colour and tactile contrast.

The creative dialogue amongst the four artists was by no means confined to the sphere of Visual Poetry. A peculiar culmination of their exchange can be seen in the sound improvisation *Zvukovoi kvadrat* (Sound Square), realized when Vitacchio and Bertola visited the Transfurist couple in Kiel, in August 2007.[73] It consisted of several parts (*Quartet I, Quartet II, In and Out, Four Solos, Two Duets*) and was created in a variety of collaborations between Rea Nikonova, Alberto Vitacchio, Carla Bertola and Serge Segay. These pieces were all based on the simultaneous, obsessive repetition of Russian, German, English and Italian words, which the artists picked from dictionaries. These verbal improvisations, performed in a Dadaist style, are from time to time intertwined with different sound effects, for instance, the crackle of a sheet of paper or the performers' emphatic sighing and gasping. This results in a disintegration of individual languages as incarnated in dictionaries. The repetition of the same sounds, or words in an alphabetical order, create not only an impression of chaos, but also has quite surreal effects. Particularly funny is the duet by Bertola and Segay, where the logical connection between sentences is completely erased. Similarly impressive is Rea Nikonova's inventive shifts from one word to another. The Kiel performance is completed by an "homage to Rea&Serge", which Vitacchio and Bertola conceived in Turin in December 2007 while they were assembling the tracks of the performance on a compact disc. Interestingly, this final work involves not only the voices of the two poets, but also the noise tapes contained in a box made by Bertola in 1992, which Segay transformed into a *Noise Book* in 2003. Having inserted into the box four small balls wrapped in a newspaper, he was able to take part in the performance despite the geographical distance, thanks to the sound effects created each time the balls rolled inside the box.

72 In Vitacchio and Bertola: "Rea Nikonova and Serge Segay: Notes on a Journey Through Art".
73 Previously, in January 1991 Bertola and Vitacchio released a cassette tape entitled *Slushaite, kushaite* (Listen, Eat!) in their collection of sound poetry, *Pâté de voix*. It contained various readings and improvisations by Nikonova, Segay and Konstriktor recorded by Gerald Janecek in Yeysk in July 1985. See Janecek: "A Report on Transfuturism", p. 141.

Conclusions: A museum without walls

In 1988, Segay began his contribution to *The Works: The Block Island Art Magazine*, edited by Brian Salzberg in Rhode Island, which also featured Italian artists such as Maggi and Baroni. Issues nos. 3 and 4 of volume 3 (1989) carried a longer piece entitled "Mail Art Glasnost" which proposed "a U.S. – U.S.S.R. Friendship Mail Art Exchange", to be initiated by Crackerjack Kid (pseud. of Chuck Welch) and Nikonova and Segay, who also provided the names and addresses of nine mail artists living in the USSR.[74]

While Segay and Nikonova were unsuccessful in persuading other Russian artists to join the Mail Art network, their international exchanges kept intensifying to the point that they could organize an International Mail Art Exhibition at the Yeysk Art School (from 2–11 January 1989) and a personal show of works by Ruggero Maggi.[75] Alongside Baroni and other prominent mail artists such as Ryosuke Cohen, Hans Ruedi Fricker and Luc Fierens, Maggi was also present in the first Mail-Art project in the USSR (*Write Yourself*) that Rea Nikonova included in the exhibition she curated in January 1989 at the Yeysk Museum. These Mail Art exhibitions showed the need to reach beyond the inner circle of Mail Art and to aim for a broader audience.

In 1973, the 22-year-old Maggi opened the Milan Art Center, a gallery strategically located in Via Fatebenefratelli, near the Brera Academy of Fine Arts and many artists' studios. It is hard to ascertain whether Giancarlo Politi, the editor-in-chief of *Flash Art* was right when he called him "the youngest gallerist in the world". However, throughout the decades, Maggi pursued an intense exhibition programme, acquainting the Milanese audience with relevant artists active in the Visual Poetry and Mail Art circles. Following Segay's initiative in Yeysk, he also organized a show of the Transfurist poet in Milan, soon after he had met him in person.

When Segay visited Italy, he met Mail Art friends there and re-elaborated his visual compositions.[76] When he was invited by Marzaduri to contribute to the zaum' conference in Venice (see above, p. 138), Segay joined Fricker's "Tourism" Mail Art project as well. For his trip to Italy, in November 1989, Segay reworked

74 Their involvement in the Mail Art network proceeded in parallel to contributions to journals: in the same year, Nikonova and Segay's names appeared amongst those of well-established artists and authors of Visual Poetry in the second series of DOC(K)S, created in 1976 by Julien Blaine.

75 "Руджеро Маджи, уже знакомый русской публике благодаря его персональной выставке в Ейском музее..." ("Ruggero Maggi, already well-known to the Russian public because of his personal show at the Yeysk museum".) Sigei: *Mezhdunarodnaia vystavka vizual'noi poezii*, p. 15.

the rubber stamp he had been using as a signature since 1986. Its text "Serge Segay – Visual Poetry" was turned into "Serge Segay in Italy: Mail Art Tourism". The importance of this change is explained by Pierre Restany: "The artist's stamp, in fact, defines in its miniaturized space the points of convergence between the two components of artistic identity: presentation and representation",[76] and consequently "acts as the highly personalized identity card of such and such a creator."[77] Thus, Segay signalled with his new rubber stamp not only his participation in the transnational project of Mail Art, but also his physical presence in the space of the Western art system. Soon enough, he put Fricker's concept of "Tourism" as "execution of the Mail Art concept"[78] into practice by visiting Maggi in Milan: "Well, I was in Italy all November and I saw Ruggero in Milano",[79] he wrote to Held on 6 January 1990. A probable consequence of their meeting was the group exhibition entitled *Rea Nikonova, Serge Segay, Dobrica Kamperelić: Visual Poetry and Mail Art*, which took place at the Milan Art Center from 31 January to 13 February 1990. Teaming up with the Serbian artist Dobrica Kamperelić (1947–2020) is particularly significant: Maggi wanted to underline their common roots in Eastern Europe, where after the fall of the Iron Curtain in 1989 artists aspired to form part of Western art networks. Segay and Nikonova's work of the 1990s was a particularly significant sign of this new trend in global art.

Explaining his *Brain Cell* Mail Art project, Ryosuke Cohen said that mail artists were building the "museum without walls"[80] that André Malraux had dreamt of, and Rea Nikonova and Serge Segay (who contributed to *Brain Cell* from 1987 to 1989) certainly shared this utopian aspiration. On the other hand, exhibiting in *real* spaces such as Maggi's art centre allowed them to interact with very specific contexts. In this respect, it is emblematic that Maggi asked them to contribute to the exhibition he conceived in 1993 for the 60th anniversary of Piero Manzoni's birth (which was also the 30th anniversary of his early death). As an homage to the conceptual artist who spent most of his life in Milan and to his *Linea di lunghezza infinita* (Line of Infinite Length, 1960), Rea Nikonova created a *Vakumnaia*

---

76 "[...] le timbre d'artiste, en effet, définit dans son espace miniaturisé des points de convergence des deux influx de l'identité artistique: présentation et représentation." Laszlo and Reynaud: *Timbres d'artistes*, p. 11.

77 "[...] agit ainsi comme la carte d'identité hautement personnalisée de tel ou tel créateur." Laszlo and Reynaud: *Timbres d'artistes*, p. 12.

78 Fricker: "About Tourism", s.p.

79 John Held papers relating to mail art. Archives of American Art, Smithsonian Institution, Washington, DC. Box 4, Folder 4. https://edan.si.edu/slideshow/viewer/?damspath=/CollectionsOnline/heldjohn/Box_0004/Folder_004.

80 Cohen: "Mail Art – Brain Cell – fractal (1997)." https://artpool.hu/MailArt/chrono/1998/BrainCell3.html.

desiatimetrovaia poema (Ten Metre Vacuum Poem) which never reached Milan and remained in her archive. In April 2014, shortly after her death, Segay made a box for it as one of his own very last works (he himself passed away in September 2014). From his early veneration for Marinetti onwards, connections to Italy accompanied him until the end of his life.

Acknowledgement: This essay originates from a question Serge Segay asked me when I visited him and Rea Nikonova in Kiel in February 2010. He was curious to know whether Carlo Belloli had passed on copies of *Poèmes pour ballerines de grand théâtre de l'URSS* to public libraries in Milan, as he had promised to do. All my gratitude goes to Vittore Baroni, Carla Bertola, Anna Boschi Cermasi, Ruggero Maggi and Alberto Vitacchio. Without their help and their promptness in replying to my questions, I would not have been able to write this essay.

Bibliography

Archival sources

John Held papers relating to Mail Art, 1947–2018, bulk 1973–2013. Archives of American Art, Smithsonian Institution, Washington, DC. Box 4, Folders 1 to 5: Segay, Serge and Rea Nikonova – Eysk, Russia, 1988–1992. https://www.aaa.si.edu/collections/john-held-papers-relating-to-mail-art-6273; finding aid: https://sirismm.si.edu/EADpdfs/AAA.heldjohn.pdf (consulted 12/12/2022).

Printed sources

Baroni, Vittore: "Iliazdic Zaumail Explained." Vittore Baroni, Rea Nikonova, and Serge Segay: *Iliazdic Zaumail: Postal Collaboration Poems.* Viareggio: Near the Edge Editions, 1995. I–II.

Baroni, Vittore, Rea Nikonova, and Serge Segay: *Iliazdic Zaumail: Postal Collaboration Poems.* Viareggio: Near the Edge Editions, 1995.

Belloli, Carlo: "Poesia audiovisuale: Note per un'estetica dell'audiovisualismo." Pino Masnata: *Poesia visiva: Storia e teoria.* Roma: Bulzoni, 1984. 206–207.

Belloli, Carlo: "Armando Mazza: Precursore 'mail art' futurista d'assalto." *Futurismo-oggi* 16:11–12 (November–December 1984): 15–20.

Belloli, Carlo: "Mail-Art: Origini, posizioni, sviluppi." *Rassegna clinico-scientifica* 59:7–8 (July–August 1983): 30–31.

Belloli, Carlo: "Préface." Serge Segay. *Poèmes pour ballerines de grand théâtre de l'URSS.* Orilla: ASFi Editions, 1990. 5.

Belloli, Carlo, ed.: *Il contributo russo alle avanguardie plastiche = Russkii vklad v plasticheskie avangardy.* Exhibition catalogue. Milano & Roma: Galleria del Levante, 27 ottobre – 27 novembre 1964.

Bennett, John M.: "The Translinguistic Collaborative Poetry of Serge Segay, Rea Nikonova and John M. Bennett." *Russian Literature* 59:2–4 (2006): 362–374.

Berghaus, Günter: "Ilya Zdanevich (Iliazd): Ambassador of Georgian Futurism." *International Yearbook of Futurism Studies* 12 (2022): 445–464.

Bertola, Carla, and Alberto Vitacchio: "For Rea and Serge." Serge-Aljosja Stommels, and Albert Lemmens, eds.: *Bookwork: Rea Nikonova & Serge Segay.* Nijmegen: LS Collection Van Abbemuseum, 2016. 334–340.

Britsch, Florian, and Peter Weiss, eds.: *Le avanguardie artistiche e la cartolina postale.* Firenze: Cantini, 1989.

Calcagni Abrami, Artemisia, ed.: *I libri di Iliazd: Dall'avanguardia russa alla scuola di Parigi.* Exhibition catalogue. Firenze: Biblioteca Nazionale Centrale, 9 aprile – 11 maggio 1991; Orosei: Chiesa di Sant'Ignazio, 19 maggio – 9 giugno 1991; Castelluccio di Pienza in Val d'Orcia: Palazzo Piccolomini, 20 luglio – 4 agosto 1991. Firenze: Centro Di, 1991.

Comberiati, Daniele: "I romanzi collettivi de 'I Dieci' negli anni Venti: Fra la fine dell'avanguardia futurista e l'anticipazione del postmoderno." *Les Lettres romanes* 65:3–4 (July 2011): 449–472.

Compton, Susan: *Russian Avant-Garde Books, 1917–1934.* London: The British Library, 1992.

Crispolti, Enrico: "La creatività 'postale' futurista." Maurizio Scudiero, ed.: *Futurismi postali: Balla, Depero e la comunicazione postale futurista.* Rovigo: Longo, 1986. 13–16.

Fricker, Hans Ruedi: "About Tourism." *Clinch* 5 (1984): s.p.

Friedman, Ken: "Foreword: The Eternal Network." Chuck Welch, ed.: *Eternal Network: A Mail Art Anthology.* Calgary, Alb: University of Calgary Press, 1995. XV–XVII.

Eco, Umberto: *Opera aperta: Forma e indeterminazione nelle poetiche contemporanee.* Milano: Bompiani, 1962.

Greve, Charlotte: *Writing and the "Subject": Image-Text Relations in the Early Russian Avant-Garde and Contemporary Russian Visual Poetry.* Amsterdam: Pegasus, 2004.

Greve, Charlotte: "Zaumland: Serge Segay and Rea Nikonova in the International Mail Art Network." *Russian Literature* 59:2–4 (2006): 446–467.

Gurianova, Nina, Gerald Janecek, Margit Rowell, and Deborah Wye, eds.: *The Russian Avant-Garde Book, 1910–1934.* New York: The Museum of Modern Art, 2002.

Held, John Jr.: *Archiving Advanced Art.* Breda: Tam-Publications, 2020.

Hildebrand-Schat, Viola: "Anarcho-Futurism Revisited: The Magazine 'Transponans'." Serge-Aljosja Stommels, and Albert Lemmens, eds.: *Bookwork: Rea Nikonova & Serge Segay.* Nijmegen: LS Collection Van Abbemuseum, 2016. 68–85.

Hock, Beáta: "'162 Artists from over 50 Countries': Artistic Networking in the Mainstream and on the Margins." Katja Castryck-Naumann, ed.: *Transregional Connections in the History of East-Central Europe.* Berlin & Boston: De Gruyter, 2021. 113–132.

Janecek, Gerald J.: "A Report on Transfuturism." *Wiener Slawistischer Almanach* 19 (1987): 123–142.

Khardzhiev, Nikolai: *Pis'ma v Sigeisk* [Letters to Sigeisk]. Amsterdam: Pegasus, 2006. Amsterdam: Pegasus, 2006.

Kukui, Il'ia: "Laboratoriia avangarda: Zhurnal 'Transponans'." [Laboratory of the Avant-Garde: The Journal *Transponans*] *Russian Literature* 59:2–4 (2006): 225–59.

Klähn, Tim: "Rea Nikonova and the Legacy of Russian Futurism." *International Yearbook of Futurism Studies* 5 (2015): 395–424.

Laszlo, Jean-Noel and Chantal Reynaud, eds.: *Timbres d'artistes.* Paris: Musée de la Poste, 1994.

Lista, Giovanni: *L'Art postal futuriste.* Paris: Place, 1979.

Marinetti, Filippo Tommaso: "Technical Manifesto of Futurist Literature." F.T. Marinetti: *Critical Writings*. Ed. by Günter Berghaus. New York: Farrar, Straus and Giroux, 2006. 107–119.

Medaglia, Francesca: " 'Lo Zar non è morto': La scrittura a più mani nel futurismo." *Fermenti: Periodico a carattere culturale, informativo, d'attualità e costume* 42:240 (2013): 50–57.

Nikonova, Rea: "Mail Art in the U.S.S.R." Chuck Welch, ed.: *Eternal Network: A Mail Art Anthology*. Calgary, Alb: University of Calgary Press, 1995. 95–99.

Nikonova, Rea: "Meine Idee ist die Überschreitung der Grenzen." Hans Ruedi Fricker: *I Am a Networker (Sometimes): Mail-Art und Tourism*. St. Gallen: Kunstverein St. Gallen, 1989. 96–97.

Nikonova, Rea: *Protsess nad Shotlandtsem* [The Trial of the Scotsman]. Trento: [Edizioni Serge Sigej in Italia], 1989.

Piscopo, Ugo: "Significato e funzione del gruppo nel futurismo." U. Piscopo: *Questioni e aspetti del futurismo: Con una appendice di testi del futurismo a Napoli*. Napoli: Ferraro, 1976. 225–244.

Salaris, Claudia, ed.: *Futurismo postale = Futurist Mail: Collezione Echaurren Salaris*. Cinisello Balsamo (MI): Silvana, 2019.

Sigei, Sergei: "Dopolneniia ko Khlebnikovu." [Additions to Khlebnikov] *Transponans* 1 (1979): 5.

Sigei, Sergei: "Fragmenty polnoi formy." [Fragments of a Full Form] *Novoe literaturnoe obozrenie* [New Literary Review] 16 (1995): 296–309. Reprinted in *Russian Literature* 59:2–4 (2006): 149–163.

Sigei, Sergei: "Kommentarii k pis'mam N.I. Khardzhieva." [Commentary on N.I. Khardzhiev's Letters] Nikolai Khardzhiev: *Pis'ma v Sigeisk* [Letters to Sigeisk]. Amsterdam: Pegasus, 2006. 173–295.

Sigei, Sergei: "Kvintessentsiia stsenizma." [The Quintessence of the Scenic] *Transponans* 11 (1982): 63–91.

Sigei, Sergei [Segay, Serge]: "Mail-Art ist die einzige Rettung." Hans Ruedi Fricker: *I Am a Networker (Sometimes): Mail-Art und Tourism*. St. Gallen: Kunstverein St. Gallen, 1989. 92–93.

Sigei, Sergei [Segay, Serge]: *Poèmes pour ballerines de grand théâtre de l'URSS*. Orillia, Ont.: ASFi Editions, 1990.

Sigei, Sergei [Segay, Serge], and Ryklin Mikhail: "O prirode vizual'noi poezii." [On the Nature of Visual Poetry] *MDP No. 2. Vizual'naia i alternativnaia poeziia* [MDP No. 2: Visual and Alternative Poetry]. Moskva: Izdanie pri Klube avangardistov, 1988. 8–17.

Sigei, Sergei, ed.: *Meil-art: K vystavke v Eiskom muzee* [Mail Art: On the Exhibition at the Yeysk Museum]. Exhibition catalogue. Eisk: Eiski Muzei, July-August 1989.

Sigei, Sergei, ed.: *Mezhdunarodnaia vystavka vizual'noi poezii* [International Exhibition of Visual Poetry]. Exhibition catalogue. Eisk: Eiski Muzei, July 1990.

Sigei, Sergei, ed.: *Transpoets: Ry Nikonova, B. Constriktor, Serge Segay, A. Nik*. Trento: [Edizioni Serge Sigej in Italia], 1989.

Solt, Mary Ellen, ed.: *Concrete Poetry: A World View*. Bloomington/IN: Indian University Press, 1968.

Stommels, Serge-Aljosja, and Albert Lemmens, eds.: *Bookwork: Rea Nikonova & Serge Segay*. Exhibition catalogue. Den Haag: Museum Meermanno – Huis van het boek, 8 oktober 2016 – 22 januari 2017. Nijmegen: LS Collection Van Abbemuseum, 2016.

Vitacchio, Alberto, and Carla Bertola: "Rea Nikonova & Serge Segay: Notes on a Journey Through Art." *Russian Literature* 59:2–4 (2006): 487–505.

Weststeijn, Willen G.: "Introduction." Nikolai Khardzhiev: *Pis'ma v Sigeisk* [Letters to Sigeisk]. Amsterdam: Pegasus, 2006. VII–IX.

Weststeijn, Willem G: "Serge Segay (1947–2014)." *International Yearbook of Futurism Studies* 5 (2015): 467–473.

Zhumati, Tatiana, and Tamara Galeeva: "The Uktuss School: Coding Changes." Serge-Aljosja Stommels, and Albert Lemmens, eds.: *Bookwork: Rea Nikonova & Serge Segay.* Eindhoven: LS Collection Van Abbemuseum, 2016. 29–33.

Zvenigorodskaia, Natalia: "Rukopisnye knigi i kollazhi Sergeia Sigeia kak sposob issledovaniia poezii russkogo futurizma." [Handmade Books and Collages by Serge Segay: A Way to Study Russian Futurist Poetry] Georgii F. Kovalenko, ed.: *Russkii kubofuturizm* [Russian Cubo-Futurism]. Sankt-Peterburg: Bulanin. 197–201.

Internet sources

Baroni, Vittore: "Memo from a Networker." https://www.lomholtmailartarchive.dk/texts/vittore-baroni-memo-from-a-networker (consulted 12/12/2022).

Cohen, Ryosuke: "Mail Art – Brain Cell – fractal (1997)." https://artpool.hu/MailArt/chrono/1998/BrainCell3.html (consulted 31/3/2023).

D'Ambrosio, Matteo: "Di come Carlo Belloli, partendo dal 'Poema preciso' marinettiano, divenne un precursore della Poesia concreta." *ZRAlt!: Rivista multimediale della Zona Rossa* 6:23–24 (Winter 2018–Spring 2019): 1–19. https://zralt.angelus-novus.it/zralt-n-23-24-inverno-2018-primavera-2019/di-come-carlo-belloli-partendo-dal-poema-preciso-marinettiano-divenne-un-precursore-della-poesia-concreta/ (consulted 12/12/2022).

Weststeijn, Willem G.: "Sergei Sigei and Aleksei Kruchenykh: Visual Poetry in the Russian Avant-Garde and Neo Avant-Garde." *Arts* 11: 5 (#98) (2022): 1–21. https://doi.org/10.3390/arts11050098. (consulted 12/12/2022).

Mikhail Pavlovets

Konstantin K. Kuzminsky as a Neo-Futurist

Abstract: Konstantin K. Kuzminsky promoted his own poetic image and established a reputation of a Neo-Futurist in the world of literature by posing as an heir and expert of the Russian historical avant-garde. In his various artistic endeavours, he implemented systematic and archival approaches to the artistic legacy of the first third of the twentieth century typical of the neo-avant-garde. Kuzminsky did not specifically focus on creating his own individual way of writing poetry, but rather tried to use in his work the whole gamut of artistic forms and paradigms characteristic of the historical avant-garde. Therefore, he experimented with transrational poetry (*zaum'*) and the extreme minimization of art forms, up to his so-called 'zero' texts, as well as with 'super-texts', which were meta-genre, meta-text and meta-medium. Kuzminsky used the same approach for expanding the thematic range of his artistic work and gradually violated more and more artistic and ethical taboos of the literary establishment of that time, thus becoming a notorious provocateur and troublemaker. *The Blue Lagoon: Anthology of Modern Russian Poetry* became the culmination of this approach. It was a nine-volume collection with an impressive compilation of names, facts and events taken from the world of unofficial literature, most of which were only known in the literary and artistic underground at the time.

Keywords: Recuperation of historical Futurism in Russia (1970s-80s), unofficial creative life in Soviet Russia (1960–80s); underground literature in the USSR, Samizdat publications, Russian émigré literature

Unofficial literary life in the USSR in the 1960s–1970s was an 'underground' phenomenon (hence the Russian term 'andegraund') and was mainly centred on the country's two cultural capitals, Moscow and Leningrad. According to the poet Viktor Krivulin, "the period from 1960 to 1965 was marked by an intensified appropriation of the Acmeist[1] (mainly in Leningrad) and Futurist (in Moscow) heritage of Russian poetry. It was a period of apprenticeship, of assimilating what had already been accumulated, of building bridges between the present and the past".[2] Howev-

1 The Acmeists were a group of poets around Nikolai Gumilev, Anna Akhmatova and Osip Mandelstam who favoured a neo-classical form of Modernism.

2 "период с 1960 по 1965 годы отмечен усиленным освоением акмеистического (по преимуществу в Ленинграде) и футуристического (в Москве) наследия русской поэзии. Это был период ученичества, усвоения уже накопленного, наведения мостов между настоящим и

https://doi.org/10.1515/9783111318394-008

er, these two strands of inheritance – Neo-Acmeist and Neo-Futurist – were assigned to these two cities by Krivulin more on the basis of myths rather than facts: here the cultural, Apollonian, occidental Leningrad/Petersburg; there the spontaneous, Dionysian, oriental Moscow. In truth, Futurist and avant-garde traditions were no less present in Leningrad than in Moscow during the 1950s and 1960s. May it suffice to mention here the Neo-Futurists of the Leningrad Philological School (especially Aleksandr Kondratov),[3] and, from the next generation of poets, Vladimir Erl' (pseud. of Vladimir Gorbunov), A. Nik (pseud. of Nikolai Axel'rod) and Boris Konstriktor (pseud. of Boris Axel'rod). Konstantin K. Kuzminsky (1940–2015), who called himself a modern Futurist or Neo-Futurist,[4] also belongs to this circle that sought to revive the heritage of the Russian historical avant-garde.[5]

The early years

Konstantin K. Kuzminsky, who as a sign of provocation usually signed his work 'KKK', is one of the most remarkable figures of the artistic underground of the period from the 1960s to the first half of the 1970s, and later of the Russian emigration to the United States. The son of a schoolteacher and an artist, he was born on 16 April 1940 and studied at the USSR's prestigious English school No. 213 in Leningrad, which contributed to the future poet's rapid entry into the bohemian circles of the cultural capital. By Soviet standards, he possessed good knowledge of English and was therefore able to establish contacts with representatives of Western culture before his emigration and to easily adapt to a Western life after leaving his home country. Kuzminsky did not finish his higher education as he dropped out as a second-year student from the Faculty of Biology and Pedology of Leningrad University and afterwards from the Department of Theatre Studies at the Leningrad

прошлым." Kalomirov (pseudonym of Viktor Krivulin): "Dvadtsat' let noveishei russkoi poesii: Predvaritel'nie zametki" [Twenty Years of the Newest Russian Poetry: Preliminary Notes], p. 246.

3 The Filologicheskaia shkola emerged in 1954 during a meeting of a literary society at the Faculty of Philology in Leningrad and included both poets and painters including Aleksandr Kondratov, Mikhail Krasil'nikov, Yuri Mikhailov, Sergei Kulle, Leonid Vinogradov, Mikhail Eremin, Vladimir Ufliand and Lev Losev. This early Neo-Futurist group challenged dominant aesthetics and defied the world of official publishing. It was amongst the very first to be labelled 'andegraund' and had a pronounced actionist (aktsionistskaia) tendency.

4 See, for example, Kuzminsky: *Roman-gazeta* [Novel-Newspaper], p. 39, as well as the testimony of Dmitry Bobyshev in his essay "Molodoi Mafusail'" [Young Methuselah].

5 For more on the definition of the concept see Smirnov: *Metaistoriia: K istoricheskoi tipologii kul'tury* [Metahistory: Towards a Historical Typology of Culture], p. 143.

Institute of Theatre, Music and Cinematography. Nonetheless, he was well-read, erudite and had an exceptional memory, which earned him the nickname "walking tape recorder".[6]

To avoid accusations of 'social parasitism' – a criminal offence in the USSR – Kuzminsky tried his hand at many professions: he worked in a container factory, a distillery and a zoo; he became a stage hand at the Mariinsky Theatre, a house painter at the Russian Museum, a handyman at the Hermitage Museum's Utility Department. He also went on geological expeditions and visited the Caucasus, Siberia, the Urals, the Far East, etc., thus financing his bohemian life style.

Kuzminsky attributed a key rôle in his creative development as a poet to contacts with the translator and poetess Tatiana Gnedich (1907–1976), who had served ten years in labour camps. After her rehabilitation in 1956, she taught a poetry translation seminar at the House of Culture in the city of Pushkin, from which many prominent figures of the Leningrad underground emerged, including Iurii Alekseev, Boris Kupriianov, Oleg Okhapkin, Galina Usova and Viktor Shirali. Kuzminsky created a personal myth around this circle and even more around his short period of service as Gnedich's literary secretary. He contrasted her and her circle with another major figure in Leningrad's literary milieu, Anna Akhmatova and the so-called 'Akhmatova's orphans', the four young poets that were part of the inner circle of the great poetess: Dmitry Bobyshev, Joseph Brodsky, Anatoly Naiman and Evgeny Rein. In many of his texts, Kuzminsky conceptualized his sharply subjective and not entirely fair opposition to the Akhmatova circle as a confrontation between two schools in Russian unofficial poetry: Neo-Acmeism and Neo-Futurism. This clash between two types of literary positioning was stylized by him as a conflict between an 'aristocratic' literary establishment (allegedly ready to compromise with official literature) and a democratic (nonconformist) bohemia. Kuzminsky fought against the former literary tendency, yet paid respect to the work of some its representatives, such as Brodsky, Bobyshev, Rein and especially Okhapkin, whose company he sought even though he considered him "the founder of Neo-Neo-Acmeism".[7]

Kuzminsky as a follower of Russian Futurism developed 'akhmatovophobia' and attacked all those whom he considered to be part of her tradition (especially

6 Trofimenkov: "Takelazhnik, poet, 'brodiachii magnitofon': Ob antologii K.K. Kuz'minskogo i G.L. Kovaleva 'U Goluboi Laguny'" [Scaffolder, Poet, 'Walking Tape Recorder': About K.K. Kuz'minskii's and G.L. Kovalev's Anthology "At the Blue Lagoon"].

7 BLA 2 A, 486. Quotations from *The Blue Lagoon: Anthology of Modern Russian Poetry* will be given with a reference to the volume and page number(s): BLA 1 = vol. 1, 1980; BLA 2 A = vol. 2a, 1983; BLA 2B – vol. 2b, 1986; BLA 3 A – vol. 3a, 1986; BLA 3B – vol. 3b, 1986; BLA 4 A – vol. 4a, 1983; BLA 4B – vol. 4b, 1983; BLA 5 A – vol. 5a, 1986; BLA 5B – vol. 5b, 1986.

women poets). This stood in marked contrast to the rather amicable relationships within the historical avant-garde in Russia. Although the Cubo-Futurists engaged in literary controversy with their predecessors and competitors,[8] they usually distinguished between literary and personal relationships and sometimes even collaborated with the objects of their attacks. Kuzminsky, however, in the eyes of many cultural figures, gradually gained a reputation of a person who was not only destroying existing conventions but went beyond all bounds of propriety and, therefore, deserved to be boycotted.

Although Kuzminsky emphasized his adherence to the doctrine of anarchism, he usually avoided political declarations or participation in political activities. His anarchism was based on a rejection of any hierarchies and the Soviet version of 'liberalism' among the intelligentsia. In the eyes of the 'liberal' part of the Soviet intellectual élite, Akhmatova seemed like a victim of the system, but for the Neo-Futurist Kuzminsky – an expert on avant-garde, experimental and provocative poetry – she was a poetess guilty of building her own hierarchies, memorializing her literary epoch and her own rôle in it, of surrounding herself with admirers and devotees.[9] As he wrote in his note in his *Blue Lagoon Anthology:*

> In my opinion, Akhmatova had a very corrupting influence on contemporary young literature, infecting it with rotten Acmeism. The sympathy for Acmeism is understandable in modern times: a kind of nostalgia for the "Silver Age". There were no Futurists in Leningrad, so people went to Akhmatova.[10]

Early on in his career, Kuzminsky recognized that his rôle would not only be that of a poet but also that of a moderator, chronicler and archivist of the current oppositional processes in the literary underground. He was ready to take on the mission of reviving the tradition of the historical avant-garde of the first third of the twentieth century, which had been interrupted in the USSR during the 1930s, as well as restoring the position of the avant-garde in the cultural value system of his own time. He wanted to revise the established canons, but not just those in official culture, but also those in the alternative scene. Kuzminsky's diverse activities

---

8 See, for example, the first manifesto of Russian Cubo-Futurism, *Poshchechina obshchestvennomu vkusu* [A Slap in the Face of Public Taste], 1912.

9 An essay by Aleksandr Zholkovsky studies the problem of this area of her activity: Zholkovsky: "Anna Akhmatova – piat'desiat let spustia" [Anna Akhmatova – Fifty Years Later].

10 "На мой взгляд Ахматова оказала весьма тлетворное влияние на современную молодую литературу, заразив ее прогнившим акмеизмом. Симпатия к акмеизму понятна по нонешним временам: своего рода, ностальгия по 'серебряному веку'. Футуристов же в Ленинграде не было, поэтому ходили к Ахматовой." Kuzminsky: "Naden'ka Poliakova, Natal'ia Grudinina, Anna Akhmatova, Tat'iana Gnedich", BLA 2B, p. 178.

in the context of the neo-avant-garde did not just focus on novelty as a fundamental criterion,[11] but also on the task of systematizing literary devices and restoring the legacy of its predecessors:

> The legacy of the historical avant-garde is posited as the fact that the post-historical avant-garde era is characterized by the co-existence, availability and legitimacy of all imaginable styles, forms and techniques, the consequence of this absolute stylistic freedom being that no particular style can now claim to be more advanced or progressive than others.[12]

Therefore, it is difficult to separate the original work of Kuzminsky, his active participation in the current literary process, and the constant documentation of his own and others' life and work, sometimes in an imaginary dialogue with future researchers. Despite the image of a person prone to *épatage* and harsh in his judgments, he had a high level of creative energy: he was a regular at the 'cult' places of the Leningrad underground (the most important being the Saigon Café and the cafeteria on Malaya Sadovaya Street),[13] attended many notable cultural events, joined tactical creative alliances while maintaining an internal independence from all established groups.

Already at the beginning of the 1960s, Kuzminsky collected poems by unofficial poets, exchanging them with Alik Ginzburg, the publisher of the first samizdat almanac *Sintaksis* (Syntax, 1959–1960), together with his friend Boris Taigin. For Be-Ta, Taigin's favourite publishing house, he prepared the first samizdat books of the poets of the Akhmatova circle, Nikolai Rubtsov and others. In 1962, for example, he organized at the café Ulybka (The Smile) the first exhibition of a group of unofficial artists (Anatoly Vasilyev, Valery Ivanov and Alexander Yudin) with poetry readings by Viktor Krivulin and Evgeny Pazukhin. Following on from these readings, Kuzminsky and Boris Taigin tried to publish the second volume of the anthology *Prisma* (Prism).[14] However, in the same year, Kuzminsky compiled a more representative *Antologiia sovetskoi patologii* (Anthology of Soviet Pathology, 1962), which also included works by Kuzminsky.

Kuzminsky considered the time before 1957 as the first period of his literary œuvre,[15] with juvenile, mostly playful poetic experiments. He correlated it with the avant-garde's interest in naïve and children's writing, saying: "As a child, I

---

11 "One thing only seems to hold fairly constant in the vanguardist discourse and that is the theme of originality." Krauss: *The Originality of the Avant-Garde and Other Modernist Myths*, p. 157.
12 Schaffner: "On the Reconciliation of Tradition and Invention in Concrete Poetry", p. 109.
13 See Valieva: *Sumerki "Saigona"* [The Dusks of "Saigon"].
14 The first volume of the anthology, which Taigin prepared alone, never came out.
15 See BLA 2 A, p. 486.

was more of a genius than now. And I was then, of course, a formalist".[16] He published the first volume of his Futurist poems in 1963 with the Be-Ta company, in a print run of one copy.[17] As can be seen from the surviving texts of that time, he operated with a mixture of rather traditional forms, in the spirit of the Russian classical poetry of the nineteenth century, and Cubo-Futurist dissonances, absurdism and vulgarity, reminiscent of, for example, David Burliuk' experiments:

Идиллия	*Idyll*
Рыгая и урча желудком,	Burping and growling with our stomachs,
Мы шли по берегу Невы.	We walked along the Neva's shores.
Глаза твои, как незабудки	Your eyes like forget-me-not flowers
Сияли, ты сказала: "Вы..."[18]	Were shining, you addressed me: 'Sir...'

Polyglossia

Kuzminsky's *Poema o Kurtybae* (A Poem about Kurtybay, 1956) was written in a mixture of the Russian and Adyghe and anticipated the poet's later polyglottism. The use of words from various languages, both authentic and artificial, became one of his hallmarks and had been anticipated in the historical avant-garde. We can recall the stylized Finnish language in Elena Guro's poem *Finliandiia* (Finland, 1913),[19] or the Turkish language in Vasily Kamensky's "ferro-concrete poem" *Konstantinopol'* (Constantinople, 1914).[20]

While such examples were infrequent in the early twentieth century, polyglossia became for Kuzminsky a favourite technique, as well as the subject of poetological reflections, for example, in *S chego ia 'zagovoril na iazykakh'?* (Why Have I Begun 'Speaking in Tongues'?, s.d.): "Charles de Coster and Hašek with their polyglossia literally stuffed me with foreignness. What was a literary device for them, turned into a method for me".[21] The poet collected dictionaries of exotic languages, for example, Tregear's *Maori-Polynesian-English Dictionary* of 1891,[22] and he creat-

16 "в детстве я был гениальнее, чем сейчас. И был я тогда, естественно, формалистом". BLA 2 A, p. 486.

17 See BLA 2 A, p. 488.

18 BLA 2 A, p. 490.

19 "Хей-тара! / Тере-дере-дере... Ху! / Холе-кулэ-нэээ". Guro: *Nebesnye verbliuzhata* [The Baby Camels of the Sky], p. 140.

20 "НАРЭ / РАМЗIЭ / АМЗА / СААДЭТЫ / ЦХАРЭ". Kamensky: *Nagoi sredi odetykh: Izdanie rossiiskikh futuristov* [Naked Among the Clad: Publication of Russian Futurists], p. 1.

21 "Шарль де Костер и Гашек, со своей полиглоссией, буквально набили меня иностранщиной, которая, у них будучи приемом – у меня вылилась в метод". BLA 2 A, p. 538.

22 See BLA 2 A, p. 538.

ed a whole body of texts that incorporated foreign words into them, ranging from individual words from one or several languages to texts entirely written in foreign tongues such as Ukrainian or English, or in a mixture of many languages. And while some of these texts are discursively intelligible and coherent, others resemble Futurist *zaum'* (transrational) poetry. In a letter written probably on 11 July 1979, Kuzminsky explained to the poet and translator Georgy Ben:

> One should write incomprehensibly, and so now I simply switched to the dialects of Zanzibar and Zambia. Otherwise, it can happen that you write some absurdity in French, and some b*tch knows French, thinks "how surreal is that?" and translates it. Of course it's surreal when I combine words not according to their meaning but according to their sound.[23]

The late 1950s and the first half of the 1960s became for Kuzminsky a period of prolific creativity that propelled him to expand the scope of his search for new forms. He gravitated towards the genre of poetry and wrote, for example, *Stekliannye guby* (Glass Lips, 1959), *Tuman* (Fog, 1959) or the monosyllabic poem *Sister Death* (1959). Moreover, he developed his own genre of a *stostrochnik* (hundred-liner), built on a purely formal limitation of their length as, for example, *Taiga* (1960) and, without a single punctuation mark, *Goluboe* (Sky-Blue, 1960). But he also wrote ordinary poems, a good 3,000 altogether, sometimes in *vers libre*, but by his own admission, these "poems, by my present standards, are nowhere near good enough".[24]

Most of these works were written in the village of Rodionovo in the Tomsk region. Typical of these was the poem *Tom'* (Tom, 1962), which "absorbed all the 'trends' of Futurism and related movements: Gorodetsky of the *Iar'* (Spring Corn) period, quotes from *Pis'ma o russkoi poezii* (Letters on Russian Poetry) by Nikolay Gumilev, Velimir [Khlebnikov] and Kruchenykh, Kamensky (especially), etc."[25] He also wrote "books on ethnography, biology, ecology, zoology, anthropolo-

---

23 "Писать надо непонятно, поэтому сейчас попросту перешел на диалекты Занзибара и Замбии. А то по-французски пишешь абсурд, а какая-нибудь бл*дь французский язык знает: как это у вас сюрреалистически получается, и переводит. Ясно, сюрреалистически, когда я слова не по значению, а по звучанию сопрягаю." Kuz'minskii and Ben: "Perepiska" [Correspondence].

24 "добрые 3000 стихов, по теперешним моим меркам – никуда не годятся". BLA 2 A, p. 476.

25 "...вобрала в себя все 'трэнды' футуризма и смежных: Городецкого (периода 'Ярь' – цитаты из 'Писем о русской поэзии' Н.С.Гумилева), Велемира [Хлебникова] и Крученых, Каменского (особенно)." *Iar'* [Spring Corn, 1906] was the first book by Sergei Gorodetsky, written before his Acmeist period and based on vernacular language and folk-song imagery. *Pis'ma o russkoi poezii* [Letters on Russian Poetry, 1923] was a collection of literary-critical works by the Acmeist poet Nikolay Gumilev.

gy, diaries of all travellers".[26] In this regard, Kuzminsky's work was at the intersection of two key neo-avant-garde trends, with their materials and vocabulary serving him as a source of inspiration: active reflection on the work of his vanguard predecessors, and utilization of his knowledge of natural sciences. Some of these poems were included by Kuzminsky in his first samizdat collection, *Assorti* (Mixed Platter, 1963), the very title of which speaks of the eclectic nature of the author's "'experiments with excrements' in the field of form over the previous four years".[27] Only some of the works included in *Assorti* were re-published by Kuzminsky, but later in his anthology *The Blue Lagoon* he reprinted a detailed review of the collection by the linguist and writer Lev Uspensky, to which he added his own comments. These works are thus a mixture of his own writings and a refraction of them through someone else's perception, as well as the author's dialogue with this perception.[28]

Versification of sound

Lev Uspensky's friendly remarks in this review were the reason for Kuzminsky to arrive at an important conclusion about his own principles of poetry, echoing his characterization of his own polyglossia: "True, I have become a purely 'sonic' poet, rejecting almost completely the 'visual' image [...], which I am incapable of 'due to blindness'. However, thanks to Lev Vasil'evich [Uspensky], the semantic context has also become extremely important".[29] According to Natalia Likhtenfeld, Kuzminsky "began to develop already in the early 1960s a theory of 'sound versification'"[30] which, apparently, formed the basis of Kuzminsky's neo-avant-garde method.

Igor' Smirnov wrote that Futurism was a precedent-setting movement for the Russian avant-garde because if gave the artistic sign the property of a material

26 "книги по этнографии, биологии, экологии, зоологии, антропологии, дневники всех путешественников". BLA 2 A, p. 495.

27 "замешал в нем все мои 'эксперименты с экскрементами' в области формы за 4 предыдущих года." BLA 2 A, p. 508.

28 See BLA 2 A, pp. 508–514.

29 "Правда, я стал чисто 'звуковым' поэтом, отринув почти полностью 'зрительный ' образ [...], к коему не способен 'по слепоте', но, Льву Васильевичу благодаря – еще и семанти[че]ский ряд чрезвычайно стал важен". BLA 2 A, p. 514.

30 "уже в начале 1960-х годов стал развивать теорию 'звукового стихосложения'. Likhtenfel'd: "Saigonavty – pliashushchie zvezdy" [The Saigonauts – Dancing Stars], https://poetograd.ru/nomer.php?id=2508.

thing.[31] Artistic 'meaning' is created not by means of *what* is articulated, but *how* it is articulated, i. e. by its vocal, graphic or mimic-gestural quality. The external, material side of the sign is identified with its ideal aspect.[32] It was this attitude towards the materialization of the written sign, towards a formal experiment that the Russian neo-avant-garde inherited from the historical avant-garde, opposing it to the attitude towards 'meaning' in neoclassical and neo-avant-garde movements (including the Neo-Acmeism of the Leningrad School of Poetry).

At the same time, the radical materialization of the written sign – including *zaum'* – was for Kuzminsky only one of his creative strategies. He did not strive for the 'purity' of the method but demonstrated the freedom to handle a wide variety of artistic forms, combining in his work the most traditional of them with the most daring experimental ones. Actually, his public image was based on his concept of *zhiznetvorchestvo* (life creation), an idea that had arisen within Symbolism and was central to Russian Futurism.[33] Kuzminsky appeared in public places in an old-fashioned bowler hat or with a shaggy Caucasian sheep hat (*papakha*) or in even more exotic attire, thus appropriating in an eclectic manner images and traditions of the past and causing conflict and confrontation with his acts of presentation. According to Bürger, "the avant-garde [...] made artistic means recognizable in their generality because it no longer chooses means according to a stylistic principle, but avails itself of them as means".[34] Consequently, Kuzminsky was amused when editors selected for publication the fragments of his works which seemed to them 'traditional' or 'classical'.[35] As the traditional character of these texts was not

---

31 "...сообщил смыслу свойство вещи, материализовал семантику художественного знака, уравнял идеологическую среду с эмпирической". Smirnov: *Khudozhestvennii smysl' i evolutsiia poeticheskikh sistem* [The Artistic Meaning and Evolution of Poetic Systems], p. 103.

32 "'Художественный смысл' – это не то, чтó артикулируется, а то, кáк артикулируется, сам звуковой, графический или мимико-жестикуляционный акт. Внешняя, материальная сторона знака отождествляется с его идеальным аспектом". Smirnov: *Khudozhestvennii smysl' i evoliutsiia poeticheskikh sistem*, p. 103 f.

33 On the concept of 'Life Creation' in the Russian avant-garde, especially Khlebnikov and Mayakovsky, see Ioffe: "Simvolicheskii kapital posmertnogo naslediia Khlebnikova i Maiakovskogo sub specie avangardnoi performativnosti skandala: Semioticheskaia pragmatika avangardnogo povedeniia i zhiznetvorchestva." [The Symbolic Capital of Khlebnikov and Mayakovsky's Posthumous Heritage in the Light of the Avant-garde Performativity of the Scandal: The Semiotic Pragmatics of Avant-garde Behaviour and Life-Creation]

34 Bürger: *Theory of the Avant-Garde*, p. 19.

35 Kuzminsky wrote about this approach to the publication of the fragments of his poem *The Tower of Babel:* "Там, посередке, имелось и псевдоклассицистическое 'Осеннее троеглавие', которое 'Континент' по тупости и безграмотности редколлегии, принял за 'диссидентское' и тиснул без спросу. [...] А мне его даже стало противно перепечатывать: уж раз понравилось им – ..." ("There, in the middle, there was also a pseudo-classical 'Autumn three-headedness', a conscious authorial choice, Kuzminsky placed them into new contexts and thus 'defamiliarized' them, making them equivalent to his most hermetic texts.

Thematic books

After a while, Kuzminsky became sceptical of the approach on which the *Assorti* collection was based, as is evident from his later correspondence with editors of his works. Instead of mixing texts of a heterogeneous nature within one collection, he cultivated "an attempt to somehow sort [the texts that are being selected] according to topics and techniques",[36] citing a list of such supertextual units:

> tower // poems for sleep (rukonog) // gratis (full) // 3 poems of hermeticism // neshtiaki (belkin, mouse) / fir-tree // 3 poems of antisemitism / birobidzhan // vazamba mtuta / concept fly [a contamination of the title of Chukovsky's children's fairy tale "The Mukha-Tsokotukha" and the word "conceptualism"] / news from a word of mouth // tat'iana? / faina // solovki / arkhangelsk / ale versh / oleanders in livadia / the livonian war // CONCEPTS / poetry of dispersion / deep underground // mother anarchy // about this.[37]

Issuing "thematic books", as the poet himself called them,[38] that is, uniting disparate works in accordance with one formal-structural or thematic principle, was not uncommon amongst neo-avant-garde poets. The fluid nature of such types of works can be detected, for example, in *Moi troitsy* (My Trinities, no later than 1975) by Aleksandr Kondratov, a Neo-Futurist poet of the above-mentioned Philological School. Kuzminsky's attempt to systematize his entire œuvre, including

---

which 'Continent', due to the stupidity and illiteracy of the editorial board, took for 'dissident' and stole without asking. [...] And since they liked it, it even became disgusting for me to reprint it.") BLA 2A, p. 530.

36 "попытку как-то рассортировать [отбираемые тексты] по темам и техникам". Letter to Asia Maizel' from 5 June 2000 in Kuzminsky: *Ne stol'ko o poetike, skol'ko – ob etike: Kniga pisem* [Not That Much About Poetics as – About Ethics: A Book of Letters], pp. 233–234.

37 "башня // стихи на сон (руконог) // гратис (полный) // 3 поэмы герметизма // нештяки (белкин, мышь) / ель // 3 поэмы антисемитизма / биробиджан // вазамба мтута / муха-концептуха / вести из известий // татьяна? / фаина // соловки / архангельск / але верш / олеандры в ливадии / ливонская война // КОНЦЕПТЫ / поэзия рассеяния / глубоко под землей // анархия мать // про ето." Kuzminsky: *Ne stol'ko o poetike*..., p. 234. Furthermore, he commented on this: "это вот была попытка вспомнить и разбить себя по "циклам", сделанная ровно 12 лет назад" ("that was an attempt to recall and break myself into 'cycles', made exactly 12 years ago"). Kuzminsky: *Ne stol'ko o poetike*..., p. 234.

38 See BLA 5B, p. 466.

not yet written texts united by one or another dominant principle,[39] was combined with the practice of building his books around a specific technique or genre similar to the collections of poetry by Genrikh Sapgir, a member of the Lianozovo School in the 1940s.[40]

Thus, the book *Gratis* (Free of Charge, 1973) is inspired by the Futurist practice of collaboration between a poet and a visual artist, in this case Konstantin Kuzminsky as author of the texts and A.B. Ivanov (unidentified artist known only by that name) as author of the drawings, who made this book look like an example of supra-syntactic *zaum'*[41] or, as the author himself defines it, "aesthetic absurdity".[42] According to Kuzminsky, "texts written in slang and in the clumsy language of the 'techies' (*iteers*[43]) were transcribed into choral melodies".[44] Apparently, the rhythmic pattern of these absurdist texts was formed by already existing melodies.[45] Another book, *Vazamba Mtuta* (1976), is a typical example of Kuzminsky's *zaum'* polyglossia. As he himself said, "I stuffed the text of *Vazamba Mtuta* with the dialects of Zanzibar, Zambia and Uganda, from the diaries of Miklouho-Maclay – I made in Papua 'A good Russian man Maclay-Miklouho'. I was immediately forgetting the meaning of the words but the sound would remain".[46]

---

39 Kuzminsky included this plan in BLA 1, pp. 235–237.

40 The Lianozovo School was one of the first underground groups in the second half of the 1940s. For more on this see Orlitskii: "Vvedenie v poetiku Sapgira: Sistema protivopostavlenii i strategiia ikh preodoleniia" [Introduction to Sapgir's Poetics: The System of Oppositions and the Strategy of Overcoming Them], pp. 324–325, 328.

41 More on that in Janecek: "A Zaum' Classification."

42 BLA 2 A, p. 296.

43 From ITR, the Russian abbreviation for 'engineering and technical worker'. Kuzminsky used this word, not without disdain, to describe representatives of the technical intelligentsia, the main audience of the bohemian underground. It served as an analogue to the 'pharmacists', the middle- and upper-class patrons of the Stray Dog cabaret (1911–1915), who liked to be seen as mingling with the bohemia and true avantgardists. See Livshits: *Polutoroglazyi strelets: Stikhotvoreniia. Perevody. Vospominaniia* [The One and a Half-Eyed Archer: Poems. Translations. Recollections], pp. 509–510.

44 "тексты, написанные сленгом и корявым языком итээров, перелагались на хоральные мелодии". BLA 2 A, p. 296.

45 A similar method of writing texts to other people's tunes was practiced by Aleksei Khvostenko, and Kuzminsky himself often wrote his lyrics to existing songs: the 'Ukrainian' part of the poem *The Tower of Babel* (*Чи Ти Кохана…*; *Are You loved…*) continues the folk song *Ой Ти Дивчина… (Oh, You Lass…)*, heard from the heroine-addressee of the poem Larisa Voitenko.

46 "надрал я текст 'Вазамба Мтута' диалектами Занзибара, Замбии и Уганды, из дневников Миклухо-Маклая – сделал на папуа 'Тамо русс Маклай-Миклухо' ('Хороший русский человек Маклай-Миклухо.') Значение слов я тут же забывал, но звучание – оставалось." BLA 2 A, p. 541.

Twijanzi janzi o katakiro
Kabaka kadzi Uwuma mtiro
Uzoga gamba mga Muiwanda
Kagehi Manwa Uchambi chongo[47]

Interesting examples are Kuzminsky's two samizdat books *Neshtiak* (1972, re-published in 1984 by his own publishing company Podval (The Cellar) in New York and *El': Vtoraia kniga neshtiakov* (Fir-Tree: The Second Book of 'Neshtiaks', 1972; re-published when Kuzminsky was living in Texas between 1976 and 1981). *Neshtiak* is a slang word that usually means either 'something very good, excellent, of the highest quality, which is a source of positive emotions' or, in a narrower sense, 'leftovers' (or even 'any food');[48] it also has a predicative usage, meaning 'good, excellent'.[49] The book *Neshtiak* consisted of seventeen works, which were united by the fact that they were all written, according to the author's commentary, when he was a patient at the Bekhterev Psychoneurological Research Institute in Leningrad. The absurd nature of the texts in the book, the very form of which was motivated by Kuzminsky's drug addiction, correlates to the well-known avant-garde technique of defamiliarization by means of irrational or incongruous images.

The form of these poems is rather close to the Futurists' 'stepladder verse' (*lesenka*), where the verse is divided into segments arranged like the descending steps of a ladder.[50] However, the absence of punctuation marks and capital letters also resembles the 'constellations' of Concrete Poetry, as well as experiments with this form by Vladimir Erl', to whom the book is dedicated and to whom Kuzminsky attributed "the healthy nature of Oberiutism and Futurism".[51] The lexical composition of the texts included in the book comprises the jargon of drug addicts or – more broadly – youth slang, medical terms (associated with the treatment of addictions – "Antabuse", "Apomorphine", "Pipolphen"); musical and literary names (Jimmy Hendrix, the Beatles, F. Scott Fitzgerald; Albert Camus, Cecil Day-Lewis), etc. Most of the texts have an agrammatical structure, the words are connected with each other more by means of paronymy or anagramming ("фиакр сел в

47 BLA 2A, p. 541.
48 Mokienko: *Bolshoi slovar' russkogo zhargona* [Large Dictionary of Russian Jargon], pp. 383–384.
49 Ibid., p. 383.
50 See Lawton and Eagle: *Russian Futurism through Its Manifestoes, 1912–1928,* p. 15.
51 "здоровое начало обериутства и футуризма". BLA 4B, p. 269. ОБэРИу – Объединение реального искусства (The Association for the Real in Art) was a short-lived avant-garde collective, founded in 1928 by Daniil Kharms and Alexander Vvedensky. It also included some Futurist writers and was notorious for its provocative activities, which in many ways foreshadowed Kuzminsky's public performances.

факир" – the fiacre sat into a fakir), which again brought Kuzminsky close to Khlebnikov and Kruchenykh.

The second book, *El': Vtoraia kniga neshtiakov* (Fir-tree: The Second Book of Neshtiaks, 1972) was a collection of minimalist poetry, for the most part 'transrational'. It employed extremely small forms, ending (like the book *Neshtiak*) with a 'single-point' work that occupies a whole page. It makes *Fir-tree* related to the book of the Ego-Futurist Vasilisk Gnedov *Smert' iskusstvu* (Death to Art, 1913), which consists of fifteen one-line, one-word and even one-letter poems. It ends with the *Poema kontsa* (Poem of the End), which consists only of the title *Poem of the End (15)* on the last page of the book[52] (and which Kuzminsky published separately in his own small press Podval in New York in 1984).[53]

Most of the texts in *Fir-tree* are based on the same technique as the first book of *Neshtiaks* – on paronymic 'attraction' (especially evident in "ребродроб / добро б / бодр", "мыш / клекочет / течь/ка/" – rib crush / good b / cheerful, mouse / scream / flow / ka /, etc.). But there are also interesting experiments with the visual appearance of the letters of a word (for example, the lowercase "a" in the word "KAZaN'" typed in capital letters allows to see the word *казнь* 'execution' inside of the name of the city), with its phonics (in the word "треух/голка" the word *треух* (a type of hat worn by Russian commoners), antinomic to *треуголка* (a type of hat worn by the aristocracy), appears through the accentuation of the South Russian pronunciation). In addition, different ways of ruining of poetic language are used: semantic (the use of *zaum'* words such as "вывр", "сарф", "мр" – vyvr, sarf, mr), grammatical ("сырк" – by cheese?), orphographic ("мыш", "Өеодор" – mouse, Theodor), up to the ultimate minimalization of the verbal form ("мр", "а / е", "ъ").

The Tower of Babel

The period of Kuzminsky's mature work began in 1967, when he returned to an active literary life after a pause that lasted from 1964 to 1966. It was in the late 1960s and the first half of the 1970s that Kuzminsky wrote his most famous poetic works, most importantly, the poem *Vavilonskaia bashnia* (The Tower of Babel, 1967–72), a programme piece of the neo-avant-garde, re-published in 1992 in the United States, about which the author wrote: "The poet fulfilled himself only in 1967–72, in the period of building the monumental poem-construction 'The

52 Gnedov: *Smert' iskusstvu: Piatnadtsat' (15) poem* [Death to Art: Fifteen (15) Poems], p. 8.
53 Gnedov: *Poema kontsa* [The Poem of the End].

Tower of Babel' of 100 pages – or 150 if you include and count the later additions."[54] This appears to have been his first attempt to create an avant-garde 'super-text' (in analogy to Khlebnikov's 'super-saga' *Zangezi)*, with which he himself was satisfied.

The Tower of Babel has an autobiographical origin: according to the author, it "began with the 'Ukrainian' chapter (*Are you loved...*) and continued for five years in the form of letters to *Madonna*, Larisa Andreevna Voitenko. It began with the 'Poem, Doomed to Be a Sacrificial Lamb', which I sacrificed for poetic unreliability and built the *Tower* from the wreckage."[55] The theme of unhappy love, as well as the other traits, brings it closer to Mayakovsky's *Oblako v shtanakh* (A Cloud in Trousers, 1915) and *Fleita-pozvonochnik* (Backbone Flute, 1915). However, it is not the similarities but the differences between Mayakovsky's and Kuzminsky's poems that enable us to see the fundamental difference between the avant-garde and the neo-avant-garde. The classical avant-garde built the artistic world according to the model of destruction / reconstruction (building a new reality on the ruins of the old world). So, the hero of the poem *A Cloud in Trousers*, having learned that his beloved prefers another man to him, rejects her understanding of love. Then follows his rejection of the art that formed her delusive idea of love, the social system in which this false art developed, and, finally, God, the creator of this reality: "Down with your love, down with your art, down with your system, down with your religion – four cries in four parts".[56] The poem ends with the hero's symbolic murder of God and the affirmation of the necessity to take the position he vacated in order to create a new world, in which there will be no place for social injustice or for a false understanding of love ("to <be able> without anguish – to kiss and kiss and kiss"[57]).

In contrast to the historical avant-garde, the neo-avant-garde undertook a heroic attempt to create a new unity, a 'super-text', seen from the perspective of the previous experience as utopian and doomed to failure. The meta-plot of the

54 "Поэт состоялся лишь в 1967–72 гг., в период строительства монументальной поэмы-конструкции 'вавилонская башня', в 100 (150) страниц – ежели включать и считать позднейшие добавления." Kuz'minskii: *Ne stol'ko o poetike...*, p. 291.

55 "Начал с главы 'украинской' (*Чи Ти Кохана...*) и продолжал в форме писем *Мадонне*, Ларисе Андреевне Войтенко, на протяжении 5 лет. Началось с 'Поэмы, обреченной на заклание', каковую я заклал, за поэтической недостоверностью, и из обломков выстроил 'Башню'." BLA 2 A, p. 521.

56 "долой вашу любовь, долой ваше искусство, долой ваш строй, долой вашу религию – четыре крика четырех частей". Maiakovskii: *Izbrannye proizvedeniia.* Vol. 1 [Selected Works. Vol. 1], p. 615.

57 "чтобы <можно> было без мук – целовать, целовать, целовать". Maiakovskii: *Izbrannye proizvedeniia.* Vol. 1, p. 171.

poem *The Tower of Babel* is love, the collapse of which leads to the collapse of the entire structure: in fact, it is the opposite of the utopian dream of love and social cohesion in *A Cloud in Trousers*. The very title of Kuzminsky's poem carries with it the idea of doom: the *Tower of Babel* that the hero-poet seeks to erect collapses not in the closing lines but in the very process of erection:

> The poet recognizes in the woman the poem he has to write. But he knows that he will not be happy with this woman, that she will never become his. And he begins a poem, the fate of which is predetermined – to become the Tower of Babel, to lead him if not to silence, then to linguistic confusion and misunderstanding: "There is no poem."[58]

Mayakovsky used the ambivalent image of a hero-poet, who is a God-Man, a theomachist ready to replace the Creator of this world with himself. He is also christomorphic, a man suffering from love, a "screaming-lipped Zarathustra".[59] Kuzminsky operated with an ambivalent image of a heroine who combines the features of the biblical Shulamite and Salome,[60] a witch and a devout woman, the hero's Darling and the Whore of Babylon. His poem is just as ambivalent, both rising and falling, thought out in a constructivist manner and devoid of any coherence. The poem also seems to be a polemic pique against (Neo-)Acmeism which operated with the architectural metaphor of culture, for example, Osip Mandelstam comparing poetry and architecture in his article *Utro akmeizma* (The Morning of Acmeism, 1919).[61] However, Mandelstam's cathedral poem *Notre-Dame* (1912), from his first collection, *Kamen'* (Stone), becomes in Kuzminsky's *The Tower of Babel* doomed never to be built, collapsing under its own weight.

The genre subtitle of *The Tower of Babel* is "poem-construction": the poem contains not only a montage of thematically heterogeneous texts, but also texts written or 'constructed' in different languages. It thereby creates a literal image of Baby-

---

58 "Поэт узнает в женщине поэму, которую ему предстоит создать. Но он же знает, что с этой женщиной ему не быть счастливым, что она никогда не станет его. И он начинает поэму, судьба которой предрешена – стать вавилонской башней, привести его если не к молчанию, то к языковой путанице и непониманию: 'Поэмы нет.'" From the unpublished text of Petr Kazarnovskii's report at the conference *Vavilonskaia bashnia poezii* [The Babel Tower of Poetry], held in Saint Petersburg on 5–6 March 2022. I thank the author for giving me an opportunity to get acquainted with the speech, now available as a video at https://www.youtube.com/watch?v=wk8CgJf0UtM.

59 "сегодняшнего дня крикогубый Заратустра!" Maiakovskii: *Izbrannye proizvedeniia*. Vol. 1, p. 160.

60 The Shulamite Maiden in the Song of Solomon was an alluring, sensual woman with refined eroticism. By contrast, Salome was a a dangerous femme fatale and a destructive temptress.

61 Mandel'shtam: *Polnoe sobranie sochinenii i pisem v trekh tomakh*. Vol. 2. *Proza* [Complete Collected Works and Letters in Three Volumes. Vol. 2. Prose], pp. 23–24.

lonian polyglossia (in addition to the four main languages of the poem – Old Russian, Russian, Ukrainian and English – it also contains pseudo-texts constructed from French, German, Spanish, Italian and Latin words). However, the rejection of the conventional grammar and syntax of these languages gives Kuzminsky's texts a certain *zaum'* quality, makes them semantically indefinite or even empty, actualizing the acoustic form of various languages instead. The disintegration of the classical form of the poem into parts, structurally related to each other but semantically heterogeneous, symbolizes the collapse of communication between the beloved and the hero, who tried to build these relationships: they can be called 'relationships' in their form, but in actual fact they are none. The form of the poem at the macro level is sustained, as a whole, by means of the structural framework of the genre; however, at the micro levels the connections are dominant not in terms of their meaning but through consonance: rhyme (which Kuzminsky has not rejected) and paronymy:

когда спицы с серпами срезают под корень неверных	when needles with sickles are cutting at the root the unfaithful
на равнинах исполненных крови и пролитой скверны	on plains full of blood and spilled filth
как каверны зияют следы неприятельских ядер	like caverns traces of enemy's cannonballs are gaping
и войска пруссаков переходят разлившийся одер	and the Prussian troops are crossing the flooded Oder river
на одре своих дум задремавший пустынник фернейский[62]	dozed off on the bed of his thoughts, the hermit of Ferney

Moreover, the montage nature of the poem is manifested in the fact that its semantically indistinct parts are juxtaposed with the parts written in accordance with quite conventional traditional poetry, to which Kuzminsky paid tribute in his early days, for example in *Poema, obrechennaia na zaklanie* (Poem, Doomed to Be a Sacrificial Lamb, 1967). However, this juxtaposition itself discredits the traditional poetic discourse and defamiliarizes it. It turns out to be only one language amongst others in the cosmos of Babylonian polyglottism. Moreover, the collapse of love/poetry turns into the collapse of this language as well.

Ilya Kukulin calls this type of montage "post-utopian": "In literary works that had the method of post-utopian montage applied in them, history turned out to be a series of breaks, and the last break, the most significant, separated it from the

62 Kuz'minskii: *Vavilonskaia bashnia: Konstruktsiia* [The Tower of Babel: A Construction], p. 23.

present".[63] In the poem, the sign of this final break is the failure both in building a coherent and internally logical and consistent literary narrative – namely, of a 'narrative poem' – and in building the relationship of the hero of the poem with the heroine-addressee of the work. An additional sign of this failure was the publication of *The Tower of Babel* in his Podval publishing house in 1992, which comprised along with the poem itself several "chapters that were not included in the tower or written later" ("Глав, не вошедших в башню, или написанных опосля").

Among those texts were several works on a historical theme, dedicated to Catherine the Great and her era, primarily her relations with favourites and her attitude towards war, including the suppression of Pugachev's Rebellion in 1775.[64] These 'chapters' are not accidentally added to the main text, which tells about the hero's unhappy love affair; they can be interpreted as Kuzminsky's further polemic with the aesthetics associated with Akhmatova and her 'school' (in her last years, Akhmatova was often compared to an Empress). Kuzminsky contrasts the hierarchical classical culture with the anarchic rebellion of the popular uprising, thereby continuing the tradition of the Russian Futurists with their cult of rebellion, as can be seen in Velimir Khlebnikov's poem *Ustrug Razina* (Razin's Boat, 1923) or Vasily Kamensky's novel *Stepan Razin* (1915). Moreover, for Kuzminsky – as well as for the Futurists – it was a masculine rebellion against female domination, which overturned the traditional binary opposition male vs. female, but did not abolish their inequality. It is no coincidence that in one of the texts written in the spirit of the Neo-Futurist Aleksandr Kondratov and dedicated to him, *Kontseptsiia Pugachevshchiny po Pushkinu i pomimo: Gishtoriia Podavleniia Pugachevskogo Bunta* (The Concept of Pugachevism according to Pushkin and Others: A Story of the Suppression of Pugachev's Rebellion, 1990). It takes the form of a list of names of those men hanged by Catherine the Great, of fictional and famous cultural figures, from the poet Oleg Okhapkin to the writer Vasily Shukshin and the scholar Sergey Averintsev. It ends like this:

63 "в произведениях, использовавших метод постутопического монтажа, история оказывалась серией разрывов, и последний разрыв, самый значительный, отделял ее от современности." Kukulin: *Mashini zashumevshego vremeni* [Machines of a Noisy Time], p. 341.
64 The Pugachev Uprising of 1773–1775, also known as the Cossack Rebellion, was a large-scale peasants' war led by Yemelyan Pugachev. It presented a challenge to the imperial administration of Catherine II., who had Pugachev executed in 1775.

Горбушкина Кукушкина	Gorbushkina Kukushkina
Овечкина Колечкина	Ovechkina Kolechkina
Собачкина и Клячкина	Sobachkina and Klyachkina
и всех превыше – Пушкина.[65]	and above all of them – Pushkina

Another important feature of Kuzminsky's works is his desire for spontaneity in the creative act. He often noted the date and the precise time of when a piece was written, and these indications show that rather voluminous texts can be written 'in one sitting', as, for example, the poem *Birobidzhan* (1974), referring to the name of a town in the Jewish Autonomous Oblast. The electronic publication indicates that it was created "from, approximately, after midnight – 07.07.15.11.74. St. Petersburg."[66] This is indeed an experience of spontaneous poetry, where the logic of the text flow is determined by rhythm and rhyme, as well as the melodic pattern of several songs, amongst which are the song *Oblaka* (Clouds, 1962) by Aleksander Galich and the Arkhangelsk folk song *Lodochka-Pomorochka*, etc., and a single creative impulse limits the possibility of selecting the content and editing the text. "'The Tower' [...] has a rigid structure, which I am dissatisfied with and I tried to overcome in my 'Birobidzhan'."[67] The poem is dedicated to the poet's lover Elena Glukhovskaya, who left him for the poet Mikhail Gendelev, who in turn became an object of hostility for him for many years. The nature of this poem allows us to note another feature of Kuzminsky's creative practices in his writing: poetry recitations and other forms of performance.

Kuzminsky regularly tested the boundaries of social conventions established by political correctness, ethics and the laws of the land. His defiantly antisocial behaviour (verbal abuse, public nudity, often in a state of intoxication) corresponds to the violation of a number of prohibitions. Many of his statements against his opponents can be perceived as xenophobic, racist, antisemitic, misogynist, homophobic, etc. Thus, the poem *Birobidzhan* was about a town in the Jewish Autonomous Oblast created in the USSR in the 1930s, but the title, as well as a number of rather riské images, more likely hints at Mikhail Gendelev's Jewish identity. However, while for the poet such defiant violations of ethical conventions were rather a means of poetic expression, they were rarely accepted by his addressees or readers. They were recognized not as artistic forms of *épatage* but as insults. The

---

65 Kuz'minskii: *Vavilonskaia bashnia*, p. 137.

66 "с, примерно, после полуночи – 7.07.15.11.74. СПБ." BLA 2 A, quoted after the electronic version of the anthology *The Blue Lagoon: Anthology of Modern Russian Poetry* at https://kkk-bluelagoon.ru/tom2a/kuzminsky5.htm, which differs slightly from the print publication.

67 " 'Башня' [...] – являет собой жесткую конструкцию, коей я недоволен, что и пытался преодолеть в своем 'Биробиджане'." BLA 2 A, p. 521.

poet seemed to be testing the limits of what is permissible and thus gained for himself an odious reputation.

Kuzminsky as an anthologist and organizer in the Leningrad underground scene

Even those who questioned Kuzminsky's poetic talent were willing to acknowledge his great organizational skills, as well as his 'obsession' with collecting and distributing works of the unofficial literary and artistic scene in Russia. As early as 1967, Kuzminsky met the writer Suzanne Massie and her husband Robert K. Massie, a historian and author of a number of books about the House of Romanov. This acquaintance grew into a long-term collaboration: Kuzminsky helped Massie to compile and publish with Doubleday in New York and Gollancz in London *The Living Mirror: Five Young Poets from Leningrad* (1972). Three of the poets – Aleksandr Kushner, Viktor Sosnora and Gleb Gorbovsky – were members of the Union of Soviet Writers, but they maintained close ties with unofficial circles, whilst the other two – Joseph Brodsky and Kuzminsky himself – represented to the Western reader underground poets from Russia.

Kuzminsky edited in 1973–74 two more anthologies of Leningrad poetry, this time in Russian: *Pervyi etap* (The First Stage) included fourteen poets who, according to the compiler's preface, represented his own "teachers or, let's say, older 'brothers in pen'."[68] *Vtoroi etap* (The Second Stage) included fourteen "friends, students or just peers".[69] Thus, Kuzminsky as compiler became a lens through which the image of modern Leningrad poetry was refracted. Kuzminsky complemented each anthology with his own highly subjective characterization of the authors included in it. In 1975, he also published an anthology of Leningrad prose by twenty-three authors, *Leprozorii-23* (Leprozorium-23) and, in the winter of 1975, he joined the editing team of the anthology *Lepta* (unpublished). After the defeat of the so-called *Bul'dozernaia vystavka* (Bulldozer Exhibition) in Moscow, which for one day (15 September 1974) showed nonconformist art and was forcefully dismantled by the authorities with water cannons and bulldozers (hence the name), the author-

68 "учителей или, скажем, старших собратьев по перьям". Amherst Center for Russian Culture, Amherst College, Konstantin K. Kuzminsky Papers, 1951–2013, Subseries 11: Zhivoe zerkalo (1972–1974), box 40, folders 1 to 4.

69 "друзей, или учеников, или просто ровесников". Amherst Center for Russian Culture, Amherst College, Konstantin K. Kuzminsky Papers, 1951–2013, Subseries 11: Zhivoe zerkalo (1972–1974), box 40, folders 1 to 4.

ities consented to an exhibition of unofficial art in Izmailovsky Park two weeks later. This inspired the Leningrad writers to attempt to publish an anthology of uncensored poetry. In total, the *Lepta* project brought together thirty-two authors but, as Kuzminsky himself recalled,

> I was not an idiot who for a single minute believed that they would allow us to publish the BOOK. But it seemed to me to be absolutely vital to have live poetic communication (whether with one another or with the public), similar to the "Stray Dog" cabaret, or to our cheerful escapades at the very beginning of the 1960s. Not to mention the fact that, stewing in the juice of individualism and being surrounded by a bunch of admirers or tolerant fellow writers – the poets had UNLEARNED how to read poetry, especially "in the limelight" of a public stage. That is why, under the brand name "LEPTA", in April-May alone, I teamed up with Krivulin and Yulia [Vosnesenskaya] to organize about fifty apartment readings.[70]

In 1970, Kuzminsky and his family moved into a new flat on Profsoiuznyi Boulevard and turned it for two and a half years into one of the main cultural venues in Leningrad. There were poetry readings, exhibitions of unofficial artists, as well as discussions about further publishing projects. The poet received his guests in a dressing gown and stretched out on a sofa. This situation – recorded in many memoirs and on photographs – became an important part of his public image and referred back to the ultimate symbol of Russian laziness in Ivan Goncharov's 'canonical' novel *Oblomov* (1859). It presented Kuzminsky as a person leading an idle lifestyle, which in itself was a challenge to the Soviet authorities (see Fig. 1).

A one-day *Eksperimental'naia vystavka grafiki i grafiki-foto* (Experimental Exhibition of Graphics and Graphics-Photos) with works of twenty-three artists, was organized by Kuzminsky in 1973 at the Faculty of Psychology of Leningrad University. Due to the success of the show, a second exhibition, *Pod parashiutom* (Under the Parachute), with works of thirteen photographers, was arranged in Kuzminsky's apartment at the end of October 1974. The visitors were greeted by Kuzminsky – as always reclining on a sofa in the centre of the room – under a parachute stretched across the ceiling. He was again at the centre of another one-day exhibition of four painters held here, *Obraz menia v sovremennom iskusstve* (The Image of Me in Contemporary Art). Such exhibitions of unofficial painting, as well as lit-

---

70 "Идиотом я не был и поверить, что нам – разрешат КНИГУ – не верил ни на минуту. Но живое поэтическое общение (между собой ли, с публикой ли) по типу 'Бродячей собаки' или наших веселых эскапад самого начала 60-х – казалось мне крайне насущным. Не говоря о том, что варясь в соку индивидуализма, в кучке поклонников или просто терпеливых собратьев по перу – поэты РАЗУЧИЛИСЬ читать стихи, тем более, "на публику". Вот почему, под маркой "ЛЕПТЫ", за апрель-май только, мною, Кривулиным и Юлией было организовано где-то с полсотни квартирных чтений." BLA 5B, p. 100.

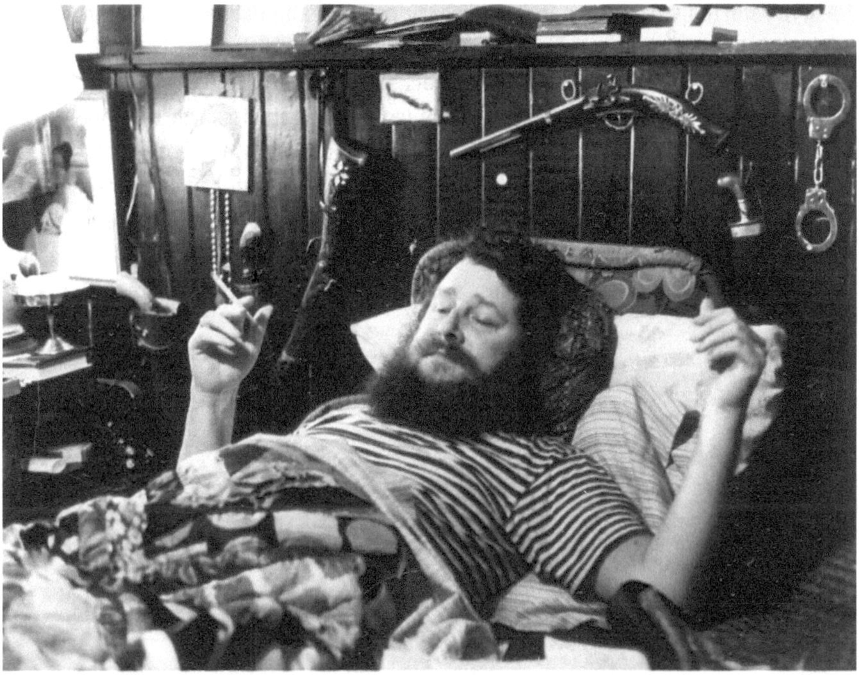

Fig. 1. Konstantin Kuzminsky on his sofa. Date and author of photograph unknown.

erary readings (no less than fifty in total), continued to be held in Kuzminsky's flat up until his emigration to the USA.

In emigration

In 1975, Kuzminsky emigrated to Vienna, where he settled for several months. He initially intended to move on to France but, in January 1976, he accepted an invitation from the Tolstoy Foundation for Russian Welfare and Culture ("Tolstovsky Farm") near Manhattan. In September 1976, he taught a postgraduate seminar on contemporary unofficial poetry in the USSR at the University of Texas at Austin. He translated into English the diary of the human rights activist and poet Julia Voznesenskaya, who was convicted in 1976 of 'anti-Soviet propaganda', advised translators of unofficial poetry and began preparatory work for the creation of a large poetry anthology. In 1979, Kuzminsky founded, together with the art critic John Bowlt, the non-profit Institute of Modern Russian Culture at Blue Lagoon in Los Angeles. In 1981, finally, Kuzminsky moved to New York, where he led a bohemian lifestyle, started various art and publishing projects and participated in art events, such as a Russian Ball in honour of David Burliuk on 29 June 1982, where he appeared in a 'birthday suit' with his buttocks and navel painted.

Kuzminsky continued to write poetry (some of it, such as the 1978 poem *Solovki*, in the spirit of the OBERIU poet Aleksandr Vvedensky) and prose, including the novel *Hotel zum Тюркен* (Hotel zum Türken, 2014)[71] which can be viewed in the context of Venedikt Erofeyev's 'poem in prose' *Moskva – Petushki* (Moscow – Petushki, 1969) and émigré prose such as Eduard Limonov's *Eto ia, Edichka* (It's me, Eddie, 1979) and Sergei Dovlatov's *Inostranka* (A Foreign Woman, 1985).

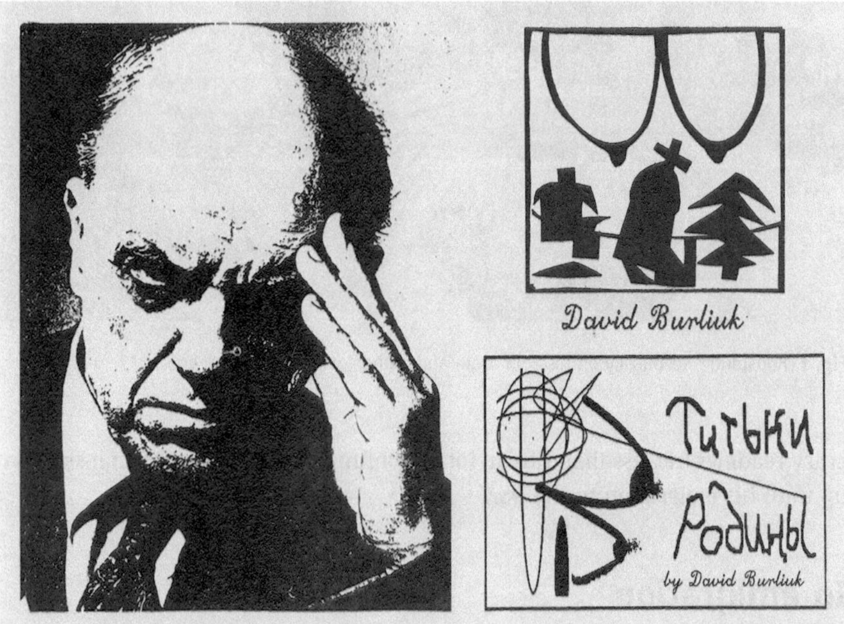

Fig. 2: David Burliuk: *Titki rodiny* (Tits of the Motherland). This handmade book with illustrations, book design and typography by Konstantin Kuzminsky was published in 1982 to commemorate the one-hundredth birthday of the Futurist poet David Burliuk. The verses were collected by Kuzminsky, Gerald Janecek and Lev Nusberg and printed in Russian and in an English translation.

In New York, it became evermore important for Kuzminsky to collect and (re-)publish unknown or little-known texts from both the historical avant-garde and con-

71 The title refers to a hotel by that name on the Obersalzberg, which served Adolf Hitler as a holiday retreat,

temporary underground authors. In his 'samizdat' publishing house Podval, he published books of his contemporaries in small print runs of usually only ten numbered copies. Most of these authors – like Kuzminsky – did not fit into the establishment of Russian émigré literature, represented by Vagrich Bakhchanian, Genrikh Khudiakov, Anri Volokhonsky, Rimma and Valerii Gerlovin. Kuzminsky also published texts of his predecessors, including Pavel Filonov, Nina Khabias, the Ego-Futurist Vasilisk Gnedov, the Cubo-Futurist David Burliuk (see Fig. 2) and the Constructivist Alexei Chicherin. His prose, as well as the extensive correspondence of that time, demonstrates his interest in unknown figures and phenomena, primarily of the Russian avant-garde of the early twentieth century.

Kuzminsky's main project, and his most famous, was the anthology *U goloboi laguni: Antalogiia noveishei russkoi poezii / The Blue Lagoon: Anthology of Modern Russian Poetry*. Published in 1980–1986 in five volumes and nine books (except for the first volume, published under the auspices of the Institute of Modern Russian Culture, they consist of two semi-volumes), the anthology had Kuzminsky at the same time as compiler, main author and commentator. We are dealing here with a 'total project' of a neo-avant-garde poet who almost single-handedly undertook the mission of summing up the 40-year experience of uncensored art (most importantly, poetry) in such a way as to, on the one hand, include it in the line of succession of the historical avant-garde of the first third of the twentieth century. On the other hand (which might not be all that obvious), the anthology placed his own œuvre, and moreover, his manifold cultural and creative activities, in the context of the Leningrad underground scene. Ilja Kukuj commented on this practice:

> In the BLA, the very texture of the book was supposed to emphasize the documentary nature of the publication, to reproduce the aesthetics of samizdat, and to give prominence to the polemical, subjective, politically incorrect commentary of the compiler. It formed a kind of corpus of unofficial culture, in which – seen from Kuzminsky's point of view – the purity of creative research was organically combined with the filth of literary and Soviet life. The intensity of Kuzminsky's artistic gesture can also be explained by the fact that, by the beginning of work on his magnum opus, he no longer felt like being a part of this literary body. The BLA became a kind of hypercompensation for Kuzminsky's exclusion from a tradition that had been organic for him.[72]

72 "В АГЛ сама фактура книги должна была подчеркнуть документальный характер издания, воспроизводящего эстетику самиздата, а полемический, субъективный, неполиткорректный комментарий составителя – своеобразную телесность неофициальной культуры, в которой, с точки зрения Кузьминского, чистота творческих исканий органично сочеталась с грязью литературного и советского быта. Интенсивность художественного жеста Кузьминского может объясняться и тем фактом, что к началу работы над своим opus magnum он уже не чувствовал себя частью этого литературного тела – АГЛ стала своего рода

The *Blue Lagoon* anthology formed part of the life of a real person, Konstantin K. Kuzminsky; it was his 'life-creating project' and his own biography (diary, memoir, notes, archive). But it can also be considered in the context of other projects closely related to it in the neo-avant-garde. They included the journal *Transponans* by Ry Nikonova and Serge Segay, the above-mentioned project *My Trinities* and the entire corpus of texts by the Neo-Futurist poet Aleksandr Kondratov. Furthermore, Kuzminsky's activity of archiving, collecting, researching and publishing resembled similar activities by other authors of the neo-avant-garde of the 1950s–1980s: Vladimir Erl', Gennady Aygi, as well as the poets, researchers and popularizers of the historical and neo-avant-garde Sergey Biryukov, German Lukomnikov and others.

The fundamental 'montage' nature of the anthology allows us to return to the idea expressed at the beginning of this essay: that in Kuzminsky's case we are dealing with a type of montage that challenges both the Soviet canon and the classical canon of the 'intelligentsia'. He gave a voice to the authors repressed by both, and thereby created an alternative canon intimately linked to the name of Velimir Khlebnikov, whom he considered a key figure of the Russian avant-garde: "Because Khlebnikov is alive. He lives in Krasovitsky, Eremin, Rivin, Khromov, Volokhonsky, Khvostenko, Bokshtein, in me, in Aronzon, Altshuler, Erl, Makrinov, Belousov, Lyon, Limonov, in thousands, in – us."[73]

Conclusion

The Neo-Futurism proclaimed by Kuzminsky was a product of the late, post-war avant-garde – the neo-avant-garde or, in Igor' Smirnov's terminology, an "avant-garde-3" that rejects "a perspectivized model of the world in favour of retrospection",[74] thus restoring the cultural gap between the past and the present, as well as Russian and world culture. Even after the publication of the *Blue Lagoon* anthology, Kuzminsky did not abandon his efforts to collect and systematize the avant-garde heritage. Together with Gerald Janecek and Aleksander Ocheretiansky, he

гиперкомпенсацией отстранения Кузьминского из органичной для него традиции." Kukuj: "Antologiia Konstantina Kuz'minskogo kak 'zhivoe zerkalo'" [Konstantin Kuzminsky's Anthology as a 'Living Mirror'], p. 18.

73 "Потому что Хлебников – жив. Жив в Красовицком, Еремине, Ривине, Хромове, Волохонском, Хвостенко, Бокштейне, во мне, в Аронзоне, Альтшулере, Эрле, Макринове, Белоусове, Лёне, Лимонове, в тысячах, в – нас." BLA 2A, p. 40.

74 "перспектированной модели мира в пользу ретроспекции". Smirnov: *Ot protivnogo: Razyskaniia v oblasti khudozhestvennoi kultury* [Of the Opposite: Researches in the Field of Literary Culture], p. 72.

prepared the anthology *Zabytyi avangard: Rossiia, pervaia tret' XX stoletiia* (The Forgotten Avant-Garde: Russia, First Third of the Twentieth Century, 1988). It can be assumed that Kuzminsky would agree with Vilen Barsky's assessment in his answers to the questionnaire which was included in the *Blue Lagoon* anthology:

> Our generation was a bridge to Western culture, to Russian culture and art of the first third of our century. I think that this was the rôle given to us by God. To restore the connection but not to fall into the abyss, like the hero of Kafka's parable *The Bridge*. That was our life: to realize ourselves – what you do in art – in the context of living culture, in the context of its true values.[75]

Kuzminsky's activity as a collector was not academic, just as his publications of rare works of the authors of the historical avant-garde were not strictly speaking scholarly editions. When Perestroika arrived in the USSR with the subsequent collapse of the country, the cultural floodgates were opened, and the very concept of a 'forgotten avant-garde' lost its meaning. There appeared alternatives to Kuzminsky's hard-to-find publications, and they had a wider circulation and were more reliable in a scholarly sense. Moreover, the literary circles to which Kuzminsky had belonged, and whose works he had popularized, became history and the subject of scholarly studies.

From 1998 until the end of his days, Kuzminsky settled in a private house he had bought in Lordville, called 'Bozhedomka' (literally God-mother, here meaning 'potter's field') by him. This hamlet in New York State on the border with Pennsylvania was far removed from the cultural world of New York City, which he had tried to conquer in the 1980s and 1990s. In this remote domicile, he continued to collect artefacts of a bygone era (manuscripts, paintings, objects of naïve art), receive guests and maintain an extensive correspondence, devoted in particular to the infrequent publication of his works in Russia. His name was increasingly associated with the past and not with the current literary process in Russia. An attempt to reprint *The Blue Lagoon* anthology in Russia stalled after the first volume, and only part of the US-American edition was sold. His poetry books were published in a print run of 50 copies, and in one of them we can read: "The

75 "Наше поколение было мостом в западную культуру, в русскую культуру и искусство первой трети нашего века. Думаю, что это и была роль, отпущенная нам Богом. Восстановить связь, но не рухнуть в пропасть, как герой притчи Кафки "Мост". Это была наша жизнь: осознать себя – то, что ты делаешь в искусстве – в ряду живой культуры, в ряду ее истинных ценностей." BLA 3B, p. 240.

fewer people who read me, the better; the main thing is that those whom I love read me".[76]

All of these frenzied creative and cultural activities indicated a widening gap between Kuzminsky and his readers, who by no means only belonged to his own generation. The recent interest in the legacy of Kuzminsky, not only as a collector and publisher of the Russian underground but also as an author of original works of art,[77] gives hope for a significant expansion of this readership. Kuzminsky's latest large-scale project was the book *Roman-gazeta* (Novel-Newspaper, 2014), created as a complement to his anthology and pursuing similar principles of montage. As a collage of materials from his extensive archive – correspondence, newspaper clippings, photographic materials, fragments from the anthology, etc. – it serves as a chronicle of the life of the author himself. It sums up all of his diverse activities and assigns a place of honour for Kuzminsky in the culture of the second half of the twentieth and the early twenty-first century.

Bibliography

Archival sources:

Konstantin K. Kuzminsky Papers, 1951–2013. Amherst Center for Russian Culture, Amherst College, Amherst, MA.

Finding aid: https://www.amherst.edu/academiclife/departments/russian/acrc/collections/archives/konstantin-k.-kuzminsky-papers (consulted 12/12/2022).

Printed sources:

Bürger, Peter: *Theory of the Avant-Garde.* Transl. Michael Shaw. Minneapolis/MN: University of Minnesota Press. 1984.

Gnedov, Vasilisk: *Poema kontsa* [The Poem of the End]. New York: Podval, 1984.

76 "чем меньше людей меня прочтет, тем лучше, главное, чтобы прочли те, кого я люблю." Kuzminsky: *Po obe storony okeana: Stikhi* [On Both Sides of the Ocean: Poems], p. 6.

77 The Amherst Center for Russian Culture at Amherst College acquired Kuzminsky's extensive archive in 2014 and held two archival seminars in 2017 and 2018. "Vavilonskaia bashnia poezii" [Babel Tower of Poetry], the first international conference in memory of Kuzminsky was held at the Akhmatova Museum (!) in Sankt Petersburg in March 2022. 2022 also saw the publication of the collection of studies and materials *Na beregakh Goluboi Laguny: Konstantin Kuz'minskii i ego Antologiia* [On the Shores of the Blue Lagoon: Konstantin Kuz'minskii and his Anthology, edited by Ilja Kukuj].

Gnedov, Vasilisk: *Smert' iskusstvu: Piatnadtsat' (15) poem* [Death to Art: Fifteen (15) Poems]. Sankt Peterburg: Peterburgskii Glashatai, 1913.

Guro, Elena: *Nebesnye verbliuzhata* [The Baby Camels of the Sky]. Sankt Peterburg: Limbus Press, 2001.

Ioffe, Dennis G.: "Simvolicheskii kapital posmertnogo naslediia Khlebnikova i Maiakovskogo sub specie avangardnoi performativnosti skandala: Semioticheskaia pragmatika avangardnogo povedeniia i zhiznetvorchestva." [The Symbolic Capital of Khlebnikov and Mayakovsky's Posthumous Heritage in the Light of the Avant-garde Performativity of the Scandal: The Semiotic Pragmatics of Avant-garde Behaviour and Life-Creation] *Kritika i semiotika* 1 (2022): 228–272.

Janecek, Gerald: "A Zaum' Classification." *Canadian-American Slavic Studies* 20:1–2 (1986): 37–54.

Kalomirov, Aleksandr [Krivulin, Viktor]: "Dvadtsat' let noveishei russkoi poesii: Predvaritel'nie zametki." [Twenty Years of the Newest Russian Poetry: Preliminary Notes] *Chasi* 22 (1979): 240–263.

Kamenskii, Vasilii: *Nagoi sredi odetykh: Izdanie rossiiskikh futuristov* [Naked Amongst the Clad: Publication of Russian Futurists]. Moskva, Rossiiskie futuristy, 1914.

Krauss, Rosalind: *The Originality of the Avant-Garde and Other Modernist Myths.* Cambridge/MA: MIT Press, 1986.

Kruchenykh, Aleksei: *Faktura slova: Deklaratsiia (Kniga 120-ia)* [The Texture of the Word: Declaration. 120th Book]. Moskva

Kukuj, Ilja: "Antologiia Konstantina Kuz'minskogo kak 'zhivoe zerkalo'." [Konstantin Kuzminsky's Anthology as a 'Living Mirror'] Ilja Kukuj, ed.: *Na beregakh Goluboi Laguny: Konstantin Kuz'minskii i ego antologiia: Sbornik issledovanii i materialov* [On the Shores of the Blue Lagoon: Konstantin Kuz'minskii and His Anthology: A Collection of Studies and Materials]. Boston/MA, & Sankt Peterburg: Academic Studies Press, 2022. 13–30.

Kukulin, Il'ia: *Mashini zashumevshego vremeni: Kak sovetskoi montazh stal metodom neofitsial'noi kul'tury* [Machines of a Noisy Time: How the Soviet Montage Became a Method of the Unofficial Culture]. Moskva: Novoe literaturnoe obozrenie, 2015.

Kuz'minskii, Konstantin, Gerald Janecek, and Aleksandr Ocheretianskii, eds.: *Zabytyi avangard: Rossiia. Pervaia tret' XX stoletiia. Sbornik spravochnykh i teoreticheskikh materialov* [The Forgotten Avant-garde: Russia. The First Third of the twentieth Century. A Collection of Reference and Theoretical Materials]. Wien: Wiener Slawistischer Almanach, 1988.

Kuz'minskii, Konstantin: *Vavilonskaia bashnia: Konstruktsiia* [The Tower of Babel: A Construction]. Brighton Beach/NY: Podval naverkhu, 1992.

Kuz'minskii, Konstantin: *Ne stol'ko o poetike, skol'ko – ob etike: Kniga pisem* [Not That Much About Poetics as – About Ethics: A Book of Letters]. Sankt Peterburg: Peterburg – XXI vek, 2003.

Kuz'minskii, Konstantin K.: *Roman-Gazeta* [Novel-Newspaper]. Lordville/NY: Poslednii Podval Naverkhu, 2014.

Kuz'minskii, Konstantin K.: *Po obe storony okeana: Stikhi* [On Both Sides of the Ocean: Poems]. Sankt Peterburg: Be-Ta, 2009.

Livshits, Benedikt: *Polutoraglazyi strelets: Stikhotvoreniia. Perevody. Vospominaniia* [The One and a Half-Eyed Archer: Poems. Translations. Recollections]. Leningrad: Sovetskii pisatel', 1989.

Mandel'shtam, Osip: *Polnoe sobranie sochinenii i pisem v trekh tomakh.* Vol. 2. *Proza* [Complete Collected Works and Letters in Three Volumes. Vol. 2: Prose]. Moskva: Progress-Pleiada, 2010.

Maiakovskii, Vladimir: *Izbrannye proizvedeniia.* Vol. 1 [Selected Works. Vol. 1]. Moskva-Leningrad: Sovetskii pisatel', 1963.

Mokienko Valerii, and Tat'iana Nikitina: *Bolshoi slovar' russkogo zhargona* [Large Dictionary of Russian Jargon]. Sankt Peterburg: Norint, 2000.

Orlitskii, Iurii: "Vvedenie v poetiku Sapgira: Sistema protivopostavlenii i strategiia ikh preodoleniia." [Introduction to Sapgir's Poetics: The System of Oppositions and the Strategy of Overcoming Them] Galina Zykova, Vladislav Kulakov, and Mikhail Pavlovets, eds.: *"Lianozovskaia shkola": Mezhdu barachnoi poeziei i russkim konkretismom* ["Lianosovo School": Between Barack Poetry and Russian Concretism]. Moskva: Novoe literaturnoe obozrenie, 2021: 322–354.

Schaffner, Anna Katherina: "Inheriting the Avant-Garde: On the Reconciliation of Tradition and Invention in Concrete Poetry." David Hopkins, and Anna Katharina Schaffner, eds.: *Neo-Avant-Garde.* Amsterdam: Rodopi, 2006. 97–118.

Shapir, Maksim: "Esteticheskii opyt XX veka: Avangard i postmodernizm." [The Aesthetic Experience of the twentieth Century: Avant-Garde and Postmodernism] *Philologica* 2 (1995): 136–143.

Smirnov, Igor': *Khudozhestvennii smysl' i evolutsiia poeticheskikh sistem* [The Artistic Meaning and Evolution of Poetic Systems]. Leningrad: Nauka, 1976.

Smirnov, Igor': *Metaistoriia: K istoricheskoi tipologii kultury* [Metahistory: Towards a Historical Typology of Culture]. Moskva: Agraf, 2000.

Smirnov, Igor': *Ot protivnogo: Razyskaniia v oblasti khudozhestvennoi kul'tury* [Of the Opposite: Researches in the Field of Literary Culture]. Moskva: Novoe literaturnoye obozrenie, 2018.

Trofimenkov, Mikhail: "Takelazhnik, poet, 'brodiachii magnitofon': Ob antologii K.K. Kuz'minskogo i G.L. Kovaleva 'U Goluboi Laguny'." [Scaffolder, Poet, 'Walking Tape Recorder': About K.K. Kuz'minskii's and G.L. Kovalev's Anthology "At the Blue Lagoon"] *Smena* [Change] 126 (1 June 1990).

Tynianov, Iurii: "O literaturnoi evoliutsii." [On Literary Evolution] Iurii Tynianov: *Poetika. Istoriia literatury. Kino* [Poetics. History of Literature. Cinema]. Moskva: Nauka, 1977. 210–281.

Valieva Iuliia, ed.: *Sumerki "Saigona"* [The Dusks of "Saigon"]. Sankt Peterburg: ZAMIZDAT, 2009.

Zholkovskii, Aleksandr: "Anna Akhmatova – piatdesiat' let spustia." [Anna Akhmatova – Fifty Years Later] *Zvezda* 9 (1996): 211–227.

Internet sources

Bobyshev, Dmitrii: "'Molodoi Mafusail': Interv'iu Yuriia Levinga." ["Young Methuselah": Interview with Yuri Leving] *Gor'kii* (7 February 2019). https://gorky.media/context/molodoj-mafusail/ (consulted 12/12/2022).

Kuz'minskii, Konstantin, and Georgii Ben: "Perepiska." [Correspondence] *Kreshchatik* [Khreshchatyk] 62 (2013). https://www.kreschatik.kiev.ua/62/35.htm (consulted 12/12/2022).

Likhtenfel'd, Natal'ia: "Saigonavty – pliashushchie zvezdy." [The Saigonauts – Dancing Stars] *Poetograd* 6 (2010): 1–3. http://www.poetograd.ru/nomer.php?id=2508 (consulted 12/12/2022).

3 Asia and Latin America

Sun-yung Park

The Post-utopian Avant-garde Poetics of the Korean 'Futurist' Min-jeong Kim

Abstract: This essay examines the avant-garde poetics of Min-jeong Kim, a representative of Korean 'futurism' in the early twenty-first century. Kim's anti-traditional poetics is full of the images based on metamorphosis and deconstruction, chains of analogies and onomatopoeia, which also formed part of the aesthetic credo of historical Futurism. In her first two collections of poems, *The Flying Hedgehog Lady* (2005) and *She Began to Feel, for the First Time* (2009), the poet depicts in a resolute and candid manner a grotesque world built on sensorial impressions, fantasies and subconscious desires. In order to break away from traditional lyricism and to capture her raw imagery at a linguistic level, Kim uses blunt and non-poetic expressions, slang words and curses, while intentionally erasing the hallowed aura of poetry through puns or tirades. She also makes poems externally unfamiliar by inserting punctuation marks, changing fonts, or by placing emphasis points over words. Furthermore, she deliberately reduces readability by using unfamiliar and drastic metaphors and images, and structures sentences like a stream of consciousness. Also in terms of contents, she seeks to escape traditional concepts of poetry, habitually thought to describe inner and outer worlds through lyrical compression. The world depicted by Kim is full of bizarre landscapes, rooted in the unconscious, in nightmares and daydreams saturated with sex, excretion and madness. Like Marinetti, she seeks to 'murder' the literary 'I' and to bring 'the ugly' into literature. Kim has expanded her unique world of poems by breaking taboos, parodying the sacred world order and subverting established hierarchies. Kim's poetry reflects the anti-traditionalist aesthetics of historical Futurism, broadens the horizons of Korean literature and has ushered in a new generation of innovative and avant-garde 'futurist' circles in her country.

Keywords: Futurism in Korean literature, labelling of literary trends, metamorphosis, deconstruction, colloquialism and obscenities in poetry

https://doi.org/10.1515/9783111318394-009

The birth of Korean 'futurism'

In contrast to the era of utopianism in the early twentieth century, when Italian and Russian Futurism were born with a great tumult through the issuing of manifestos, 'futurism'[1] in South Korea was born quietly in the post-utopian era of the early twenty-first century,[2] by the pen of a young literary critic, Hyeok-ung Kwon (b. 1967).[3]

At the end of the twentieth and the beginning of the twenty-first century, a feeling of depression and disillusionment became dominant in South Korea, largely due to the so-called 'IMF crisis', a financial calamity caused by a severe foreign exchange shortage and the near default of the South Korean central bank in December 1997. In the face of the new millennium, words such as 'apocalypse' or 'utopia' had lost their meanings amongst ordinary people, who had seen many historical calamities before. Meanwhile, from the early 2000s onwards, 'young' poets in their thirties, who had witnessed a series of chaotic processes after reaching the age of maturity, began to publish great numbers of radical poems with new contents and forms completely different from those of previous generations.

As unconventional, experimental and avant-garde works began to fill literary magazines, the critic and poet Hyeok-ung Kwon (b. 1967) used the word 'miraepa' (futurists) in his essay "Miraep'a – 2005, chŏlmŭn shiindŭl" (Futurists – 2005, Young Poets) to characterize poets such as Seok-won Jang (b. 1969), Byeong-seung Hwang (1970–2019), Min-jeong Kim (b. 1976) and Hyung-jin Yoo (b. 1974). Although these poets had not yet published their first book and were criticized in the papers for writing meaningless and frivolous nonsense, Hyeok-ung Kwon assured the public that they "would write the Korean poetry of the future".[4] While some critics of the new generation expressed their support for Hyeok-ung Kwon, his attempts to

---

1 South Korean 'futurists' are different from the historical Futurists in that they never formed a group. They came into existence when a critic referred to them by this name, regardless of the poets' self-image and intentions. Therefore, when referring to South Korean 'futurists' in the 2000s, inverted commas will be used.

2 The first section, "The birth of Korean 'futurism'" summarizes, revises and supplements my essay "Miraep'a hyŏnsangŭi unmyŏnge kwanhan sogo: 20segi rŏshia miraep'awa 21segi han'guk 'miraep'a'rŭl chungshimŭro" [A Study on the Destiny of the Futurist Phenomenon: Focussing on Russian Futurists in the 20th Century and Korean 'Futurists' in the 21st Century], pp. 307–309 and pp. 328–344. For an English-language introduction to Korean Futurism see Cho: "Futurism in Korea: From the Historical to the Postmodern Avant-garde" and Cho: "Korea."

3 The Korean practice to place surnames before given names is inverted here to follow English-language publication practices used in other essays of the Yearbook.

4 Kwon: *Miraep'a: Saeroun siwa shiinŭl wihayŏ* [Futurism: For New Poetry and Poets], p. 149.

confer unconditional legitimacy to the young rebels irritated other critics, who valued lyricism in poetry and came to stand against him.[5] Consequently, 'futurism' provoked heated debates in the Korean literary world.

When Hyeok-ung Kwon decided to define the poetic qualities and characteristics of South Korean poets in the twenty-first century as 'futurist', he clearly had the historical movement – especially the Italian group around F.T. Marinetti – in mind. Indeed, to emphasize the dynamism of their works, he referred to the number of legs of a running horse, which was often used by Italian Futurists.[6] He gave the first section of his book the sub-heading 'The number of legs of a running horse is not 4 but 20', and called the sixth and final section 'The number of legs of a running horse can be 4 or 20'.

In another essay of 2005, "Sangsaŭi nori" (The Plays of Similarities), Kwon did not use the term 'futurist' when characterizing the authors who "are embodying a new aesthetics of our time".[7] But he underlined that the works of Ki-seok Ham (b. 1966), Haeng-sook Kim (b. 1970), Min-ha Lee (b. 1967), Geun-hwa Lee (b. 1976), Yeon-ho Cho (b. 1969) and Eon Kim (b. 1973) were "free and independent from the pressures of established languages and aesthetic traditions".[8] In the same year, Hyeok-ung Kwon published a collection of critical essays, *Miraep'a: Saeroun siwa siinŭl wihayŏ* (Futurism: For New Poetry and Poets), which included the two articles mentioned above. At the beginning of the book, he expressed his infinite affection ('preferentiality', as he wrote) for the young 'futurists' and announced that he would invest the future of his criticism in these poets and their poetry.[9]

Of course, discussions related to Futurism had appeared intermittently in Korean literary circles in the twentieth century, but Korean poets had never been clearly categorized as 'Futurists'. That is, if the term 'Futurist' or 'Futurism' was mentioned in the history of Korean literature before 2005, it was related only to a small number of poets and critics.[10] This limited reception of Futurism was due to a certain delay with which the movement itself became known in Korea. When Marinetti's manifesto *Le Futurisme* was published in 1909 in the newspaper

5 Among the critics supporting the 'futurists' one should mention Jang-uk Lee, Hyeong-cheol Shin and Su-i Kim, whereas critics with an anti-'futurist' proclivity were represented by Bong-jun Goh, Dae-hyeon Park, Myeong-won Lee, Gyeong-su Lee, Sang-il Ha, Myeong-cheol Goh and Gi-don Hong.

6 "A running horse has not four legs, but twenty." Boccioni, et al.: "Futurist Painting: Technical Manifesto", p. 64; Boccioni, et al.: "The Exhibitors to the Public", p. 108.

7 Kwon: *Miraep'a: Saeroun siwa shiinŭl wihayŏ*, p. 128.

8 Ibid.

9 Ibid., p. 9. This book was so successful that it was selected as 'Excellent Literature Book' by the Korean Culture and Arts Committee in 2006.

10 See Cho: "Futurism in Korea: From the Historical to the Postmodern Avant-garde."

Le Figaro, the full text was translated into Japanese right away.[11] In contrast, Futurism was only introduced in 1924 to literary circles in Korea – then under Japanese colonial rule – by Young-hee Park (1901–1950), and its concept was then analysed in more details in 1929 by Ju-dong Yang (1903–1977). Thereafter, Gi-rim Kim (1908–?), Sang Yi (1910–1937) and Ji-yong Jeong (1902–1950), who were advocates of Modernist literature in Korea, and Hwa Im (1908–1953), a poet belonging to KAPF (Korea Artista Proleta Federatio, the Esperanto name of the Proletarian Federation of Korean Artists), expressed an interest in machine culture, in speed and dynamism in works written under the influence of Italian Futurism. This, however, was only one aspect of their literary œuvre, soon to be replaced by other tendencies. For this reason, Futurism never developed in Korea into a fully-fledged movement with organized groups and partisan magazines.

When, in the early 2000s, debates were raging in Korea regarding a new generation of 'futurists', the poets themselves had little chance to be properly heard. In autumn 2007, the quarterly magazine *Siro yŏnŭn sesang* (The World Opened with Poetry) published a special section entitled "Miraep'aŭi chagi chindangwa miraep'aŭi mirae" (Futurists' Self-Diagnosis and Futurists' Future). The nine poets who were interviewed expressed that this process of pigeonholing and categorizing their works was not at all welcome. Min-jeong Kim, who was considered the most representative of the 'futurists', then and now, expressed her dissatisfaction in her critical essay "Uridŭrŭn kŭjŏ arŭmdaun pulgudŭril ppun: Shi andapshigo" (We Are Just Beautiful Cripples: On Poetry).

> At that moment, the mobile phone rings unexpectedly.
>
> Hey, this is me, let me ask you one thing. When I took an urgent call from a novelist close to me, I could see the faces of persons through the jumbled loud voices gossiping on the phone. Do you know whether OOO, who writes poetry, is a futurist or not? What? That's annoying. [...] Although this is not a situation where I should be angry, I can't stand the growing irritation. It is as if I had been pricked by a thorn, and I pour out words as they come into my mind. Is it a *kye?*[12] Did I join it voluntarily or am I the leader of the *kye?* Why do you include me in them despite the fact that I am not one who received the money first and ran away? That's not what it means. I know, I am sorry to be angry, but if you have time to figure out who is in a group or not, read the poems properly. [...]
>
> At that moment, I received another phone call. It was a person asking for a review: 'Please write a critique of something you cannot sympathize with, some appraisal of a poem or

---

11 See Zanotti: "Japan", pp. 628–629.

12 The *kye* is a traditional private credit system popular among Koreans, whose members contribute a modest amount of money to a joint pool and take turns to receive a lump sum share when needed. Each member receives the 'pot' on a rotating basis until all members have received their payout.

> an argument promoted by some critic.' I have nothing to say. No, I think you have something to say. What can I say when they say that they read the poems as they are? I am not interested in what they say. But people talk about futurists frequently. When did the poets come together and admitted it? It is not 'Poets of all nations, unite!' [...]
>
> I wish that people would stop the stupid needlework that puts us, buttons of various colours, on one coat. Unless it is sensible workmanship worth looking at, I am not grateful for it at all. We're buttons, we're just beautiful cripples, aren't we?[13]

The quoted remarks of Min-jeong Kim suggest that she was strongly opposed to critics attaching the label 'futurism' to poets of dissimilar directions. The fact that 'futurism' caused heated debates in Korean poetic circles is beyond question. However, it is difficult to provide a definite answer to the question of whether the Korean 'futurists' possessed a truly Futurist substance. Unlike the Italian and Russian Futurists of the early twentieth century who poured out countless manifestos and declarations with the name of their association emblazoned on them, the Korean 'futurists' in the early twenty-first century emerged from the effusions of one critic concerning a number of poets who had never used the term themselves. Nevertheless, these 'futurists' of the early twenty-first century are already engraved in the history of Korean literature, and Min-jeong Kim has been treated as their representative. Therefore, in the following sections of this essay I shall examine the twenty-first century Korean 'futurists' through the poetical lens of Min-jeong Kim.

Min-jeong Kim as a representative South Korean 'futurism'

According to the critic Bong-jun Goh, who discussed and summarized the phenomenon of 'futurism' in Korean literary circles, the so-called 'futurist' poets operated with three distinct concepts: "different [i. e. experimental] lyricism" (according to Jang-uk Lee), "fantasy" (according to Haeng-sook Kim) and "subconscious desire" (according to Hyeok-ung Kwon and Su-i Kim).[14] The poet who demonstrated these to a great extent was no other than Min-jeong Kim. She was born in Incheon in 1976, graduated from the Department of Creative Writing at Chung-Ang University in Seoul, and then completed graduate studies at the same university. She made her poetic debut in 1999 when "Pŭllaek nanaŭi kkum" (Black Nana's Dream) and nine other poems won the *Munye Chungang* New Author Literary

---

13 Kim: *Kaksŏrhago,* [Anyway,], pp. 161–163. The comma behind *Kaksŏrhago* forms part of the title.
14 Goh: *Tarŭn moksoridŭl* [Other Voices], pp. 216–217.

Award. In 2005, she published her first collection of poems, *Narŭnŭn kosŭmdoch'i agassi* (The Flying Hedgehog Lady), which showed clear 'futurist' characteristics. Her second book of poems, *Kŭnyŏga ch'ŏŭm, nŭkkigi shijak'aetta* (She Began to Feel, for the First Time), which can be said to be "a reminiscence or sequel of *The Flying Hedgehog Lady*",[15] followed in 2009. Thereafter, she published a collection of prose works, *Kaksŏrhago,* (Anyway, 2013), and two other volumes of poems that show differences in tone and topics from her previous works: *Arŭmdapko ssŭlmoŏpkirŭl* (To Be Beautiful and Useless, 2016) and *Nŏŭi kŏginŭn chakko naŭi yŏginŭn k'ŏsŏ uridŭrŭn heŏjinŭn chungimnida* (We Are Breaking Up Because Your 'There' Is Small and My 'Here' Is Large, 2019). She received the In-hwan Park Literary Award in 2007, the Contemporary Poetry Award in 2016, and the Sang-hwa Lee Poetry Award in 2018.

Apart from being a poet, Kim has been active as a publisher, manager and editor-in-chief. After working with many magazines and publishing houses, she became an editor at Munhaktongne, one of Korean mainstream literary publishing houses, and is currently the CEO of Nanda Publishing House, an affiliate of Munhaktongne. She has thus pursued a successful career and is now credited with having edited well over 500 books.

The literary critic Su-i Kim pointed out that Korean poetical circles around the year 2005 were "experiencing strange pleasures and chaotic feelings when confronted with unfamiliar speeches and unpredictable irregularities of young poets".[16] These characteristics certainly apply to Min-jeong Kim, and they were already present in her first anthology, *The Flying Hedgehog Lady* (2005), one of the most notable collections of poems in 2005. The book portrays the grotesque world of women who indulge in their fantasies and dreams, and experience frightening nightmares, characterized by Hyeok-ung Kwon as "a comic theatre of cruelty" which "unfolds scenes that adopt the documentary style of *Mondo Cane:*[17] body amputation, sex with dead bodies, ubiquitous abusive language, long descriptions of diseases, incest, cannibalistic monsters, rotten objects, masturbation, excrements, masochism and sadism, fetishism and exhibitionism, murder, rape, adultery, gluttony, torture, domestic violence and bestiality abound in each and

---

15 Lee: "Ppanhago shishihago an chillinŭn kŭnyŏŭi iyagi: Kim Min-jeong, 'Kŭnyŏga ch'ŏŭm, nŭkkigi shijak'aetta' (Munhakkwajisŏngsa, 2009.12)" [The Plain, Trivial and Boring Story of Her: Min-jeong Kim's 'She Began to Feel, for the First Time' (Munhakkwajisŏngsa, December 2009)], p. 42.

16 Kim: *Sŏjŏngŭn chinhwahanda* [Lyricism Evolves], p. 68.

17 *Mondo cane* (A Dog's Life, 1962) was a commercially successful Italian film that provides glimpses into cultural practices around the globe. It featured strange rituals filmed in a lurid and shocking manner.

every poems".[18] The cruel yet comical world drawn by the poet through the constant intersection of reality and fantasy conjures up a very unpleasant and grotesque world that has overturned the Korean poetic tradition, where lyricism is regarded as being of paramount importance.

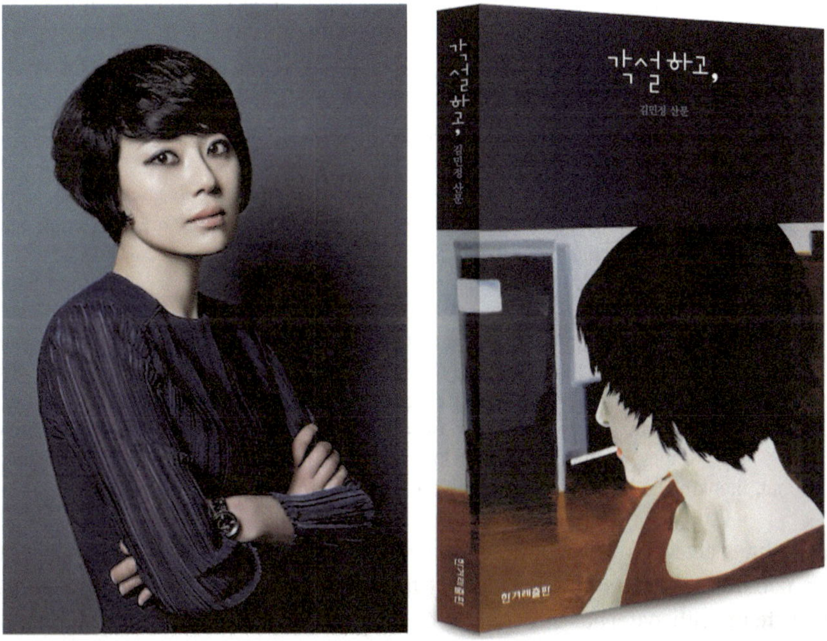

Fig. 1a: The poet Min-jeong Kim (date of photograph unknown). **Fig. 1b:** Cover of her collection of essays *Kaksŏrhago,* (Anyway,) published by Han'gyŏre ch'ulp'an in 2013.

In "Hwang Byeong-seung hyŏnsanggwa miraep'aŭi mirae" (The Byeong-seung Hwang Phenomenon and the Future of the Futurists), Sang-il Ha, an executive editor of the literary magazine *Onŭrŭi munyebip'yŏng* (Today's Literary Criticism), deals with what he considers to be the biggest problem of the 'futurists': their inability to communicate with their readers due to the abstruseness of their poems.

> The poems are getting more and more difficult. The poems have been considered to be much more difficult than works in prose, due to their metaphorical phraseology. Their rhetoric reach extreme states which even critics, who are professional readers, can hardly under-

18 Kwon: *Miraep'a: Saeroun shiwa shiinŭl wihayŏ*, pp. 160–161.

> stand. In fact, it is not an exaggeration to say that our poets have lost the small number of readers who have maintained an interest in poetry, and are now in a state of crisis.[19]

The perplexing quality of 'futurist' poetry has also been pointed out by various other critics with an anti-'futurist' proclivity. Min-jeong Kim is aware of readers' reactions to her poems, and her response to them is as uncompromising as her poems. She humorously describes the shock that must be felt by readers who "read her poems only superficially", as Hyeok-ung Kwon said, when she evokes her dialogues with her father in the essay "Soyoesŏ koyoro: Shironirapshigo" (From Disturbance to Silence: A So-called Criticism of Poems):

> Why is my daughter a 'flying hedgehog lady'? Read it carefully. My dad, who listens to me, immersed himself in my poems, even drawing lines under the verses. I don't know what you're talking about, but these works are truly funny. But are they really poems? If they are funny, that is great. My dad, who had enjoyed giving his daughter's collection of poems to his friends, had to look at their apathetic facial expressions all the time. They condemn me a lot. They say, "Why don't you give her a sound beating at home? Does Min-jeong have a mental problem? She seems to have associated with many men, so you better have her get married quickly. By the way, are all of these stories true? …" So, what did you say? You sons of a bitch, you know nothing. Hehe, you did well, but from now on, say the following: Stop prattling, and mind your own business! Father with redoubled courage, I would say that, thankfully, I began writing poems because of you.[20]

These lines give us an idea of how Min-jeong Kim reacted to readers' responses to her poems. Her father made an effort to understand her esoteric works and to read them with paternal affection. This attitude contrasts with the reactions of his acquaintances, who neither feel nor want to explore the poems in depth. Similarly, readers may try to understand the poems with an open mind or fail to engage with the characteristics of her texts. Since the majority of readers will fall into the latter category, Kim came to admire her father's "redoubled courage" and to despise her critics. In *The Flying Hedgehog Lady*, she humorously expressed her gratitude to her parents for enabling her to become a poet:

> My oven, my bread, my mumbling mouth,
> Dad Yeon-hoe Kim, mom Eun-suk Yang
> Who baked me so that I can eat myself until satiated,
> Thanks to you, I am so full.[21]

---

19 Ha: "Hwang Byeong-seung hyŏnsanggwa miraep'aŭi mirae" [The Byeong-seung Hwang Phenomenon and the Future of the Futurists], p. 81.

20 Kim: *Kaksŏrhago*, pp. 150–151.

21 Kim: *Narŭnŭn kosŭmdoch'i agassi* [The Flying Hedgehog Lady], p. 5.

When reviewing Kim's first collection of poems, the literary critic and professor of Korean literature Gye-sook Kang considered the average reader's inclination to interpret the poems as realistic depictions of life and warned them that such superficial readings should be avoided. She wrote: "If we read Min-jeong Kim's poems in a reductive manner and restrict them to the horizon of a rational reality with things actually occurring with mathematical probability, all we can get from them is discomfort and embarrassment that put cultural traditions, moral conventions and the language of common sense to shame."[22] Min-jeong Kim, who "despises beautifully resonant poems and hates to follow the logical order of events and objects",[23] creates literary works that are full of "irregularities, exceptions, fragments and coincidences".[24]

Kim's works quoted above demonstrate the non-traditional quality of the poet's writing. Although South Korean 'futurists' were unhappy about the fact that they were grouped together under the banner of Futurism, their aesthetic credo and strategy of anti-traditionalism was in fact very similar to the fight against conventions and dogmas by the historical Futurists in Italy and Russia. This was also the reason why the critic Hyeok-ung Kwon decided to call the non-traditional avant-garde poets of the twenty-first century 'futurists'. In other words, even though Kim did not directly link her work with historical Futurism, she shared the basic attitude of Korean twentieth-century poets who wrote poetry under the influence of historical Futurism (for example, Gi-rim Kim, Sang Yi, Ji-yong Jeong and Hwa Im). She certainly shared Marinetti's assertion of "Courage, boldness, and rebellion" in his *Foundation and Manifesto of Futurism* (1909),[25] and pursued similar strategies as those proclaimed in the *Technical Manifesto of Futurist Literature* (1912). In Kim's poetry, there are many disordered chains of analogies, onomatopoeia and examples of unusual typography. For example, in "Majimak sŏlchŏn" (The Last Verbal Battle), a poem depicting an unreal and grotesque conversation between a father and a daughter in the process of burying a patriarchal and violent father, the sound of closing the coffin echoes throughout the poem:

> (Teong, Teong, Teong)
> My daughter, it seems someone has come, isn't this a knock on the door?

22 Kang: "K'okkirirŭl naengjanggoe nŏnnŭn kŏmŭn Nana: Kim Min-jeong, 'Narŭnŭn kosŭmdoch'i agassi' (Yŏllimwŏn, 2005)" [Black Nana that Puts an Elephant into a Refrigerator: Min-jeong Kim, 'The Flying Hedgehog Lady' (Yŏllimwŏn, 2005)"], p. 393.

23 Kim: "Kongbaegŭi anmu" [Blank Choreography], p. 125.

24 Ibid., p. 125.

25 Marinetti: "The Foundation and Manifesto of Futurism", p. 13.

(Teong, Teong, Teong)
It is nailing sound, don't worry, father, this door will never, ever, open again.
(Teong, Teong, Teong)
Come on, my daughter, apply some blood to the doorpost.
(Teong, Teong, Teong)
There's no blood to do that, father.
[...]
(Teong, Teong, Teong)
The coffin has been lowered into the grave now. Father, now shut up and go to sleep.[26]

Min-jeong Kim fought more actively than anyone else in Korea to break down the 'masculinity' and the male-centred worldview prevalent in historical Futurism, most famously captured in Marinetti's call to scorn woman.[27] Although Kim's typography fell short of the most radical experiments undertaken by the historical Futurists, she produced unusual page layouts by changing fonts or alternating font sizes or using italics for emphasis. In the poem "Yongyong chukketchi" (You Are Irritated by Death, Aren't You?), the typical closing phrase of Korean ghost stories ("Do you still see me as OO?") and its variations were emphasized using the Gothic font (in Korea, this looks similar to the Arial font in English). In the poem "Tŭlgae pŭrabo tŭlkkae" (Wild Dog Bravo Perilla), the barking of dogs was changed here and there into Italics in order to separate it from the poem's narrative: "*Seethes, seethes further, woof woof wild dog barking,* one second before 0 o'clock when the pendulum sticks out its tongue and long molars like straws for red bean sherbets are felt on each biceps of people holding dumbbells, *seethes, seethes further, woof woof wild dog barking.*"[28] In the poem "Kajaebal tallin chipkebŏlleŭi pangmun" (Visit of an Earwig with Crayfish-feet), the font sizes were adjusted to distinguish between reality (grandmother and I, lying down after taking some sleeping pills) and fantasy (visit of and conversation with the earwig). The result is somewhat comical: "But thump thump door-hitting sound, boom boom, door-striking sound... Who is there? ... I am an earwig, please let me in.[29] I drilled a hole of a pebble size on the centre of the attic door."[30] It is also noteworthy that Kim often places emphasis points over certain words,[31] for example in the poem *Nanŭnya*

26 Kim: *Narŭnŭn kosŭmdoch'i agassi*, pp. 68–69.

27 Marinetti: "The Foundation and Manifesto of Futurism", p. 14.

28 Kim: *Narŭnŭn kosŭmdoch'i agassi*, p. 48.

29 The reduced font size is in the original.

30 Kim: *Narŭnŭn kosŭmdoch'i agassi*, p. 41.

31 Due to the nature of East Asian scripts, using bold to indicate emphasis makes their characters rather unreadable, especially at smaller font sizes. Therefore, emphasis points are used, similar to using an underline in Western languages for creating an emphasizing effect. However, in Korea,

"*p'oltchak*" (I Am "Jumping"): "The rope spins The rope that spins by itself without anyone spinning the rope slices the thick flesh of the cabbage well while splitting the air I am "jumping" by myself."[32]

In the following section, I shall examine how Kim's avant-garde poetry overturned the existing norms in Korean poetry and how the two collections published in the early phase of her career contributed to the rise of a form of poetry in Korea that critics now generally refer to as 'futurist'.

Metamorphosis and deconstruction in Min-jeong Kim's poetry

In the aforementioned essay "From Disturbance to Silence: A So-called Criticism of Poems", Min-jeong Kim reveals her poetics and lists the persons who enabled her, the eldest daughter in a family of four girls, to write poems in her distinctive, lively style. She mentions her parents who made her develop into a precocious child; the doctor who diagnosed her with 'depression' at the age of seven due to 'stress overload'; the married female teacher at the music academy who was blinded by love and ran away with a bachelor tuner; the Korean language teacher who led the 'sensitive' high school girl into the world of poetry; a senior student at university who taught her to introduce the serious 'father' theme into her poems and to experiment with it in a manner that pleases her. Furthermore, she pays homage to the 'cockroaches' (i.e. words with 'dirty' meanings), which she attached with scotch tape to her science observation diary and which, unintentionally, frighten her class teacher. And, above all, she takes delight in describing her reaction towards people who attacked her poems for not being poetic at all:

> One day, when I was called by name and looked back, well, there were poems. I was in a playful mood and suggested to my friends to play freeze tag, saying, "Stop right there." My play with poems had been a mess from the very beginning. Experiencing all of the reversals between *freeze* and *stop*, between the tagger and the hiding child at moments when the hiding child nearly seemed to be caught but in the end was not caught, I could free myself a little from my obsession with poems. Every time I was asked to recite a poem, my head and heart became as tangled as an iron scrubber. Since all kinds of scratches are a natural procedure, I, with my tattered spirit, had to spend the whole night giving birth to words, riding words and killing words. [...] Therefore, let me tell you: your poems are not poems. In that

both bold and emphasis points are used for the emphasizing effect. The latter is considered old-fashioned today and bold is comparatively more common. Kim used emphasis points rather than bold to enhance the visual effect of the page.

32 Kim: *Narŭnŭn kosŭmdoch'i agassi*, p. 146.

> case, are my poems novels? Your poems with so many words are certainly not poems. In fact, they are poems full of omissions.[33]

This excerpt shows that Min-jeong Kim's prose writing style is far from being neat. It is almost impossible to find sentences with lyricism and beautiful expressions (something that readers usually expect in prose works written by poets). Ingenious associations can frequently be observed in her poems (for example comparing her head and heart to a 'tangled iron scrubber'), as well as puns such as "giving birth to words, riding words and killing words", which play with the homonyms 'mal' (language, word) and 'mal' (horse).

Min-jeong Kim's poems seem to have been written casually and recklessly, for which they were subjected to severe criticism: "These poems cannot be poems because they have no depth or system of thought."[34] However, according to what she stated in an interview with the critic and a close friend of hers, Hyeong-cheol Shin, her poems were born through meticulous conception and planning: "I calculate[35] a lot. […] When writing poems, I also act as a fashion consultant. This is how I coordinate my poems: When I wear a vintage trench coat, I hold a luxury bag and I tend to create poems while questioning the overall picture to myself. […] I am a bitch who conducts a process of adding or subtracting from poems with a firm mind."[36] At the same time, Kim uses colloquial speech (for example referring to herself as a "bitch"). Even in interviews, her speech habits appear as coarse as the words in her poetry and prose works. Kim is trying to abolish all conventions traditionally attached to the concepts of 'poetry' or of 'the poet' in a manner that is similar to what the Russian Futurists called "a slap in the face of public taste" (*Poshchechina obshchestvennomu vkusu*) in a manifesto published in December 1912.[37]

The avant-garde nature of Kim's poetry can be explained through the concepts termed 'metamorphosis' and 'deconstruction'. The poet is transforming non-poetic things or occurrences into poetry, but still letting them sound coarse and vulgar. To

33 Kim: *Kaksŏrhago*, pp. 149–150.

34 Ibid., p. 163.

35 She repeatedly uses this expression 'calculation' to suggest that her planning is like a mathematical operation. In other words, she is planning her poems in great detail by adding or subtracting words.

36 Shin: "24kae tanŏro mandŭn sajŏn: Hwang Byeong-seunggwa Kim Min-jeongŭi kyŏngu" [A Dictionary Made of 24 Words: The Case of Byeong-seung Hwang and Min-jeong Kim], pp. 292–293.

37 The manifesto was published in the brochure *Poshchechina obshchestvennomu vkusu: Stikhi, proza, stat'i*. Moskva: Kuz'min, 1912, an anthology with contributions by David and Nikolai Burliuk, Wassily Kandinsky, Velimir Khlebnikov, Aleksei Kruchenykh, Benedikt Livshits and Vladimir Mayakovsky.

get away from the control and compression that are emphasized in traditional lyric poetry, she focusses on images and words that have a distinctly raw quality, using non-poetic vocabularies taken from slang and profane language, while intentionally erasing the aura of poetry by employing puns and curses. She also makes poems look unfamiliar by abolishing punctuation, by changing fonts or by placing emphasis points over words, as mentioned above.

The following example shows a poem with abolished punctuations, the repeat sign (:‖) taken from music scores, alternating font type and bold for emphasis effect as well as a lack of line breaks like in prose texts:

고통에 찬 빨래 되기
—나는 안 닮고 나를 닮은 검은 나나들 5

낮에도 여자는 늘 세탁중이네 피칠 두른 살에 지져진 얼룩들이 남아 영 지워지질 않네 회전하는 드럼통 안에도 흉터처럼 얼룩들 남아 닦고 또 닦아도 아이 참 이 씨부럴 놈의 얼룩들 지워지질 않고 도돌이표 도돌이표로 다시 밤마다 :‖

Kot'onge ch'an ppallae toegi
– Nanŭn an tamko narŭl talmŭn kŏmŭn nanadŭl 5

Najedo yŏjanŭn nŭl set'akchungine p'ich'il turŭn sare chijyŏjin ŏlluktŭri nama yŏng chiwŏjijil anne hoejŏnhanŭn tŭrŏmt'ong anedo hyungt'ŏch'ŏrŏm ŏlluktŭl nama takko tto takkado ai ch'am ssiburŏl nomŭi ŏlluktŭl chiwŏjijil ank'o todorip'yo todorip'yo tashi **pammada :‖**[38]

Becoming the Laundry Full of Pain
– I Don't Resemble, but Black Nanas that Resemble Me 5

The woman is always doing the laundry during the day The stains worn on the flesh covered in blood remain and are not erased at all The fucking stains remain like scars in the rotating drum and are made by repeat sign, by repeat sign **every night :‖**

In addition, Kim reduces readability by introducing unfamiliar metaphors and letting sentences erupt like in a stream of consciousness. She describes her uniqueness as a poet in the essay "We Are Just Beautiful Cripples" by referring to her honesty as a 'weapon' which allows her to write bravely, without hesitation and filter, all that which she wishes to communicate.

> I use honesty like a weapon, which is not unusual but maybe different, so they [the critics] say. Without any sort of 'pretending' to write sublimely and beautifully in a classical and tra-

---

38 Kim: *Narŭnŭn kosŭmdoch'i agassi*, p. 66.

> ditional way, […] I reveal every detail, including even the weak points that can make me look like a sort of fool or wimp.[39]

Kim's indifference and disregard for the 'sublime' and the 'beautiful' in a classical and traditional sense allows her to be bold (in her words, 'honest') and to embrace, both in form and content, the vulgar and ugly aspects of life. Kim's poetics, which can be called 'an aesthetics of ugliness', reminds us of Marinetti's repeated demand to introduce 'the ugly' into literature, for example in his *Technical Manifesto of Futurist Literature:* "Indeed, we use all the ugly sounds, all the expressive cries of the violent life that surrounds us. Bravely, we bring the 'ugly' into literature."[40]

Slang, obscene language and punning in Min-jeong Kim's poetry

What shocks readers the most in Min-jeong Kim's language is the offensive vocabulary derived from slang, insults and obscene expressions. This non-poetic everyday language seems to have been inserted without undergoing a process of literalization and poetization. Kim's poems were therefore subjected to severe criticism, going as far as denying her the right to call her works 'poetry'. Jang-uk Lee, who wrote the introduction to Kim's first poetry collection, *The Flying Hedgehog Lady,* explains her language as follows:

> The idioms employed in this collection of poems are raw and are taken from discourses existing outside the genre of poetry. Those idioms can be found everywhere, at home, on the street, at school, in hospitals, on buses and subways; but above all, they are part of our subconscious, like a nightmare that is about to burst. These terms are in many cases colloquial and, as if they were natural, embrace obscene language, slang and swear words. […] Everyday language has intruded upon her poems without any poetic correction or filters. This vocabulary seems radical when employed in a genre called 'poetry', but is extremely common outside in the streets. Therefore, this collection of poems does not 'reflect' life and the world through the grammar of the genre but uses the rough vocabularies of the street and the unconscious, borrowed here for a moment. This is the case not only with vocabularies. Just open this collection of poems at any point and look at the images and sentences that have been formed by using this lexicon.[41]

39 Kim: *Kaksŏrhago*, p. 163.

40 Marinetti: "Technical Manifesto of Futurist Literature", p. 113.

41 Lee: "Kŭ yŏjaŭi angmong" [That Woman's Nightmare], pp. 152–155.

According to this critic, the roots of Kim's poetry in a fantasy world can already be detected in the title of the anthology *The Flying Hedgehog Lady.* The animal referred to here, which uses its spiky quills to defend itself against its environment, is not, realistically, 'flying'. It is a fantasy animal, yet ultimately grounded in reality transformed by means of poetic language. A noteworthy point is that the poet, by her own admission, inserted the slang words, curses and obscenities according to a schema, or what she herself calls 'calculations'. The sex-related vocabulary ("genitals", "egg", "labia minora", "penis", "testicles", "semen", "sperm", "clitoris", "pubic region", "masturbation", "swollen nipples", etc.) has as a counterpart provocative curses ("Damn me") and slang expressions ("fucking fast crawling tortoise"; "You evil bitch, you bitch should be beheaded posthumously, you should be struck dead by a lightning, bitch") or sexual slurs ("Your genitals taste of MSG *Miwon*"). Therefore, Kim's poems cannot but shock a reader who is accustomed to and expects the conventional beauty of lyric poetry. Kim's poems are brusque, explicit and crude; and they lack filters or embellishments.

Another feature in Kim's poetry that catches readers' eyes is the use of puns, which include imitations of vocal sounds or playing with homonyms. It is largely because of this punning that the violent or horrific scenes come across as 'comic' or 'humorous'. In a review of Kim's first book of poems, the critic Gye-suk Kang highlighted the poet's unbridled word play, applied to a practical joke often employed by recruitment managers: 'How to put an elephant into a refrigerator?' / 'Open the refrigerator door. Put the elephant into the refrigerator. Close the refrigerator door.'

> This pun, which cannot be a real situation given the size of an elephant, is a sort of word game that induces laughter by ignoring the social contract established between the signifier and the signified, and by simply reversing the realistic context established between the sign and the referents. [...] Readers come to find that there is a commonality between the poet's phraseology and the 'rhetoric of the elephant' in terms of a formal aesthetics. Min-jeong Kim's 'Black Nana' would probably put the elephant into the refrigerator as follows. 'Open the refrigerator door. Saw the elephant into pieces. Grind the pieces with a mixer. Put the ground pieces into the refrigerator. Close the refrigerator door.' The act of sawing an elephant to pieces, grinding the pieces with a mixer and putting the ground pieces into the refrigerator has nothing to do with an actual event in reality. The language used here is not an imitative language that communicates facts. It functions as a medium for a word game and a game of signifiers.[42]

42 Kang: "K'okkirirŭl naengjanggoe nŏnnŭn kŏmŭn Nana: Kim Min-jeong, 'Narŭnŭn kosŭmdoch'i agassi' (Yŏllimwŏn, 2005)", pp. 390–391.

Gye-suk Kang emphasizes here the playfulness of Min-jeong Kim's language and argues that it "leads poetry into an indeterminate borderland that is neither real nor unreal, that is, into a world of fantasy".[43] Punning was one of Kim's major strategies and caused the poet Byeong-seung Hwang to consider her to be "a master of puns".[44] Kim used phonetic word play, for instance, in the title of the first poem in her first collection of poems, "Naega kŭrin kirin kŭrim kirim" (Admiring a Painting of a Giraffe Drawn by Me),[45] or at the end of this first collection in a poem playing with the homophones 'ŭmmo' (pubic hair) and 'ŭmmo' (conspiracy), "Ŭmmo han t'ŏrŏk soge sesang modŭn ŭmmoga ta sumŏ ittŭshi" (As All the Conspiracies in the World Are Hidden in One Pubic Hair).

In the second collection of poems, *She Began to Feel, for the First Time,* which already alludes to sexual codes in its title, Kim mixed puns with obscenities, as in "Ŭmmoranŭn irŭmŭi ŭmmo"[46] (Conspiracy Named Pubic Hair), "Chŏtiranŭn irŭmŭi chot" (A Dick Named Bosom), "P'enisŭranŭn irŭmŭi p'eisŭ" (A Face Named Penis).[47] Many other titles use similar devices, such as "Hwadunya hwat'unya" (Topic or Korean Playing Cards), "Gobiranŭn irŭmŭi gobi" (Crisis Named Gobi), "Opparanŭn irŭmŭi oba" (Over Named Brother), "Namp'yŏniranŭn irŭmŭi namŭi p'yŏn" (A Man on the Other Person's Side Named Husband), "Poksuranŭn irŭmŭi aksu" (A Handshake Named Revenge) and "Ttongkko peibi" (Anus Baby; with echoes of "Don't Go Baby"). Min-jeong Kim explained her interest in puns as follows: "When my mom first learned to send text messages on her phone, she accidentally wrote 'haengbok' (surrender) instead of 'hangbok' (happiness). This was before my first collection of poems was published, and I kept the fact in my memory for a long time. What can I do when it comes back to me repeatedly, despite the fact that I try to suppress my reminiscence? I shall not do it anymore."[48]

Although puns decreased in Kim's subsequent poetry books, they did not stop altogether. For example, in "The Poet's Words" in her third collection, *To Be Beautiful and Useless*, she plays with homonyms:

> Without *shi* [poems]
> I wanted *shijip* [a collection of poems] too much.

---

43 Ibid., p. 393.

44 Shin: "24kae tanŏro mandŭn sajŏn: Hwang Byeong-seunggwa Kim Min-jeongŭi kyŏngu", p. 290.

45 In fact, it is a variation of a well-known Korean tongue-twister.

46 Here, and in the following, I use regular type and italics to stress the punning with similar sounds.

47 In this collection of poems, titles that actively utilizes puns ('OO(i)ranŭn irŭmŭi ▲▲ [▲▲ named OO]') were used quite frequently (in 12 out of 60 poems).

48 Shin: "24kae tanŏro mandŭn sajŏn: Hwang Byeong-seunggwa Kim Min-jeongŭi kyŏngu", p. 290.

Wanting is *pyŏk* (癖) [habit]
Even if that *pyŏk* [habit] is not this *pyŏk* (壁) [wall]
Since *mun* (文) [literature] is a *mun* (門) [door]
I want to open it one more time.

This is the 3rd time, and
33 poems.

Because *sam* [3] is *samsam* [attractive].[49]

The poet is trying here to make her text funny by using seemingly illogical puns based on homophones, and then enhances the reader's comprehension by adding Chinese characters to the text. By using the number 3, she writes about her 3rd book of poetry composed of 33 poems. However, there is no similarity between '3' (sam) and 'attractive' (samsam), except for the phonetic similarity of 'sam'. The poet makes her readers laugh by arbitrarily connecting them.[50]

The fourth collection of poems, *We Are Breaking Up Because Your 'There' Is Small and My 'Here' Is Large*, is composed of 44 poems, many of them using puns, as in the first poem, "1wŏl 1il iryoil – Koktu 1" (1 January 1 Sunday – Phantom 1):

I saw *tokki* [an ax] and *t'op* [a saw] during the day
I saw *kkwŏng* [a pheasant] and *t'okki* [a rabbit] at night.

I would not write *ssibal* [fucking] in poems, and
Would not write *cholla* [damn on] on the snow. [...]

While drinking *ssukch'a* [mugwort tea]
I heard *Ssuktaemŏri* [a song of pansori *Ch'un-hyang*].[51]

In addition, the poet tried to revolutionize the formal avant-garde nature of her poetry by erasing the boundaries between poetry and prose. She intentionally ignored the rules concerning line breaks and used commas arbitrarily, for example

49 Kim: *Arŭmdapko ssŭlmoŏpkirŭl* [To Be Beautiful and Useless], p. 5. Text in round brackets are Kim's additions, text in square brackets are mine.
50 The Chinese characters are in the original. In Korea, illogical and somewhat unfunny puns based on phonetic similarities like these are called 'ajae gag [uncle's gag]'). I added the number 3 to the text so that non-Korean readers can understand the lines more easily.
51 Kim: *Nŏŭi kŏginŭn chakko naŭi yŏginŭn k'ŏsŏ uridŭrŭn heŏjinŭn chungimnida* [We Are Breaking Up Because Your 'There' Is Small and My 'Here' Is Large], p. 9. The poet intentionally uses words 'there'/'here' and 'small'/'large' to imply sexual organs.

"In the, end *ae* (love)" instead of "In the end *ae* (love)" and "right, and, wrong" instead of "right and wrong". In the poem "Kot'onge ch'an ppallae toegi – Nanŭn an tamko narŭl talmŭn kŏmŭn nanadŭl 5" (Becoming the Laundry Full of Pain – I Don't Resemble, but Black Nanas that Resemble Me 5), the repeat sign :‖, taken from music scores, is used to emphasize the recurring nature of an event. In addition, fonts were changed to lend emphasis to certain words: "The Women is always doing the laundry during the day The stains worn on the flesh covered in blood remain and are not erased at all The fucking stains remain like scars in the rotating drum and are made by repeat sign, by repeat sign **every night:‖**".[52]

Fantasy and reality in Min-jeong Kim's poetry

The avant-garde nature of the linguistic and formal dimensions in Kim's poetic works breaks away from traditional Korean lyricism, which treats compression and moderation as virtues and aims at reflection and contemplation. Kim's unlimited fantasy and maximized sense of the bizarre and grotesque delved into the world of the unconscious, conjured up nightmares, broke sexual taboos, and thus shocked many readers. The root cause of this gruesome and fragmented world was the poet's own wounds, lived out in her world of imagination as a revenge for the grief and anguish experienced at home or in school. As the poet herself acknowledged, the majority of poems in *The Flying Hedgehog Lady* depict a world in which reality has been transformed into fantasy by means of 'flying'. In the end, the "carnivalesque chaos of infinite violence"[53] occurring in the absence of causality of events can be seen as the poet's own desperation: "In my first collection of poems, when I got hurt, I constantly screamed that I was in pain. Frankly speaking, there was a sort of anticipation that somebody would come running to protect me."[54]

Kim's debut piece and one of her most representative works, "Black Nana's Dream", can be said to sum up her entire first collection in that it deals with the author's divided poetic selves and the fantasy worlds they created in her mind. *The Flying Hedgehog Lady* consists of 54 poems. The first part is entitled 'Their Märchen'[55] (17 poems), the second 'Black Nana's Dream' (17 poems), and

52 Kim: *Narŭnŭn kosŭmdoch'i agassi*, p. 66. The change of font is in the original.

53 Kang: "K'okkirirŭl naengjanggoe nŏnnŭn kŏmŭn Nana: Kim Min-jeong, 'Narŭnŭn kosŭmdoch'i agassi' (Yŏllimwŏn, 2005)", p. 397.

54 Shin: "24kae tanŏro mandŭn sajŏn: Hwang Byeong-seunggwa Kim Min-jeongŭi kyŏngu", p. 276.

55 She uses the German word for fairy tale, meaning that women's lives in poems resemble the cruel fate of their sisters in fables and legends.

the third 'I Am Jumping' (20 poems). As can be seen from the title of the first part of the collection, the poetic subject is always a woman, and the genre is that of the fairy tale, which can eliminate the boundaries of the poetic world. Interestingly, the 'Nana' presented in Part 2 can be viewed as a proper noun,[56] but it seems more correct to understand it as a plural (*Na* + *Na*) of the first person singular pronoun in Korean (*Na*). The poetic subject of the entire collection is indeed changed from 3rd person plural/They (Part 1) into 3rd person singular or 1st person plural/ Black Nana (Part 2), and 1st person singular/I (Part 3), indicating that the poetic process takes the form of a sinking into the world of the lyrical 'I's.

The poet, who struggled to discover the "I within me" and to find "the complete I of me"[57] through the writing of her poetry, presents in her poetry countless lyrical alter egos, all of them suffering and screaming when confronted with painful situations and hurtful events. As the readers journey from the first poem, "Admiring a Painting of a Giraffe Drawn by Me", to the last poem, "As All the Conspiracies in the World Are Hidden in One Pubic Hair", they discover endless variations of the author's lyrical 'I's. This break-up or break-down of the author's representative egos bears close similarity to what Marinetti demanded in 1912: "In literature, eradicate the 'I'",[58] repeated in 1913 in his warnings "against the obsession with the 'I', which the poets have described, sung about, analyzed, and spewed up until the present day",[59] and repeated again in 1916: "In the new Futurist lyricism, which expresses geometrical splendors, our literary 'I' is burnt up and destroys itself in the superior vibrancy of the cosmos."[60] In Kim's words, this multi-layered 'I' is conjured up in the lines:

> You are standing in the window, which has not been cleaned after an egg broke on it
> Forever there, weeping with the rusty water of the panties covering you
> My angel
> It's fucking me in the layered mirror stained with my tortured search for grace[61]

---

56 In French, the word means 'young girl', 'girlfriend', sometimes 'mistress', and in colloquial speech also 'babe', 'chick', 'moll', 'piece of ass', 'pussy', etc.

57 These are quotes from Kim's poem "In Search of the 'Complete' I of me" and interview after the winning of a prize in the poem sector of the 21th *Munye Chungang* New Author Literary Award: "I wanted to find the 'I' within me. From the moment I began writing poetry, the question 'What indeed is the 'I'?' has never left my mind. I came to think that the 'I' who is dreaming, the 'I' who woke up and the 'I' who got up and write are different beings and that my ego consists of not one but several 'I's who are completely different from each other." Goh: *Tarŭn moksoridŭl*, p. 227.

58 Marinetti: "Technical Manifesto of Futurist Literature", p. 110.

59 Marinetti: "Destruction of Syntax – Untrammeled Imagination – Words-in-Freedom", pp. 124–125.

60 Marinetti: "Dynamic, Multichanneled Recitation", p. 194.

61 Kim: *Narŭnŭn kosŭmdoch'i agassi*, p. 12.

The birth of the 'I within me' is implied through the sexual associations of the words 'egg' and 'panties'; but also the division of the 'me' can be infinitely changed and multiplied through a 'layered mirror'. The 'you' and 'my angel', which are in a place that can hardly be reached, are revealed as 'fucking me in the layered mirror'. Her torturing quest to achieve 'grace' has 'stained' the mirror, and gazing into it makes her aware of her repeated failures.

This passage reveals that Kim's contortion of various alter egos depicts a (postmodern) investigation of the self that goes beyond Marinetti's exhortation to do away with the Romantic subject in poetry. Although both Marinetti and Min-jeong Kim focussed their attention on the eradication of the literary 'I', this poetic ego possesses different properties due to the different epochs in which they were operating. Marinetti was opposed to the Romantic literary ego and the lone genius, who lives in an ivory tower. He promoted instead a resilient and strong 'creative ego' who is able to collaborate with other Futurist geniuses in order to improve the world. Marinetti proclaimed the need to annihilate the poetic 'I' and to develop a new understanding of individualism that superseded psychological parameters. He sought to abolish the conventional psychology of the Romantic, self-expressive author and establish a new 'lyrical sensibility' that is able to express the essence of matter.

This abolition of the literary 'I' was not the same as the dissolution of the ego (another complex issue in Futurism). Marinetti did not want to abolish the ego but to foster strong individuals bonded together by their common interests, ideals and needs. The literary 'I's of Italian and Russian Futurists, who lived in the era of utopianism, was linked to confident and courageous individuals who tried to overthrow the real world in order to create a bright future. Korea's 'futurists', on the other hand, including Min-jeong Kim, lived in the post-utopian era with weak and timid 'I's who could only dream of overthrowing the real world in the fantasy domain of literature.

Kim's poems portray with rough brushstrokes a world full of lyric personas "who went out of the body and are attached to the ceiling" ("Black Nana's Dream"). The author's "blue second self"[62] is borrowed from Sarah Kirsch ("Wanjŏnhan kyŏngni" [Complete Isolation]),[63] and the hardships and wounds are suf-

62 Ibid., p. 121.

63 Sarah Kirsch (pseud of Ingrid Bernstein, 1935–2013) was a German lyric poet, whose works express loneliness, isolation, grief and pain as an existential condition of the human race. In 1993, a collection of poems by Sarah Kirsch was translated into Korean by the Germanist and poet Sangbae Park. Min-jeong Kim is likely to have encountered Sarah Kirsch's poems, themes and techniques thanks to this collection. Kim subsequently paid attention to the German poet's feminism, and the theme of the divided self (the double) is repeatedly reflected in her poems.

fered by diverse selves such as beaten wives and girls who are sexually harassed or ravaged, and girls who are subject to violence at school or at home. The woman who appears to have been raped in the poem "Kot'onge ch'an ppallae ppalgi: Nanŭn an tamko narŭl talmŭn kŏmŭn nanadŭl 1" (Doing the Laundry Full of Pain – I Don't Resemble, but Black Nanas that Resemble Me 1), for instance, "wanted to burn the smell of my flesh that did not go away even after wiping it off with a scrubber", but in the end abuses her own body every night while doing the laundry, because the smell "kept growing".[64] On the other hand, some of the poetic selves mercilessly and cruelly plot revenge. For example, in the poem "Naega nal challa kupko innŭn pam p'unggyŏng" (Night Scenery Where I Cut and Bake Myself), the 'I' is sadistically dismantled, and in "Salsujebi kkŭrinŭn ai" (The Child Who Boils Hand-pulled Flesh Soup), the "I-already-dead" boils "the hand-pulled mom-and-dad flesh soup" and "scoops up while keeping puffing" and "chews the flesh".[65]

Although women often appear as poetic subjects in Min-jeong Kim's poems, these words should not simply be understood as narratives from a female perspective. In "Kim Jong-min ajŏssi" (Uncle Jong-min Kim), the figure of a dead uncle is depicted as infinitely changing and proliferating in Seoul's subway line 1: "Even though he was not a twin, the uncle was not one person because the bodies of those, who sat on the seat where the uncle sat, were instantly changed into the body of the uncle [...] Whoo, ha, hoo, ha, huh, Uncle Jong-min, why is the number of you increasing all the time?"[66] When a male narrator, such as the "owner of seasoned fried chicken joint *Urijip* [My House]" and "boys selling eyeballs on the snowy street", appear in other poems, these figures are not solely representing men either. As if the poet was wary of her poetry being interpreted as offering female narratives, in the last poem of her first collection she emphasizes that she recounts a "most obvious old story" that is "the story of all of us".[67] In other words, she wants to emphasize that the suffering of various protagonists (not only humans, but also animals and plants) is the story of all beings who share similar histories of suffering: "The most obvious old story, it is the story of all of us. The sad thing to me is that one day, when I was a pair of tweezers, hair was not completely pulled out. So, I was abandoned. My mom was giving birth to me again then."[68]

---

64 Kim: *Narŭnŭn kosŭmdoch'i agassi*, p. 58.
65 Ibid., p. 72.
66 Ibid., pp. 122–123.
67 Ibid., p. 151.
68 Ibid., p. 151.

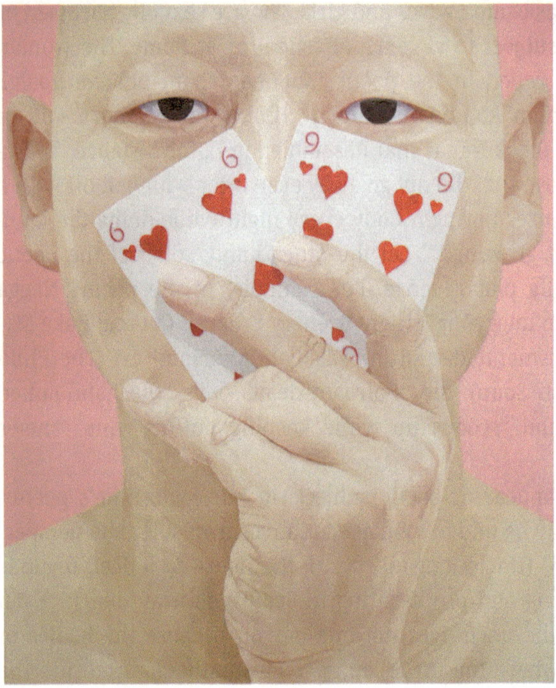

Fig. 2: Ung-pil Byeon: *Self-portrait as a Man _ <6♡9>* (2010).

As mentioned above, the poetic subjects of the entire collection gradually submerge into the world of the first-person poetic self, and the boundary between 'I' and 'you' eventually collapses. Kim's perception of the essence of human existence became a model for other artists. For example, in 2010, she collaborated with the painter Ung-pil Byeon on a book project for the crossover exhibition *Kŭrimedo pulguhago* (Despite the Painting),[69] dedicated to a fusion of art and literature. Byeon's oil painting *Self-portrait as a Man _ <6♡9>* (it has no Korean title) interpreted a poem by Kim, "Chŏtiranŭn irŭmŭi chot" (Dick Named Bosom), in which the painter embodies the similarity between 'chŏt' (bosom) and 'chot' (dick), using the shapes of the numbers 6 and 9. Before the exhibition (held at Interalia Art Space, Seoul, 5 March – 1 April 2010), they published a book entitled *Kŭrimedo pulguhago* (Despite the Painting), in which Min-jeong Kim presented Ung-pil Byeon as a person with countless egos, as a being in a state of metamorphosis, eventually

69 The title uses a pun based on the phonetic similarity between 'kŭrŏmedo pulguhago' (nevertheless) and 'kŭrimedo pulguhago' (despite the painting).

breaking down the boundary between 'you' and 'me' to arrive at an understanding of male and female as a 'we':

> This is a boy. [...] Yes, this is a girl. [...] Yes, this is a young man. [...] Yes, this is a married man. [...] Yes, this is a married woman. [...] Yes, this is a grandfather. [...] Yes, this is my great-grandmother. [...] Yes, it is me, it is you, it is us. As such, we who are me and you and everyone at the same time, I will call us Byeon.[70]

In her second collection of poems, Kim continued her contemplation on the existence of human beings in a state that encompasses both life and death. *She Began to Feel, for the First Time* consists of 4 sections: Part 1 'Small Events' (16 poems), Part 2 'Mumble, Mumble' (15 poems), Part 3 'God Is in Footnotes' (14 poems) and Part 4 'Flying Poems About a Running Woman' (15 poems). Here, the poet pushes metamorphosis and deconstruction to the extreme and expanded the use of fantasy as a weapon: "In the first collection of poems I did everything with a person termed 'I', such as gnawing and tearing things apart to eat. Thereafter, I felt content, because there was no limit to what I could try afterwards."[71] Kim comments on her progression as a poet as follows: "If my first collection of poems was said to be flying, the second collection of poems was walking. When, for the first time, I stamped my foot onto the ground, I could see people, but how could I know what they were like? I should just live as a person."[72]

The poet still emphasizes that the events depicted in her second collection of poems can be shared by everyone. In "Face Named Penis", three themes termed 'So this is an extremely plain story', 'Therefore, a very boring story' and 'But a story that we will never tire of' are marked in the Gothic font to let readers understand that the stories are universal. Also in the poem "Nabi chungdokcha" (Butterfly Addict), the content is not limited to *one* woman, but depicts the lives of *all* women. After seeing "a woman carrying a cow on her shoulder", that is, a woman who carries food such as milk for her family,[73] the last line says: "décalcomanie that does not run out of",[74] indicating that the lives of women, who are traditionally in charge of food in families, are extremely repetitive. In this poem, the word "repeat

70 Lee, et al.: *Kŭrimedo pulguhago* [Despite the Painting], p. 145.

71 Ibid., p. 187.

72 Shin: "24kae tanŏro mandŭn sajŏn: Hwang Byeong-seunggwa Kim Min-jeongŭi kyŏngu", p. 271.

73 Min-jeong Kim repeatedly likens women to cows because both produce milk.

74 Décalcomanie is a process of transferring pictures or designs printed on specially prepared paper to materials such as glass or metal. In the early twentieth century, many French firms specialized in this reproduction technique.

sign", which is almost synonymous with "décalcomanie", supports this interpretation.

As the titles of the poems "Nŭl kŭrŏn kongshik" (Always Such Formula) and "Hŭnhaeppajin rep'ŏt'ori" (A Banal Repertoire) in this second collection suggest, Kim's poetry is rooted in our daily lives where isolation, alienation, violence and absurdity are common. But in her poetry, such troublesome and unpleasant experiences become even more nightmarish because, in Gye-sook Kang's words, "Mi-jeong Kim is rolling out the hell of reality before us, telling us to open our eyes wide and to look at it clearly."[75] After all, as the critic Min-jeong Kim herself said about the poet Min-jeong Kim in a book review: "A courageous poet is a poet who describes pain as pain and lack as lack."[76]

Confronting the demand that 'poetry should be like this or that', Kim ridicules, transforms and deconstructs the stable and familiar world and erects a new one where contradictions and unsteadiness are exposed. In addition, she creates an awareness of the dark and awkward side of things. This is the very reason why Kim's poems cannot be considered entertaining, although the poet herself always emphasized the 'fun' aspects of her works. Chan Lee compared Kim's poems with Mikhail Bakhtin's concepts of the 'carnivalesque' and 'grotesque realism' in *Tvorchestvo Fransua Rable i narodnaia kul'tura Srednevekov'ia i Renessansa* (Francois Rabelais and Folk Culture of the Middle Ages and the Renaissance, 1965). He argues that, despite these superficial characteristics, the other side of Kim's poetry should also be considered: "If you cannot stomach the poet's heavy introspection and ethical struggles hidden behind Kim's carnivalesque, grotesque realism and black humour, you may read only one half of this collection of poems."[77]

When her poems were judged to be too long, cumbersome, radical and destructive ("they have an intense smell of an amateur"[78]), the poet Seung-ho Choe (b. 1954) gave her this advice: "Kill the gardener in you, get rid of all those who want to prune you."[79] Mi-jeong Kim could use metamorphosis and deconstruction as means to twist or parody the sacred, the status quo and established hierarchies, to indulge in fantasies, dreams and fairy tales while expanding her own unique world of poetry. However, the Korean 'futurist' poet was different from the histor-

75 Kang: "K'okkirirŭl naengjanggoe nŏnnŭn kŏmŭn Nana: Kim Min-jeong, 'Narŭnŭn kosŭmdoch'i agassi' (Yŏllimwŏn, 2005)", p. 340.

76 Kim: "Natsŏn hokŭn nalsŏn imijiŭi k'anibal: Kim Min-jeong shijip 'Narŭnŭn kosŭmdoch'i agassi'", p. 249.

77 Lee: "Mihaktŭl, segyerŭl mannanŭn shiinŭi p'ŭrijŭmdŭl" [Aesthetics, Prisms of Those Poets Who Examine the World], p. 351.

78 Kim: *Kaksŏrhago*, p. 154.

79 Ibid.

ical Futurist poets in the early twentieth century, who mostly dreamed up utopias to become realities in the near future. The Korean 'futurist' poets, including Min-jeong Kim, were living in a post-utopian era, when all hopes for the future had evaporated. Nevertheless, the critic Gyeong-su Lee commended the creative methods of the Korean 'futurists' by explaining that Kim's way of revealing everything without hiding anything was "a strategy that a poet, who writes (has no choice but to write) non-poetic poetry in the non-poetic era, can adopt".[80]

The future of a Korean 'futurism' that actually existed and did not exist at all

As discussed at the beginning of this essay, the Korean 'futurists' were not an organized group but appeared on the scene when a critic referred to them by that label. Poems written in this 'futurist' style were submitted until the mid-2010s in the annual spring literary contests, which are said to reflect contemporary literary trends.[81] In addition, since the works of Min-jeong Kim were already treated in universities as being representative of 'futurism', they quickly entered the history of Korean literature. However, it should be pointed out that the tag 'futurism' functions in Korean literary circles as a general noun rather than a technical term related to the historical Futurists in Italy and Russia, who defined themselves as *futuristi* / *futuristy* in their proclamations and manifestos.[82] In Korea, the label 'futurism' was attached to young poets who wanted to break away from traditional poetry and reform the literary genre with regard to content and form. It is ironic that the number of so-called 'futurist' poets continued to grow in a country where no Futurist group of poets ever existed. In this regard, it seems helpful to quote an interview Min-jeong Kim gave to the press after the publication of the fourth collection of poems in 2019:

> Q. If you were asked 'what do you think of the word futurist' or 'what do you think when Min-jeong Kim's poetry is characterized with the word 'futurist', what would you answer?
>
> A. 'Futurism' is a label that both opened up and narrowed down my opportunities. There were many misunderstandings about, and equally many understandings of, the term 'futur-

80 Lee: "Ppanhago shishihago an chillinŭn kŭnyŏŭi iyagi: Kim Min-jeong, 'Kŭnyŏga ch'ŏŭm, nŭkkigi shijak'aetta' (Munhakkwajisŏngsa, 2009.12)", p. 43.
81 Park: "Miraep'a hyŏnsangŭi unmyŏnge kwanhan sogo: 20segi rŏshia miraep'awa 21segi han'guk 'miraep'a'rŭl chungshimŭro" [A Study on the Destiny of the Futurist Phenomenon: Focussing on Russian Futurists in the 20th Century and Korean 'Futurists' in the 21st Century], p. 330.
82 Ibid., p. 337.

> ism', but I think that the definition and the category of an 'ism' reduced the meaning and brought about results quite different from what was intended. I think that all poets in Korea belong to this group, if the 'ism' is removed from 'futurism'. Except for the 'ism', how many different Korean poems can be implied by the word 'future'? Well, in that sense, what word would perfectly fit it? I agree, this is a difficult problem. [...] Whenever I was asked a question about 'futurism', I responded instead with a phrase from Su-gyeong Heo's poem: "I am a car in a state of sorrow, but with a wheel that believes in progress." I think Korean poetry has rolled along like that, and I want it to roll along as such. This may be a trivial answer, but please understand.[83]

Meanwhile, Dong-gyu Hwang (b. 1938), an elder lyric poet in Korea, expressed dissatisfaction with the name 'miraepa' (Futurist), as it could be confused with the historical Futurists, and presented a new term 'sumtongpa' (Windpipist).

> Futurism is the name of an Italian art movement in the early 20th century. It is not advisable to give today's Korean poets a name that already exists. Rather, I would like to call them *Sumtongpa* (Windpipists) in the sense that a group of young poets, including Byeong-seung Hwang, open the windpipe of the Korean poetical circles.[84]

Irrespective of whether the term *miraepa* or *sumtongpa* is chosen, the poets reacted negatively against being grouped together and pigeonholed by others. Nonetheless, as the example of Min-jeong Kim demonstrates, 'futurism' was a label that stuck and"opened up and narrowed down" a poet's opportunities. It is clear that thanks to 'futurism', which became a fashion in the early twenty-first century, the entire Korean poetical world had an opportunity to contemplate more deeply the essence of poetry. This, in turn, has broadened the horizon of the Korean literary world. As Byeong-seung Hwang said, "making things that are not poems into poems and widening the area of poetic things" is the duty of a poet. Therefore, the young generation of poets should also "widen the area of poetic writing by means of multifaceted experiments".[85] Won Lee (b. 1968), a poet who wrote a commentary on Kim's third collection *To Be Beautiful and Useless*, evaluates her works as follows:

> Even at the time of writing this, I still really don't know Min-jeong Kim. But I do know one thing: she is a poet who wants to write poems in a manner that was never practised before. She is a person who sought to 'invent' a form of love that was not yet in existence but was

---

83 Kim: "Tŭlkkŭrŭmyŏ pujibulshikkan ssodajinŭn kŏt... Kŭgŏshi shi" [What Boils and Involuntarily Pours... That's Poetry].

84 [Anon.]: "30taeŭi pallan... miraep'a anin sumt'ongp'a" [The Rebellion of the Poets in Their 30s... not Futurists, but Windpipists].

85 Shin: "24kae tanŏro mandŭn sajŏn: Hwang Byeong-seunggwa Kim Min-jeongŭi kyŏngu", p. 272.

> locked up inside her. [...] Since Min-jeong Kim exists, the history of contemporary Korean poetry became like a 'beautiful and useful' fishing net thrown into the distant sea.[86]

The poet Jun Park (b. 1983) commented on Kim's fourth collection *We Are Breaking Up Because Your 'There' Is Small and My 'Here' Is Large* with the following words: "I hope that everyone welcomes the publication of this collection of poems. With her, our 'there' [i. e. existence], which would be literature, life or death, has grown wider and larger. With her, the boundary of the poet has been broadened so beautifully. 'There' we can 'jump' at any time [i. e. where the poetic world expands, we can also broaden our aesthetic horizons]."[87] Jun Park's remarks do not only apply to Min-jeong Kim. Since the horizon of Korean poetry has already widened sufficiently in the early twenty-first century thanks to the 'futurists', we can expect the emergence of more innovative and avant-garde 'futurists' in the near future.

Bibliography

[Anon.]: "30taeŭi pallan ... miraep'a anin sumt'ongp'a." [The Rebellion of the Poets in Their 30s .... not Futurists, but Windpipists] *Chosŏn Ilbo* [Korean Daily], 14 August 2006. https://www.chosun.com/site/data/html_dir/2006/08/14/2006081470085.html (consulted 30/12/2021).

Boccioni, Umberto, Carlo Carrà, Luigi Russolo, Giacomo Balla, and Gino Severini: "Futurist Painting: Technical Manifesto, 11 April 1910." Lawrence Rainey, Christine Poggi, and Laura Wittman, eds.: *Futurism: An Anthology.* New Haven/CT: Yale University Press, 2009. 64–67.

Boccioni, Umberto, Carlo Carrà, Luigi Russolo, Gino Severini, and Giacomo Balla: "The Exhibitors to the Public, February 1912." Lawrence Rainey, Christine Poggi, and Laura Wittman, eds.: *Futurism: An Anthology.* New Haven/CT: Yale University Press, 2009. 105–109.

Cho, Kyoo Yun: "Futurism in Korea: From the Historical to the Postmodern Avant-garde." *International Yearbook of Futurism Studies* 6 (2016): 3–21.

Cho, Kyoo Yun: "Korea." Günter Berghaus, ed.: *Handbook of International Futurism.* Berlin & Boston: De Gruyter, 2019. 648–655.

Goh, Bong-jun: *Tarŭn moksoridŭl* [Other Voices]. Seoul: Somyŏngch'ulp'an, 2008.

Ha, Sang-il: "Hwang Byeong-seung hyŏnsanggwa miraep'aŭi mirae." [The Byeong-seung Hwang Phenomenon and the Future of the Futurists] *Onŭrŭi munyebip'yŏng* [Today's Literature Criticism] 64 (February 2007): 81–97.

Kang, Gye-sook: "K'okkirirŭl naengjanggoe nŏnnŭn kŏmŭn Nana: Kim Min-jeong, 'Narŭnŭn kosŭmdoch'i agassi' (Yŏllimwŏn, 2005)." [Black Nana that Puts an Elephant into a Refrigerator:

86 Lee: "Shijip Kim Min-jeong" [A Collection of Poems Named Min-jeong Kim], p. 110.

87 Park: "Urido p'oltchak" [We Are Also Jumping], p. 131. Jun Park writes his commentary metaphorically, alluding to the word 'there' from the title of Min-jeong Kim's fourth collection and the word 'jump' from the subtitle of her first collection of poetry.

Min-jeong Kim, 'The Flying Hedgehog Lady' (Yŏllimwŏn, 2005)] *Shilch'ŏnmunhak* [Practical Literature] 79 (August 2005): 390–400.

Kim, In-hwan: "Kongbaegŭi anmu." [Blank Choreography] Min-jeong Kim: *She Began to Feel, for the First Time.* Seoul: Munhakkwajisŏngsa, 2009. 116–130.

Kim, Mi-jeong: "Natsŏn hokŭn nalsŏn imijiŭi k'anibal: Kim Min-jeong shijip 'Narŭnŭn kosŭmdoch'i agassi'." [Carnival of Strange or Cutting Images: Min-jeong Kim's Collection of Poems 'The Flying Hedgehog Lady'] *Shiwa segye* [Poetry and World] 11 (September 2005): 245–256.

Kim, Min-jeong: *Arŭmdapko ssŭlmoŏpkirŭl* [To Be Beautiful and Useless]. Paju: Munhaktongne, 2016.

Kim, Min-jeong: *Kaksŏrhago,* [Anyway,]. Seoul: Han'gyŏre ch'ulp'an, 2013.

Kim, Min-jeong: *Kŭnyŏga ch'ŏŭm, nŭkkigi shijak'aetta* [She Began to Feel, for the First Time]. Seoul: Munhakkwajisŏngsa, 2009.

Kim, Min-jeong: *Narŭnŭn kosŭmdoch'i agassi* [The Flying Hedgehog Lady]. Paju: Yŏllimwŏn, 2005.

Kim, Min-jeong: *Nŏŭi kŏginŭn chakko naŭi yŏginŭn k'ŏsŏ uridŭrŭn heŏjinŭn chungimnida* [We Are Breaking Up Because Your 'There' Is Small and My 'Here' Is Large]. Seoul: Munhakkwajisŏngsa, 2019.

Kim, Su-i: *Sŏjŏngŭn chinhwahanda* [Lyricism Evolves]. Seoul: Changbi, 2006.

Kim, Yu-tae: "Tŭlkkŭrŭmyŏ pujibulshikkan ssodajinŭn kŏt... Kŭgŏshi shi." [What Boils and Involuntarily Pours... That's Poetry.] *Maeilgyŏngje* [Daily Business News], 2 January 2020. https://www.mk.co.kr/news/culture/view/2020/01/6184/ (consulted 27/12/2021).

Kwon, Hyeok-ung: *Miraep'a: Saeroun shiwa shiinŭl wihayŏ* [Futurism: For New Poetry and Poets]. Seoul: Munhakkwajisŏngsa, 2005.

Lee, Chan: "Mihaktŭl, segyerŭl mannanŭn shiinŭi p'ŭrijŭmdŭl." [Aesthetics, Prisms of Those Poets Who Meet the World] *Sŏjŏngshihak* [Lyric Poetics] 26:4 (November 2016): 348–362.

Lee, Gyeong-su: "Ppanhago shishihago an chillinŭn kŭnyŏŭi iyagi: Kim Min-jeong, 'Kŭnyŏga ch'ŏŭm, nŭkkigi shijak'aetta' (Munhakkwajisŏngsa, 2009.12)." [The Plain, Trivial and Boring Story of Her: Min-jeong Kim's 'She Began to Feel, for the First Time' (Munhakkwajisŏngsa, December 2009)] *Platform* 20 (March 2010): 42–43.

Lee, Jang-uk: "Kŭ yŏjaŭi angmong." [That Woman's Nightmare] Min-jeong Kim: *The Flying Hedgehog Lady.* Paju: Yŏllimwŏn, 2005. 152–171.

Lee, Won et al.: *Kŭrimedo pulguhago* [Despite the Painting]. Paju: Munhaktongne, 2010.

Lee, Won: "Shijip Kim Min-jeong." [A Collection of Poems Named Min-jeong Kim] Min-jeong Kim: *To Be Beautiful and Useless.* Paju: Munhaktongne, 2016. 87–110.

Marinetti, Filippo Tommaso: "Destruction of Syntax – Untrammeled Imagination – Words-in-Freedom." F.T. Marinetti: *Critical Writings.* Ed. by Günter Berghaus. New York: Farrar, Straus and Giroux, 2006. 120–131.

Marinetti, Filippo Tommaso: "Dynamic, Multichanneled Recitation." F.T. Marinetti: *Critical Writings.* Ed. by Günter Berghaus. New York: Farrar, Straus and Giroux, 2006. 193–199.

Marinetti, Filippo Tommaso: "Technical Manifesto of Futurist Literature." F.T. Marinetti: *Critical Writings.* Ed. by Günter Berghaus. New York: Farrar, Straus and Giroux, 2006. 107–119.

Marinetti, Filippo Tommaso: "The Foundation and Manifesto of Futurism." F.T. Marinetti: *Critical Writings.* Ed. by Günter Berghaus. New York: Farrar, Straus and Giroux, 2006. 11–17.

Park, Jun: "Urido p'oltchak." [We Are Also Jumping] Min-jeong Kim: *We Are Breaking Up Because Your 'There' Is Small and My 'Here' Is Large.* Seoul: Munhakkwajisŏngsa, 2019. 125–131.

Park, Sun-yung: "Miraep'a hyŏnsangŭi unmyŏnge kwanhan sogo: 20segi rŏshia miraep'awa 21segi han'guk 'miraep'a'rŭl chungshimŭro." [A Study on the Destiny of the Futurist Phenomenon: Focussing on Russian Futurists in the 20th Century and Korean 'Futurists' in the 21st Century]

Hanyangdae at'aejiyŏkyŏn'gusent'ŏ [Asia-Pacific Research Center, Hanyang University], ed.: *Paengnyŏnŭi maehok: han'gugŭi chisŏng rŏshiae kkŭllida* [A Hundred Years of Fascination: Korean Intellectuals Were Attracted by Russia]. Seoul: Minsogwŏn, 2017. 307–350.
Shin, Hyeong-cheol: "24kae tanŏro mandŭn sajŏn: Hwang Byeong-seunggwa Kim Min-jeongŭi kyŏngu." [A Dictionary Made of 24 Words: The Case of Byeong-seung Hwang and Min-jeong Kim] *Chaŭmgwa moŭm* [Consonants and Vowels] 8 (May 2010): 265–303.
Zanotti, Pierantonio: "Japan." Günter Berghaus, ed.: *Handbook of International Futurism.* Berlin & Boston: De Gruyter, 2019. 628–647.

Claudio Palomares-Salas and Ángel Díaz Miranda

The Infrarealist Movement and its Futurist Roots

Abstract: The members of Infrarealism, a neo-avant-garde literary movement founded in Mexico in the mid-1970s, considered themselves to be the inheritors of historical avant-garde groups such as Dada, Surrealism and Mexican Stridentism. It is logical to assume that Futurism also played an important rôle in shaping the movement's ideas; however, their connection has barely been explored. This essay investigates how Futurism influenced first Infrarealism and then the poetry and prose of Roberto Bolaño, who acquired international renown as a novelist after Infrarealism disbanded. We argue that Futurism was at the centre of Infrarealist sensibility and activity, if not in an explicit then at least in an implicit manner, with the intention of showing that Infrarealism was a clear example of Neo-Futurism, but one that re-elaborated Futurist concepts from a Latin American perspective.

Keywords: Futurism in Mexico, Stridentism (1921–1927), Infrarealism (1974–1978), Roberto Bolaño, Mario Santiago Papasquiaro, art and life, art and political activism, aeropainting

The birth of Infrarealism

In the 1970s, the Mexican State was trying to regain some credibility and support after its disastrous handling of the 1968 student movement that resulted in the massacre of hundreds of students, first in 1968 and then in 1971.[1] As part of a complex strategy of conciliation, the governments of Luis Echeverría (1970–1976) and José López Portillo (1976–1982) provided generous support to writers and artists, particularly those who could rally oppositional forces against political institutions.[2] The State's intention was to motivate an attitude favourable to the authorities and

1 The first massacre took place in the Tlatelolco square in Mexico City on 2 October 1968. The second, known as the Corpus Christi Massacre, or El Halconazo, occurred on 10 June 1971, also in Mexico City. These bloodbaths had profound and lasting effects on the Mexican political, social and cultural imaginary. See Poniatowska: *Massacre in Mexico*; Taibo: *'68: The Mexican Autumn of the Tlatelolco Massacre*; Pensado and Ochoa: *México Beyond 1968.*

2 See Schmidt: *The Deterioration of the Mexican Presidency*; Mabire: *Políticas culturales y educativas del Estado mexicano.*

https://doi.org/10.1515/9783111318394-010

to prevent the left-leaning sectors of the population from overtly contesting its decisions. The Mexican literary scene, led at the time by Octavio Paz, benefited greatly from the government's strategy by accepting public posts and jobs, scholarships and fellowships, spaces in print and visual media, publishing options, etc. It is in this context that, in 1975, a group of young poets living in the Mexican capital formed the Infrarealist movement in direct opposition to the State and the dominant literary scene, which they saw as a 'mafia' or as a corrupt caste.

The Infrarealists were steadfast in their desire to be marginal and sought to operate outside the official cultural sphere. They actively tried to propose – or rather to impose – a vision of art, literature and culture that responded to their specific concerns, experiences and values. The Infrarealists' aim was difficult to achieve, particularly in a country like Mexico, where the State had hegemonic power and its decisions affected all aspects of social, political and cultural life. The Infrarealists' efforts, like those of so many avant-garde movements before them, remain an example of courage and ingenuity, and as testimony to the artistic and political sensitivity of part of the Mexican youth of the time, a sensitivity that they shared with the Futurists' rebellion against antiquated mores in the early twentieth century.

The leaders of the Infrarealist movement were the Mexican poet Mario Santiago Papasquiaro and Chilean writer Roberto Bolaño, who lived in Mexico City from 1968 to 1977.[3] Both were strongly influenced by nineteenth-century French poetry (Arthur Rimbaud, Charles Baudelaire, Comte de Lautréamont), by historical European avant-gardes such as Dada and Surrealism (André Breton, Philippe Soupault, Antonin Artaud, Marcel Duchamp); by Mexican Stridentism (Manuel Maples Arce, Arqueles Vela, Germán List Arzubide),[4] by the American Beat Generation of the 1950s (Allen Ginsberg, William S. Burroughs, Herbert Huncke, Lucien Carr and Jack Kerouac) and by contemporary Latin American movements of the neo-avant-garde of the 1960s and 70s, such as the Hora Zero movement in Peru. In their

3 Other members of the group, as enumerated by Rubén Medina, were Chileans Bruno Montané Krebs and Juan Esteban Harrington; the Peruvian José Rosas Ribeyro and the Argentine Claudia Kerik; the Mexicans Mara Larrosa, José Peguero, Rubén Medina, Cuauhtémoc Méndez, Ramón Méndez, María Guadalupe Ochoa Ávila, Jorge Hernández Piel Divina, Geles Lebrija, Victor Monjarás and José Vicente Anaya. A second generation of Infrarealist poets includes Pedro Damián Bautista, Edgar Artaud Jarry, Mario Raúl Guzmán, Eduardo Guzmán Chávez and Rafael Catana. See Medina: "Infrarealism", p. 14.

4 Stridentism (*estridentismo)* was the first Mexican avant-garde movement, lasting from 1921 to 1927. Its name was derived from 'estridente', denoting a raucous or shrill noise. The word appeared in many of Marinetti's poems and manifestos. On Stridentism see Schneider: *El estridentismo o Una literatura de la estrategia*, Gallo: "Wireless Modernity" and Rashkin: *The Estridentista Movement in Mexico.*

works and discussions, the Infrarealists acknowledged the influence of these movements on their conception of art, poetry and life, but their indebtedness to Futurism failed to be sufficiently acknowledged.

Futurism, acting as a foundation of all subsequent historical avant-garde movements, affected Infrarealism in at least three instances: 1) in the manifestos written by Roberto Bolaño and Mario Santiago Papasquiaro; 2) in the idea of a lived poetry that transforms both art and society; and 3) in the extra-literary attitudes (i. e., sabotage of literary events) with which the Infrarealists sought to subvert the Mexican literary establishment of the 1970s.

After positioning Infrarealism as a neo-avant-garde movement, we discuss in this essay their principal manifestos and how their notion of heroism relates to Marinetti's *beaux gestes libertaires.* We then analyse some of Bolaño's works and how they celebrate speed and dynamism in a Futurist manner. Finally, we examine his interest in and poetic evocation of Futurist Aeropainting. We thus try to show that Futurism, although not openly recognized as a source of inspiration for Infrarealism, played a major rôle in the group's manifestos, literary writings and actions, and that certain aspects of Marinetti's programme had a lasting influence on Latin American artists and writers after the Second World War.

From Futurism to Infrarealism

It could be argued that the name Infrarealism has a Neo-Futurist origin. Rubén Medina, himself a member of the Infrarealist group and one of its most important historians, has explained that "the name Infrarealism stood for the group's efforts to represent the whole reality (an infra-world) that lies beyond the range of hegemonic regimes of perception."[5] Supposedly, the term was derived from the Soviet writer Georgy Gurevich's short story *Infra Drakon: NF rasskaz* (Beneath Drakon: A Science-Fiction Story).[6] The nomenclature of the movement, then, has its origin in a text in which two of the pillars of the Infrarealist ethos converge: social revolution, manifested in the Soviet imaginary within which Gurevich was writing, and Futurism, manifested in the science fiction and the apology of technology present in his text.

On 20 February 1909, Filippo Tommaso Marinetti published *The Foundation and Manifesto of Futurism* in the Parisian newspaper *Le Figaro.* After that, a series

5 Medina: "Infrarealism", p. 10.

6 First published in *Znanie-sila* 12 (1958), pp. 30–33, translated into English as "Infra Draconis" in the anthology *Soviet Science Fiction* (1962).

of Futurist manifestos aimed to motivate artists to transform not only painting, music, theatre, architecture and cinema, but also everyday life: cuisine, clothing, sexual behaviour, etc. Futurism developed a form of packaging and selling social and aesthetic ideas in a manner that had never been seen before: "Marinetti's inexhaustible exuberance and ingenuity, his tremendous joy of life, and his generosity to people of different cultures and countries caused him to be called the 'Caffeine of Europe'."[7] Throughout the twentieth century, hundreds of artists and writers tried, each in their own way, to imitate Marinetti's capacity to convince, shock, disturb and transform the realms of art, politics and social life. Like Marinetti and the Futurists, the Infrarealists in Mexico actively worked to shake up the artistic establishment. In the 1970s, in Mexico City, Mario Santiago Papasquiaro and Roberto Bolaño followed in Marinetti's steps and proposed to their Mexican contemporaries a new way of understanding art and life. They wanted to see poets acting as catalysts for social change and as self-appointed messengers of truth in all aesthetic matters. These ideas were promoted with the same impetus and hope, and with the same passion for polemics, as Marinetti had done, although with much more modest results in terms of efficacy and decisiveness.

Infrarealism's main impact did not come from the texts they issued, as was the case with other avant-garde movements. Their literary production, besides the unavoidable appeal of their original manifestos, often lacked the substance necessary to make an impression, not because a malicious literary establishment conspired against them, but because the texts themselves were not considered convincing by the critics, the public or their literary peers. Since the late 1990s, however, Infrarealism has gained notoriety, not because the movement affected in any significant way the Mexican literary scene, but because Roberto Bolaño based one of the most influential novels of the second half of the twentieth century, *Los detectives salvajes* (The Savage Detectives, 1998) on it. Yet, as an example of Neo-Futurism, the movement deserves to be studied as part of the Latin American neo-avant-garde, which in its own way aimed at reviving the social and artistic experiments of their early twentieth-century ancestors.

The Infrarealists published four manifestos: Mario Santiago Papasquiaro's *Manifiesto infrarrealista* (Infrarealist Manifesto, 1975); José Vicente Anaya's *Manifiesto infrarrealista: Por un arte de vitalidad sin límites* (Infrarealist Manifesto: For a Vital and Unlimited Art, 1975); Roberto Bolaño's *Déjenlo todo, nuevamente* (Leave It All, Once More, 1976; see Fig. 1a) and *Las fracturas de la realidad: Manifiesto infrarealista* (Fractures of Reality: Infrarealist Manifesto, 1977). None of them directly acknowledges Futurism; yet attitudes and ideas that were typical of Futur-

7 Wynne: "F.T Marinetti and Futurism", p. 108.

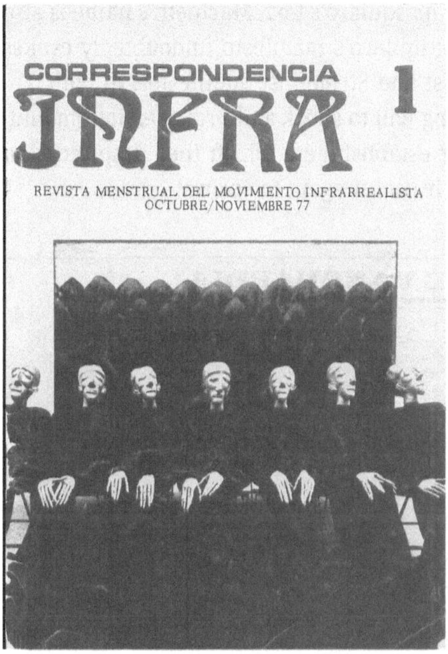

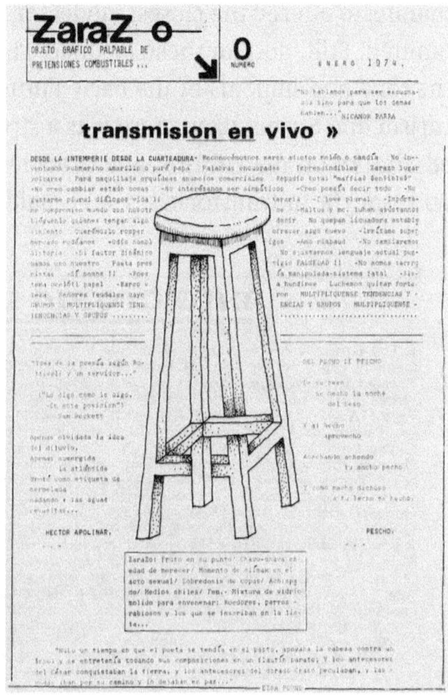

Fig. 1a: Cover of *Correspondencia infra: Revista menstrual del movimiento infrarrealista* 1 (October – November 1977), where Roberto Bolaño's manifesto *Déjenlo todo, nuevamente* (Leave It All, Once More, 1976) was published. **Fig. 1b.** Mario Santiago Papasquiaro's one-off periodical *ZaraZo: Objeto gráfico palpable de pretensiones combustibles* (ZaraZo: Palpable Graphic Object of Combustible Pretensions), no. 0, January 1974.

ism can be found in all of them. These attitudes were often passed to them indirectly, via other avant-garde movements, above all Mexican Stridentism.

At the end of his *Manifiesto infrarrealista,* for example, Mario Santiago Papasquiaro offers a list of names that evoke the "Directorio de vanguardia" (Avant-Garde Directory) found in Manuel Maples Arce's first Stridentist manifesto, *Actual No. 1* (Actual No. 1; see Fig. 2), released in Mexico City in December 1921. Maples Arce's text included the names of poets and painters associated with the European and Latin American historical avant-garde, including several Italian Futurists, whom the Stridentists considered relevant to their works. In turn, more than fifty years later, Mario Santiago Papasquiaro offered his own list of names presumably to legitimize Infrarealism in the eyes of his contemporaries. This list comprised Antonin Artaud, Alfred Jarry, André Breton, William S. Burroughs, Allen Ginsberg, Jack Kerouac, Franz Kafka, Jean Luc Godard, César Vallejo and José Revueltas, amongst several other important figures of twentieth-century art and literature. Curiously, Maples Arce's name is absent from the list, even though his manifesto offered the closest model for Papasquiaro's text. Marinetti's name is also omitted. Still, despite these lacunae, Papasquiaro's manifesto undoubtedly evokes the tone and impetus of the early Futurist and Stridentist manifestos. In both, Futurism and Stridentism, there was a strong will to shock and provoke. Both mounted attacks on the cultural and academic establishment which they despised, and both sought to transform art and make it useful again to society.

DIRECTORIO DE VANGUARDIA

Rafael Cansinos Assens.-Ramón Gómez de la Serna.-Rafael Lasso de la Vega.-Guillermo de Torre.-Jorge Luis Borges.-Cleotilde Luisi.-Vicente Ruiz Huidobro.-Gerardo Diego.-Eugenio Montes.-Pedro Garfias.-Lucía Sánchez Saornil.-J. Rivas Panedas.-Ernesto López Parra.-Juan Larrea.-Joaquín de la Escosura.-José de Ciria y Escalante.-César A. Comet.-Isac del Vando Villar.-Adriano del Valle.-Juan Las.-Mauricio Bacarisse.-Rogelio Buendía.-Vicente Risco.-Pedro Raida.-Antonio Espina.-Adolfo Salazar.-Miguel Romero Martínez.-Ciriquiain Caitarro.-Antonio M. Cubero.-Joaquín Edwards.-Pedro Iglesias.-Joaquín de Aroca.-Loeón Felipe.-Eliodoro Puche.-Prieto Romero.-Correa Calderón.-Francisco Vighi.-Hugo Mayo.-Bartolomé Galíndez.-Juan Ramón Jiménez.-Ramón del Valle Inclán.-José Ortega y Gasset.-Alfonso Reyes.-José Juan Tablada Diego M. Ribera.-D. Alfaro Siqueiros.-Mario de Zayas.-José D. Frías.-Fermín Revueltas.-Silvestre Revueltas.-P. Echeverria Atl.-J. Torres García.-Rafael P. Barradas.-J. Salvat.-Papasseit.-José María Yenoy.-Jean Epstein.-Jean Richard Bloch.-Pierre Brune.-Marie Blanchard.-Corneau.-Farrey.-Fournier.-Riou.-Mme. Ghy-Lohem.-Marie Laurencin.-Dunozer de Segongac Honneger.-Georges Auric.-Ozenfant.-Albert Gleizes.-Pierre Reverdy.-Juan Gris.-Nicolás Beauduin.-William Speth.-Jean Paulhan.-Guillermo Apollinaire.-Cypien Máx.-Jacob.-Jorge Braque.-Survage.-Coris.-Tritst Tzara.-Francisco Picabia.-Jorge Ribemont.-Dessaigne.-Renée Dunan.-Archipeuko.-Soupault.-Bretón.-Poul Eduard.-Marcel Duchamp.-Frankel.-Sernen.-Erik Satie.-Elie Faure.-Pablo Picasso.-Walter Bonrad Arensberg.-Celine Arnauld.-Walter Pach.-Bruce.-Morgan Roussel.-Marc Chagall.-Herr Baader.-Max Ernest.-Christian Schaad.-Lipchitz.-Ortíz de Zárate.- Correia d'Araujo.- Jacobsen.-Schkold Adam Fischer.-Mme. Fischer.-Peer Kroogh.-Alf Rolfsen.-Jeauneiet.-Piet Mondrian.-Torstenson.-Mme. Alika.-Ostrom.-Geline.-Salto.-Weber.-Wuster.-Kokodika.-Kandinsky.-Steremberg (Com. de B. A. de Moscou).-Mme. Lunacharsky.-Erhenbourg Taline.-Konchalowsky.-Machkoff. Mme. Ekster.-Wlle Monate.- Marewna.- Larionow.- Gondiarowa.- Belova.-Sontine Daiibler.-Doesburg.-Raynal.-Zahn.-Derain.-Walterowua Zur Mueklen.-Jean Coeteau.-Pierre Albert.-Birot.-Metsinger.-Jean Charlot.-Maurice Reynal.-Pieux.-F. T. Marinetti.-G. P. Lucinni.-Paolo Buzzi.-A. Palazzeschi.-Enrique Cavacchioli.-Libero Altomare.-Luciano Folgore.-E. Cardile.-G. Carrieri.-E. Mansella Fontini.-Auro d'Alba. Mario Betuda.-Armando Mazza.-M. Boccioni.-C. D. Carrá.-G. Severini.-Balilla Pratella.-Cangiullo.-Corra.-Mariano.-Boccini.-Fessy.-Setimelli.-Carli.-Ochsé.-Linati.-Tita Rosa.-Saint-Point.-Divoire.-Martini.-Moretti.-Pirandello.-Tozzi.-Evola.-Ardengo.-Sarcinio.-Tovolato.-Daubler.- Doesburg.- Broglio.-Utrillo.-Fabri.-Vatrignat.-Liege.-Norah Borges.-Savory.-Gimmi Vang Gogh.-Grunewald.-Derain.-Cauconnet.-Boussingautl.-Marquet.-Gernez.-Fobeen.-Delaunay.-Kurk Scchwiters. - Heyniche. - Klem.- Zirner.- Gino.-Galli.- Bottai.- Cioccatto.- George Bellows.-Giorgio de Chirico.- Modigliani.- Cantarelli.- Soficci.- Carena.-etc.

Fig. 2: The "Directory" at the bottom of Manuel Maples Arce's Stridentist manifesto *Actual no. 1* (The Current: no. 1, 1921).

The Futurism-Infrarealism relationship becomes apparent, for example, when we look at the tenth point of the Futurist Manifesto: "We wish to destroy museums, libraries, academies of any sort, and fight against moralism, feminism, and every kind of materialistic, self-serving cowardice […]. We wish to free our country from the stinking canker of its professors, archaeologists, tour guides, and antiquarians." [8] Using a similar incendiary rhetoric, both Mario Santiago Papasquiaro and Roberto Bolaño mounted their own attacks on the cultural institutions they considered to be decadent and corrupt. In his manifesto, Santiago Papasquiaro sought "TO CONVERT LECTURE HALLS INTO SHOOTING RANGES"[9], while Bolaño

8 Marinetti: *Critical Writings*, p. 14.

9 Papasquiaro: "Infrarealist Manifesto", p. 25. "CONVERTIR LAS SALAS DE CONFERENCIAS EN STANS DE TIRO." Caps in the original.

requested: "Look for it, not only in the museums is there shit".[10] Santiago Papasquiaro wrote that: "BEETHOVEN, RACINE & MICHELANGELO STOPPED BEING THE / MOST USEFUL / THE MOST AMPHETAMENIC, THE MOST NOURISHING",[11] a statement that resembles Maples Arce's rejection of outdated models in the fifth point of his *Actual no. 1:* "¡Chopin a la silla eléctrica!" (Chopin to the electric chair!)[12]

It must be noted that both Maples Arce's denunciation of Chopin and Santiago Papasquiaro's dismissal of Beethoven are echoes of Marinetti's dismissals of western musical traditions. In *Noi rinneghiamo i nostri maestri simbolisti, ultimi amanti della luna* (We Renounce our Symbolist Masters, the Last of All Lovers of the Moonlight, 1911), for example, he argued against "a romantic sentimentalism, dripping with moonlight" and declared: "Against a nostalgic, sentimental, or erotic moonlight, we finally exalt an unjust and cruel heroism such as will tame the all-conquering zeal of the motor."[13] Alternatively, in *Il teatro di Varietà* (The Variety Theatre Manifesto, 1913), he asked his followers to "liven up the works of Beethoven, Wagner, Bach, Bellini, and Chopin by inserting Neapolitan songs. [...] Play one of Beethoven's symphonies backward".[14] It is clear, then, that Beethoven's *Moonlight Sonata* was to the Futurists what Chopin's nocturnes were to the Estridentistas, and that the Infrarealists' rejection of Beethoven and Michelangelo was inspired by Futurism. Writing in the 1970s, however, the Infrarealists' rebuttal of classical or Romantic models appears rather anachronistic; paradoxically, their argumentation did not project into the future, but rather harked back to avant-garde sensitivities of the early twentieth century.

In another indirect reference to Futurism, Bolaño cites, in *Déjenlo todo, nuevamente,* a fragment of Kurt Schwitters' sound poem *Ursonate* (1932): "To subvert the daily reality of current poetry. The chaining that leads to a circular reality of the poem. A good reference: crazy Kurt Schwitters. Lanke trr gll, or, upa kupa arggg, become the official line, phonetic researchers codifying the howl."[15] Schwitters' work was indebted to Marinetti's influential *Zang Tumb Tuuum* (1914).[16] As it is

---

10 Bolaño: "Leave It All, Once More", p. 28. "Busquen, no solamente en los museos hay mierda."
11 Papasquiaro: "Infrarealist Manifesto", p. 25. "BEETHOVEN, RACINE & MIGUEL ÁNGEL DEJARON / DE SER LO MÁS ÚTIL / LO MÁS ANFETAMÍNICO, LO MÁS ALIMENTICIO."
12 Maples Arce: "Actual No. 1", p. 269.
13 Marinetti: *Critical Writings*, pp. 45–46.
14 Ibid., p. 191.
15 "Subvertir la realidad cotidiana de la poesía actual. Los encadenamientos que conducen a una realidad circular del poema. Una buena referencia: el loco Kurt Schwitters. Lanke trr gll, o, upa kupa arggg, devienen en línea oficial, investigadores fonéticos codificando el aullido." Bolaño: "Leave It All, Once More", p. 32.
16 On Schwitters' debts to Marinetti see Puineuf: "Quicksands of Typography", pp. 66–68.

well known, Marinetti drew on onomatopoeia as one of the ways to invigorate language and to enhance the effect of Words-in-Freedom.[17] In *Zang Tumb Tuuum*, for example, one can find lines such as these:[18]

TRITURATO ROSSO ROSSO STRIATO SUSSULTANTE
urrrrrraaaaah urrrrraaaah
vincere vincere gioia gioia vendetta massacrare continuare
tatatatatatatatatatatatata
FINE DISPERAZIONE PERDUTO NIENTE–DA–FARE INUTILE
immergersi freschezza dilatarsi aprisi ammollirsi dilatarsi
plum plamplam pluff pluff frrrrrr
sterco–di–cavallo orina bidet ammoniaca odore–tipografico
ETERNO SOLE A RIPETIZIONE 20.000 PROIETTILI AL MINUTO
urrrrrrraaaaaaaaaaa
gioia gioia gioia gioia ancora ancora vendetta
tatatatatatatatatatatata
RICOMINCIARE INUTILE INUTILE NON C'È MEZZO
vuoi nuotare fibra di 2 millimetri
pluff plaff plaff gottgott gluglu
ammoniaca odor–di–donna–matura ascelle tuberosa cadavere

CRUSHED RED RED STREAKED STARTLING
Hoorrrrrraaaaay Hoorrrrrraaaaay
win win joy joy revenge massacre continue
ratatatatatatatatatatatatata
END DESPAIR LOST NOTHING-TO-DO POINTLESS
plunging freshness expanding opening-out softening
Plop pllop plof plof frrrrr
Horse-dung urine bidet ammonia print-shop-smell
ETERNALLY REPEATING SUN 20,000 BULLETS-PER-MINUTE
Hoorrrrrraaaaay
joy joy joy joy again again revenge
ratatatatatatatatatatatatata
STARTING OVER POINTLESS POINTLESS NO WAY OUT
wanna swim 2 millimeter fibre
Plof plop plop gulp chug
Ammonia mature-woman-scent armpits tuberose corpse

Marinetti's use of onomatopoeia could be considered a precursor of Schwitters' *Ursonate* (Sonata in Primordial Sounds, 1923–1932), which contains lines such as: "Lanke trr gll / pe pe pe pe pe / Ooka ooka ooka ooka."[19] By referencing Schwitters, Bolaño reveals that although passing through the filter of posterior artists (in this case Kurt Schwitters), Infrarealism's sensibility and artistic references were coming from Futurism.

Marinetti used aviation as a central metaphor in his poetry. In 1919, the Futurists created the "aerial theatre" performed at airports, and many Futurists were

17 See Marinetti: "Technical Manifesto of Futurist Literature", *Critical Writings*, pp. 107–119 and "Destruction of Syntax – Untrammeled Imagination – Words in Freedom", *Critical Writings*, pp. 120–131.

18 Marinetti: *Zang tumb tuuum*, pp. 146–147, reprinted in *Teoria e invenzione futurista*, pp. 744–745. The English translation has been taken from *International Yearbook of Futurism Studies* 2 (2012), pp. 177–178.

19 Schwitters: "Lanke trr gll....", s.p.

involved in decorating the newly built airports in Italy with Futurist frescos.[20] Futurist aerial art also served as an inspiration for one of the most innovative graphic projects of the 1930s, *Aeroporto della rivoluzione futurista delle parole in libertà poesia pubblicitaria* (Airport of the Futurist Revolution in Words-in-Freedom Advertising Poetry, 1939).[21] Papasquiaro's sentence "TO SHAKE THE HIPS OF THE PRESENT WITH EYELASHES BATTING / FROM THE AIRPORTS OF THE FUTURE"[22] may have been an ingenious way to suggest, albeit in a disguised way, Futurism's infatuation with aviation. Read in this way, the sentence could imply a glance at (and a questioning of) the present from a *past* Futurist perspective.

Although allusions to Futurism are not explicit in the Infrarealists' manifestos, there is no doubt that the Futurist ethos inhabits their texts and proclamations. As already mentioned, the dialogue established between Infrarealism and the historical avant-gardes includes Dada, Surrealism and Stridentism. As Futurism appeared a few years before Dada and more than a decade before Stridentism and Surrealism, it is considered a foundation of all subsequent avant-gardes, and every movement that followed was indebted to it in one way or another. Throughout the twentieth century, manifestos that sought to propose a new way of seeing, writing, thinking and being, revisited – often not deliberately – proposals made by F.T. Marinetti, Umberto Boccioni, Carlo Carrà, Giacomo Balla, Gino Severini and other Futurists. Infrarealism was no exception.

Santiago Papasquiaro's first avant-garde creation, the one-off periodical *ZaraZo: Objeto gráfico palpable de pretensiones combustibles* (ZaraZo: Palpable Graphic Object of Combustible Pretensions, no. 0, Jan 1974; see Fig. 1b) explained the organizing principle behind Infrarealism as "the unification of art and life".[23] Later, in his *Manifiesto infrarrealista*, he urged to "TRANSFORM ART / TRANSFORM DAILY LIFE [...] TO RETURN TO ART THE NOTION OF A PASSIONATE & CONVULSIVE / LIFE."[24] The same idea occurred in Roberto Bolaño's *Déjenlo todo, nuevamente:* "Our ethics is the Revolution, our aesthetics, Life: one-single-thing.[25] This idea,

20 See Berghaus: "Fedele Azari and Futurist Aerial Theatre", pp. 485–494.

21 Published as a special issue of *Campo grafico: Rivista di estetica e tecnica grafica* 7:3–5 (March–May 1939).

22 "MOVERLE LAS CADERAS AL PRESENTE CON LOS / OJOS PESTAÑEANDO / DESDE LOS AEROPUERTOS DEL FUTURO." Papasquiaro: "Infrarealist Manifesto", p. 25.

23 See Medina: "Infrarealism", p. 10, and Cobas Carrai: "'La estupidez no es nuestro fuerte", pp. 11–29.

24 "TRANSFORMAR EL ARTE / TRANSFORMAR LA VIDA [...] DEVOLVERLE AL ARTE LA NOCIÓN DE UNA VIDA APASIONADA & CONVULSIVA." Papasquiaro: "Infrarealist Manifesto", p. 31.

25 "Nuestra ética es la Revolución, nuestra estética la Vida: una-sola-cosa." Bolaño: "Leave It All, Once More", p. 31.

shared by the Infrarealists as a whole, is perhaps the movement's most evident debt to Futurism.

Peter Bürger has suggested that the "attempt to organize a new life practice from a basis in art" was a central demand of the European historical avant-garde.[26] Although the desire to reintegrate art into the praxis of life and to transform bourgeois society once and for all proved unattainable, the idea of art-as-action had an enduring influence on subsequent art movements and groups, including Mexican Infrarealism. Futurism, although largely ignored by Bürger, was the first avant-garde movement to propose this radical transformation of art and society. As Günter Berghaus has explained: "The Futurists sought to remodel life as an artwork and to reintegrate art into the praxis of life. Futurist aesthetics aimed at a transformation of humankind in all its physiological, psychological and social aspects. Art was no longer restricted to be a *reflection* of reality, instead it sought to *create* new realities on the basis of a unified theoretical concept."[27] In a similar way, the Infrarealists aspired to an aesthetic transformation of Mexican society in all its physiological, psychological and social aspects: "TO SHOW THAT EVERYTHING IS ART THAT EVERYBODY / CAN DO IT [...] TO GET PEOPLE OUT OF THEIR DEPENDENCY AND PASSIVITY / TO SEEK UNPRECEDENTED MEANS OF INTERVENTION & OF DECISION IN THE WORLD / TO DEMISTIFY / TO BECOME AGITATORS".[28] In other words, they desired to become Futurists ... although with a delay of almost seven decades.

---

26 Bürger: *Theory of the Avant-garde*, p. 49.

27 Berghaus: "The Futurist Conception of Gesamtkunstwerk and Marinetti's Total Theatre", pp. 285–286. See also the following passages from Marinetti: *Critical Writings:* "I am telling you that *lyricism* is that most rare *capacity for inebriating oneself with life* and *inebriating life with our selves.* The ability to transform the muddy waters of life that envelop and flow through us, into wine", p. 123; "I proposed a swift lyricism, brutal and immediate, a lyricism which to all our predecessors would have seemed antipoetical, a telegraphic lyricism that bears not the slightest hint of books but, as much as possible, the taste of life", p. 127.

28 "MOSTRAR QUE TODO ES ARTE Y QUE TODO MUNDO PUEDE HACERLO [...] SACAR A LA GENTE DE SU DEPENDENCIA & / PASIVIDAD / BUSCAR MEDIOS INÉDITOS DE INTERVENCIÓN & DE / DECISIÓN EN EL MUNDO / DESMITIFICAR / CONVERTIRSE EN AGITADORES." Papasquiaro: "Infrarealist Manifesto", pp. 25–26.

Heroism and the *beaux gestes libertaires*

In several Futurist manifestos, Marinetti advocated "a methodical, everyday heroism".[29] Furthermore, he thought he could "liberate the world", having "established the religion of the manifest Will and everyday Heroism as the norm".[30] The idea of the artist as a "heroic citizen"[31] was at the centre of the Futurist programme of renewal. The same attitude was shared by the Infrarealists, for they also saw themselves as heroes who could liberate Mexican poetry from the stagnation caused by institutionalized mediocrity. Bolaño writes: "A new lyricism begins to grow in Latin America, to brace itself in ways that never ceases to surprise us. The entry to the material is the entry to adventure: the poem as a journey and the poet as hero revealing heroes".[32] A few lines later, Bolaño reiterates his message: "I repeat: The poet as hero revealing heroes, as a fallen red tree announcing the beginning of the forest".[33] The Futurists and Infrarealists were both convinced of their own indispensability and destiny as heroes of the cultural scene, as the only ones capable of effecting change and proposing new paths for the modern artist or writer, or as Santiago Papasquiaro puts it:

> AT THIS TIME MORE THAN BEFORE THE ARTISTIC PROBLEM CANNOT BE CONSIDERED AS AN INTERNAL STRUGGLE OF TENDENCIES / BUT RATHER AS A TACIT STRUGGLE (ALMOST DECLARED) BETWEEN THOSE WHO, CONSCIOUSLY OR NOT, SUPPORT THE SYSTEM OR AIM TO CONSERVE AND PROLONG IT / AND THOSE WHO, ALSO IN A CONSCIOUS FASHION OR NOT, WISH TO MAKE IT EXPLODE.[34]

---

29 Marinetti: *Critical Writings*, p. 23. In other manifestos he spoke of "the desire for danger and day-to-day heroism", "adventurous instincts, taking risks, and heroism" and "a life that is free, full of adventure, vitality, and a habitual heroism". See Marinetti: *Critical Writings*, pp. 44, 54, 60.
30 Marinetti: *Critical Writings*, p. 39.
31 Ibid., p. 64.
32 "Un nuevo lirismo, que en América Latina comienza a crecer, a sustentarse en modos que no dejan de maravillarnos. La entrada en materia es ya la entrada en aventura: el poema como un viaje y el poeta como un héroe develador de héroes." Bolaño: "Leave It All, Once More", p. 30.
33 "Repito: el poeta como héroe develador de héroes, como el árbol rojo caído que anuncia el principio del bosque." Bolaño: "Leave It All, Once More", p. 30.
34 "EN ESTA HORA MÁS QUE ANTERIORMENTE, EL PROBLEMA ARTÍSTICO NO PUEDE SER CONSIDERADO COMO UNA LUCHA INTERNA DE TENDENCIAS / SINO SOBRE TODO COMO UNA LUCHA TÁCITA (CASI DECLARADA) ENTRE QUIENES DE MANERA CONSCIENTE O NO ESTÁN CON EL SISTEMA Y PRETENDEN CONSERVARLO Y PROLONGARLO / Y QUIENES TAMBIÉN DE MANERA CONSCIENTE O NO QUIEREN HACERLO ESTALLAR." Papasquiaro: "Infrarealist Manifesto", p. 26.

The Infrarealists, of course, like the Futurists, wished to make it explode.[35]

Perhaps one of the most Futurist aspects of the Infrarealist movement was the vigour with which they confronted the Mexican literary establishment of the 1970s. The movement was seduced by the idea of escaping the hierarchies of the Mexican literary world and of instituting a break with everything that had gone before. Ironically, rather than innovating, they continued the "tradition of rupture" discussed by Octavio Paz in relation to the Latin American obsession with 'the modern'.[36] The Infrarealists attacked the most recognized literary figures of the day and were famous for sabotaging literary readings and poetry workshops.[37]

At first, Octavio Paz was praised for challenging the governmental repression in Tlatelolco. Starting in the 1970s, that praise was transformed into harsh criticism. The younger generation of poets, writers and cultural critics began to challenge his paternalistic and authoritative position. The Infrarealists felt that Paz was too close to institutions of political power and monopolized literary culture, not only in Mexico City, but throughout the country. They felt that there was no access to public funds or leadership positions without Paz's endorsement. He was deemed to be out-of-touch with new developments and no longer politically acceptable.[38]

Perhaps the clearest testimony to the contempt that the Infrarealists felt for the institutionalization of poetry in Mexico can be seen in Roberto Bolaño's novel *Los detectives salvajes* (The Savage Detectives, 1998), where Octavio Paz appears a dozen times as a fictional character. Although at the end of the novel it is possible to see Arturo Belano, Roberto Bolaño's alter ego in the novel, conceding a certain respect towards Paz as a poet, most passages of *Los detectives salvajes* reveal the Infrarealists' rejection of the writer. In a passage in which Luis Sebastián Rosado (a fictitious character based on the Mexican literary critic José Joaquín Blanco) converses with the Infrarealist poet Piel Divina (based on the Mexican poet Jorge Hernández Piel Divina), the latter reveals a plan which, if it had been carried

35 Examples of similar Futurist rhetoric can be found in Marinetti: *Critical Writings:* "The destructive act of the libertarian", p. 14; "Exaltation of the anarchists' acts of destruction", p. 18; "A group of young men who are utterly rebellious and destructive, who are fed up with adoring the past, sick of academic pedantry, bursting with the desire for fearless originality, and positively gasping for a life that is free, full of adventure, vitality, and a habitual heroism", p. 60; "We see ourselves as the destructive nitric acid that it would be well to throw over all political parties, as they are in a state of putrefaction", p. 61.

36 See Paz: "La tradición de la ruptura", pp. 15–37. See also "Boicot a Octavio Paz y a David Huerta", pp. 69–71.

37 See Madariaga: *Bolaño Infra 1975–1977*, pp. 47–64.

38 By contrast, José Revueltas and Efraín Huerta were amongst the Mexican poets and writers who were respected by the Infrarealists.

on, would have accorded Infrarealism a much more prominent place in the history of Mexican literature:

> For a moment, I admit, the idea of a terrorist act passed through my mind. I saw the visceral realists [i. e.the Infrarealists] getting ready to kidnap Octavio Paz, I saw them breaking into his house (poor Marie-José, all that broken china), I saw them emerging with Octavio Paz gagged and bound, carried shoulder-high or slung like a rug, I even saw them vanishing into the slums of Netzahualcoyotl in a dilapidated black Cadillac with Octavio Paz bouncing around in the trunk.[39]

This passage, although fictional, is reminiscent of Marinetti's adoration of the *beaux gestes libertaires* which he turned into a fundamental principle of Futurist art. Again and again, he praised "the destructive act of the libertarian"[40] and advocated "the violent incursion of life into art"[41] by "introducing the fist into the struggle for art".[42] In Marinetti's view, artists should be "happy-go-lucky fire raisers"[43] and produce works that have the effect of "a well-primed grenade over the shattered heads of our contemporaries".[44] In his speech of 1910, *Necessità e bellezza della violenza,* he advanced the idea that "the destructive acts of the anarchist perhaps represent an absurd yet beautiful hankering after the ideal of a justice."[45]

In another passage of the novel, the character of Luis Sebastián Rosado unequivocally links Infrarealism to Stridentism by applying to the former a critique from Carlos Monsiváis, one of the most prominent Mexican cultural and literary critics:

> Monsiváis said it first: disciples of Marinetti and Tzara, their noisy, outrageous, overwrought poems did battle in the realm of simple typographic arrangement, never rising above the

39 Bolaño: *The Savage Detectives*, p. 155. The original reads: "Por un momento, no lo niego, se me pasó por la cabeza la idea de una acción terrorista, vi a los real visceralistas preparando el secuestro de Octavio Paz, los vi asaltando su casa (pobre Marie-José, qué desastre de porcelanas rotas), los vi saliendo con Octavio Paz amordazado, atado de piés y manos y llevado en volandas o como una alfombra, incluso los vi perdiéndose por los arrabales de Netzahualcoyotl en un destartalado Cadillac negro con Octavio Paz dando botes en el maletero." Bolaño: *Los detectives salvajes*, p. 171.
40 Marinetti: "The Foundation and Manifesto of Futurism" in *Critical Writings*, p. 14.
41 Marinetti in an interview with Carlo Albertini, "On the Subject of Futurism", in *Critical Writings*, p. 143.
42 Marinetti: "Futurism's First Battles", in *Critical Writings*, p. 151.
43 Marinetti: "The Foundation and Manifesto of Futurism", in *Critical Writings*, p. 15.
44 Marinetti: "Preface to Mafarka the Futurist", in *Critical Writings*, p. 32.
45 Marinetti: "The Necessity and Beauty of Violence", in *Critical Writings*, p. 61. For more on Marinetti's anarchist iconoclasm see Berghaus:"Violence, War, Revolution: Marinetti's Concept of a Futurist Cleanser for the World" and "La 'violenza stavolgente e incendiaria': Uno stumento di igiene per il mondo. Guerra e rivoluzione nel pensiero di Filippo Tommaso Marinetti."

> level of childish entertainment. Monsi [i. e. Monsiváis] was talking about the stridentists, but the same goes for the visceral realist [i. e. the Infrarealists]. No one paid attention to them and they opted for indiscriminate assault.[46]

Bolaño synthesizes here the way in which members of the Mexican literary establishment saw the Infrarealists in the 1970s: as something of a marginal group with a latent violent streak. This is exactly how the newspapers viewed the Futurists at the time. For example, Carlo Albertini introduced his interview with Marinetti in the Neapolitan magazine *La Diana* in January 1915 with the words:

> The Futurists relish the struggle, it being their first principle. [...] They love war, which stimulates all latent energies. They desire action, which represents life. [...] "The Futurist serate," F.T. Marinetti wrote to me in one of his most recent letters, "mean precisely the violent incursion of life into art. Artists, alive at last, and no longer up in their ivory towers, despising aestheticism, asking to participate, like workmen or soldiers, in the progress of the world." This, in few words, is the essence of Futurism.[47]

History shows that the Futurists, in the long run, balanced the *pars destruens* with the *pars construens*, i. e., the "will to destroy and renew",[48] treating destruction as a preparatory action for rebuilding society on a dynamic basis. In the end, the explosive ideas of Futurism made a profound contribution to art and literature, just as the destructive ideology of Infrarealism served Roberto Bolaño in the preparatory phase of *Los detectives salvajes.*

Bolaño's poetic celebration of speed and dynamism

The influence of Futurism is perceptible in Roberto Bolaño's poetry following his involvement with the Infrarealist movement. This is particularly apparent in *El burro* (The Donkey, 1994), in two brief and untitled poems from the collection *La universidad desconocida* (The Unknown University, 2007) and in the poem *El gu-*

46 Bolaño: *The Savage Detectives*, p. 155. The original reads: "Monsiváis ya lo dijo: Discípulos de Marinetti y Tzara, sus poemas, ruidosos, disparatados, cursis, libraron su combate en los terrenos del simple arreglo tipográfico y nunca superaron el nivel de entretenimiento infantil. Monsi está hablando de los estridentistas, pero lo mismo se puede aplicar a los real visceralistas." Bolaño: *Los detectives salvajes*, p. 152.
47 Marinetti: "On the Subject of Futurism: An Interview with 'La Diana'" in *Critical Writings*, pp. 143–144.
48 Marinetti: "An Open Letter to the Futurist Mac Delmarle", in *Critical Writings*, p. 104.

sano (The Worm, 1994).[49] *El burro* combines the well-known Futurist celebration of speed (see Fig. 3) with a subtle nod to homoerotic escape. The donkey in question is a motorcycle which the poetic persona – Bolaño – and his rescuer – Mario Santiago – use to leave behind both Mexico City and the Mexican nation:

> Sometimes I dream that Mario Santiago
> Comes looking for me on his black motorcycle.
> And we leave behind the city and as
> The lights are disappearing,
> Mario Santiago tells me we're dealing with
> A stolen bike, the last bike
> Stolen to travel through the poor
> Northern lands, towards Texas,
> Chasing an unnameable dream,
> Unclassifiable, the dream of our youth.[50]

Bolaño's use of the trope of leaving the city behind on a motor vehicle evokes Futurist poems such as Marinetti's *À l'automobile* (To My Pegasus, 1905; also known as *All' automobile da corsa* [Ode to a Racing Car]) and especially Bruno Giordano Sanzin's *Tra le braccia della Dea Velocità* (In the Arms of the Goddess of Speed, 1924). In *À l'automobile,* Marinetti compares his car to the mythical winged horse Pegasus in several horse-related metaphors.[51] The steel Pegasus is "pulling at the bit with strident teeth!" and freedom is achieved once the brakes are let go: "I finally release / your metallic bridle, / and voluptuously you rush / into Infinite freedom!"[52] The idea of the motorcycle as a symbol of freedom is also present in Sanzin's Futurist poem *Tra le braccia della Dea Velocità* where he writes:

---

49 Bolaño won literary prizes with his poetry, which he then reworked and submitted elsewhere. Both *El burro* and *El gusano* appeared in *Los perros românticos* (The Romantic Dogs,1994), but they were probably written much earlier.

50 "A veces sueño que Mario Santiago / Viene a buscarme con su moto negra. / Y dejamos atrás la ciudad y a medida / Que las luces van desapareciendo / Mario Santiago me dice que se trata / De una moto robada, la última moto / Robada para viajar por las pobres tierras / Del norte, en dirección a Texas, Persiguiendo un sueño innombrable, / Inclasificable, el sueño de nuestra juventud." Bolaño: *The Romantic Dogs*, p. 121.

51 In the fourth line of the poem, the car transforms into a winged horse ready to be freed.

52 Marinetti: "To My Pegasus", pp. 425–427. The original reads: "Dieu véhément d'une race d'acier, / Automobile ivre d'espace, / qui piétines d'angoisse, le mors aux dents stridentes! / [...] Je lâche enfin tes brides métalliques et tu t'élances, / avec ivresse, dans l'Infini / libérateur! ..." Marinetti: "À l'automobile", p. 11. The poem's title changed numerous times. It was first published as "À l'automobile" in *Poesia* 1:7 (August 1905), p. 11, then reprinted as "À mon Pégase" in *La Ville charnelle*, pp. 169–172, then reprinted as "À l'automobile de course" in *I poeti futuristi. Con un proclama di F.T.*

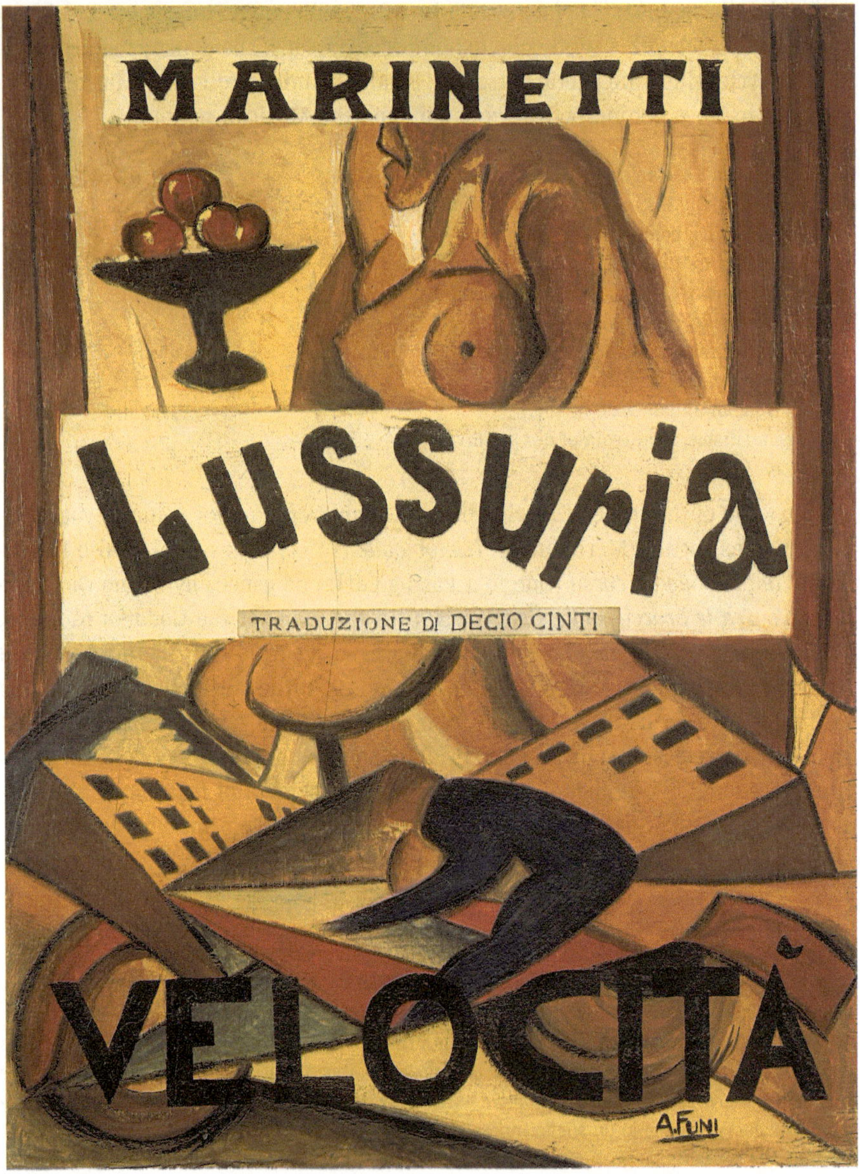

Fig. 3: The cover of *Lussuria velocità* (Lust Speed), Milano: Modernissima, 1921, an Italian translation of F.T. Marinetti's *La Ville charnelle* (The Carnal City), Paris: Sansot, 1908. It contains the poem *All' automobile da corsa* (Ode to a Racing Car, 1908) and the manifesto *La nuova religione-morale della velocità* (The New Ethical Religion of Speed, 1916).

> I would like to launch it [the motorcycle] immediately at high speed, but the heavily populated city streets prevent me from doing so. When, finally, the last houses have disappeared behind me, I press with unspeakable delight the accelerator with the index finger of my right hand.[53]

Bolaño also presents the idea of the motor vehicle as means to achieve personal freedom.[54] The motorcycle in *El burro* is used as a symbol of individuality and of adventurous escape from the constraints of the narrow streets of Mexico City. However, it is also a subtle critique of modernity since the poets' trip is not only about achieving speed, but also about the characters' grieving for the loss of youth:

> The dream of our youth,
> Which is to say the bravest of all
> Our dreams. And put that way
> How could I deny myself a ride on that fast black
> Northern bike, breaking out on those roads
> Long ago traveled by Mexican saints,
> Mendicant Mexican poets,
> Taciturn leeches from Tepito
> Or la colonia Guerrero, all on the same path,
> Where times are mixed up and confused,
> Verbal and physical, yesterday and aphasia.[55]

In *El burro*, Bolaño mixes his personal conception of time with the speed longed for by the Futurists. Shapes are blurred, and time is perceived in its own way, underscoring the Futurist maxim that "Speed destroys the laws of gravity, it makes the values of time and space subjective".[56] Marinetti anticipated the phenomenon

---

Marinetti e uno studio sul verso libero di Paolo Buzzi. Milano: Edizioni futuriste di "Poesia", 1912, pp. 324–326, then reprinted in *Der Sturm* 3:109 (May 1912), p. 36.

53 "Vorrei lanciarla subito a grande velocità, ma le vie cittadine intensamente popolate me lo impediscono. Quando finalmente le ultime case sono sparite dietro a me, premo con indicibile voluttà l'acceleratore coll'indice della mano destra." Sanzin: "Tra le braccia della Dea Velocità." *L'aurora* 6 (June 1924), p. [1]. Reprinted in *Bruno G. Sanzin aeropoeta futurista triestino*, p. 35.

54 This idea also dominated Stridentist poetry. Maples Arce's poem 80 H. P., for example, suggests a dizzying journey in a car that ends up leaving behind iconic Mexico City neighbourhoods such as Tacubaya, San Angel and Mixcoac. See Maples Arce: "80 H.P." in Schneider: El estridentismo, pp. 548–549.

55 Bolaño: "The Donkey", in *The Romantic Dogs*, pp. 120–121. "El sueño de nuestra juventud, / Es decir el sueño más valiente de todos / Nuestros sueños. Y de tal manera / Cómo negarme a montar la veloz moto negra / Del norte y salir rajados por aquellos caminos / Que antaño recorrieran los santos de México, / Los poetas mendicantes de México, / Las sanguijuelas taciturnas de Tepito / O la colonia Guerrero, todos en la misma senda, / Donde se confunden y mezclan los tiempos: / Verbales y físicos, el ayer y la afasia."

56 Marinetti: "The New Ethical Religion of Speed", *Critical Writings*, p. 257.

of a collapsed time-space nexus and mentions the motorcar as a sign of technological advances that will renew "human sensibility".[57] Moreover, he predicted that technological advances would have a decisive and everlasting influence on people's experience of reality and affect their modes of perception:

> Futurism is based on the complete renewal of human sensibility brought about by the great discoveries made by science. Anyone who today uses the telegraph, the telephone, and the gramophone, the train, the bicycle, the motorcycle, the automobile, the ocean liner, the airship, the airplane, the film theatre, the great daily newspaper (which synthesizes the daily events of the whole world), fails to recognize that these different forms of communication, of transport and information, have a far-reaching effect on their psyche.[58]

Bolaño, like Marinetti, was both in awe of and perplexed by modernity, but he feared that a Futurist espousal of progress would lead poets (and people in general) to their demise. In an untitled two-verse poem from *La universidad desconocida*, he returned to the Futurist trope of a speeding motor vehicle, but this time the automobile is associated with death: "Death is an automobile / with two or three distant friends."[59] Bolaño's sombre evocation of the automobile in these lines goes against the Futurist grain. After all, Marinetti recounts in *The Foundation and Manifesto of Futurism* (1909) that it was thanks to his own desire for speed and subsequent car crash that the Futurist movement was born. In the fictionalized account Marinetti emerges from his overturned car to dictate the manifesto. Marinetti sees his close encounter with death as a rebirth for himself and for poetry.[60] Bolaño, on the other hand, constantly employed the image of the car as an omen of death.[61]

In another untitled poem also from *The Unknown University*, he reused the same image and expands it so as to include the faces of his companions:

> Death is an automobile with two or three distant friends. Faces
> I can't forget: cerulean, cold, just one step away from dusk.[62]

Bolaño then recycles the image of the automobile and places it in Mexico City so as to localize issues of speed, memory and death:

---

57 Marinetti: "Destruction of Syntax", *Critical Writings*, p. 120.

58 Ibid., p. 120.

59 Bolaño: *The Unknown University*, p. 273. "La muerte es un automóvil con dos o tres amigos lejanos."

60 Marinetti: "The Foundation and Manifesto of Futurism", pp. 11–13.

61 See also the poem "Bólido" (Roadster) in *The Romantic Dogs*, p. 103.

62 "La muerte es un automóvil con dos o tres amigos lejanos. Rostros / que no puedo olvidar: cerúleos, fríos, a un paso tan sólo del atardecer." Bolaño: *The Unknown University*, p. 577.

> Death is an automobile out driving the avenues of Mexico City
> Uselessly searching for your house: a carbon trail, a carbon
> tail, carbon fingers sinking into darkness. Death
> is R.B. and L.J.'s lips in the backseat of a minibus: now I know
> no one escapes those avenues. I'll leave it as collateral:
> the end of my childhood.[63]

Readers of Bolaño's prose are accustomed to his strategy of repetition, variation and expansion of previously used texts and characters. It is clear here that this method is related to a drive to *work through* personalized memories, even if fictitious. Bolaño is also framing contemporary Latin American subjects as tied to a modernity that is in equal parts violent and unsettling. The only way forward is to memorialize the poetic voice's coming of age by documenting it as a poem or "leav[ing] it as collateral". It is through constant temporal shifts that Bolaño single-handedly moved Futurist aesthetics into the field of traumatic memory. This is achieved through the repeated use of the speed metaphor, frequently materialized in the form of the automobile.

Another example of Bolaño's reliance on the trope of the automobile comes from one of his better-known poems, *El gusano* (The Worm, 1993). At first glance, it describes a haggard character from Mexico's northern border who is afflicted with mental health issues and endorses violence. It then turns into a meditation on the poet's younger self defending poetry as an act of bravery. Mario Santiago also appears in the poem as an embodiment of the poet facing modernity and is once again linked to illegal activities and a moving vehicle:

> Sunsets observed Mario Santiago pass by,
> Up and down, frozen stiff, in the backseat
> Of a contrabandist's car. Sunsets
> Of infinite white and infinite black.[64]

In these lines, Mario Santiago witnesses from the backseat of a car, trapped in a sort of atemporal loop, the merging of violence with the landscape. The poem posits Santiago as living permanently in that position, always travelling as contraband,

---

63 "La muerte es un automóvil en marcha por las avenidas de Ciudad de México / buscando inútilmente tu casa: una estela de carbón, una cola de / carbón, unos dedos de carbón que se hunden en la oscuridad. La muerte / son los labios de R.B. y L. J. en el asiento posterior de un pesero: ahora sé / que de esas avenidas no escapa nadie. Te lo dejo como prenda: / el final de mi infancia." Bolaño: *The Unknown University*, p. 577.

64 "Los atardeceres que vieron pasar a Mario Santiago, / arriba y abajo, aterido de frío, en el asiento trasero / del coche de un contrabandista. Los atardeceres / del infinito blanco y del infinito negro." Bolaño: *Poesía reunida*, p. 380.

permanently marked as a marginal subject. The reader can sense the proximity to death by the description of being paralysed by the cold and by the mention of possible, binary infinities. At the end of the poem, the lyric character resembles the character of "The Worm". The binary system established first with Santiago's ominous sunsets is resolved through a series of resemblances between the memory of a young Bolaño and the current "Worm".

Bolaño was a poet with sceptical views about Latin American modernity. He applied Futurist poetics and aesthetics to his critique by collapsing the past into the present in his poems. The Futurists fused forms to show how speed changes visual perspective. Bolaño underscored issues of memory by fusing time and space and resorting to the tools he adapted from European avant-garde movements, especially Futurism.

Distant Star and Futurist aeropainting

Bolaño's novel *Estrella distante* (*Distant Star*, 1996) anticipated the author's preoccupations with sexuality and violence. The erosion and transformation of poetry advanced by this novel was then developed further in *Los detectives salvajes* (The Savage Detectives, 1998) and in the posthumous *2666* (2004). A "distant star" is a pleonasm, a rhetorical device often employed in poetry. Bolaño imbues the phrase with a double meaning: the star stems from the Chilean flag that becomes pleonastically distant in exile and is, in turn, a reference to the mysterious character of Carlos Wieder, the hero of the novel.

The story begins in the months before the Chilean military coup of 1973, where Wieder had assumed a false identity and frequented poetry workshops in Concepción, Chile. The name he adopted, "Alberto Ruiz-Tagle", becomes, when abbreviated, an acronym for art (ART). The novel's plot reveals that the character was also a military pilot, poet and a serial killer of women. Wieder was protected by the State in the early years of Pinochet's rule and serves in the novel as an emblematic representative of the dictatorship. When the character disappears from Chile, the novel is told from the viewpoint of an anonymous narrator, who has been living in Spain for some time. Previously, he was a member of the very poetry workshops that Wieder frequented. More than twenty years later, in the mid-1990s, he is asked by a private detective to help find the serial killer whom he first met in Chile. During the final scene of the novel, they encounter an aged Wieder in a coastal town of Spain. The pair may or may not have executed him. The search becomes an allegory for the aftermath of post-coup trauma and exile.

The character Carlos Wieder produces within the novel a series of paradoxes that become clearer when we connect him to both Futurism and to the internationally renowned Chilean poet Raúl Zurita. The Italian literary and artistic movement functions as a palimpsest or hidden trace in the novel, while Zurita is a Latin American reference point. Zurita was a founding member of CADA (Colectivo Acciones de Arte), a group of neo-avant-garde artists and writers who organized and carried out a series of complex and intellectually sophisticated performances in Pinochet's Chile. The poet himself was involved in acts of auto-mutilation, public masturbation and the hiring of five small aircraft to disseminate leaflets with encrypted anti-Pinochet verses.[65] On 2 June 1982, Zurita performed one of what he called 'poetry-actions', in which five planes drew lines of a poem with smoke over New York's blue sky. The poem is entitled "LA VIDA NUEVA" (a reference to Dante Alighieri *La vita nuova*). It was documented on video and later in photographs. The poem and pictures were included in Zurita's book *Anteparaíso* (The Anteroom of Paradise, 1982).[66]

In a similar yet disturbingly different way, Bolaño's novel has Wieder using the support of the Chilean State for projecting verses into the sky by means of smoke emitted from a military aeroplane: all the lines that he writes into the sky have a pseudo-religious quality as they make use of biblical verses in Latin.[67] Wieder's brutal and fanatic nature made him an emblem of Pinochet's régime. The relationship between the character and Zurita's "art actions" turns him into a kind of distorted doppelgänger, or a concave mirror reflection. Chiara Bolognese[68] astutely points out that "Bolaño's determination to choose an aviator poet as a character has a double meaning: on the one hand, he pays homage to Zurita,

65 This resonates with Gabriele D'Annunzio dropping thousands of propaganda leaflets in the colours of the Italian flag over Vienna (August 1918), and Guido Keller performing a similar feat when, in a stunt flight over the parliament building in Rome, he distributed thousands of flyers in defence of the Fiume government (November 1920). See Berghaus: *Italian Futurist Theatre*, p. 487.

66 Below is the poem in Jack Schmitt's 1986 translation, *Anteparadise: A Bilingual Edition:* "MY GOD IS HUNGER / MY GOD IS SNOW / MY GOD IS PAMPA / MY GOD IS NO / MY GOD IS DISILLUSIONMENT / MY GOD IS CARRION / MY GOD IS PARADISE / MY GOD IS PAMPA / MY GOD IS CHICANO / MY GOD IS CANCER / MY GOD IS EMPTINESS / MY GOD IS WOUND / MY GOD IS GHETTO / MY GOD IS PAIN / MY GOD IS / MY GOD LOVE." *Anteparadise*, p. 1.

67 The text reads: "IN PRINCIPIO ... CREAVIT DEUS ... CAELUM ET TERRAM." "TERRA AUTEM ERAT INANIS ... ET VACUA ... ET TENEBRAE ERANT ... SUPER FACIEM ABYSSI ... ET SPIRITUS DEI ... FEREBATUR SUPER AQUAS ..." In his second loop Wieder continues: "DIXITQUE DEUS ... FIAT LUX ... ET FACTA EST LUX ... ET VIDIT DEUS ... LUCEM QUOD ... ESSET BONA ... ET DIVISIT ... LUCEM AC TENEBRAS." Bolaño: *Distant Star*, pp. 25–28. The pilot ends his performance with an imperative and ominous verse "LEARN". Bolaño: *Distant Star*, p. 29.

68 Bolognese is the first critic to understand and write about the importance of Raúl Zurita's poetry in Bolaño's work. I want to extend my gratitude and thank her for making her studies available to me.

and on the other, he takes a dig at him when he has Wieder write biblical verses, a choice that parodies Zurita's messianism."[69]

After the initial, unprompted aerial performance, Wieder is asked by some high-ranking military officers to participate in more "ceremonies and commemorations".[70] These were designed to be exclusive events for members of the military high brass and the business élites. Wieder's airshows turned out to be increasingly popular as the new authoritarian régime was solidifying. For example, he drew a star near an airstrip and, some days later at El Cóndor[71]Air Force Base, he wrote a poem naming all his victims. The spectators assumed-they were the names of his girlfriends. In Santiago de Chile, he wrote more biblical verses, and, over the Bío-Bío river, he drew a large Chilean flag with the aid of two commercial pilots.

Moreover, after a brief period when, in a show of endurance, he flew on his own to the Antarctic, he again wrote poems into the sky: "Death is friendship ... death is Chile ... death is love ... death is growth ... death is communion ... death is cleansing ... death is my heart ... take my heart."[72] As Bolognese makes clear in her analysis, these verses parody Zurita and, in an effect in polarity, strengthen the Pinochet ideology.[73]

In his desire to create a new form of poetry in Chile, Wieder subscribed to the tenets proclaimed in the *Manifesto of Futurist Aeropainting* (1931).[74] Some of its key points become distorted in the mind of the serial killer: 1. "The shifting perspectives of flight constitute an absolutely new reality which has nothing in common with reality as traditionally constituted by a terrestrial perspective;" and 2. "The elements of this new reality are unstable and are constructed by perpetual mobility."[75]

Wieder understood the first two points to justify and validate his murderous urges and their 'poetization' in the sky. Point 9 of the manifesto underscores what Wieder believed to be his duty: the creation of an art that gives way to "a new extraterrestrial plastic spirituality".[76] The events that Wieder sparked off resemble

69 Bolognese: "Roberto Bolaño y Raúl Zurita: Referencias cruzadas", p. 262.

70 Bolaño: *Distant Star*, p. 31.

71 The name of the military base is a reference to 'Plan Cóndor' or 'Operación Cóndor', a United States-backed plan of anti-Communist repression across Latin America.

72 Bolaño: *Distant Star*, pp. 80–82.

73 Bolognese: "Roberto Bolaño y Raúl Zurita: Referencias cruzadas", p. 262.

74 The *Manifesto dell'aeropittura* was published in different versions, the best known being "Manifesto della aeropittura" in the catalogue *Prima mostra di aeropittura dei futuristi.* Roma: La Camerata degli Artisti, 1931.

75 Balla et al.: "Manifesto of Aeropainting", p. 283.

76 Ibid., p. 284.

what Futurist Fedele Azari had in mind when he transformed the experience of flight into paintings, poems and aerial art. He also wrote plays to be performed by aeroplanes in which the machines would personify the characters and loudspeakers would transmit the dialogues.[77] Even though Wieder does not go that far, the murderous character uses his aeroplane as a giant pen to write poems onto the canvas of the sky.

More importantly, Wieder is connected to Futurism by way of a subtle, yet important, reference: *Distant Star*'s anonymous narrator informs us that the spectators of Wieder's aerial feats "understood or thought they understood the pilot's will, and they knew that although they couldn't make head or tail of it, they were witnessing a unique event, of great significance for *the art of the future*."[78] That art of the future cannot be anything other than a corrupted form of Futurism.

Conclusion

By 1978, Infrarealism had disbanded. Roberto Bolaño had left Mexico in 1977 and settled in Spain, where he became one of the most influential fiction writers at the end of the twentieth century.[79] It quickly became clear that Infrarealism would not succeed in transcending its brief moment of activity in the Mexican capital. As with so many avant-garde movements, reality would soon prove too complex for the fanciful aspirations expressed in the manifestos to be accomplished. The members of the group, apart from Bolaño, failed to produce texts that earned themselves a place in the history of Mexican literature. Even now they are considered marginal. Nevertheless, from the perspective of Futurism Studies, Infrarealism has an assured place as an heir to the movement launched by Marinetti in 1909.

As we have demonstrated in this essay, the influence of Futurism was not openly recognized by the members of Infrarealism, and yet in both its manifestos and actions, as well as in the ensuing poetry and prose of Roberto Bolaño, the Futurist heritage can clearly be discerned. Infrarealism should therefore occupy a place in the history of the Neo-Futurist avant-gardes, for it represents a perfect ex-

---

77 See the chapter "Fedele Azari and Futurist Aerial Theatre" in Berghaus: *Italian Futurist Theatre, 1909–1944*, pp. 485–494.

78 Bolaño: *Distant Star*, p. 82, our italics.

79 As was the case with so many avant-garde movements, there was neither a document nor a proclamation that declared an end to the Infrarealist movement. Although the original members continued their poetic work besides their regular work, we might consider 1978 as marking the end of the initial and most important phase of the movement.

ample of the powerful and lasting influence of Futurism on subsequent generations of Latin American artists and writers.

Bibliography

Anaya, José Vicente: "Por un arte de vitalidad sin límites." *Nada utópico nos es ajeno: Manifiestos infrarrealistas.* León: Tsunun, 2013. 43–49. English translation "For a Vital and Unlimited Art." *Chicago Review* 63:3–4 (Winter-Spring 2020): 10–13.

[Anon.]: "Boicot a Octavio Paz y a David Huerta." *Unomásuno* (Mexico City), 25 January 1980: 16. Reprinted in *Nada utópico nos es ajeno: Manifiestos infrarrealistas.* León: Tsunun, 2013. 69–71.

Balla, Giacomo, et al.: "Manifesto of Aeropainting (1929)" Lawrence S. Rainey, Christine Poggi, and Laura Wittman, eds.: *Futurism: An Anthology.* New Haven/CT: Yale University Press, 2009. 283–286

Berghaus, Günter: "Fedele Azari and Futurist Aerial Theatre." G. Berghaus: *Italian Futurist Theatre, 1909–1944.* Oxford: Clarendon Press, 1998. 485–494.

Berghaus, Günter: "La 'violenza stavolgente e incendiaria': Uno stumento di igiene per il mondo. Guerra e rivoluzione nel pensiero di Filippo Tommaso Marinetti." F. T. Marinetti: *Necessità e bellezza della violenza: Discorso futurista.* Con un saggio critico di Günter Berghaus. Napoli: Diana, 2021. 35–144.

Berghaus, Günter: "The Futurist Conception of Gesamtkunstwerk and Marinetti's Total Theatre." Franciska d'Elhoungne Hervai, and Dávid Falvay, eds.: *"Sul fil di ragno della memoria": Studi in onore di Ilona Fried.* Budapest: Eötvös Loránd Tudományegyetem, 2012. 283–302.

Berghaus, Günter: "Violence, War, Revolution: Marinetti's Concept of a Futurist Cleanser for the World." *Annali' italianistica* 27 (2009): 23–71.

Bolaño, Roberto: "Déjenlo todo, nuevamente: Primer manifiesto del movimiento infrarrealista." *Correspondencia infra: Revista menstrual del movimiento infrarrealista* 1 (October –November 1977): 5–11. English translation "Leave It All, Once More." *Chicago Review* 60:3 (2017): 28–36.

Bolaño, Roberto: "The Donkey." *The Romantic Dogs 1980–1998.* Trans. Laura Healy. New York: New Directions, 2008. 121–124.

Bolaño, Roberto: "The Worm." *The Romantic Dogs 1980–1998.* Trans. Laura Healy. New York: New Directions, 2008. 17–23.

Bolaño, Roberto: *Distant Star.* Trans. Chris Andrews. London: The Harvill Press, 2004.

Bolaño, Roberto: *Los detectives salvajes.* Barcelona: Anagrama, 1998.

Bolaño, Roberto: *Poesía reunida.* Madrid: Alfaguara, 2018.

Bolaño, Roberto: *The Savage Detectives.* Trans. Natasha Wimmer. New York: Farrar, Straus and Giroux, 2007.

Bolaño, Roberto: *The Unknown University.* Trans. Laura Healy. New York: New Directions, 2013.

Bolognese, Chiara: "Roberto Bolaño y Raúl Zurita: Referencias cruzadas." *Anales de literatura chilena* 11:14 (December 2010): 259--272.

Bürger, Peter: *Theory of the Avant-Garde.* Trans. Michael Shaw. Minneapolis/MN: University of Minnesota Press, 1984.

Cobas Carrai, Andrea: 'La estupidez no es nuestro fuerte': Trés manifestos del infrarrealismo mexicano." *Osamayor: Graduate Student Review* 17 (2006): 11–29.

Gallo, Rubén: "Wireless Modernity: Mexican Estridentistas, Italian and Russian Futurism." *International Yearbook of Futurism Studies* 2 (2012): 141–170.

Gurevich, Georgy: "Infra Draconis." *Soviet Science Fiction.* Trans. Violet L. Dutt. New York: Collier Books, 1962. 151–172.

Mabire, Bernardo: *Políticas culturales y educativas del Estado mexicano de 1970 a 1997.* México: El Colegio de México, Centro de Estudios Internacionales, 2003.

Madariaga, Montserrat: *Bolaño Infra 1975–1977: Los años que inspiraron 'Los detectives salvajes'.* Santiago de Chile: Red Internacional del Libro, 2010.

Maples Arce, Manuel: "80 H. P." Luis Mario Schneider, ed.: *El estridentismo: La vanguardia literaria en México.* México: UNAM, 2013. 548–549.

Maples Arce, Manuel: "Actual No. 1. Hoja de vanguardia." Luis Mario Schneider, ed.: *El estridentismo: La vanguardia literaria en México.* México: UNAM, 2013. 3–13.

Marinetti, Filippo Tommaso: "À l'automobile." *Poesia* 1:7 (August 1905): 11. Reprinted as "À mon Pégase." F.T. Marinetti: *La Ville charnelle.* Paris: Sansot, 1908. 169–172. Reprinted in F.T. Marinetti: *Scritti francesi.* A cura di Pasquale A. Jannini. Milano: Mondadori, 1983. 346–348.

Marinetti, Filippo Tommaso: "Destruction of Syntax – Untrammeled Imagination – Words-in-Freedom." *Marinetti: Critical Writings.* Ed. by Günter Berghaus. New York: Farrar, Straus and Giroux, 2006. 120–131

Marinetti, Filippo Tommaso: "Technical Manifesto of Futurist Literature." *Marinetti: Critical Writings.* Ed. by Günter Berghaus. New York: Farrar, Straus and Giroux, 2006. 107–119.

Marinetti, Filippo Tommaso: "The Foundation and Manifesto of Futurism." *Marinetti: Critical Writings.* Ed. by Günter Berghaus. New York: Farrar, Straus and Giroux, 2006. 11–17.

Marinetti, Filippo Tommaso: "To My Pegasus." Lawrence S. Rainey, Christine Poggi, and Laura Wittman, eds.: *Futurism: An Anthology.* New Haven/CT: Yale University Press, 2009. 425–427.

Marinetti, Filippo Tommaso: "We Renounce Our Symbolist Masters, the Last of All Lovers of the Moonlight." *Marinetti: Critical Writings.* Ed. by Günter Berghaus. New York: Farrar, Straus and Giroux, 2006. 43–46.

Marinetti, Filippo Tommaso: *Zang tumb tuuum.* Milano: Edizioni Futuriste di "Poesia", 1914. Reprinted in F.T. Marinetti: *Teoria e invenzione futurista.* A cura di Luciano De Maria. Milano: Mondadori, 1968. 559–710.

Medina, Ruben: "Infrarealism: A Latin American Neo-Avant-Garde, or The Lost Boys of Guy Debord." *Chicago Review* 60:3 (2017): 8–22.

Papasquiaro, Mario Santiago: "Manifiesto infrarrealista." *Nada utópico nos es ajeno: Manifiestos infrarrealistas.* León: Tsunun, 2013. 37–41. English translation "Infrarealist Manifesto." *Chicago Review* 60:3 (2017): 25–27.

Paz, Octavio: "La tradición de la ruptura." O. Paz: *Los hijos del limo.* Barcelona: Seix Barral, 1990. 15–37.

Pensado, Jaime M., and Enrique Ochoa: *México Beyond 1968: Revolutionaries, Radicals, and Repression During the Global Sixties and Subversive Seventies.* Tucson/TX: The University of Arizona Press, 2018.

Poniatowska, Elena: *Massacre in Mexico.* Trans. Helen R. Lane. New York: Viking Press, 1975.

Puineuf, Sonia de: "Quicksands of Typography: The Futurist Experience in Central Europe during the 1920s." *International Yearbook of Futurism Studies* 1 (2011): 61–84.

Rashkin, Elissa: *The Estridentista Movement in Mexico: The Avant-Garde and Cultural Change in the 1920s.* Lanham/MD: Lexington Books, 2009.

Sanzin, Bruno Giordano: "Tra le braccia della Dea Velocità." *L'aurora* 6 (June 1924). [1]. Reprinted in *Bruno G. Sanzin aeropoeta futurista triestino.* A cura di Paolo Sanzin e Enrica Mezzetta. Milano: Educatt, 2014. 35.

Schmidt, Samuel: *The Deterioration of the Mexican Presidency: The Years of Luis Echeverría.* Tucson/TX: University of Arizona Press, 1991.
Schneider, Luis Mario: *El estridentismo o Una literatura de la estrategia.* México: Conaculta, 1997.
Schwitters, Kurt: "Lanke trr gll…." *Merz* 6 (October 1923): s.p. Reprinted as "lanke tr gl: Skerzo aus meiner soonate in uurlauten." *Documents internationaux de l'esprit nouveau* 1 (1927): 45.
Taibo, Paco Ignacio: *'68: The Mexican Autumn of the Tlatelolco Massacre.* Trans. Donald Nicholson-Smith. New York: Seven Stories Press, 2019.
Wynne, Marjorie G., and Luce Marinetti Barbi: "F.T Marinetti and Futurism." *The Yale University Library Gazette* 57:3–4 (1983): 104–137.
Zurita, Raúl: *Anteparadise: A Bilingual Edition.* Trans. Jack Schmitt. Berkeley/CA: University of California Press, 1986.

Odile Cisneros

Russian Futurism and Brazilian Avant-garde Poetry: Incorporation, Translation, Convergence

Abstract: This article critically examines the incorporation of Futurist principles in post-war avant-garde poetry and poetics in Brazil starting in the 1950s. The brothers Haroldo and Augusto de Campos and their fellow poet Décio Pignatari, founders of the Concrete Poetry movement in Brazil, fashioned their practice after historical avant-garde movements, including Italian, French and Russian strands of Futurisms. They discussed principles such as the abolition of syntax, the foregrounding of the materiality of language, and the interaction of the verbal and nonverbal in their early theoretical writings. In a turn towards more political participation, they explored the work of Vladimir Mayakovsky and other Futurist poets. The effort produced two collections of translations, *Poemas de Maiakóvski* (Mayakovsky's Poems, 1967) and *Poesia russa moderna* (Modern Russian Poetry, 1968), authored in collaboration with the scholar of Russian literature, Boris Schnaiderman. As a later form of that reception, in the exhibition *Transfutur* (Kassel 1990; Berlin, 1992), several generations of Brazilian, Soviet, and German-language poets converged on a common interest in Russian Futurism. The connections of Brazilian avant-garde poetry and Russian Futurism are examined through three main projects and moments: an incorporation of principles in the early phase of Brazilian poetry; a wholesale effort at translation and transcreation of Russian modern and Futurist poetry; and a collaborative exhibition of Visual Poetry commonly inspired by Russian Futurism.

Keywords: Concrete Poetry, Haroldo de Campos, Augusto de Campos, Décio Pignatari, Boris Schnaiderman, Filippo Tommaso Marinetti, Vladimir Mayakovsky, Velimir Khlebnikov, *Transfutur*

Introduction

In an essay on the neo-avant-gardes in the post-war period, Anna Katharina Schaffner discussed the case of the *Noigandres* group, the brothers Augusto and Haroldo de Campos and their fellow poet Décio Pignatari, founders of Brazilian Concrete Poetry. She probed the extent to which they recuperated, continued and developed techniques pioneered in the first decades of the past century and examined their

https://doi.org/10.1515/9783111318394-011

claims that they had incorporated, and even radicalized, such techniques. Schaffner concludes that the avant-garde tradition had been sublated in their work: "It is both cancelled and preserved, it is negated, assimilated and continued, and ultimately raised to a different level."[1]

With Schaffner's conclusion as a starting point, I examine in this essay the presence of the tradition of Futurism, especially Russian Futurism, in this post-war avant-garde poetry and poetics in Brazil. The topic suggests many questions, for instance, how did the Brazilian protagonists of Concrete Poetry learn about historical Futurism? What relationship did they establish to that tradition? Which ideas stemming from historical Futurism were deemed relevant to their debates and projects? How was Futurism assimilated and developed further, including by subsequent generations?

Covering a time span from the mid-1950s to the present day, I explore how the followers of Concrete Poetry responded to Futurism. I shall focus on three main themes: incorporation, translation and convergence. I first look at the way Futurism was invoked in and incorporated into the manifesto *Plano-piloto para poesia concreta* (Pilot Plan for Concrete Poetry, 1958) and other early theoretical writings collected in *Teoria da poesia concreta* (Theory of Concrete Poetry, 1965). I then turn to the translation of Russian Futurist poetry by members of the Concrete Poetry movement, which yielded the collections *Poemas de Maiakóvski* (Mayakovsky Poems, 1967) and *Poesia russa moderna* (Modern Russian Poetry, 1968), groundbreaking volumes that put such poetry (back) into circulation. Finally, I discuss how the new generation of Brazilian, Russian and German-language poets practising Visual or Concrete Poetry converged on a shared interest in Russian Futurism in the exhibition *Transfutur* (Kassel, 1990; Berlin, 1992). These projects attest to the post-war Brazilian avant-gardes' continued and productive engagement with the legacy of Russian Futurism, an activity that, far from mere imitation, constitutes a creative endeavour in its own right.

Critical incorporation: Italian Futurism

The brothers Augusto and Haroldo de Campos and their friend Décio Pigantari developed one of the most dynamic forms of experimental poetry to emerge in the post-war period. Around the same time as when they began publishing the Little Magazine *Noigandres* in São Paulo in 1952, the Swiss-Bolivian Eugen Gomringer launched a similar poetic experiment. Upon learning about each other's work,

1 Schaffner: "Inheriting the Avant-Garde", p. 112.

both parties agreed on the term 'Concrete Poetry' to describe their writing.[2] Both traced their sources to the historical avant-gardes of the late nineteenth and early twentieth centuries. Schaffner notes that the *Noigandres* poets' "literary experiments are firmly anchored in a selective genealogy of historic and intertextual references and predecessors."[3] Indeed, the members of the *Noigandres* group saw themselves as heirs and continuators of a constellation of avant-garde and Modernist poets that included Stéphane Mallarmé, Ezra Pound, James Joyce, E.E. Cummings and Guillaume Apollinaire. In this panorama, Futurist poets do not figure prominently, but the *Plano-piloto*, their founding document, declares that the "historical cycle of verse (as formal-rhythmical unit) is closed",[4] a phrase that recalls the past-abolishing stances of Dada and Futurism. In 1961, however, the devotees of Concrete Poetry reissued the *Plano-piloto*, this time appending a phrase by the Russian Futurist Vladimir Mayakovsky as postscript: "Without revolutionary form, there is no revolutionary art."[5]

That gesture overtly affiliated Concrete Poetry to Russian Futurism. From that point onwards, Mayakovsky and other Russian Futurists would become tutelary figures for Augusto and Haroldo de Campos. The two brothers would extensively discuss and translate them in collaboration with their friend and teacher, the scholar of Russian literature Boris Schnaiderman. This incorporation of Mayakovsky prompts several questions. What motivated his inclusion into their manifesto and pantheon of chosen predecessors? What appeal did Futurism hold for debates on Concrete Poetry? What aspects fit or did not fit within the programme of its followers? How did the partisans of Concrete Poetry extend their vague affiliation with Italian and French avant-garde tendencies to a warm embrace of the Russian brand?

The followers of Concrete Poetry were certainly acquainted with Marinetti. Italian Futurism had played a key, somewhat polemical, rôle in *Modernismo*, the avant-garde that flourished in Brazil in the 1920s, so much so that it came to be called 'futurismo paulista' (São Paulo Futurism) by some.[6] Scholars have discussed

2 Marjorie Perloff points out that "in 1953, the Brazilian-born Swedish poet Öyvind Fahlström published a 'Manifesto for Concrete Poetry' under the title *Hipy papy bithithdthuthda bthuthdy*, a version of 'Happy Birthday' he took from A. A. Milne's *Winnie-the-Pooh*". Perloff: "Iconic Fallacy", s.p. It is doubtful that there was any direct contact between Fahlström and the Brazilian followers of Concrete Poetry.

3 Schaffner: "Inheriting the Avant-Garde", p. 104.

4 H. Campos, et al.: "Pilot Plan for Concrete Poetry", p. 217.

5 The exact source of this quotation is not noted in the "Pilot Plan".

6 See Fabris: *O futurismo paulista.*

that presence and Marinetti's two visits to Brazil in 1926 and 1936,[7] although they also note that Italian Futurism was not always well understood in Brazil, since only a limited number of Marinetti's writings circulated there, and many writers and artists became acquainted with Futurism in Paris through French writers and artist who were critical of or hostile to Marinetti. This highly biased French view of Futurism put a certain stamp on the reception of Futurism in Brazil.[8] One of the earliest texts by the *Noigandres* group mentioning Futurism is Augusto de Campos's "Pontos – periferia – poesia concreta" (Points – Periphery – Concrete Poetry, 1956), where he acknowledges both Dada and Futurism's historical importance and quotes Marinetti's opposition to the typographic harmony of the page in his *Manifesto tecnico della letteratura futurista* (Technical Manifesto of Futurist Literature, 1912),[9] Augusto de Campos did not fail to recognize the key rôle these tendencies played in the development of Concrete Poetry, but remained critical:

> And it will be possible to discern in the "wireless imagination", in the "words in freedom", in the drastic condemnation of the adjective something like the olfactory premonition of a poetic renewal that they, the Futurists, would not manage to crystallize, but to which they did not fail to contribute enough: with their own immolation.[10]

Augusto de Campos assessed the Futurist contribution as inferior to Mallarmé's experiments, or even Apollinaire's calligrams, which he deemed "less frenetic and more organized."[11] In the manifesto-like "Poesia concreta" (Concrete Poetry, 1956), Augusto de Campos stated that, alongside Mallarmé, Joyce and Cummings, Futurist-Dadaist experimental attempts were, albeit on a secondary level, "at the root of the new poetic procedure, which tends to impose itself over the conventional organization whose formal unit is the line of verse (Free Verse included)."[12] Haroldo de Campos's "Olho por olho a olho nu" (An Eye for an Eye in Daylight, 1956) also declares a lukewarm affiliation with Futurism and Dada, listing them at the end of their "Paideuma":

7 See, for instance, Schnapp and Rocha: "Brazilian Velocities" and Berghaus: "A Cultural Icon of Ill-Repute".
8 See Aguirre et al.: *Futurism in Latin America.*
9 For brevity's sake, authors and titles of individual pieces included in *Teoria da poesia concreta* will be mentioned in the main text, but footnote references will be to the volume. A. Campos et al.: *Teoria da poesia concreta,* p. 21
10 A. Campos et al.: *Teoria da poesia concreta,* pp. 20–21. All translations from Portuguese-language sources, unless otherwise specified, are mine.
11 Ibid., p. 21
12 Ibid., p. 44.

and, why NOT, the FUTURISTS? -- "process of total light" against
the DADAISTS? -- the "*black-out*" of history --
v a l i d a t i o n
of the positive contingent of those "isms" with respect
to the OBJECTUAL or CONCRETE poetic expression
neotypography, "wordsinfreedomism", wireless imagination,
simultaneity, sonorism, etc. etc.
etc. etc.
w
i
t
h
respect to their FUNCTION NOT
simply as psychology BUT
as phenomenology
of
composition[13]

e pq NÃO os FUTURISTAS? — "processo de luz total" contra
os DADAISTAS? — o "black-out" da história:
v a l i d a ç ã o
do contingente positivo desses "ismos" em função
da expressão poética OBJETAL ou CONCRETA
neotipografia, "paroliberismo", imaginação sem fio,
simultaneísmo, sonorismo, etc etc
etc etc
e
m
FUNÇÃO de uma NÃO
apenas psicologia MAS
fenomenologia
da composição

Haroldo de Campos's poem is a witty attempt at visually demonstrating the elements he drew from Futurist aesthetics – different font sizes, typographic symbols and space as a structuring device. Although identified with Futurism, the "process of total light" alludes to Pound's ideogrammic method, whereby the Chinese ideograms for sun and moon, when printed side by side, are made to stand for the abstract idea of 'light' or 'brightness'.[14] The reference to the 'black-out' of history is less clear, although it may refer to the Dadaists' abolition of the past as well as its own self-destructive aim, or its embrace of the irrational. Overall, the contributions of both movements were validated, but less on the semantic and emotive (psychological) levels, than on the structural (phenomenological) level.

13 Ibid., p. 47.
14 Kimpel and Eaves: "Pound's 'Ideogrammic Method' as Illustrated in Canto XCIX", p. 205.

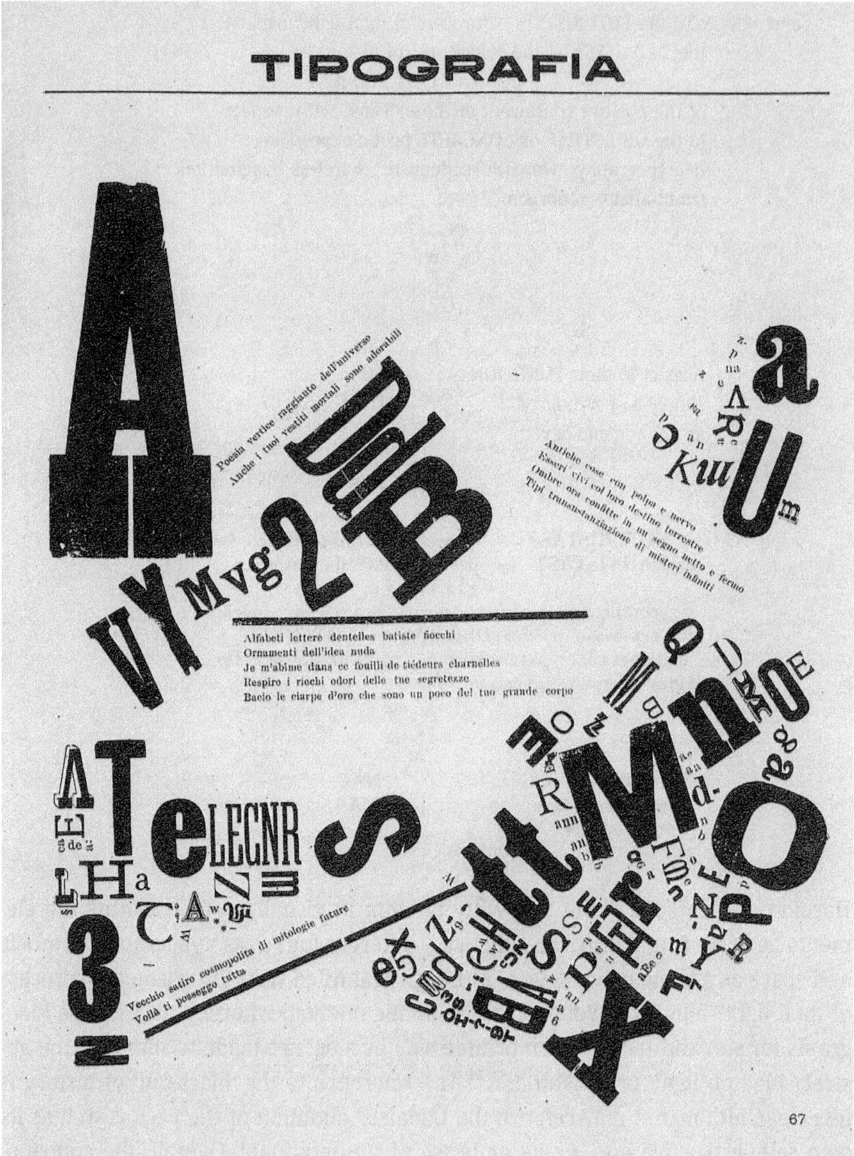

Fig. 1: Ardegno Soffici's poem "Tipografia" (Typography") from *BÏF§ZF+18: Simultaneità, Chimismi lirici* (BÏF§ZF+18: Simultaneity and Lyrical Chemistry, 1915).

In "Aspectos da poesia concreta" (Aspects of Concrete Poetry, 1957), Haroldo de Campos further developed his ideas on the contribution of specific historical figures linked to Futurism. He deemed Apollinaire's theoretical formulations on the ideographic poem "fecund and prophetic", but for him the calligrams "got lost in pictography".[15] Discussing Ardegno Soffici's poem "Tipografia" (Typography; see Fig. 1) from *BÏF§ZF+18: Simultaneità, Chimismi lirici* (BÏF§ZF+18: Simultaneity and Lyrical Chemistry, 1915), Haroldo de Campos claims that the letters, typographical symbols and numbers "serve as mere 'décor' to the presentation of traditionally structured stanzas in asymmetrical layout."[16] The Dadaists fared even worse: Haroldo de Campos saw them as preaching "pure idiocy" and "artistic chaos", with the exception of Tristan Tzara's "Note to the Bourgeois" added to his "L'Amiral cherche une maison à louer" (The Admiral Looks for a House to Rent, 1916), which links the poem's simultaneity to Cubism, Mallarmé, Apollinaire and Marinetti. Marinetti's *Technical Manifesto of Futurist Literature* is praised for its "vivifying impulses", however, Haroldo de Campos also points out that Futurism's inability to create works with a "minimum of constructive organization" was the product of their "descriptive cinematics, [...] subjectivist freneticism, [and] excessive romanticism hypostatized in the machine."[17]

Décio Pignatari, the son of Italian immigrants and *confrère* of the Campos brothers, was more sympathetic to things Italian. He was fluent in the language and, in December 1957, published translations of Italian Futurist poetry in a series curated by the poet Mário Faustino for the Sunday supplement of the *Jornal do Brasil.*[18] The works included "simultaneities" from Marinetti's *Il poema africano della Divisione "28 Ottobre"* (African Poem of the Division "28 October", 1937), and passages from *Il club dei simpatici* (The Club of the Friendly Ones, 1931), which he compared to Oswald de Andrade's *Manifesto antropófago* (Cannibalist Manifesto, 1928). Pignatari also translated works by Francesco Cangiullo, the creator of pentagram poems, Antonio Bruno and Benedetta Cappa's *Viaggio di Gararà: Romanzo cosmico per teatro* (Gararà's Journey: Cosmic Novel for the Theatre, 1931). All of these examples show that Futurism resonated with the *Noigandres* group, but mainly insofar as it had the same synthetic-ideographic orientation as Concrete Poetry.

Alongside Pignatari's translations, Faustino, a poet friendly to the *Noigandres* group, offered an appraisal that could well sum up their attitude. He acknowledged Futurism's merit in instilling an anti-past attitude that made artistic renewal pos-

15 A. Campos et al.: *Teoria da poesia concreta*, p. 97.

16 Ibid., p. 97.

17 Ibid., p. 97

18 Faustino and Pignatari: "Futurismo, IV: Marinetti e Soffici", p. 5. There is precious little scholarship on the discussions of Futurism in Faustino's didactic column "Poesia – Experiência", a fascinating series aimed at introducing avant-garde tendencies to general audiences in Brazil.

sible. Their experiments, he argued, also contributed to Joyce's prose and to the poetry of Eliot and Pound, but he claimed that Cubism was more influential for poetry. Moreover, besides criticizing Marinetti for his connections with Fascism, Faustino, in an echo of Haroldo de Campos's statement quoted above, faulted Futurism for an absence of "final products" that could justify its transformation from avant-garde into an authentic literary school. Futurism, in his view, lacked "poets and poems that, in time, become integrated to the human and aesthetic experience of poetry."[19] Still, the fact that Faustino devoted five editions of his newspaper column "Poesia – Experiência" (Poetry – Experience) to Italian Futurism bespeaks his admiration for how the movement "awakened artistic consciousness everywhere – including Brazil."[20]

Marinetti's movement had a significant impact in Russia, although Russian Futurism was largely developed from indigenous sources.[21] Like in Russia, Futurism had a rather patchy and often highly biased reception in Brazil,[22] but was warmly embraced by the *Noigandres* group. Below, I chart the affinities of the partisans of Concrete Poetry with, and divergences from, Russian Futurism in their early theoretical writings. I also discuss the eventual embrace and incorporation of Mayakovsky and other poets. Before embarking on that discussion, I provide a brief sketch of Russian Futurism and its points of contact and divergence with the Italian movement.

Interlude: Italian Futurism vs. Russian Futurism

Although Italian Futurism clearly predated and probably influenced Russian Futurism, the overall label obscures the variety of local expressions. As Anna Lawton explains, Cubo-Futurism has often been identified with Russian Futurism as a

19 Ibid., p. 7.

20 Ibid., p. 7.

21 See the two entries by Henryk Baran and Christina Lodder on Russian literature and painting in the *Handbook of International Futurism* (2018), pp. 764–823.

22 See João Cezar de Castro Rocha's entry on Brazil in the *Handbook of International Futurism* (2018), pp. 336–351. The epithet 'Futurist' could mean many things in Brazil and was by no means always based on knowledge of primary sources (literary works, paintings, manifestos). Many Brazilians received their information from second-hand sources in Paris or Lisbon, who were often negatively disposed towards Futurism. In Brazil, like in other Latin American countries, "Futurism began a 'second life' that had little in common with what Marinetti and his colleagues had originally outlined in their manifestos and works of art." Berghaus: "Marinetti's 'Futurisme mondial': Propaganda and Reality", p. 106. For more on this uneven reception see Aguirre et al.: *Futurism in Latin America*.

whole, but many other groups prior to the Russian Revolution, namely, *Ego-futurizm* (Ego-Futurism; founded in 1911, *Mezonin poezii* (Mezzanine of Poetry and *Tsentrifuga* (Centrifuge), "played an important rôle in shaping Russian Futurism into a complex and vital movement."[23] In these various groups, issues of locality and quite possibly class[24] played an important rôle in their differentiation as Russian Futurists sought to carve out a space of their own. Ego-Futurism, a more cosmopolitan and urban approach, "was particularly sensitive to foreign influences and suggestions".[25] Meanwhile, the group formed in 1910 by the three brothers, David, Vladimir and Nikolai Burliuk, along with Benedikt Livshits and Velimir Khlebnikov, called itself 'Gileia' (Hylaea), the Greek name for the southern region of Russia and home to the Scythians, a nomadic people of antiquity with whom the founders of the movement felt a close affinity. Their identification with the premodern Slavic past was unique and distinct from Italian Futurism and was significantly linked with their theories. Two miscellanies of works, *Sadok sudei* (A Trap for Judges) and *Studiia impressionistov* (Studio of the Impressionists), appeared in 1910. In 1912, Vladimir Mayakovsky and Aleksei Kruchenykh joined the group, and together they issued their most famous and bombastic manifesto, *Poshchechina obshchestvennomu vkusu* (A Slap in the Face of Public Taste, 1912). They vigorously attacked the old guard of the Symbolists and recommended: "Throw Pushkin, Dostoevsky, Tolstoy, etc., etc., overboard from the ship of Modernity."[26]

Despite these quasi-Marinettian proclamations, Gabriella Imposti argues that the Russians differed significantly from the Italians and sought to express this in their attempt to replace 'Futurists' with 'Futurians': "The differences between Italian and Russian Futurism were emphasized from the very beginning by Velimir Khlebnikov, and they have been affirmed by many scholars since. To underline the distinctions, Khlebnikov created, on the basis of Slavonic lexical units, the word 'Budetlianin', as an antithesis to the 'Latin' word 'Futurist'."[27] The goal of the Russian Futurists was not just to cancel the past (by destroying museums and burning libraries, as Marinetti famously proclaimed), but to reshape it through the action

---

23 Lawton: *Russian Futurism Through its Manifestoes, 1912–1928*, p. 11.

24 Marjorie Perloff notes that most Russian avant-gardists stemmed from middle or lower-middle class families, and that this fact influenced their attitude toward the modern city as "a citadel to be stormed". Perloff: *The Futurist Moment*, p. 126.

25 Lawton: *Russian Futurism Through its Manifestoes, 1912–1928*, p. 25.

26 Ibid., p. 51.

27 Imposti: "The First World War in Italian and Russian Futurism: F.T. Marinetti, Vladimir Mayakovsky and Velimir Khlebnikov", p. 296

of the future on the past.[28] Overcoming the weight of tradition was perceived in strictly linguistic terms as a struggle between outdated forms of expression and the new forms being created. The Russians saw the wholesale recreation of language as one of the most important projects of any avant-garde movement. Kruchenykh characterized the formal revolution as a need for "entirely new words and a new way of combining them."[29]

Examples of this radical linguistic experimentation, the main driving force of the Russian movement, are Kruchenykh and Khlebnikov's 'beyond sense poetry' (*zaum'*) or 'transrational language' (*zaumnyi iazyk*) and Kruchenykh's 'shiftology' (*sdvigologiia).* Lawton notes that *zaum'* first appeared in Kruchenykh's essay *Novye puti slova* (New Ways of the Word, 1913), although he had already published three poems in transrational language in *Pomade* (1913), "Dyr bul shchyl" being the most famous one. Lacking "formal training in poetics, [he] had no aesthetic inhibitions and was able to carry the idea of the self-sufficient word to extravagant lengths."[30] Kruchenykh and Khlebnikov had an intense collaboration, yet they disagreed on their conception of *zaum'*. Khlebnikov wanted to reveal the "primeval meaning of existing word roots, expressed through consonantal sounds rather than conventional semantics", a "universal language based on similar-sounding roots", whereas Kruchenykh sought "spontaneous, non-codified language" or "raw verbal material" exemplified by the utterances of "Russian religious sectarians who in moments of ecstasy [spoke] in foreign tongues or non-existent idioms."[31]

The Russian Futurists' linguistic investigations also had a distinctly nationalist character. Rather than adopting an international avant-garde vocabulary, they focussed their research on the possibilities of the Russian language, devising new words based on Russian morphemes, suffixes and prefixes. Khlebnikov's famous, often quoted poem *Zakliatie smekhom* (Incantation by Laughter, c.1907–08; see below) is the most patent example. Khlebnikov coined words that 'sounded' Russian because they were based on Russian morphemes.[32] In an essay comparing dif-

---

28 The concept of a 'deep past' to be rediscovered played a major rôle in this Futurist link between archaeology and modernity. See Kunichika "Primitivism and Scythianism in Russian Futurism."

29 Nicholls: *Modernisms*, p. 127.

30 Lawton: *Russian Futurism Through its Manifestoes, 1912–1928*, p. 13.

31 Ibid., p. 13.

32 Penetrating Khlebnikov's verbal universe is an adventure that the concrete poets attempted in their translations, as I discuss below. And for anyone interested in the linguistic logic of this "adamic effort to recreate poetic language", Ronald Vroon's monograph *Velimir Xlebnikov's Shorter Poems: A Key to the Coinages* is indispensable.

ferent translations of that poem, Nils Åke Nilsson points out that the poem's devices had nothing to do with Marinetti's onomatopoeia, but rather with a Russian trend of "Neo-Primitivism" that had emerged after 1905.[33] The interest of these poets was the rescue of a Russian mythology and the 'Asiatic'[34] past of their country. Nilsson mentions that the Hylaea Futurists were interested in charades, incantations, spells, laments, and *lubki* (primitive woodcuts), and some of Khlebnikov's poems "do not simply imitate known records of genuine incantations", but there are clear connections with the genre-repetitions, the sound play, and a certain 'secret' aspect of the content.[35]

Finally, it would be remiss not to mention the many collaborations between poets and painters which produced an explosion of hand-crafted Futurist books (see Fig. 2). These partnerships (especially Goncharova, Larionov, Zdanevich and Rozanova) have been studied by many scholars.[36] Lawton notes, that, like the whole avant-garde, the Cubo-Futurists had a "synesthetic understanding of art [that] produced [...] some remarkable results. While roughing up the texture of the text to make it 'palpable' through an unorthodox use of the verbal material, they also performed a typographical revolution."[37] These partnerships would continue and expand in Futurism's Constructivist phase.

33 Nilsson: "How to Translate Avant-Garde Poetry", p. 133. Lawton also notes that "the basic trait that distinguished the Cubo-Futurists from the Italians was an underlying archaism, a leaning towards a primitivism of forms and often of themes (water nymphs, bogeymen, and other figures of Slavic folklore are at home in Khlebnikov's poems). Their search for the 'word as such' was a voyage backward to a prehistoric age, where words sprouted like fragrant flowers in the virgin human soul." Lawton: *Russian Futurism Through its Manifestoes, 1912–1928*, p. 18. Neo-Primitivism also extended into the fine arts, where between 1909 and 1912 it developed a new pictorial language rooted in the native traditions of popular print and icon paintings. See Lodder: "Russia: Fine Arts."

34 Lawton writes: "The return to the origins of language [...] accounted for an ostentatious emphasis on their 'Asian soul' and their claim to be the proud descendants of the Scythian warriors, or more simply, for their sense of *narodnost'*, their spiritual ties with the Russian land and its people (folk songs and tales, naïve paintings, icons, and medieval miniature books are all part of the Cubo-Futurists' cultural baggage)." Lawton: *Russian Futurism Through its Manifestoes, 1912–1928*, p. 18.

35 Nilsson: "How to Translate Avant-Garde Poetry", p. 134.

36 See, amongst others, Rowell and Wye: *The Russian Avant-Garde Book;* Perloff: *Explodity;* Compton: *Russian Avant-garde Books;* Kovtun: *Russkaia futuristicheskaia kniga:* Gurianova: *Livres futuristes russes = The Russian Futurists and Their Books.*

37 Lawton: *Russian Futurism Through its Manifestoes, 1912–1928*, p. 14.

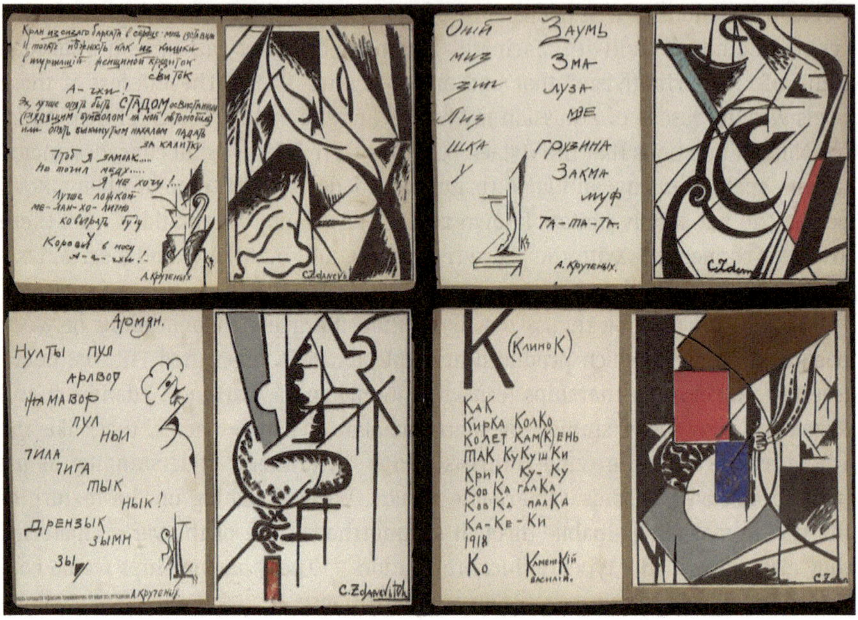

Fig. 2: Four double-pages from Vasilii Kamenskii, Aleksei Kruchenykh, and Kirill Zdanevich: *1918*. Tiflis: s.n., 1917.

Hylaea vs Concrete Poetry

The section above offers a general panorama of some of the main trends that characterized Hylaea and Russian Cubo-Futurism up until the October Revolution in 1917, which radically transformed Russian society, arts and culture. From that point onwards, Russian Futurism vigorously incorporated Constructivist aesthetics. Before launching into that discussion, it is worth exploring the connection between Hylaea and Concrete Poetry. If, as Lawton argues, "Concrete poetry is based on the principle of 'the word as such'",[38] to what extent did Hylaea and the Russian Cubo-Futurists match the aesthetics of Concrete Poetry? The focus on the word as object was indeed near and dear to the advocates of Concrete Poetry. In one of the earliest references to Russian Futurism found in "Evolução de formas: Poesia concreta" (Evolution of Forms: Concrete Poetry, 1957), Haroldo de Campos quotes the Italian Slavist Ettore Lo Gatto on Khlebnikov and other Russian Futurists, praising them as poets who "exalt[ed] the 'value of the word in all its

38 Ibid., p. 9.

metamorphic manifestations, as a primordial element above any type of content.'"[39] Valuing the word as a 'metamorphic' building block of poetry over and above its semantic 'content' is a notion that fit the 'verbi-voco-visual' focus of Concrete Poetry, where sound, visuality and semantics were intrinsically fused and equally valued. The mention of organization by 'phonetic analogy' is also a point of contact with Concrete Poetry. Augusto de Campos describes how "phonetic elements help in the creation of relationships between words, working as factors-of-proximity-and-similarity and establishing a kind of electromagnetic current that attracts or repels words."[40]

Despite these coincidences, there are also many aspects that separate the practitioners of Concrete Poetry from the Hylaea Futurists. Rarely did the devotees of Concrete Poetry attempt to fashion new words out of Portuguese or Latin roots like Khlebnikov did with his Russian vocabulary. In a key essay, "A moeda concreta da fala" (The Concrete Coin of Speech, 1957), Augusto de Campos spells out some of the reasons. Whereas poetry should seek to renew "the concrete coin of speech, worn out and rendered counterfeit by discursive language", Augusto de Campos argues, it should not aim at creating an "entire vocabulary, lexicon and syntax 'ab ovo'", given the highly undesirable "semantic intransitivity" that that would entail.[41] Even the case of Joyce, whose "panorama of all flowers of speech" is based on "a high-pressure amalgam and compression of words [...] borrowed from various languages", a "literary 'esperanto'" of sorts, would not be a viable model for Concrete Poetry: the speed of communication they sought with their poetry demanded "clarity and objectivity."[42] Their experiments focussed more on nominalization and verbification of words, where words count as both verbs and nouns, or count as pseudo-verbs because of their form, as in the following poem by Pignatari:

caviar o prazer	to caviar the pleasure
prazer o porvir	to pleasure the future
porvir o torpor	to future the torpor
contemporalizar[43]	to contemporize

Here the nouns *caviar, prazer, porvir* (to caviar, to pleasure, to future) are 'verbified' but also act as object nouns of the infinitive, flowing into the portmanteau

39 A. Campos et al.: *Teoria da poesia concreta*, p. 50.
40 Ibid., pp. 121–122.
41 Ibid., pp. 116 and 115.
42 Ibid., p. 115.
43 Ibid., p. 126.

verb *contemporalizar* (contemporize). Kruchenykh's transrational, spontaneous and non-codified approach to language likewise does not fit the emphasis on a "rigorously organizing consciousness" in Concrete Poetry.[44] In this early phase, the partisans of Concrete Poetry would have cringed at the thought of a 'transrational' poetry born out of automatism or linked to 'primitive' impulses. Haroldo de Campos specifically decried the conception of poetry as a mystical state, or any form of primitivism, or artisanal mysticism.[45] In "Da fenomenologia da composição à matemática da composição" (From the Phenomenology of Composition to the Mathematics of Composition, 1957), he hammers home the point that Concrete Poetry rejects "organic structures" in favour of "mathematical structures", seeking instead "a verbal planned structure" that possesses the "clarity of symbolic logic."[46]

While the practitioners of Concrete Poetry did manipulate, deform, and transform words for effect, they mostly did so through cuts and splices in the style of E.E. Cummings. As Haroldo de Campos notes, their objective was to "preserve the integrity of the word".[47] Moreover, regarding the visual aspect of the linguistic sign, early Concrete Poetry was almost never written in longhand, like much of *zaum'* poetry in early Russian Futurist books, or with any form of artisanal or craft approaches or hand gestures that would confer a certain expressivity to the linguistic sign. Haroldo de Campos states: "The concrete poem [...] is composed directly on the typewriter: the fixed spacing and the regularity of the fonts allows, with this instrument, typical of modern man, a greater control of the elements at play than would evidently occur in a handwritten piece."[48]

Although the poetics of Russian Futurism had the potential to offer interesting ideas to the practitioners of Concrete Poetry, given that both movements placed a strong emphasis on the materiality of the poetic word, there were also clear differences between the two approaches. In particular, the Futurist transrational poetry of the Hylaea group was anchored in a vision of a mythical, prehistoric past, which ran counter to the identification of Concrete Poetry with rational construction, modern industrial techniques and mass media. This is no surprise, given the entirely different historical contexts in which they were operating.

---

44 Ibid., p. 51.

45 Ibid., pp. 103–04

46 Ibid., p. 93. Mathematics, of course, was also a fundamental aspect of Khlebnikov's poetry and history. See Kamenskii: "Khlebnikov e i matematici", and more recently Vroon: "Matematika ili mistika: K voprosu o nauchnosti istoriosofskikh vzgliadov Velimira Khlebnikova" and Imposti: "Khlebnikov and Science: Time, Space and the Fourth Dimension."

47 A. Campos et al.: *Teoria da poesia concreta*, p. 94.

48 Ibid., p. 104.

Political engagement: Translating Mayakovsky and the 'participatory leap'

Our discussion of the coincidences and divergence between Hylaea Futurism and Brazilian Concrete Poetry in the years 1955 to 1959 is, for the most part, theoretical. The argument is not that the *Noigandres* poets knew and deliberately rejected some aspects of Hylaea Futurism. The Campos brothers had only limited knowledge of Russian Futurism, which they became acquainted with through scholarly sources such as Lo Gatto, works by Formalist critics published in France, or poetry translations into French or Spanish. The "Pilot Plan" also mentions Sergey Eisenstein's notions of the ideogram and montage, concepts they knew through the English edition of *Film Form.*[49] The encounter with the poetry of Vladimir Mayakovsky, however, changed everything. As I noted above, in 1961, the *Noigandres* group reissued the "Pilot Plan" and added as postscript the phrase "Without revolutionary form, there is no revolutionary art", attributed to Mayakovsky.[50] That same year, Haroldo de Campos published his translation of Mayakovsky's poem "To Sergey Yesenin", written after Yesenin's suicide.[51] This publication was the beginning of a wider collaborative effort to translate and critically engage with Russian Futurism and Russian poetry overall.

Before discussing the translations, it is perhaps worth asking what attracted Haroldo de Campos and his fellow poets to Mayakovsky and to this phase of Russian Futurism. The answer involves matters of geopolitics, artistic temperament and aesthetic form. Geopolitically speaking, both avant-gardes shared a desire to

---

49 José Lino Grünewald, a supporter of Concrete Poetry, translated Eisenstein's essay "The Cinematographic Principle and the Ideogram" from the English version in *Film Form.* A. Campos et al.: *Teoria da poesia concreta*, p. 187.

50 "Sem forma revolucionária não há arte revolucionária." Although no source was given, the phrase has been repeated endlessly in Brazilian scholarship. The original actually reads quite differently: "Только взрыв Революции Духа очистит нас от ветоши старого искусства [...] Революция содержания социализм – анархизм немыслима – без революции формы – футуризма." "Otkrytoe pis'mo rabochim." *Gazeta futuristov* 1 (15 March 1918), p. 1. Reprinted in Maiakovskii: *Polnoe sobranie sochinenii.* Vol. 12. *Stat'i, 1917–1930.* Moskva: Gosudarstvennoe izdatel'stvo khudozhestvennoi literatury, 1959, pp. 8–9. "Only an explosion of the Revolution of the Spirit will purge us of the rags of the old art [...] The revolution of content – socialism, anarchism – is inconceivable without the revolution of form – Futurism." See Jangfeldt: *Majakovskij and Futurism*, pp. 18–29.

51 Originally published as "Maiacóvski em português: Roteiro de uma tradução" in *Revista do livro*, it was later reworked as "O texto como produção (Maiakóvski)" in his book of essays *A operação do texto* (Textual Operation, 1976), later reissued as *A reoperação do texto* (Textual Reoperation, 2013).

unite revolutionary ideals with innovative aesthetics. The Russian Futurists constituted as a group before 1917, realized that the October Revolution had catapulted Russia into a new social and political reality, and thus they "welcomed the Bolsheviks and a short-lived alliance was forged between them."[52] In the early 1960s, Brazil faced an economic and political crisis that eventually led to the 1964 military coup. This key historical moment led to stock-taking and re-evaluation on the part of poets.[53] Concrete Poetry had thus been perceived as a practice with, at best, a non-committal political attitude. In "A situação atual da poesia no Brasil" (The Current Situation of Poetry in Brazil, 1961), Pignatari announced Concrete Poetry's imminent "content-semantic-participatory leap."[54] By this he meant that Concrete Poetry, at the time of the military coup in Brazil, relinquished its politically neutral position, "leapt" into a more politically engaged mode and aligned itself with leftist activism. Pignatari spoke subtly of the need to combine (liberal) political ideas with an exploration of formal innovation in poetry. In the face of the rise of what they saw as reactionary politics and poetics in post-war Brazil, translating Mayakovsky, hailed as the poet of the Russian Revolution, became part of that "participatory leap" in which they united a leftist position with experimental form. Both Campos brothers began studying Russian with Boris Schnaiderman at the University of São Paulo with the explicit goal of translating Mayakovsky. Augusto de Campos recalls that, shortly after, "in the middle of the military dictatorship", they published "for the first time in Brazil a collection by the great poet translated directly from the Russian."[55]

Temperamentally and formally, Mayakovsky had more in common with the apostles of Concrete Poetry than the Hylaea Futurists, especially in the years after the October Revolution. His later works[56] embodied the urban, rational and typographic ideals of professional book publishing (as opposed to the primitiv-

52 Nicholls: *Modernisms*, p. 132.

53 Simon: "Projetos alternativos/confronto de poéticas" p. 170.

54 "Pulo conteudístico-semântico-participante". Pignatari: "A situação atual da poesia no Brasil", p. 117.

55 Maiakóvski: *Poemas*, p. 15. In 1956, in Rio de Janeiro, Emílio Carrera Guerra published a 56-page volume of translations of Mayakovsky's poems entitled *Poemas*. A copy is housed in the rare books section of Brazil's National Library. The catalogue entry lists the publisher as Philobiblion, Civilização Brasileira, in Rio de Janeiro and notes the print run was only 300. I am unsure if the translations were directly from the Russian.

56 Primitivist style elements can be found in some of his earlier books, such as the lithographed *Ia* (I, 1913) or the illustrations in *Vladimir Maiakovskii: Tragedia* (Vladimir Mayakovsky: A Tragedy, 1914). For more on Mayakovsky and Primitivism see Richter: *Literary Primitivism: Its Function in the Early Works of Vladimir Mayakovsky and Other Russian Cubo-Futurists*. Ph.D. Dissertation. Toronto: University of Toronto, 1998.

ist, lithographed and self-made books of the early Futurist group). The Cubo-Futurists, Lawton notes, directed their gaze "to the buzz and bustle of the contemporary metropolis", and even though "Mayakovsky's urban landscapes are often nightmarish settings",[57] he did not disavow the urbanism derived from Italian Futurism.[58] Concrete Poetry remained firmly grounded in the experience of cities such as São Paulo and Brasília, the new Brazilian capital inaugurated in 1960, which showcased avant-garde urban design and architecture.[59] Moreover, as Schnaiderman argues, rationalism underlies Russian Futurism's preoccupation with constructing a poetic work as a system, an attitude present in the "Third Order" of Mayakovky's unfinished poem, *Piatyi Internatsional* (The Fifth International, 1922):

Я поэзии одну разрешаю форму: краткость, точность математических формул.[60]	I for poetry allow one form only: brevity, exactness of mathematical formulas.[61]

The devotees of Concrete Poetry had a strong commitment to rational design. Nowhere is this more explicit than in "Construir e expressar" (Constructing and Expressing, 1959), where Pignatari writes: "Poets should silence their personal and demagogic whining and try to construct poems worthy of the new times, worthy of the rationally planned and produced industrial objects."[62] This commitment also entailed employing the language of the 'common man', avoiding both the discursive and the metaphorical characteristics of outdated forms of poetry. In this respect, they too agreed with Mayakovsky. In "Contexto de uma vanguarda" (Context of an Avant-garde, 1963), Haroldo de Campos quotes Mayakovsky's essay "The Workers and Peasants Do not Understand You", published in *Novyi Lef* in January 1928, where the Futurists are exhorted "to organize the comprehension of a book" because the favourable mass reception of literary works can only be the result of "our struggle" rather than "the books of some literary genius."[63]

57 Lawton: *Russian Futurism Through its Manifestoes, 1912–1928*, p. 25.
58 Schnaiderman, *A poética de Maiakóvski*, p. 24.
59 A. Campos et al.: *Teoria da poesia concreta*, p. 151.
60 Maiakovskii: "Piatyi internatsional. 8 chastei. Chast' pervaia: Prikaz № 3." *Polnoe sobranie sochinenii.* Vol. 4. *1922 – fevral' 1923.* p. 108.
61 Mayakovsky: *Mayakovsky*, p. 156.
62 A. Campos et al.: *Teoria da poesia concreta*, p. 125.
63 Ibid., p. 152. See V.V. Maiakovskii: "Vas ne ponimaiut rabochie i krest'iane." *Novyi Lef* 2:1 (#13) (January 1928), pp. 37–41.

Finally, formally speaking, Mayakovsky's embrace of professional typography and modern printing techniques held great appeal for the supporters of Concrete Poetry. In "Maiakóvski e o construtivismo" (Mayakovsky and Constructivism, 1962), Haroldo de Campos stresses the parallel between Mayakovsky's innovative poetic art and the path of renewal pursued by visual artists such as Alexander Rodchenko, Vladimir Tatlin and, especially, El Lissitzky in his design for Mayakovsky's *Dlia golosa* (For the Voice, 1923). Haroldo de Campos calls Lissitzky's book design "a veritable reading score – with corresponding solutions and inventions at the typographical level", which tries to reproduce the phonic values of Mayakovsky's poetry.[64] He praises Lissitzky's "graphic humour", including "all the finesse of the structural layout", the bare geometric Constructivist pagination as well as his invention of the "marginalia-index", a clever visual design that introduces each poem and announces the following ones using keywords and a topical visual emblem on the right-hand side of the page (see Fig. 3).[65]

Ultimately, for Mayakovsky, Constructivist principles were not just compositional technique but rather an all-embracing attitude towards art and life. Haroldo de Campos mentions how Mayakovsky, in a chronicle written in Paris around 1922, stated that Constructivism should encompass the "formal work of the artist as a necessary engineering for the configuration of our entire practical life."[66] Constructivism as an international movement expressed itself primarily in non-utilitarian graphic works, based on abstract tectonic forms and spatial structures developed by Vladimir Tatlin, El Lissitzsky or Naum Gabo. However, Constructivism also became a significant aspect of Russian Futurism during its Productivist phase, when artists applied their artistic form building to practical projects and switched to engineering and design, thus removing the borders between art and life. This idea resonates with the last paragraph of the *Plano-piloto:*

> Concrete Poetry: total responsibility before language. Total realism. Against a subjective and hedonistic poetry of expression. To create precise problems and to solve them in terms of sensible language. A general art of the word. The poem-product: useful object.[67]

---

64 Maiakóvski: *Poemas*, p. 237.

65 Ibid., p. 238.

66 Ibid., p. 240. "Конструктивизм должен стать высшей формальной инженерией всей жизни. Конструктивизм в разыгрывании пастушеских пасторалей – вздор." Aseev, et al.: "Kogo predosteregaet Lef?" p. 10. The quote can be found in Maiakovskii: *Polnoe sobranie sochinenii.* Vol. 12. *Stat'i, 1917–1930.* Moskva: Gosudarstvennoe izdatel'stvo khudozhestvennoi literatury, 1959, p. 49.

67 H. Campos, et al.: "Pilot Plan for Concrete Poetry", p. 219.

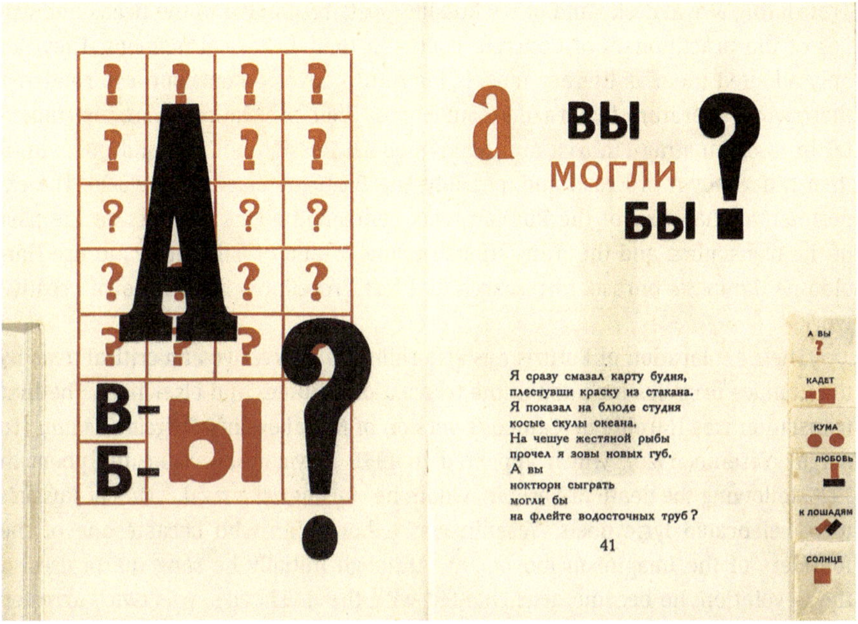

Fig. 3: Mayakovsky's poem "A vy mogli by?" (Could You?, 1913) in *Dlia golosa* (For the Voice, 1923), designed by El Lissitzky. On the right are the cut-in thumb tabs similar to those in an address book, serving as an index system.

Although Mayakovsky and other Futurists were shunned by subsequent Soviet literary historians, Haroldo de Campos, writing in 1962, noted that, in the post-Stalinist thaw, something fundamental of that tradition remained in the air "awaiting, necessarily, a revival."[68] Half a world away, in Brazil, the partisans of Concrete Poetry participated in that revitalization: their translations, or 'transcreations' of Mayakovsky and other Russian poets, as well as their critical reflections, creatively engaged with Russian Futurism and brought it back into circulation. Writing about world literature as an international exchange of texts, David Damrosch argues that

> works become world literature by being received into the space of a foreign culture, a space defined in many ways by the host culture's national tradition and the present needs of its own writers. [...] The receiving culture can use the foreign material [...] as a positive model for the future development of its own tradition [...]. World literature is thus always as much about the host culture's values and needs as it is about a work's source culture.[69]

68 Maiakóvski: *Poemas*, pp. 240–241.

69 Damrosch: "World Literature, National Contexts", p. 514.

Translating Mayakovsky and other Russian poets responded to the needs and values of the practitioners of Concrete Poetry in their historical moment. They not only adopted them as literary models for future development, but also rendered them world literature for Brazilian audiences. Their translations were instrumental in disseminating Futurist and other modern Russian authors and poets until then little known in Brazil and, possibly, the Portuguese-speaking world. The experimental character of the Russian texts demanded equal boldness on the part of the translators, and the translations became a kind of 'laboratory', to use Haroldo de Campos's phrase, to research and test procedures for their own creative work.

Their exploration of Futurism is also reflected in creative and critical texts by the Campos brothers included in the translation volumes and elsewhere. The first translation was Haroldo de Campos's version of Mayakovsky's *Sergeiu Eseninu* (To Sergey Yesenin, 1926), which appeared in 1961. Mayakovsky wrote the poem in 1926, following the death of Yesenin, whom he considered a rival.[70] One of Russia's most celebrated lyric poets, Yesenin was a bohemian who became one of the founders of the Imaginism movement. Although initially he sang the praises of the Revolution, he became disenchanted with the Bolsheviks, was twice arrested in 1923 and interrogated by the secret police. He struggled for a while with alcoholism and mental illness and, in 1925, committed suicide in a hotel, leaving behind a farewell poem, reportedly written with his own blood. Mayakovsky's elegy is a sobering response to Yesenin's poem, taking stock of his life and death.

Given that the advocates of Concrete Poetry insisted on the abolition of the line of verse as a structural unit, Haroldo de Campos's choice of "To Sergey Yesenin" as his first stab at translating Mayakovsky may seem surprising. After all, belonging to a less experimental phase, the poem is written in lines and makes use of traditional elements such as rhythm and rhyme. In the commentary that accompanied his translation,[71] Haroldo de Campos painstakingly details his choices and strategy. For one, when he began the translation, Haroldo de Campos had only been learning Russian for a scant three months, so he availed himself of the existing Spanish and German translations of this poem; moreover, he judged the work to be one of the most important creations of Mayakovsky's mature phase, and Mayakovsky himself had chosen it as an example for his essay on poetics, *Kak delat' stikhi* (How Are Verses to Be Made?, 1926).[72]

---

70 See Jangfeldt: *Mayakovsky: A Biography*, pp. 355–360.

71 It later developed into the essay "Text as Production (Maiakóvski)", included in his essay collection *Operation of the Text*.

72 H. de Campos, "O texto como produção (Maiakóvski)", pp. 48–49. For an English translation, see *How Are Verses Made?*

Haroldo de Campos's commentary tried to align Mayakovsky as much as possible with Concrete Poetry. "To Sergey Yesenin" uses trochee patterns but not consistently, and the lines are spaced out on the page. One of Haroldo de Campos's first assertions regarding this feature is that Mayakovsky is a "spatial poet" and the poem is a "reading score".[73] While this staggering of the lines into shorter segments was useful when speaking to large crowds in a kind of oratorical poetry favoured by Mayakovsky,[74] for Haroldo de Campos this feature constituted rather a kind of 'montage', quoting Eisentein's observation that Mayakovsky did not write in lines but rather in cinematic 'shots'.[75] Haroldo de Campos also stresses Mayakovsky's disregard for strict metrical rules and his heterodox approach to rhyme, concluding that 'economy' was a fundamental rule of all his aesthetic production, with logical connections established by an 'ideogrammic-analogical' montage.[76] Mayakovsky, when seen from this perspective, begins to look as if he had been an apostle of Concrete Poetry.

Haroldo de Campos's complex description of his translation method bears out his assertion that he followed in his own translation work Mayakovsky's cues in *How Are Verses to Be Made?* He paid special attention to the phonic affinities that Mayakovsky tried to establish between words, even though it meant deviating from the semantics, as in this line:

> Gdié on, / Brónzi zvon / íli granita gran?
> Onde / o som do bronze / ou o grave granito?[77]
>
> Where is it / bronze reverberant / or granite grand?[78]

Haroldo de Campos explains that he sought to avoid the literal meaning of *gran* (facet, edge, corner), keeping instead the alliteration and the solemn tone of the passage, where 'granite' and 'bronze' allude to a yet–unbuilt monument to the dead poet. Haroldo de Campos's translation, published in 1961, was followed in September 1962 by a co-translation of the poem "Letter to Tatiana Yakovleva" with Boris Schnaiderman, accompanied by Haroldo de Campos's article "Maiakóvski e o construtivismo", discussed above. More translations of poems by Khlebni-

---

73 H. de Campos, "O texto como produção (Maiakóvski)", p. 55.

74 The Futurist art of recitation did not only determine the form of Marinetti's poetry and manifestos, but also much of Mayakovsky's poetic output. See Palmer: "Mayakovsky's Voices: Futurist Performance and Communication in Verse."

75 H. de Campos, "O texto como produção (Maiakóvski)", p. 57.

76 Ibid., pp. 57–60.

77 Ibid., p. 75

78 Mayakovsky: *Mayakovsky*, p. 348.

kov, Mayakovsky and Yevtushenko appeared in December 1962. Finally, in 1967, the three collaborators published the book-length *Poemas de Maiacóvski* (Poems by Mayakovsky), and Schnaiderman authored *A poética de Maiakóvski* (Mayakovsky's Poetics, 1971), a critical edition and translation of some of Mayakovsky's key prose writings with a scholarly introduction.

The selection of Mayakovsky's poems reflects a desire to bring the experimental nature of his poetics to the fore. In his introduction, "Maiakóvski: Evolução e unidade" (Mayakovsky: Evolution and Unity, 1967), Schnaiderman lays bare the criteria that guided the choices of the group. He explains how the reception of Mayakovsky's work was often selective, with certain portions being rejected wholesale. Pasternak admired the pre-revolutionary work and disdained everything else except for *Vo ves' golos* (At the Top of My Voice, 1930); Soviet critics, for their part, rejected the works of his early period as 'formalist' and 'Futurist'.[79] Schnaiderman argues instead that

> Mayakovsky's œuvre should be considered in its entirety [with a] connecting thread that joins the early to the late poetry [...] The Futurist Mayakovsky [...] is the same as the poet of the Revolution, conscious and defiant, [and] the poems he wrote on the eve of his death are branded with the same original and highly elaborate poetic devices he deployed from 1912 on.[80]

Although Schnaiderman's preference for Futurism is clear – 36 of his translated poems stem from the pre-1918 phase versus 14 pieces from the post-Revolutionary period – the selection bears witness to "the continuity and permanence in Mayakovsky's œuvre".[81] Schnaiderman briefly but carefully comments on each choice and his translation strategies. Augusto de Campos also reveals that he and his brother Haroldo were very interested in Mayakovsky's Cubo-Futurist poems because "they revealed a hidden face of the poet: his furious craft, expressed in offensive images, unexpected verbal play and odd, startling rhymes",[82] which they tried to bring out in their own versions. In the end, they sought to convey "Mayakovsky's modernity [and] active presence, even in our day and age."[83]

---

79 Maiakóvski: *Poemas*, p. 32.
80 Ibid., p. 32.
81 Ibid., p. 33.
82 Ibid., p. 277.
83 Ibid., p. 47

Expanding the field: modern Russian poetry

Barely one year after *Poemas de Maiacóvski* (titled *Maiakóvski: Poemas* in subsequent editions), the Campos brothers and Schnaiderman brought out an anthology entitled *Poesia russa moderna* (Modern Russian Poetry, 1968), featuring an entire phalanx of Russian poets (not just the Futurists). The anthology received rave reviews even outside of Brazil.[84] The initial list of 24 poets was increased to 27 in subsequent editions, and the selection of poems was substantially expanded: for the second edition, the translators added 40 new poems.[85] The most recent includes 16 new translations and a 1991 dossier of Visual Poetry from the more recent generations, edited by Schnaiderman, some of which were included in the exhibition *Transfutur*, discussed below.

Although *Poesia russa moderna* is wide-ranging, it is clearly centred on the Hylaea and Cubo-Futurists. It includes works by David Burliuk, Vasily Kamensky, Wassily Kandinsky, Velimir Khlebnikov, Aleksei Kruchenykh, Iliazd (pseud. of Ilya Zdanevich) and Mayakovsky. It also comprised other contemporaries, such as Anna Akhmatova, Boris Pasternak, Osip Mandelstam, Marina Tsvetaeva, Sergey Yesenin, and poets from the Soviet era (Yevgeny Yevtushenko, Andrei Voznesensky, Gennady Aygi). Khlebnikov, acknowledged as prophetic, "unlike anything that came before him",[86] is prominently featured with a selection of 19 poems, a count second only to Mayakovsky. Although his *zaum'* experiments were not much incorporated into Concrete Poetry, translating his seemingly untranslatable poems became a challenge and an opportunity for poetic experimentation, as we can see in Haroldo de Campos's version of Khlebnikov's iconic *Incantation by Laughter*.

Incantation by Laughter is undoubtedly Khlebnikov's most celebrated poem. Vladimir Markov, the first historian of Russian Futurism, notes that it was ridiculed in numerous magazines and articles, but when Mayakovsky began reciting it in public, it charmed the critics, including Chukovsky, for whom it signalled

---

84 At the time, the Slavist Victor Terras wrote: "The Campos brothers and Boris Schnaiderman] have produced a volume of which we, in the English-speaking world, must be envious [...] We have very little in English that can be compared to [...] the de Campos brothers' translations of a whole galaxy of Russian poets from Blok to Voznesenskij [...] There is a sustained effort to reproduce the acoustic patterns of the original [...] All of which makes for a remarkably successful effort at introducing modern Russian poetry to what must be an almost virgin audience." Terras: "Review of 'Poesia russa moderna'", p. 508.

85 A. de Campos et al.: *Poesia russa moderna*, p. 29.

86 Ibid., p. 20.

the beginning of Futurism in Russia.[87] It is a "poetic exploration of the possibilities of morphological derivations inherent in the Russian language."[88] Nilsson points out that, rhythmically, the original has a trochaic pulse (one strong tonic syllable and one weak atonic syllable in a row), and, in phonic terms, one of the most interesting features is the dominance of open front vowels (as opposed to closed or dark vowels), which gives the sound of the poem a certain lightness.[89] From a morphological perspective, Nilsson highlights the creation of neologisms from the roots *smekh, smei* ('laughter') and suffixes and prefixes.[90] Haroldo de Campos's version, printed exceptionally facing the original,[91] follows a similar pattern:

Ride, ridentes!
Derride, derridentes!
Risonhai aos risos, rimente risandai!
Derride sorrimente!
Risos sobrerrisos – risadas de sorrideiros risores!
Hílare esrir, risos de sobrerridores riseiros!
Sorrisonhos, risonhos,
Sorride, ridiculai, risando, risantes,
Hílariando, riando,
Ride, ridentes!
Derride, derridentes![92]

Hlahla! Uthlofan, lauflings!
Hlahla! Ufhlafan, lauflings!
Who lawghen with lafe, who hlaehen lewchly,
Hlahla! Ufhlofan hlouly!
Hlahla! Hloufish lauflings lafe uf beloght lauchalorum!
Hlahla! Loufenish lauflings lafe, hlohan udaufly!
Lawfen, lawfen,
Hloh, hlouh, hlou! luifekin, luifekin,
Hlofeningvim, hlofeningum.
Hlahla! Uthlofan, lauflings!
Hlahla! Ufhlofan, lauflings![93]

Open and front vowels dominate, the phoneme /i/, in particular, and there is an absence of nasal or closed vowels. He uses words with roots that relate to the Portuguese verb *rir* ('laugh'), and others within the same semantic field – *sorrir, risonho, derrisório, ridículo, hilário* – using suffixes (*-ente, -mente, -ante*) and prefixes (*de-, es-, so-, sobre-*) as well as endings that correspond to the imperative of verbs in Portuguese (*risandai*). His morphological choices create semantic variants which add images: by coincidence, *ridente*, an adjective for someone who laughs,

87 See Markov: *Russian Futurism*, p. 8.
88 Markov: *Russian Futurism*, p. 7.
89 Nilsson: "How to Translate Avant-Garde Poetry", pp. 136–137.
90 Ibid., p. 136.
91 Only very few of the poems include the Russian original, and in the case of *Incantation by Laughter*, a facsimile of the first 1910 edition is reproduced with a note that comments on the visual effect of the original typography. A. de Campos et al.: *Poesia russa moderna*, p. 118.
92 A. de Campos et al.: *Poesia russa moderna*, p. 119.
93 Khlebnikov: *Collected Works*. Vol. 3. *Selected Poems*, p. 30. The original was first published in 1910 in *Studiia impressionistov* and can be found in Khlebnikov: *Sobranie sochinenii*. Vol. 2. *Tvoreniia*, 1906–1916, p. 35.

also contains *dente* (tooth), which visually suggests an open-mouth grin. Haroldo de Campos respected the poetic structure of the original, especially the first two lines that are also repeated at the end. The translation is a real tour de force when we compare it with less accomplished versions into other languages.[94]

The translation of these texts provided a precious linguistic 'laboratory' for the Campos brothers, who implemented their experimentation and findings in other creative texts. Augusto de Campos, for example, authored visual poems inspired by Rodchenko's profile portrait of Mayakovsky, *Profilograma 1* (Profilegramme, 1966; See Fig. 4a) and *Chuva oblíqua de Maiakóvski* (Mayakovsky's Oblique Rain, 1982; see Fig. 4b).

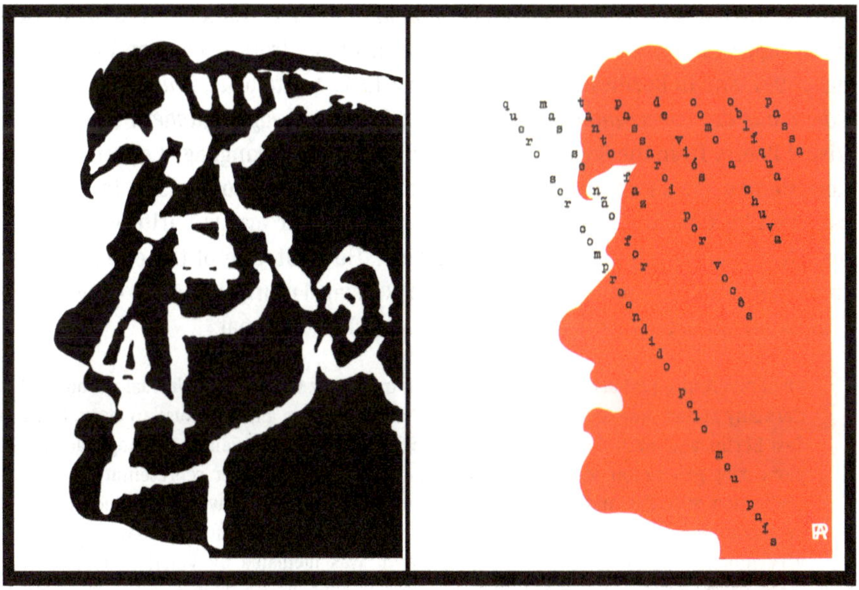

Fig. 4a: Augusto de Campos: *Profilograma 1: Pound / Maiakóvski* (1966). Screen printing based on a Portrait of Mayakovsky by Alexander Rodchenko (1940) and a drawing of Ezra Pound by Henri Gaudier-Brzeska (1916). **Fig. 4b.** Augusto de Campos: *Chuva oblíqua de Maiakóvski* (Mayakovsky's Oblique Rain, 1982).

He also reworked some of his translations of Khlebnikov, Mayakovsky and Mandelstam as visual poems and included them in his poetry collections *Despoesia* (Unpoetry, 1994) and *Não poemas* (Non-Poems, 2003). As recently as 2019, Augusto de Campos published *Esses russos* (Those Russians), a chapbook with his own lav-

94 See Nilsson: "How to Translate Avant-Garde Poetry", pp. 140–150.

ish visual elaborations and transcreations of 'ferroconcrete' poems by Kamensky and Iliazd, among others.

Convergence: *Transfutur*

The last edition of *Poesia russa moderna* includes a note about the *Transfutur* exhibition, perhaps the last major chapter in the productive engagement between Brazilian avant-garde poets and the legacy of Russian Futurism. A joint project by the German curator and poet Friedrich Block, the Brazilian artist and poet André Vallias and the Russian-language poet Valeri Scherstjanoi (born to a Lithuanian mother in Kazakhstan as Valerii Mikhailovich Sherstianoi and living in Germany since 1971), the exhibition took place in Kassel from December 1990 to January 1991, and in Berlin from June to August 1992. A catalogue, *Transfutur: Visuelle Poesie aus der Sowjetunion, Brasilien und deutschsprachigen Ländern* (Transfutur: Visual Poetry from the Soviet Union, Brazil and German-language Countries, 1990), documented the show that included 36 poets from three contexts. It featured essays by Block, Vallias and Scherstjanoi, by the graphic artists Carlfriedrich Claus and Karla Sachse, and by the publisher Peter Huckauf. One of the objectives was to "honour the tradition they shared with Russian Futurism".[95] This convergence was as serendipitous as it was significant. Block recalls that:

> I had met André [Vallias] – a great artist, poet, translator, designer, intellectual – who lived in Germany at that time and our friend Valeri Scherstjanoi, an amazing Russian artist, living in East Berlin, and kind of reincarnation of Russian Futurism. We wanted to bring together the pioneering generation of concrete and visual poetry with younger representatives like the generation of André and myself […] to reflect the impact of the avant-garde-movements of the early twentieth century on our personal interest in experimental poetry, and we were very much inspired by Russian Futurism as it was mediated by Valeri and others like Serge Segay, Rea Nikonova and Boris Konstriktor from Russia, who formed the group of 'Transfurists' […] the name of this group, which also participated in 'Transfutur', also lent some motivation for the title of the show.[96]

The three contexts converged in this exhibition, not only through bonds of friendship but also through historical roots. As Block notes, these three geographical regions were key to experimental poetry in the twentieth century: Brazil and German-speaking countries represent "the beginnings of Concrete Poetry in the fifties, and the Russian [context] is a fundamental contribution to the poetic revo-

95 Block: *Transfutur*, p. 1.
96 Block: Personal communication, 18 May 2020.

lution that took place internationally since the turn of the century: Russian FUTURism."[97] Besides bringing together Visual Poetry from Brazil, German-speaking countries, and the Soviet Union (in the final year of its existence), *Transfutur* also spanned several generations: from the last living representative of the Russian avant-garde, the OBERIU poet Igor Bakhterev, to the Concrete Poetry generation from Brazil, Germany and Austria, to younger poets influenced by these avant-gardes.[98] The Campos brothers and Pignatari, along with Vallias were part of the Brazilian cohort, as were younger poets and visual artists such as Arnaldo Antunes, Lenora de Barros, Betty Leirner and Walter Silveira, to name but a few. While not all had a direct connection to Russian Futurism, many were influenced by the *Noigandres* group. As Block argues regarding how the reception of a trend can be generative: "The avant-gardes live from the traditions they develop further."[99] Case in point is the work of Vallias, one of the organizers and a digital poet and artist. Vallias's "A encantação pelo riso" (Incantation by Laughter, 2003), a digital animation of Haroldo de Campos's translation of Khlebnikov's *Incantation by Laughter*,[100] with sound, text and 3D graphic maps of the rhythm, is an "inter-semiotic translation (from textual to audiovisual and textual signs) [...] a verbivocovisual interpretation of a poem."[101] It constitutes a vivid example of how a tradition that emerged in Russia in the early twentieth century could live on in twenty-first century Brazil. Because Vallias visually 'translates' Haroldo de Campos's transcreation of Khlebnikov, we could say it is Russian Futurism to the third degree.

Conclusion

The Brazilian representatives of Concrete Poetry effectively recovered and continued the project of the historical avant-garde, drawing lessons from it for their own practices. In their theoretical writings from the 1950s, they discussed the poetics of Italian and Russian Futurisms, incorporating some of their insights while dismissing others. Italian Futurism was familiar to them from sources and translations available in Brazil, while Russian Futurism was accessible initially only through second-hand sources. While not all principles of early Russian Futurism were suit-

97 Block: *Transfutur*, p. 1.
98 Vallias: Personal communication, 9 May 2020.
99 Block: *Transfutur*, p. 2
100 Available in https://www.youtube.com/watch?v=bC9mXDUSMqo.
101 Wiese: "A poesia digital de André Vallias", p. 50.

ed to their aesthetics of Concrete Poetry, they eventually found inspiration in the work of Vladimir Mayakovsky, after learning Russian to explore his work further.

Rehabilitated after the post-Stalinist thaw, Mayakovsky's Constructivist poetics and revolutionary stance came to breathe new life into the Brazilians' experimental programme for Concrete Poetry. In collaboration with Boris Schnaiderman, a scholar of Russian language and literature, they translated and commented on the work of Mayakovsky, a project that led them to a wider interest in Russian Futurist and avant-garde poetry. Their pioneering volumes of poetry translations or transcreations have been in print in expanded forms since the 1960s, attesting to their continued vitality and topicality. This translation practice was both a creative endeavour that provided a laboratory for literary experimentation and brought Russian Futurism to Brazilian audiences as an instance of world literature. The exhibition *Transfutur* was witness to the impact of their work on the newer generations of poets, who converged in a common interest in Russian Futurism which, astonishingly, found a lasting legacy in Brazil.

Bibliography

Aguirre, Mariana, Rosa Sarabia, Renée M. Silverman, and Ricardo Vasconcelos, eds.: *International Yearbook of Futurism Studies.* Vol.7. *Futurism in Latin America.* Berlin & Boston: De Gruyter, 2017.

Aseev, Nikolai, Boris Arvatov, Osip Brik, Nikolai Chuzhak, Boris Kushner, Vladimir Maiakovskii, and Sergei Tret'iakov: "Kogo predosteregaet Lef?" *Lef: Zhurnal levogo fronta iskusstv* 1:1 (March 1923): 10–11.

Baran, Henryk: "Russia: Literature." Günter Berghaus, ed.: *Handbook of International Futurism.* Berlin & Boston/MA: De Gruyter, 2018. 764–798.

Berghaus, Günter: "A Cultural Icon of Ill-Repute: Marinetti and Brazilian Antifascism." *International Yearbook of Futurism Studies* 7 (2017): 250–259.

Berghaus, Günter: "Marinetti's 'Futurisme mondial': Propaganda and Reality." Jurij Lileev, Yvonne Pörzgen, and Mario Zanucchi, eds.: *Europäische Avantgarden um 1900: Kontakt – Transfer – Transformation.* Paderborn: Brill Finck, 2021. 85–112.

Block, Friedrich W., André Vallias, and Valeri Scherstjanoi, eds.: *Transfutur: Visuelle Poesie aus der Sowjetunion, Brasilien und deutschsprachigen Ländern. Ein Katalogbuch.* Kassel: Jenior & Pressler, 1990.

Campos, Augusto de, Haroldo de Campos, and Boris Schnaiderman, eds.: *Poesia russa moderna.* São Paulo: Perspectiva, 6th edn 2019.

Campos, Augusto de, Haroldo de Campos, and Décio Pignatari: *Teoria da poesia concreta.* São Paulo: Livraria Duas Cidades, 2nd edn 1975.

Campos, Augusto de: *Despoesia.* São Paulo: Perspectiva, 1994.

Campos, Augusto de: *Esses russos: Extraduções.* Londrina: Galileu, 2019.

Campos, Augusto de: *Não poemas.* São Paulo: Perspectiva, 2009.

Campos, Haroldo de, et al.: "Pilot Plan for Concrete Poetry." H. de Campos: *Novas: Selected Writings.* Ed. by Antonio Sergio Bessa, and Odile Cisneros. Evanston/IL: Northwestern University Press, 2007. 217–19.

Campos, Haroldo de: "O texto como produção (Maiakóvski)." H. de Campos: *A reoperação do texto.* São Paulo: Perspectiva, 2013. 47–94.

Compton, Susan: *Russian Avant-garde Books, 1917–34.* Cambridge/MA: MIT Press, 1993.

Damrosch, David: "World Literature, National Contexts." *Modern Philology* 100:4 (2003): 512–531.

Fabris, Annateresa: *O futurismo paulista: Hipóteses para o estudo da chegada da vanguarda ao Brasil.* São Paulo: Perspectiva, 1994.

Faustino, Mário, and Décio Pignatari: "Futurismo, IV: Marinetti e Soffici." *Suplemento dominical do Jornal do Brasil* (Rio de Janeiro), 15 December 1957.

Faustino, Mário, and Décio Pignatari: "Futurismo, V: Cangiullo, Antonio Bruno, Benedetta." *Suplemento dominical do Jornal do Brasil* (Rio de Janeiro), 22 December 1957.

Gurianova [Gourianova], Nina Al'bertovna, ed.: *Livres futuristes russes = The Russian Futurists and Their Books.* Paris: La Hune, 1993.

Imposti, Gabriella Elina: "Khlebnikov and Science: Time, Space and the Fourth Dimension." *International Yearbook of Futurism Studies* 8 (2018): 189–212.

Imposti, Gabriella Elina: "The First World War in Italian and Russian Futurism: F. T. Marinetti, Vladimir Mayakovsky and Velimir Khlebnikov." *International Yearbook of Futurism Studies* 6 (2016): 269–301.

Jangfeldt, Bengt: *Majakovskij and Futurism, 1917–1921.* Stockholm: Almqvist and Wiksell, 1976.

Jangfeldt, Bengt: *Mayakovsky: A Biography.* Chicago/IL: University of Chicago Press, 2014.

Kamenskii, Vasilii: "Khlebnikov e i matematici." *Rassegna sovietica* 17:3 (1966): 86–118.

Khlebnikov, Velimir. *Collected Works.* Vol. 3. *Selected Poems.* Cambridge/MA: Harvard University Press, 1997.

Khlebnikov, Velimir. *Sobranie sochinenii.* Vol. 2. *Tvoreniia, 1906–1916.* Leningrad: Izdatel'stvo pisatelei v Leningrade, 1930.

Kimpel, Ben Drew, and Thomas Cary Duncan Eaves: "Pound's 'Ideogrammic Method' as Illustrated in Canto XCIX." *American Literature* 51:2 (1979): 205–237.

Kovtun, Evgenii Fedorovich: *Russkaia futuristicheskaia kniga.* Moskva: Kniga, 1989. 2nd edn 2014.

Kunichika, Michael: "Primitivism and Scythianism in Russian Futurism." *International Yearbook of Futurism Studies* 6 (2016): 302–327.

Lawton, Anna, and Herbert Eagle: *Russian Futurism Through Its Manifestoes, 1912–1928.* Ithaca/NY: Cornell University Press, 1988.

Lodder, Christina: "Russia: Fine Arts." Günter Berghaus, ed.: *Handbook of International Futurism.* Berlin & Boston/MA: De Gruyter, 2018. 798–823.

Maiakovskii, Vladimir Vladimirovich: "Piatyi internatsional. 8 chastei. Chast' pervaia: Prikaz № 3." V.V: Maiakovskii: *Polnoe sobranie sochinenii.* Vol. 4. *1922 – fevral' 1923.* Moskva: Gosudarstvennoe izdatel'stvo khudozhestvennoi literatury, 1957. 107–134.

Maiakovskii, Vladimir Vladimirovich: *Poemas.* Ed. by Boris Schnaiderman, Augusto de Campos, and Haroldo de Campos. São Paulo: Perspectiva, 2017.

Maiakovskii, Vladimir Vladimirovich: *Poemas.* Trans. by E. Carrera-Guerra. Rio de Janeiro: Philobiblion, Civilização Brasileira, 1956.

Markov, Vladimir: *Russian Futurism: A History.* Washington/DC: New Academia, 2006.

Mayakovsky, Vladimir: "How Are Verses Made?" *How Are Verses Made? With Cloud in Trousers and To Sergey Esenin.* Trans. by George Malcolm Hyde. Bristol: The Bristol Press, 1990. 42–90.

Mayakovsky, Vladimir: *Mayakovsky.* Ed. by Herbert Marshall. London: Dobson, 1965.
Nicholls, Peter: *Modernisms: A Literary Guide.* New York: Palgrave Macmillan, 2nd edn, 2009.
Nilsson, Nils Åke: "How to Translate Avant-Garde Poetry: Some Attempts with Xlebnikov's 'Incantation by Laughter.'" Nils Åke Nilsson, ed.: *Velimir Chlebnikov: A Stockholm Symposium, April 24, 1983.* Stockholm: Almqvist & Wiksell International, 1985. 133–150.
Palmer, Isobel: "Mayakovsky's Voices: Futurist Performance and Communication in Verse." *International Yearbook of Futurism Studies* 9 (2019): 157–187.
Perloff, Marjorie: "Writing as Re-Writing: Concrete Poetry as Arrière-Garde." *Ciberletras: Revista de crítica literaria y de cultura* 17 (2007). https://www.lehman.cuny.edu/ciberletras/ (consulted 26/05/2022).
Perloff, Marjorie: *The Futurist Moment: Avant-Garde, Avant Guerre, and the Language of Rupture.* Chicago/IL: University of Chicago Press, 1986.
Perloff, Nancy: *Explodity: Sound, Image, and Word in Russian Futurist Book Art.* Los Angeles/CA: Getty Research Institute, 2016.
Pignatari, Décio: "A situação atual da poesia no Brasil." D. Pignatari: *Contracomunicação.* São Paulo: Ateliê, 2004. 99–119.
Richter, Victoria: *Literary Primitivism: Its Function in the Early Works of Vladimir Mayakovsky and Other Russian Cubo-Futurists.* Ph.D. Dissertation. Toronto: University of Toronto, 1998.
Rocha, João Cezar de Castro: "Brazil." Günter Berghaus, ed.: *Handbook of International Futurism.* Berlin & Boston: De Gruyter, 2019. 336–351.
Rowell, Margit, and Deborah Wye: *The Russian Avant-Garde Book, 1910–1934.* New York: Museum of Modern Art, 2002.
Schaffner, Anna Katharina: "Inheriting the Avant-Garde: On the Reconciliation of Tradition and Invention in Concrete Poetry." David Hopkins, ed.: *Neo-Avant-Garde.* Amsterdam: Rodopi, 2006. 97–117.
Schnaiderman, Boris: *A poética de Maiakóvski através de sua prosa.* São Paulo: Perspectiva, 1971.
Schnapp, Jeffrey T., and João Cezar de Castro Rocha: "Brazilian Velocities: On Marinetti's 1926 Trip to South America." *South Central Review: The Journal of the South Central Modern Language Association* 13:2–3 (1996): 105–156.
Simon, Iumna Maria: "Projetos alternativos/confronto de poéticas." *Revista iberoamericana* 43:98–99 (1977): 169–181.
Terras, Victor: "Review of 'Poesia Russa Moderna', by H. de Campos & A. de Campos." *The Slavic and East European Journal* 13:4 (1969): 507–508.
Vroon, Ronald: "Matematika ili mistika: K voprosu o nauchnosti istoriosofskikh vzgliadov Velimira Khlebnikova." Korneliia Ichin, ed.: *Nauchnye konceptsii XX veka i russkoe avangardnoe iskusstvo.* Belgrad: Izdatel'stvo filologicheskogo fakul'teta Belgradskogo universiteta, 2010. 43–74.
Vroon, Ronald: *Velimir Xlebnikov's Shorter Poems: A Key to the Coinages.* Ann Arbor/MI: Michigan Slavic Publications, 1983.
Wiese, Maíra Borges: *A poesia digital de André Vallias.* Tese de Doutorado. Coimbra: Universidade de Coimbra, 2012.

4 Music, Sculpture and Architecture

Esther Schmitz-Gundlach

Back to the Future of *The Art of Noises:* The After-Life of Futurism in Twentieth-Century Music

Abstract: By exploring the aesthetic implications of historical Futurism, this essay offers an approach to Neo-Futurist tendencies in the music of subsequent decades. From 1913 onwards, the manifestos published by Luigi Russolo (1885–1947) on music and the construction of noise-producing instruments (*intonarumori*) contributed to the emancipation of noise as musical material and set an aesthetic impulse that was significant for the music history of the twentieth century. However, Futurism's rôle in this development was underestimated for a long time, largely because of the movement's affiliation with Fascism and because Futurist manifestos were given a superficial interpretation by contemporary composers. The intention of this essay is to extrapolate, with reference to historical Futurism, aesthetic criteria for a type of music that can be considered to exhibit a Neo-Futurist tendency. Starting from this, the Futurist definition of noise as musical material will be shown in its consequences for modes of production and reception in later periods. Futurist musical aesthetics focussed on a scientific approach to acoustic material. In the second half of the twentieth century, the modes of production and reception of music developed further, in parallel to the availability of technical possibilities of sound production. This process will be exemplified in this essay by composers who had different attitudes towards Futurism: some were positively or negatively disposed towards it; others adopted some but rejected other features of Russolo's demand for a separation of noise from its sources of inspiration (such as the metropolis, the street and the factory). In any case, Russolo paved the way for musical abstraction, a transformation that was shaped significantly by technologies of sound production and reproduction. Edgard Varèse (1883–1965), John Cage (1912–1992), Pierre Schaeffer (1910–1995) and György Ligeti (1923–2006) developed compositional practices that gave noise a musical form and created works that became examples of a music that ultimately turned noise into abstract sounds.

Keywords: Luigi Russolo, Edgard Varèse, John Cage, Pierre Schaeffer, György Ligeti, *L'arte dei rumori* (The Art of Noises), liberation of sound, noise, silence, enharmony, micropolyphony, sound objects, electronic music, *musique concrète*

https://doi.org/10.1515/9783111318394-012

On the final page of *L'arte dei rumori* (The Art of Noises, 1916), Luigi Russolo demanded that "noise must become a primary material in the moulding of a work of art".[1] This attitude implied a completely new approach to music, to its material, structure, production, reception and, thereby, its institutions. For subsequent composers aligned to various twentieth-century neo-avant-garde movements, Futurism was included in the canons of predecessors, but each had a different view on how its musical theories were to be evaluated. So, how are we to relate a form of music that was the result of highly individual experiences and compositional practices to its inspirational impulses, and how are we to determine whether these works can be termed 'Neo-Futurist'? The very fact that Futurism missed out on the actual production of new music, due to the lack of cooperation with visionary composers, and thus never became part of a tradition that could be deemed a 'school', should make us direct our attention to the movement's overall *potential* as an inspirational force of musical aesthetics. At the outset, I shall offer some definitional criteria that allow us to examine the potential of musical Futurism for subsequent generations of composers. Subsequently, these criteria will be applied to concepts and musical practices developed by Edgard Varèse, John Cage, Pierre Schaeffer and György Ligeti.

Converting sound into music

At the turn of the century, Ferruccio Busoni offered in his *Entwurf einer neuen Ästhetik der Tonkunst* (Sketch of a New Aesthetic of Music, 1907) a poetically veiled definition of sound: "This child – it floats on air! It touches not the earth with its feet. It knows no law of gravitation. It is wellnigh incorporeal. Its material is transparent. It is sonorous air. It is almost Nature herself. It is – free."[2] These words illuminate how the composer attempted to create a bridge between music on the one hand and natural science and technology on the other. He sought to expand twentieth-century music and to emancipate it from all established notions of form and content. It was becoming obvious to him that sound needed to escape the perception of its physical origin in order to be 'freely' available as autonomous material. Only thus would an expanded definition of music become a possibility in later generations. A further prerequisite for developing a new musical aesthetic was the availability of instruments that could produce and reproduce the full spec-

1 "Il rumore deve divenire un elemento primo da plasmare per l'opera d'arte." Russolo: *L'arte dei rumori*, p. 176. Translation is mine, unless otherwise noted.

2 Busoni: *Sketch of a New Esthetic of Music*, p. 4; *Entwurf einer neuen Ästhetik der Tonkunst*, p. 13.

trum of sounds and noises. For Luigi Russolo and composers who came into contact with Futurism, either as contemporaries or later on, this was a vision they passionately yearned to put into practice.

Whereas the Futurist composers Francesco Balilla Pratella (1880–1955), Franco Casavola (1891–1955) and Silvio Mix (1900–1927) failed to make a long-term impact outside Italy, Luigi Russolo (1885–1947) was regarded by the neo-avant-garde as a pioneer, due to his *Art of Noises* manifesto (1913) and the booklet of the same name published in 1916.[3] His concepts and those of his older colleague Pratella,[4] especially the guiding principles of simultaneity, dynamism and synthesis of sense impressions gained from contemporary urban life, became a source of inspiration for composers of the post-war period. In contrast, reflections on 'movement' and 'stasis' by the Futurist painters were not deemed significant for later avant-garde music; it was only John Cage who discovered that 'silence', ultimately, does not exist.

Umberto Boccioni's comprehensive conceptions of pictorial dynamism and simultaneity, which were based on the absolute and relative movement of objects,[5] anticipated this development in music. In 1914, he described painting as: "In reality,

3 Russolo's first manifesto was included in the collection *I manifesti del futurismo* (1914) and was translated into French by Jules Ecorcheville in "Le Futurisme ou le bruit dans la musique" in the *Revue musicale SIM* in 1913. A German version appeared as "Die Kunst der Geräusche als Fortentwicklung des modernen Orchesters" in *Melos* 7 (1928). The Russian translations of 1913–14 (in *Maski* 7–8, Mikhail Engelhardt's *Futurizm* and Vadim Shershenevich's *Manifesty ital'ianskogo futurizma*) had a remarkable effect, both in professional circles and in amateur ensembles, as Konstantin Dudakov-Kashuro has shown in "Noise Music in Russian Futurism." After the First World War, an English translation appeared in Slonimsky: *Music since 1900* (New York: Norton, 1937), followed by one by Robert Filliou (New York: Something Else Press, 1967). There was also a French version by Maurice Lemaître (Paris: Masse, 1954), and Christa Baumgarth included a German one in her *Geschichte des Futurismus* (Reinbek: Rowohlt, 1966). The 1916 booklet contained the manifesto of 1913 as an introductory chapter, followed by ten essays on various aspects of noise music. The text was only translated after the Second World War into French (Lausanne: L'Âge d'Homme, 1973), English (New York: Pendragon Press, 1986) and half a dozen other languages.

4 Pratella's *Manifesto dei musicisti futuristi* (1910) was reprinted several times and quickly translated into French (*Manifeste des musiciens futuristes*, 1911), English (*Manifesto of Futurist Musicians*, 1912) and Russian (in Mikhail Engelhardt's *Futurizm* and Vadim Shershenevich's *Manifesty ital'ianskogo futurizma*, both 1914). His second manifesto, *La musica futurista: Manifesto tecnico* (1911) was published, amongst others, in Pratella: *Musica futurista* (Bologna: Bongiovanni, 1912), in *I manifesti futuristi* (Firenze: Lacerba, 1914) and in Pratella: *Evoluzione della musica dal 1910: Valorizzazioni* (Milano: Istituto Editoriale Italiano, 1918), but not translated at the time into French, English or German. See Pratella: *Edizioni, scritti, manoscritti musicali e futuristi*, pp. 395 ff.

5 Boccioni: "Pittura e scultura futuriste: Dinamismo plastico", p. 145 ff. English translation by Agin and Versari in Boccioni: *Futurist Painting Sculpture: Plastic Dynamism*, p. 111 ff.

however, nothing is immobile in our modern intuition of life."[6] Art that wants to keep up with modern life has to depict everything that is in motion, even that which appears to be immobile. The Futurist painters' intuitive search for "the *single form that expresses continuity in space*"[7] and "that conceives the world as the endless succession of a multiplicity in evolution"[8] gave rise to the "*concept of the dynamic continuity* as sole form".[9] Boccioni's intention was to comprehend the inherent forces of objects in motion and to find "a form that's the expression of this new absolute – *speed*".[10]

Futurist painting and sculpture aimed to replace "the ancient features of enumeration, stasis, and silence" with "those of simultaneity, speed, and noise".[11] In his manifesto *La pittura dei suoni, rumori, odori* (The Painting of Sounds, Noises, and Smells, 1913), Carlo Carrà defined silence as it had been represented in the arts up until then, namely as static. By contrast, sounds, noises and smells were shown to be dynamic, and "these plastic polyphonic, polyrhythmic, and abstract wholes correspond to the necessity for an internal enharmonic relation."[12] All motion takes place in time; and music, as an art which is only executed temporally, accomplishes the same by means of sounds.

6 "In realtà però non c'è nulla di immobile nella nostra moderna intuizione della vita." Boccioni: "Pittura e scultura futuriste: Dinamismo plastico", p. 146; *Futurist Painting Sculpture: Plastic Dynamism*, p. 112.

7 "Questo succedersi […] vi giungiamo attraverso la ricerca intuitiva della *forma unica che dia la continuità nello spazio.*" Boccioni: "Pittura e scultura futuriste: Dinamismo plastico", p. 149; *Futurist Painting Sculpture: Plastic Dynamism*, p. 115. Emphasis by Boccioni.

8 "L'esponente di una sensibilità che va concependo il mondo come un succedersi infinito di una verità in evoluzione." Boccioni: "Pittura e scultura futuriste: Dinamismo plastico", p. 153; *Futurist Painting Sculpture: Plastic Dynamism*, p. 119.

9 "Al più moderno concetto impressionista di suddivisione, di ripetizione, di abbozzo delle immagini, noi sostituiamo il *concetto della continuità dinamica* come forma unica." Boccioni: "Pittura e scultura futuriste: Dinamismo plastico", p. 149; *Futurist Painting Sculpture: Plastic Dynamism*, p. 115. Emphasis by Boccioni.

10 "Cioè si tratta di trovare una forma che sia l'espressione di questo nuovo assoluto: *la velocità.*" Boccioni: "Pittura e scultura futuriste: Dinamismo plastico", p. 147; *Futurist Painting Sculpture: Plastic Dynamism*, p. 113. Emphasis by Boccioni.

11 "Tornando all'essenza plastica della pittura e scultura futuriste, si può affermare che agli antichi caratteri di enumerazione, di statica e di silenzio si vanno sostituendo nell'opera d'arte in generale dei caratteri di simultaneità, di velocità e di rumore." Boccioni: "Pittura e scultura futuriste: Dinamismo plastico", p. 153; *Futurist Painting Sculpture: Plastic Dynamism*, p. 119.

12 "Questi insiemi plastici, polifonici e poliritmici astratti risponderanno a necessità di enarmonie interne." Carrà: "La pittura dei suoni, rumori, odori", p. 16; "The Painting of Sounds, Noises, and Smells", p. 158.

As far as Pratella was concerned, sound material, when translated into music, transformed this idea of continuity with the help of so-called ‘enharmony’, or ‘enharmonic mode’, a potentially infinite subdivision of the octave,[13] and of the harmonic equality of every conceivable interval. Potentially, this led to the abolition of consonance and dissonance[14] and thus to the concept of “polyphony in an absolute sense”.[15] Just like Pratella’s call for polyrhythmic freedom and the abolition of thematic development through rhythmic modulation, these concepts would only be realized in the music of later generations.

Luigi Russolo, who was initially involved in Futurism as a painter, transferred these demands to a new type of music, the *arte dei rumori* (art of noises). Analogous to Boccioni’s postulate for Futurist painting that it should originate from “the central nucleus of the object”,[16] Russolo sought to achieve, with the resources available to him at the time, a more precise generation of the ‘core’ qualities of sound and noise and to give expression to his “hope of a new acoustic spirit”.[17] Seen from a global perspective, however, Russolo’s position in re-determining music as sound remained ambiguous or ambivalent. Ambiguous because he gave the mechanical sound instruments that he had been constructing since 1913 programmatic names;[18] and ambivalent because his vision of a new type of music produced by machines operated with a skilful intonability of sound (hence the name *intonarumori*): “Thus, the motors and machines of our industrial cities can one day be given pitches, so that every workshop will become an intoxicating orchestra of noises.”[19]

---

13 “Noi futuristi proclamiamo quale progresso e quale vittoria dell’avvenire sul modo cromatico atonale, la ricerca e la realizzazione del *modo enarmonico.* Mentre il cromatismo ci fa unicamente usufruire di tutti i suoni contenuti in una scala divisa per semitoni minori e maggiori, l’enarmonia, col contemplare anche le minime suddivisioni del tono, oltre al prestare alla nostra sensibilità rinnovata il numero massimo di suoni determinabili e combinabili, ci permette anche nuove e più svariate relazioni di accordi e di timbri.” Pratella: “Manifesto tecnico della musica futurista”, p. 200; “Futurist Music: Technical Manifesto”, p. 81. Emphasis by Pratella.

14 “Dichiaramo inoltre inesistenti i valori di consonanza e di dissonanza.” Pratella: “Manifesto tecnico della musica futurista”, p. 200; “Futurist Music: Technical Manifesto”, p. 81.

15 “Con la fusione dell’armonia e del contrappunto, creare la polifonia in un senso assoluto, non mai usato fino ad oggi.” Pratella: “Manifesto tecnico della musica futurista”, p. 203; “Futurist Music: Technical Manifesto”, p. 84.

16 “Una costruzione centripeta che partendo dal nucleo centrale dell’oggetto con direzioni centrifughe di forma si legava all’ambiente solido o gassoso.” Boccioni: “Pittura e scultura futuriste: Dinamismo plastico”, p. 155; *Futurist Painting Sculpture: Plastic Dynamism*, p. 120.

17 Lombardi: “Luigi Russolo und die Musikalisierung des Geräuschs”, p. 91.

18 Russolo: *L’arte dei rumori*, p. 133; *The Art of Noises*, p. 28.

19 “Così i motori e le macchine delle nostre città industriali potranno un giorno essere sapientemente intonati, in modo da fare di ogni officina una inebriante orchestra di rumori.” Russolo: *L’arte dei rumori*, p. 134; *The Art of Noises*, p. 29.

However, the music which Russolo conceived did not completely break away from the semantics of the industrialized city. It is therefore understandable that defining the glorified sounds of the modern metropolis as 'music' exposed him to the accusation of being an 'imitator'. Russolo, of course, rejected this allegation and emphasized that noise as musical material transcended its original source of inspiration. Russolo clearly stipulated the intention to achieve 'absolute' rather than 'imitative' sounds: "It will not be through a succession of noises imitative of life but through a fantastic association of the different timbres and rhythms that the new orchestra will obtain the most complex and novel emotions of sound."[20] He wanted his acoustic products to be autonomous, modifiable material; thus, his definition of music as an *Art of Noises* anticipated a later concept of music as a sound structure. It presupposed a liberation of hearing in the sense that it facilitated a perception of the surrounding sounds as 'aesthetic'. This process of aestheticization expanded the pool of acoustic material to be used in musical compositions. Now that noise was deemed 'pleasant',[21] a new scientific and technical approach became possible.

Aiming "to give pitches to these diverse noises, regulating them harmonically and rhythmically",[22] Russolo began to produce sound material in a laboratory setting.[23] This was when his research advanced to a more profound understanding of the physical laws of noise. Russolo anticipated the composition principles of future generations: "*The rhythmic motions of a noise are infinite. There always exists, as with a pitch, a predominant rhythm,* but around this there can be heard numerous other, secondary rhythms."[24] However, compared to the way in which equivalent sounds would later be conceived, Russolo's approach in 1913 did not yet integrate sound and noise into his conception of music: he wanted to substitute sounds with noise, and the orchestra of classic-romantic instruments with an orchestra made up of *intonarumori.*[25]

And yet, despite this propagation of an abstract use of noise, Russolo did not completely defeat the notion of imitation, because Futurism assigned the function

20 "Non sarà mediante una successione di rumori imitativi della vita, bensì mediante una fantastica associazione di questi timbri vari, e di questi ritmi vari, che la nuova orchestra otterà le più complesse e nuove emozioni sonore." Russolo: *L'arte dei rumori*, p. 134; *The Art of Noises*, p. 29.
21 See Russolo: *L'arte dei rumori*, p. 131; *The Art of Noises*, p. 25 f.
22 "Noi vogliamo intonare e regolare armonicamente e ritmicamente questi svariatissimi rumori." Russolo: *L'arte dei rumori*, p. 132; *The Art of Noises*, p. 27.
23 See Russolo: *L'arte dei rumori*, p. 136; *The Art of Noises*, p. 32.
24 "*I movimenti ritmici di un rumore sono infiniti. Esiste sempre, come per il tono, un ritmo predominante,* ma attorno a questo altri numerosi ritmi secondari sono pure sensibili." Russolo: *L'arte dei rumori*, p. 133; *The Art of Noises*, p. 28. Emphasis in the original.
25 See Russolo: *L'arte dei rumori*, p. 133; *The Art of Noises*, p. 28.

of mediality to noise. As far as music was concerned, it was to function as a symbolic vehicle for a life in an accelerated environment of the future shaped by machines and developed by means of technology.

From Futurism to the neo-avant-garde

Instead of attempting to establish direct links between post-war composers and Futurism,[26] it makes more sense to determine to what extent the legacy of Futurist aesthetics, as outlined above, influenced the music of subsequent generations. For a start, this method is based on the assumption that from the theory and practice of Futurist music, only the writings of Luigi Russolo received any international media coverage and were, at least in part, known to later composers. We also have to bear in mind that reception can be a complex and contradictory process that includes both acceptance and denial. In addition, it is difficult to identify Neo-Futurist traits in neo-avant-garde music that has long broken away from tonality and has increasingly gone its own divergent ways.

Whilst Russolo, thanks to his scientific perspective on the ways humans react to noise in an urban environment and due to his construction of the *intonarumori*, became a pioneer of modern experimental music, his compositions which could have showcased his noise-generating instruments never progressed very far. The liberation of noise music from mere imitation, which Russolo had tirelessly demanded,[27] became much easier for composers after the Second World War because they could enjoy the fruits of an infinite diversification of available musical material. Noise finally became, as Russolo had requested, "autonomous and malleable material".[28] It is therefore necessary to determine whether the innovations in neo-avant-garde music drew inspiration from the scientific view of sonic phenomena promoted by Russolo, and whether these new types of music finally broke away from the imitative use of noise and its mimetic agenda.

In addition, the reception of Futurist music in the second half of the twentieth century was hampered by the movement's perceived rôle in the political developments of Italy. Music is always a mirror of its era, and Futurist music was a reaction to the rise of the machine in the industrial age, and the uses that were made of

---

26 I attempted this in my volume *Musikästhetische Konzepte des italienischen Futurismus und ihre Rezeption durch Komponisten des 20. Jahrhunderts*, which I have updated for this essay.

27 See Russolo: *L'arte dei rumori*, p. 133; *The Art of Noises*, p. 27 ff.

28 "E poichè liberato così il rumore dalle necessità che lo producono, noi lo dominiamo, trasformandone a voler nostro il tono, l'intensità e il ritmo, lo sentiamo subito divenire materia autonoma, malleabile." Russolo: *L'arte dei rumori*, p. 176; *The Art of Noises*, p. 87.

technology in the armed conflicts of the twentieth century. Futurism's rôle in the history of noise music was often ignored because Fascism and the Second World War interrupted a continuous line of development spanning the twentieth century. The dedication at the beginning of his booklet *The Art of Noises* (1916) reveals Russolo's unreserved enthusiasm for war: "To my dear and great Futurist brothers Marinetti, Boccioni, Piatti, Sant'Elia, Sironi, who during the taking of Dosso Casina, on the flanks of the Altissimo mountain, enjoyed with me the exhilarating noisy enharmony of our 149."[29] In 1913, in his first manifesto, he deliberately ignored the fact that guns are made for the purpose of killing other human beings when he reflected on "the newest noises of modern war" that could be experienced in the Bulgarian War (1912–13), and the musical inspiration to be drawn from "the orchestra of a great battle".[30]

The generation which survived the Second World War was shocked by the Futurists' aestheticization of war, by their eulogies of monstrous machinery invented for the extermination of millions of people. Whatever Russolo's merits as a theorist may have been, he was not deemed worthy of being installed as a precursor of a modern tradition in music. The younger generation of composers wanted 1945 to be the 'Year Zero'[31] for music in Europe, and this term was certainly applicable to serial and electronic music.[32] However, composers never start from scratch; consciously or unconsciously, neo-avant-garde composers complemented their engagement with dodecaphony with the use of noise as musical material, as longed for by Luigi Russolo and Edgard Varèse. The second generation of avant-garde musicians welcomed, in particular, the new technical possibilities that had developed in the field of electronic music and had become widely available in the radio or recording studios. Consequently, composers developed new ways of dissecting and modifying the components of sound. Thus, a new type of music emerged that displayed various kinds of overlap with historical Futurism, on the basis of the following criteria:

- A tie-in with the scientifically-based perspective of the musical material
- A continuation of the definition of musical material relating to 'sound'
- At a compositional level, the journey of noise, or sound, respectively, towards abstraction

29 "Ai cari e grandi fratelli futuristi Marinetti, Boccioni, Piatti, Sant'Elia, Sironi, che durante la presa di Dosso Casina, su fianchi dell'Altissimo, godevano con me l'esaltante enarmonismo rumorista dei nostri 149." Russolo: *L'arte dei rumori*, p. 129. The 149 was a heavy cannon that formed the backbone of the Italy artillery during the First and Second World War.

30 See Russolo: *L'arte dei rumori*, pp. 131–132; *The Art of Noises*, p. 16.

31 See Dibelius: "Moderne Musik nach 1945", p. 23.

32 See Riethmüller: "Ausklang: Die 'Stunde Null' als musikgeschichtliche Größe", p. 325.

- A forward-looking, open-minded attitude towards the musical potential of technical innovation
- The uptake, processing and realization of phenomena such as speed, simultaneity and synthesis, with the aid of musical parameters, strengthened by technological developments and tangible on an aesthetic level.

Edgard Varèse's *Art-Science*

At the beginning of the twenty-first century, Edgard Varèse (1883–1965) is rated as a towering artistic force in twentieth-century music.[33] Born in Paris, he moved to New York in 1915, lived in Paris from 1928–1933 and returned to New York in 1933. In 1950, he was a guest lecturer at the *Darmstädter Ferienkurse für Neue Musik* (Darmstadt Summer Courses for New Music), and was in contact with Pierre Boulez, Pierre Schaeffer, Le Corbusier and Iannis Xenakis, among others. In the 1950s, he worked on his *Poème électronique* and was able to realize it at the 1958 Brussels World's Fair. His contribution to the emancipation of noise in a musical context made him one of the most important figures between the generations of Futurists and the neo-avant-garde. He probably learned about Futurism through his friendship with Ferruccio Busoni in Berlin in 1913,[34] but his relationship with Futurism remained, at least on the surface, negative, or, according to some sources, ambivalent. It has been suggested that this was so because he lacked knowledge, or possibly understanding, of Futurist writings. His deprecating references to the Futurists as being merely imitating the noises of life suggest that, at the time, he was not interested in finding out more about them. In 1929 Varèse met Russolo in person and considered using the *Russolophon* in his orchestra.[35] As transpired from an interview with the *New York Telegraph* in 1916, he shared with the Futurists an interest in the expansion of the musical languages and new instruments, but

33 See Nanz: "Edgard Varèse: Die Orchesterwerke", p. 568.

34 See Stenzl: "'Sklavisch reproduzierte Alltäglichkeit': Varèse und der italienische Futurismus", p. 144. Although Busoni valued Boccioni as a painter and in 1912 acquired his painting *La città che sale*, he distanced himself emphatically from the Futurist movement as a whole: "I have never attached myself to a sect – Futurism, a movement of the present time could have no connection with my arguments." Busoni: *The Essence of Music and Other Papers*, p. 17.

35 See Stenzl: "'Sklavisch reproduzierte Alltäglichkeit': Varèse und der italienische Futurismus", p. 146. The Fondazione Russolo – Pratella in Varese possesses a letter by Varèse to Russolo of 4 July 1930, in which the former stated: "C'est avec le plus vif intérêt que j'ai entendu et étudié le 'Russolophone'. Je suis sûr que les possibilités qu'il offre et la facilité de son maniement lui assureront dans un bref délai sa place à l'orchestre."

he distanced himself from the idea of reproducing sounds from the everyday world:

> Our musical alphabet must be enriched. We also need new instruments very badly. In this respect Futurists (Marinetti and his bruiteurs) have made a serious mistake. New instruments must be able to lend varied combinations and must not simply remind us of things heard time and time again. Instruments, after all, must only be temporary means of expression. Musicians should take up this question in deep earnest with the help of machinery specialists. In my own work I have always felt the need of mediums of expression. I refuse to limit myself to sounds that have already been heard. What I am looking for is new mechanical mediums which will lend themselves to every expression of thought and keep up with thought.[36]

Lectures given by Varèse in the USA from 1936 onwards suggest an aesthetic affinity with the ideas and style of Futurist manifestos. At this point, his demands were no longer new, but rather matured convictions based on the idea of a form of music that was in tune with contemporary scientific and technical developments. He shared the anti-dogmatic, avant-garde attitude of artists who made use of novel means of expression to reflect the new developments of the time: "It is the artist who crystallizes his age – who fixes his age in history."[37] His radical attitude was combined with an admiration of technical progress, also in the field of music, and the adoption of an experimental, scientific approach: "On the threshold of beauty science and art collaborate."[38] Varèse called for artistic developments to align themselves with technical progress[39] and hoped for a time "when new instruments will allow me to write music as I conceive it".[40] However, contrary to Futurism, he entertained a certain respect for tradition which, in his view, offered useful tools for his compositional practice.

Varèse translated Russolo's concept of the 'musicalization of sound'[41] into a 'liberation of sound' that did not treat sound and noise as antithetical units, but as integral components of a musical chord (*Klang*). As far as he was concerned, there was only *Klang:* "Sound is the material of music. [...] Ever since music came into existence, it has been sound. Just as humans, sound is something that

36 Varèse: *Varèse: A Looking-Glass Diary*. Vol. 1, p. 123.
37 See Varèse: "Music as an Art-Science", p. 200.
38 Varèse: "New Instruments and New Music", p. 196.
39 This is how Varèse speaks of "the very newness of the mechanism of life" in "New Instruments and New Music", p. 196.
40 Ibid., p. 197.
41 Lombardi: "Luigi Russolo und die Musikalisierung des Geräuschs", p. 85.

can only exist in the atmosphere."[42] Like Boccioni and Prampolini, who wrote extensively on the atmospheric structure of the Futurist work of art, Varèse considered the spatial dimension of sound to be a fundamental and integral element of the musical work of art; he even defined music "as bodies of intelligent sounds moving freely in space".[43]

Varèse's imaginative language to characterize his ideas of music poses a few problems due to the fact that Italian, French, German and English do not have an overlapping terminology to describe sonic phenomena. As far as his American audience was concerned, he explained his choice of words during a lecture at Yale University in 1962 as follows:

> As far back as the twenties, I decided to call my music "organized sound" and myself, not a musician, but "a worker in rhythms, frequencies, and intensities." Indeed, to stubbornly conditioned ears, anything new in music has always been called noise. But after all what is music but organized noises? And a composer, like all artists, is an organizer of disparate elements.[44]

From the beginning of his career, Varèse's choice of musical language was already inspired by technology. Equally the way in which it heralded the music of future generations: his statements threw the previous interpretation of musical parameters into disarray.[45] At the same time, the etymology of the term 'organization' indicated a radically different way of thinking about the microstructures of sound.[46] Russolo took a decisive step by differentiating between sound (suono) and noise (rumore) and developing from them what he called 'suono-rumore', that is, a noise that could be tuned. *The Art of Noises* transcends what had traditionally

---

42 See Charbonnier: "Entretiens avec Edgard Varèse", p. 35: "E. V. [Edgard Varèse]: [...] Le matériau de la musique est le son. [...] Depuis que la musique existe, c'est du son. Le son, comme l'homme, est une chose qui ne peut vivre, exister, que dans le domaine atmosphérique."

43 Varèse: "Spatial Music", p. 204.

44 Varèse: "The Electronic Medium", p. 207.

45 See Charbonnier: "Entretiens avec Edgard Varèse", p. 25: "G. C. [Georges Charbonnier]: Quand avez-vous commencé à organiser des sons? E. V. [Edgard Varèse]: Je ne sais pas. J'étais un peu le clown de la classe de contrepoint et de fugue. Si je faisais une fugue, je la bâclais en quelques heures. Assez ingénieusement. Naturellement il n'y avait pas une goutte de musique dedans. Pour moi la fugue n'a rien à voir avec la musique. C'est n'est pas une composition, c'est une exercice. Un exercice fermé sur lui-même. Je faisais des gammes, je n'organisais pas des sons. Pas même des notes. Quant aux sons, à vrai dire, j'ai toujours pensé à les organiser."

46 See Varèse: "New Instruments and New Music", p. 198: "Not only will the harmonic possibilities of the overtones be revealed in all their splendor, but the use of certain interferences created by the partials will represent an appreciable contribution. The never-before-thought-of use of the inferior resultants and of the differential and additional sounds may also be expected.'

been called 'music', and this required, on the part of the composer, constant research in the field of acoustics.

The terms 'Klang' or 'son organisé' brought into focus Varèse's interpretation of music as autonomous and absolute. This rooted him in the tradition of 'absolute' music, in line with his interpretation of Busoni's adage that "music was born free; and to win freedom is its destiny."[47] Consequently, in terms of his own compositions, he developed an understanding of the œuvre not as an individually-accomplished execution of a traditional, given form, but as a result of a process where 'form' and 'content' are identical. And yet, music was not to be free from the influences of its time. Varèse wanted to create a type of music which, in aesthetic terms, corresponded to the developments in the modern world. Compositional processes should avoid all semblance of being tonally reproductive or superficially depicting modern phenomena, yet accomplish, via abstraction, a realization of the inner structures of sound. His works demonstrate a heterogeneity of materials, styles and techniques, and reveal a search for maximum contrasts in the integration of divergent elements that are representative of his era.[48]

In the heterogeneity of sound elements, however, rhythm can offer, according to Varèse, an 'element of stability' and "unrelated metrical simultaneity".[49] This idea was a continuation of Pratella's demand that thematic development should be replaced with rhythmic modulation. Varèse intended a "movement of sound-masses"[50] to replace linear counterpoint and the "entire work" to develop in its acoustic appearance "a melodic totality".[51] Formally, this totality would display an external shape and an internal structure. This is reminiscent of Boccioni's statements regarding the movement of objects. Varèse defined 'shape' as an organic process based on his view that "there is an idea, the basis of an internal structure, expanded and split into different shapes or groups of sound constantly changing in

47 "Frei ist die Tonkunst geboren und frei zu werden ihre Bestimmung." Busoni: *Entwurf einer neuen Ästhetik der Tonkunst*, 2020 edn, p. 4. Varèse referred to this in "Ferruccio Busoni: A Reminiscence", published on the occasion of a Columbia University event "A Commemoration of Edgard Varèse": "In 1907, still in my early twenties I went to Berlin, where I spent most of the next seven years, and had the good fortune of becoming (in spite of the disparity of age and importance) the friend of Ferruccio Busoni, then at the height of his fame. I had read his remarkable little book, *A New Esthetic of Music*, a milestone in my musical development, and when I came upon, 'Music is born free; and to win freedom is its destiny,' it was like hearing the echo of my own thought." See Varèse: "Ferruccio Busoni: A Reminiscence", in *Columbia University Forum* 9:2 (Spring 1966), p. 20 and *Varsity Graduate* (University of Toronto) 13:1 (December 1966), p. 73.

48 See Nanz: "Edgard Varèse: Die Orchesterwerke", p. 561.

49 Varèse: "Spatial Music", p. 205.

50 Varèse: "New Instruments and New Music", p. 197.

51 Ibid., p. 197.

shape, direction, and speed, attracted and repulsed by various forces. The form of the work is the consequence of this interaction."[52] Varèse aimed at revealing "the phenomena of penetration or repulsion" and something which he called 'sound projection', namely "that feeling that sound is leaving us with no hope of being reflected back, a feeling akin to that aroused by beams of light sent forth by a powerful searchlight – for the ear as for the eye, that sense of projection, of a journey into space."[53] This projection also included acoustic arrangements for the creation of various acoustic 'perspectives' through 'zones of intensities'[54] where the differentiation of timbres is an integral part of 'shape'. Whilst the idea of 'penetration' in the transmutation of moving sound masses is reminiscent of Futurism, the phenomenon of acoustic projection, as described by Varèse, also prefigured the acoustic illusions by György Ligeti.

The 'new musical apparatus' envisioned by Varèse for the execution of his music is a "sound-*producing* machine (not a sound-*reproducing* one)",[55] with the ability "to emit sounds of any number of frequencies".[56] For instance, his use of sirens in *Amériques* (1918–21), influenced by experiments by Hermann Helmholtz,[57] did not imitate the function of a siren in the mundane world, but was used to realize a smooth glissando, "a kind of continuous flowing curve that instruments could not give me".[58] Varèse's sonic experiments were opposed to the Futurists' supposedly imitative style. Instead of using descriptive elements in the depiction of the modern city as resounding symphony, Varèse anticipated a musical vision of the machine that transcends everything that humans can achieve. He wanted to create music of every possible pitch, scale, timbre, volume, harmony, or rather a combination of all these. Rhythms were to be executed independently and under the guidance of a time measure. After years of longing for electronic possibilities of producing and arranging sound with a spatial acoustic dimension, Varèse discovered towards the end of his life a balance between the human and mechanical factors in music: "The machine can give out only what we put into it."[59] The person who guides it remains, as does the person who composes.[60]

---

52 Varèse: "Rhythm, Form and Content", p. 203.
53 Varèse: "New Instruments and New Music", p. 197.
54 Ibid., p. 197.
55 Varèse: "Music as an Art-Science", p. 200. Emphasis in the original.
56 Varèse: "New Instruments and New Music", p. 197f.
57 Varèse: "Spatial Music", p. 205.
58 Varèse: "The Electronic Medium", p. 207.
59 Varèse: "Rhythm, Form and Content", p. 202.
60 Varèse: "The Electronic Medium", p. 208.

John Cage and the 'All-Sound Music of the Future'

John Cage (1912–1992) interpreted sound in a manner that radically expanded its very limits. However, unlike Russolo, for whom the pre-modern past was entirely silent ("la vita antica fu tutta silenzio"),[61] Cage took the view that humanity is permanently surrounded by noises. Cage's vision of a new music dates back to 1937, when he conceived of *The Future of Music: Credo.*[62] Already the title nods in the direction of Futurist manifestos, in particular Russolo's *Art of Noises,*[63] and bears witness to Cage's delight in provocation and iconoclasm. Whereas Russolo had rooted *The Art of Noises* in the world of inspiration,[64] Cage eliminated the quasi-religious moment from the traditional interpretation of music in order to establish his own point of departure: humankind is immersed in the sonic field of multifaceted noises and is fascinated by it, provided that the attitude is one of conscious listening. Cage located this fascination in the attention one pays to the noises of contemporary technology, and, as their counterpart, those in Nature.[65] As a result, the *Credo* presented a streamlined version of Luigi Russolo's 1913 manifesto. In both cases, the expansion of the concept of music is rooted in the listening experience, but Cage, unlike Russolo, detached the production of music from the idea of specially constructed instruments. He treated the sounds themselves as musical instruments, always available and adjustable with the aid of recording technologies.[66]

---

61 Russolo: *L'arte dei rumori*, p. 129; *The Art of Noises*, p. 23.

62 According to Cage, it goes back to a conversation in 1937 during a meeting with the Seattle Arts Society, but it was put into writing in 1958. See Cage: "Silence: Lectures and Writings", p. 3.

63 Cage read Russolo's *The Art of Noises* around 1935 and counted it amongst the ten books which had the most profound impact on his thinking. See Kostelanetz: "John Cage", p. 138. In a text from January 1946, he deplored the lack of knowledge that musicians had of Russolo's sound art: "In several of its important aspects, modern music of the twenties is now known only by hearsay. The Italian 'Art of Noise' established by Luigi Russolo has totally disappeared; in memory it is mistakenly associated with Marinetti." John Cage in a review of *Bad Boy of Music*, published as "Recent Books: The Dreams and Dedications of George Antheil" in *Modern Music* 23 (1946) and reprinted in Kostelanetz: "John Cage", p. 73.

64 "L'Arte dei rumori [...] attingerà la sua maggiore facoltà di emozione nel godimento acustico in sé stesso, che l'ispirazione dell'artista saprà trarre dai rumori combinati." Russolo: *L'arte dei rumori*, p. 133; *The Art of Noises*, p. 28.

65 "The sound of a truck at fifty miles an hour. Static between the stations. Rain." Cage: "The Future of Music: Credo", p. 3.

66 Cage: "The Future of Music: Credo", p. 3.

Cage's criticism of existing devices for electronic sound production was that they were still aiming at imitation, and his use of Varèse's term 'organization of sound'[67] for the music of the future took Russolo's idea a step or two further. By becoming an 'instrument' itself, noise must serve the production of music, and not the creation of imitative effects. Similar to Varèse, Cage yearned for electronic sound production to replace the mechanical principle. By interlinking music and technology, the composer gains control over sound parameters, overtone structures, frequencies, amplitudes and duration.[68] This, too, begins with the listening experience, an approach again adopted from Russolo, and the perceived sounds are then 'captured', 'controlled' and 'used'.[69] The electronic apparatus, which permits both production and reproduction, serves as a medium and establishes a direct link between the 'organizer of sound'[70] and the work, thus rendering the performer obsolete. Furthermore, this type of music production will, in the future, allow the musician to surpass what is possible by manual means alone.[71]

Cage wanted a break with tradition because he rejected the history of music as an art of expression. Whereas Varèse's term 'sound' imbued all acoustic phenomena with the same potential of being 'musical', Cage was determined to expand the word even further. His musical material included 'silence', because that which is considered 'silence' is ultimately always noise and has therefore the potential of being developed musically. Whereas Varèse composed with the aim of transforming imagined sounds, Cage's mechanized aesthetic of the 'organization' of sounds led to the suspension of musical aesthetics inherited from the Romantics. His music was not to serve any longer as an expression of the composer's imagination, but was to be based on aleatoric principles. Although traditional notions of 'composition' when seen from this perspective also involved that which can be termed 'technical' (i. e., the 'arrangement' of music according to formal laws), his 'organization of sound' was technical in the spirit of the twentieth century. It did not serve gods or express emotions or communicate preconceived ideas. Sound was, finally, understood as *L'art pour l'art*, or 'sound for its own sake'. Whilst 'organization' is usually intended to make sounds available as well as to structure them, Cage demonstrated in his most radical work, *4'33"* (1952), that he intended it merely to provide an artistic frame for a musical performance, where art is generated by chance alone. Here, the 'musical instruments' are the noises of the environment.

---

67 See Ibid., p. 3.

68 Ibid., p. 4.

69 "We want to capture and control these sounds, to use them not as sound effects, but as musical instruments." Ibid., p. 3.

70 Ibid., p. 5.

71 Ibid., p. 5.

For the listener, however, the work is experienced according to Cage's interpretation of music in his *Credo:* "Wherever we are, what we hear is mostly noise. When we ignore it, it disturbs us. When we listen to it, we find it fascinating."[72] The performance situation in *4'33"*, at least in terms of its intention, forces the listener to switch from an unconsciously filtering-out of ambient sounds to a mode of consciously listening to the environment because what had been expected (a piano recital) is not taking place. This demonstrates how the Futurist principle of 'creative destruction'[73] can be truly fulfilled: *4'33"* negates the previous perception of music on all levels, that of the musical work of art and its genesis, the rôles of composer, performer, instrument and material, and ultimately its effect on the listener.

Sound and technology in Pierre Schaeffer's *Musique concrète*

Whereas the Futurists used sound material partly because of its semantic connotations ("the motors and machines of our industrial cities can one day be given pitches, so that every workshop will become an intoxicating orchestra"),[74] the founder of *musique concrète*, Pierre Schaeffer (1910–1995), strove to give sounds an abstract quality in the sense of detaching them from their original context and handling them as objects with a musical quality.[75] According to Schaeffer's definition, *musique concrète* took the opposite approach to traditional composition

72 Ibid., p. 3.

73 For example, Marinetti wrote in *Le Roi Bombance:* "Creazione! Distruzione! Rigenerazione! Ciò che voi chiamate 'la morte' non è che uno degl'innumerevoli mutamenti la cui successione costituisce la Vita!" Marinetti: *Teatro.* A cura di Giovanni Calendoli. Vol. 2, p. 247; and a few years later: "Dopo la distruzione dell'antico bene e dell'antico male, noi creiamo un nuovo bene." Marinetti: "La nuova religione-morale della velocità", in Marinetti: *Teoria e invenzione futurista*, p. 132.

74 "Così i motori e le macchine delle nostre città industriali potranno un giorno essere sapientemente intonati, in modo da fare di ogni officina una inebbriante orchestra di rumori." Russolo: *L'arte dei rumori*, p. 135; *The Art of Noises*, p. 29.

75 "Si j'extrais un'élément sonore quelconque et si je le répète sans me soucier de sa forme, mais en faisant varier sa matière, j'annule pratiquement cette forme, il perd sa signification; seule sa variation de matière émerge, et avec elle le phénomène musical. Tout phénomène sonore peut donc être pris (tout comme les mots du langage) pour sa signification relative, ou pour sa substance propre. Tant que prédomine la signification, et qu'on joue sur elle, il y a littérature et non musique. Mais comment est-il possible d'oublier la signification, d'isoler l'en-soi du phénomène sonore? Deux démarches sont préalables: Distinguer un élément (l'entendre en soi, pour sa texture, sa matière, sa couleur). Le répéter. Répétez deux fois le même fragment sonore: il n'y a plus événement, il y a musique." Schaeffer: "A la recherche d'une musique concrète", p. 21.

process, which proceeds from the abstract, mental conception of music and links it, via notation, to concrete, instrumental performances. By contrast, *musique concrète* starts from real, 'concrete' sound material and achieves through experiments abstract musical structures of sound objects without taking recourse to a score that would outline the sounds to be produced in performance.[76] Schaeffer approached his material not as a composer but as a graduate in mathematics and physics. Although he denied that he had any knowledge of Russolo's writings in 1948, his aesthetics and methods reveal considerable overlap with Futurist thinking on music.[77] Having experienced war and having been shaped by an aesthetization of technology, Schaeffer touched upon subjects which were also part of the Futurist canon: primitivism, violence and technology. He considered his *musique concrète* to be 'wild' yet 'sophisticated'[78] and the product of "a time that in itself is violent and out of joint, a time of the atom and the rocket, of violence and furious speed."[79] The experimental spirit of his compositional method stood in contrast to everything that had existed before. His music explored the key question of whether the 'technical revolution' in music merely needed new apparatuses in order to 'make music' *as before,* or whether it led to the "discovery of new types of music which we are *not yet able to make, much less to hear*".[80] Schaeffer favoured

76 See Schaeffer: "A la recherche d'une musique concrète", p. 35.

77 Schaeffer referred in 1952 to the Futurists as precursors of noise music, without mentioning Russolo, Pratella or *The Art of Noises* by name, and called their creation of noise music by means of instruments a cul-de-sac: "En fait, les Italiens, avec Marinetti, ont été des précursors, il y a 20 ans de cela. Mais il s'agissait de concerts de bruits directs, conduisant, comme on l'a vu, à une impasse." Schaeffer: "A la recherche d'une musique concrète", p. 31. In 1954, the editor of the French translation of Russolo's manifesto, Maurice Lemaître, accused Schaeffer of being untruthful. He felt that the overlaps in terms of content meant that Schaeffer must have known Russolo's manifesto. See Lemaître: "L'Art des bruits: Manifeste futuriste 1913", p. 15 f. Schaeffer reacted to Lemaître's criticism in 1959, in an essay for the Biennale di Venezia magazine, in which he emphasized that he had not had any knowledge of his precursors when he began his research into noise in 1948. See Schaeffer: "La galleria sotto i suoni ovvero il futuro anteriore", p. 66.

78 "Une langue inconnue, [...] une musique 'autre': étrangère, insolite ou sauvage. Par sauvage, on comprend bien que nous n'évoquons pas telle musique exotique – toujours fort élaborée." Schaeffer: *La Musique concrète,* p. 10.

79 "C'était bien là la musique de l'époque, elle-même brutale et bouleversée, époque de l'atome et de la fusée, de la puissance et de la vitesse, des éléments eux aussi déchaînés." Schaeffer: *La Musique concrète,* p. 9.

80 "La révolution technique qui atteint la musique apporte-t-elle, en effet, de nouveaux moyens de 'faire de la musique', *comme auparavant,* ou bien nous mène-t-elle à la découverte de nouvelles musiques, que nous ne savons pas encore faire, et encore moins entendre?" Schaeffer: *La Musique concrète,* p. 7. Emphasis by Schaeffer.

the second option. His music was subject to a “dialectic of the unexpected”,[81] and the musician was no longer a person with a diploma in Musical Studies, but a ‘sound engineer’.[82]

After two years of research, in the programme for the first concert of the *musique concrète* (1950), Schaeffer highlighted the importance of technology for his music,[83] but also defined it as provisional and unfinished. The “musician-engineer who was able to elicit something from the humming of the machines” had “a right to take over”,[84] just like Russolo once hoped for composers and “innovative musicians” (*musicisti innovatori*).[85] However, the acoustic material that Schaeffer offered in response to the “musical element [that was] set a priori”[86] was medialized differently from the way it was done in Russolo’s time: recorded and manipulated on records and tapes, it only existed thanks to technical devices. The technical prerequisites offered by the radio led beyond Russolo: Schaeffer’s ‘sound objects’ were not generated and modulated by conventional instruments but, in reverse of the traditional composition process, they started from concrete, real, recorded materials and became abstract through the technical processing and modification of the sounds.

The creation of this type of music highlights the process of exploration and assumes that the sound object detaches itself from the semantics of its origin. Like Russolo, Schaeffer saw the beginning of this process in the listening experience of human beings, who are surrounded by an environment of constant background noises. He therefore saw a “potential for development as well as a limitation of any new music” in the “resources of the ear”; the development of a new musical conception takes place with the help of systematic aural perception of sounds.[87]

The ability to perceive the abstract quality of sound objects presupposes a ‘reduced’ hearing of the original sources. This type of listening should be practised so that the musician can learn to handle apparatuses for sound manipulation. Similar to what Russolo had already described in 1916 for the change of sound pitch in the

---

81 “dialectique du fortuit”. Schaeffer: *La Musique concrète*, p. 11.

82 Schaeffer: “A la recherche d’une musique concrète”, p. 17.

83 “Nous avons pris l’outil que la technique nous avait donné.” Schaeffer: *La Musique concrète*, p. 12.

84 “L’ingénieur musicien, s’il a pu arracher quelque chose au ronron des machines, a droit aussi à la relève.” Schaeffer: *La Musique concrète*, p. 12.

85 Russolo: *L’arte dei rumori*, p. 174; *The Art of Noises*, p. 85.

86 “C’est donc poser *a priori* un certain musical.” Schaeffer: *La Musique concrète*, p. 38.

87 “Primauté de l’oreille. – Le potentiel d’évolution, en même temps que les limites, de toute musique nouvelle, tient aux ressources de l’oreille.” Schaeffer: *La Musique concrète*, p. 29.

intonarumori, Schaeffer discovered in his sound experiments of 1948 how the indexical value, namely the association of the sound with its origin, can be reduced or even cancelled. When several sounds are layered, they become abstract musical material and assume independent tonal properties. Although this may correspond to the 'research character' postulated by Schaeffer, works such as the *Cinq études de bruits* (Five Noise Studies, 1948) still reveal the sources of the material used. Schaeffer tried to distinguish himself from composers of electronic music by giving preference to 'concrete' (real) acoustic sources and rejecting the exclusive use of electronic sound devices; the equal value of all sound on the level of sound production has thus not yet been reached.

Liberation by electronic means: György Ligeti's conception of 'Klang'

György Ligeti (1923–2006) attested to the post-war generation that they were "fed up with all of these 'neo-' and 'going-back to'" trends and that they had "a deep mistrust of the achievements of the fathers, indeed of everything conventional".[88] His escape in 1957 from the cultural isolation in Stalinist Hungary led him to Cologne, one of the most important centres of new music. He was a profound connoisseur of the works of his predecessors as well as his contemporaries, yet, at the same time, he rejected the "new academisms"[89] of the post-war years because it showed many signs of wear and tear. He wanted to subject each musical work to an individual shaping process in order to realize a tonal conception that was radically geared towards the future. Such a work would not be developed on the basis of formal models, but rather based on its own rules. The driving forces behind Ligeti's creative work were independence and constant change: "We must permanently renew our material; not only the methods, but the entire musical imagination.[90]

Ligeti had an open-minded attitude towards his predecessors and recommended studying their works so that newly emerging music could reach the same level

88 "Die Elite dieser Jüngsten hatte die Nase voll von allem 'Neo-' und 'Zurück zu' [...]. Wie alle Nachkriegsgenerationen hegten sie tiefes Mißtrauen gegen die Errungenschaften der Väter, ja gegen alles Herkömmliche." Ligeti: "Die Vorbereitungen zur zweiten Revolution in der Neuen Musik", p. 80.

89 Ligeti: "Musik auf neue Art gedacht: Sechzehn Jahre 'das neue werk'", p. 215.

90 "Wir müssen unser Material ständig erneuern – nicht nur die Methoden, vielmehr die ganze musikalische Vorstellung." Ligeti: "Musik auf neue Art gedacht: Sechzehn Jahre 'das neue werk'", p. 215.

of excellence.[91] He considered Gustav Mahler, Claude Debussy and Anton Webern to have fostered a new musical poetics; he gladly received impulses from Charles Ives' combination of heterogeneous musical elements; he admired Edgard Varèse's tectonic layering of sounds.[92] In his treatise *Über elektronische Musik* (On Electronic Music, 1961), Ligeti cited Luigi Russolo's experiments and instruments among the precursors of electronic music, alongside Varèse's pure noise composition *Ionization* (1929–31).[93] From the confrontation with the music of his contemporaries, Ligeti arrived at aesthetic positions that were breaking new ground in his own compositions. By studying the extremes of John Cage's aleatoric music and the most recent development of twelve-tone and serial music, he came to the conclusion that a total implementation of the serial principle would, ultimately, cancel the notion of seriality itself: "Basically, there is no difference between automatic results and random products: The totally determined becomes equal to the totally indeterminate."[94] After analysing and testing the possibilities of an electronic form of producing sound, he recognized its limits and moved away from the sine wave generator. This, however, did not apply to the aesthetics of the most differentiated sound that emerged from it.

Ligeti's realization that the "form of sounds, that is, their internal structure, is not necessarily a given entity any longer"[95] was revolutionary for the time. The internal structuring of sound by means of the technical possibilities offered in an electronic studio and the subsequent experimental work with them allowed Ligeti to apply those structures to the compositional process of instrumental music, without taking any recourse to electronic means. Along the way, he expanded the definitions of 'sound' to include 'so-called musical sounds', so-called "because there is no such thing as pure musical sound; all musical sounds have a noise compo-

91 Ligeti: "Neue Wege im Kompositionsunterricht", p. 132.

92 Ligeti: "Musik auf neue Art gedacht: Sechzehn Jahre 'das neue werk'", p. 201ff.

93 Ligeti: "Über elektronische Musik", p. 126. It needs to be noted here that this text by Ligeti was originally published in 1961 under the German title "Musik von anderen Planeten: Zur Geschichte und Gegenwart der elekronischen Musik". It is not known which of Russolo's manifestos Ligeti had knowledge of at that time.

94 "Grundsätzlich gibt es keinen Unterschied zwischen automatischen Ergebnissen und Zufallsprodukten: Das total Determinierte wird dem total Indeterminierten gleich." Ligeti: "Wandlungen der musikalischen Form", p. 92.

95 "[...] führten zu der Vorstellung, daß die Form der Klänge, d.h. ihr interner Aufbau, nicht notwendig mehr gegeben ist." Ligeti: "Musik auf neue Art gedacht: Sechzehn Jahre 'das neue werk'", p. 202.

nent."[96] Likewise, there is no such thing as 'pure noise'. All sounds produced in music are 'artificial': "What we hear in electronic music is also vibration of the air; so it can equally be considered 'Nature'."[97]

Ligeti changed his concept of music when he gained new insights into the working methods of an electronic studio. Exposed to sounds in their constitutional make-up, he began to think in terms of sound structures which, in place of melody or harmony, placed the traditionally barely perceptible or imperceptible by-products of sound production at the centre of composition and musical design. The electronic studio revealed to him the inner structure of acoustic phenomena and made it obvious to him that every sound consists of a characteristic, individual spectrum of timbres.[98] This paved the way for his realization that sound is not predetermined or fixed by the acoustic character of a traditional instrument. From now on, sound was for him the result of compositional construction.

When the WDR Studio für elektronische Musik (Studio for Electronic Music in the West German Radio Station) was founded in Cologne in 1951, it was the first of its kind in the world and gave rise to a novel way of producing music. Karlheinz Stockhausen arrived at the Studio in March 1953, and was its director from 1963 to 1989. Composers from all over the world, including György Ligeti and Mauricio Kagel, embarked on pilgrimages to Cologne to use the Studio's unique facilities. Ligeti's insights into the possibilities of splitting and layering sounds were subsequently transferred to the composition of instrumental and vocal music. Russolo's belief that "every noise has a pitch, some even a chord, which predominates among the whole of its irregular vibrations"[99] was taken up by Ligeti when he worked on sonic sub-structures using conventional instruments, but now Ligeti structured the individual sound as a synthesis of a multitude of individual voices. In *Apparitions* (1958/59) and *Atmosphères* (1961), which were created as a direct result of these experiences in the electronic studio, Ligeti found for the first time a method of composition in which sonic events are constitutive of the form. He declared that everything which had previously – that is, before the arrival of elec-

---

96 "Ich sage sogenannter musikalischer Klang, weil es reinen musikalischen Klang nicht gibt – alle musikalischen Klänge haben einen Geräuschanteil." Ligeti: "Musik auf neue Art gedacht: Sechzehn Jahre 'das neue werk'", p. 213.

97 "Prinzipiell gibt es keinen Unterschied zwischen elektronisch und instrumental oder vokal erzeugten Klängen. Die Instrumentalmusik als 'natürlich', die elektronische hingegen als 'technisch-artifiziell' zu bezeichnen, ist irreführend. [...] Schließlich ist das, was wir bei elektronischer Musik hören, ebenfalls Vibration der Luft, also genauso 'Natur'." Ligeti: "Auswirkungen der elektronischen Musik auf mein kompositorisches Schaffen", p. 88.

98 Ligeti: "Über elektronische Musik", p. 123.

99 *"Ogni rumore ha un tono, talora anche un accordo che predomina nell'insieme delle sue vibrazioni irregolari."* Russolo: *L'arte dei rumori*, p. 132; *The Art of Noises*, p. 27. Emphasis by Russolo.

tronic technology – existed below or at the border of the acoustic perception[100] was musical material.

Through extreme differentiation of the orchestral sound, Ligeti created sonic structures of “supersaturated polyphony”.[101] He chose this term because the sound of orchestral instruments taken as a whole is intensified by the extreme layering of individual sounds in the manner of a sine wave in electronic music, although it is not a pure sine wave but rather the complex sound of the respective instruments. The term that is nowadays used for this procedure is ‘micropolyphony’. Ligeti’s composed sound consists, as it were, in a vertical section of the multitude of individual orchestral voices, and appears horizontally as a noise structure in which changes are so subtle that the individual voice is imperceptible in the context of the dense (‘supersaturated’) sound of the orchestra.

The harmonic function of the intervals lies beyond the limits of human auditory perception, yet the minute changes in the tonal structures have a form-shaping effect.[102] Essential principles drawn from electronic sound generation and transferred to instrumental and vocal composition arrive at a “blurring limit” (*Verwischungsgrenze*)[103] as well as the generation of a new kind of sound quality, which Ligeti called “movement colour” (*Bewegungsfarbe*).[104] As an acoustic consequence of the extreme differentiation of the sound, supplemented by the finest dynamic gradations, the individual instruments no longer function as in classical music; they are submerged in a multifaceted fabric, where the musical shapes are not created from single tones, harmonies or rhythms, but rather from the interactions of distinctive elements that have largely lost their individual character. The resulting timbre is neither that of a classical orchestral nor that of electronic

---

100 Ligeti remarks that tone sequences are audible only when they are longer than 50 msec; shorter intervals are perceived as simultaneous. See Ligeti: “Auswirkungen der elektronischen Musik auf mein kompositorisches Schaffen”, p. 88.

101 Ligeti: “Über meine Entwicklung als Komponist”, p. 119.

102 See Ligeti’s notes on *Apparitions* in Dibelius: “György Ligeti: Eine Monographie in Essays”, p. 21.

103 “Diese Differenzierung ermöglicht mir, durch plötzliches Ein- und Aussetzen von klanglichen Ereignissen unterhalb der Verwischungsgrenze arbeiten zu können, wodurch diskontinuierliche Vorgänge in unserer Wahrnehmung kontinuierlich erscheinen.” Ligeti: “Auswirkungen der elektronischen Musik auf mein kompositorisches Schaffen”, p. 89.

104 See Ligeti’s notes on *Lux aeterna:* “Wenn aber genügend viele instrumentale oder vokale Stimmen, die in ihrer Bewegung minimal gegeneinander verschoben sind, gleichzeitig verlaufen, so kann das Resultat dieser Verschiebung durchaus unterhalb der Grenze von 1/20 Sekunde liegen. Derart entsteht aus rhythmischen Konfigurationen eine Art Klangfarbe – ich nenne sie ‘Bewegungsfarbe’ –, die sich qualitativ von den spezifischen Klangfarben der einzelnen Instrumente beziehungsweise der menschlichen Stimme unterscheidet.” Ligeti: “Über ‘Lux aeterna’”, p. 239.

music. Individual voices lie below the threshold of what he called "blurring limit" (see above), up to the point of the rhythm's dissolution into simultaneity. These structures, called 'sonorities' (*Sonoritäten*)[105] no longer receive their form-shaping function from the intervals' relationships to each other, but through "movements and internal changes"[106] within the sound complex, and by entering into a relationship with other sonorities.

For *Apparitions*, Ligeti conceived two characteristic sonorities to realize his musical ideas, which he associated with "delicate sounding textures" (*zarte, klingende Texturen*),[107] the function of which he described as 'states', and with "firmer sound groups" (*festere Klanggruppen*)[108] that function as 'events'. Both groups work together in an almost process-like manner.[109] The changes of the first tonal group are triggered by the appearance of the sounds of the second group, with a tilting of the form at the dynamic climax of the first movement, triggered by the sound of a "metallic explosion"[110] created in combination of different sounds.

Ligeti realized with the help of micropolyphony a kind of Neo-Futurist vision of a music inspired by technology. He re-defined the relationship between human beings and machines in the field of music and went beyond the point of electronic sound production longed for by previous composers. The new electronic technology had an effect on his composition of instrumental music. Here, as in the time of historical Futurism, technical progress led to a broadening of knowledge about sound phenomena and gave rise to a new conception of music. In Ligeti's case, due to the advanced technical possibilities at his disposal, this was no longer restricted to the world of sound, but extended to the 'deep structures' of sound.

Conclusion

My investigation into the work of composers who focussed on the expansion of sound suggests that the potential for Neo-Futurist tendencies in the music of the

105 Ligeti: "Über *Apparitions*", p. 174.

106 Ibid., p. 174.

107 Ligeti: "Zustände, Ereignisse, Wandlungen: Bemerkungen zu 'Apparitions'", p. 171.

108 Ibid., p. 171.

109 "Die Zustände werden dabei von plötzlich eintretenden Ereignissen unterbrochen und verändern sich unter deren Einfluß, und umgekehrt: Die veränderten Zustände haben auch eine gewisse Wirkung auf die Art der Ereignisse, denn diese müssen stets von neuartiger Prägung sein, um den veränderten Zustand weiter verändern zu können. Auf diese Weise entsteht eine unablässige Wandlung." Ibid., p. 173.

110 Ibid., p. 173.

neo-avant-gardes was rooted in Russolo's demand for the definition and handling of sound as a musical raw material. Responses to historical Futurism in the post-war period varied amongst individual composers, but in each case a 'reshaping' of noise on an aesthetic level bore comparison with Futurist notions of a new kind of musical production with sounds.

The composers' aesthetic re-evaluation of sound led to an ever-expanding conception of music, to the point that music could be treated as a mere 'sonic structure'. This re-interpretation advanced the goal of abstraction, that is, composing with the 'core' of sound free of external associations. Declaring sound to be musical material also required a new listening attitude and assigned to the audience a new rôle in the musical communication process. Edgard Varèse pointed ahead to the coming generation when he defined music as 'organized sound' and declared his intention of liberating sound from internal imagination, from the limitations of the tonal system and from established forms of instrumentation. Varèse's closeness to Futurism is recognizable in his search for a new musical 'alphabet', for new instruments, for an aesthetics that drew inspiration from science and technology. He functioned as a mediator between the historical and the neo-avant-garde in his pursuit of an autonomous music, as well as in his rôle as an experimental sound researcher.

Russolo's demand for 're-shaping' sounds into a work of art required new kinds of alliances with technology. Instrumental music has always been linked to sound-producing devices, thus making it 'artificial'.[111] The skills required to organize sounds link music with the "techniques of the body".[112] Music as a medium acts as a mirror of its time. The all-inclusive expansion of the concept of music to include noise took inspiration from the machine as both a thematic and structural subject. Noise became available for musicalization only after emancipating itself from its origins, and the process of sound creation, reproduction and finally production was closely connected to the aestheticization of the machine and human – machine interaction. Technology affected the conception and production of music through the ways in which the relationship between man and machine was expressed. This ranged from the glorification of the machine by Russolo and his Futurist friends to a programmatically infused machinolatry in Arthur Honegger's *Pacific 231* (1923), to Varèse's yearning for new technologies that enable the real-

---

111 Ligeti: "Über elektronische Musik", p. 123.

112 "Le corps est le premier et le plus naturel instrument de l'homme. Ou plus exactement, sans parler d'instrument, le premier et le plus naturel objet technique, et en même temps moyen technique, de l'homme, c'est son corps. […] Avant les techniques à instruments, il y a l'ensemble des techniques du corps." Mauss: "Les Techniques du corps", p. 372.

ization of new and universal concepts of music, or to Ligeti's evocation of acoustic illusion as a result of his experiments with electronic technologies.

Cage's musical work demonstrates that the relationship between human beings and technology in the field of art cannot be completely abolished through the use of chance. The individual producing a work of art is only making a detour here: without humans neither technology nor art exist. The musical work of art continues to be conceived and organized by an individual and then brought forth by means of technology. At the time of Ligeti and other composers, technology made it possible to understand the microstructures of sound and to develop from this an almost microscopically refined, highly complex composition technique that allowed the creation of new sound forms. In 1957, Ligeti recognized the creative potential of synthetic sound production, and thus unleashed a musical revolution. He transcended electronic, serial music by composing new instrumental music with the help of microstructures derived from electronic music. Technology thus had the effect of revolutionizing the way he thought about music as a sonic structure. The radiant power of the machine was directed towards a method of composition that made use of traditional instruments in the creation of music inspired by the sonic structures generated in the electronic studio.

The extensive knowledge concerning the structures of sound, which the Futurists accelerated with their investigation into sound and noise led not only to new forms of sound production, but also to new form-giving processes in the compositional praxis. Working with the sonic interior substance, this type of music realized features that Futurism had declared to be benchmarks: simultaneity, asymmetry, heterogeneity and rhythm. While Russolo believed that the old instruments had to be replaced by new ones, Ligeti with his compositional methods arrived at solutions that corresponded to Russolo's demand for "a fantastic association of the different timbres and rhythms" with which "the new orchestra will obtain the most complex and novel emotions of sound".[113] Ligeti's abstract sound structures were free from any association with the sounds of everyday life and were produced by the rich timbre of traditional musical instruments. By allowing the audience at the première of *Apparitions* and *Atmosphères* to succumb to the illusion that they were listening to electronic music,[114] Ligeti unintentionally succeeded in creating a musical fiction of the machine.

---

113 "Non sarà mediante una successione di rumori imitativi della vita, bensì mediante una fantastica associazione di questi timbri vari e di questi ritmi vari, che la nuova orchestra otterrà le più complesse e nuove emozioni sonore." Russolo: *L'arte dei rumori*, p. 134; *The Art of Noises*, p. 29.
114 When *Apparitions* was premièred in Cologne in 1960 and *Atmosphères* in Donaueschingen in 1961, many listeners believed that the orchestral sound was electronically manipulated or that

Although avant-garde music was directed towards the future, if we look at it from a historical perspective, its 'traditional' aspects cannot be ignored. Whereas before, 'sound' was understood in opposition to 'noise', the neo-avant-garde accomplished the desired aesthetic expansion by treating both as musical material and integrating them into the cosmos of simultaneously sounding, overlapping *Klänge* (chords).[115] Based on the definition of noise as musical material, what could be considered Neo-Futurist is the detachment of noise from its original sonic environment and the adoption of technology as a potential stimulus of musical creativity.

The relationship between man and machine, which was one of the great themes of twentieth-century music, continues to be topical in the twenty-first century, especially with regard to the rôle of the individual in the generation of music experiences. To what extent the "euphoric expectations of the future", defined by Franco Berardi as the cultural "motor of modern expansion" from "Faust to Marinetti",[116] can be realized in music is still up for discussion. But in the 1950s, when the neo-avant-garde explored the possibilities and limits of the interplay between technology and music, there were many individually negotiated Neo-Futurist tendencies in the vacillating methodologies employed by the composers discussed in this essay.

Acknowledgements: I would like to thank Günther Rötter and Roger Dretzler for their judicious advice during my studies.

Bibliography

Berardi, Franco: "Zukunft: Erschöpfung." *Kunstforum International* 267 (May 2020): 112–117.

Boccioni, Umberto: "Futurist Painting Sculpture (Plastic Dynamism)." U. Boccioni: *Futurist Painting Sculpture: Plastic Dynamism.* Ed. by Richard Agin, and Maria VersariLos Angeles: Getty, 2016. 57–158.

Boccioni, Umberto: "Pittura e scultura futuriste: Dinamismo plastico." U. Boccioni: *Gli scritti editi e inediti.* A cura di Zeno Birolli. Vol. 1. Milano: Mimesis, 2011. 75–204.

Busoni, Ferruccio: *Entwurf einer neuen Ästhetik der Tonkunst.* Herausgegeben von Martina Weindel. Wilhelmshaven: Noetzel, 2001.

Busoni, Ferruccio: *The Essence of Music and Other Papers.* London: Rockliff, 1957.

---

loudspeakers were secretly transmitting an electronic tape. See Ligeti: "Musik und Technik: Eigene Erfahrungen und subjektive Betrachtungen", p. 252.

115 The German term with its derivatives such as Gleichklang, Klangfarbe and Klangfülle have no direct equivalent in the English language.

116 Berardi: "Zukunft: Erschöpfung", p. 117.

Cage, John: "Recent Books: The Dreams and Dedications of George Antheil." *Modern Music* 23:1 (Winter 1946): 78–79. Reprinted in Richard Kostelanetz, ed.: *John Cage: An Anthology.* New York: Da Capo Press, 1991. 73–74.

Cage, John: "The Future of Music." J. Cage: *Silence: Lectures and Writings.* London: Boyars, 2009. 3–6.

Carrà, Carlo: "La pittura dei suoni, rumori, odori. Manifesto futurista." Carlo Carrà: *Tutti gli scritti.* A cura di Massimo Carrà. Milano: Feltrinelli, 1978. 16–21. English translation: "The Painting of Sounds, Noises, and Smells." Lawrence Rainey, Christine Poggi, and Laura Wittman, eds.: *Futurism: An Anthology.* New Haven/CT: Yale University Press, 2009. 155–158.

Charbonnier, Georges: *Entretiens avec Edgard Varèse* [1955]. Paris: Belfond, 1970.

Dibelius, Ulrich: *György Ligeti: Eine Monographie in Essays.* Mainz: Schott, 1994.

Dibelius, Ulrich: *Moderne Musik nach 1945.* München: Piper, 1998.

Donhauser, Peter: *Musikmaschinen: Die Geschichte der Elektromusik.* Berlin: Vergangenheitsverlag, 2019.

Drees, Stefan: "Dokumentation – Labor – Verzauberung: Punktuelle Beobachtungen zur Geschichte des elektroakustischen Komponierens." *Neue Zeitschrift für Musik* 175:2 (March 2014). 12–19.

Dudakov-Kashuro, Konstantin: "Noise Music in Russian Futurism." *International Yearbook of Futurism Studies* 6 (2016): 94–118.

Kostelanetz, Richard, ed.: *John Cage.* London: Allen Lane and The Penguin Press, 1971.

Ligeti, György: "Auswirkungen der elektronischen Musik auf mein kompositorisches Schaffen." G. Ligeti: *Gesammelte Schriften.* Hg. von Monika Lichtenfeld. Vol. 2. Mainz: Schott, 2007. 86–94.

Ligeti, György: "Die Vorbereitungen zur zweiten Revolution in der Neuen Musik." G. Ligeti: *Gesammelte Schriften.* Hg. von Monika Lichtenfeld. Vol. 1. Mainz: Schott, 2007. 79–83.

Ligeti, György: "Musik auf neue Art gedacht: Sechzehn Jahre 'das neue werk'." G. Ligeti: *Gesammelte Schriften.* Hg. von Monika Lichtenfeld. Vol. 1. Mainz: Schott, 2007. 201–216.

Ligeti, György: "Musik und Technik: Eigene Erfahrungen und subjektive Betrachtungen." G. Ligeti: *Gesammelte Schriften.* Hg. von Monika Lichtenfeld. Vol. 1. Mainz: Schott, 2007. 237–261.

Ligeti, György: "Neue Wege im Kompositionsunterricht." G. Ligeti: *Gesammelte Schriften.* Hg. von Monika Lichtenfeld. Vol. 1. Mainz: Schott, 2007. 131–156.

Ligeti, György: "Über 'Apparitions'." G. Ligeti: *Gesammelte Schriften.* Hg. von Monika Lichtenfeld. Vol. 2. Mainz: Schott, 2007. 174.

Ligeti, György: "Über elektronische Musik." G. Ligeti: *Gesammelte Schriften.* Hg. von Monika Lichtenfeld. Vol. 1. Mainz: Schott, 2007. 123–130.

Ligeti, György: "Über 'Lux aeterna'." G. Ligeti: *Gesammelte Schriften.* Hg. von Monika Lichtenfeld. Vol. 2. Mainz: Schott, 2007. 236–243.

Ligeti, György: "Über meine Entwicklung als Komponist." G. Ligeti: *Gesammelte Schriften.* Hg. von Monika Lichtenfeld. Vol. 2. Mainz: Schott, 2007. 119–122.

Ligeti, György: "Wandlungen der musikalischen Form." G. Ligeti: *Gesammelte Schriften.* Hg. von Monika Lichtenfeld. Vol. 1. Mainz: Schott, 2007. 85–105.

Ligeti, György: "Zustände, Ereignisse, Wandlungen. Bemerkungen zu 'Apparitions'." G. Ligeti: *Gesammelte Schriften.* Hg. von Monika Lichtenfeld. Vol. 2. Mainz: Schott, 2007. 170–173.

Ligeti, György: *Apparitions.* Wien: Universal Edition, 1971.

Lombardi, Daniele: "Luigi Russolo und die Musikalisierung des Geräuschs." Irene Chytraeus-Auerbach, and Georg Maag, ed.: *Futurismus: Kunst, Technik, Geschwindigkeit und Innovation zu Beginn des 20. Jahrhunderts.* Berlin: LIT, 2016. 77–93.

Marinetti, Filippo Tommaso: "La nuova religione-morale della velocità." *L'Italia futurista.* 1:17 (11 May 1916): 2. Reprinted in F.T. Marinetti: *Teoria e invenzione futurista.* Milano: Mondadori, 1968. 111–

118. 2nd edn 1983. 130–138. English translation "The New Ethical Religion of Speed." F. T. Marinetti: *Critical Writings.* Ed. by Günter Berghaus. New York: Farrar, Straus and Giroux, 2006. 253–259.

Marinetti, Filippo Tommaso: *Le Roi Bombance: Tragédie satirique en quatre actes, en prose.* Paris: Société du Mercure de France, 1905. Italian translation *Re Baldoria: Tragedia satirica in quattro atti, in prosa.* Milano: Treves, 1910. Reprinted in F. T. Marinetti: *Teatro.* A cura di Giovanni Calendoli. Vol. 2. Roma: Bianco, 1960. 1–253.

Mauss, Marcel: "Les Techniques du corps." *Journal de psychologie normale et pathologique* 32:3–4 (15 March – 15 April 1936): 271–293. Reprinted in Marcel Mauss: *Sociologie et anthropologie.* Paris: Presses Universitaires de France, 8 edn. 1983. 363–386.

Nanz, Dieter A.: *Edgard Varèse: Die Orchesterwerke.* Berlin: Lukas, 2003.

Pratella, Francesco Balilla: "Manifesto tecnico della musica futurista." Milano: Redazione di "Poesia", 1911. Reprinted in Stefano Bianchi: *La musica futurista: Ricerche e documenti.* Lucca: Libreria Musicale Italiana, 1995. 199–203. English translation "Futurist Music: Technical Manifesto." Lawrence Rainey, Christine Poggi, and Laura Wittman, eds.: *Futurism: An Anthology.* New Haven/CT: Yale University Press, 2009. 80–84.

Pratella. Francesco Balilla: *Edizioni, scritti, manoscritti musicali e futuristi.* A cura di Domenico Tampieri. Ravenna: Longo, 1995.

Riethmüller, Albrecht: "Ausklang: Die 'Stunde Null' als musikgeschichtliche Größe." Albrecht Riethmüller, ed.: *Geschichte der Musik im 20. Jahrhundert, 1925–1945.* Laaber: Laaber, 2006. 317–328.

Russolo, Luigi: *L'art des bruits: Manifeste futuriste 1913.* Introduction de Maurice Lemaître. Paris: Richard-Masse, 1954.

Russolo, Luigi: *L'arte dei rumori.* Milano: Edizioni Futuriste di "Poesia", 1916. Reprinted in Gianfranco Maffina, ed.: *Luigi Russolo e l'arte dei rumori: Con tutti gli scritti musicali.* Turin: Martano 1978. 129–177.

Russolo, Luigi: *The Art of Noises.* Translated from the Italian with an introduction by Barclay Brown. New York: Pendragon Press, 1986.

Schaeffer, Pierre: "La galleria sotto i suoni ovvero il futuro anteriore." *La Biennale di Venezia: Arte, cinema, musica, teatro* 9: 36–37 (July-December 1959). 65–71.

Schaeffer, Pierre: *À la recherche d'une musique concrète.* Paris: Éditions du Seuil, 1952.

Schaeffer, Pierre: *La Musique concrète.* Paris: Presses Universitaires de France, 1967.

Schmitz-Gundlach, Esther: *Musikästhetische Konzepte des italienischen Futurismus und ihre Rezeption durch Komponisten des 20. Jahrhunderts.* München: M-Press Martin Meidenbauer Verlag, 2007.

Stenzl, Jürg: "'Sklavisch reproduzierte Alltäglichkeit': Varèse und der italienische Futurismus." Felix Meyer, and Heidy Zimmermann, eds.: *Edgard Varèse: Komponist. Klangforscher, Visionär.* Mainz: Schott, 2006. 142–148.

Varèse, Edgard: "Ferruccio Busoni: A Reminiscence." *Columbia University Forum* 9:2 (Spring 1966): 20. Reprinted in *Varsity Graduate* (University of Toronto) 13:1 (December 1966): 73–74.

Varèse, Edgard: "Music as an Art-Science." Elliott Schwartz, and Barney Childs, eds.: *Contemporary Composers on Contemporary Music.* New York: Holt, Reinhart and Winston, 1967. 198–201.

Varèse, Edgard: "Rhythm, Form and Content." Elliott Schwartz, and Barney Childs, eds.: *Contemporary Composers on Contemporary Music.* New York: Holt, Reinhart and Winston, 1967. 201–204.

Varèse, Edgard: "Spatial Music." Elliott Schwartz, and Barney Childs, eds.: *Contemporary Composers on Contemporary Music.* New York: Holt, Reinhart and Winston, 1967. 204–207.

Varèse, Edgard: “New Instruments and New Music.” Elliott Schwartz, and Barney Childs, eds.: *Contemporary Composers on Contemporary Music.* New York: Holt, Reinhart and Winston, 1967. 195–198.
Varèse, Edgard: “The Electronic Medium.” Elliott Schwartz, and Barney Childs, eds.: *Contemporary Composers on Contemporary Music.* New York: Holt, Reinhart and Winston, 1967. 207–208.
Varèse, Louise: *Varèse: A Looking-Glass Diary.* Vol. 1. *1883–1928.* London: Poynter, 1973.

Tenley Bick

Postcolonial Retro-Futurism: Alessandro Ceresoli's *Linea Tagliero* Prototypes

Abstract: In 2009, Italian artist Alessandro Ceresoli (b. 1975) moved to Asmara, Eritrea, and began working with a local glassware manufacturer. This resulted in a series of six structural objects: the *Linea Tagliero Prototipi* (Tagliero Line Prototypes). Inspired by local Italian modern architecture remaining from Fascist colonization, the series quotes Giuseppe Pettazzi's aeroplane-shaped Fiat Tagliero service station (1938), widely recognized as a Futurist building, in a way that mimics and destabilizes its Futurist (and futuristic) design. The unsettlingly alluring series of 'Italian' design objects and furniture items, all made by Eritrean glassworkers (as was glassware under Fascist occupation), navigates violent histories of Italian colonialism and cultural heritage, problematizing histories of Italian Modernism. Upon these premises, this essay examines the series' treatment of the Pettazzi station and broader subversion of Futurist languages of time, technology and aviation associated, in the late 1930s, with Italian chemical warfare and genocide in East Africa. Tracing these works' mirrorings, doublings and inversions of the building, their reflection of aero-Futurist aesthetics and position as prototypes for an unfulfilled line of 'Italian' goods, I argue that the *Linea Tagliero* Prototypes enact a postcolonial Neo-Futurism. Through analysis of Ceresoli's artist book, *Ritorno al futuro* (Back to the Future, 2011), I demonstrate that the series models more specifically what I name and theorize as 'postcolonial Retro-Futurism' (and 'retrofuturism'): a critical return to a historical version of Futurism, in this case colonial, third-wave Italian Futurism, through which new histories and futures emerge, and to a historical ideation of the future, potentially found in other historical and geographical contexts.

Keywords: Italian Modernist architecture in East Africa; Fascist colonialism; Giuseppe Pettazzi's Fiat Tagliero service station (1938); centre-periphery trade relations; aero-Futurism; furniture design; ceramics and glass works; postcolonial Retro-Futurism (retrofuturism); Asmara

https://doi.org/10.1515/9783111318394-013

Introduction

In 2009, Italian artist Alessandro Ceresoli (born 1975 in Romano di Lombardia) flew to the East African city of Asmara, Eritrea, with an open-ended travel plan. Two months into his stay in 'Piccola Roma', as the Red Sea coastal city and former colonial metropolis in Italy's East African project is often referred to, Ceresoli began working in collaboration with Indigenous artisans at Jumbo Glass Vetreria, a local glassware manufacturer that still retains the Italian word for glassmaking in its name. Itself a complex trace of Italian colonialism in name, Jumbo Glass also uses machines that were originally imported from Italy, and the owner employs Italian practices from the period of colonial rule in Eritrea (1890–1947).[1]

Ceresoli, as I discuss below, is an artist who produces works about colonialism in East Africa and its aftermaths, using a variety of (mostly two-dimensional) media, but he had never worked in glass. The collaboration between the Italian artist, who designed and helped execute the works, and the Eritrean glass workers who were responsible for their construction (and, according to the artist, innovation thereof), resulted in a series of six structural objects: three low-profile cantilevered tables (Prototypes 01–03); a pedestal vanity and wall mirror (Prototype 04); a taller accent table illuminated with red neon (Prototype 05); and an azure-blue double-cylinder floor lamp (Prototype 06). After completion, the works were the object of a nearly two-year effort to transport them from Eritrea to Italy, due to, as per the press release for their subsequent exhibition, "the autocratic and totalitarian policies of the Eritrean government."[2]

Protracted difficulties in shipping the objects were eventually resolved, after which they were the first Eritrean glass works to be exported from the country. After their shipment to Italy, they subsequently comprised the content of the artist's show in Milan at Galleria Francesca Minini, entitled *Ritorno al futuro* (Back to the Future, 9 January–5 March 2011; see Fig. 1).

1 This period officially began in 1890, when Eritrea was declared Italy's *colonia primogenita* or first-born colony; Italian colonialism in the region is better known, however, through the period of colonial expansion under Fascism, when Asmara was part of the multi-state colony *Africa Orientale Italiana* (Italian East Africa, 1935–1941). AOI consolidated following Italy's second military conquest of Ethiopia, from 1935 to 1936, and included Eritrea, areas of Ethiopia and Somalia. It formally ended in 1947, the date of the *Trattato di Pace* by which Italy renounced its colonies. For a brief review of Italian commercial purchase, military occupation of and colonial history in Eritrea, see the first section of Fuller: "Italy's Colonial Futures: Colonial Inertia and Postcolonial Capital in Asmara." The press release for Ceresoli's exhibition *Ritorno al futuro* (2011) used the date 1880, the earliest date of land purchase, as the start date of Italian colonialism in the region.

2 Minini: "Alessandro Ceresoli", s. p.

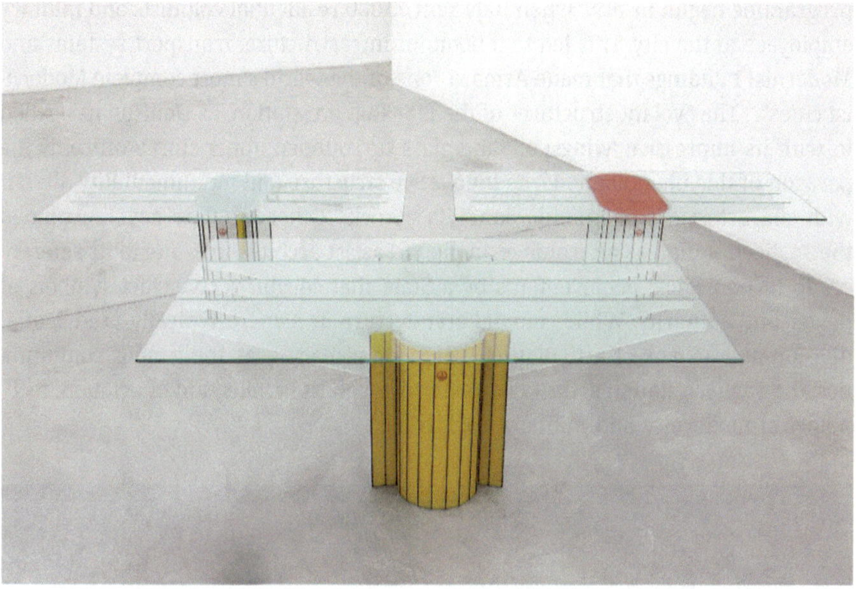

Fig. 1: Alessandro Ceresoli: *Linea Tagliero – Prototipo 01*, with (in the back) *Prototipo 02* and *Prototipo 03* (all 2009), during the exhibition *Ritorno al futuro* at Francesca Minini in Milan (2011).

Collectively entitled the *Linea Tagliero Prototipi* (Tagliero Line Prototypes), the series of geometric furniture items, reminiscent of Italian Art Déco of the 1930s, was inspired by Fascist Modernist architecture in Asmara that remains from colonial rule. More specifically, the imaginary *Tagliero Line* (imaginary, in the sense that the eventual real line of objects that might follow prototypes was never produced), quotes the aeroplane-shaped Fiat Tagliero automobile service station by the architect Giuseppe Pettazzi (1907–2001), a building from 1938 that has become famous in recent years, especially amidst efforts to preserve Italian Modernist architecture in Asmara (see Fig. 2).

Ceresoli and Pettazzi's service station in Asmara

Designed for Fiat's Eritrea-based dealer in then Italian East Africa, the now-iconic building is known for its cantilevered reinforced-concrete 'wings', each measuring an impressive fifteen metres or forty-nine feet, which made the service station appear as if an (Italian) aeroplane were alighting on Eritrean soil, then colonial terrain that was part of the Italian Empire. The building, as architectural historian Edward Denison has noted, was part of a concentrated colonialist construction programme begun in 1935, when Italy sent 70,000 residential colonists and military employees to the city. This led to a boom of infrastructure, transport systems and Modernist buildings that made Asmara "one of the world's most complete Modernist cities".[3] The "volant structure" of the Fiat Tagliero station, as Denison has called it, with its impressive 'wingspan' and glass-surrounded upper-storey office, is the paragon of this phenomenon;[4] its innovative structure and monumentality align it with characteristics of Antonio Sant'Elia's work.[5] Other scholars have positioned the Tagliero station as an iconic example of Fascist architecture, due to its references to technological achievements by a State that sought to construct symbols of power and authority. While colonial architecture in Asmara typically used spatial division as a means of articulating Italian supremacy over Indigenous communities, the Tagliero station articulates power through its recollection of aviation, technological modernity and military warfare.[6]

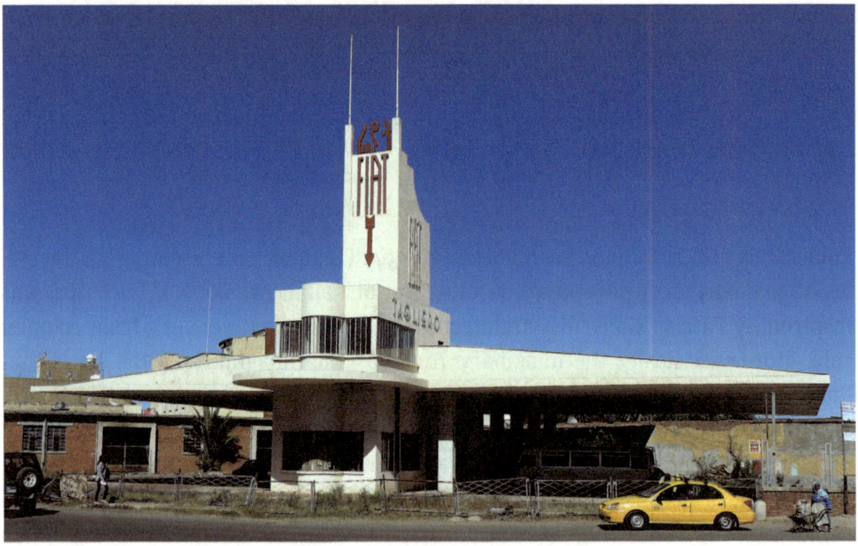

Fig. 2: Giuseppe Pettazzi: *Fiat Tagliero Service Station* (1938).

The two-storey station was inspired by Futurist *architettura aerea* and its related manifestations of a Futurist *aerovita* (aeropainting, aeropoetry, aerosculpture and

3 Denison: "Fiat Tagliero Service Station", pp. 134–135.

4 Ibid.

5 De Seta: *Architettura futurista*, pp. [3] and [5].

6 Scarlett: "Preserved for whom: Reappraising Asmara's Colonial-Era Architecture", pp. 184–185.

aeromusic), associated with technological achievement and at times with imperial conquest.[7] The building exemplifies Italy and Italian Futurism's fascination with aviation, emerging in the early twentieth century when it seized the popular and artistic imaginary of the country and its new avant-garde, becoming *aeromania* by the 1930s.[8] Marinetti celebrated aeroplanes in countless manifestos, from *La fondazione e manifesto del futurismo* (The Foundation and Manifesto of Futurism, 1909) to *L'aeropittura dei bombardamenti: Manifesto futurista* (Aeropaintings of Bombings: Futurist Manifesto, 1940). He described their use by Italian colonial military in the first air raids in military history during the Libyan or Italo-Turkish War (1911–12), as "the most beautiful aesthetic spectacle" he had ever seen.[9] Decades later, during the Second World War, Futurists would again celebrate Italian aerial bombing, as in Ennio Concini's collection of poems, *Aeropoesie futuriste di bombardamenti* (Futurist Aeropoems of Bombings, 1941).[10] The Fiat Tagliero service station, when related to such bellicose aspects of Futurist production of the 1930s and 1940s, begs complicated questions from contemporary viewers, as can be seen in Ceresoli's *Linea Tagliero* project.

The *Linea Tagliero* Prototypes mimic the Futurist (and futuristic)[11] design of the colonial-era Fiat station through mirroring, doubling and skewed reproduction, altering forms and translating them into objects for a house interior. The objects are made of transparent mirrored glass and are sometimes illuminated with neon lighting housed inside the structures. They hint at the design elements of the Tagliero building in terms of material, colour and aesthetic. With Ceresoli's references in mind, for instance, the grouping of a trio of low-profile glass tables reads like a formation of aeroplanes (see Fig. 1). The frame of an ornate wall mir-

7 See the *Manifesto futurista dell'architettura aerea* by F.T. Marinetti, Angiolo Mazzoni and Mino Somenzi (1934). For an overview of Futurist architecture of the 1930s, see Sabatino: "Architecture", pp. 75–79.

8 Günter Berghaus has estimated the *aero* genres also helped to popularize Futurism, given the popular appeal of aviation under the régime. See Berghaus: *Futurism and Politics*, p. 247.

9 "Fu il più bello spettacolo estetico della mia vita." F.T. Marinetti: Letter to Aldo Palazzeschi, January 1912, in Marinetti and Palazzeschi: *Carteggio con un'appendice di altre lettere a Palazzeschi*, p. 61. Marinetti also closes the founding manifesto with a reference to aeroplanes: "Eventually, they will find us, [...] far away in the country, huddling anxiously together beside our airplanes." Marinetti: *Critical Writings*, p. 16. On the topic of flight and aero-Futurism, see Berghaus: "Futurism and the Technological Imagination Poised between Machine Cult and Machine Angst", pp. 12–14; on *aeromania*, Fascism and aero-Futurism, see Pizzi: *Italian Futurism and the Machine*, pp. 222–225.

10 For a reproduction of the cover of this book, which features aeroplanes dropping bombs, see Berghaus: *Futurism and Politics*, plate 15.

11 Ceresoli describes the Fiat Tagliero station as "la futuristica stazione di benzina" (the futuristic petrol station). See Ceresoli: *Ritorno al futuro*, s. p.

ror (Prototype 04; see Fig. 3a) is composed of curved segments of glass; closer comparison with the Tagliero station reveals that the mirror recapitulates and *mirrors* the side-view of the station's spire. In yet another work (Prototype 06), a cylindrical floor lamp recapitulates the windowed second storey of the station and its viewing deck (see Fig. 3b). The unsettlingly alluring series of revivalist 'Italian' furniture items and design objects made by Eritrean workers (as were glassworks in Eritrea under Fascism) are all marked with the logo of the Eritrean company. They are not unlike the geometric furniture usually offered by Jumbo Glass.[12] Clearly marked logos stand in opposition to the propagandistic use of glass in Fascist visual and material culture, which included glass sheets engraved with miniature fasces (see Fig. 4a).

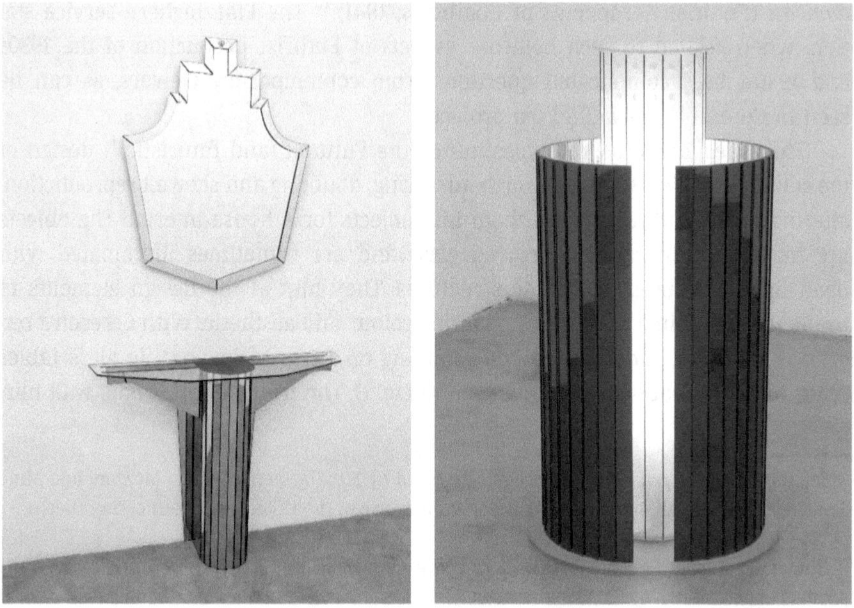

Fig. 3a: Alessandro Ceresoli: *Linea Tagliero – Prototipo 04*, 2009. Glass, mirror, 2 parts, 86 x 116.2 x 31.6 cm / 105.7 x 84.5 cm. **Fig. 3b.** Alessandro Ceresoli: *Linea Tagliero – Prototipo 06*, 2009. Glass, mirror, white neon, 101.6 x 53.3 x 40.6 cm.

Ceresoli's prototypes therefore navigate violent histories of Italian colonialism, Modernism and cultural heritage. They do so through a problematization of tem-

12 See, for example, their display at the Eritrean National Festival in 2014 "ERiTV Eritrea: Reportage Asmara, 20 August 2014".

porality and identity, and through a questioning of the history of Italian Modernism as a distinctly colonial project. More specifically, they disrupt the project of Futurist Modernism during the years of the Italian Empire (established in 1936) in colonial architecture and built environments. From this perspective, I argue that they enact a postcolonial critique of Futurism through what I am calling a 'postcolonial Retro-Futurism / retrofuturism'. This term has two meanings. By 'Retro-Futurism', I mean the critical return to a historical (and in this case, colonialist) version of second-wave Futurism, enacted here by means of re-deployment, deconstruction and extension in the *Linea Tagliero* Prototypes.

While Retro-Futurism should be understood as a version of Neo-Futurism, insofar as it revives Futurism's visual languages at a later date, beyond the historical scope of its reference, I am specifically using the Latin prefix *retro* (meaning 'back', 'backwards') to describe this form of revival as a going-backward. The action and aesthetic that it enacts extend the history of Futurism by going back to it, opening it up and offering new histories and future possibilities yet to come. By retrofuturism, instead, I mean the critical return and seemingly analeptic redeployment of an atavistic historical 'futurism' in a general view of or concern with the future. This lower-case 'retrofuturism' might be found in other geographical and historical contexts.[13] In this essay, I use both versions of the term, as they are both pertinent to Ceresoli's series. A brief overview of Ceresoli's work will help us to situate the *Linea Tagliero* Prototypes as extensions of Ceresoli's interest in Futurism, Asmara's architecture, Italian colonialism in East Africa and the aftermath of these histories.

Ceresoli's art: East Africa, colonialism and *fumetti* revisited

After studying at the Brera Art Academy in Milan, Ceresoli showcased his work in a number of galleries and museums in Italy in the late 1990s and early 2000s. Most notable was his 2003 solo exhibition at the Castello Sforzesco in Milan, where he presented a video work based on Umberto Boccioni's concluding "farewell" oil painting (*gli addii*) in his famous triptych, *Stati d'animo* (Ceresoli used the first version of 1911). For this project, Ceresoli filmed vague sculptural forms meandering under water; they resemble the drifting figures in Boccioni's painting, where fig-

13 The lower-case retrofuturism is in line with recent scholarship on modernism as opposed to (Eurocentric) Modernism, and therefore to the multiplicity of modernisms (or futurisms), as well. This dual usage is also merited because Ceresoli uses both Futurism and futurism, in his texts, with the latter referring to a general futuristic vision of the future.

ure and environment seem to fuse into one another.[14] Ceresoli arose to wider renown in 2007 with his solo debut at the prestigious Galleria Francesca Minini, where he exhibited a series of large black monochrome paintings meant to evoke the underworld.[15] In 2009, the artist made a series of works on black paper, featuring illustrative scenes of East African wildlife and natural environs, captioned with narratives about the history of colonialism in the region. Some were given titles derived from prominent figures in the fight for Eritrean Independence (such as the leader of the Eritrean Liberation Front, Hamid Idris Awate). They recall the graphic aesthetic and layout of Italian comic books (*fumetti*), which often served as colonial propaganda during the years of Italy's colonization of North and East Africa. The materials that Ceresoli used in this series, however, impede rather than facilitate the easy visual and narrative legibility, as well as the graphic impact associated with *fumetti* and other graphic-narrative mass media. One work from the series, entitled *Bloody Thirty Years* (2009), narrates Asmara's emergence as a "colonial metropolis" in the 1930s, describing the "fascination with Asmara's architecture" and ongoing conflicts in the region, such as the (then) ongoing border conflict between Eritrea and Ethiopia. Its caption states:

> Asmara boomed in the 1930s as a colonial metropolis. The reason for this boom was Italy's expansionist policies toward Ethiopia and the ensuing war using lethal gas weapons. Thus, the fascination of Asmara's architecture and urban planning was confronted with the Fascist era, race divisions, and the avangarde [sic] claims of modernism. Eritrea was annexed by Ethiopia in 1961, which again caused a bloody 30 years liberation war resulting in the Independence of Eritrea in 1991[.] In 1998 a border dispute with Ethiopia led to the Eritrean-Ethiopian war in which thousands of soldiers from both countries died. The war ended in 2000 with the signing of the Algiers agreement, but was rejected from Ethiopia[.] Today the border question remains in dispute.

Ceresoli continued this project after completing the *Linea Tagliero* Prototypes in 2010 in two bodies of work: a short film on nationalism, régimes, and propaganda, *She's the One*, whose first half focusses on the Fiat Tagliero station and Italian Fascist-era Art Déco Modernist architecture in Asmara, and whose second half showcases the Miss Eritrea beauty pageant;[16] and a series of sixteen *fumetti*-inspired images, shown at the Centro di Cultura Contemporanea Strozzina in Florence in 2011. In this exhibition, dedicated to emerging talents in Italian art, Ceresoli narrated

---

14 Bonvicini: "Alessandro Ceresoli," *Giovani artisti italiani*, https://www.giovaniartisti.it/gm/2003/english/09.htm.

15 Caruso: "Alessandro Ceresoli Milano Francesca Minini." *Exibart* online review.

16 Ceresoli discusses the film in these terms in his interview with A12. Alessandro Ceresoli, interview by A12, *Flash Art*, s. p.

the story of Alice Auma, the Acholi leader of a late-1980s resistance movement against the Ugandan president at the time, Yoweri Musaveni.[17] One panel reproduced a Wikipedia article on Auma, telling us that she was a "spirit-medium" who channelled a dead Italian soldier, Lakwena (meaning 'Messenger'), by which name she is also known.

A final work in glass that accompanied the 2011 exhibition of the *Linea Tagliero* Prototypes in Milan merged the black drawings with the glassworks made in Eritrea. *Jumbo*, from 2009, is a blackened squarish panel of glass, covered in a raised text in Tigrinya (the language predominantly spoken in Eritrea and the Tigray region). Propped up slightly askew against the wall of the gallery, the glass sheet is held in place by an organic mass of material on the floor: a black clay body that acts as a sculptural foot. The work sits uncomfortably between the elegantly pristine Prototypes and the carefully installed two-dimensional works hanging on the gallery walls. Beige cracks appear to have shattered the tempered surface along the right-side edge of the panel; crawling across the sheet from right to left, they lend the work an aesthetic of survival, as if it had endured a fire or other disaster. The text is punctuated by a series of important dates in Eritrea's fight for independence; it ends with the beginning of the Eritrean-Ethiopian War in 1998–2000, also mentioned in *Bloody Thirty Years*, which, effectively, lasted until the countries signed a peace agreement in 2018. As the text is difficult to see on the blackened panel and because Italian viewers, as the general audience of the exhibition, were not normally able to read the predominantly Tigrinya text, the work enacts a visual *withholding* of precise meaning. Ultimately, the work symbolically functions as a sign of refusal, rejecting subjugation by foreign powers.

Ceresoli's Prototypes clearly build on his long-term interest in Futurism, Asmara's architecture and Italian colonialism in East Africa. When situated within the trajectory of Ceresoli's practice, we can see that the *Linea Tagliero* series emphasizes the colonialist ideology that underpins the works of some second-wave Futurists who were also active in Mussolini's Imperialist projects.

17 See Behrend: "The History & Ethnogenesis of the Acholi", pp. 23–29.

Futurist aesthetics of the technological: Aviation in the arts and the 'Italianization of the Mediterranean'

Futurism scholarship has underscored the movement's dedication to the aesthetics of the technological world. Futurism's machine aesthetics were, in many cases, *aesthetic* rather than *functional*, with a particular focus on the spatial, perceptual and psychically transformative experience of "kinetic velocity";[18] and "the thrill of speed."[19] In the period of second-wave Futurism, air travel was connected to military might and, from 1935 onwards, Imperial conquest. Several artists in the later period of Futurism were deeply involved in promoting Fascist politics. Marinetti specifically was a vocal champion of the Ethiopian invasion and colonial war in East Africa, which he celebrated in *Il poema africano* (1937) with the words: "Writers and artists of Italy / I would brutally tell you there is nothing better you can do than fight for Italy in Abyssinia."[20] Although he was also known for his repeated criticism of the régime, his public appearance was, as Günter Berghaus judged, like that of "a chameleon, adapting to the ever-changing circumstances of the regime" and showing a "rather ambivalent character".[21] Whereas close study of Futurists' participation in the invasion of East Africa and celebration of the Italian Empire sheds light on what Ernesto Ialongo has called a "less savory, bellicose, and ultimately Fascist side of Futurism",[22] Marinetti's complex relationship to Africa was also one of identification (beyond his connection to it by birth, in Alexandria, Egypt), as Lucia Re has argued: the invasion of Ethiopia may have offered Italians an "opportunity to re-Africanize themselves, even as they Italianize Ethiopia."[23]

18 Mather: *Futurist Conditions: Imagining Time in Italian Futurism*, pp. 1 and 5.

19 Terrosi: "Futurismo e postumano", p. 264. The original Italian reads: "l'ebbrezza della velocità." Translations, unless otherwise noted, are mine.

20 Marinetti: *Il poema africano della divisione "28 ottobre"*, p. 24. The original Italian reads: "Scrittori e artisti d'Italia / Vi potrei dire brutalmente che non vi è nulla di meglio da fare che combattere per l'Italia in Abissinia". Also see Re: "'Barbari civilizzatissimi': Marinetti and the Futurist Myth of Barbarism", p. 361.

21 Berghaus: *Futurism and Politics: Between Anarchist Rebellion and Fascist Reaction, 1909–1944*, pp. 277–307, quotations on pp. 289 and 290.

22 Ialongo: "Filippo Tommaso Marinetti: The Futurist as Fascist", p. 394.

23 Re: "'Barbari civilizzatissimi'", p. 364.

The aesthetic support that Futurism lent to Fascism in the 1930s is perhaps best exemplified by the bellicose version of *aeropittura*.[24] *Aeropittura*, which celebrated the "shifting perspectives of flight",[25] constituted the primary inspiration of Pettazzi's original design for the station, which emphasizes the aeroplane motif of the building's architectural structure. The bellicose strand was one of several in the heterogeneous terrain of *aeropittura*, which included, among others, a "cosmic, stratospheric, biochemical" version, a mystical version, and one focussed on regional landscapes, as described by Marinetti.[26] Indeed, *aeropittura di guerra* (war aeropainting) was recognized in 1935 by the régime as a key part of Fascist aesthetics.[27]

Aviation and views of the earth seen from above already featured in some Futurist paintings of the 1920s, such as Fedele Azari's *Prospettive di volo* (Flying Perspectives, 1926), exhibited at that year's Venice Biennale.[28] *Aeropittura*, however, took off in the 1930s, as artists such as Tato (Guglielmo Sansoni), Giacomo Balla, Gerardo Dottori, Tullio Crali and others took an interest in the genre, which celebrated mobility, speed and technology. Some sought to give viewers a sensation of visual "shock and awe" and military "invincibility",[29] as Emily Braun has argued in an essay on *aeropittura* as a zenith of artistic devotion to aviation, specifically to military aviation; through this devotion, the Futurists "fantasized their dominion of the air."[30] For these Futurists, aerial perspective could provide voyeuristic enjoyment of Futurist urbanism, spatial superiority and power, which, in the context of Italian colonialism, in some cases asserted racial primacy as well.[31]

These ideals became closely connected to the colonial exigencies after Mussolini's proclamation of the Italian Empire in May 1936. While the Futurists had long celebrated war and technology, by the 1930s, certain members of the movement positioned *aeropittura* as an agent of Italian Imperialism. The *aero* genres were, as Berghaus has demonstrated, "a way for many artists to ingratiate themselves

---

24 Marinetti identified these strands in 1934. See Marinetti: "L'aeropittura futurista inizia una nuova êra della plastica", pp. 11–12.

25 Marinetti et al.: "Manifesto of Aeropainting", p. 283. The original Italian reads: "le prospettive mutevoli del volo".

26 Key primary texts on *aeropittura* include Somenzi: "Aeropittura e aeroscultura (Manifesto tecnico futurista)" from 1928, and Marinetti: "Prospettive del volo e aeropittura", which was the first version of the "Manifesto della aeropittura" [sic], from 1929.

27 Berghaus: *Futurism and Politics*, p. 234.

28 Pizzi: *Italian Futurism and the Machine*, p. 226.

29 Braun: "Shock and Awe", p. 272.

30 Ibid., p. 269.

31 These ideas relate to scholarship on racial superiority and the Tagliero station in Italian colonial Asmara, for example Cianfarani: "The Fascist Legacy in the Built Environment", p. 30.

with the regime. [They] offered plenty of scope for the promulgation of Fascist ideology".[32] For Marinetti, the *aero* genres, as well as Futurist urbanism and architecture, were closely connected to what he called the "Italianizzazione del Mediterraneo" (the Italianization of the Mediterranean), Mussolini's and Italian Fascism's imperial goal.[33]

On 3 November 1936, approximately one year after Italy's invasion of Ethiopia and five months after Mussolini's declaration of the Italian Empire, the second national exhibition of mural décor for Fascist buildings in Italy and Africa (*II Mostra nazionale di plastica murale per l'edilizia fascista in Italia e in Africa*), organized by the *Movimento futurista*, opened in Rome. For the Futurists, colonial architecture was to be inspired by the work of Antonio Sant'Elia. On the occasion of the exhibition, the manifesto *La plastica murale futurista* (Futurist Mural Décor, 1934) was re-published as a leaflet, bringing its aim for "aviator life, sensibility, and perspectives" to Fascist buildings in the Italian Empire.[34] This was the context in which Pettazzi's station was built. Although the architect was not recognized as a Futurist by the movement itself, the building consolidated the Imperial values that certain Futurists aligned themselves with, through its engagement of both bellicose *aeropittura* and the aviation-inspired aesthetics and sensibility desired for Fascist colonial architectural décor.

Glassmaking in colonial Eritrea and the Fascist project of techno-industrial modernity

Explicitly quoting the described mechanical aesthetics of aero-Futurism, Ceresoli's *Linea Tagliero* Prototypes resonate with two visual languages or forms: techno-modernism on the one hand, and the artisanal object, which might be used at home, on the other, as the artist himself has emphasized.[35] For Ceresoli, the artisanal quality of the works comes from their little imprecise 'defects' that distinguish the objects and distance them from industrial products. In 2010, Andrea Balestrero, a member of architectural collective A12, noted in an interview with Ceresoli a merger of architectural and sculptural design in the *Linea Tagliero* Pro-

32 Berghaus: *Futurism and Politics*, p. 247.

33 Marinetti: "Formula letteraria artistica del futurismo nel suo trentennale."

34 Marinetti, et al.: *Un manifesto polemico: La plastica murale futurista* (1934). The original Italian reads: "vita, sensibilità e prospettive aviatorie."

35 Balestrero: "Alessandro Ceresoli", pp. 1–8.

totypes.[36] Five years later, in the exhibition *Nero su bianco* (Black on White, 2015), curated by Lyle Ashton Harris, Robert Storr and Peter Benson Miller at the American Academy of Rome, one of the Prototypes and *Bloody Thirty Years* were shown in a section dedicated to "the colonial legacy."[37] I propose that we read these works in two ways: 1) as visual echoes of colonial techno-modernist aesthetics of second-wave Italian Futurism, and 2) as design objects, which are recognizable as objects for everyday use,[38] whose little imperfections and therefore artisanal quality (characteristics that Ceresoli associates with Eritrean culture) undermine the 'Italian' manufacture of their historical referents. In both ways they are driven by 'gestalts' – in the sense that the contemporary Italian writer and activist Franco 'Bifo' Berardi has used the term to refer to systems that structure vision and power – of empire and commodity aesthetics, in this case, linked to *italianità*.[39] How do these 'gestalts' attract us and how do they fail in these works? How does the series engage with and destabilize these 'gestalts'? How do they relate to the temporal structure of retrofuturism / Retro-Futurism that they deploy?

We might find an answer to these questions when asking ourselves what kind of design objects these works actually are. Their distinctive aesthetic recalls Italian and international Modernist design, while their material evokes an industrial history that is closely connected to Italian Fascist colonial planning. Toward the end of the Second World War, British reports on the former Italian colonies cited glass-making as a 'promising' industry in Eritrea, imported by Italy; England, which occupied Eritrea after the dissolution of Italian East Africa, hoped to develop an export trade.[40] Prior to the colonial period, glassware was imported to Eritrea as a luxury good; during colonialism, glass (along with matches, buttons and leather goods) was one of several "import substituting manufacturing industries"[41] shipped in by the Italians. The industrial machines they brought remained after the end of Fascist colonial rule, although industry abated. Now held at the Istituto Luce, photographic albums of Italian glassworks in Asmara, such as Sava Mirenghi Industria del Vetro, depict Eritrean and Italian working with machinery.[42] As for Jumbo Glass, it retains what appears to be the Italian Fascist architecture for *vetre-*

---

36 Ibid.

37 Harris, Storr and Miller: *Nero su bianco*, pp. 76–79.

38 Ceresoli refers to the table in the series as an 'oggetto riconoscibile, chiaro e di uso comune' (clear, recognizable object for everyday use). Alessandro Ceresoli, interview by A12, *Flash Art*, s. p.

39 Berardi: *Futurability: The Age of Impotence and the Horizon of Possibility*, pp. 103–104.

40 See, for example, M. E. P.: "The Italian Colonial Empire: A Note on Its Rise and Fall—II", p. 265.

41 Araya: "Colonialism and Natural Economy: The Eritrean Case", pp. 168 and 171.

42 See, for example, photos of colonial glass factories in the Fototeca IsIAO. Images of the Sava Mirenghi Glass Industry workers can be found on p. 19, f. 82, of an album on Sava Mirenghi.

rie in colonial Asmara. This history differed from the context of Italian North Africa. Tripoli, for example, already had a school for arts and crafts by the late nineteenth century (1898), under Ottoman rule.[43] In Libya, Italian colonists under Giovanni Volpi sought to preserve, study and 'restore' Indigenous practices to more authentic methods in Tripoli, where jewellery making was a mainstay.[44]

Industry was a cornerstone of Italian Fascism. Periodicals dedicated to different materials and to reporting on all of their uses and advancements proliferated during the *ventennio.* The *Federazione nazionale fascista degli industriali del vetro e della ceramica* (National Fascist Federation of the Industries of Glass and Ceramics) published a monthly journal, *Il vetro* (Glass, Rome, 1938–1943; see Figs. 4 a and b). The Fascist administration photographed glassworks extensively, both at home and in their overseas territories (*l'Oltremare*).[45] During the same period, the International Style in architectural Modernism celebrated the technological achievement of glass-enclosed buildings and skyscrapers. At the same time, in Italy's case, however, Modernist architecture under Fascism often embraced a reduced material repertoire, in which glass was only a part.[46] Doing so was a way to support traditional Italian materials and craftsmanship (and *italianità*) and to position national culture within the field of international Modernism.[47]

Ceresoli's use of neon illumination within the structures lends them a visual aesthetic of radiant, geometric, multi-coloured light that hints at the interests of first-wave Futurism, while his references to Pettazzi's station firmly recall the aero-aesthetics of second-wave Futurism (underscoring strands that had Imperialist, Fascist associations). The lightness of the material – by which I mean the visual weight, transparency and luminosity – confers a Futurist aesthetic of radiant interpenetration and electric light technology. At the same time, the works find analogous objects in the context of modern furniture design in the mid-twentieth

43 Di Pasquale: "La scuola di arti e mestieri di Tripoli in età coloniale (1911–1938)", p. 401.

44 McLaren: "The Italian Colonial appropriation of Indigenous North African Architecture in the 1930's", p. 166.

45 For more on Italian colonial documentation of Asmara through the *Società Africana d'Italia* and the Istituto Italiano per l'Africa e l'Oriente or IsIAO, see Palma: "Sleeping Memory in Italian Archives: Historical Photographs of Asmara and Italy's Controversial Relationship with its Colonial Past", p. 89.

46 Panzini: "Pines, Palms, and Holm Oaks: Historicist Modes in Modern Italian Cityscapes", p. 129.

47 Coloured-glass panelling that was common in colonial architecture in Asmara might be understood as reminiscent of artisanal mosaics that were revived in the period as part of Italian Fascist modernity. This seems especially important given the primacy of murals to Futurist contemplation of colonial architecture. For current research on the 'return to craft' under Fascism and the proliferation of glass mosaic in Futurist murals of the period, see Lindeman: "Plastica murale, Arte polimaterica, and Futurist Materials of Empire."

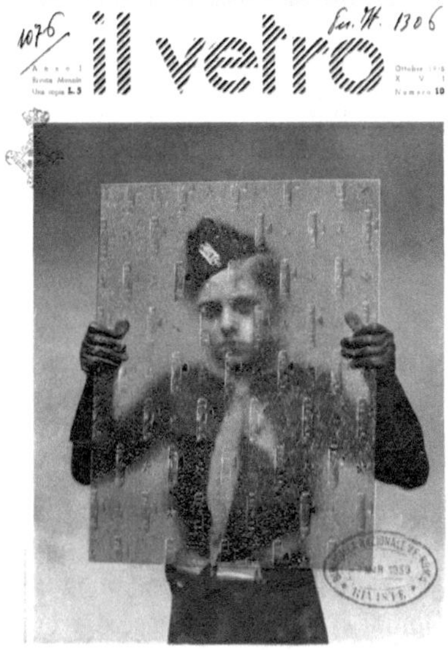

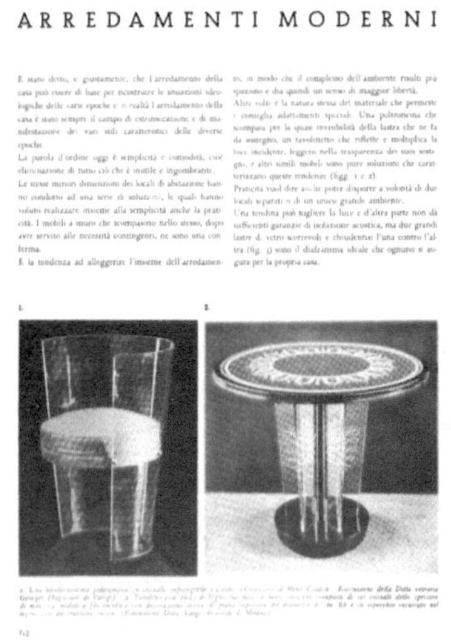
ARREDAMENTI MODERNI

Fig. 4a: Cover of *Il vetro: Rivista mensile* 16:10 (October 1938), showing a boy holding up a piece of glass with *Littorio* fasces reported on in the journal. **Fig. 4b:** An illuminated glass table is the paragon of modern furniture, in the Fascist journal *Il vetro: Rivista mensile* 16:2 (February 1938). The caption reads: "Tavolino con fusto di legno lucidato in nero, sostegni composti di sei cristalli dello spessore di mm. 12 molati con decorazione incisa" (Small table with black-lit wood shaft, supports composed of six highly polished glass sheets, each 12 mm thick, with incised decoration).

century. For example, *Prototipo 05* resembles illuminated mirror glass tables, e.g., those produced by Ditta Luigi Brusotti di Milano, touted in Fascist glass magazines as "modern furnishings" (*arredamenti moderni*, see Fig. 4b). Ceresoli's works combine national and international Modernisms, not dissimilar to Futurism's navigation of ultranationalism and internationalism (the terrain of Imperialism). He thus highlights the contradiction between Marinetti's desire to Africanize Italians, at a time when Mussolini sought to Italianize African regions.[48]

We might find another Futurist precedent for Ceresoli in the little-known "luminous" sculptural objects of Futurist architect and set designer Luciano Baldessari (1896–1982), such as the columnar *Luminator* (1929), amongst other prismatic,

48 On Marinetti as ultra-nationalist and internationalist, see Berghaus: *Futurism and Politics*, p. 290. On re-Africanization, see Re: "'Barbari civilizzatissimi': Marinetti and the Futurist Myth of Barbarism", p. 364.

pyramidal and cylindrical forms in transparent materials and other media, one of the surviving prototypes for which he used as a coat rack. Baldessari showed extensively with international Modernists but never joined the Fascist Party. This, in effect, hindered his career and he left Italy in December 1939.[49] With Baldessari in mind, Ceresoli's work makes us think not only of Fascist Futurism but also of the diminished histories of an a-Fascist Futurism, for which they offer a future that might have been.

Postcolonial re-codings: Ceresoli's *Ritorno al futuro*

Ceresoli's artist's book *Ritorno al futuro* (see Fig. 5) offers a poly-temporal model of histories and futures that provides further insight into the stakes of the *Linea Tagliero* Prototypes. Varied chronologies frame the many visual correspondences we find in the book between vernacular and colonial architecture. These correspondences complicate familiar attempts to neatly narrate what is Italian and Eritrean, and which Modernism and modernity belongs to whom. The book, for example, includes photographs of Italian colonial architecture (especially of the late 1930s), such as the Commercial Building (1938) at Fenkil Street, designed by architect Lucio Masakili, and the Alfa Romeo building (1937–38, architect unknown), whose façade is still marked by two fasces as sculptural decoration. Now in disrepair, Ceresoli juxtaposes these structures with scenes of everyday life and vernacular architectural decoration. Readers of the book will find images of the following: signs for the removed monument to fallen Italian colonial soldiers at their defeat by Ethiopia in the 1887 Battle of Dogali, held near Massawa; graveyards (Italian and Eritrean); and images of stray cats, recapitulated in the relief image of a leopard standing in profile, plant life growing underneath it, marking old Fascist decorations on building facades in a kind of visual slant rhyme for the Capitoline wolf. One photograph captures pink and black shapes painted on an exterior plastered wall. These shapes are echoed in Ceresoli's works: the first prototype in the series is decorated with a painted dark-pink ovoid form, marking the intersection between base and tabletop.

We might consider this mark to be a postcolonial re-coding of both Italian Modernist (specifically Fascist, Futurist) form and Asmara as an Italian-built environment. In another example, a photograph of brightly coloured weavings on bedframes, printed on the side of one page, finds its echo on the verso of its facing

49 On Baldessari and his "luminous objects", see De Seta: *Architettura futurista*, [pp. 18–19].

page, in a patterned wall of coloured glass in the rear of a bowling alley. In another example still, white crenellated Coptic crosses that mark local graves are juxtaposed with images of elaborately frosted cake designs and doilies that decorate bakery windows. Yet again, scenes of sun-bleached animal bones respond to a painted interior mural featuring a gazelle and baobab tree; we see a photograph of the latter on another page, thereby extending this visual correspondence between Ceresoli's images. In a final example, the turquoise blue of a vintage Italian car is captured in a display platform painted the same colour that showcases concrete sculptures of leopards, an example of local wildlife and a national symbol found on Eritrean coins (see Fig. 5).

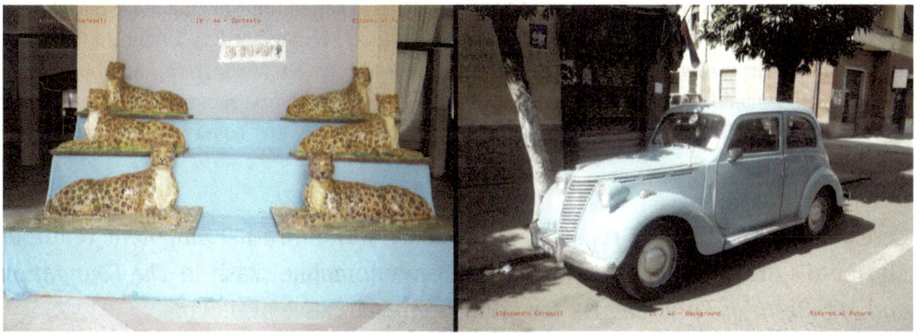

Fig. 5: Alessandro Ceresoli: *Ritorno al futuro* (Milano: Mousse, 2011), pp. 10–11.

Ceresoli's project ultimately undermines nationalist narratives and a worldview closely connected to European colonialism. Asmara is captured as a space of visual dialogue and polysemy that corrodes the forceful iconography, visual dominance and totalitarian ideology of Italian Fascism. *Ritorno al futuro* does not give us the future envisioned by Fascism. It disrupts Fascism's modernist, genocidal 'utopia' by being distinctly postcolonial and celebratory of the Eritrean vernacular and local subsumption of 'Italian' heritage.

The book's only two-page images, spanning the bifold, include photographs of Pettazzi's Tagliero station and of the transporting of Ceresoli's works from Asmara to Milan via the *Linea Messina* shipping line. These images emphasize the *double entrendre* between *line* as design set and *line* as transit route, not to mention the visual and geographical expanses of the station's wings and the cross-Mediterranean shipping path captured by the bifold image.

In addition to these visual cues is Ceresoli's retrospective narrative of travelling to Asmara and seeing streets and buildings from his taxi window. Framing *Ritorno al futuro*, the narrative reads as a colonial travelogue that echoes the human desire for travel but also the Eurocentric (and European Modernist) fetishization of Africa. Marinetti's primitivist fascination with Africa appeared in countless Futurist writings.[50] Similarly, Ceresoli says that he was drawn by a "mysterious instinct" to Asmara and then had a six-month "stay in Africa"[51] (the potentially generalizing refence to 'Africa' seems to imply that he travelled elsewhere on the continent; yet, he did not leave Eritrea.) Ceresoli's text begins:

> I don't know exactly what I was seeking, but a mysterious instinct led me to Asmara, the crowded capital of Eritrea. It was four in the morning and after getting through customs I waited for over two hours, for a person who never showed up. My trip began with an episode that, after the fact, seems like a leitmotiv [sic] of the whole experience, which began in this city and ended thousands of miles away. In the six months of my stay in Africa, hidden, I had the subtle sensation of waiting (perhaps in vain) for thoughts, people, revelations. At the time I didn't know that the waiting would become a surreal gap in time, lasting more than a year. Getting back to that night spent in restless expectation, I remember [...]. I went [to the hotel] from the airport by taxi, staring through the window at fragments of streets and buildings. I can still remember some of the signs. Everything about those first moments of dawn is very vague now. But I still have some flashbacks, clear fragments that come to the surface in my memory.[52]

Ceresoli's text ultimately reads as a markedly slowed, rather impotent redux of Marinetti's own account of his rebirth in an automobile crash in *The Foundation and Manifesto of Futurism.* He too situates his narrative at dawn:

> "Let's be off! See there, the Earth's very first dawn! Nothing can equal the splendor of the sun's red sword slicing through our millennial darkness, for the very first time!" [...] A furious

50 Some of the studies on this topic include: Mikkonen: "Artificial Africa in the European Avant-Garde: Marinetti and Tzara", pp. 391–407; Contini: *Le Afriche di Marinetti: Viaggio nelle pagine africane del 'barbaro futurista'*; and Tomasello: "Marinetti: Tra territorio del mito e l'estetizzazione dell'Africa," pp. 83–120. On Marinetti's interest in the Black Atlantic, see Marzioli: "Cannibalizing the Black Atlantic in F.T. Marinetti's Interwar Writing," pp. 547–572.

51 Balestero: "Alessandro Ceresoli", pp. 1–8.

52 "Non so esattamente cosa stavo cercando ma un istinto misterioso mi ha portato ad Asmara, la popolata capitale dell'Eritrea. Erano le quattro del mattino e, passata la dogana, ho attesa per oltre due ore una persona che non è mai arrivata. Il mio viaggio inizia con un episodio che, a posteriori, è stato il leitmotiv di questa esperienza, cominciata in questa città e finita a migliaia di chilometri di distanza. Nei sei mesi di permanenza in Africa, nascosta, ho avuto la sottile sensazione di aspettare (forse invano) pensieri, persone, rivelazioni. Allora ero ignaro che l'aspettare sarebbe diventato un intervallo di tempo surreale durato oltre un anno. [...] Ritornando a quella notte avvolta d'attesa e di inquietudine, ricordo [...] Ho percorso il tragitto dall'aeroporto alla pensione in taxi, scorgendo dal finestrino frammenti di strade, palazzi, ricordo qualche scritta. Tutto è molto vago ora di quelle prime luci dell'alba. Ma di allora ho alcuni flashback, distini frammenti che emergono dalla mia memoria." Ceresoli: *Ritorno al futuro*, unattributed English translation, p. 43; original Italian, p. 2.

> gust of madness tore us out of ourselves and hurled us along roads as deep and plunging as the beds of torrents. Every now and then a feeble light, flickering behind some windowpane, made us mistrust the calculations of our all-too-fallible eyes. [...] I swung the car right around sharply, with all the crazy irrationality of a dog biting its own tail. Then suddenly a pair of cyclists came toward me, gesticulating that I was on the wrong side, dithering about in front of me like two different lines of thought, both persuasive but for all that, quite contradictory. Their stupid uncertainty was in my way ... How ridiculous! What a nuisance! ... I braked hard and to my disgust the wheels left the ground and I flew into a ditch... O mother of a ditch, brimful with muddy water! [...] How I relished your strength-giving sludge that reminded me so much of the saintly black breast of my Sudanese nurse...When I got myself up – soaked, filthy, foul-smelling rag that I was – from beneath my overturned car, I had a wonderful sense of my heart being pierced by the red-hot sword of joy![53]

Yet, Ceresoli is uncertain where Marinetti is bombastic in his conviction; Ceresoli endures long unexpected delays and waiting times where Marinetti experiences unbridled, dangerous speed. Ceresoli then narrates his encounter with the Tagliero station and how it endured in his memory:

> Like the memory of those first moments after my arrival, I also carry with me an image that has taken on the character of a sort of symptom, or a premonition. To my great surprise, and with the sense of enchantment that can only accompany a revelation, during that taxi ride I saw what had brought me – now I can say it with certainty – all the way to Asmara: the futuristic gas station from 1938, "Fiat Tagliero." The Impression, though vague, was of having found the initial fragment that would lead me to put together what, almost two years later, would be completed with the show in Milan. Intense, dazzling, like an [sic] flash of intuition, this image filled me with a sense of happiness, for a few seconds.[54]

The artist describes here, first with fervour and excitement, and then seemingly with sudden regret, what we might call a mode of mnemonic perception. In this case, the visual primacy of the Tagliero station in his first encounter results in an "impression" of its image upon him, which thereafter serves as a "symptom" or "premonition."[55] For Ceresoli, that is, a visual memory of Asmara constitutes

53 Marinetti: "The Foundation and Manifesto of Futurism," pp. 12–13.

54 "Così come il ricordo dell'attesa dei primi istanti dell'arrivo, mi è rimasta impressa un'immagine che è diventata una sorta di sintomo o premonizione. Con grande sorpresa e con l'incantesimo che solo le rivelazioni sembrano possedere, durante il percorso ho visto quello che – ora lo posso dire con certezza – mi aveva condotto fino ad Asmara: la futuristica stazione di benzina del 1938 'Fiat Tagliero'. L'impressione, anche se vaga, era di aver trovato il tassello iniziale che mi avrebbe portato a comporre quello che quasi due anni dopo, avrei ultimato con la mostra a Milano. Intensa, folgorante, come fosse un'illuminazione, quest'immagine, per qualche secondo mi riempì di una sensazione di felicità." Ceresoli: *Ritorno al futuro*, unattributed English translation, p. 43; original Italian, p. 2.

55 Ceresoli: *Ritorno al futuro*, p. 2.

the generative encounter for the series. This mode of perception aligns with what Bifo has discussed in his recent essays on power, automation and vision. For Bifo,

> power [is] the temporary condition of implementation of a selection among many possibilities. I call power a regime of visibility and invisibility: the exclusion of different possible concatenations from the space of visibility. A form emerges from many possible forms, then it turns into a gestalt, a format of perception of the surrounding reality. The gestalt is a perceptual code: a form that generates forms. This is power.[56]

Bifo's view of capitalism as a "semiotic gestalt" resembles Ceresoli's impressions of Asmara: what he *recognizes* is less the symbol of Italian Fascist modernity than a visually attractive Italian Modernist building, a dizzying, awe-inspiring experience for viewers.[57] In the resulting series, however, the symbolic function of the Fascist building is alluded to in the title; it asks us to consider the histories of this late, colonial version of the Italian avant-garde, specifically of those Futurists of the late 1930s to 1940s who endorsed the Italian Empire. This version of the avant-garde now reads as if it is characterized by an *arretratezza*, a 'backwardness', a retrofuturism, as Ceresoli would describe late-Fascist colonial architecture more generally. In the interview by A12 in *Flash Art*, Ceresoli commented on Fascist-era Rationalist architecture, such as that of Gruppo 7, often celebrated for its aesthetic innovation: "The architecture of the regime in Eritrea does nothing but evoke an Italianness that aspires to the avant-garde but expresses itself with backwardness."[58] In written correspondence to me, Ceresoli expanded on this point: '[What I said] meant to underscore that the real architectonic innovation, often erroneously connected to Fascism, was proposed and realized by the same architects who had distanced themselves from the régime."[59]

Some of Ceresoli's views align with outdated readings of first-wave Futurism that see its emulation of the visual effects of mechanical media in non-mechanical, conventional media (painting, e. g.) as "too literal, almost backward". Such a discursive construction of *retardataire* Futurism, as David Mather has described it, finds

---

56 Berardi: *Futurability: The Age of Impotence and the Horizon of Possibility*, pp. 103–104.

57 Braun: "Shock and Awe: Futurist 'Aeropittura' and the Theories of Giulio Douhet", p. 272.

58 "L'architettura di regime in Eritrea non fa altro che evocare un'italianità che ambiva all'avanguardia ma si esprimeva con arretratezza." Alessandro Ceresoli, interview by A12, *Flash Art*, s. p.

59 "Dunque, la mia frase voleva sottolineare che la vera innovazione architettonica spesso collegata erroneamente al fascismo, è stata proposta e realizzata dagli stessi architetti che hanno preso le distanze dal regime." Alessandro Ceresoli, e-mail correspondence with me, 15 April 2020. Ceresoli referred here to the early innovative work of Rationalist architecture collective Gruppo 7, for example, before Fascism became a totalitarian regime. The later architecture associated with Fascism at its peak, for Ceresoli, was "a monumental and political rationalism, with a decidedly inferior design quality."

that in "having accelerated to meet the demands of the modern world, they arrived too late or not at all".[60] But Ceresoli's works do not position all Futurists as retrograders in their use of conventional media, or as flawed in the practical execution of the ideas expressed in their theoretical statements. The retrofuturism they describe in Futurism comes into view via a postcolonial critique: by illuminating anew its connections to the régime and to Italian colonialism. Whether it was or not, the Tagliero station is positioned as a precedent of late-colonial Futurism for Ceresoli's postcolonial Retro-Futurism, which models the legacy of second-wave Futurism associated with Fascism and the Italian Empire as a 'weak Futurism'.[61] This critique is made even more powerful by dint of the visual irony between Ceresoli's grounded objects and the station's impressive 'futuristic' architectural achievement in its massive, seemingly unsupported wingspan. The Italianness evoked by Ceresoli's Retro-Futurist (and retrofuturist) objects, therefore, redoubles this backwardness: the backwardness of late-Futurism and late colonial Modernism (better known in Le Corbusier's work in Africa, including urban plans and buildings in North and East Africa), and the backwardness, perhaps, of continuing to be enthralled with Italian Modernist architecture in Asmara today.

Sean Anderson has discussed the timing of colonial architecture in Asmara with an awareness of the then-future construction of the Italian Empire, contingent upon what he calls a "reframing of the modern for the Italian colonies".[62] The goal for Italian urban planning and modern architecture was to create a "visible campaign to build a forward-looking image".[63] In Ceresoli's series, then, colonialism's future is positioned as an encounter with and recollection of a Futurist vision that has since passed, both politically and formally. Ceresoli's use of what is now historical Futurism (politically and formally) is explored along the series, fashioned as a line of prototypes in the style of second-wave Italian Futurism (1920–1944), which itself had already become a Retro-Futurism of sorts, to *primo futurismo* (1909–1915).[64] Here, we have indeed a prototype, a mechanical and aes-

---

60 Mather: *Futurist Conditions*, p. 4.

61 I borrow 'weak Futurism' from Fisher: "Futurism and Radio", pp. 246–247.

62 Anderson: *Modern Architecture and Its Representation in Colonial Eritrea: An In-visible Colony, 1890–1941*, p. 83.

63 Ibid., p. 84.

64 Cesare De Seta has noted the complexity of naming second-wave Futurism, as "second-generation" Futurism or "Neo-Futurism", although he dismisses the importance of terminology. Instead, he cites the fact that architects knew they would have to continue to "come to terms with Futurism", whether or not they were associated with the movement for significant periods. See De Seta: *Architettura futurista*, p. [6].

thetic model from which an eventual reproducible copy might be made: an unfulfilled *antecedent* to something that has not yet or perhaps never will come.

Postcolonial 'chronophobia':[65] Pettazzi's petrol station and Fascist architecture in Eritrea

Examination of these issues requires an overview of Italian Modernist architecture in Eritrea and what Ceresoli (and others) have interpreted as 'Futurist'. The Pettazzi station, among other coeval structures highlighted in Ceresoli's artist's book, aligned with the technological model of Italian modernity advanced under Fascism. The station's cantilevered roof spans over one hundred feet; positioned at a key crossroads in Asmara, it seems to have just alighted or to be about to depart. In the context of 1938, it could be seen as a reminder of Italian aerial warfare that had massacred tens of thousands in Libya, Eritrea and Ethiopia. As Cianfarani has argued, for local Indigenous communities it was connected with both race terror and Italian race supremacy.[66] This was not exceptional: Fascist building programmes (engineering and architectural) in colonial cities, and the "quasi-Futurist mechanization" of cities they enacted, as Sean Anderson has noted, were often aligned with ideas of Italian and European racial superiority.[67] The station is, however, one of the few Italian buildings realized in Africa that are deemed to be 'Futurist'.[68] To this day, it remains a marvel of technological achievement in architecture, a symbol of Italian occupation of East Africa and the Italian-ness of Asmara as a colonial city.

65 I use this term as invoked by Pamela Lee in her book *Chronophobia: On Time in the Art of the 1960s.*

66 Cianfarani: "The Fascist Legacy in the Built Environment", p. 30.

67 Anderson: *In-visible Colonies: Modern Architecture and Its Representation in Colonial Eritrea, 1890–1941* (2006), pp. 140–141, quotation p. 141.

68 Berghaus: "Futurist Utopias", pp. 489–90. Other examples of Italian colonial modern architecture in Asmara include commercial, mixed use, public and residential buildings by the architects Aldo Burzagli, Roberto Capellano, Antonio Vitaliti and Giuseppe Arata. While Asmara is frequently referred to in popular and scholarly discourse alike as a city of Futurist architecture, these examples (aside from Pettazzi's station) are more in line with Italian Art Déco Modernism than Futurist architectural forms. This list of modern Italian buildings and architects in Asmara comes from Sean Anderson's excellent study on Italian modernist architecture, *Modern Architecture and Its Representation in Colonial Eritrea.* On *architettura aerea*, which declared the addition of aviation to Sant'Elia's 1914 "Manifesto dell'architettura futurista", see Marinetti, Mazzoni, and Somenzi: "Manifesto futurista dell'architettura aerea", p. 3. For more on architecture in second-wave Futurism, see Godoli: *Il futurismo: Guida all'architettura moderna* and Sabatino: "Architecture".

In the years after the Second World War, films and other media addressed Italy's colonial past, focussing on the (European) modern temporality that remains attached to Asmara in the context of Africa. In the 1950s, amidst Italy's "long decolonization" of East Africa (a process that would last until 1960),[69] as Pamela Ballinger has described this period, documentary footage of Italian cinemas, schools and other areas of East Africa was common. One film, the documentary feature *Una lettera dall'Africa* (A Letter from Africa, 1951), produced by Leonardo Bonzi for Istituto Nazionale Luce, is particularly noteworthy. The film takes the form of a road trip from Tripoli, beginning on the Fascist coastal highway, the *strada litoranea*, all the way to Mogadishu. As the car traverses the expanse of Italy's recently lost colonies in North and East Africa, it gives viewers a cinematic tour of Italy's former colonies. From the perspective of the passenger in an Italian car (itself a sign of Italian industry brought by colonialism), we see railways, automobiles and streets mark the entrance to Asmara, while the narrator announces: "Asmara, sogno d'Italia" (Asmara, dream of Italy). The end of the Fascist colonial state of AOI in 1941 may have been the end of the Italian Fascist dream in East Africa, but as historian Nicola Labanca would later write: "Il sogno dell'impero era sfumato" (The dream of Empire had faded). However, as the narrator tells us, many colonists remained.[70] The narrator's wistful delivery exemplifies Italian colonial nostalgia or *mal d'Africa.*[71]

The cinematic medium perhaps underscores the neo-colonial scopophilia of not only being close to, but *seeing* an Italian colonial city again. This is distinct from "temporal loss as remedied by geographical repositioning", as Rhiannon Noel Welch has read *mal d'Africa.*[72] The narrator of the film provides us with the timeline of the colonial cultivation of Asmara and nearby Massawa, lauding Asmara for "always conserving the noble air of the garden city".[73] Images of Italian architecture and urbanism function as visual testimony for the viewer. The con-

69 Ballinger: *The World Refugees Made: Decolonization and the Foundation of Postwar Italy*, p. 19.
70 Labanca: *Oltremare: Storia dell'espansione coloniale italiana*, p. 210. Fourteen thousand Italians were enrolled in schools in Asmara at the time.
71 On Italian oral recollections of fond memories in the colonies, see Fuller: "Italy's Colonial Futures," n. p.
72 Welch: "Here and Then, There and Now: Nation Time and Colonial Space in Pasolini, Oriani and Marinetti", p. 628.
73 In the original soundtrack: "Asmara conservò sempre la sua aria signorile di città giardino." *Una lettera dall'Africa,* directed by Leonardo Bonzi, with Manulo Lualdi (Istituto Nazionale Luce, 1951), colour, 1:10.05.

cern here is chronological: the filming relays an anxiety about the prospective aging of these colonial 'gifts' to East Africa.[74]

Recent scholarship on Fascist colonial architecture in Asmara by Sean Anderson (2016) and Francesco Cianfarani (2020) situate Pettazzi's work as part of the 'civilizing' and fear-inducing modernity of Italian colonial architecture.[75] These critical works stand in contrast to other publications on Asmara as 'Africa's secret modernist city' or 'Africa's jewel of modernity' that subjugate African modernity to colonial (Eurocentric) modernity.[76] Marco Tagliafierro has argued that the *Linea Tagliero* Prototypes elucidate the historiographic marginalization of Eritrean communities to histories of Modernism but nevertheless reinscribe readings of Eritreans as having only "been touched by it".[77]

Pettazzi's station was built only two years after the end of Italy's second Ethiopian invasion, in which the Italian air force murdered thousands in chemical warfare. The Italian station-as-aeroplane was an architectural marvel associated with Fascist militarism and technological achievement in aviation.[78] The Tagliero station was built in the same year as Italo Balbo, then Governor of Italian North Africa in Libya, visited Eritrea; footage of his landing was documented and screened by the Giornale Luce newsreel on 18 May 1938. Today, it might also be associated with a failed Imperial project and the aesthetics of aero-Futurism in the field of architecture. This vision, however atavistic, nevertheless dazzled Ceresoli in his visit in 2009, and he is not alone in his interest in this symbol and its history. Mia Fuller has referred to the distinctive endurance of the Italian "refashioning" of Asmara as an extreme case of "colonial inertia" and adds: "Asmara's colonial architecture and urban layout are so unchanged today that they remain uncannily close to the Italian image in which they were designed."[79] The colonial inertia, or put differently, coloniality of Pettazzi's building, persists.[80]

---

74 Leonardo Bonzi, with Manulo Lualdi, *Una Lettera dall'Africa* (Istituto Nazionale Luce, 1951), colour, 1:10.05.

75 Anderson: *Modern Architecture and Its Representation in Colonial Eritrea: An In-visible Colony, 1890–1941*; Cianfarani: "The Fascist Legacy in the Built Environment", p. 30.

76 See, for example, Denison, Ren and Gebremedhin: *Asmara: Africa's Secret Modernist City*; and Visscher, photography by Boness: *Asmara: Africa's Jewel of Modernity*.

77 Tagliafierro: "Alessandro Ceresoli, Franesca Minini", p. 30.

78 In her discussion of Italian success in aviation, Braun notes the RAI was the only such air force outside of Great Britain. See Braun: "Shock and Awe", p. 269, and Arcangeli: "Guidonia, City of the Air: A Lost Identity", p. 213.

79 Fuller: "Italy's Colonial Futures", s. p.

80 I use 'coloniality' here in the sense of enduring colonial power, after the fact, as defined by Mignolo: *Local Histories/Global Designs: Coloniality, Subaltern Knowledges, and Border Thinking*.

Known in Italy and East Africa as *Piccola Roma* or 'Little Rome', since the period of Italian (liberal and Fascist) colonial rule (1890–1947), the city (and now UNESCO World Heritage Site) is distinguished by Italian Modernist architecture, infrastructure and urban design that dates to the early decades of the twentieth century, following the city's transition from military outpost to capital of Italy's East African territories in 1899, and by 1939 to the largest "'Italian town' of the Italian empire", as Ceresoli's quotation of Wikipedia in his artist's book tells us.[81] Asmara fell as a colonial city on 1 April 1941, during the demise of AOI.[82]

Retro-Futurism: Echoes of Pettazzi in the *Linea Tagliero* Prototypes

Tabletops in the series (in Prototype 01, of which there are variations in Prototypes 02–05) visually and structurally echo the Fiat station's wing-shaped roof, which has made it an icon of Futurist and Italian Modernist architecture in East Africa.[83] In Ceresoli's adaptation, however, a key element has been inverted. The horizontally elongated, triangular beams that help *suspend* the load of the cantilevered wings and anchor them to the central structure of the Fiat station, now *uphold* the cantilevered surface (tabletops) from below. This is the case in all of the Prototypes that quote this architectural element (five of the six). The visual magic of the building, with its seemingly impossible wide wingspan, is gone. While the Fiat station seems to have just alighted on the ground, still in motion (a suggestion amplified by the arrow of the Fiat sign pointing downwards), the *Linea Tagliero* Prototypes, by contrast, seem to have just opened their wings, which require (visually legible) support from below. The station and association with Futurism it embodies (that is, Fascist Futurism) have been inverted by Ceresoli's objects: the Prototypes, so to speak, turn Futurism on its Fascist head.

This correspondence is also recapitulated in the colour palette of Ceresoli's series. The Prototypes are made of cut rectangular and geometric facets of sky-blue, white, goldenrod-yellow, mint and brick-red glass. Ceresoli's palette is taken from the colours of accents on the original Tagliero building and surrounding pavement, and views of the blue sky seen through the glass. One can detect the correspondence between the pavement that is grounding the central structure of the building and the saturated pink oblong shape in the rear prototype, the first

81 Tecle-Misghina: *Asmara, an Urban History*, pp. 38–42.
82 Labanca: *Oltremare*, p. 210.
83 The measurement comes from Cianfarani: "The Fascist Legacy in the Built Environment", p. 30.

in the series. These colours recall the palette and environmental semiotics of red earth (*terra*), blue sky and sea (*cielo, mare*), and yellow sand and sun often seen in Italian colonial industrial design and advertisements. These colours are also found in print advertisements for Fascist exhibitions, as in a display card designed by Ugo Giammusso and Corrado Mancioli for the colonial exhibition of the *Prima mostra triennale delle Terre Italiane d'Oltremare* (First Triennial Exhibition of Overseas Italian Territories), held in Naples in 1940. In that image, a sandaled, green, patinated-copper foot of an animated Roman colossus, trailed by his blood-red cape, steps across the blue strip of the sea onto the yellow sands of Italian Africa.[84] With this colonial palette in mind, Ceresoli's works seem to offer strange echoes of the promises of the colonies as natural resources, as spaces of terrestrial conquest and environmental health. They also echo the connection between Italian industry and colonial environments, suggested by visual media and propaganda in Fascist Italy. As design objects themselves, they also underscore the commoditization of the colony as a natural domain (devoid of people) waiting to be occupied.

These formal and symbolic correspondences, inversions and mirrorings underscore the temporal operations the series enacts: from history to present, from historical Futurism to present Retro-Futurism, and from colonial Futurism to postcolonial Retro-Futurism. The contemporary prototypes (for absent future models) navigate former colonial fantasy. They get to what Rhiannon Noel Welch has called the "discursive afterlife of Italian colonialism", with a critical approach to this legacy.[85] As prototypes, they posit mass-produced objects that show us what will come. As a discrete set of unique objects, however, presented as works of art to be gazed upon, they reposition the colonial project referred to, as being ultimately unfulfilled. The works also undermine the colonial logic of glass production and working in Asmara. On every object, we see the logo of Jumbo Glass. Ceresoli documented the construction of the works undertaken by his Eritrean collaborators. Describing the process of sending the structures to Italy as an odyssey, he remarked: "This problematic and slow-going cooperation gave life to a contemporary odyssey, where bureaucratic cavils, customs problems, interruptions and hiccups in communication temporarily blocked the transport of the objects from Africa to Europe."[86]

84 I thank Emily Braun, whose inclusion of this display card in her previously cited essay on *aeropittura* brought my attention to this work.

85 Welch: "Nation Time and Colonial Space in Pasolini, Oriani and Marinetti", p. 628.

86 The original Italian reads: "Questa cooperazione, problematica e lenta, ha dato vita ad un'odissea contemporanea, dove cavilli burocratici, problemi doganali, comunicazioni interrotte e a sin-

The difficulty of exporting the works from Eritrea to Italy outlined by Ceresoli in the above passage invites us to consider the series' commentary on historical colonial logics of economy. The machines, materials, and practices for glassmaking were historically imported by Italy *into* colonial Eritrea to avoid the expense of having to import glass *from* Italy for the Italian colonists living in Eritrea. Ceresoli's objects were made on the site of a colonial-era glassworks in Asmara, and Ceresoli had to transport them out of Eritrea 'back' to Italy after he returned there. He had some difficulty in doing so. Such a postcolonial repatriation of Italian colonialism registers an inversion of power. The problem of getting 'Italian' objects made by Eritreans in Asmara, with practices and machines inherited from Italian colonial industry, highlights the severance of Asmara as a peripheral city from Italy, its former centre.[87]

Two works by contemporary artists who have also addressed histories of Italian Fascism in East Africa exemplify the range of artistic approaches today to Italian colonial Futurism, that is, the range of approaches to this Retro-Futurism. First, the series *Asmara Dream* (2006–2008) by contemporary Italian photographer Marco Barbon (b. 1972) captures the Tagliero station in soft focus, in one of the fifty-one images that reflect on Asmara as a colonial fantasy and 'new Rome in Africa'. While Barbon also sees the series as a "triple dream", in which the second and third are Eritrean independence from Ethiopia and emigration to "better futures beyond [Eritrea's borders]", colonial utopia is allowed to continue unchecked, in a city that is perceived to be marked by "the suspension of time and history."[88]

By contrast, the work of Wu Ming 2 and Palermo-based artistic collective Fare Ala has addressed Italian colonialism more broadly from this period with regard to military aviation, race terror and chemical warfare. In an intervention from their project *Viva Menilicchi!* (Long Live Menelik! 2018), made for the European biennial *Manifesta 12*, in Palermo, they posted in advertising spaces documentary images of the horrifically blistered hands, faces and wounded bodies of Ethiopian victims of Italian chemical warfare, organized by the General Vincenzo Magliocco, the general in charge of Fascist Italy's air force in East Africa, still honoured in Palermo's street names. The violent images of Fascist terror in Africa interrupt the amnesia for colonialism perpetuated in Italy. As they show passers-by images of aero-mili-

ghiozzo, hanno bloccato temporaneamente il trasporto delle opere dall'Africa all'Europa." Ceresoli: *Ritorno al futuro*, n. p. Unattributed translation.

87 I thank Brian McLaren for his suggestion to think about histories of artisanal industry and potential inversion of imports/exports in the former colonies.

88 Barbon, untitled and undated statement, *Asmara Dream* (2006–2008): www.marcobarbon.com/work/the-ruse-ay2wd.

tary genocide in Italian colonialism, Wu Ming 2 and Fare Ala offer us an opportunity to contemplate that which is unseen for many in the Tagliero station.

Postcolonial Retro-Futurism: An ending, an opening

By this point, I have established that the *Linea Tagliero* Prototypes' Retro-Futurist vision is invested in both materials and the image of flight. Glass products could be artworks in international Modernism or signs of Imperial identity in Fascist Italy. Ceresoli's translation of the Pettazzi station into a series of objects for domestic interiors no longer projects the 'invincibility' associated with Italian aviation in Fascist times.

Ceresoli's glass prototypes tenuously fashion the postcolonial present in tension with the retrofuturism that persists in Asmara. 'Colonial inertia' is one way to read this enduring vision of Asmara as an 'Italian' city. Indeed, for many, this is what makes Asmara a world cultural heritage site. As we gaze into and through the mirrored and transparent surfaces of Ceresoli's series, his prototypes ask us to reflect on their history, on Italy and Eritrea's histories, and on the damages, fantasies and afterlives of the Italian Empire. As we reflect on these histories, we reflect on ourselves and on the attraction these objects invoke in us.

What I would like to propose, however, is the following: what happens through postcolonial Retro-Futurism, in this case, is not only a critical reflection on the politics of history and the futures these histories have imagined. Exporting Ceresoli's *Linea Tagliero* Prototypes from Eritrea to Italy also symbolically exports the future (and a certain version of Futurism) imagined during Fascist times back to the former metropole and centre of the Italian Empire from whence it came. Ceresoli's objects insist on a re-designing of the Future that the Tagliero station represented in East Africa under Fascism. The works suggest that these retrofutures failed; no objects will follow from these tests. They are prototypes that enact the failure of second-wave Futurism and of the Italian Empire. Postcolonial Retro-Futurism shows us that going back to the Future means precisely that other futures have been realized and will continue to unfold.

Bibliography

Anderson, Sean: *In-visible Colonies: Modern Architecture and Its Representation in Colonial Eritrea, 1890–1941.* Ph.D. Dissertation. Los Angeles/CA: University of California, 2006.

Anderson, Sean: *Modern Architecture and Its Representation in Colonial Eritrea: An In-visible Colony, 1890–1941.* Abingdon: Routledge, 2016.

Araya, Mesfin: "Colonialism and Natural Economy: The Eritrean Case." *Northeast African Studies* 13:2–3 (1991): 165–190.

Arcangeli, Luca: "Guidonia, City of the Air: A Lost Identity." Kay Bea Jones, and Stephanie Pilat, eds.: *The Routledge Companion to Italian Fascist Architecture. Reception and Legacy.* 212–227. Abingdon: Routledge, 2020.

Balestrero, Andrea: "Alessandro Ceresoli: Interview for A12." *Flash Art* [Italian edition] 43:286 (August–September 2010): 1–8.

Ballinger, Pamela: *The World Refugees Made: Decolonization and the Foundation of Postwar Italy.* Ithaca/NY: Cornell University Press, 2020.

Barbon, Marco: Untitled and undated statement, *Asmara Dream* (2006–2008): https://www.marcobarbon.com/work/the-ruse-ay2wd.

Behrend, Heike: *Alice Lakwena & the Holy Spirits: War in Northern Uganda, 1986–97.* Oxford: Currey; Kampala: Fountain Publishers; Nairobi: EAEPl; Athens/OH: Ohio University Press, 1999.

Berardi, Franco 'Bifo': *Futurability: The Age of Impotence and the Horizon of Possibility.* London: Verso, 2017.

Berghaus, Günter: "Futurist Utopias." *International Yearbook of Futurism Studies* 5 (2015): 486–501.

Berghaus, Günter: *Futurism and Politics: Between Anarchist Rebellion and Fascist Reaction, 1909–1944.* Providence/RI: Berghahn Books, 1996.

Bonvicini, Gyonata: "Alessandro Ceresoli." *Giovani artisti italiani* (September 2009): https://www.giovaniartisti.it/gm/2003/english/09.htm.

Caruso, Ambra: "Fino al 17 III 2007, Alessandro Ceresoli Milano Francesca Minini." *Exibart* (20 February 2007): https://www.exibart.com/milano/fino-al-17-iii-2007-alessandro-ceresoli-milano-francesca-minini/.

Ceresoli, Alessandro: *Ritorno al futuro.* Milano: Mousse, 2011.

Ceresoli, Alessandro. E-mail correspondence with Tenley Bick. 15 April 2020.

Cianfarani, Francesco: "The Fascist Legacy in the Built Environment." Kay Bea Jones, and Stephanie Pilat, eds.: *The Routledge Companion to Italian Fascist Architecture: Reception and Legacy.* Abingdon: Routledge, 2020. 10–53.

Concini, Ennio: *Aeropoesie futuriste di bombardamenti.* Roma: Edizioni futuriste di "Poesia", 1941.

De Seta, Cesare: *Architettura futurista.* Milan: Daverio, 1990.

Denison, Edward: "Fiat Tagliero Service Station." *Architectural Design* 76:6 (2006): 134–135.

Denison, Edward, Guang Yu Ren, and Naigzy Gebremedhin: *Asmara: Africa's Secret Modernist City.* London: Merrell, 2003.

ERiTV Eritrea: "ERiTV Eritrea: Reportage Asmara, 20 August 2014," YouTube, https://www.youtube.com/watch?v=Y_lPNmRScYA.

Fisher, Margaret: "Futurism and Radio." Günter Berghaus, ed.: *Futurism and the Technological Imagination.* Amsterdam: Rodopi, 2009. 229–263.

Fuller, Mia: "Italy's Colonial Futures: Colonial Inertia and Postcolonial Capital in Asmara." *California Italian Studies* 2:1 (2011): 1–18.

Godoli, Ezio: *Il futurismo: Guida all'architettura moderna.* Roma: Laterza, 1983.

Harris, Lyle Ashton, Robert Storr, and Peter Benson Miller, eds.: *Nero su bianco.* Exhibition catalogue. Rome: American Academy in Rome, 26 May – 19 July 2015. Rome: Nero, 2015.

Ialongo, Ernesto: "Filippo Tommaso Marinetti: The Futurist as Fascist, 1929–1937." *Journal of Modern Italian Studies* 18:4 (2013): 393–418.

Il vetro rivista mensile. Rome (1938–1943).
Labanca, Nicola: *Oltremare: Storia dell'espansione coloniale italiana.* Bologna: Il Mulino, 2002.
Lee, Pamela M.: *Chronophobia: On Time in the Art of the 1960s.* Cambridge/MA: MIT Press, 2004.
Lindeman, Ashley: "Plastica murale, Arte polimaterica, and Futurist Materials of Empire." Ashley Lindeman: *L'Arte Murale: Modern Italian Muralism in the Age of Fascism, 1932–1945.* Ph.D. Dissertation. Tallahassee/FL: Florida State University, 2022. 124–168.
M. E. P.: "The Italian Colonial Empire: A Note on Its Rise and Fall. Pt. 2." *Bulletin of International News* 21:7 (1 April 1944): 258–266.
Marinetti, Filippo Tommaso: "L'aeropittura dei bombardamenti: Manifesto futurista." *Agenzia A. L. A.* 11:16 (7 December 1940): 1–2.
Marinetti, Filippo Tommaso: "L'aeropittura futurista inizia una nuova êra della plastica." *Stile futurista* 1:2 (August 1934): 11–12.
Marinetti, Filippo Tommaso: "Formula letteraria artistica del futurismo nel suo trentennale." *Agenzia A.L.A.* 9:57 (9 February 1939): 1.
Marinetti, Filippo Tommaso: "Le Futurisme." *Le Figaro* (20 February 1909). Reprinted in Giovanni Lista, ed.: *Le Futurisme: Textes et manifestes, 1909–1944.* Ceyzérieu: Champ Vallon, 2015. 87–97. English translation: "The Foundation and Manifesto of Futurism." F.T. Marinetti: *Critical Writings.* Ed. by Günter Berghaus. New York: Farrar, Straus and Giroux, 2006. 11–17.
Marinetti, Filippo Tommaso: *Il poẹma africano.* Milano: Mondadori, 1937.
Marinetti, Filippo Tommaso: "Prospettive del volo e aeropittura." *La gazzetta del popolo* (Torino), 22 September 1929.
Marinetti, Filippo Tommaso, and Aldo Palazzeschi: *Carteggio con un'appendice di altre lettere a Palazzeschi.* A cura di Paolo Prestigiacomo. Milano: Mondadori, 1978.
Marinetti, Filippo Tommaso, Angiolo Mazzoni, and Mino Somenzi. "Manifesto futurista dell'architettura aerea." *Sant'Elia* 2:3 (1 February 1934): 3.
Marinetti, Filippo Tommaso, Alfredo Ambrosi, Cesare Andreoni, Benedetta (Cappa-Marinetti), Fortunato Depero, Gerardo Dottori, Fillìa, Pippo Oriani, Bruno Munari, Enrico Prampolini, Mino Rosso, Tato: "Un manifesto polemico: La plastica murale futurista." *La gazzetta del popolo* (1 December 1934) and *Stile futurista* 1:5 (December 1934): 3. Reprinted as "La plastica murale futurista: Manifesto." *2ª mostra nazionale di plastica murale per l'edilizia fascista in Italia e in Africa.* Milano: Edizioni futuriste di "Poesia", 1936. 3–6.
Marinetti, Filippo Tommaso, Enrico Prampolini, Mino Somenzi, and Tato (Guglielmo Sansoni): "Manifesto della aeropittura." *Prima mostra di aeropittura dei futuristi.* Roma: La Camerata degli Artisti, 1–10 febbraio 1931. Roma: Palombi, 1931. 3–9. Reprinted in Marinetti: *Teoria e invenzione futurista.* A cura di Luciano De Maria. Milano: Mondadori, 1968. 169–171. 2nd edn 1983. 197–201. English translation: "Manifesto of Aeropainting." Lawrence Rainey, Christine Poggi, and Laura Wittman, eds.: *Futurism: An Anthology.* New Haven/CT: Yale University Press, 2009. 283–286.
Marzioli, Sara: "Cannibalizing the Black Atlantic in F.T. Marinetti's Interwar Writing." *Interdisciplinary Literary Studies* 23:4 (2021): 547–572.
Mather, David: *Futurist Conditions: Imagining Time in Italian Futurism.* London: Bloomsbury, 2020.
McLaren, Brian: "The Italian Colonial appropriation of Indigenous North African Architecture in the 1930's." *Muqarnas* 19 (2002): 164–192.
Mikkonen, Kai: "Artificial Africa in the European Avant-Garde: Marinetti and Tzara." Sascha Bru, et al., eds.: *Europa! Europa? The Avant-Garde, Modernism and the Fate of a Continent.* Berlin: De Gruyter, 2009. 391–407.

Mignolo, Walter D.: *Local Histories / Global Designs: Coloniality, Subaltern Knowledges, and Border Thinking.* Princeton/NJ: Princeton University Press, 2012.

Panzini, Franco: "Pines, Palms, and Holm Oaks: Historicist Modes in Modern Italian Cityscapes." *Studies in the History of Art* 78. Symposium Papers LV: Modernism and Landscape Architecture, 1890–1940. Washington/DC: National Gallery of Art, 2015. 117–136.

Pizzi, Katia: *Italian Futurism and the Machine.* Manchester: Manchester University Press, 2019.

Re, Lucia: "'Barbari civilizzatissimi': Marinetti and the Futurist Myth of Barbarism." *Journal of Modern Italian Studies* 17:3 (2012): 350–368.

Sabatino, Michael: "Architecture." Günter Berghaus, ed.: *Handbook of International Futurism.* Berlin & Boston: De Gruyter, 2019. 69–87.

Scarlett, Matthew: "Preserved for whom: Reappraising Asmara's Colonial-Era Architecture." Kay Bea Jones, and Stephanie Pilat, eds.: *The Routledge Companion to Italian Fascist Architecture: Reception and Legacy.* Abingdon: Routledge, 2020. 179–190.

Tagliafierro, Marco: "Alessandro Ceresoli, Francesca Minini." *Artforum* 49:8 (April 2011): 30.

Tecle-Misghina, Belula: *Asmara: An Urban History.* Rome: Nuova Cultura, 2014.

Terrosi, Roberto: "Futurismo e postumano." Federico Luisetti, and Luca Somigli, eds.: *A Century of Futurism: 1909–2009.* Special issue of *Annali d'Italianistica* 27 (2009): 263–273.

Tomasello, Giovanna: "Marinetti: Tra territorio del mito e l'estetizzazione dell'Africa." G. Tomasello: *L'Africa tra mito e realtà: Storia della letteratura coloniale italiana.* Palermo: Sellerio, 2004. 83–120.

Visscher, Jochen, and Stephen Boness: *Asmara: Africa's Jewel of Modernity.* Berlin: Jovis, 2016.

Welch, Rhiannon Noel: "Here and Then, There and Now: Nation Time and Colonial Space in Pasolini, Oriani and Marinetti." *Italica* 91:4 (Winter 2014): 625–653.

5 Artist Statements

Artur R. Sztukalski and Guillaume Touissant

Transfuturism Manifesto

Introduction:

In 1909 Filippo Tommaso Marinetti founded Futurism, one of the most seminal art movements ever. It declared an absolute necessity to discard tradition in its broad sense (as it stifled the emancipating streak in the human species), to redefine the cognitive horizon and the aesthetic canons relying on dynamism and simultaneity of perception, to develop a new axiology allowing solely for what awaits humankind in the future, and uncompromising submission to emanations of the future. Many of its postulates, however correct, were subsequently negated, to a considerable extent, by opportunistic activities of Marinetti, shamefully deluded by successful applicability of politics to the transformation of the state mechanism while either forgetting or ignoring the issue of the developed mentality of a human as the subject and the prime object of the expected system transformation.

That is the reason why a hundred years later we, the Transfuturists, seek both to restore those ideas to their former glory and to give them a new quality taking into account the reality at hand and the prospects of the future.

We proclaim as follows:

1. Our primary aim is a comprehensive transgression of self-awareness, consisting of permanently challenging both theoretically and practically the concept, any form of identity and collective identification, and the customarily and culturally justified rules of maintenance of interpersonal relationships stipulating that an individual is unconditionally accountable to a specific social unit, community, nationality, or the humankind in general.

2. We reject any ties to existing religious, philosophical or political systems. We despise the socially acceptable constraints on personal freedom to choose one's gender, and the public obsession with maintaining interstate borders and culture barriers. Unlike the Italian progenitors, we perceive patriotism and war as extremely undesirable atavisms to be eliminated from the intellectual and behavioural sphere of human activity as soon as possible.

3. We see no threat in acceleration of dissemination of information, computer technologies, artificial intelligence, or transhumanism. Conversely, we see them as an opportunity for final questioning and reckoning of the existing continuum of the cultural achievement encumbered by the baggage of bodily needs, procreation,

https://doi.org/10.1515/9783111318394-014

self-preservation instinct, sensuality, hedonism, compulsion of memory, and futile striving for oneness with nature.

4. We embrace Bauman's liquid modernity, which exteriorises the form of social emanations of biological and physical phenomena such as entropy, autoimmunisation, wave-particle duality, or quantum fluctuations. Thus, we confirm our orthodox counter-culture origin and see the act of suicide as logical culmination of the transgression.

5. For our primary aim to be attained, we propound that the symmetry of the ontological dualism be questioned, and point at the unquestionable primacy of transcendence over evanescence and material imperfection, at the primacy of human imagination and advanced self-awareness over senses determining perception of the ubiquitous world, which in fact is merely a phantasmagorical entity.

6. We are convinced that it is art that is the catalyst for the process of transformation of mentality. While its existence relies on the imperfection of the senses, art is the only vehicle within the material world for one to break through to the metaphysical, and then to head for Hegelian dialectic and philosophical speculation, eventually making it possible for the dominating role of the so-called empiric ego to degrade.

7. The redeeming quality of art should be its ability to blur the line between the illusion of truth and obvious manifestation of mystification. This should be accompanied by an abiding passion for creating and perceiving, by participation in a unique act of communication, and first and foremost, by conviction of the power of an alchemic creation transmuting an abstract figment of imagination into a material entity that has an impact on experienceable reality. We only affirm two art movements: body art in visual arts and bruitism in music.

8. The aim of body art should be the objectification of the human body by reducing it to an imperfect organic shell. The body only serves as a plastic material for expressing thought (philosophical speculation) and strengthening the conviction of the rift between instability and worthlessness of matter, and transcendence.

9. Much like our Italian predecessors, most importantly Luigi Russolo, it is in noise alone that we see the potential for one to open to what it is real, that is to what is transcendental, and thus, to what facilitates the transgression of one's constraints. Unlike the author of The Art of Noises, however, we believe that bruitism should be entirely free from mimesis. The role of a Transfuturist composer should not be to mimic nature, including acoustic man-made urban and technological environment, but to create a speculative extrasensory reality where noise will go beyond the musical or sonic connotations that are assigned to it for the thought of the artist to be conveyed.

10. We also reject the Aristotelian catharsis infecting human creativity. Any manifestation of art driven by the desire of self-purification of the artist compul-

sively struggling with decadence, sexual obsessions, suffering, and alienation effectively validates the obsolescence, futility, and intellectual uselessness of art. Having watched the continuous degeneration of the neo-avantgarde, whose immanent part is the extensive scene of industrial music, despite certain clear formal and aesthetic similarities, we emphatically dissociate ourselves from that art movement remaining ever faithful to the Art-Life-Action-Death doctrine.

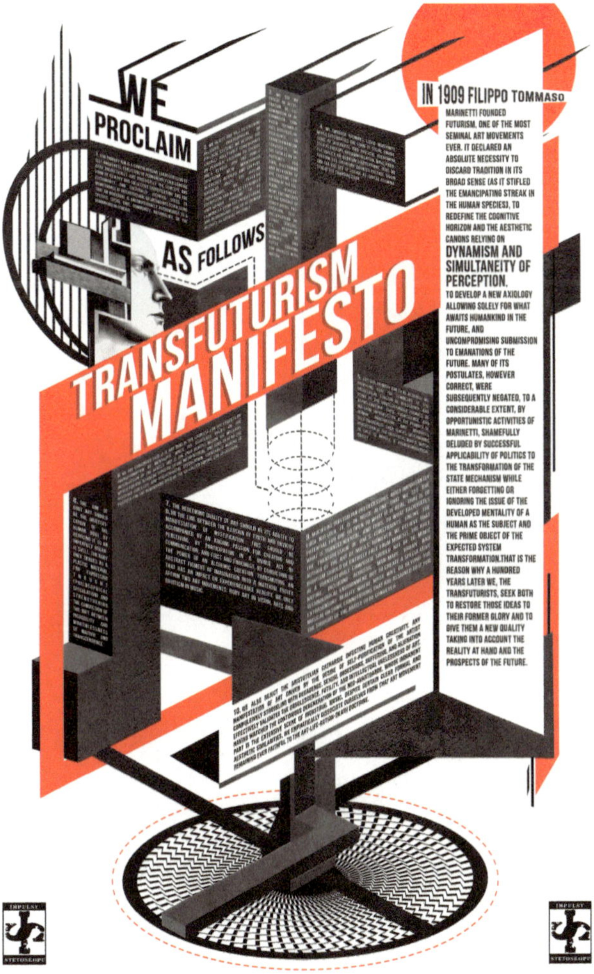

sively struggling with [illegible] successors suffering into Menuhunci[illegible] [illegible]

Giovanni Fontana

From Words-in-Freedom to Epigenetic Poetry: Evolutions in Futurist Recitation and Performance

At the dawn of the last century, Marinetti's Words-in-Freedom (*parole in libertà*), together with free expressive spelling, multilinear lyricism, the typographical revolution, onomatopoeic sounds and other polemical and technology-driven innovations opened up new paths for poetry. Marinetti launched his concept of Words-in-Freedom in 1912 in the *Manifesto tecnico della letteratura futurista* (Technical Manifesto of Futurist Literature) and discussed it in a broader manner in the manifesto *Distruzione della sintassi – Immaginazione senza fili – Parole in libertà* (Destruction of Syntax – Untrammelled Imagination – Words-in-Freedom, 1913). This theoretical framework had a strongly synaesthetic orientation and introduced an extra-verbal dimension to poetry. Marinetti envisaged compositions in which 'languages' of different extractions can act simultaneously in a syncretic and contrapuntal key.

In practice, words, sound and images can be interwoven in the most diverse ways in a fabric which goes far beyond the genre of conventional poetry. In their continuous attempts at expression through maximum force and depth, Words-in-Freedom are naturally transformed into **AUTO-ILLUSTRATIONS** by means of freely expressive orthographical and typographical forms, the synoptic tables of lyrical values, and typographically shaped analogies.[1]

This new type of poetry based on Words-in-Freedom will "break through the boundaries of literature, striding away toward painting, music, and the art of noise, constructing a marvellous bridge between the word and the real object."[2] Furthermore, the *parole in libertà* "have the function of rendering the facial ex-

1 Marinetti: "Geometrical and Mechanical Splendor and Sensitivity Toward Numbers", p. 139. "Le parole in libertà, in questo sforzo continuo di esprimere colla massima forza e la massima profondità, si trasformano naturalmente in auto-illustrazioni, mediante l'ortografia e tipografia libere espressive, le tavole sinottiche di valori lirici e le analogie disegnate." "Lo splendore geometrico e meccanico e la sensibilità numerica", p. 89.

2 Marinetti, et al.: "The Futurist Cinema", p. 262. "Le parole in libertà [...] rompono i limiti della letteratura marciando verso la pittura, la musica, l'arte dei rumori e gettando un meraviglioso ponte tra la parola e l'oggetto reale." "La cinematografia futurista", p. 120.

https://doi.org/10.1515/9783111318394-015

pressions and other gestures of the narrator."[3] The different graphic symbols in typography correspond to the tones, volumes and registers of the declaimer.

In Marinetti's poetry declamations, the sonority of the text is heightened in a vocal spectacle charged with tension and dynamics that spills over into the audience. The performances could be aggressive or ironic or playful, but they were always provocative to the point of triggering violent reactions from the audience. The declamation of *parole in libertà* and, in particular, that of *tavole parolibere* (Free-Word Tables), was strongly conditioned by the verbal-visual character of the texts, which in turn conditioned the reading procedures. We can speak here of an 'opto-phonetic' dimension of the text. Marinetti said that the poet as declaimer is "intuitively laying down new laws and creating novel and unforeseen horizons in the Words-in-Freedom that he interprets."[4] He is thus referring to the declaimer's willingness to use improvisation in order to enhance the dynamics and the vitality of the stage action.

Marinetti condemned traditional methods of declamation and instead proposed a completely different approach to the text. He wanted modern, dynamic acting and a use of voice that went beyond any pre-established timbre, tonal and rhythmic scheme. He sought to find elements that corresponded to the new poetic forms. His *parole in libertà* and *tavole parolibere* became veritable scores, which other Futurists developed in their own idiosyncratic manners: Giacomo Balla called them "rumoristica plastica", Fortunato Depero "verbalizzazione astratta" and "onomalingua", Francesco Cangiullo "poesia pentagrammata", and so on. These verbal-graphic scores included musical signs, arithmetical formulas, words in dialects, obsolete words, neologisms, deformed or foreign words.

These poetic compositions were set up as visual spectacles made to resonate in the mind of the reader (see Figs. 1a and 1b). From there, they were to find expression in an act of declamation, which Marinetti outlined in his manifesto *La declamazione dinamica e sinottica* (Dynamic, Multichannelled Recitation, 1916). It specified that the Futurist declaimer must be an inventor and tireless creator and must decide:

> instinctively, at every moment, the point at which the tone-adjective and the atmospheric adjective have to be spoken and repeated. Since there aren't any precise indicators in the Words-

3 Marinetti: "Geometrical and Mechanical Splendor and Sensitivity Toward Numbers", p. 139 "L'ortografia e la tipografia libere espressive servono inoltre ad esprimere la mimica facciale e la gesticolazione del narratore." "Lo splendore geometrico e meccanico e la sensibilità numerica", p. 89.

4 Marinetti: "Dynamic, Multichanneled Recitation", p. 196. "Egli collaborerà coll'autore parolibero, gettando intuitivamente nuove leggi e creando nuovi orizzonti imprevisti nelle parole in libertà che egli interpreta." "La declamazione dinamica e sinottica", p. 108.

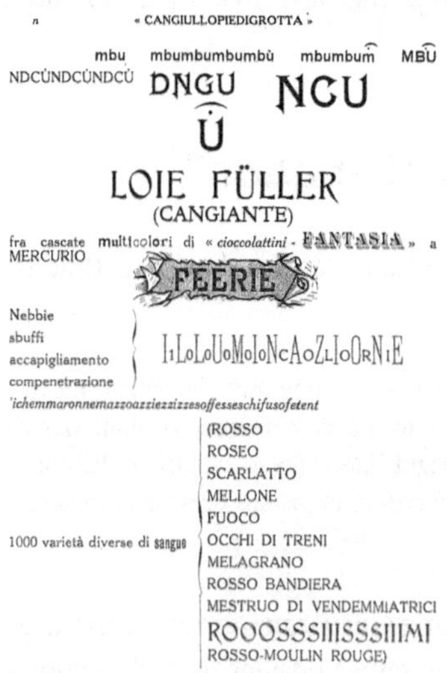

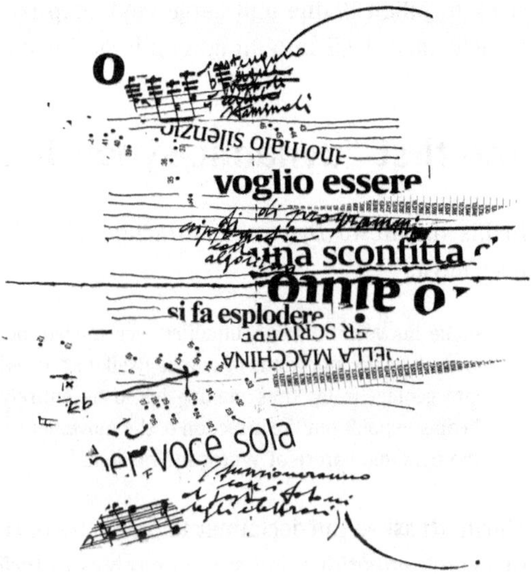

Fig. 1a: A page from Francesco Cangiullo: *Piedigrotta*. Milano: Edizioni futuriste di “Poesia”, 1916.
Fig. 1b: Score for Giovanni Fontana’s sound poem *Per voce sola* (For Solo Voice, 2005).

> in-Freedom, he must follow his own inclinations, taking the greatest care to attain maximum geometrical splendor and numerical sensibility. In this way, he will work closely with the author who uses Words-in-Freedom, intuitively laying down new laws and creating novel and unforeseen horizons in the Words-in-Freedom that he interprets.[5]

Therefore, the *parole in libertà* constitute a sort of flexible score and allow the declaimer to phonically free the vibrations and dynamism of the text. In short, the typographical revolution, which had modernized printed texts by making them more complex and multidirectional, had in fact introduced a system of notation that had to be decoded, making the relationship between the page and the declaimer more active. The phonetic dimension, the gestural language and the scenic background became the hinges of poetry transformed into ‘action poetry’, anticipating the *poésie-action* of the second half of the twentieth century (from Bernard Heid-

5 Marinetti: “Dynamic, Multichanneled Recitation”, p. 196. “… istintivamente ad ogni istante il punto in cui l’aggettivo-tono e l’aggettivo atmosfera deve essere pronunciato e ripetuto. Non essendovi, nelle parole in libertà, nessuna indicazione precisa, egli deve seguire in ciò soltanto il suo fiuto, preoccupandosi di raggiungere il massimo splendore geometrico e la massima sensibilità numerica. Così egli collaborerà coll’autore parolibero, gettando intuitivamente nuove leggi e creando nuovi orizzonti imprevisti nelle parole in libertà che egli interpreta.” “La declamazione dinamica e sinottica”, pp. 107–108.

sieck to Julien Blaine and Serge Pey). Step by step, the new style of declamation transformed itself into an authentic performance art.

The first "dynamic-synoptic declamation"

In his manifesto *Dynamic, Multichannelled Recitation*, Marinetti wrote that the poet must:

> make his voice metallic, liquefied, vegetalized, be turned to stone and electrified, fusing it with the very vibrations of matter itself, expressed by means of Words-in-Freedom. Gesticulate geometrically, thus making his arms entirely rigid like railway signals or lighthouse beams to point out the direction of the movement of forces or of pistons or wheels, to express the dynamic nature of Words-in-Freedom. [6]

Marinetti asked the declaimer to make use of strange instruments and props, draw theorems, equations and synoptic tables of lyrical values on blackboards, conquer the scenic space with gestures and movements, employ special lighting, etc. The breadth and complexity of these propositions suggest that the declaimer must engage in constant experimentation.

A first demonstration of what this new style should look like was given in Rome, at the Galleria Sprovieri, on 29 March 1914.[7] "With a firm, husky, pounding voice, a face gathered in a contraction of energy and violence, an imperious silhouette",[8] Marinetti recited *Piedigrotta* by Francesco Cangiullo, accompanied by instruments and Balla, Depero, Sironi and Sprovieri as supporting actors. The newspapers of the time characterized this soirée as an exhilarating event with a convulsive and festive atmosphere. The hall was lit by red lamps that enhanced

---

6 Marinetti: "Dynamic, Multichanneled Recitation", p. 196. "Avere una gesticolazione geometrica, dando così alle braccia delle rigidità taglienti di semafori e di raggi di fari per indicare le direzioni delle forze, o di stantuffi e di ruote, per esprimere il dinamismo delle parole in libertà. Avere una gesticolazione disegnante e topografica che sinteticamente crei nell'aria dei cubi, dei coni, delle spirali, delle ellissi, ecc." "La declamazione dinamica e sinottica", pp. 106–107.

7 A detailed analysis of this and similar events is given in Berghaus: *Italian Futurist Theatre*, pp. 233–244. Further elucidation on the manifesto *Dynamic, Multichannelled Recitation* and its complicated publication history can be found on pp. 172–175.

8 "[...] con voce ferma, acciaccata, martellante, viso raccolto in una contrazione di energia e di violenza, sagoma imperiosa." Sgabelloni: "Come le signorine Tofa, Putipù, Triccaballacche e Scetavajasse si produssero nel putiferio del putiputipù." The review in *Il giornale d'Italia* of 31 March 1914 has been reprinted in Cangiullo: *Piedigrotta* (1978 edn), pp. VIII-XI and, together with Sprovieri's detailed recollection of the event, partially translated in Berghaus: *Italian Futurist Theatre*, pp. 235–237.

the dynamic values of a backdrop painted by Balla. The troupe of artists wore fantastical paper hats. Greatly admired was the colourful vessel that Balla carried on his head. Each artist played a traditional Neapolitan instrument,[9] while Cangiullo occasionally improvised music on a piano.

An anonymous author wrote in *Lacerba* that the Futurists were organizing in their Roman gallery "spettacoli di gaia e strabiliante poesia" (performances of joyful and amazing poetry).[10] Amongst the most original was *Discussione di due critici sudanesi sul futurismo* (Discussion Between Two Sudanese Critics on Futurism) by Marinetti, Cangiullo and Balla. The journalist Pietro Sgabelloni described it in these terms:

> And the chaotic orchestra of sounds, colours, shapes, smells, flavours, contacts, convulsions of laughter, of exploding and seething and blazing joy grows, grows, grows, while hour by hour the young ladies Tofa, Putipù, Triccaballacche, Scetavajasse come out of their infernal bedlam and give, by means of their sounds, the living sensations of the jubilant, maddening, intoxicating, blinding, suffocating, noisy and deafening feast of Piedigrotta.[11]

The rediscovery of Futurist recitation in the 1960s

With the rediscovery of Futurist theatre and drama in the 1960s, a new generation of poets and performers discovered the particular style of recitation the Futurists had developed in the 1910s: the dynamic forms of gesture and stage presence, the strength of the impact on the audience, the dynamics of movement, the presence of the voice as an affirmation of the body, the explosion of sounds based on shattered and harsh linguistic matter. Since the early 1960s, a significant sector of poetry had established complex relationships between writing and the fine arts, defined as 'intermediality' by the Fluxus artist Dick Higgins.[12] Here, the confines of the page are

---

9 *Piedigrotta* was a poetic evocation of the Neapolitan folk festival of the same name, in which various forms of self-made instruments are used, often as cacophonic as their exotic names: Putipù, Scevatajasse, Triccaballacche etc.

10 [Anon.]: "Piedigrotta futurista", p. 110.

11 "E la caotica orchestra di suoni, di colori, di forme, di odori, di sapori, di contatti, di convulsioni di riso, di gioia esplodente e ribollente e lapillante e fiammeggiante cresce, cresce, cresce, mentre ad ora ad ora le signorine Tofa, Putipù, Triccaballacche, Scetavajasse escono dalla loro bolgia infernale e danno, per mezzo dei loro suoni, le sensazioni vive della tripudiante, folleggiante, ubriacante, accecante, soffocante, rumoreggiante ed assordante festa di Piedigrotta." Sgabelloni: "Come le signorine Tofa, Putipù, Triccaballacche e Scetavajasse si produssero nel putiferio del putiputipù."

12 Higgins' "Intermedia" first appeared in 1966 in the *Something Else Newsletter.*

violated and the figure of the poet is confronted with the need to explore spatially the poem's linguistic intersections, contaminations and synaesthetic interrelations. Even though not mentioned by Higgins, the links to Futurism are more than evident. Marinetti clearly opened up a performative dimension to the neo-avant-garde.[13]

The Total Work of Art was a fundamental theme in nineteenth-century art and was rediscovered by the Futurists as an area of lively and invigorating research.[14] It became a testing ground for innovative personalities, a laboratory of disorderly and risk-taking artists. The path towards a re-definition of the multidimensional work of art in a perspective of general renewal was pursued by various painters, poets, musicians and stage performers. Also in literature, the techniques of verbal-visual writing contributed to the creation of synaesthetic artworks that brought to fruition the enormous potential of the interconnection of signifiers in different aesthetic languages. Texts left the domain of the book, underwent gestural, spatial and musical cross-codification and opened themselves up to tactile, olfactory and gustatory sensations. They developed, according to the poet Adriano Spatola, "verso la poesia totale" (towards total poetry).[15]

My research is certainly in tune with these principles and converges on interdisciplinarity and intermediality, where poetry places the voice at its centre and adopts a form that has the quality of 'notations' (see Figs. 2a and 2b). The voice intervenes in the text as if it were an underdeveloped, unfinished object that requires the process of recitation to become alive and reach its communicative goal.[16] After all, the poet is, in reality, the one who is the creator. And with this conviction, I can well share Luigi Pareyson's concept of formativity, defined as "the inseparable nexus of invention and production: to form means to do, but such a doing that, while doing, invents the way of doing: to perform, to realize, *poiein*, but not something predetermined according to a prearranged rule, but something that is invented by doing it, according to a rule that is discovered in the course of doing."[17]

---

13 The question of how much knowledge Fluxus artists had of Futurism has been discussed in Berghaus: "Tomas Schmit: A Fluxus Farewell to Perfection. An Interview" and Berghaus "Happening and Fluxus."

14 See Berghaus: "The Futurist Conception of Gesamtkunstwerk."

15 See Spatola: *Verso la poesia totale.*

16 This very much correlates with Paul Zumthor's theory of orality in *Langue, texte, énigme* (1975), *Introduction à la poésie orale* (1983), *La Poésie et la voix dans la civilisation médiévale* (1984) and *La Lettre et la voix* (1987).

17 Pareyson: *Esistenza e persona*, p. 209.

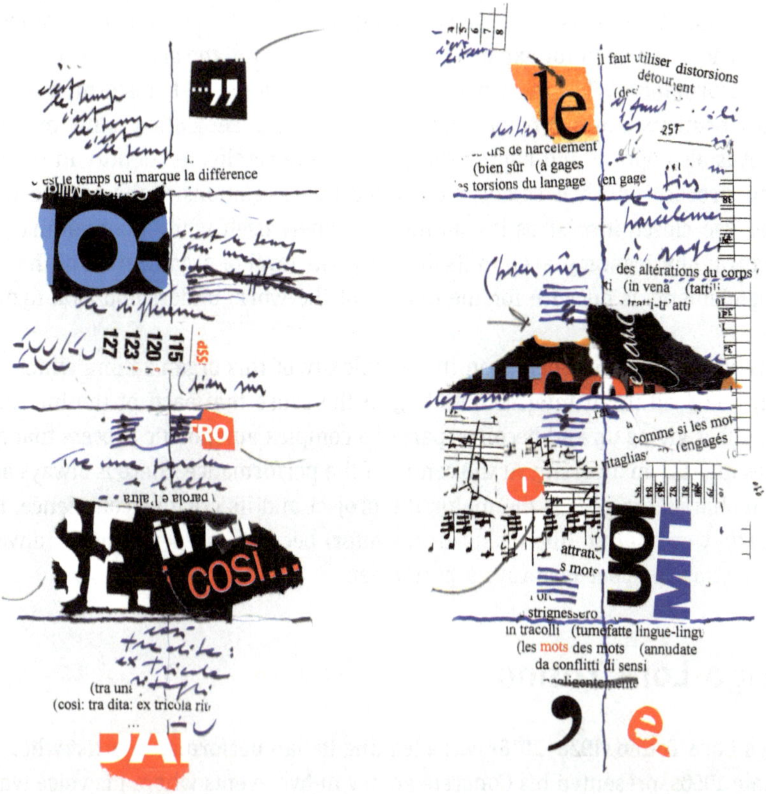

Fig. 2a: Giovanni Fontana's sound poem *Partition 1* (2006). **Fig. 2b:** Giovanni Fontana's sound poem *Partition 2* (2006).

Form and method, therefore, converge in a performative moment governed by the *φωνή* (phōnḗ, an articulated sound), or rather: the music of speaking that enhances the plane of the signifier and at the same time unleashes an enormous force. The 'action poem' is capable of involving different elements as it expands beyond the page. It contains a complex structure and incorporates all those elements that must or can, in one way or another, enter 'the situation'. If poetry is a living organism, it develops its potentialities only in relation to its performative setting.

Indeed, every organism needs to choose its own environment, all the more so since the organism in question is distinctly self-(re)productive (autopoietic) and open to dimensions other than those of the page. Inside the covers of a book, the text pulsates with inner life. This pulsation (and here we are talking about phonic and rhythmic values entrusted primarily to the textual composition) presses outwards. This process is similar to what happens when composing music. There is a need for expansion from the score into the space-time dimension of a performance. What the score contains *in nuce* must be transformed into material vibrations that can be perceived by our senses. Perception is not only auditory; it is also optical and haptic. The text or score retains its identity in the autopoietic process, which is essentially defined by its relations to the outside world, but is also closed insofar as it continues to renew itself while maintaining all its structural physiognomy, even in its diversity. The level of organization of the interacting elements is decisive for the quality of the work, understood as a dynamic system.

Obviously, much depends on the complexity of this organization, which must always be read in an intermediate key, in the sense that each of the interacting elements is giving up and becomes part of a complex autopoietic process that guarantees identity in diversity. At the centre of the performance, there is always a person in charge: the poet is the motor, the project and its creative conscience. He is the *artifex* or *ποιητής* (the maker or inventor) because the performer is always a poet, just as the poet is always a performer.

Arrigo Lora Totino

Arrigo Lora Totino (1928–2016) was a leading Italian performance artist who, since the late 1950s, presented his Concrete Poetry in live events where his voice was accompanied by noise, movement and gestures. In 1966, he created with the musician Enore Zaffiri and the painter Sandro De Alexandris the Studio di Informazione Estetica dedicated to research into the interrelations between poetry, art and electronic music. To promote knowledge of the work undertaken by his predecessors in the historical avant-garde, he published in 1978 *Futura: Historical-critical Anthology of Sound Poetry* with Cramps Records in Milan, where he presented on seven 33 rpm records the voices of the most interesting sound poets of the twentieth century, including examples of Futurist declamation (Filippo Tommaso Marinetti, Francesco Cangiullo, Giacomo Balla, Fortunato Depero, Farfa) and *zaum'* poetry readings (Vladimir Mayakovsky, Velimir Khlebnikov, Vasily Kamensky, Aleksei Kruchenykh, Ilya Zdanevich).

Arrigo Lora Totino writes that "in a Free-Word Table, the word – decomposed and recomposed by laws of phonic accentuation – is fixed in an optical dynamic organization that is equivalent to a phonic dynamism, in an audiovisual image of splendidly geometric plasticity."[18] Lora Totino, who was a true link between Futurism and Concrete Poetry, sound and performance poetry, was a convinced supporter of optophonic values. On a poetic level, he revisited every aspect of Futurist creativity and was greatly inspired by the visual quality of the *tavole parolibere.* In order to make the relationships between word, image, body and gesture more complex, he conceived of 'mimo-declamations' that fostered phono-gestural languages, and 'gymnastic poetry' that asserted the physical aspects of the poet's body. His attempts to synthesize text and action made him rediscover Anton Giulio Bragaglia's 'photodynamism.' It was in 1976 that he created his own *fotodinamiche simultanee* (simultaneous photodynamics; see Fig. 3b), re-opening the dialogue between Bragaglia and the Futurists more than sixty long years after *Fotodinamismo futurista* (Futurist Photodynamism, 1913).[19]

Arrigo Lora Totino drew attention to the complex relationships that exist between the dynamism of the body in space, the scenic construction of the image and its rhythm, the performer's sense of gesture and its theatricality, between the narrative element and its presentation in time and space. But there was more, because Lora Totino borrowed for his poetic purposes Bragaglia's synthesis of movement and spirit of the gesture, the essence of motion and the signification of time. Like Bragaglia, he launched phonemes in the impalpable flash of a gesture and in an intercoded perspective.

If Bragaglia had a clear awareness of the absolute modernity of his project that anticipated intermedia techniques of the 1960s and 70s, Arrigo Lora Totino amplified this vision and made photodynamism function in connection with verbal 'gestures'. In his visual poems, he inserted them freely into the page, or at its bottom by way of a caption, in order to draw attention to the parallelism of image and word or their mutually supportive interpenetration (see Fig. 3).

Lora Totino demonstrated how word and image can be dynamically linked by fusing gestural performance, photography and verbal-visual writing in a constructive process that summarizes and merges times and modes, bodies and places. This becomes evident on the image level due to the vibrant effects of the crossings and transparencies; but it is equally evident on the verbal level due to the alliterative games that bring to the fore the typographically compressed sonority, enhancing its effects in a counterpoint amplified synaesthetically by figurative oscillations and tremors. These poetic works are masterful syntheses of creative gestures

18 Lora Totino: "Poesia da ascoltare", p. 24.

19 The booklet had three editions, with 48 pages and 16 images in 15 plates outside the text. It was attacked in *Lacerba* of 27 September 1913 in a notice of the Futurist painters Boccioni, Carrà, Russolo, Balla, Severini and Soffici.

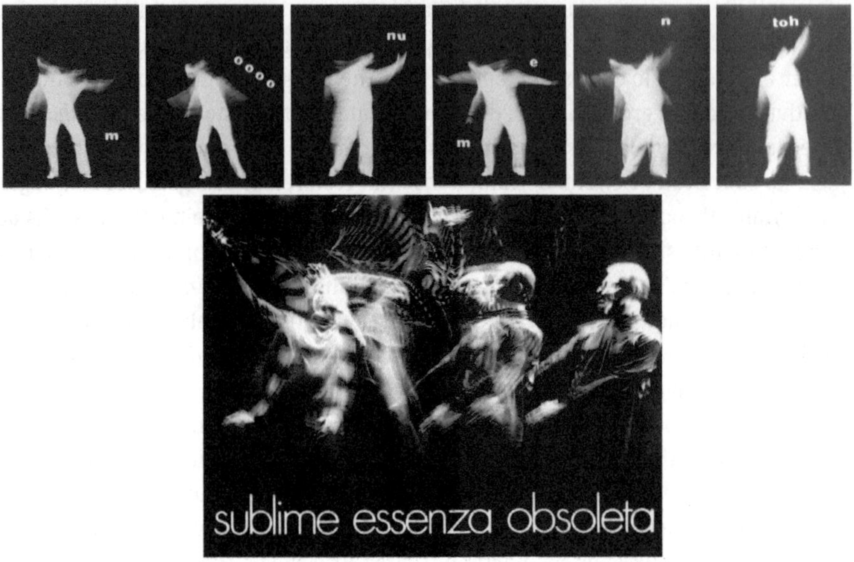

Fig. 3: Arrigo Lora Totino performing his *Fotodinamiche simultanee* series (1975–76). Top: *Monument-oh* (1975). Bottom: *Sublime essenza obsoleta* (1976).

and emblems of poetic research into intermedia, which had already begun in the 1910s with Futurist sound poetry.

The poet and his voice: Towards an epigenetic form of poetry

The poetry of space and time will always revolve around vocality. The declaimer's voice goes beyond the dynamic charge of writing a poetic text and beyond the infinite range of relationships that exist between writing and other linguistic universes. The vital energy of the voice and its poietic qualities determine and structure sounds that catalyse other elements in a multidimensional fabric of interconnections, just as the Futurists had shown in the 1910s. Seen from this perspective, the text must be conceived as an integrated polytext produced by a body vibrating in sympathy with other sound sources. As such, it is fundamentally different from traditional poetry that rests buried in a book. A truly Futurist (or Neo-Futurist) poem will have to live in a space-time dimension and will be a medium for intersections (contaminations?) with other arts. Its structure is polyphonic, intermedial and interlinguistic.

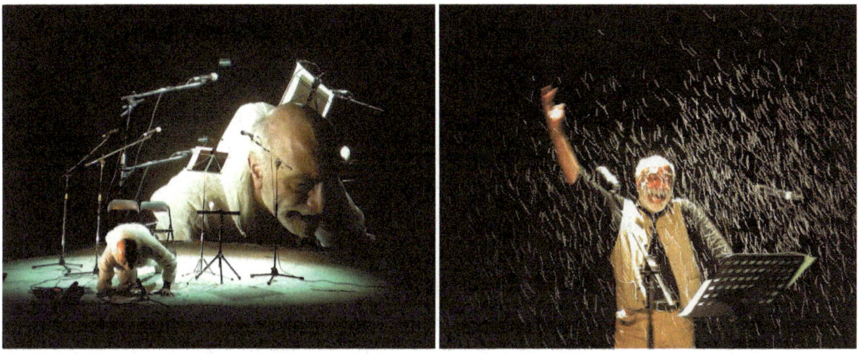

Fig. 4a: Giovanni Fontana performing *Epigenetic Poetry* in Rome, Centrale Preneste (Teatro per le Nuove Generazioni), 12 February 2011. Photo by Marco Palladini. **Fig. 4b:** Giovanni Fontana performing *Hypervox* at the Mixed Media Art Festival *East Wind – West Wind* in Shanghai, Hi-Shanghai Creative Zone, 5 November 2005. Photo by Bernard François.

In addition to the metric and sound values of the verse, it is necessary to consider the complementary aspects of the acoustics of the body and its creative force. The poem must be based on action languages that are not a mere summation of the subsidiary languages involved. The written text, on the other hand, is a pre-text which in its graphic or typographic form contains metamorphic germs capable of realizing the complexity of the text beyond the page. This allows a search for new relationships between text and intermedial performative spheres, with the intention of constructing poetry that is multidirectional, multivalent, pluripotential, polycentric, multilateral, polyrhythmic and multisonant. Such an 'expanded poetry' is not inward-looking and can evoke the most disparate territories, as long as the contamination of systems is the bearer of antagonistic components, and the interpenetration of separate universes is deaf to the sirens of institutional strictures (e.g., getting caught up in a maelstrom of television, art gallery and book market). It is a poetry that, starting from an Urtext, is able to reconstruct itself in a continuous mirroring.

The poet thus becomes a polyartist; he appropriates electronic and videographic practices, cinema, photography, the universe of sound art, the theatrical medium and the kinetic domain of rhythmic movement. He acts poietically, using all techniques, all supports, all spaces. He seeks to bring his own body back into the creative sphere, linking his gesture and his voice to the new technologies fed by the energetic substratum of electronic media. All of this constitutes the foundation of a new poetic attitude which broadens and denudes the boundaries of poetry and establishes tensions between a variety of systems. The interpenetration of separate universes and the use of new media bundles the boundless energies offered by science and technology. It connects them to the energies of memory and body through a different conception of the materiality of language. The poet's voice is a motor that re-reconnects us to the vanished realm of orality. At the same time, thanks to digital tools of sound synthesis, it places itself at the forefront of a new and unheard vocality.

Today's technologies make it possible to amplify the imperceptible sounds of the body. They can capture the most hidden *flatus* and generate from it new vocal universes. We have therefore moved on from Marinetti's concept of onomatopoeic sounds as "one of the most dynamic elements in Futurist poetry"[20] (which was naïve in many ways) to a digitized hypervox, which opens up new acoustic horizons for language. Far removed from any archaic mimetic effects, we can speak of an electrophonic and numerical 'mask' behind which sound is articulated as one of the fundamental aspects of language. In a truly hyperpoetic form, a poem evolves within itself. It is a poem in the making that does not renounce its origins in a text-image and shows itself to be different.

A poem starts from a text (a pre-text) and expands in space-time; it then returns to the pre-text, enriched with experiences and memories. Each time it is a new experience, but it is always the same game of tossing and turning. A formal nexus of invention and production adds and removes voices and gestures, disassembles words and continuously reconfigures them in an act of *poiesis* that is always ready for different suggestions, for the construction of different actions in view of different re-writings.

The polyartist is therefore the creator and the actant. Thanks to his gesture, to his energy, to his continuous pressure, the poetic organism undergoes successive processes of re-organization, and the following multidirectional itineraries are all subjected to a progressive modelling of the spatio-temporal evolutionary phases. In parallel to 'epigenetic' processes in biology, by which heritable modifications in gene function occur without a change in the sequence of the DNA, we can speak here of 'epigenetic poetry'.[21]

Translated by Günter Berghaus

20 Marinetti: "Futurist Dance", pp. 210–211

21 See Fontana: "La poesia epigenetica: Urtext in espansione."

Bibliography

[Anon.]: "Piedigrotto futurista." *Lacerba* 2:7 (1 April 1914): 110.

Berghaus, Günter: "Tomas Schmit: A Fluxus Farewell to Perfection. An Interview." *The Drama Review* 38:1 (Spring, 1994): 79–97.

Berghaus, Günter: "Happening and Fluxus." G. Berghaus: *Avant-garde Performance: Live Events and Electronic Technologies.* London: Palgrave Macmillan, 2005. 79–131.

Berghaus, Günter: "The Futurist Conception of Gesamtkunstwerk." Franciska d'Elhoungne Hervai, and Dávid Falvay, eds.: *"Sul fil di ragno della memoria": Studi in onore di Ilona Fried.* Budapest: Eötvös Loránd Tudományegyetem, 2012. 131–150.

Berghaus, Günter: *Italian Futurist Theatre, 1909–1944.* Oxford: Clarendon Press, 1998.

Bragaglia, Anton Giulio: *Fotodinamismo futurista.* Roma: Nalato, [1913].

Cangiullo, Francesco: *Piedigrotta, col manifesto sulla declamazione dinamica sinottica di Marinetti.* Milano: Edizioni futuriste di "Poesia", 1916. Reprint Firenze: Studio per Edizioni Scelte, 1978.

Fontana, Giovanni: "La poesia epigenetica: Urtext in espansione." G. Fontana, ed.: *Epigenetic Poetry.* Ravenna: Montanari, 2020. 30–53.

Lora Totino, Arrigo: "Poesia da ascoltare." Dietrich Mahlow, and A. Lora-Totino, eds.: *Poesia concreta: Indirizzi concreti visuali e fonetici.* Venezia: La Biennale, 1969. 19–49

Higgins, Dick: "Intermedia." *Something Else Newsletter* 1:1 (1966): 1–6. Reprinted in *Leonardo: Journal of the International Society for the Arts, Sciences and Technology* 34:1 (February 2001): 49–54.

Higgins, Dick: *Horizons: The Poetics and Theory of the Intermedia.* Carbondale/IL: Southern Illinois University Press, 1987

Marinetti, Filippo Tommaso: "Distruzione della sintassi – Immaginazione senza fili – Parole in libertà." F.T. Marinetti: *Teoria e invenzione futurista.* A cura di Luciano De Maria. Milano: Mondadori, 1968. 57–70. 2nd edn Milano: Mondadori, 1983. 65–80. English translation "Destruction of Syntax – Untrammeled Imagination – Words-in-Freedom." F.T. Marinetti: *Critical Writings.* Ed. by Günter Berghaus. New York: Farrar, Straus and Giroux, 2006. 120–131.

Marinetti, Filippo Tommaso: "Lo splendore geometrico e meccanico e la sensibilità numerica." F.T. Marinetti: *Teoria e invenzione futurista.* A cura di Luciano De Maria. Milano: Mondadori, 1968. 84–92. 2nd edn 1983. 98–107. "Geometrical and Mechanical Splendor and Sensitivity Toward Numbers." F.T. Marinetti: *Critical Writings.* Ed. by Günter Berghaus. New York: Farrar, Straus and Giroux, 2006. 135–142.

Marinetti, Filippo Tommaso: "Manifesto della danza futurista." F.T. Marinetti: *Teoria e invenzione futurista.* A cura di Luciano De Maria. Milano: Mondadori, 1968. 123–130. 2nd edn 1983. 144–152. English translation "Futurist Dance." F.T. Marinetti: *Critical Writings.* Ed. by Günter Berghaus. New York: Farrar, Straus and Giroux, 2006. 208–217.

Marinetti, Filippo Tommaso: "Manifesto tecnico della letteratura futurista." F.T. Marinetti: *Teoria e invenzione futurista.* A cura di Luciano De Maria. Milano: Mondadori, 1968. 40–54. 2nd edn 1983.46–62. English translation "Technical Manifesto of Futurist Literature." F.T. Marinetti: *Critical Writings.* Ed. by Günter Berghaus. New York: Farrar, Straus and Giroux, 2006. 107–119.

Marinetti, Filippo Tommaso, Bruno Corra, Emilio Settimelli, Arnaldo Ginna, Giacomo Balla, and Remo Chiti: "Cinematografia futurista: Manifesto." *L'Italia futurista* 1:10 (15 November 1916): 1. Reprinted in F.T. Marinetti: *Teoria e invenzione futurista.* A cura di Luciano De Maria. 2nd edn Milano: Mondadori, 1983. 138–144. English translation "The Futurist Cinema." F.T. Marinetti: *Critical Writings.* New York: Farrar, Straus and Giroux, 2006. 260–265.

Pareyson, Luigi: *Esistenza e persona.* Genova: Il Melangolo, 2002.

Sgabelloni, Pietro: "Come le signorine Tofa, Putipù, Triccaballacche e Scetavajasse si produssero nel putiferio del putiputipù." *Il giornale d'Italia*, 31 March 1914.

Spatola, Adriano: *Verso la poesia totale.* Salerno: Rumma, 1969. 2nd edn Torino: Paravia, 1979.

Marcella Giulia Lorenzi

The Future of Futurism in Digital Photography

Introduction

The turn of the twentieth century saw great revolutions in thought related to new understandings of the physical world, of technology, of the psychology of perception, along with an artistic sensibility that grappled with these new issues. In particular, Albert Einstein changed the ways in which scientists and artists understood the universe, shifting the view from a static and rigid description of physics on the basis of the Galilean framework, with space and time separated and immutable, to a new vision in which both came to be inextricably interlinked in a four-dimensional new entity, called space-time. Guillaume Apollinaire declared in 1913:

> Today scientists no longer limit themselves to the three dimensions of Euclid. The painters have been led quite naturally, one might say by intuition, to preoccupy themselves with the new possibilities of spatial measurement which, in the language of modern studios, are designated by the term: the fourth dimension. Regarded from the plastic point of view, the fourth dimension appears to spring from the three known dimensions: it represents the immensity of space eternalizing itself in all directions at any given moment. It is space itself, the dimension of the infinite.[1]

On the other hand, and at the same time, technology was rapidly changing the world. New devices and means of communication such as the telegraph, radio, aeroplanes and cameras were also contributing to a change of perspective on time and space. In a sense, the world was being crossed by a new wind, by a new reality: velocity. It entered the artistic consciousness and caused Marinetti

1 Apollinaire: *The Cubist Painters: Aesthetic Meditations*, p. 12 "Les nouveaux peintres, pas plus que leurs anciens ne se sont proposés d'être des géomètres. Mais on peut dire que la géométrie est aux arts plastiques ce que la grammaire est à l'art de l'écrivain. Or, aujourd'hui, les savants ne s'en tiennent plus aux trois dimensions de la géométrie euclidienne. Les peintres ont été amenés tout naturellement et, pour ainsi dire, par intuition, à se préoccuper de nouvelles mesures possibles de l'étendue que dans le langage des ateliers modernes on désignait toutes ensemble et brièvement par le terme de quatrième dimension. Telle qu'elle s'offre à l'esprit, du point de vue plastique, la quatrième dimension serait engendrée par les trois mesures connues : elle figure l'immensité de l'espace s'éternisant dans toutes les directions à un moment déterminé. Elle est l'espace même, la dimension de l'infini." *Les Peintres cubistes: Méditations esthétiques*, pp. 15–16.

https://doi.org/10.1515/9783111318394-016

to proclaim in his *Foundation and Manifesto of Futurism* that "this wonderful world has been further enriched by a new beauty, the beauty of speed."[2]

New spaces, new technology, new science: they all contributed to making the future something less remote and more directly perceived in the collective imagination. The new age that emerged in the early twentieth century was one of motion, speed and dynamism, leading to new forms of perception and visualization. Representations of the world and the ways objects were portrayed changed from an exhibition of static objects to interactive works of art that made "the spectator live in the center of the picture".[3]

Umberto Boccioni wrote on the relations between Futurist art and the new science in his book *Pittura scultura futuriste (Dinamismo plastico)* (Futurist Painting and Sculpture: Plastic Dynamism, 1914):

> The most recent scientific hypotheses, the endless possibilities offered to us by chemistry, physics, biology, and all of science's discoveries, the life of the infinitesimally small, the fundamental unity of the energy that gives us life, everything pushes us to establish analogies in the world of artistic sensibility with these new and marvelous natural conceptions. [...] And we artists? [...] Let's convince ourselves that if this infinite, this imponderable, this invisible is becoming increasingly an object of investigation and observation, it's because, in the mind of the moderns, some marvelous sense is being awakened within the unknown depths of consciousness.[4]

Other Futurist artists shared this new artistic vision of a new world with cars, bicycles, trains and a world in motion. As a consequence, Umberto Boccioni, Carlo Carrà, Giacomo Balla, Gino Severini and Luigi Russolo created in their works an imagery that not only expressed movement, but made it central to their work. And in a long series of manifestos they established one of the main rules of Futurist painting, music, architecture, dance, photography and cinema: abolishing traditional perspective in favour of simultaneous visions able to capture dynamism.

---

2 Marinetti: "The Foundation and Manifesto of Futurism", p. 13 "La magnificenza del mondo si è arricchita di una bellezza nuova: la bellezza della velocità." "La fondazione e manifesto del futurismo." 1st edn 1968, p. 10; 2nd edn 1983, p. 10

3 Balla et al.: "The Exhibitors to the Public", p. 103.

4 Boccioni: *Futurist Painting Sculpture (Plastic Dynamism)* , p. 156. "Le ultime ipotesi scientifiche, le incommensurabili possibilità offerteci dalla chi mica, dalla fisica, dalla biologia e da tutte le scoperte della scienza, la vita dell' infinitamente piccolo, l'unità fondamentale dell'energia che ci dà la vita, tutto ci spinge a creare delle analogie nella sensibilità plastica con queste nuove e meravigliose concezioni naturali. [...] E noi artisti? [...] Convinciamoci che se questo infinito, questo imponderabile, questo invisibile, diventa sempre più oggetto d'indagine e di osservazione è perchè nei moderni qualche senso meraviglioso va destandosi nelle profondità sconosciute della. coscienza.." Boccioni: "Pittura scultura futuriste (Dinamismo plastico)", pp. 201–203,

As a consequence, an 'aesthetic of velocity' generated a truly dynamic art where motion involved both the object depicted and the space in which it is displayed. Futurism differed from Cubism in the way it superimposed multiple views from different viewpoints rather than adopt the effect of a single glance. Futurist paintings embedded a fourth dimension into two-dimensional canvases, thus achieving, as Boccioni said, "to synthesize the unique forms of continuity in space."[5]

The Futurist sought to capture in their works of art the ideas of motion itself, and to represent it with a great emotional impact as being formed by a continuous sequence of movement. The introduction of the fourth dimension of space-time was pursued through perceptive solutions that drew on new technologies related to the development of photography and cinematography.

Futurism and photography

Anton Giulio Bragaglia, a photographer associated with the Futurist movement, wanted to create a form of imagery that refused to make use of the medium of photography as a passive way of depicting reality. He experimented with various techniques of incorporating the perception of vital energy into his images, for example using slow shutter speeds to record people in motion. He called this type of photography 'photodynamism'.[6]

Crucial to both Bragaglia and the Futurist painters was the notion that a work of art should show the continuity of motion of a subject over a period of time, rather than a series of sharp images taken in sequence, as had previously been done in the scientific photography of Eadweard Muybridge and Etienne-Jules Marey ('chronophotography').[7]

Bragaglia wanted to construct an "algebra of movement".[8] The Futurist painters had begun to work on this idea, for example, with their concept of 'absolute' and 'relative' motion. Absolute movement was the general direction in witch a subject was moving, and relative movement was the internal movement of the subject,

5 Boccioni: *Futurist Painting Sculpture (Plastic Dynamism)*, p. 206. "Voglio sintetizzare le forme uniche della continuità nello spazio." This was the title of a painting shown in December 1913 in the *Esposizione di scultura futurista del pittore e scultore futurista Boccioni*, held in the Galleria Futurista in Rome. See p. 27 in the catalogue,.
6 See his booklet *Fotodinamismo futurista.* Roma: Nalato, [1913].
7 See Braun: "Giacomo Balla, Anton Giulio Bragaglia, and Etienne-Jules Marey" and Braun: *Picturing Time: The Work of Etienne-Jules Marey 1830–1904.*
8 Bragaglia: "Futurist Photodynamism", p. 372.

for example the turning wheels of a car or the swinging arms of a person, movements that are independent of the absolute movement. This eventually led to a full acceptance of photography by the Futurist movement in the *Manifesto della fotografia futurista* by Marinetti and Tato in 1930,[9] in which they declared their aim of "extending the possibilities of the science of photography into pure art"[10] by means of a series of new forms of composition related to a new way of perceiving contemporary reality.

Digital photography and the "Future of Futurism"

Photography, as the name says, is all about light. The word comes from the Greek words φωτός ('photos'; light) and γράφος ('graphos'; writing, drawing), meaning 'drawing with light'. A photographer is someone who uses light to draw pictures. Photography, therefore, is not about objects or people or scenery, but rather about how light can reveal those things. The effect of light on a light-sensitive material (film or an electronic device) creates an image. An object can be lighted so that it almost disappears or so that it is virtually three-dimensional. Colour photography is a relatively recent invention, where not only the intensity of the light, but also the colour of the light affects an image.

One century later, some statements from the Futurist manifestos appear to be chiming with contemporary digital photography techniques and applications. The recent developments in this field, in particular through the technique known as 'painting with light', and generating variations on the basis of similar ideas, have indeed refreshed the legacy of Futurism, not least because these new ideas have been linked up with Bragaglia's concept of 'algebra of movement'.

Rick Doble, a visual artist exploring and experimenting with time, motion (space-time) and light with digital photography, including light painting, states:

> Photography may be the visual Art best suited to creating still images of subjects in time. This is because a photograph is made by recording an object (via the lens) over time (by opening the shutter for a specific duration). Therefore, a photographic exposure is a combination of space and time, a recording of Space and Time.[11]

9 The long process of accepting photography as a valid Futurist art has been analysed by Braun: "Photography".

10 Marinetti and Tato: "Futurist Photography", p. 393.

11 Doble: *The Everything Digital Photography Book*, p. 125.

The capabilities of digital photography can make use of all of these ideas about movement in a fashion that the Futurists could only dream about. 'Light painting', also known as 'light drawing', is a photographic technique in which exposures – usually at night or in a darkened room – are made by moving a light source or by moving the camera. In the former case, light can either be used to selectively illuminate parts of the subject or to 'paint' a picture by shining it directly into the camera lens. Light painting requires a sufficiently slow shutter speed, usually a second or more. Like night photography, it has grown in popularity since the advent of digital cameras. Flash lights or light pens can also be used to project an image on Charge Coupled Devices (CCD). They allow the conversion of photons into electron charges, which are then converted into an image. Light painting by moving the camera is the antithesis of traditional photography. At night, or in a dark room, the camera can be taken off the tripod and used like a paintbrush. An example is using the night sky as the canvas, the camera as the brush and cityscapes (amongst other light sources) as the palette (see Figs 1a and 1b). Putting energy into moving the camera by stroking lights, making patterns and laying down backgrounds can create abstract artistic images. A variety of light sources can be used. Manual focus is often used since autofocus systems may not perform well in low light. In addition, photographers often use a slow film speed or low film sensitivity (ISO setting) on a digital sensor to minimize grain (or digital noise) and increase exposure tolerance. When moving the camera, longer exposures can create more intricate images.

Yet to photograph a space-time image is quite complex. For example, the correct shutter speed to depict motion varies considerably, depending on the motion of the subject and the artistic intentions of the photographer. In addition, there are many other variables to movement. And to record this kind of imagery successfully, the photographer must have a tool that allows instant display of the imagery just taken so that adjustments can be made based on that feedback. This very powerful capability is provided by digital photography.

The term 'Generative Art' refers to how art is made and does not take into account why it was made or what the content of the artwork is. In Generative Art, the creative process counts just as much as the results (the 'work'). Also because the results of each generative process are endless variations belonging to the same idea, it is a continuously unique process. The results are 'light paintings', produced in a Generative Art process.

Digital photographers who are interested in the depiction of movement have tried to add what the Futurist called an 'algebra of movement'. Photography knows two fundamental kinds of movement: subject movement and camera movement. It also adds a third kind of movement which is the combination of subject and camera movement, for example panning a camera with a moving subject. The Futu-

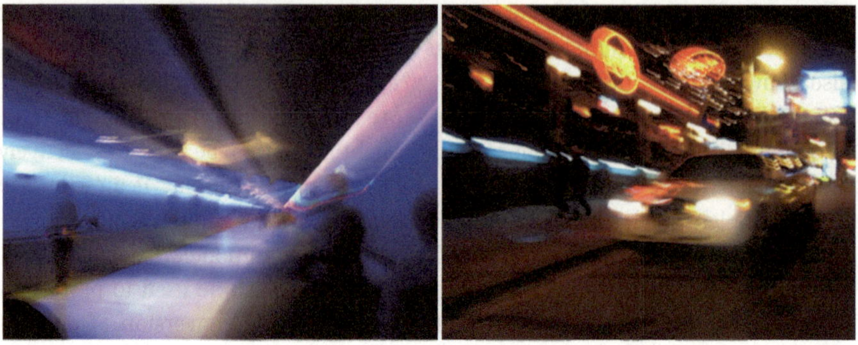

Fig. 1a: *Passage in SpaceTime* (2007). **Fig. 1b:** *Photodynamism of a Limo in Niagara Falls* (2007). Two photographs by Marcella Giulia Lorenzi.

rists' notion of absolute and relative movement is part of subject movement and works very agreeably with other photographic considerations when it comes to taking pictures of a subject in motion (see Figs. 2a and 2b).

Some digital photographers have added other aspects of subject movement to their ideas. These different types of subject movement can be defined thus:

1. Regular movement (like that of a train, that moves at a fairly steady pace in a predetermined direction);
2. Predictable movement (like a dancer doing a traditional dance, repeating the same steps but not in exactly the same spot);
3. Irregular movement (when some movements are repeated, but in an irregular fashion, such as a dancer who moves in a free-form manner).
4. Erratic movement (the movement of a singer on a stage or a child playing with a dog can be hard to predict, however, scenes such as these can yield exciting and unusual imagery).
5. Camera movement (carried out by the camera itself depicting motion from the photographer's point-of-view). This type of imagery has been called 'painting with light' and also 'camera painting'. It is essentially a new art form that has become practicable with the advent of digital photography and leads to dynamic abstract imagery much like the abstract work of the Futurists.

The Futurist could only imagine what technology is nowadays capable of doing: many features of digital cameras can easily be utilized to obtain a variety of artistic outcomes that resemble those the Futuristic had aimed for and worked towards.

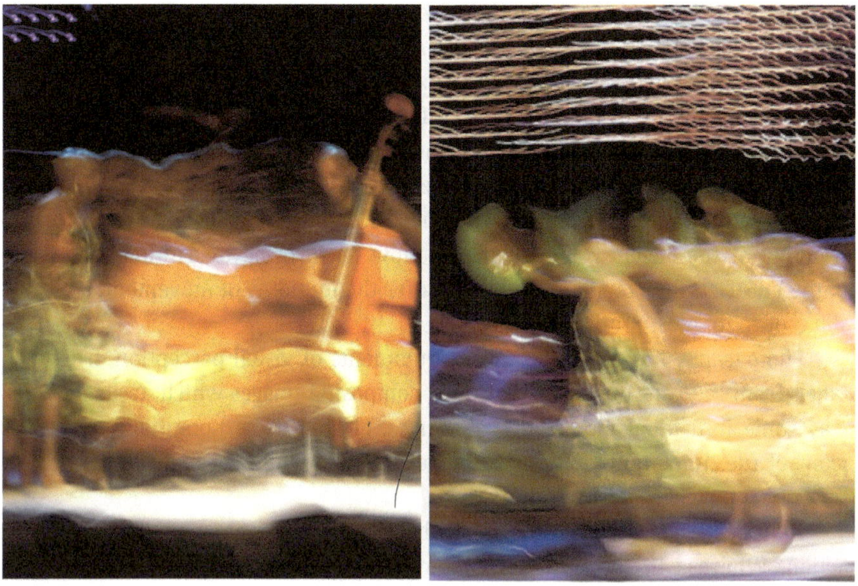

Fig. 2a & b: Photodynamic portraits of Dee Dee Bridgewater singing and dancing with a green fan during a Jazz concert (2010). Two photographs by Marcella Giulia Lorenzi.

1. LCD Monitor: It gives an immediate feedback, helping digital photographers to learn how to photograph objects in motion.
2. Low Cost: Taking pictures of movement, by necessity, requires many test shots. Digital photographers can now shoot hundreds of pictures without worrying about the cost, as in the past.
3. Stabilizing Control: It allows photographers to execute shots with handheld cameras at very low shutter speed. This means that photographs of subject movement by itself, for example, can be accurately captured without any or with minimal camera shake.
4. Exchangeable Image File Format Data: It is an invaluable new digital tool that lets a photographer go back to data recorded by most digital cameras and embedded in the photographic image. It allows a review of settings such as shutter speed and to learn from and build on that information.
5. Expressive Control: While digital photography is a technical craft, it is also an expressive medium. Images reflect the photographers' personalities and their artistic visions. As a result, the world in motion can be both accurately recorded and also depicted in an expressive and individual manner.

In their 'futuristic' struggle, the Futurists made the prediction that "there might come a time in which the picture might not be enough, its immobility, its childish means will be an anachronism in the dizzying movement of human life! Other values will rise, other evaluations, other feelings of which we conceive the boldness..."[12] Many of these predictions have come true in recent times, meaning that the torch has been passed from the Futurists to a new generation of artists in the twenty-first century. The technology of digital photography and an understanding of the 'algebra of movement' allow us to bring to fruition the visions of the Futurists and, one hundred years after the founding of movement, to realize some of their most ambitious aims.

Photography has the ability to hold moments of visual perception, fragments taken from the continuous flow of time, composing images which accurately portray some individual moments of our lives, elected to be potentially significant icons of the time and place. For example, the following figure shows the generation of geometric patterns from light:

New paradigms are going beyond the classic conceptions of time, place and action. Whereas in the past the contents of a work of art has conventionally been defined by its frame, in today's multimedia tools we have become accustomed to the simultaneity of many 'windows'. This means that in the near future visual communication will enhance the interactive 'transparency' of various forms of data, and many images can overlap in the same framework.

Digital photography almost symbolically expresses these features of today's viewing experience. It recollects the projected image from the lens on an optical sensor that settles the recovery delay to a computer memory, under the form of digital data, which at a later stage can be treated for a technical or creative interpretation, finally allowing the transmission on the Word-Wide-Web or the consultation of files encoded as a database. Once again, thanks to photography, our mind can switch between the memory of the visible and the visible memory.

Bibliography

Apollinaire, Guillaume: *Les Peintres cubistes: Méditations esthétiques.* Paris: Figuière, 1913. English translation *The Cubist Painters: Aesthetic Meditations.* New York: Wittenborn, 1944.

12 Boccioni: *Futurist Painting Sculpture (Plastic Dynamism)*, p. 157. "Verrà un tempo forse in cui il quadro non basterà più. La sua immobilità, i suoi mezzi infantili saranno un anacronismo nel movimento vertiginoso della vita umana! Altri valori sorgeranno, altre valutazioni, altre sensibilità di cui noi non concepiamo l'audacia..." Boccioni: "Pittura scultura futuriste (Dinamismo plastico)", p. 203.

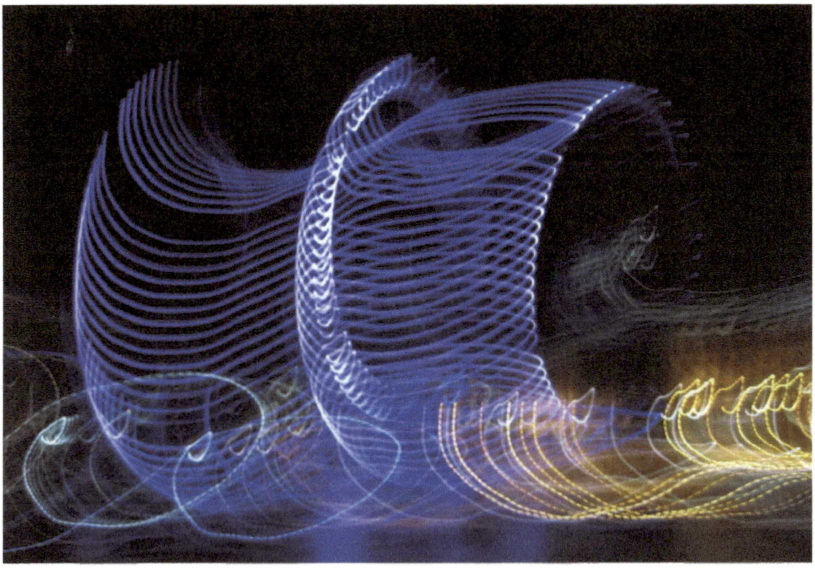

Fig. 3: Generation of Light Waves (2009). Photograph by Marcella Giulia Lorenzi.

Boccioni, Umberto, Carlo Carrà, Luigi Russolo, Gino Severini, and Giacomo Balla: "Gli espositori al pubblico." U. Boccioni: *Scritti sull'arte.* Milano: Mimesis, 2011. 13–21. English translation "The Exhibitors to the Public, February 1912." Lawrence Rainey, Christine Poggi, and Laura Wittman, eds.: *Futurism: An Anthology.* New Haven/CT: Yale University Press, 2009. 105–109.

Boccioni, Umberto: *Pittura scultura futuriste (Dinamismo plastico).* Milano: Edizioni Futuriste di "Poesia", 1914. Reprinted in Umberto Boccioni: *Scritti sull'arte.* Milano: Mimesis, 2011. 75–204. English translation: *Futurist Painting Sculpture (Plastic Dynamism).* Los Angeles/CA: Getty Publications, 2016. 57–158.

Bragaglia, Anton Giulio: "La fotografia di movimento: La fotografia futurista." *Noi e il mondo* 3:4 (April 1913): 358–364.

Bragaglia, Anton Giulio: *Fotodinamismo futurista.* Roma: Nalato, [1913]. Reprint Torino: Einaudi, 1970. 2nd edition 1980. Partial English translation "Futurist Photodynamism (1911)." *Modernism/Modernity* 15:2 (April 2008): 363–379.

Braun, Marta: "Giacomo Balla, Anton Giulio Bragaglia, and Etienne-Jules Marey." Vivien Greene, ed.: *Italian Futurism 1909–1944: Reconstructing the Universe.* New York: Guggenheim Museum, 2014. 95–103.

Braun, Marta: "Photography." Günter Berghaus, ed.: *Handbook of International Futurism.* Berlin & Boston/MA: De Gruyter, 2015. 215–230.

Braun, Marta: *Picturing Time: The Work of Etienne-Jules Marey 1830–1904.* Chicago/IL: University of Chicago Press, 1992

Briani, Giulio: "I futuristi e la fotodinamica." *Atti della Accademia roveretana degli agiati. A. Classe di scienze umane, lettere ed arti,* serie VII, vol. 5, A 245 (1995): 253–287.

Doble, Rick, Marcella Giulia Lorenzi, and Mauro Francaviglia: "Motion and Dynamism: A Mathematical Journey through the Art of Futurism and Its Future in Digital Photography." *Aplimat: Journal of Applied Mathematics and Engineerings* 3:1 (2010): 65–78.
Doble, Rick, Marcella Giulia Lorenzi, and Mauro Francaviglia: "The Future of Futurism." Celeste Soddu, ed.: *Generative Art: Proceedings of GA2009 (XII Generative Art Conference), Milano: Politecnico di Milano, 14–17 December 2009.* Milano: Domus Argenia, 2010. 377–385.
Doble, Rick: *The Everything Digital Photography Book.* Holbrook/MA: Adams; Northam: Roundhouse, 2002. 2nd edn Boston/MA: Adams Media, 2008.
Esposizione di scultura futurista del pittore e scultore futurista Boccioni. Roma: Galleria Futurista, dicembre 1913.
Lorenzi, Marcella Giulia, and Mauro Francaviglia: "Art & Mathematics: Motion and Fourth Dimension, the Revolution of XX Century." *Aplimat: Journal of Applied Mathematics and Engineerings* 1:2 (January 2008): 97–108 (2008).
Lorenzi, Marcella Giulia, and Mauro Francaviglia: "Painting with Light: Generative Artworks or 'Setting in Motion' the Fourth Dimension." Celestino Soddu, ed.: *Proceedings of the 10th Generative Art Conference GA2007.* Milano: Alea Design, 2007. 350–360.
Lorenzi, Marcella Giulia, Mauro Francaviglia, and Rick Doble: "Futurism, Geometry of 'Photodynamism ' and Digital Photography." Nathan Selikoff, and Robert W. Fathauer, eds.: *Bridges Coimbra 2011 : Mathematics, Music, Art, Architecture, Culture.* Phoenix/AZ: Tessellations, 2011. 459–462.
Marinetti, Filippo Tommaso: "La fondazione e manifesto del futurismo." F. T. Marinetti: *Teoria e invenzione futurista.* A cura di Luciano De Maria. Milano: Mondadori, 1968. 7–14. 2nd edn 1983. 7–14. English translation "The Foundation and Manifesto of Futurism." F. T. Marinetti: *Critical Writings.* Ed. by Günter Berghaus. New York: Farrar, Straus and Giroux, 2006. 11–17.
Marinetti, Filippo Tommaso, and Tato [pseud. of Guglielmo Sansoni]: "La fotografia futurista: Manifesto." *Il futurismo: Rivista sintetica illustrata* 22 (11 January 1931). English translation "Futurist Photography." F. T. Marinetti: *Critical Writings.* Ed. by Günter Berghaus. New York: Farrar, Straus and Giroux, 2006. 392–393.

Lindsay Brandon Hunter

The Infinite Wrench: An Ensemble Member Reflects on the Theatre Company 'The Neo-Futurists' During and After Greg Allen's Tenure

Abstract: Connections between historical Futurism and The Neo-Futurist performance ensembles founded by Greg Allen in Chicago in 1988 have always been rather loose. Still, the recent histories of those ensembles illuminate a shift in that relationship, and in particular to The Neo-Futurists' commitment to speed, boldness, and force. This essay examines variations to the performance ensemble's long-running flagship show, *Too Much Light Makes the Baby Go Blind*, including the 2016 re-tooling of the ensemble's weekly offering of short plays from *Too Much Light* into *The Infinite Wrench*. As a member of the New York ensemble who performed intermittently from 2004 to 2016, I recognized key features of the shows that might resonate with imaginaries of Futurism. Those aesthetic qualities – irreverence, dynamism, brevity, unruliness – sometimes had ethical implications, as when the groups' engagement with boldness risked transgressing against audience consent. Ethical concerns also came to the fore when founding director Greg Allen unexpectedly cancelled the Chicago ensemble's rights to perform *Too Much Light* in 2016, invoking the desire to combat Fascism as a rationale. The ongoing transformation of the performance ensembles hence signals a compelling change in their responses to the preoccupations of Futurism, as their relationship to its legacy continues to mean different things in evolving contexts.

Keywords: The Neo-Futurists (theatre ensembles in Chicago, New York, San Francisco), audience participation, power structures in collaborative ensembles, theatre and politics, Futurism and Fascism

Introduction: Neo-Futurist performance between speed and violence

When I speak to students about my time with The Neo-Futurists, a group of performance ensembles first established in Chicago in 1988 by Greg Allen, they often ask what relationship the company had with the Italian Futurists of the early twentieth century. My own work with The Neo-Futurists, who stage late-

https://doi.org/10.1515/9783111318394-017

night, experimental work in decidedly unpretentious venues, began in 2004 in the New York branch of the company. As a new artist in the ensemble, my impression was that even indirect references to Futurism within the company were pretty rare, and that Futurism's influence could be recognized only in elusive and diffuse ways. It seemed to me then, as it does now, that any likeness or perceived genealogy connecting the work of The Neo-Futurists with historical Futurism consisted largely in the ensembles' commitments to the qualities of brevity, rapidity, randomness and a bold frankness, which itself implied a kind of disdain for something so seemingly bourgeois as theatrical illusion.

In their book *Ensemble-made Chicago*, Chloe Johnston and Coya Paz Brownrigg describe The Neo-Futurists' work in terms that might do something to elucidate those commitments for anyone unfamiliar with The Neo-Futurists' long-running weekly shows. The authors narrate the experience of an audience member navigating a circuitous route to an unconventional theatre space, after which

> you'll be told to get into one of two lines, and when you step up to the front, you roll a six-sided die to determine how much you'll pay to enter the space. You're then ushered into a small room where someone wearing sunglasses and headphones will loudly demand that you tell them your name and then write something entirely different on the name tag they hand you. Only then do you enter the theatre itself. About one hundred sixty people are crowded into the narrow room; no audience member is more than fifteen feet from the playing area. There is no backstage, and when the performers are not performing, they generally sit in the audience. Above the stage is a clothesline, with thirty pieces of paper (labeled one through thirty) hanging on it. Someone comes to the stage to welcome you, to introduce you to the cast, to set the ground rules. [...] They warn you that there's no fourth wall here – be ready for the performers to enter the audience and treat you like a fellow human.[1]

In this narrative, Johnston and Paz Brownrigg foreground signature peculiarities of The Neo-Futurists, like the attachment to randomness and unpredictability signified by the throwing of dice to determine the price of admission. They also communicate the generalized lack of regard for decorum (the headphones, the yelling, the misnaming) and illusionary artifice (the playing space has no backstage, performers sit amid the audience during the show and engage in frank exchanges with them) that characterizes The Neo-Futurists' work. The authors go on to catalogue the show's composition: thirty short plays, each around two minutes long, some brand-new as of that week, all listed by number and title on a menu handed to each audience member; the numbered titles correspond to the numbers hanging on a clothesline over the stage. Those short pieces are performed in no more than sixty minutes, the hour counted down inexorably by a darkroom clock that buzzes

1 Johnston and Paz Brownrigg: *Ensemble-Made Chicago*, p. 111.

when time is up, whether all thirty plays have been performed or not. At the beginning of the show, an ensemble member winds up the clock's timer, and from that point forward

> it feels like anything could happen. The audience yells. A performer runs on stage, pulls down a number, reads the title, and that's the play that you'll see next. One moment, a performer stands in a spotlight and tells you a heartfelt story about their grandmother's funeral. The next, the performers are spraying you with water guns. Before you catch your breath, you are listening to an elaborate musical number about local politics and parking meters. The audience might be invited onstage to dance with the cast. Sometimes a title tells you everything you need to know about a play. In [the short play] *A Battle of Wills, A Measure of Patience, A Solution We Can Live With, And Some Dehydrated Fruit*, an adult channels their inner toddler while eating raisins. Next, a man might appear in a full-body spandex suit, carving a milk carton open to retrieve a rubber rat. . . . Sometimes a performer will step over your seat, sometimes they will ask you for money, sometimes they will whisper a secret. One thing is certain – a late-night show at the Neo-Futurists embraces the random, the unpredictable, the unrepeatable.[2]

The Neo-Futurists' break with norms of bourgeois theatre is, perhaps, recognizable as a gentle echo of the more passionate Futurist dismissal of history, tradition, or its conventions in favour of innovation. Specifically, their work might be visible as one answer to Marinetti's call, as early as 1913, for a theatre that "feeds on the rapidly passing events of the moment" and forbids actors "to fall into stagnation or to repeat themselves".[3] Whether or not The Neo-Futurists share Marinetti's "deep contempt for the theater of today",[4] their works pointedly reject any performance that – again in Marinetti's words – "wavers between historical reconstruction (pastiche or plagiarism) and photographic reproductions of our daily lives", proving "finicky, slow, analytic, and watered down – in fact, entirely worthy of the age of the oil lamp". [5] The Neo-Futurists' continual unpredictability and rapid turnover of new, short, experimental material is more easily legible as "born like us into the age of electricity."[6]

However, the words from Marinetti I recall running into most frequently (which is to say, the only citation from an actual Futurist I can remember from the days I was working regularly with the ensemble), are the same ones as those quoted by Johnston and Paz Brownrigg in their description of an evening of performance by The Neo-Futurists. They stem from the 1909 *Foundation and*

2 Ibid., p. 112.
3 Marinetti: "The Variety Theatre," p. 185.
4 Ibid., p. 185.
5 Ibid., p. 185.
6 Ibid., p. 185.

Manifesto of Futurism: "We believe that this wonderful world has been further enriched by a new beauty, the beauty of speed."[7] Certainly, an appetite for speed is a relatively easy characteristic of The Neo-Futurists' aesthetic to appreciate. The ensembles' late-night shows – first performed under the title *Too Much Light Makes the Baby Go Blind* and, later, in a revised version as *The Infinite Wrench* – are largely defined by the overwhelming quickness and concomitant exercises of chance that govern the material's genesis, performance and withdrawal from the repertoire. The short plays that make up each evening's performance are written and rehearsed in a rapid fashion, usually in the week before they first appear on stage, where they run for a few weeks before being cut from the show, sometimes never to be presented again. Each piece is set up, performed and struck in a matter of minutes, using a defiantly do-it-yourself, show-the-seams aesthetic. If the plays that compose the show drag on or if the audience shirks its responsibility to keep up the evening's pace (by shouting out new play numbers as soon as the previous play concludes), they may not get to see all the titles listed on that evening's menu.

This kind of brashness and disruptive energy might be the most visible sign of a Futurist preoccupation with violence,[8] albeit in an attenuated form fit for the theatre. This indirect resonance – one so watered-down as to be better described, maybe, as an aura or a vague reminder – between The Neo-Futurists' confident, energetic lack of propriety and the historical Futurists' aesthetic regard for aggression[9] is admittedly more difficult to pin down. Johnston and Paz Brownrigg describe the good-natured semi-bedlam of The Neo-Futurists' *Too Much Light Makes the Baby Go Blind* as "chaotic", referencing both its pace and its unpredictable but ultimately rather harmless spirit of disruption: "Performers yelled at the audience, the audience yelled at the performers", they write of the show's boisterous energy. "Performers threw tortillas at the audience, the audience threw tortillas back."[10]

Airborne tortillas admittedly feel a long way from venerating warfare as "the sole cleanser of the world", per Marinetti.[11] And yet both my experience and Johnston and Paz Brownrigg's description feature toy versions of weapons: from my

7 Marinetti: "The Foundation and Manifesto of Futurism", p. 13.

8 For a discussion of Marinetti's concept of violence see Berghaus: "Violence, War, Revolution: Marinetti's Concept of a Futurist Cleanser for the World."

9 "There is no longer any beauty except the struggle. Any work of art that lacks a sense of aggression can never be a masterpiece. Poetry must be thought of as a violent assault upon the forces of the unknown with the intention of making them prostrate themselves at the feet of mankind." Marinetti: "The Founding and Manifesto of Futurism", p. 14.

10 Johnston and Paz Brownrigg: *Ensemble-Made Chicago*, p. 112.

11 Marinetti: "The Foundation and Manifesto of Futurism", p. 14.

time as an ensemble member, I remember performing in a short play in which we ordered audience members to leave the theatre to perform some kind of errand while their accompanying partners remained hostage on stage, guarded by performers with water guns, like the ones Johnston and Paz Brownrigg refer to in their description of an evening with The Neo-Futurists. Vital to the situation was the threat of an actual soaking (that is, if the audience member did not comply with the performer's 'orders'). "Can we do that?" I recall one ensemble member asking, "can we really do that to them?" The answer, at the time, was: yes, we can. Exploring the limits of the power performers have over their audiences – that is, the power to make audience members *do* things, to cause them to feel things, to apply pressure, to discomfit them publicly – was part and parcel of what was presumed to be Futurist, in however attenuated a fashion, about The Neo-Futurists' style. Although such acts might not qualify as 'violence', they do represent an intrusive behaviour carried out by charismatic performers who were just audacious enough to 'super-soak' you if you refused to do what they asked.

In interviews, the group's founder, Greg Allen, has pointed to aspects of Italian Futurism that read as assertive, even antagonistic – in, for example, its desire for speed and rupture – as inspirational to him as he developed The Neo-Futurists' signature aesthetic. Allen cites the Futurists' didactic manifestos, their "fiery rhetoric", as attractive to him as he forged his own theatrical style.[12] At Oberlin, as a college student, he had helmed a group of students called "The Automatons", who performed Italian Futurist material to comic effect.[13] Allen describes himself trying to write "the great American play" as an emerging artist – and then, finding himself unsuccessful, turning instead to "the brevity, and kind of the *harshness*, the shock of these Italian Futurist plays" for inspiration.[14] Eventually, he came up "with the idea of combining the Italian Futurist plays – brevity, structure to a certain degree – with my own short pieces" and "my own aesthetic".[15] Citing a desire to "wipe away all artifice", Allen's early work arose from his desire for a kind of theatre that felt more immediate and muscular, which prioritized bold-

---

12 "Pop Matters: Interview with Neo Futurists Founder Greg Allen." Online Posting. You Tube, 28 March 2011.

13 John Pierson: *The Neo Interviews.* This online collection of interviews with Greg Allen and Neo-Futurist ensemble members, past and present, created in 2009, is cited in Glenn: *Baby's First Steps: A Microhistory of the Chicago Neo-Futurists*, p. 13

14 "Pop Matters: Interview with Neo Futurists Founder Greg Allen." Online Posting. You Tube, 28 March 2011.

15 Ibid.

ness, delighted in the unexpected and derogated illusion in favour of self-evident action.

In 1987, at the Organic Theatre in Chicago, Allen staged an evening of his own short plays under the title *Too Much Light Makes the Baby Go Blind*, the same title he would later give The Neo-Futurists' long-running flagship show.[16] In October 1988, he auditioned performers to produce an evening of works under that title, including both material of his own and plays written by the new performers. According to Max Glenn, this run, at Chicago's Stage Left theatre, began to attract local audiences, and in June 1989 first sold out its house.[17] In 1992, the group acquired a small 154-seat theatre and renamed it The Neo-Futurarium. This venue served as their new theatrical home for a show that continues (in spirit if not in name) to this day. Additional ensembles were established in New York (briefly in 1995 and again in 2004), San Francisco (2014) and London (in 2016, under the name Degenerate Fox). The titles of the weekly shows have varied: the London ensemble uses *The Dirty Thirty*, and the US ensembles changed the name of their weekly show from *Too Much Light Makes the Baby Go Blind* to *The Infinite Wrench* in 2017, a decision that shall be discussed at more length below. However, at their core they are all similar evenings of performance: thirty very short plays performed within 60 minutes, using an aesthetic that revels in rapid change, games of chance, and the abjuring of theatrical illusion or the pretence of a fourth wall. Interaction with audiences (who are typically young and boisterous) is encouraged. Although the ensembles have also developed additional works and have performed them in other time slots, the weekly hour-long, late-night show that began decades ago as *Too Much Light Makes the Baby Go Blind* constitutes The Neo-Futurists' greatest legacy and comprises the foundation of their public identity. The Chicago ensemble characterizes their work as a "fusion of sport, poetry, and living newspaper", with a predilection for measured chaos and point-blank directness over decorum that seeks to "embrac[e] those unreached or unmoved by conventional theater."[18]

Some of The Neo-Futurists' efforts to 'reach' or 'move' audiences may not be particularly kind – for instance, the water-gun play. Although I described it as "intrusive behaviour" rather than "violence," there is no denying that its effects on audience members are actual and real. In another short play I recall from the New York ensemble in 2007, a cast member placed a pair of noise-isolating head-

16 Milkovich, cited in Glenn: *Baby's First Steps: A Microhistory of the Chicago Neo-Futurists*, p. 15
17 Glenn: *Baby's First Steps: A Microhistory of the Chicago Neo-Futurists*, p. 20.
18 Chicago Neo-Futurists: "Mission." https://neofuturists.org/mission.

phones centre stage on a black cube and informed the audience that any one of them could retrieve the headphones and put them on. The performer then announced that he was going to sing a song of his own composition, one that detailed the plot of a Harry Potter novel that had just come out, effectively broadcasting 'spoilers' to an audience that predictably included many fans who had eagerly anticipated the book but not yet read it. When he began to sing (rather lustily), cries rang out from the audience; many people clamped their hands over their ears. I cannot recall if anyone made it to the stage to put on the headphones, but I do remember the friend who had accompanied me to the show telling me that she had found the threat – of upsetting an audience by gratuitously spoiling the finale of a beloved series of fiction – rather distasteful. For her, it exemplified a complaint she had long had about The Neo-Futurists' work: "It's not, like, *edgy*, to do that to people", she said, gesturing toward the company's occasional experiments with low-stakes authoritarianism. "It's just condescending." She did not use the term, but I suspect she meant that revealing the ending of a highly anticipated piece of fiction was a 'dick move' – that is, the kind of obstreperous mischief generally considered not serious enough to forbid, even though it might be unfriendly, unkind, or just plain mean.[19] Like the threat of the water guns, this performer's action was more obnoxious than violent, but unmistakably used the position of the stage to exert power over the audience.

Patriarchy and power plays

The Neo-Futurists are known for their decades-long presence in Chicago; even more so than the longevity of the other ensembles in New York and San Francisco. Despite their particularly enduring tenure in their city's performance scene, a potentially existential disruption occurred in 2016, when founding director Allen, who holds the rights to *Too Much Light Makes the Baby Go Blind*, declined to renew the rights held by The Neo-Futurists to perform the show in Chicago (although not in New York or San Francisco). The decision came as a surprise to the working ensembles. In a press release, Allen explained the move as a reaction to Donald Trump's ascent to the US presidency, and proposed to re-open *Too Much Light* with a new ensemble "comprised entirely of people of color, LTBQ+ [sic], ac-

19 The colloquial term 'dick move', added to the Oxford English Dictionary in 2019, is defined there as 'an obnoxious, devious, or stupid decision or course of action, typically one which undermines or causes harm to another person.' See the Oxford English Dictionary, online edition of 2019: https://public.oed.com/updates/new-words-list-june-2019/. Accessed 22.11.2022.

tivist/artist women, and other disenfranchised voices". He professed a desire to "rebrand the show with a new diverse ensemble that embraces a specifically socially activist mission", in order to better "combat the tyranny of censorship and oppression".[20] Painting Trump's election as a compellingly dire wake-up call, Allen described his retraction of the performance rights to *Too Much Light* in starkly moral terms: "I could no longer stand by and let my most effective artistic vehicle be anything but a machine to fight Fascism", he explained.[21]

Despite the urgency for larger political action that Greg Allen implied in his announcement, his statement lacked any serious engagement with anti-fascist strategies, even in the most general sense. In fact, the document focussed almost exclusively on Allen himself, his unilateral decision and his individual accomplishments. It communicated no political plans other than the vague promise of "rebooting" the show, hiring a new cast, and of undertaking "a specifically political message and fundraising mission" that is not even loosely described, in order to support unspecified "organizations fighting for civil rights".[22] The press release relentlessly highlights Allen's individual achievements but includes no promise from him to share power with the diverse artists that he proposes will create a "rebrand[ed]" Neo-Futurist show. Neither does it offer any recognition of the contributions made by the manifold artists (many of them women, queer folks and people of colour) who had long been active constitutive members of The Neo-Futurists and had performed *Too Much Light* every week for many years. His decision appeared to many ensemble members not as a social justice crusade, but a real 'dick move': a self-aggrandizing exercise of authority that affirmed Allen's personal standing at the cost of working artists, all under the pretence of "fight[ing] Fascism".[23]

Indeed, many working members of The Neo-Futurists read Allen's press release with suspicion and criticized the seeming lip service it paid to social justice. Soon after Allen's announcement, both Kurt Chiang, then the Chicago ensemble's artistic director, and Megan Mercier, a past artistic director, made statements noting the existing company's significant diversity and political engagement, the very elements Allen promised to foster through 're-branding' the company. Chiang

---

20 Press release embedded in Vire: "Greg Allen Pulls 'Too Much Light' from Chicago's Neo-Futurists."

21 Allen, quoted in Vire: "Greg Allen Pulls 'Too Much Light' from Chicago's Neo-Futurists." For a response from scholars in Fascism Studies to "the complex relationship between fascism, the politics of Donald Trump, and the wider MAGA movement", see "Debate: Donald Trump and Fascism Studies." *Fascism: Journal of Comparative Fascist Studies* 10:1 (June 2021): 1–15.

22 Allen, quoted in Vire: "Greg Allen Pulls 'Too Much Light' from Chicago's Neo-Futurists."

23 Ibid.

noted that the Chicago ensemble had "entered into negotiations [with Allen] in good faith" to renew the company's rights to perform *Too Much Light,* and were caught unawares by his announcement.[24] In a blog post, Mercier described the active company's makeup in November of 2016 as "comprised almost entirely of artists who identify as queer and gender non-conforming, people of color, [and] artist/activist women", noting that "[i]n revoking the rights to the Chicago Neo-Futurists' flagship show, Greg Allen directly revokes employment opportunities from the very demographic he claims to be so passionate about employing."[25] Both Mercier and Chiang made note of the fundraising and outreach activities in which the ensemble was already engaged, which supported local non-profit organizations, and Mercier described the ensemble's work as specifically "bold, diverse, risky, and – without question – *highly* political."[26] Moreover, despite a claimed desire to "giv[e] space and voice to marginalized people in the predominately white, patriarchal Chicago theater community",[27] Allen's revocation of the licence to perform *Too Much Light* removed power and opportunity from a diverse ensemble – as Mercier notes – and attempted to concentrate it in the hands of the individual white patriarch who owned the rights. Allen, after all, refers to himself in the press release as the "Father of Neo-Futurism", a moniker similar to the one featured prominently on his website at the time of the announcement, where he credited himself as "the Founding Father of Neo-Futurism" (since then amended to "Founder").[28]

Although Allen's revocation of the rights to perform *Too Much Light* in Chicago was a move he himself linked to Trump's 2016 election, it followed years of difficult relationships with the ensemble and its board of directors, in which Allen's behaviour and his continued future with the company was a consistent point of tension. Mercier also noted that Allen's "threat" to withdraw the rights from the Chicago company had "loomed since the end of 2011, when Greg was democratically removed from the active ensemble" in light of "repeated behaviors of abuse [and] harassment" which, Mercier alleges, had been ongoing "for years".[29] Allen's revocation of the rights from only the Chicago ensemble, where his relationship with the resident company was most strained, and not the New York or San Francisco

24 Chiang, quoted in Vire: "Greg Allen Pulls 'Too Much Light' from Chicago's Neo-Futurists."

25 Mercier: "Donald Greg Allen Trump." This is a rebuttal to Allen's similarly worded statement quoted on page 383–384.

26 Ibid.; emphasis in the original.

27 Allen, quoted in Vire: "Greg Allen pulls 'Too Much Light' from Chicago's Neo-Futurists."

28 Vire: "Greg Allen Pulls 'Too Much Light' from Chicago's Neo-Futurists."

29 Mercier: "Donald Greg Allen Trump."

ensembles, revealed that the change was more an act of pique than one of conscience. It made it clear that his moral pretence applied only to one city's ensemble, while the others could continue to license his "most effective artistic vehicle" and to carry on with the same work they had long been doing, while paying him royalties to do so.

Mercier recognized "parallels" between Trump's and Allen's personae and actions, in the form of harassment, manipulation and "abuse of power", but also in the self-interested "dishonest[y]" of his press release, which read to her (and many of us) as a disingenuous cover for actions that effectively consolidated his own power. Honesty (and its lack) has a particular value for The Neo-Futurists, who sometimes equate their frankness and disregard for theatrical illusion with the qualities of veracity and truthfulness. Johnston and Paz Brownrigg write that the group's "emphasis on truth is a cornerstone of its aesthetic", so much so that an individual play called *Honestly*, which features a performer's honest answers to audience questions on a bare stage, in a sort of 'ask-me-anything' format, remains "one of the most popular and enduring *Too Much Light* plays".[30] Allen's personal website continues to feature a text, *Neo-Futurism in a Nutshell*, which many ensemble members are familiar with as a succinct explanation of The Neo-Futurists' rejection of illusion and its embrace of candour as an alternate theatrical strategy: "You are who you are. Your name is your name. Your age is your age. Your appearance, physical condition, and way of speaking, as well as your personal history and life experiences are none other than your own."[31] This explicit lack of pretence – and, in many cases, subsequent predilection for vulnerability and exposure – was a hallmark of The Neo-Futurists in performance. Allen's decision to shut down the Chicago run of *Too Much Light* appeared to many artists who knew him and his history with the ensemble as not only self-centred, but, as Mercier puts it, "in direct opposition to the tenets of Neo-Futurism founded by Greg and his original company" and practiced by the extant ensembles to the present day.[32]

In other words, it was a real 'dick move' – in the sense of the OED, both 'undermin[ing]' and somewhat 'devious', 'caus[ing] harm' even if it appears merely 'obnoxious'. Allen's revoking of the Chicago branch's performance rights constituted a self-aggrandizing exercise of authority that affirmed his personal standing at the cost of working artists, made worse by his attempt to mask his self-interest under the pretence of "fight[ing] Fascism'.[33] Given that pretence, it is certainly no-

30 Johnston and Paz Brownrigg: *Ensemble-Made Chicago: A Guide to Devised Theater*, p. 114.

31 Allen: *Neo-Futurism in a Nutshell.*

32 Mercier: "Donald Greg Allen Trump."

33 Allen, quoted in Vire: "Greg Allen Pulls 'Too Much Light' from Chicago's Neo-Futurists."

table and nearly outrageous to consider the ways in which – as the title of Mercier's post references – Allen's actions *resembled* the strongman techniques of Donald Trump, impeding the work of resistance to power while affirming the centrality, authority and legacy of a single patriarch over the decades-long work undertaken by a multifaceted, collaborative ensemble.

Allen's relish for his central, foundational rôle in The Neo-Futurists is illustrated by his penchant for referring to himself as a 'father figure'. He remained for thirty years a key representative of Neo-Futurism in US-American theatre, persisting as a charismatic figure even after other Neo-Futurists took over artistic direction of the ensemble. After Allen was succeeded as artistic director in Chicago (in 2004, by Genevra Gallo-Bayiates), he acknowledged that he saw the Neo-Futurists as being fundamentally his creation, despite its collaborative, evolving nature and the input of many other artists over the ensuing decades: "It's always a dilemma, because it's my baby … How much do I let go of the rights and let other people do the show?"[34] Allen even referred to himself as "a benevolent dictator" and received criticism from ensemble members for the extent to which he sought to control the company's work, even as he idealized its workings as "egalitarian".[35]

"Benevolent dictator" are Allen's own words – as is, somewhat uncomfortably, the invocation of Mussolini in his press release, in which he describes Neo-Futurism as an "updating of Italian Futurism, a movement which, ironically, was created by artists who later supported Mussolini".[36] In this reference, Allen draws on associations that might link Neo-Futurism to Fascism, via the Neo-Futurists' debts to popular readings of history that enduringly connect Futurism to Mussolini.[37]

34 Allen, quoted in Felshman: "A Neo-Futurist Never Looks Back."

35 Glenn: *Baby's First Steps: A Microhistory of the Chicago Neo-Futurists*, pp. 23 and 3.

36 Allen, quoted in Vire: "Greg Allen Pulls 'Too Much Light' from Chicago's Neo-Futurists."

37 I am indebted to Günter Berghaus for his clarification in a personal communication, dated 26 August 2022: "To speak of Italian Futurism as a movement 'created by artists who later supported Mussolini' is historical nonsense, as some of them were already dead by the time Mussolini came to power. This is the original group according to Marinetti: Gian Pietro Lucini, Paolo Buzzi, Corrado Govoni, Federico De Maria, Enrico Cavacchioli, Libero Altomare, Giuseppe Carrieri, Mario Puccini, Enrico Cardile, Luciano Folgore, Mario Bétuda. Only 3 of them gave half-hearted support to Fascism." For an in-depth discussion of the conflictual relationship between Futurism and Fascism, and on the Futurists' "anarchist and anti-authoritarian convictions," see Berghaus: *Futurism and Politics: Between Anarchist Rebellion and Fascist Reaction, 1909–1944*; Berghaus: "The Futurist Political Party"; Berghaus: "Violence, War, Revolution: Marinetti's Concept of a Futurist Cleanser for the World." In his most recent book, *Necessità e bellezza della violenza: Discorso futurista* (Napoli: Diana Edizioni, 2021), Berghaus also edited Marinetti's most revolutionary speech, *The Necessity and Beauty of Violence*, given in 1910 in three meetings halls of the anarcho-syndicalist Left.

Berghaus points out ways in which Allen's dealings with The Neo-Futurists stand in marked contrast to Marinetti's interaction with his Futurist followers:

> Although Marinetti tended to behave like a messianic leader, it also needs to be stressed that he never acted like a general who sought to keep close control on his remote garrisons. In the Severini – Delmarle dispute, of July 1913, Marinetti made it absolutely clear that he did not consider himself to be a "Pope of Futurism" but rather the leader of a "broad Church" that could accommodate both dogmatists and dissidents. […] In fact, it is to his credit that he never attempted to impose a monolithic ideology on the movement and that he maintained amicable relationships even with those who professed rather heterodox ideas or operated under the label of 'Independent Futurists'. Throughout the 1910s, Marinetti reiterated again and again that he did not want Futurism to be a uniform and homogenous school or "little church", but rather a multi-faceted expression of a desire to radically overhaul the artistic and political system.[38]

In that sense, Allen's 'dick move' – his decision to excommunicate a Chicago ensemble with whom he could no longer find agreement in order to reify his authority and maintain his legacy – registers not only as a betrayal of his colleagues, but of a Futurist interest in anarchic dissent.[39]

Although the dynamics of paternalism, authority, and what Mercier terms "abuse of power" threaded through Allen's history with The Neo-Futurists has nothing to do with Fascism per se, Allen's professed zeal to oppose Donald Trump (which he shorthands as "fighting Fascism") keeps awkward company with reports of Allen's own "bullying and intimidation", as Mercier characterizes it.[40] While comparing Allen's flexing of his authority to political authoritarianism might feel rather glib, the extent to which his actions demonstrate a bent toward the consolidation of power is telling.

Authority, provocation, challenge

It is more common to think of performers exercising power over audiences – by making them feel things, for instance – as theatrical, or even virtuosic, than it is to consider it sadistic or controlling (or condescending, as my friend suggested). I have felt a kind of analogous thrill when performing with The Neo-Futurists; that is, one that comes from holding a kind of authority over audience members, especially in a performance that encourages or even requires their participation.

---

38 Berghaus: "Zenitism and Futurism: International Networks in the Historical Avant-Garde", p. 229.

39 I am grateful to editor Dalila Colucci for suggesting this figure of double betrayal.

40 Mercier: "Donald Greg Allen Trump."

The liberties I have taken in that position, however small in scale, might nevertheless register to some as a series of 'dick moves': the times I mocked an audience member, even if I thought I did so gently, or wilfully shocked someone by making an intensely personal revelation or invoking a real-life tragedy without warning. Perhaps worse, given The Neo-Futurists' regard for truthfulness, I once consciously and gleefully (if secretly) lied during *Honestly*, the play mentioned by Johnston and Paz Brownrigg as being emblematic of Neo-Futurism, even though my only job in the play was to tell the unvarnished truth in response to audience questions.

These examples might not be very impressive as instances of transgression, but I have to admit that I have not been a particularly provocative Neo-Futurist. Still, as I hope the water gun example from the beginning of this essay or the spoiling of the Harry Potter novel illustrates, for a performance group with a history of valuing provocation, or even instrumentalizing it, the wielding of authority is likely to be particularly charged, even when stakes are low.

To give an example: when I first joined the New York ensemble, I particularly loved taking part in the audience-naming ritual described by Johnston and Paz Brownrigg above. I volunteered for it every week. Wearing headphones playing very loud music, I would yell at audience members: "Hey, what's your name?" And although I could never hear the answer, I would write down a word of my choosing with a black marker pen on an adhesive 'hello-my-name-is ...' sticker and hand each one of them their new name. I particularly liked it when an audience member unfamiliar with the ritual tried to correct me, repeating their actual name slowly while trying to hand me back the name tag that dubbed them 'Honeydew' or 'Friendster' or 'RACCOON'. I liked this job because I could listen to music before the show, but also because it involved the excitement of transgression on a very small scale, with only benign effects. It was delicious to indulge in this minor affront to a paying audience. It was not until years later that I began to reflect on the power dynamic inherent in renaming someone I did not know, how the impulse to reassign identities to a line of approaching people, from a position of relative authority – even in play – might be something other than 'benign'.

During my first year in the ensemble, a fellow cast member proposed a play that involved him sitting on the lap of an audience member, one whom he planned to choose without seeking consent. Not asking permission was purposeful; as the performer described it, the play was intended to discomfit, in a way that could not be achieved or would be neutralized by a prior solicitation of consent. To him, the act was a minor affront, a benign encroachment. Another ensemble member who was in the show that week and I both objected to the play's inclusion in the upcoming performance. The performer who proposed the piece was clearly frustrated with our objection, seeing his invasion of an audience member's space as a tried-and-true Neo-Futurist technique, in line with the water gun, the Harry Potter spoilers, and maybe even the airborne tortillas. It was intended not as a performance that *risked* making someone in the audience uncomfortable, but as a purposeful design that attempted to ensure it. This was years before open discussions regarding consent and trauma-informed processes became a professional standard in (at least some) theatrical spaces, and all of us struggled to find language for exactly what we were campaigning for and objecting to. The play did not run, but we were not able to talk very productively about why this was the case.

In the more than fifteen years since I joined the New York ensemble, this, maybe more than anything else, is what I can observe having changed: The Neo-Futurists might make fewer 'dick moves', at least intentional ones. The Neo-Futurist celebration of speed and boldness could occasionally make *Too Much Light* feel – to me, at least – troublingly forceful, at risk of celebrating dominance, imposition, or other tribulations that can trickily, troublingly resemble supremacy. The show seems now to have been tempered, made more responsive, and stage-audience relationships are more good-humoured. While Neo-Futurism was never an authoritarian régime, it has predictably suffered from and enacted the kinds of injustices that not only surround it within dominant culture, but which can multiply when a group has a specific desire for muscular force, boldly applied without apology or consent.

In *Neo-Futurism in a Nutshell,* Allen observes that the "Neo-Futurism" he wants to see in performance not only "embraces the actual world around us" but "drags it kicking and screaming onto the stage where everyone can observe its hideous beauty and wrestle with its unfathomable contradictions".[41] It is *the world* he characterizes as kicking and screaming, not the audience, and certainly not the performers. Still, his lionizing of forceful, coercive actions – dragging, kicking, grappling – perhaps reminds us that consent was not necessarily valued as part of the aesthetic championed by Allen at the outset of his career. It might, however, be part of what emerges as the ensembles continue to evolve, in the absence of their founder, to meet a contemporary moment that calls artists to enact care for whole communities rather than prioritize individual or institutional acts of force and imposition.

Conclusion: Urgency and slowing down

The Neo-Futurists' weekly late-night show did not end when Allen communicated his plan to refuse the Chicago ensemble the rights to perform *Too Much Light*

41 Allen: *Neo-Futurism in a Nutshell.*

Makes the Baby Go Blind. All three of the US ensembles responded to Allen's decision by ending their runs of *Too Much Light*, and opening in its place a newly titled, but very recognizable late-night Neo-Futurist show: *The Infinite Wrench.* Like its predecessor, *The Infinite Wrench* is made up of thirty short plays staged in sixty minutes.[42] The new show maintains most of *Too Much Light*'s hallmarks – it features a menu of thirty plays, a darkroom clock, a clothesline full of numbers, and perhaps more importantly, the same bold and frank aesthetic – and adds some additional ones (chiefly, the titular 'wrenches', a series of one-night-only rules that can affect the progression of the evening's performance). As Justin Hayford of the *Chicago Reader* wrote two years into the newly-titled run, "To see the difference between the Neo-Futurists' *Too Much Light Makes the Baby Go Blind* [...] and the Neo-Futurists' *The Infinite Wrench*, you have to squint awfully hard."[43] The show has changed its title, but not really altered its form or energy. Speaking of the work of the Chicago ensemble, Hayford observes that

> most importantly, the ingenuity and engagement of the work not only remains but has deepened. With only the occasional misstep into poetic opacity, the ensemble maps thorny social, psychological, and political terrain with foolishness and ferocity. And watching a dozen or so people sprint for an hour, setting up and tearing down plays they've barely had time to rehearse, is exhilarating and vital.[44]

It would seem that speed and dynamism, perhaps two legible inheritances from Marinetti, persist as hallmarks of The Neo-Futurists. As for the 'anti-fascist machine' Allen promised to create out of *Too Much Light*, it never materialized, at least not in Chicago. The Neo-Futurist ensembles, however, continued to engage politically, even in the face of the global COVID-19 health crisis. In 2020, the shows in San Francisco, New York and Chicago had to change drastically in light of precautions and prohibitions imposed by the pandemic on public gatherings. For The

---

42 The show's new title is drawn from Mina Loy's *Feminist Manifesto* of 1914, which contains the lines "Women if you want to realize yourselves – you are on the eve of a devastating psychological upheaval – all your pet illusions must be unmasked – the lies of centuries have got to go – are you prepared for the wrench – ?" Loy: "Feminist Manifesto", p. 92. The Neo-Futurists' invocation of Loy, a feminist associated with Futurism between 1914 and 1917, attempts to apply Futurist zeal to a more defensible cause – that is, Loy's assault on the oppression of women – despite Loy's legacy being troubled by her embrace of eugenics and dubious racial theory. Loy's words handily couple feminism to the Futurist enthusiasm for upheaval which The Neo-Futurists light-heartedly borrowed: "NO scratching on the surface of the rubbish heap of tradition will bring about Reform, the only method is Absolute Demolition." Loy: "Feminist Manifesto", pp. 92–93.

43 Hayford: "Two Years after Greg Allen Pulled Too Much Light, the Neo-Futurists Continue with The Infinite Wrench."

44 Ibid.

Neo-Futurists, these changes meant some fundamental re-figuring as they pondered a transition to distanced and digitally mediated forms: what would become of their trademark chaotic energy without an audience's live interaction? It also meant considering new ways of producing art within and for communities that suffered acute, sustained, unrelenting crisis. In Chicago, the weekly show was offered online as "30 digital plays in 60 analog minutes" through Patreon, a membership platform that enabled the company to get paid for their individually recorded short plays. A viewer could navigate through a menu, or set the list of plays to shuffle, and then enjoy them in a sequenced or random order. Setting a timer for 60 minutes to limit the viewing (in the spirit of the live-presented show) was optional, as artistic director KR Riiber explained: "Fuck it. We are in uncertain hellish times and you can watch all the plays you want."[45]

The New York ensemble produced a live-streamed – that is, not pre-recorded – version of the show entitled *CyberWrench*, which used the Twitch platform to allow viewers to interact with performers via the 'chat' function. They also produced an audio series called *Hit Play*, which functioned like a sort of mix tape of short audio plays. The San Francisco ensemble, too, streamed their work on a regular basis. Each of the companies managed to produce a significant amount of new work and continued to support artists financially at a time when many theatres ceased production. They did so in ways consistent with the spirit of their aesthetics and their mission, including The Neo-Futurists' drive to respond to the political and social demands of the moment. In September 2020, Riiber told the *Chicago Tribune* that The Neo-Futurists "are used to creating new material every single week so we are able to respond to events with immediacy. When our community experiences either a victory or a tragedy, people come to our theatre to hear an honest response to those events",[46] even when the physical theatre is translated into online space.

I have not been an active part of the Neo-Futurists for many years, but I understand the company's recent shifts as evidence of a significant, ongoing project: to steward the companies' continual response to a changing theatrical, social and political landscape. That commitment is core to The Neo-Futurists' mission to produce "ever-changing" theatre, even (especially) when it means displacing a patriarchal model in order to respect better the collaborative and distributed processes that have long helped The Neo-Futurists to flourish. Such a shift can only help the ar-

45 Quoted in Reid: "All Your Home's a Stage."
46 Quoted in Jones: "The Neo-Futurists Have Created the Most Successful Online Shows of the Pandemic."

tists respond to the complexity and urgency of the contemporary world's catastrophes – not only pandemic, but climate change, late capitalism, white supremacy.

I spoke with Rob Neill, a current ensemble member and one of two artistic directors (with Kyra Sims) of the New York company, about how the times were changing The Neo-Futurists and their work. He described specific shifts in the ways that the New York ensemble's online work integrated the audience in the absence of the raucous interaction that characterized the live shows. In their *Cyber-Wrench* productions, the performers invited and integrated the audience's input, including the order in which the plays are to be performed, via the relatively slower and quieter function of live online chat, requiring the velocity and volume of The Neo-Futurists' in-person audience interaction to give way to other registers. Neill described to me the company's attempts to develop means of interacting with audiences online that was not merely an attenuated form of live engagement, but one that "illuminate[d] different types of agency". "Are we giving them things to do and not just using them as a prop?" he asked, suggesting it not only as a question about how performers and audiences can engage through media platforms, but as one suited to fostering more ethical interactions overall".[47] As an example, Neill pointed to the audio series *Hit Play*, in which the asynchronous means of presentation constrained the ways in which performers could act on their audience. Anything the performers asked listeners to do or consider was, in the podcast, both optional and anonymous, an invitation rather than a demand at water-gun point.

Overall, Neill painted a picture of Neo-Futurism circa 2020 as not only media-delivered, but perhaps less enamoured of the 'dick move' that it had been. It was a portrait of provocations carefully considered rather than ebulliently thrown at the audience, with less dependence on harsh rhetorics and aesthetics that work via aggression. He observed that when the world outside the theatre is so resolutely and transparently violent, the world inside it needs new tools and practices. Although at times, he admitted, "the better art comes from conflict and fight",[48] perhaps these are not those times.

It is, perhaps, an era for re-evaluating the purpose and the effects of bold energy in the theatre, at least the sort that asks for kicking and screaming and coercive action, without concern or care for how privilege and power work in performance. It might be a useful time to find strength and potency in careful engagement – or even care itself – rather than in the intoxicating effects of speed, the tool which The Neo-Futurists most obviously borrow from the Italian Futurists. As philosopher and activist Bayo Akomolafe and feminist religious lead-

---

47 Neill: Personal Interview.

48 Ibidem.

er Marta Benavides recently declared in an open letter: "The time is very urgent – we must slow down."[49] While rapid response to contemporary events may always be a core Neo-Futurist technique, it might be performers' dedication to care and community – to a responsiveness that takes consideration, not just speed, to enact – that make it most workable as a Fascism-fighting machine.

Bibliography

Printed sources

Berghaus, Günter: *Futurism and Politics: Between Anarchist Rebellion and Fascist Reaction, 1909–1944.* Providence/RI: Berghahn Books, 1996.

Berghaus, Günter: "The Futurist Political Party." Sascha Bru, and Gunther Martens, eds.: *The Invention of Politics in the European Avant-garde, 1905–1940.* Amsterdam: Rodopi, 2006. 153–182.

Berghaus, Günter: "Violence, War, Revolution: Marinetti's Concept of a Futurist Cleanser for the World." *Annali d' italianistica* 27 (2009): 23–71.

Berghaus, Günter: "Zenitism and Futurism: International Networks in the Historical Avant-Garde." Bojan Jović, and Irina Subotić, eds.: *Sto godina časopisa Zenit: Zbornik radova = A Hundred Years of the 'Zenit' Magazine 1921–1926–2021: Collection of Essays.* Kragujevac: Galerija RIMA; Beograd: Institut za književnost i umetnost, 2021. 227–253.

"Debate: Donald Trump and Fascism Studies." *Fascism: Journal of Comparative Fascist Studies* 10:1 (June 2021): 1–15.

Glenn, Max D.: *Baby's First Steps: A Microhistory of the Chicago Neo-Futurists.* M.A. Thesis. Columbus: OH: Ohio State University, 2014.

Johnston, Chloe, and Coya Paz Brownrigg: *Ensemble-Made Chicago: A Guide to Devised Theater.* Evanston/ IL: Northwestern University Press, 2019.

Loy, Mina: "Feminist Manifesto." Alex Danchev, ed.: *100 Artists' Manifestos from the Futurists to the Stuckists.* London: Penguin Books, 2011. 92–95.

Marinetti, Filippo Tommaso: "The Foundation and Manifesto of Futurism." F. T. Marinetti: *Critical Writings.* Ed. by Günter Berghaus. New York: Farrar, Straus and Giroux, 2006. 11–17.

Marinetti, Filippo Tommaso: "The Variety Theater." F. T. Marinetti: *Critical Writings.* Ed. by Günter Berghaus. New York: Farrar, Straus and Giroux, 2006. 185–192.

Internet sources

Akomolafe, Bayo, and Marta Benavides: "The Times Are Urgent: Let's Slow Down." B. Akomolafe: *Writings.* https://www.bayoakomolafe.net/post/the-times-are-urgent-lets-slow-down. Accessed 18 July 2022.

49 Akomolafe and Benavides: "The Times are Urgent: Let's Slow Down."

Allen, Greg: *Neo-Futurism in a Nutshell.* https://www.neogregallen.com/neo-futurism-in-a-nutshell/. Accessed 18 July 2022.

Chicago Neo-Futurists: "Mission." https://neofuturists.org/mission/. Accessed 18 July 2022.

Felshman, Jeffery: "A Neo-Futurist Never Looks Back." *Chicago Reader,* 5 May 2005. http://chicagoreader.com/news-politics/a-neo-futurist-never-looks-back/. Accessed 18 July 2022.

Hayford, Justin: "Two Years after Greg Allen Pulled Too Much Light, the Neo-Futurists Continue with 'The Infinite Wrench'." *Chicago Reader,* 7 December 2018, http://chicagoreader.com/arts-culture/two-years-after-greg-allen-pulled-too-much-light-the-neo-futurists-continue-with-the-infinite-wrench/. Accessed 18 July 2022.

Jones, Chris: "The Neo-Futurists Have Created the Most Successful Online Shows of the Pandemic." *Chicago Tribune*, 10 September 2020. https://www.chicagotribune.com/entertainment/theater/chris-jones/ct-ent-neo-futurist-chicago-theater-f-all-2020–20200910-h3lujip3qbgfnk64lrb3miiria-story.html. Accessed 18 July 2022.

Mercier, Megan: "Donald Greg Allen Trump." *Rubberneck Whiplash*, 30 November 2016. https://rubberneckwhiplash.tumblr.com/post/153890925206/donald-greg-allen-trump. Accessed 18 July 2022.

"New Words List June 2019." *Oxford English Dictionary.* https://public.oed.com/updates/new-words-list-june-2019/. Accessed 18 July 2022.

Reid, Kerry: "All Your Home's a Stage." *Chicago Reader,* 27 March 2020. http://chicagoreader.com/arts-culture/all-your-homes-a-stage/. Accessed 18 July 2022.

Vire, Kris: "Greg Allen Pulls 'Too Much Light' from Chicago's Neo-Futurists." *Time Out Chicago*, 30 November 2016. https://www.timeout.com/chicago/blog/greg-allen-pulls-too-much-light-from-chicagos-neo-futurists-113016. Accessed 18 July 2022

Other sources

Neill, Rob: Personal Interview. 18 July 2021.

Section 2: **Reports**

Günter Berghaus

EAM2022 in Lisbon: The Global Expansion of Futurism in the 1910s and 1920s

In 2007, the European Network for Avant-Garde and Modernism Studies (EAM) was founded as a consequence of several scholarly meetings in Copenhagen, Ghent, Reykjavik, Stockholm and Tromsø, concerned with the multifaceted strands of Modernist forms of expressions in the late-nineteenth and early-twentieth centuries. The first edition of the association's bi-annual conference series, EAM2008 (*Europa Europa*), offered a platform for scholars to meet and discuss their research into the avant-garde in Europe within a global setting. Subsequent meetings focussed on *High and Low* (2010, Poznan), with a section on "Futurism in East and Central Europe",[1] *Material Meanings* (2012, Canterbury), *Utopia and (Im)Possible Life* (2014, Helsinki),[2] with a section on "The Futurist Utopia in North-European Countries",[3] *Quest/Investigation* (2016, Rennes), with a section on "The Futurist Fusion of Artistic and Scientific Inquiry"[4] and *Realisms* (2018, Münster). As EAM2020 (Leuven) on the theme of *Crisis* had to be cancelled due to the Corona crisis, it was with great anticipation that some 250 members of the association descended on Lisbon for the eighth edition on the theme of *Globalising the Avant-garde.*

Futurism always featured prominently at EAM meetings, but in the past the focus was nearly always directed towards Europe. With hindsight, the name of the association was badly chosen.[5] Although initially we were only a small group of scholars based in Europe, we were quickly complemented by colleagues from the Unites States of America. My repeated calls to invite researchers from Africa, Asia and Latin America and to expand the remits of the programme to include non-Western forms of Modernism[6] never found much response. I am therefore

1 Published in 2011 as a special issue of the *International Yearbook of Futurism Studies.*

2 See Berghaus: "Futurist Utopias."

3 Selected papers on Finland, Denmark, Lithuania, Latvia, Estonia and Iceland were published in the 2015 edition of the *International Yearbook of Futurism Studies.*

4 Selected papers on "Futurism and Science" were published in the 2018 edition of the *International Yearbook of Futurism Studies.*

5 In 2005/06, the idea of EAM arose out of the Nordic Network of Avant-Garde Studies when it wanted to extend its activities to other parts of Europe. Now that members also come from other continents, the name should be changed to International Association of Modernism and Avant-garde Studies (IAMAS).

6 See Berghaus: "Futurist Utopias", pp. 493–494.

https://doi.org/10.1515/9783111318394-018

glad to report that EAM2022 in Lisbon finally changed this emphasis on Europe. There were more non-Western colleagues present than ever (although many of them hold academic posts in the USA) addressing an ever-widening geographical range of topics, even including the Arctic region (in a fascinating paper on Inuit Modernism). The two keynote lectures by Paul Wood on "The Globalisation of the Avant-garde: A User's Manual" and Ming Tiampo on "Transversal Modernism/s: Lateral Networks and Multidirectional Avant-garde/s" (see Fig. 1) engaged, albeit in rather contrary fashions, with the complex interactions between centre and periphery in the fields of Modernism and the avant-garde.

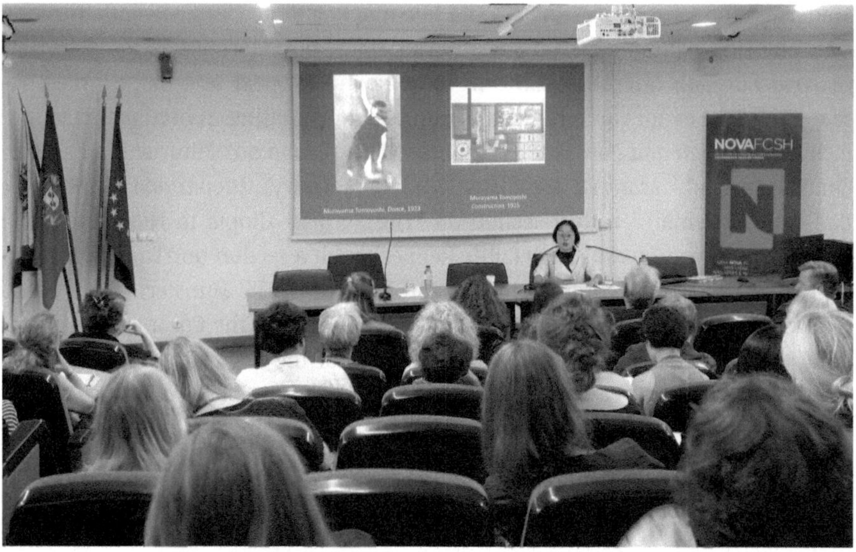

Fig. 1: Ming Tiampo in her keynote address discussing the work of Tomoyoshi Murayama (1901–1977), who participated in *The Great Futurist Exhibition* at Israel Ber Neuman's Graphisches Kabinett in Berlin in February-March 1922. Marinetti gave him a copy of his Tactilism manifesto, which Murayama translated and distributed in Japan in 1923.

Futurism was discussed in various sections, some of which will be highlighted here. *Shifting Futures* included Tiit Hennoste (University of Tartu) discussing Estonian Futurism, especially its contrasting attitudes to modern urban life and technology vs. indigenous rural life and pagan mythology. Giulia Beatrice (Bibliotheca Hertziana, Rome) investigated the network of encounters, transnational influences and cultural exchanges between the Futurist movement in Egypt and the local artist community in Alexandria and Cairo. Ana-Maria Milčić (Courtauld Institute of Art, London) offered a novel approach to the Futurist activities in occupied Fiume

(1919–1920) by juxtaposing canonical Futurist texts with forgotten sources by local Fiuman artists and townspeople who spoke Croatian or Hungarian. Drawing on postcolonial theories of identity, she showed how the Futurists' approach to an international revolution was entrenched in Italian imperialism.

Eastern Visions included a paper by Olga Isaeva (University of Bonn) on the Japanese avant-garde seen from a transcultural perspective, in which David Burliuk's visit to Japan in 1920–22 was analysed. In a section on *Symbolist Networks*, Thea Santangelo (Free University Berlin) discussed "Marinetti on the Threshold between Symbolism and Futurism", in which she showed how the Late-Symbolist magazine *Poesia* became the mouthpiece of the newborn Futurist movement and how traces of Symbolism continued to play a rôle in Marinetti's *Mafarka le futuriste* and *Roi Bombace.* Andrea van der Smissen, a musicologist from the University of Vienna, investigated in "Tactilism: The Art of Immersion" the global reception of *Il tattilismo: Manifesto futurista* (Tactilism: A Futurist Manifesto, 1921), in which Marinetti propagated an aesthetic experience rooted in an immersive sensory realm. Her main focus was on the Hungarian avant-gardist István Tiszay, who lived in Italy between 1923 and 1926. After his return to Budapest, he founded a tactile theatre and propagated a changed rôle of sound and composition for the music of the future. Iwona Boruszkowska (Jagiellonian University, Krakow) focussed in "Abolishing Borders: Avant-Garde Figure of a Nomadic Beyonder" on Aleksander Wat's Futurist prose poem *JA z jednej strony i JA z drugiej strony mego mopsożelaznego piecyka* (Me from One Side and Me from the Other Side of My Pug Iron Stove, 1919) and glossolalic *namopaniki* (sound poems employing morphemes from various tongues, including fake-languages) that destabilize identity through intertextual dissolution and overlapping soundscapes. Abigael van Alst (Catholic University Leuven) gave a paper on *La Création du monde* by Blaise Cendrars, Fernand Léger, Darius Milhaud and Jean Börlin, in which she analysed the twenty-minute ballet performed by the Ballets Suédois at the Théâtre des Champs-Élysées in Paris (1923), inspired by African sculpture, American jazz, the dances of whirling dervishes and Futurist designs. Scholarship has paid much attention to the primitivist aesthetic of this mechanical ballet, and Van Alst demonstrated how primeval, prehistoric and futuristic elements merged to announce the birth a new humanity.

At the beginning of 2022, I was in touch with four Russian Futurism scholars to discuss their contributions to the conference. Soon after the Russian invasion of Ukraine on 24 February 2022 it became clear that they would not be able to travel to Lisbon. They were therefore given a special section, entitled *Russian Futures*, with remote access via Skype technology. It was chaired by Natalia Smolianskaia and went very well, with plenty of questions and a short discussion. The online panel began with a paper by Anna Shvets (Moscow State University) on "Futurism and Scandal: Going Global or Not?", which focussed on the poetic activities of the Cubo-Futurist circle in Saint Petersburg and analysed how author-reader communication impacts on the social-aesthetic experience of a work of art. She discussed Marinetti's legacy of engineering scandals and of shocking audiences out of their complacency by enticing the spectators to take an active part in a performance. This violation of norms made the headlines and managed to broadcast the ideas behind Futurism to a wider public. In Italy, Russia and in other parts of the world, it fostered a creative engagement of audiences with the communicative experiments of the avant-garde and caused a transformation of the spectator into a co-producer of a performance.

Irina Sirotkina, who has recently been appointed Honorary Senior Research Fellow at University College London, spoke on "Dance and the Futurists". She painted a broad picture of the cross-pollination between café-culture of the 1910s and demonstrated that the spirit of protest against bourgeois sentiments was characteristic of both Italian and Russian Futurist performances. Dances were usually incorporated into evenings of poetry recitation and so-called 'serate'. As the Futurists rejected ballroom dance, with the exception of Tango, they produced pantomime dances that mimicked the movements and rhythms of machines. In Russia they created the new genre of 'slovoplastika' in which poetry recitals were accompanied with gestures and body movements. Over time, this developed into 'plastichesky', a form of early modern dance, which flourished in Russia in the 1920s.

Ekaterina Lazareva (State Institute for Art Studies, Moscow) investigated "Italian Futurism's Exhibition History in an International Context". She showed how Marinetti's attempts to endow his movement with an international, global character – especially in the *Free International Futurist Exhibition* in Rome (1914) – was not without opposition, as he himself had to experience in 1914 in Russia, where his proselytizing campaigns were considered patronizing and colonialist. Lazareva showed how, in the 1970s to 90s, Italian Futurism gained kudos in the international art world and came to be recognized as the cradle of many contemporary art trends. The exhibition *Futurism & Futurisms* (Venice, 1986) was a remarkable attempt to evaluate Futurism beyond national borders; *Futurism 1909–1944: Art, Architecture, Performance, Literature, Advertising* (Rome, 2001) showed the movement's contribution to a broad spectrum or artistic disciplines; and *Italian Futurism 1909–1944: Reconstructing the Universe* (New York, 2014) presented its full history from 1909 to 1944.

The largest thematic panel of the 2022 conference, extending over three sessions, was "The Global Expansion of Futurism in the 1910s and 1920s", coordinated and convened by Günter Berghaus (see Figs. 2a and 2b). Futurism is generally considered to have been the first avant-garde movement. Emerging more or less simultaneously in Italy and Russia, the version promoted by F.T. Marinetti quickly became a major factor in artistic debates in the early 1910s. The founding manifesto of 1909 was translated into many languages and published in countless periodicals in Europe, Asia and the Americas. After a ground-breaking touring exhibition in 1912–13, a large number of artists produced works in Futurist style or, more frequently, works that reveal an intense study of Futurist aesthetics.

In the past decades, scholars have examined how Futurist ideas and stylistic features entered the artistic languages in many countries around the world. What has been less investigated is how writers and artists used the stimulus of Italian or Russian Futurism to develop their own Modernist ideas and to merge the newly arriving concepts with indigenous traditions. The panel in Lisbon scrutinized this dialectic process of rejection and absorption in a global perspective by revisiting countries that only recently emerged as nation states. Marinetti's call "We wish to destroy museums, libraries, academies of any sort"[7] could not be heeded here because there were no traditions and institutions present that needed to be destroyed. Speakers investigated the relations between centre and periphery that determined how new artistic trends in European capitals were responded to in the former colonies and how Futurist machine culture interacted with indigenous (often folkloristic) traditions, thus giving rise to Futurist forms of 'primitivism'.

Tcharne Sawyer (The University of Notre Dame, Sydney) began the day with a presentation on " 'Futurist Rot': Futurism's Artistic Reception in Australia", which truly offered an itinerary into a *terra incognita.* Her paper clearly stood out because, so far, nobody has ever undertaken a thorough and comprehensive investigation into the reception of Futurism in Australia. Sawyer not only surveyed the press responses in the 1910s but also analysed a host of Australian artists (especially Frank Hinder, Dorrit Black and Roger Kemp) who, in one way or another, responded to ideas crossing the Indian Ocean from Italy. Barbara Meazzi (Université Côte d'Azur, Nice) directed attention to "Pettoruti, le futurisme et l'Argentine". The artist lived in Italy, in Argentina and from 1952/53 in Paris. Although he repeatedly insisted that he was not a Futurist, he certainly belonged to the Futurist sphere of influence and entertained amicable relations to Futurists such as Alberto Sartoris and Enzo Benedetto. Meazzi analysed Pettoruti's autobiography in which he said about the Futurists that "I was with them and took their side, [but] accompanying them did not mean for me accepting their conceptions".[8] Meazzi showed in her

7 Marinetti: "The Foundation and Manifesto of Futurism", p. 14.

8 "[...] estaba con ellos y tomaba su partido [...] Acompañarlos, no significaba para mí aceptar sus concepciones." Pettoruti: *Un pintor ante el espejo*, p. 116.

paper that Pettoruti, despite his proviso, was much closer to Futurism than he would admit. Patrícia Silva (University of Coimbra) discussed in "Futurism in Portugal and the Avant-garde Metaphysics of Raul Leal and Fernando Pessoa" the multifaceted forms of Futurism that appeared on the pages of *Portugal futurista* (1917), a periodical that gave expression to a combination of avant-garde impulses with *arrière-garde* Symbolist stances. She analysed the local nuances of Portuguese Futurism, in particular the group's highly original, unorthodox responses to core aesthetic issues of the avant-garde, the metaphysical syncretism underpinning the Raul Leal's attempt to turn Futurism into a new religion and the hermetic poetry of Fernando Pessoa. Mariana Pinto dos Santos (New University, Lisbon) addressed the topic of "Primitivism and Futurism in Portugal". She demonstrated that Marinetti's movement was not exclusively embracing technology and progress but also, paradoxically, propagated a regression either to infancy or to an 'uncivilized' past. This Primitivism / Futurism paradox was explored here within the Portuguese context. Pinto dos Santos showed how the circulation of information about Italian Futurism led to hybrid interpretations and practices, encompassing eroticism, folk art and an exoticized image of Africa in works by Santa-Rita Pintor, Amadeo de Souza-Cardoso, Almada Negreiros, Fernando Pessoa and Raul Leal.

The second morning session began with Bojan Jović (Institute for Literature and Arts, Belgrade) speaking about "Absorption and Transmutation of Futurism in Serbian Literature in the 1910s and 1920s". He discussed two lines of Futurist transformation in Serbia. The first sought to explore the depths of the human soul and to unite the poet's spirituality with the cosmos, prompting a pronounced drive towards myths and the art of prehistoric times. The second focussed on dynamism, speed, energy, power of the machine and the vitality of modern urban life. Emilia David (University of Pisa) discussed in her paper "Tristan Tzara's Shift from Symbolism to Futurism to Dadaism, 1912–1916" how the young writer adopted Futurism thanks to his roots in Symbolism, an aesthetic he shared with Marinetti. David then examined the network of cultural relations forged by the Romanian writer between the young Dada group in Zurich and members of the Futurist movement in Rome, Naples and Mantua, demonstrating that Tzara continued to be open to Futurist influences, in particular with regard to the graphic and typographic features of his poetry and the tactics employed in his performance practice. Erwin Kessler (Romanian Academy, Bucharest) spoke on another Romanian artist, M.H. Maxy, and his brand of Futurism promoted in the periodicals *Integral, Contimporanul, 75HP* and *Punct. Integral* was particularly open to Futurism and dedicated its twelfth issue nearly entirely to the Italian movement. Maxy's close collaborator Ernest Spirt, however, propagated the need to move beyond the Italian models and to progress from Futurism to Integralism. Sonia de Puineuf (Independent Scholar, Brest) in her paper "The Typographic City: A Futurist Ideal of the Modern Urban Environment?" examined the omnipresence of typographical signs on illuminated billboards. These sophisticated advertisements underlined the growing importance of typography in urban settings and the transposition of Words-in-Freedom into the field of architecture.

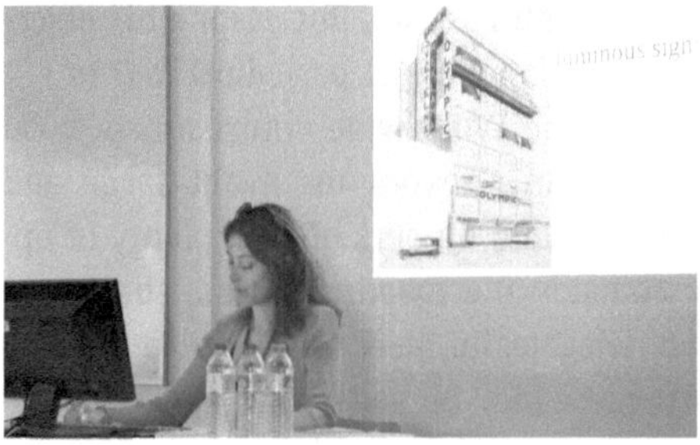

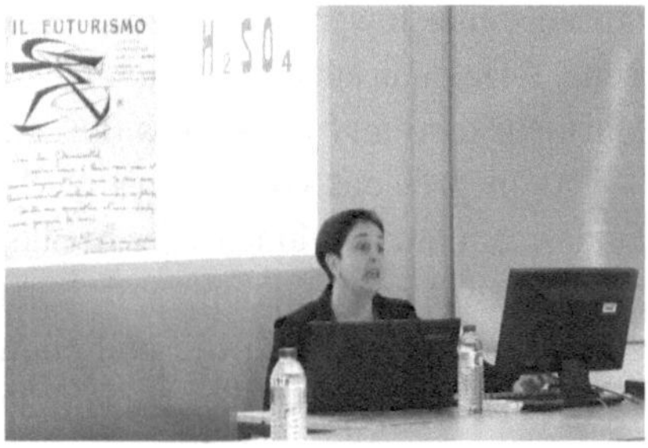

Fig. 2a: Sonia de Puineuf presenting examples of the Futurist 'Typographic City'. **Fig. 2b:** Bela Tsipuria discussing Marinetti's letters to Ilya Zdanevich.

The afternoon session opened with Vera Faber (University of Oslo) addressing "The Network of Futurism in Odessa". The paper focussed on the group Iugo-LEF (The Southern Left Front of the Arts), which formed in Odessa in 1924. The five issues of their periodical of the same name featured texts in Russian, Ukrainian and Yiddish and laid emphasis on political agitation. Their graphic components emulated principles of Constructivist design rather than the Futurist style of typography. Nonetheless, early Futurist practices were perpetuated in a certain way in Leonid Nedolya's manifestos, Semyon Kirsanov's neologisms and sound experiments and Leonid Chernov's social provocations. Helena Čapková (Ritsumeikan University, Osaka) discussed in "Václav Fiala and David Burliuk: Transnational Futurism in Japan" how these two artists fleeing the devastations of post-Revolutionary Russia contributed to the 'leap into the future' in Japanese modern arts. Fiala's Futurist work produced in Japan is yet to be discovered, and Čapková's research contextualized his œuvre beyond his collaboration with Burliuk.

Bela Tsipuria (Ilia State University, Tbilisi) investigated the reception of Futurist poetics in 1990s Georgia. After the collapse of the USSR, a younger generation of poets reconstructed the Georgian Futurist experience in the 1910s and 20s, reintroduced Futurist texts and paintings to modern audiences and created works in the spirit of historical Futurism. She discussed a number of poets who translated Marinetti's writings and whose works were clearly inspired by the group H_2SO_4: Dato Barbakadze, Karlo Kacharava, Irakli Charkviani and the avant-garde grouping The Reactive Club. Tsipuria demonstrated in her paper that, even after decades of cultural isolation, a cultural transformation can be achieved by harking back to the Futurist avant-garde in the early twentieth century. Finally, Jindřich Toman (University of Michigan, Ann Arbor) revisited the conflictual relationship between the Czech and Italian leaders of the avant-garde. The two men first met in 1922, and in several essays Teige paid homage to the Futurists, considering them precursors of the avant-garde and of modern art in general. At the same time, he took a distanced stance towards Marinetti's association with Fascism. But despite his objections, Teige dedicated in February 1929 a whole issue of his periodical *ReD* to F.T. Marinetti *a světový futurismus* (F.T. Marinetti and Worldwide Futurism).

As in previous conferences of the European Network for Avant-Garde and Modernism Studies, long coffee breaks, lunches and dinners offered plenty of opportunity for conversations and debates outside the meeting rooms. The warm Mediterranean climate of Lisbon allowed delegates to meet on a shaded terrace, where benches and tables laden with Portuguese food invited everyone to combine the *prodesse* with the *delectare*. This setup will indeed be a hard act to follow at the next EAM meeting planned to take place at the Jagiellonian University in Krakow in 2024.

Bibliography

Berghaus, Günter: "Futurist Utopias." *International Yearbook of Futurism Studies* 5 (2015): 486–497.

Berghaus, Günter, ed.: "Futurism and Science." *International Yearbook of Futurism Studies* 8 (2018): 189–324.

Berghaus, Günter, ed.: *Futurism in Eastern and Central Europe.* Special issue of the *International Yearbook of Futurism Studies* 1 (2011).

Marinetti, Filippo Tommaso: "The Foundation and Manifesto of Futurism." F.T. Marinetti: *Critical Writings.* Ed. by Günter Berghaus. New York: Farrar, Straus and Giroux, 2006. 11–17.

Pettoruti, Emilio: *Un pintor ante el espejo.* Buenos Aires: Libreria Histórica, 2004. English edn *A Painter before the Mirror.* Translated by Christina Soares Gache. Buenos Aires: StockCero, 2006.

Leandro Pasini

Futurism and the Brazilian Week of Modern Art (1922): Some Thoughts Prompted by the *Centenário da Semana de 22*

Abstract: The centenary of the Week of Modern Art has been an occasion for both celebrating and reassessing Brazilian Modernism. Although it should have been an occasion to revisit its contradictory ties to international avant-gardes, including its Futurist trigger, the centenary's main focus has been on the rôle of São Paulo in the national culture of the 1920s. Furthermore, there has been a debate on who formed part of Brazilian Modernism and how this affects our present culture. This essay aims at extending our focus beyond the São Paulo – Rio de Janeiro axis, adding a number of works from provincial centres that show the proliferation of 'Futurism' in several Brazilian states. It also revisits a number of long forgotten or undervalued figures in the history of Brazilian Modernism and discusses new research into their rôle in their acceptance or rejection of the terms 'Futurism' and 'Futurist'. Furthermore, it discusses the use of the term 'Futurism' in a satirical manner by the adversaries of Modernism, the links of these terms to the controversial innovations promoted by the Week of Modern Art, and the need to arrive at a reevaluation of Futurism in the debates on cultural modernity in Brazil.

Keywords: The Week of Modern Art in São Paulo (1922); Centenary of the Week of Modern Art (2022); Futurism in Brazil; Brazilian Modernism; Centre–Periphery; Lima Barreto, Graça Aranha, Menotti del Picchia; parodies and satires of Futurism

Introduction

Era uma vez o moderno (Once upon a Time, there Was Modernity) was a comprehensive exhibition about Brazilian Modernism at the Centro Cultural FIESP and the Instituto de Estudos Brasileiros (10 December 2021 – 29 May 2022), mounted to celebrate the centenary of the Week of Modern Art held in São Paulo in 1922.[1] In its press release, there is a very brief reference to Futurism that tells us that the painter Tarsila do Amaral informed her friend Anita Malfatti in 1920 about her first encounters with modern art and, "in particular, with the Italian Fu-

1 See Reiner and Bagolin: *Era uma vez o moderno.*

https://doi.org/10.1515/9783111318394-019

turism of Boccioni, which at the time scandalized her".[2] Although Boccioni's sculpture *Unique Forms of Continuity in Space* had been placed at the entrance room of the Centro Cultural (see Fig. 1), the altogether modest presence of Futurism in such a monumental event was typical of how, over the past two years, Marinetti's movement has been approached in Brazil.

In the centenary's countless events, debates and publications, one rarely came across any noteworthy references to Futurism, even though everyone acknowledges the movement's importance in the early phase of Brazilian Modernism. Given this scanty attention paid to Futurism in the 2022 celebration, I shall address in this report some of the issues brought forth by the centenary and relate them back to the debates on Futurism one hundred years ago. In particular, I shall address the need to recover secondary or forgotten characters such as Afonso Henriques de Lima Barreto, Paulo Menotti del Picchia and José Pereira da Graça Aranha and to investigate their relation to Futurism and Modernism. I also wish to question São Paulo's position as a hotbed of Modernist culture, to highlight the need to extend our geographical focus when discussing modern culture in Brazil and to bring the north-east and north of Brazil into our critical horizon.

To understand the reasons for why Futurism has been given such inadequate attention in the current revisionist drive on Brazilian Modernism, we must look back at the way the Futurist aesthetic was confronted in the early part of the twentieth century. Mirhiane Mendes de Abreu has ascertained that, initially, "São Paulo absorbed the word 'Futurism' and linked it to the semantics of absurdity and extravagance. Later, the term 'Modernism' replaced it to denote any battle against constraining structures."[3] But then, she explains, "by the end of the 1920s, the word 'Futurism' could no longer excite anybody" and by the mid-1930s, "Marinetti's movement had [...] lost all function."[4] In an article called "Em defesa dos ismos" (In Defence of the Isms),[5] Bruna Della Torre pays more attention to the historical avant-gardes and emphasizes the international dimension of the Week of Modern Art, but she fails to make any mention of Futurism. She defends Brazilian Modernism and its best-known epiphanies, Oswald de Andrade's *Manifesto antropófago* of 1928 and Mário de Andrade's novel *Macunaíma* (1928). It should be noted, though, that if the '-isms' need a defence, it is because they have been disregarded or down-

---

2 "Tarsila do Amaral, está lendo uma carta datada de 1920, na qual, de Paris, na França, ela escreveu para Anita Malfatti, relatando os seus primeiros encontros com a arte moderna, em particular, com o futurismo italiano de Umberto Boccioni que então a escandalizou." [Anon]: "Exposição 'Era uma vez o moderno' [1910–1944]."

3 Abreu: "Between Letters and Memoirs: Behind the Scenes of Futurism in Brazil", p. 284.

4 Ibid., p. 283.

5 Della Torre: "Em defesa dos ismos."

played in the exhibitions, publications and events commemorating the centenary of the Week of Modern Art.

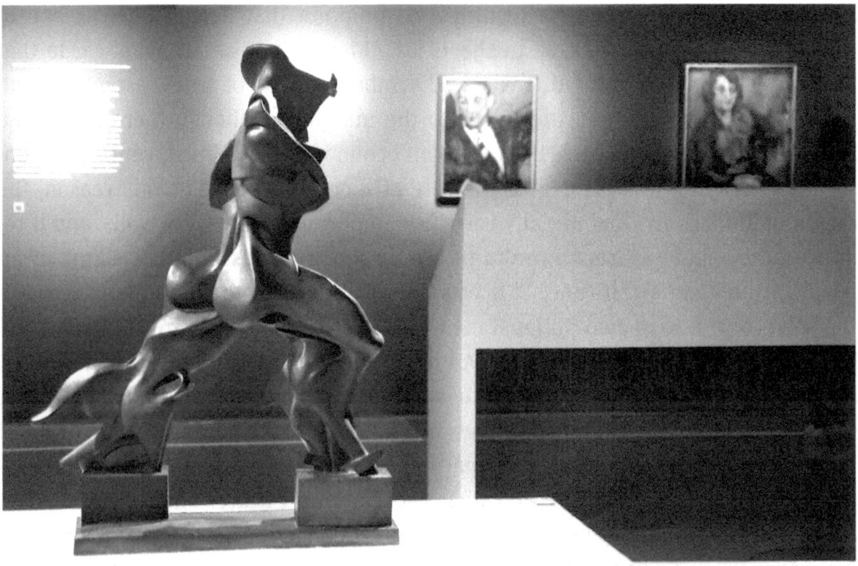

Fig. 1: Umberto Boccioni's sculpture *Forme uniche della continuità nello spazio* (Unique Forms of Continuity in Space, 1913) in the exhibition *Era uma vez o moderno* (Once upon a Time, there Was Modernity) at the Centro Cultural Federação das Indústrias do Estado de São Paulo. On the wall behind, two portraits by Anita Malfatti: *O homem amarelo* (The Yellow Man, 1915–16) and *A estudante russa* (The Russian Student, 1915).

Paulo Roberto Pires gives us another hint about the current apathy concerning the relation between Futurism and Modernism in Brazil. He argues that the embrace of Futurism by the cosmopolitan élite in Brazil was a cover for marketing a self-image by means of an "advertising rhetoric of the 'new'".[6] Thus, according to Pires, the words 'Futurism' and 'Futurist' in the first years of Brazilian Modernism were "an important and valuable asset in the relations between intellectuals and their sponsors, who felt a certain need to promote their cosmopolitan aspirations".[7] By portraying the adoption of Futurism in Brazil as an advertising stunt,

6 "[...] retorica publicitaria do 'novo'." Pires: "O século modernista que ia ser futurista: Sobre manchetes, vanguardas e o consenso de 22", p. 326.

7 "[...] um ativo importante e valioso nas relações entre os intelectuais e seus mecenas, que se sentem de alguma forma contemplados em seus anseios cosmopolitas." Pires: "O século modernista que ia ser futurista: Sobre manchetes, vanguardas e o consenso de 22", pp. 331–332.

Pires both admits the local value of Marinetti's practices and denounces its espousal as a "pact between the happy few, equals amongst themselves".[8]

One should note, however, that Pires' commitment to demystifying Brazilian Modernism repeats the false historical assumption that São Paulo was one of the Brazilian cultural centres in the 1920s: "Modernism, as an avant-garde that emerges closely tied to the financial and symbolic capital of a new establishment, irradiated its beliefs from the centre to the margin".[9] Although there can be no doubt that São Paulo, in the 1920s, was an economic and political centre, it is entirely misleading to ascribe to it the rôle of a cultural hub. For this reason, the Week of Modern Art had initially very little impact outside its city walls, and it required the input of Graça Aranha in Rio de Janeiro to assume the status of an event of *national* significance.[10] It was only in the 1950s that São Paulo came to be seen as of one of two national centres, largely due to a group of intellectuals from the University of São Paulo (Antonio Candido, Paulo Emilio Salles Gomes, Décio de Almeida Prado, etc.) who sought to continue the artistic legacy of Mário de Andrade, because they saw in him not only an innovative writer and poet, but also an intellectual who had made a vital contribution to the process of building a comprehensive and inclusive national culture. Furthermore, there was the São Paulo group of poets who promoted Concrete Poetry (Haroldo de Campos, Augusto de Campos and Décio Pignatari). In their work as literary critics and theorists they re-evaluated Oswald de Andrade – until then almost forgotten as an irreverent and polemical minor figure – and his concept of Anthropophagy.[11] Yet, throughout the 1920s, no-one considered São Paulo to be a city with a cultural significance comparable to that of Rio de Janeiro.

One of the causes of Futurism's relative absence in the current debate on the Week of Modern Art relates to the avant-garde's proclaimed rupture with its immediate predecessors and coeval institutions. In recent years, the dominant narratives of Brazilian Modernism have been challenged by a positive valuation of 'traditional' cultures, especially the popular, the Afro-Brazilian, the indigenous and the

8 "[...] um pacto de poucos, iguais entre si." Pires: "O século modernista que ia ser futurista: Sobre manchetes, vanguardas e o consenso de 22", p. 342.

9 "Vanguarda que nasce inseparável do capital financeiro e simbólico de um novo establishment, o modernismo irradiou seus princípios do centro para a margem." Pires: "O século modernista que ia ser futurista: sobre manchetes, vanguardas e o consenso de 22", p. 325.

10 See Pasini: *Prismas modernistas: A lógica dos grupos e o modernismo brasileiro*, pp. 30–31.

11 On Haroldo and Augusto de Campos and their fellow poet Décio Pignatari as founders of the Concrete Poetry movement in Brazil, see in this volume of the Yearbook Odile Cisneros's essay "Russian Futurism and Brazilian Avant-garde Poetry: Incorporation, Translation, Convergence" (pp. 253–283).

regional, to name but a few. The result is a questioning of the avant-garde's future-oriented aesthetics, now seen to be the outcome of an intellectual, social, gender and racial élite that excluded large sections of Brazilian society.

Denouncing the socio-economic position of the figures considered to be the key representatives of Brazilian Modernism has led to a revision of the Week of Modern Art. Also the exclusion of indigenous people has been highlighted several times and summed up by Lilia Moritz Schwarcz in her statement "The profile of people participating [in the Week of Modern Art] was, by the way, very homogeneous. With the exception of Mário [de Andrade], the event gathered young, white, cosmopolitan males, all descendants of wealthy families."[12] Ironically, the current revisionist drive is not completely exempt from repeating the failures of the past. It is interesting to note that although social and racial minorities now have wider representation in political and cultural organizations (after all, a hundred years have passed), some of the most radical critics of the social exclusiveness of the Modernist movement are characterized by precisely the same social markers. Two of the institutions promoting a revision of the dominant narratives of Brazilian Modernism – the Instituto Moreira Salles and Instituto Itaú Cultural – are both associated with major banks in Brazil. Thus, a considerable amount of criticism of the social, racial and cultural limitations of the Week of Modern Art has been launched by the same national élites that dominated the cultural scene in São Paulo one-hundred years ago.

A black (anti-) Modernist: Lima Barreto and Futurism

The idea of a plurality of Brazilian Modernisms opened up spaces for authors who had been overseen in previous decades. One of the figures often presented as a counterpoint to the *Semana de 22* is the novelist Afonso Henriques de Lima Barreto, whose untimely death in 1922 did not prevent him from becoming an icon of an 'alternative modernity' in Brazil. Lima Barreto wrote a series of novels between 1909 and 1919, including *Recordações do escrivão Isaías Caminha* (Memories of the Scrivener Isaias Caminha, 1909), *Vida e morte de M. J. Gonzaga de Sá* (Life and Death of M. J. Gonzaga de Sá, 1919), as well as *Clara dos Anjos* (written 1922, published 1948) and the unfinished autobiographical *Cemitério dos vivos* (Grave-

12 "O perfil de seus integrantes, aliás, era bastante homogêneo; a exceção de Mario, ali se reuniam jovens brancos, cosmopolitas e provenientes de famílias de posse." Schwarcz: "O negrismo e as vanguardas nos modernismos brasileiros: Presença e ausência", p. 306.

yard of the Living, written 1919–20, publ. 1956). His interest in the Russian novel, especially Fyodor Dostoyevsky, gave his writings an angry and rebellious tone, used to denounce the prejudices of race and class, which he himself fell victim to. Barreto's novels combine an affective commitment with a Realist style closer to journalism (one of his means of income) than the *belles lettres.* This stylistic choice contrasted with stilted literary style of well-established writers such as Henrique Maximiano Coelho Neto, one of the main targets of the Modernists. Barreto's lively language stood in opposition to established literary norms. His historical position as an author ahead of his time[13] is largely based on the fact that he was a black writer fighting racism, the First Republic's oligarchy and wealth based on slave labour.

Lilia Moritz Schwarcz and Pedro Meira Monteiro assert the image of an unruly author, who was a "reader of the Russian [novelists] and the European avant-gardes, a subscriber of French magazines."[14] They also argue that his opposition to the literary status quo was not only grounded in his aesthetic convictions but also attached to new social agendas, especially those of the lower classes.[15] However, Barreto's position was not exempt from paradoxes. Although he was a critic of the Brazilian Academy of Letters, he tried three times to become a member of that conservative institution.[16] This fact alone demonstrates Barreto's tortuous literary career, oscillating between antagonism to the establishment and a search for recognition from official institutions.

It is against this background that Barreto's response to the 'Futurists' of São Paulo should be read. His articles published in the magazine *Careta* (The Grimace) sought to ridicule Futurism as nonsense and trickery. Taking as its subject the launching of a magazine called *Vida literária* (Literary Life) by the 'Futurist' Sérgio Buarque de Holanda, Barreto admitted that he did not really understand the meaning of Futurism. The author then invented a dialogue with a grocer who explains to him that a client, after having refused to pay his bill, argued that he did so because he was a 'Futurist', which meant that he would only care about his debts in the future. The second article engaged in a more serious debate about 'Futurist' ideas in São Paulo and in Rio de Janeiro.[17] As a matter of fact, modernity in the capital city Rio de Janeiro during the first two decades of the last century was a

13 See Oliveira: "Lima Barreto, modernidade e modernismo no Brasil", p. 114.
14 "[...] leitor dos russos e das vanguardas europeias, assinante de revistas francesas." Schwarcz and Monteiro: "Sérgio com Lima: Um encontro inusitado em meio aos modernismos", p. 43.
15 See Schwarcz and Monteiro: "Sérgio com Lima: Um encontro inusitado em meio aos modernismos", p. 43.
16 Ibid.
17 See Barreto: "O futurismo"; Chrispim (pseud. of Lima Barreto): "Futurismo.".

blend of modernizing drives and of various forms of popular culture, often slandering and satirizing Futurism, as Sobrinho Neto's investigations into the periodical *Careta* have shown.[18] At that time, the competition between the capital of the Republic and São Paulo) as the most industrialized city in the country caused Barreto to discredit the latter's intellectual class for trying to make people believe that Futurism was their discovery. In "O futurismo", he referred to Futurism as a subject that had been known in Rio de Janeiro for decades:

> Do these honourable young men really think that we did not know anything about this thing called Futurism? People have been talking about it for twenty years or more, and there is not a single person reading these cheap French magazine or despicable Italian publications who does not know the buffooneries of 'il Marinetti'.[19]

Even though Barreto asserts his long-standing knowledge of the subject, his final verdict is one of "sincere antipathy against the grotesque 'Futurism' which, in the end, is nothing but brutality, crudeness and, above all, scatology."[20] Regarding the European avant-gardes, Barreto was a conservative with a pronounced lack of comprehension of Marinetti's movement. In fact, his conclusions are in sharp contrast to the image of Barreto as a well-informed and up-to-date intellectual, advocated by Schwarcz and Monteiro. However, the possibility of a new image of Brazilian Modernism, and of Futurism's presence in it, should not be restricted to the accurate use of the labels 'Futurism' and 'Futurist', but rather take into consideration the artistic and literary productivity that these words prompted at the time. Barreto's intervention constitutes a curious and interesting moment in the mapping of the polemics surrounding Futurism in the history of Brazilian Modernism.

---

18 Neto: "Modernismo, futurismo e polêmicas literárias na revista 'Careta' (1909–1922)."

19 "Esses moços tão estimáveis pensam mesmo que nós não sabíamos disso de futurismo? Há vinte anos, ou mais, que se fala nisto e não há quem leia a mais ordinária revista francesa ou o pasquim mais ordinário da Itália que não conheça as cabotinagens do 'il Marinetti'." Barreto: "O futurismo", p. 10.

20 "[...] minha sincera antipatia contra o grotesco 'futurismo', que no fundo não é senão brutalidade, grosseria e escatologia, sobretudo esta." Barreto: "O futurismo", p. 10. See also Abreu: "Between Letters and Memoirs: Behind the Scenes of Futurism in Brazil", p. 275.

Futurism in São Paulo and Rio de Janeiro: Misunderstandings and achievements

In the 1920s and 20s, the labels 'Futurism' and 'Futurist' served as a leaven for the diffusion and nationalization of Modernism in Brazil. The terms were not only used to delineate artistic and cultural platforms, but served as markers for all kinds of things deemed extravagant, excessive or outré: "The word 'Futurist' became synonymous with something new, out-of-the-ordinary, as madness. Everything that was done outside of tradition was considered Futurist. There was Futurist furniture, women's hats, ice cream, dishes, and jazz music."[21] Apparently, misconceptions and misjudgements followed these words wherever they occurred. Forgotten figures such as José Pereira da Graça Aranha, or underestimated ones such as Paulo Menotti del Picchia pushed the lexical ambiguity to a limit while, at the same time, using them as an artistic and cultural mobilizing force. Yet, each context had its specific traits, and the polysemy could manifest quite different qualities in different quarters. The idea of a *futurismo paulista* troubled the press between 1920 and 1922 as it stood for an incendiary assault against enshrined Brazilian authors and a staunch vindication of the idea of novelty. Oswald de Andrade and Menotti del Picchia, in particular, embodied this attitude, that is, "the peremptory tones or the provocation of Futurist cultural agitation."[22] Above all, Menotti del Picchia's Futurist activism was characterized by a polemical and grandiloquent tone, usually ill-informed and confused when dealing with characteristic traits of Marinettian aesthetics.

Menotti del Picchia had a regular column in the São Paulo newspaper *Correio paulistano*, in which, between 1920 and 1922, he often promoted the so-called 'futurismo paulista'.[23] Ana Paula Freitas Andrade discussed Menotti del Picchia's contradictory relation to Futurism and explained that his defence of the 'new' and attacks on the 'old' often implied intellectual confusion, since he "didn't properly clarify the criteria and aesthetic operations to be explored."[24] In fact, his column

21 "A palavra futurista tonou-se sinonimo de coisa nova, fora do comum, de maluquice para os bem-pensantes e tradicionalistas. Tudo que saia fora da tradicao era futurista. Havia mobilia, chapeus para senhoras, sorvete, louca, musica de jazz futuristas." Moraes: *Testemunha ocular: Recordaçoes*, pp. 185–186.

22 See Lista: "The Activist Model; or, The Avant-Garde as Italian Invention", p. 22.

23 See Picchia: *O gedeão do modernismo.*

24 "[...] não esclarecia muito bem os critérios e operações estéticas a serem explorados". Andrade: "A primeira bandeira futurista, avanguardia e verdamarelismo", p. 10

on 'Futurism' carried all sorts of reinterpretations[25] to reach his goal to promote São Paulo as the most important city in the country.[26] This became explicit in 1926, when he launched the nationalist *Verde-amarelo* group,[27] which included as its members Cassiano Ricardo and Plínio Salgado, both of them supporters of a xenophobic nationalism.

Two quotations will suffice to show the vagaries of Menotti del Picchia's campaign. On 8 November 1921, in an article on *Futurismo paulista*, he wrote: "Indeed, Oswald [de Andrade], Guilherme [de Almeida], Menotti [del Picchia], Mário de Andrade are not Futurists in the scholarly, dogmatic sense of the group that enthroned Marinetti, this genial fetish. They are, nonetheless, Futurist in the wider sense, meaning reactionary,[28] up-to-date, daring."[29] Yet, on the second day of the Week of Modern Art (15 February 1922; see Fig. 2b), when the most intense confrontation with the audience took place, Menotti del Picchia declared: "The term 'Futurist', with which people wrongly labelled us, we accepted because it was a public challenge. The aggressive cusp of this verbal prow shattered like a battering ram on the glacial Carrara marble of ruling Parnassianism. We are not, we never were 'Futurists'."[30] Notwithstanding Menotti del Picchia's misconceptions, his constant changes of positions and limited understanding of Futurist aesthetics were paradoxically convenient. After all, his activism did not aim at informing his audiences about the ideals and artistic achievements of Italian Futurism; his main objective was to promote the Modernist group in São Paulo by means of shock and confrontation. Thus, in the centre of an opportunistic muddle, one can find a certain logic and method.

A similar kind of disoriented behaviour can be found in another key figure in the development of Brazilian Modernism, José Pereira da Graça Aranha. He played

25 See Picchia: *O gedeão do modernismo*, p. 180.

26 Fabris: "Um futurismo singular: Menotti del Picchia", pp. 32–33.

27 The group's name evoked the colours of the Brazilien flag. Its members "favoured electing São Paulo as the nation's new model whilst divesting Rio de Janeiro of that same rôle." Mattos. "Heavenly Heights, or Reign of the Dangerous Classes?", p. 294.

28 In the 1920s, the word 'reactionary' meant 'revolutionary'.

29 "Oswald, Guilherme, Menotti, Mário Andrade, de facto, não são 'futuristas' no sentido escolástico, dogmático, do grupo que enthronizou o fetiche genial que é Marinetti. São, porém, 'futuristas' no largo sentido reacionário, atual, ousado." Menotti del Picchia; "O futurismo paulista." *Correio paulistano*, 8 November 1921, p. 5. Reprinted in Picchia: *O gedeão do modernismo*, p. 294

30 "O termo futurista, com que erradamente a etiquetaram, aceitamo-lo porque era um cartel de desafio. Na geleira de mármore de Carrara do parnasianismo dominante, a ponta agressiva dessa proa verbal estilhaçava como um aríete. Não somos, nem nunca fomos 'futuristas'." Picchia: "Arte moderna: A conferência do Dr. Menotti del Picchia no Municipal…" *Correio paulistano*, 17 February 1922, p. 2. Reprinted in Picchia: *O gedeão do modernismo*, p. 328.

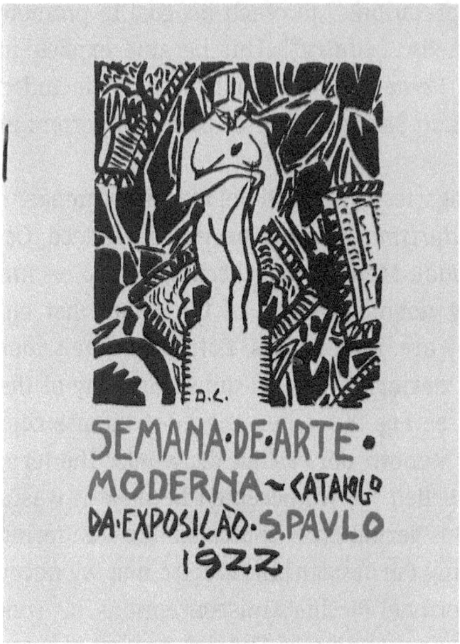

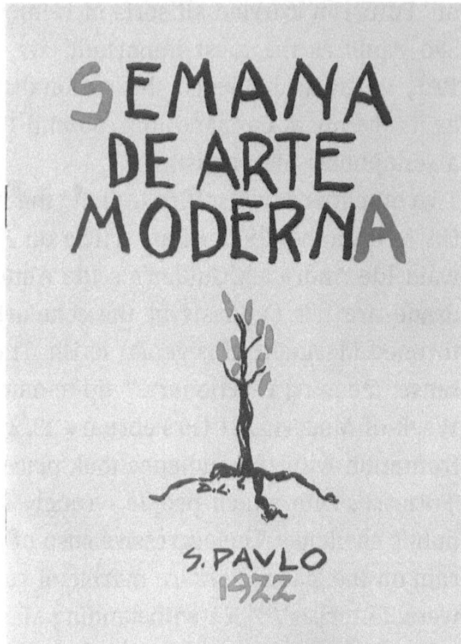

Fig. 2a: Catalogue of the exhibition at the *Semana de arte moderna* at the Teatro Municipal, São Paulo, 11–18 February 1922. **Fig. 2b:** Programme of the second day of the *Semana de arte moderna*, 15 February 1922.

a major rôle during Marinetti's visit to Brazil in 1926[31] and took advantage of the emotive terms 'Futurism' and 'Futurist' without showing any deep understanding of their original context. When Marinetti landed in Rio de Janeiro to deliver a series of lectures in the capital of the Republic and in São Paulo, he was greeted by an entourage of Brazilian Modernists led by Aranha. Author of the opening lecture of the Week of Modern Art (13 February 1922), he was also a member of the Brazilian Academy of Letters. Apart from various novels, he had published the philosophical tract *A estética da vida* (Aesthetics of Life, 1921), in which he displayed a vitalist concept of the modern world. He had also contributed an introduction to a collection of essays, *Espírito moderno* (The Modern Spirit, 1925) and the anthology *Manifestos de Marinetti e seus companheiros* (Manifestos by Marinetti and His Compan-

31 For an extensive discussion of this visit see the essays in the special issue of the *International Yearbook of Futurism Studies* 7 (2017) on *Futurism in Latin America*; Barros: *O pai do futurismo no país do futuro: As viagens de Marinetti ao Brasil em 1926 e 1936*; Rocha: "Manifestos: A estética, a politica, as polêmicas e o legado"; Rocha and Schnapp: "Brazilian Velocities: On Marinetti's 1926 Trip to South America"; Rocha: "Brazil".

ions, 1926).[32] Acting from the start as the Brazilian Modernist leader, Graça Aranha had a foothold in Rio de Janeiro in a group that included Ronald de Carvalho and Renato Almeida.

Graça Aranha had his distinguished position increasingly contested by the leaders of the Futurist group in São Paulo, Oswald de Andrade and Mário de Andrade. The latter was named "The Pope of Futurism"[33] in a marketing strategy of the newspaper *A noite* (The Night). In 1925, he created a column called "Mês futurista" (Futurist Month) which, at Mário de Andrade's request, was later changed to "Mês modernal" (The Modernist Month). Nevertheless, it was Graça Aranha who performed the most influential gesture for the national spread of Modernism in Brazil. On 19 June 1924, he gave a lecture on *O espírito moderno* (The Modern Spirit) within the walls of the Brazilian Academy of Letters, challenging this institution to become Modernist or to perish. The event was followed by a turbulent quarrel between academicians and Modernists who, at the end, carried Graça Aranha on their shoulders out of the building. The Academy refused Aranha's modernizing project and, as a result, he officially resigned his membership. The rousing performance in the hallowed halls of the academy had a similarly shocking effect as some of Marinetti's public lectures, as the Italian writer acknowledged in this brief biographic sketch:

> Ex-Minister of Brazil in Paris during the war, famed novelist and playwright of *Canaã* and *Malazarte*, he was appointed as a grand academician, tried to revolutionize the Academy, did not entirely succeed and resigned, thus earning for himself prestige and the title of leader of Brazilian Futurism.[34]

Because the Week of Modern Art took place in São Paulo, it had little national resonance in the rest of the country, both in 1922 and in the immediate years that fol-

---

32 This collection opens with Graça Aranha's essay on "Marinetti e o futurismo", previously published in *A pátria* (Rio de Janeiro) on 16 May 1926. The back cover states "Editor N. Viggiani", but Niccolò (Niccolino) Viggiani did not act as an 'editor' in the conventional sense of the word. He was a theatrical impresario and event manager who had contracted Marinetti to give a series of lectures on his Brazil trip in 1926 and had launched this anthology as part of a publicity campaign to garner interest in the visit. The book reprints some manifesto leaflets – all in French – and sections of *Le Futurisme: Revue synthétique illustrée*, nos 1, 2, 7.

33 See the interview "Assim falou o papa do futurismo: Como Mario de Andrade define a escola que chefia." *A noite* (Rio de Janeiro), 12 December 1925.

34 "Ex-ministro del Brasile a Parigi durante la guerra, romanziere e autore dramatico illustre di Chanaan e di Malazarte, venne nominato grande accademico, tentò di rivoluzionare l'accademia, non vi riusci perfettamente e diede le sue dimissioni, conquistandosi così il prestigio e il titolo di capo del futurismo brasiliano." Marinetti: "Velocità brasiliane", p. 137.

lowed. By contrast, Graça Aranha's break with literary legitimacy in Rio de Janeiro gave him a national level of notoriety, with the news of his resignation reaching all cities in the country.[35] Fifteen years after the Week of Modern Art, in the then very distant city of Cuiabá, capital of the state of Mato Grosso, the first local Modernist group launched the "Graça Aranha Manifesto", demonstrating the national reach of Graça Aranha's lecture/performance in the Brazilian Academy of Letters. Nonetheless, in the closed circle of the Modernist groups in São Paulo and Rio de Janeiro, the prestige of Mário de Andrade and Oswald de Andrade increased, while Graça Aranha fell into oblivion. When Sérgio Buarque de Holanda drew up a balance sheet of the changes that had occurred in the intellectual landscape of Brazil over the ten years between 1916 and 1926, Aranha was assigned to the "generation which those who live have long forgotten".[36] Graça Aranha's last effort to maintain his status came when he historicized his rôle as 'leader of Brazilian Modernism' in his collection of essays entitled *The Modern Spirit.* He also tried to mirror himself in the *capo* of Italian Futurism when he led an entourage of Brazilian intellectuals to welcome Marinetti during his visit in 1926.

Nowadays, little critical attention is paid to Graça Aranha or to the crucial rôle he played in the first years of the Modernist movement in Brazil. His activity in Rio de Janeiro complemented the Week of Modern Art and started a process of 'decentralization' in the Brazilian literary establishment. Facing a disrupted literary field based in the Capital Rio de Janeiro, the other nuclei of cultural production in the country achieved a certain degree of autonomy. In the northern state of Pará, for example, the reaction to São Paulo's rise of importance in cultural matters was one of amazement and bewilderment:

> From an intellectual point of view, it seemed impossible that an old political cadre were falling apart. It was really appalling to watch the old imperial court and then capital of the Republic losing its position as the intellectual showcase of the country to a 'province' such as São Paulo.[37]

35 See Sant'Anna: *História do modernismo em Alagoas (1922–1932)*, p. 107.

36 "As figuras mais representativas desse espírito acadêmico e mesmo as melhores (como é o caso dos nomes que citei) falam uma linguagem que a geração dos que vivem esqueceu há muito tempo. Holanda: "O lado oposto e os outros lados", p. 9.

37 "Não era possível que, do ponto de vista intelectual, um velho quadro político brasileiro estivesse desmoronando. Era mesmo estarrecedor assistir à antiga corte imperial e depois capital da República perdendo o espaço de vitrine intelectual do país para uma 'província' como São Paulo." Figueiredo: *Os vândalos do apocalipse e outras histórias: Arte e literatura no Pará dos anos 20*, p. 27.

The pivotal moment when the cultural centre began to cede importance to 'minor' and even 'provincial' cities inaugurated a lively and interesting development, from which a few examples should be mentioned here.

The spread of Futurism from centre to periphery

A decentralized reception of Futurism in Brazil could already be observed at the very beginning of the movement. As Patricia Peterle and Aline Fogaça have shown, the first Brazilian translations of the *Foundation and Manifesto of Futurism* appeared in the city of Natal (Rio Grande do Norte) on 5 June 1909 in the newspaper *A republica*, and then in Salvador (Bahia) on 30 December of the same year in the periodical *Jornal de noticias.*[38] Furthermore, the misunderstandings of the words 'Futurism' and 'Futurist' were a powerful stimulus for the nationwide spread of the Modernist movement. Linked to the general ideas of 'novelty' and 'eccentricity', these buzzwords emerged in the popular culture of various Brazilian cities: in Pernambuco, Austro-Costa (pseud. of Austriclínio Ferreira Quirino) compared Recife in the early morning to 'a Futurist poem' (*O Recife da madrugada é um poema futurista,* 1923), and in Bahia, a "Mlle. Futurismo" featured in *Poema instantâneo*" (Instantaneous Poem, 1929) by José Alves Ribeiro.

The relative backwardness of the north-eastern states of Brazil in comparison with São Paulo and Rio de Janeiro led intellectuals from the periphery to ask themselves what relevance a Futurist aesthetics, focussed on the machine and on urban industrialization, could have in their environment. In Alagoas (another north-eastern state), the Modernist poet Jorge de Lima mocked in a speech of July 1927 a famous local poet: if Futurism has large factories, metropolises and skyscrapers as its theme, how could "the sweet lyric poet of Church Street" comprehend such things, assuming that he had never "seen buildings taller than those of Commerce Street [of three stores maximum]?"[39] This mismatch of Futurist aesthetics in a backward civilization was also felt in another north-eastern state, Ceará. Although its capital Fortaleza possessed a budding industrial base, its intellectuals felt that

38 Fogaça: *As traduções esquecidas: O manifesto do futurismo em Natal e Salvador*; Peterle and Fogaça: "The Reception of Italian Futurism in Brazilian Periodicals: 1909, 1922 and after"; Peterle and Cechinel: "Manifesto futurista no Brasil: Traduções e polêmicas."

39 "Como poderia, meus amigos, como poderia Ranulfo Goulart, este doce lírico da rua da Igreja interpretar todas estas coisas assombrosamente grandes e pavorosamente ágeis se o nosso mavioso parnasiano jamais viu sobrados mais altos que aqueles da rua do Comércio?" Quoted in Sant'Anna: *História do modernismo em Alagoas (1922–1932)*, p. 61.

"a 'Futurist' poet in this land would really look like a fool or would make fun of himself."[40]

The new art and literature were widely propagated all over the country after the Week of Modern Art and rarely fitted into the local contexts of underdeveloped parts of Brazil, where – like Futurism – they caused both bewilderment and derision. Satire and parody of the extravagances of modern poetry and painting sprang up everywhere and, paradoxically, became an integral part of the history of Brazilian Modernism. Two cases may suffice to illustrate this fact.

The periodic press in Ceará polemicized for and against Futurism in the 1920s, for example the *Estâncias futuristas* (Futurist Stanzas, 1923) by Arthunio Vales (pseud. of Antônio Sales), *Literatura sem futuro* (Literature without Future, 1923) by J. Bernardo (pseud. of Eurico Pinto) and *Distâncias futuristas* (Futurist Distances, 1923) by Conde de Messejana (pseud. of Terêncio Guedes Filho).[41] Rodrigo de Albuquerque Marques has documented the activities of Antônio Sales, a former leader of a prestigious literary group in Ceará called 'Padaria espiritual' (Spiritual Bakery). Although Ceará's first Modernist group appeared only in 1927,[42] Sales took notice of the movement in Rio de Janeiro shortly after the Week of Modern Art and returned to Ceará with the intention of opposing the influx of foreign and national absurdities in the fields of art and literature. To this end, he published a series of "humorous poems that dealt blows against 'Marinetti's heirs' and turned out to unleash controversies in the local press about the attempts at aesthetic renewal."[43] From the few satires recovered by Marques, I should like to quote two excerpts. In "Futurist Stances XVIII", Futurism is reduced to the automatism of a machine ("I prepare my Kodak / to take a picture. / I choose a spot; / Clic! Clac!/Done!"), and another poem advertised the author's name as an inveterate critic of newfangled poetics: "Look at Antônio Sales, / Carrying books and magazines ... / Certainly thinking awful things / About my *Futurist Stanzas*").[44]

40 "Um poeta 'futurista' nestas terras ou passaria mesmo por louco ou faria pilhéria de si mesmo." Marques: *A nação vai à província: Do romantismo ao modernismo no Ceará*, p. 170.

41 See Nobre: *Modernism no Ceará (1922–1931)*, p. 167.

42 Marques: *A nação vai à província: Do romantismo ao modernismo no Ceará*, pp. 175–184.

43 "[...] poemas de humor que desferiam golpes contra os 'herdeiros de Marinetti' e que findaram por criar uma pequena polêmica na impressa local sobre as tentativas de renovação estética." Marques: *A nação vai à província: Do Romantismo ao Modernismo no Ceará*, p. 158. Marques informs us that another intellectual, Cruz Filho, translated for the journal *O Nordeste* (The Northeast), in 1923, "Marinetti's Futurist Manifesto, besides pointing out the foundations of the new proposal." See Marques: *A nação vai à província: Do romantismo ao modernismo no Ceará*, p. 162.

44 "Preparo o meu Kodak/para tirar um instantâneo./Escolho um ponto;/Clic! Clac!/Pronto! (...) Olhem o Antônio Sales,/Levando livros e revistas.../Certo, vai pensando horrores/Dessas minhas Es-

In another northern state, Pará, Edgar Proença was interested in Futurism and created a pseudonym, Duque do Guajará, to publish, in 1924, a series of poems entitled *Fagulhas futuristas* (Futurist Sparks) in the Belém newspaper *A semana* (The Week).[45] Taking Futurist aesthetics mainly as provocation and extravagance, Duque do Guajará tried to advocate the use of onomatopoeia and neologisms and write in phonetic Portuguese to achieve a sort of poetical purity that would communicate via the sound of the spoken word. In "Futurist Sparks II", he describes his persona in non-normative Portuguese: "You know, my dear, that I am phonetic, / frenetic, impressionistic, neurasthenic, etc."[46] With satirical intent, both Ceará's and Pará's cases cited here demonstrate how the spread of 'Futurism' and 'Futurist' went along and sometimes foreshadowed the debates about Modernism in Brazil.

Conclusion

If the knowledge of the works of Marinetti and his group played a secondary rôle in the spreading out of Brazilian Modernism across the nation, the methods employed by the Brazilian Modernists in this process were similar to those of the Italian Futurists who somehow inspired them. The terms 'Futurism' and 'Futurist' were intimately linked to polemics and cultural defiance, although the practice of boisterous soirées in the style of the Italian *serate*[47] was not introduced in Brazil. Nonetheless, these rowdy events in Italy served as a blueprint for the battle between innovators and traditionalists as could be seen in the second day of the Week of Modern Art and in Graça Aranha's lecture at the Brazilian Academy of Letters.

The organization of more or less articulated groups followed the activist model in Italy,[48] where, within a few years, Futurism spread from Milan, Florence and

tâncias Futuristas." Marques: *A nação vai à província: Do romantismo ao modernismo no Ceará*, pp. 166–167.

45 Figueiredo: *Os vândalos do apocalipse e outras histórias: Arte e literatura no Pará dos anos 20*, pp. 80–81.

46 "Sabes, meu caro, que sou fonético, / frenético, impressionético, neurastenético, etc." Quoted in Figueiredo: *Os vândalos do apocalipse e outras histórias: Arte e literatura no Pará dos anos 20*, p. 82.

47 On the form and practice of this genre see Berghaus: "The Beginnings of a Futurist Performance Art: The Early Serate."

48 On the crucial function of group identity and cohesion see Viazzi: "Il futurismo come organizzazione: Tecniche e strumenti di gruppo" and Piscopo: "Significato e funzione del gruppo nel futurismo."

Rome to the furthest corners of the peninsula. Dozens of local cells pursued artistic programmes often only vaguely related to the ideas proclaimed by Marinetti. Similarly, Futurism found diverging responses in the major and minor cities in Brazil. But its presence in the debates on a new aesthetics for a new age could be felt everywhere, as the research quoted in this essay demonstrates.

For this reason, it must be considered a missed opportunity that the centenary of the Week of Modern Art did not adequately reflect the stimulating rôle of Futurism in the history of Brazilian Modernism. The impact of Marinetti's movement in Brazil is still a neglected aspect that needs to be recovered and reassessed. Further research on the connections between Brazilian Modernism and the Italian avant-garde could trace influences which might reconfigure both the local and the cosmopolitan axes of Brazilian Modernism.

Bibliography

Abreu, Mirhiane Mendes de: "Between Letters and Memoirs: Behind the Scenes of Futurism in Brazil." *International Yearbook of Futurism Studies* 7 (2017): 267–287.

Aguirre, Mariana, Rosa Sarabia, Renée M. Silverman, and Ricardo Vasconcelos, eds.: *Futurism in Latin America.* Special issue of *International Yearbook of Futurism Studies* 7 (2017). Berlin: De Gruyter, 2017.

Andrade, Ana Paula Freitas: "A primeira bandeira futurista, avanguardia e verdamarelismo." *Nossa América: Revista do memorial da América Latina* (São Paulo) 58 (2022): 9–17.

Andrade, Gênese de, ed.: *Modernismos 1922-2022.* São Paulo: Companhia das Letras, 2022.

Andrade, Oswald de: "Manifesto antropófago." *Revista de antropofagia* 1:1 (May 1928): 3 and 7.

Aranha, Graça: "Marinetti e o futurismo." *A patria* (Rio de Janeiro), 16 May 1926. Reprinted as "Prefacio de Graça Aranha." *Manifestos de Marinetti e seus companheiros.* Rio de Janeiro: Pimenta de Mello, 1926. 3–10. Graça Aranha: *Obra completa.* Ed. by Afrânio Coutinho. Rio de Janeiro: Aguilar, 1969. 863–869.

Barros, Orlando de: *O pai do futurismo no país do futuro: As viagens de Marinetti ao Brasil em 1926 e 1936.* Rio de Janeiro: E-Papers, 2010.

Barreto, Afonso Henriques de Lima: "O futurismo." *Careta* 15:735 (15–22 July 1922): 10. Reprinted in Maria Eugênia Boaventura: *22 por 22: A Semana de Arte Moderna vista pelos seus contemporâneos.* São Paulo: EDUSP, 2000. 323–324. Felipe Botelho Corrêa Lima Barreto: *Sátiras e outras subversões: Textos inéditos.* São Paulo: Companhia das Letras, 2016. 310–311.

Berghaus, Günter: "The Beginnings of a Futurist Performance Art: The Early Serate." G. Berghaus: *Italian Futurist Theatre, 1909–1944.* Oxford: Clarendon Press, 1998. 85–155.

Boaventura, Maria Eugênia, ed.: *22 por 22: A Semana de Arte Moderna vista pelos seus contemporâneos.* São Paulo: Editora da Universidade de São Paulo, 2008.

Bosi, Alfredo: *História concisa da literatura brasileira.* São Paulo: Cultrix, 1997.

Chrispim, João [pseud. of Lima Barreto]: "Futurismo." *Careta* 15:720 (8 April 1922): 30. Reprinted in Maria Eugênia Boaventura: *22 por 22: A Semana de Arte Moderna vista pelos seus contemporâneos.* São Paulo: EDUSP, 2000. 387–390.

Fabris, Annateresa: "Um futurismo singular: Menotti del Picchia." *MODOS: Revista de história da arte* (Campinas) 2:1 (2018): 29–48.

Fabris, Annateresa: *O futurismo paulista: Hipóteses para o estudo da chegada da vanguarda ao Brasil.* São Paulo: Perspectiva, 1994.

Figueiredo, Aldrin Moura: *Os vândalos do apocalipse e outras histórias: Arte e literatura no Pará dos anos 20.* Belém: IAP, 2012.

Fogaça, Aline: *As traduções esquecidas: O manifesto do futurismo em Natal e Salvador.* Florianópolis: Universidade Federal de Santa Catarina, 2012.

Holanda, Sérgio Buarque de: "O lado oposto e os outros lados." *Revista do Brasil* (Rio de Janeiro) NF 3 (15 October 1926): 9–10.

Lista, Giovanni: "The Activist Model; or, The Avant-Garde as Italian Invention." *South Central Review* 13: 2/3 (Summer-Autumn1996): 13–34.

Marinetti, Filippo Tommaso: "Velocità brasiliane." *South Central Review: The Journal of the South Central Modern Language Association* 13:2–3 (Summer-Fall 1996): 135–138.

Marques, Rodrigo: *A nação vai à província: Do romantismo ao modernismo no* Ceará. Fortaleza: Imprensa Universitária, 2018.

Moraes, Rubens Borba de: *Testemunha ocular: Recordaçoes.* Brasília: Briquet de Lemos, 2011.

Neto, Joachin de Melo Azevedo Sobrinho: "Modernismo, futurismo e polêmicas literárias na revista 'Careta' (1909–1922)." *Saeculum: Revista de história* 37 (July-December 2017): 111–125.

Nobre, Thiago da Silva: *Modernismo no Ceará (1922–1931): Práticas letradas, cotidiano e experiência estética.* Porto Alegre: Editora Fi, 2022

Oliveira, Irenísia Torres de: "Lima Barreto, modernidade e modernismo no Brasil." *Terceira margem* (Rio de Janeiro) 16 (January-June 2007): 95–112.

Pasini, Leandro: *Prismas modernistas: Alógica dos grupos e o modernismo brasileiro.* São Paulo: Editora da Universidade Federal de São Paulo, 2022.

Peterle, Patricia, and Aline Fogaça: "The Reception of Italian Futurism in Brazilian Periodicals: 1909, 1922 and after." *International Yearbook of Futurism Studies* 4 (2014): 328–359.

Peterle, Patricia, and Fernanda Moro Cechinel: "Manifesto futurista no Brasil: Traduções e polêmicas." *In-Traduções: Revista do Programa de Pós-graduação em Estudos da Tradução da UFSC* 4 (2011): 10–18.

Picchia, Menotti del: "Arte moderna: A conferência do Dr. Menotti del Picchia no Municipal." *Correio paulistano*, 17 February 1922. 2. Reprinted in Menotti del Picchia: *O gedeão do modernismo.* Rio de Janeiro: Civilização Brasileira, 1983. 327–334.

Picchia, Menotti del: *O gedeão do modernismo.* Introdução, seleção organização e notas Yoshie Sakiyama Barreirinhas. Rio de Janeiro: Civilização Brasileira; São Paulo: Civilização Brasileira; Secretaria de Estado da Cultura, 1983.

Pires, Paulo Roberto: "O século modernista que ia ser futurista: Sobre manchetes, vanguardas e o consenso de 22." Gênese de Andrade, ed.: *Modernismos 1922–2022.* São Paulo: Companhia das Letras, 2022. 323–347.

Piscopo, Ugo: "Significato e funzione del gruppo nel futurismo." U. Piscopo: *Questioni e aspetti del futurismo: Con una appendice di testi del futurismo a Napoli.* Napoli: Ferraro, 1976. 225–244.

Reiner, Fabrício, and Luiz Armando Bagolin, eds.: *Era uma vez o moderno.* Exhibition catalogue. São Paulo: Galeria de Arte do Centro Cultural FIESP, 10 December 2021–29 March 2022. São Paulo: Serviço Social da Indústria do Estado de São Paulo, 2022

Rocha, João Cézar de Castro, and Jeffrey Schnapp: "Brazilian Velocities: On Marinetti's 1926 Trip to South America." *South Central Review* 13: 2/3 (Summer-Autumn, 1996): 105–156.

Rocha, João Cézar de Castro: "Brazil Manifestos: A estética, a política, as polêmicas e o legado." Gênese de Andrade, ed.: *Modernismos 1922–2022.* São Paulo: Companhia das Letras, 2022.
Rocha, João Cézar de Castro: "Brazil." Günter Berghaus, ed.: *Handbook of International Futurism.* Berlin/Boston: De Gruyter, 2019. 336–351.
Sant'Anna, Moacir Medeiros de: *História do modernismo em Alagoas (1922–1932).* Maceió: Editora da Universidade Federal de Alagoas, 1980.
Schwarcz, Lilia Moritz, and Pedro Meira Monteiro: "Sérgio com Lima: Um encontro inusitado em meio aos modernismos." *Revista brasileira de história* 36:73 (September-December 2016): 41–62.
Schwarcz, Lilia Moritz: "O negrismo e as vanguardas nos modernismos brasileiros: Presença e ausência." Gênese de Andrade, ed.: *Modernismos 1922–2022.* São Paulo: Companhia das Letras, 2022. 297–322.
Viazzi, Glauco: "Il futurismo come organizzazione: Tecniche e strumenti di gruppo." *Es: Rivista quadrimestrale* 3:5 (September-December 1976): 36–60.

Online sources

[Anon]: "Exposição Era uma vez o moderno[1910–1944]." https://www.ieb.usp.br/exposicao-era-uma-vez-o-moderno-1910-1944/ (consulted 04/08/2022).
Della Torre, Bruna: "Em defesa dos ismos." https://blogdaboitempo.com.br/2022/02/18/em-defesa-dos-ismos-1922-2022/ (consulted 16/08/2022).

Simona Cigliana

Anton Giulio Bragaglia: The Archive of a Visionary

The exhibition *Anton Giulio Bragaglia: L'archivio di un visionario*, curated by Claudia Palma for the National Gallery of Modern and Contemporary Art in Rome, provided an opportunity to present GNAM's recent acquisition of the papers the artist left behind after his death in 1960. This immense patrimony of documents is of fundamental importance not only for the reconstruction of Bragaglia's life and œuvre, but also for the study of the avant-garde, of Italian Futurism and of the history of the performing arts in Italy.

The exceptional size of this personal archive derives from the artist's breadth of interests, the multifaceted personality behind it, and his decades-long intellectual and entrepreneurial career. Anton Giulio Bragaglia was a theorist and essayist, a critic, stage designer, theatre and film director, an impresario, author of numerous publications on the history of dance and theatre, an editor of several periodicals. He was an experimenter who operated on parallel planes: on the one hand intellectual-theoretical reflection, on the other practical implementation of his artistic visions. He was a tireless promoter of cultural events and conceived of artistic research as a territory that went beyond established traditions or current trends. By not adhering to any artistic school, he could involve some of the most prominent protagonists of the international scene in his projects, thus opening the Italian art world up to other European currents, even during the years of Fascism, when 'imported' cultural novelties were frowned upon or met with hostility.

A life in cinema and photography, journalism and theatre

A.G. Bragaglia was born in 1890 in Frosinone, a small town some 75 kilometres south-east of Rome. From a very young age, he was present in the capital, where he began his career at the age of sixteen by working as an assistant in one of the first Italian film production companies, Cines, of which his father Francesco was administrative director. Soon, he was a regular guest at the Caffè Aragno, the most famous artistic haunt in Rome, and became actively involved in Roman intellectual circles.

At the age of twenty-one, attracted by the belligerent demands expounded by the Futurist painters in their manifestos, he entered the field of photography and,

https://doi.org/10.1515/9783111318394-020

together with his brothers Arturo and Carlo Ludovico, undertook studies of the flow of movement in a number of visual syntheses that he christened *fotodinamiche* (photodynamics). The premises and conceptual implications of these long-exposure shots were set out in the brochure *Fotodinamismo futurista,* of which three editions appeared in 1913.[1] It was a polemical book perfectly in line with the combative style of Marinetti's movement and constitutes the first theoretical text on avant-garde photography. As the many citations and reprints of excerpts in anthologies testify, it is still considered a significant contribution to twentieth-century visual aesthetics.

Bragaglia presented his photographic work as being entirely in line with the Futurist spirit, but he was immediately contradicted by Boccioni and his entourage, despite the fact that Bragaglia was supported by Marinetti, who sponsored an exhibition of photodynamic images at the Pichetti gallery in Rome (1912). Boccioni complained on 4 September 1913 in a letter to the owner of the Futurist gallery in Rome, Giuseppe Sprovieri:

> *I write to you on behalf of my Futurist friends and request* that you rule out any contact with Bragaglia's photodynamics. It is a presumptuous uselessness that harms our aspirations of overcoming the *schematic or successive* reproduction of stillness and motion [...] Imagine, then, if we need the graphomania of a positivist photographer of dynamism [...] His little book seemed to me, and equally to my friends, to be plainly monstrous. Grotesque prosopopoeia and infatuation with the non-existent.[2]

A few days later, a "Notice" appeared in *Lacerba* in which the entire group of painters, with the addition of Ardengo Soffici, disavowed Photodynamics and announced that it had "absolutely nothing in common with Plastic Dynamism" and pertains "exclusively" to innovations in the field of photography.[3] Nonetheless, Bra-

1 In the critical literature on Futurism, one can also find phantom editions of 1911 and 1912, due to the announcement of a "saggio 'Fotodinamismo' sulla nuova arte della fotografia" in the magazine *L'artista* 1:5 (December 1911). The booklet contained 48 pages and 15 plates outside the text and was announced as having been published a day ago ("È uscito ieri") in the Futurist magazine *Lacerba* on 1 July 1913, p. 147.

2 "*Mi raccomando, te lo scrivo a nome degli amici futuristi,* escludi qualsiasi contatto con la fotodinamica del Bragaglia. È una presuntuosa inutilità che danneggia le nostre aspirazioni di liberazione dalla riproduzione *schematica o successiva* della statica e del moto [...] Immagina dunque se abbiamo bisogno della grafomania di un fotografo positivista del dinamismo [...] Il suo libercolo mi è sembrato, e così agli amici, semplicemente mostruoso. Grottesca la prosopopea e l'infatuazione sull'inesistente." Drudi Gambillo and Fiori: *Archivi del futurismo*, vol. 1, p. 288.

3 "Noi Pittori futuristi dichiariamo che tutto ciò che si riferisce alla fotodinamica concerne esclusivamente delle innovazioni nel campo della fotografia. Tali ricerche puramente fotografiche non

gaglia's Photodynamics made the trajectory of gestures visible, highlighted their simultaneous passage through space and time, and expressed the essence of movement, not unlike an idea expressed in the *Technical Manifesto of Futurist Painting:* "The gesture that we want to reproduce will no longer be a moment in the universal dynamism which has been stopped, but the dynamic sensation itself, perpetuated as such."[4]

Following this brush with the Futurist group of painters, Bragaglia threw himself into a series of new ventures. At the outbreak of the First World War, he began a successful career in journalism, initially working for the daily newspaper *Il fronte interno* (The Domestic Front) and soon becoming its editor-in-chief. As a result of this, he was exempted from military service in the First World War. At the same time, he founded the pantheist-inspired monthly magazine *La ruota* (The Wheel), to which leading writers from Italy and abroad contributed.

In 1916, Bragaglia began publishing *Cronache d'attualità* (Chronicles of Current Affairs), a magazine on 'art, science, music, decorative arts, politics, literature, theatre, opera, operetta, modern industries, cinematography, café-concerts, fashions, sport, finance'.[5] In the course of its six years of existence, he managed not only to obtain the collaboration of well-established authors but also to offer space to a younger generation of writers such as Aldo Palazzeschi, Federigo Tozzi and Rosso di San Secondo; composers such as Gian Francesco Malipiero, Ildebrando Pizzetti and Francesco Balilla Pratella; artists such as Carlo Carrà, Pablo Picasso, Filippo De Pisis, Fortunato Depero and Giorgio de Chirico, who in their essays and illustrations presented some of the most innovative ideas of their time.

Also in 1916, Bragaglia founded, together with Emidio De Medio, a film company, Novissima Film, and in the space of just over a year shot three feature films: *Thaïs* (1916), *Perfido incanto* (The Evil Spell, 1917) and *Il mio cadavere* (My Corpse, 1917), with sets created by Enrico Prampolini. The films worked with abstract settings and surreal effects, thus anticipating European experimental cinema, in particular German Expressionism.[6] Bragaglia considered cinema to be a new art, the only one that can capture the rhythm of movement and the complexity of modern

---

hanno assolutamente nulla a che fare col Dinamismo plastico da noi inventato." Boccioni et al.: "Avviso", p. 211.

4 Boccioni et al.: "Futurist Painting: Technical Manifesto", p.64.

5 See the cover of *Cronache d'attualità* 1:6 (30 August 1916).

6 On Bragaglia's cinematic œuvre see Wanda Strauven's entry on cinema in Berghaus: *Handbook of International Futurism*, pp. 101–115, the special issue on Anton Giulio Bragaglia of *Bianco e nero: Rivista del Centro Sperimentale di Cinematografia* 26:5–6 (May-June 1965), and the essays by Marcus: "Anton Guilio Bragaglia's 'Thaïs', Re: "Futurism, Film and the Return of the Repressed", Re: " 'Thaïs': A Different Challenge to the Stars".

life. He therefore explored with great enthusiasm the possibilities of the medium. Although, once again, he was moving within the wider sphere of Futurism, he was not amongst the signatories of the manifesto on *Cinematografia futurista* (Futurist Cinema).[7]

Indeed, Bragaglia's vision of and passion for the avant-garde always extended beyond the boundaries of Futurism. His curiosity drove him to explore every cultural novelty and to provide innovative artists with a platform. For this purpose, he created his Casa d'Arte Bragaglia, an exhibition space in the centre of Rome, run together with his brother Carlo Ludovico and financed from the proceeds from his photographic studio. The gallery consisted of four rooms, a salon and a wide corridor, and from the end of 1918 to June 1921 hosted more than seventy exhibitions, publicized through the *Bollettino della Casa d'Arte Bragaglia* (Bulletin of the Bragaglia Art Workshop).[8]

The first exhibition was by Giacomo Balla (October 1918), followed by those of Giorgio de Chirico and Mario Sironi in 1919. In 1920, Filippo De Pisis made his debut there; then came, amongst others, Julius Evola and the Dadaists, Michele Cascella and Marcello Dudovich. The gallery's exhibition horizon was international, with solo shows of Klimt and Schiele, artists from Russia (Ossip Zadkine, Léon Zack), Switzerland (Johannes Itten), Poland (Henryk Glicenstein), Germany (Franz Maria Jansen, Jakob Steinhardt, Max Beckmann), the Netherlands (Annie Cottrau Fokker) and the USA (John Decker).

Bragaglia's Casa d'Arte was a centre of lively agitation that promoted innovative ideas and often unleashed fierce controversies. In 1922, it moved into the underground premises of Palazzo Tittoni, where the rests of the ancient Baths of Septimius Severus, reaching to Via degli Avignonesi, had been discovered. In this vast catacomb, five art galleries were established: one for retrospectives, one for modern art, one for decorative art, one for graphic art, one for Futurist art. They were complemented by an experimental theatre, a dance hall and a bar for artists and visitors. Virgilio Marchi, Prampolini, Balla, Melchiorre Melis and Depero worked on the architecture and décor of the spaces. They opened to the public on 22 April 1922 with three exhibitions dedicated to Umberto Boccioni, Edoardo Dalbono and the ceramist Fedele Cappelletti.

In the following years, these premises hosted shows by many Futurists such as Francesco Cangiullo, Antonio Sant'Elia, Ivo Pannaggi, Emilio Notte, Depero and Prampolini, as well as representatives of Magical Realism (Antonio Donghi, Riccar-

7 See Verdone and Berghaus: " 'Vita futurista' and Early Futurist Cinema."

8 See Bragaglia: "Una 'battaglia in favore dell'arte': Centosessantatré esposizioni alla Casa d'Arte Bragaglia" and the documentation in Verdone et al.: *La Casa d'arte Bragaglia, 1918–1930.*

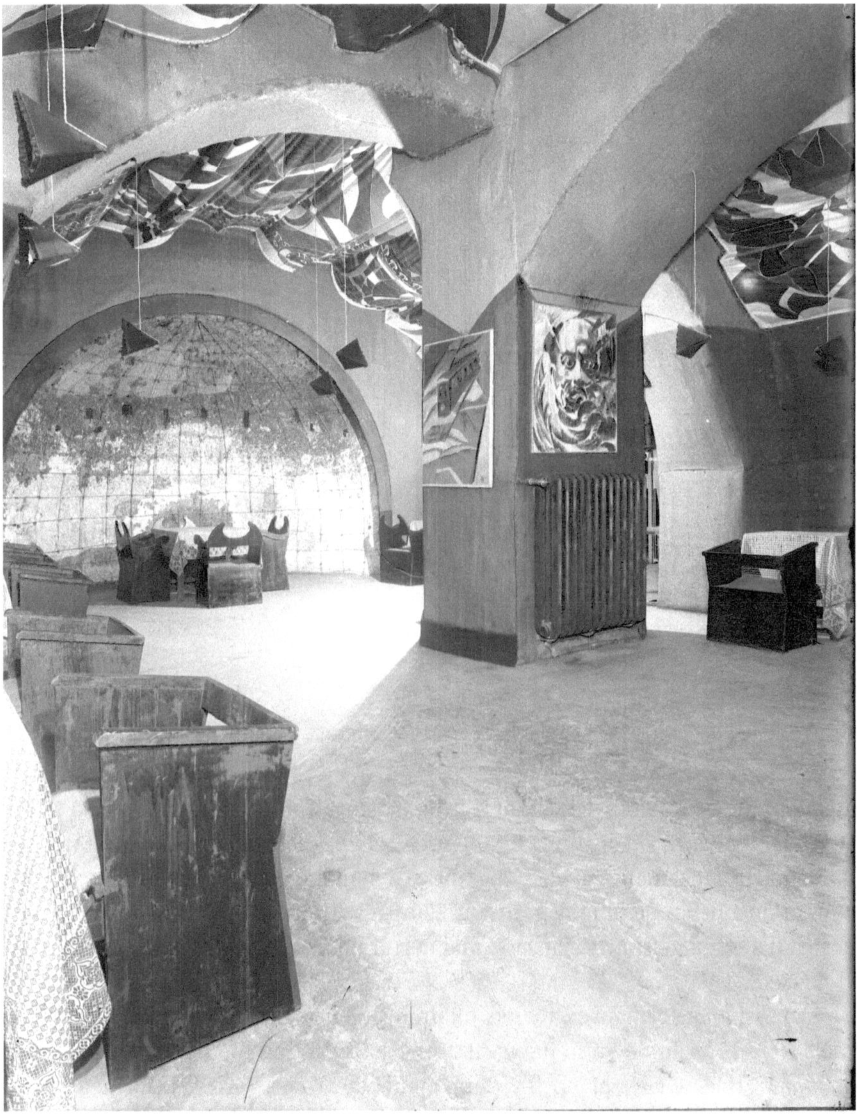

Fig. 1: The club rooms adjacent to the Teatro degli Indipendenti.

do Francalancia, Cipriano Efisio Oppo, Carlo Socrate, Francesco Trombadori) and Italian Expressionism (Mario Mafai, Marino Mazzacurati, Scipione, Antonietta Raphaël). The Russian colony in Italy was represented by Vladimir Abramovich Bobermann, Grigorii Ivanovich Shiltian (aka Gregorio Sciltian) and Pavel Andreevich Mansurov.

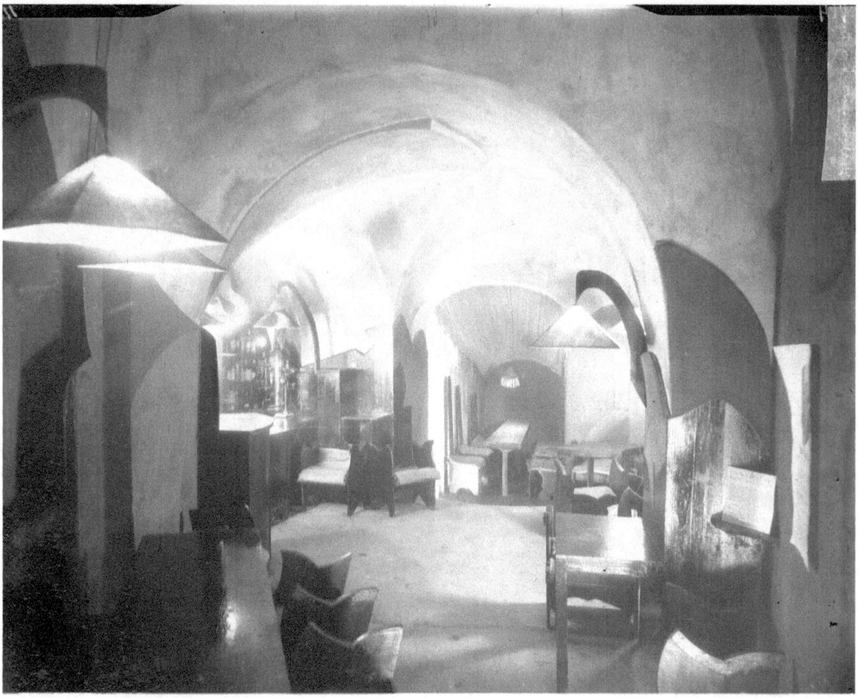

Fig. 2: The club rooms adjacent to the Teatro degli Indipendenti.

Equally intense was the activity of the Teatro degli Indipendenti,[9] annexed to the Casa d'Arte, which opened on 18 January 1923 with *Siepe a Nord Ovest*, Massimo Bontempelli's dramatic debut. The theatre building was designed by Virgilio Marchi and had a seating capacity of 200. This futuristic, multifunctional venue hosted plays, mime shows, concerts and performances by well-known international dancers.[10]

After the performances, thanks to an ingenious system of winches, the raked stalls were brought down to the level of the stage, and in the flattened space thus obtained tables were set up for dinner and the room was transformed into a restaurant and nightclub (see Figs. 1 and 2). It was frequented by artists, writers,

9 See Bragaglia: "Cronologia degli spettacoli allestiti al Teatro Sperimentale degli Indipendenti di Roma diretto da Anton Giulio Bragaglia 1922–1936" , Bragaglia: "Dalla 'Casa d'arte' agli 'Indipendenti'" and Alberti, et al.: *Il Teatro Sperimentale degli Indipendenti, 1923–1936.*

10 Bragaglia became a major promoter of the European 'free dance' movement. See Taddeo: "Il posto del corpo: Anton Giulio Bragaglia teorico di danza tra le due guerre."

critics, journalists, many intellectuals of different orientations and even high officials of the régime, including Giuseppe Bottai and Galeazzo Ciano.

Bragaglia founded his own company, the 'Compagnia Spettacoli Bragaglia', premièred many Italians play, such as Pirandello's *L'uomo dal fiore in bocca* (The Man With the Flower in His Mouth) and others by Corrado Alvaro, Orio Vergani, Rosso di San Secondo, Antonio Aniante, Ardengo Soffici, Riccardo Bacchelli, Italo Svevo, Achille Campanile, as well as Marinetti's *Bianco e Rosso* (White and Red; prem. 4 April 1923), *Fantocci elettrici* (Electric Dolls; prem. 28 May 1925) and *Il suggeritore nudo* (The Naked Prompter; prem. 12 December 1929). From outside Italy, authors then little known or completely unknown in Italy, such as Wedekind, Schnitzler, Jarry, Shaw and Strindberg, were presented. Bragaglia's formula of a *teatro teatrale* was that of a stage that "speaks to the intellect through the united paths of the eyes and ears",[11] where the rôles of author and actor are re-dimensioned and where painting, sculpture, sound and lighting contribute equally to the unfolding of the dramatic action. Multiple, mobile and interchangeable scenery, coloured and suggestive lighting, performers depersonalized by masks, and many other innovative devices successfully competed with contemporaneous Futurist experiments such as Prampolini's production of Achille Ricciardi's *Teatro del colore* (Theatre of Colours, 1920), the tours of the *Teatro della sorpresa* (Theatre of Surprise, 1924) and *Il nuovo teatro futurista* (The New Futurist Theatre, 1924) or the *Teatro novatore* (Innovatory Theatre, 1927) in Turin and *Théâtre de la pantomime futuriste* (Futurist Mime Theatre, 1927) in Paris.[12]

Unlike many Futurists, Bragaglia nurtured a lively interest in the heritage of the Italian theatre tradition, which he studied with an anthropological aptitude. His historical papers explored many forms of popular theatre, the commedia dell'arte, and much more. It is precisely this combination of experimentalism and traditionalism that characterized his *Del teatro teatrale, ossia Del teatro* (About Theatrical Theatre, that is The Theatre, 1929), a book that dwells on the dramatic value that different scenic, costume and lighting solutions can assume. It also outlines the concept of an unconventional director who combines in a single person the different functions of manager, set designer and choreographer, orchestrating all processes on stage.

The activity of the Teatro degli Indipendenti came to an end in 1932, when the Casa d'Arte moved to new premises in Piazza Mignanelli where, for another twen-

11 "Il teatro parla all'intelletto per le vie riunite degli occhi e degli orecchi." Bragaglia: *Del teatro teatrale, ossia Del teatro*, p. 22.

12 For a detailed discussion of these theatre productions see Berghaus: *Italian Futurist Theatre, 1909–1944*, pp. 347–359, 359–372, 437–439, 449–462.

ty years or so, it operated under the name Bragaglia Fuori Commercio (Bragaglia Out-of-Commerce). Bragaglia was a personal friend of the Duce and dedicated to him his book *Il teatro della rivoluzione* (The Theatre of the Revolution, 1929). In 1937, he became director of the Teatro delle Arti, which he managed until 1943.[13] Now operating within the orbit of the Fascist régime, Bragaglia continued to give space to young playwrights and, above all, to support authors that had been ostracized by the Ministry of Popular Culture, e.g. Eugene O'Neill, of whom he was the first Italian supporter. Other such seemingly 'impossible feats' were the staging of Bertolt Brecht and Kurt Weill's *Dreigroschenoper* (Threepenny Opera) at the Teatro dei Filodrammatici in Milan in 1930, in a translation by Alberto Spaini and Corrado Alvaro. Albeit purged of political content and with a changed title imposed by Mussolini (La veglia dei lestofanti; i.e The Swindlers' Vigil), it was nonetheless an innovatively presented 'jazz comedy'.[14] In 1940 followed *Bodas de sangre* (Blood Wedding) by Federico Garcìa Lorca, a republican shot in Spain four years earlier by the Franco régime, of which the Italian Fascists had been supportive allies.

After the war, Bragaglia alternated his activity as an opera director (at the Teatro La Fenice in Venice, the Teatro S. Carlo in Naples and the Teatro Massimo in Palermo) with that of scholar, publishing several significant books such as *Le maschere romane* (The Roman Masks, 1947) and *Storia del teatro popolare romano* (History of Roman Popular Theatre, 1958). He also founded the Piccolo Teatro del Ridotto in Venice and the Piccolo Teatro in Bari, wrote theatre reviews for numerous national and foreign newspapers and, invited by UNESCO, represented Italy at international theatre congresses. In 1959, he was elected president of the National Association of Artists and Set Designers, shortly before dying in July 1960.

The Bragaglia Archive at GNAM

Anton Giulio Bragaglia left behind a vast archive with materials that document almost fifty years of an extremely rich and diverse life path. His artistic pursuits were always accompanied by an intense intellectual engagement in close collaboration with significant personalities of the cultural world in the first half of the twentieth century. This conspicuous heritage, for various reasons, has long remained inaccessible to scholars. The artist's direct heir, Antonella Vigliani, initially

13 See Calendoli: *Il teatro delle arti: Lo Sperimentale di Stato di Anton Giulio Bragaglia 1937–1943.*
14 See the advertising brochure, with cover by Vinicio Paladini: *Bragaglia presenta La veglia dei lestofanti. Commedia Jazz. Spettacolo sonoro.*

allowed the artist's papers to be accessed by scholars as part of the activities of a Centro Studi Bragaglia (Bragaglia Study Centre), but then suspended almost completely the consultation of documents after some of them had been stolen. The materials, which she had jealously guarded until 2000, were then divided amongst Bragaglia's grandchildren and begun to emerge on the antiquarian book market, risking being dispersed.

Finally, a niece obtained the co-heirs' shares and re-ordered the legacy – if not in its entirety, at least for the most part – and initiated the process of placing it in the tutelage of a public institution. After many complications and refusals, her plans bore fruits when, in 2019, the Galleria Nazionale d'Arte Moderna e Contemporanea acquired the material and began with the digitization of the archive. The purchase of the Bragaglia collection was part of the museum's new acquisition policy initiated by director Cristiana Collu, who had for some time been engaged in the expansion and valorization of the historical donations in its possession. These include, amongst others, those of Mario Broglio and the magazine *Valori plastici*, the painters Giacomo Balla, Adolfo De Carolis and Giulio Aristide Sartorio, Emanuele Cavalli and Giuseppe Capogrossi.

The Bragaglia archive consists of approximately 172 linear metres of box files, containing correspondences, musical scores, scripts sent to him by various writers, drawings, graphic works and stage sketches, playbills and programmes for the Teatro degli Indipendenti and other theatres managed by Bragaglia, directorial books for the plays staged by him, press reviews, many photographs, manuscript notes for articles, lectures and books. In addition, there are 110 linear metres of books concerned with theatre history, dance and set design.

After two years of inventorying and cataloguing, these materials have been arranged in eight series: Correspondence, Writings, Scripts, Theatrical Iconography, Photographs, Thematic Iconography, Press Reviews and Library. Each is subdivided into chronological or thematic subsections, and all can be accessed via the GNAM website, Historical Funds, at https://opac.lagallerianazionale.com/gnam-web/fondi/tree/IT-GNAM-ST0027–000001.

The 'Correspondence' and 'Iconography' series have been digitized (about 18,000 files) and can be consulted online. Descriptive files exist for the 'Writings' and 'Copies' sections, and 'Press Reviews' and 'Library' are still in the process of cataloguing. As for the posters, brochures, sheet music and the extensive corpus of graphic designs (caricatures, sketches, woodcuts, gouaches), much work still remains to be done, also in terms of their inventory, not least because some of the material has only been transferred to GNAM on loan, and the ownership of the images still remains with the heirs.

For the time being, there are no plans to publish a descriptive catalogue on paper. Even the exhibition held in 2021 did not result in the printing of a catalogue.

However, the publication of a volume dedicated to an in-depth study of Bragaglia's artistic career, to be edited by Chiara Stefani, is impending.

Bibliography

Alberti, Alberto Cesare, Sandra Bevere, and Paola di Guilio, eds.: *Il teatro sperimentale degli indipendenti, 1923–1936.* Roma: Bulzoni, 1984.

Berghaus, Günter: *Italian Futurist Theatre, 1909–1944.* Oxford: Clarendon Press, 1998.

Boccioni, Umberto, Carlo Carrà, Luigi Russolo, Gino Severini, and Giacomo Balla: "La pittura futurista: Manifesto tecnico." U.Boccioni: *Scritti sull'arte.* Milano: Mimesis, 2011. 7–11. English translation "Futurist Painting: Technical Manifesto, 1910." Lawrence Rainey, Christine Poggi, and Laura Wittman, eds. *Futurism: An Anthology.* New Haven /CT: Yale University Press. 2009. 64–67.

Boccioni, Umberto, Giacomo Balla, Carlo Carrà, Gino Severini, Luigi Russolo, and Ardengo Soffici, "Avviso." *Lacerba* 1:19 (1 October 1913): 211.

Bragaglia, Anton Giulio: "Lettera sul teatro a Benito Mussolini." A.G. Bragaglia: *Il teatro della rivoluzione.* Roma: Edizioni Tiber, 1929. 5–14.

Bragaglia, Anton Giulio: *Bragaglia presenta "La veglia dei lestofanti". Commedia Jazz. Spettacolo sonoro.* Roma: Rotocalco Grafia Il Bragaglia per Tutti, 1930.

Bragaglia, Anton Giulio: *Del teatro teatrale, ossia Del teatro.* Roma: Edizioni Tiber, 1929.

Bragaglia, Anton Giulio: *Fotodinamismo futurista.* Roma: Nalato, [1913]. Reprint ed. by Antonella Vigliani Bragaglia. Torino: Einaudi, 1970. Second edition 1980. English translation "Futurist Photodynamism (1911)." *Modernism / Modernity* 15:2 (April 2008): 363–379.

Bragaglia, Anton Giulio: *Le maschere romane.* [Roma]: Colombo, 1947.

Bragaglia, Anton Giulio: *Storia del teatro popolare romano.* [Roma]: Colombo, 1958.

Bragaglia, Antonella Vigliani: "Cronologia degli spettacoli allestiti al Teatro Sperimentale degli Indipendenti di Roma diretto da Anton Giulio Bragaglia 1922–1936." *Maske und Kothurn: Internationale Beiträge zur Theater-, Film- und Medienwissenschaft* 12:4 (1966): 414–418.

Bragaglia, Carlo Ludovico: "Dalla 'Casa d'arte' agli 'Indipendenti'." C. L. Bragaglia: *Bragaglia racconta Bragaglia.* Milano: All'Insegna del Pesce d'Oro, 1997. 73–78.

Bragaglia, Carlo Ludovico: : "Una 'battaglia in favore dell'arte': Centosessantatré esposizioni alla Casa d'Arte Bragaglia." C. L. Bragaglia: *Bragaglia racconta Bragaglia.* Milano: All'Insegna del Pesce d'Oro, 1997. 85–90.

Calendoli, Giovanni, ed.: *Il teatro delle arti: Lo Sperimentale di Stato di Anton Giulio Bragaglia 1937–1943.* Vol. 1–3. Roma: Ente Nazionale di Assistenza e Previdenza, 1991–1994.

Drudi Gambillo, Maria, and Teresa Fiori eds: *Archivi del futurismo.* Vol. 1–2. Roma: De Luca, 1958–1962.

Marcus, Millicent: "Anton Giulio Bragaglia's Thaïs, Or The Death of the Diva + The Rise of the Scenoplastica = The Birth of Futurist Cinema." *South Central Review* 13:2–3 (Summer-Fall 1996): 63–81.

Marinetti, Filippo Tommaso, Bruno Corra, Enrico Settimelli, Arnaldo Ginna, Giacomo Balla, and Remo Chiti: "Cinematografia futurista." *L'Italia futurista* 1:10 (15 November 1916): 1.

Re, Lucia: "Futurism, Film and the Return of the Repressed: Learning from 'Thaïs'." *Modern Language Notes* 123:1 (January 2008): 125–150.

Re, Lucia: "'Thaïs': A Different Challenge to the Stars." Rossella Catanese, ed.: *Futurist Cinema: Studies on Italian Avant-garde Film.* Amsterdam: Amsterdam University Press, 2017. 161–178.

Strauven, Wanda: “Cinema.” Günter Berghaus, ed.: *Handbook of International Futurism.* Berlin & Boston: De Gruyter, 2019. 101–115.

Taddeo, Giulia: “Il posto del corpo: Anton Giulio Bragaglia teorico di danza tra le due guerre.” *Danza e ricerca: Laboratorio di studi, scritture, visioni* 5:4 (2013): 57–115.

Verdone, Mario, ed.: *Anton Giulio Bragaglia.* Special issue of *Bianco e nero: Rivista del Centro Sperimentale di Cinematografia* 26:5–6 (May-June 1965). Roma: Bianco e Nero, 1965.

Verdone, Mario, and Günter Berghaus: “ ‘Vita futurista’ and Early Futurist Cinema.” Günter Berghaus, ed.: *International Futurism in Arts and Literature.* Berlin & New York: De Gruyter, 2000. 398–421.

Verdone, Mario, Francesca Pagnotta, and Marina Bidetti: *La casa d’arte Bragaglia, 1918–1930.* Roma: Bulzoni, 1992.

Lisa Hanstein

Rosa Rosà / Edith Arnaldi / Edyth von Haynau (1884–1978): A Woman Photographer and Her Futurist Inspiration

Editha Johanna Ida von Haynau was born on 11 November 1884 in Vienna as the only daughter of Ernst von Haynau and Harriet Mautner von Markhof, an aristocratic family in Austria.[1] On a cruise to the North Cape in 1907 she met the Italian writer Ulrico Arnaldi (1878–1956), whom she married a year later. They settled in Rome and had four children, born between 1909 and 1915.[2] The artist became known in Futurist circles under the pseudonym Rosa Rosà and published two drawings in the Florentine magazine *L'Italia futurista.* In several articles she concerned herself with gender issues and engaged in the debate on Marinetti's provocative book, *Come si seducono le donne* (How to Seduce Women, 1917), always highlighting the positive change of women's rôles in the wake of the nascent feminist movement.[3] Between 1917 and 1919, she illustrated works by the Futurist writers Bruno Corra, Arnaldo Ginna and Mario Carli,[4] and in 1918 published her own novels *Una donna con tre anime* (A Woman with Three Souls, 1918) and *Non cè che te: Una donna con tre anime e altre novelle* (There's Nothing but You: A Woman with Three Souls and Other Short Stories, 1919). Unfortunately, most of her oil paintings, pastels, watercolours, portraits, lithographs, illustrations and ceramics from this period are considered lost. Preserved are only her coloured drawings for Ernst Roenau's fairy tale books *Das persische Papageienbuch* (The Persian Parrot Book, (1922) and *Tausend und eine Nacht* (The Arabian Nights, 1923). Extant are also the oil painting *Anticolana alla fonte* (Anticolana at the Source, c.1935), an

1 This is the birth name as it appears on her death certificate, see Proietti: *Edith von Haynau*, p. 12, but there are different name variants. Before adopting the pseudonym 'Rosa Rosà' in 1917, she was known as Edyth von Haynau; after her Futurist phase, she signed her works and letters 'Edyth Arnaldi'. Contemporary publications, however, usually list her as 'Edith Arnaldi'. I shall use in this essay her common civil name, Edyth von Haynau.

2 See the bio-bibliographic note in Claudia Salaris' reprint of *Una donna con tre anime*, p. 27.

3 Rosa Rosà: "Le donne del posdomani": Rosa Rosà: "Risposta a Jean-Jacques", Rosa Rosà: "Le donne cambiano finalmente". Marinetti seems to have liked her argumentation, as he reprinted the last two essays in the second editon of his book (Rocca S. Casciano: Cappelli, 1918).

4 See Corra: *Con mani di vetro*; Corra: *Sam Dunn è morto*; Ginna: *Le locomotive con le calze*; Carli: *Notti filtrate.*

https://doi.org/10.1515/9783111318394-021

early portrait by an unknown hand (see Fig. 1b), an untitled painting and 12 calendar pages.[5]

From 1933 to 1954, Von Haynau was also active as a photographer, after which she returned to writing historical novels, such as *Eterno mediterraneo* (The Eternal Mediterranean, 1964) and *Il fenomeno bisanzio* (The Byzantium Phenomenon, 1970), under her married name Arnaldi. She participated in various exhibitions[6] and was active as an artist and illustrator until old age. A presumably autobiographical work remained unfinished and unpublished. She died in Rome on 3 October 1978.

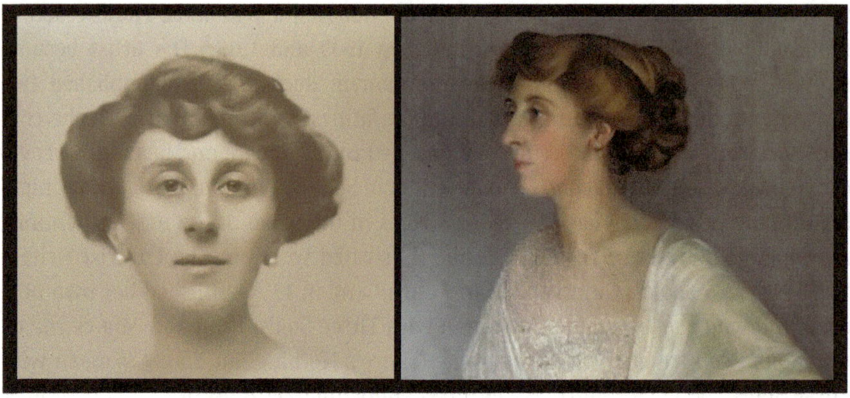

Fig. 1: Two portraits of Edyth von Haynau, early 1910s.

Edyth von Haynau as a photographer

Edyth von Haynau's interests as a photographer have recently come to light when more than 10,800 negatives and 232 prints emerged on the art market. Ferruccio Malandrini bought the material after 1986 and then sold part of it to the Archivio Storico Fratelli Alinari in Florence and another to the Archivio Malandrini in

5 The painting *Anticolana alla fonte* is now in the possession of the Civico Museo d'Arte Moderna e Contemporanea di Anticoli Corrado. Other works preserved in her family are currently investigated by me.

6 For more information on her exhibition activities see Hanstein "Edyth von Haynau: A Viennese Aristocrat in the Futurist Circles of the 1910s", for exhibitions of her photographs see Hanstein "Edith Arnaldi: Fotografa! = Edith Arnaldi: Photographer!" as well as Hanstein "The Eye of a Modern Woman: Edyth von Haynau as Photographer", forthcoming.

Siena.[7] These purchases became known to the general public through the exhibition *Fotografe! = Women Photographers*,[8] which juxtaposed artists from the early years of photography with contemporary women photographers[9] and testified that Von Haynau's engagement with the medium went far beyond that of an amateur. As early as the 1930s, she participated with her photographs in exhibitions, had some of them published in catalogues, and in two cases even received awards.[10]

The recent exhibition in Florence contained two separate sections dedicated to the sisters Marion and Wanda Wulz and Edith Arnaldi. The latter part included some 232 original photographs, which show studies of women from the Ciociara area in southern Italy and northern Hungary from the period 1934 to 1937, as well as around 20 negative prints, which document Von Haynau's numerous journeys and her interest in people and physical environments.[11] From this broad spectrum of Von Haynau's work as a photographer, two from the negative collection of the Archivio Malandrini (Fondazione Monte dei Paschi di Siena)[12] will be presented on the following pages, as they reflect aspects of Futurist aesthetics.

In the photograph *Trionfo durante il Palio* (Triumph during the Palio; see Fig. 2), the viewer looks from an elevated point of view at the Sienese horse race, the Palio, for which the central Piazza del Campo is twice a year transformed into a racecourse. In this important cultural event, ten of the city's seventeen *contrade* (districts) compete against each other. The image here shows the moment of victory, charged with emotion. Using multiple exposures, Von Haynau shows both the horse of the Contrada della Torre (Tower District) at the finish line and the moment immediately afterwards, when the cheering members of the Contrada jump towards the winner, hug each other and wave flags to celebrate their victory. Their movements are blurred and out of focus, and mix in with those of the speeding horses. The picture combines the climax of the race with the subsequent catharsis after the triumphant victory. It conveys to the viewer an emotionally charg-

7 Some of the works can be consulted online: the Fondazione Alinari per la fotografia made 164 photographs freely available (https://www.alinari.it/it/esplora-immagini?query=Edith+Arnaldi) and the Archivio Malandrini in Siena 189 negatives (Archivio Malandrini: https://opereweb.fondazionemps.it/Malandrini.aspx).

8 Held at the Villa Bardini and Fortezza di Belvedere from 18 June – 2 October 2022. See the catalogue edited by Emanuela Sesti and Walter Guadagnini.

9 Edith Arnaldi's works were juxtaposed with Marina Caneve's large-format photographs.

10 See Hanstein "Edith Arnaldi: Fotografa! = Edith Arnaldi: Photographer!", p. 30.

11 See Sesti and Guadagnini: *Fotografe* and Hanstein: "The Eye of a Modern Woman: Edyth von Haynau as Photographer", forthcoming.

12 The collection consists of 189 negatives, of which 65 scenes relating to the Palio in Siena in August 1939 are particularly interesting.

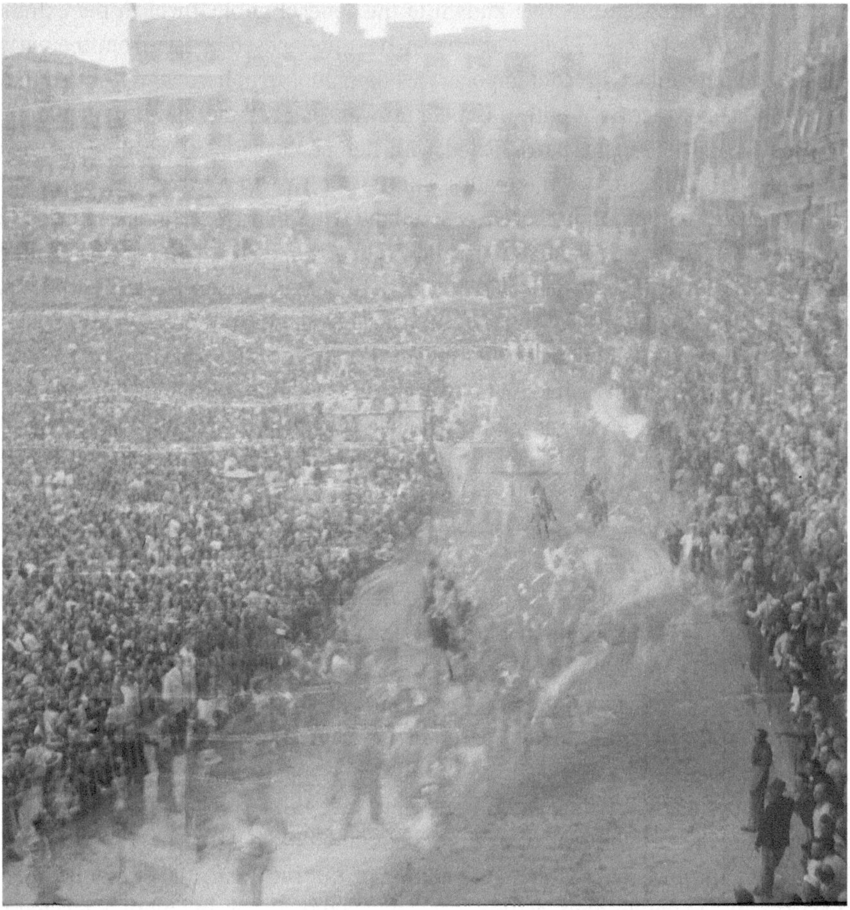

Fig. 2: Edith Arnaldi: *Trionfo durante il Palio* (Triumph during the Palio, 1939)

ed and dynamic atmosphere and offers an exciting synthesis of what has been seen, experienced and remembered on that day.

Such dissolution of solid outlines and decomposition of outer forms by both light and movement can also be found in the first phase of Futurism. In their technical manifesto of 1910, the Futurist painters declared that "movement and light destroy the materiality of bodies" and that "universal dynamism must be rendered in painting as a dynamic sensation".[13] The idea was taken up by Anton Giulio Bra-

13 Boccioni, et al.: "Futurist Painting: Technical Manifesto", p. 66. "Che il moto e la luce distruggono

gaglia in his booklet *Fotodinamismo futurista* (Futurist Photodynamism, 1913), where he explained how dynamism and the inner state of mind of people portrayed could be made visible:

> We want to render what is not seen on the surface: we want to register the living sensation of a particular reality's deep expression, and we are seeking its sensation of movement because that is rich with magnificent, hidden depths and multiple emotive sources that render it unspeakable and ungraspable.[14]

Motion came to be seen as a pure trajectory, a trace in space intended to capture the inner essence of the object. All of these aspects of Futurist art and theory are evident in Edyth von Haynau's *Trionfo durante il Palio*. In addition, this image also visualizes the eleventh point of the manifesto *La fotografia futurista* (Futurist Photography, 1930) by superimposing at the moment of victory "transparent and semitransparent images of people and concrete objects with their semiabstract phantoms [... and] with the simultaneous effect of dream memories."[15]

The shot *Via Santa Caterina* (see Fig. 3) shows the street of the same name in Siena from different perspectives through the overlay of multiple exposures. On the one hand, the different positions depict the moment when a horse returns to the stables of its *contrada*, as it strides up a slight incline towards an archway. On the other hand, in the same place, there is a group of people slightly shifted to the bottom left, above whose heads the horse seems to be floating. A further image plane allows a flag to appear weightlessly on the horse's left flank and a road sign in the middle of its tail. The dynamic image structure is further emphasized by the strong light and shadow contrasts.

The different levels interpenetrate and there is a "simultaneity of object + environment + atmosphere", as formulated by Umberto Boccioni.[16] In this synthesis of different moments and detached objects, Von Haynau succeeds in implementing

---

la materialità dei corpi [...] Che il dinamismo universale deve essere reso come sensazione dinamica." "La pittura futurista: Manifesto tecnico", p. 11.

14 "Futurist Photodynamism", p. 366. "Vogliamo rendere ciò che superficialmente non si vede: vogliamo ricordare la più viva sensazione della espressione profonda di una realtà e cerchiamo infatti quella movimentista perchè è ricca di magnifiche, riposte, profondità e di molteplici fonti emotive per le quali è fatta indicibile e inafferrabile." Bragaglia: *Fotodinamismo futurista*, pp. 10–11.

15 Marinetti and Tato: "Futurist Photography", p. 393. "La sovrapposizione trasparente e semitrasparente di persone e oggetti concreti e dei loro fantasmi semiastratti con simultaneità di ricordo sogno." Marinetti: *Teoria e invenzione futurista*, 1st edn p. 168; 2nd edn p. 196.

16 Boccioni: *Futurist Painting Sculpture (Plastic Dynamism)*, p. 136. "Simultaneità di oggetto + ambiente + atmosfera." Boccioni: *Pittura scultura futuriste: Dinamismo plastico*, p. 265.

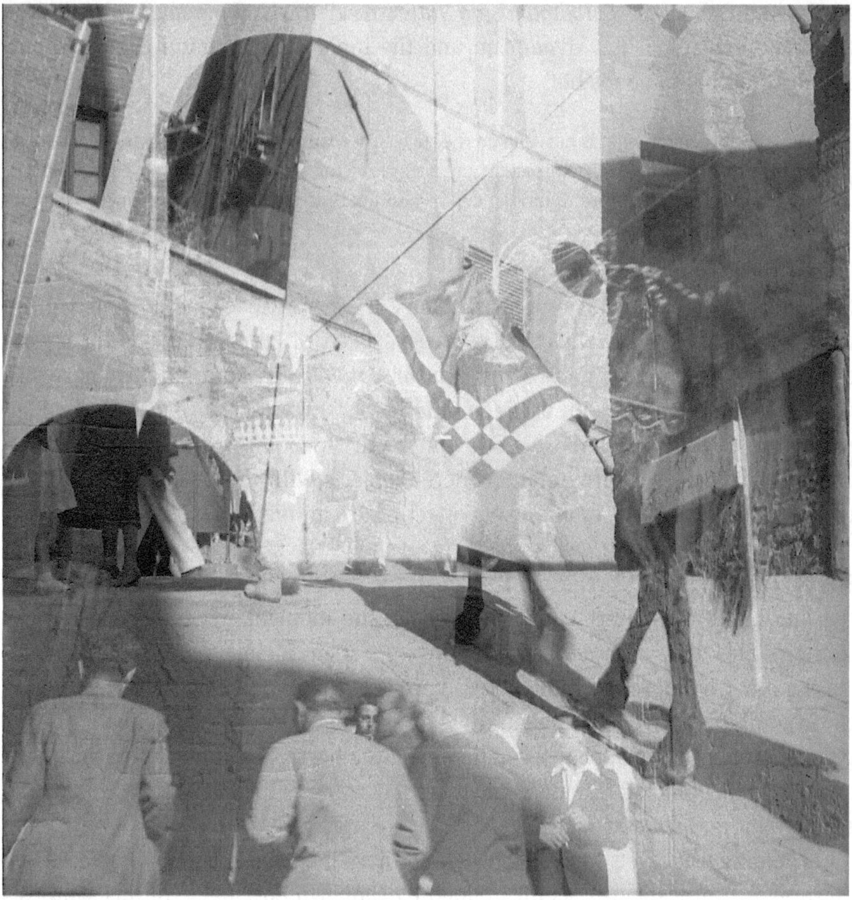

Fig. 3: Edith Arnaldi: *Via Santa Caterina* (Saint-Catherine's Street, 1939).

the fourth point of the *Manifesto of Futurist Photography*, namely "Diffracted images of some parts of human or animal bodies, either in isolation or joined together again in the wrong order." The sixth point of the manifesto, "the fusion of images taken from below with those taken from above" is also applied by changing the viewer's position. The immense size of the horse compared to the minuscule people under its hooves is reminiscent of point nine, the "dramatic disproportioning of moving and static objects", while the fluid transitions between the people, their environment, the horse and the objects take up the idea of point ten, "the desired or violent interpenetration of moving and static objects".[17]

The two images reproduced in Figs. 2 and 3 differ significantly from other photographs taken by Von Haynau. Some of these have a documentary character,[18] others testify to the photographer's love of experimentation or can be seen as pioneering humanistic photography in Italy.[19] Due to the visualization of the principles of Futurist aesthetics in *Trionfo durante il Palio* and *Via Santa Caterina*, these works by Edyth von Haynau show that her alter ego Rosa Rosà had not been entirely buried by the 1930s. These two images should therefore be given a place of honour in the chronicles of Futurist photography.

Acknowledgements: I should like to express my sincere gratitude to the Fornari family for giving me access to the Edyth von Haynau estate preserved in their archive.

Bibliography

Arnaldi, Edyth: *Eterno mediterraneo.* Roma: Sepa, 1964.

Arnaldi, Edyth: *Il fenomeno bisanzio.* Milano: Pan, 1970.

Boccioni, Umberto, Carlo Carrà, Luigi Russolo, Gino Severini, and Giacomo Balla: "La pittura futurista: Manifesto tecnico." Reprinted in Umberto Boccioni: *Scritti sull'arte.* Milano: Mimesis, 2011. 7–11. English translation "Futurist Painting: Technical Manifesto, 1910." Lawrence Rainey, Christine Poggi, and Laura Wittman, eds.: *Futurism: An Anthology.* New Haven/CT: Yale University Press, 2009. 64–67.

Boccioni, Umberto: *Pittura scultura futuriste: Dinamismo plastico.* Milano: Edizioni Futuriste di "Poesia", 1914. English translation *Futurist Painting Sculpture (Plastic Dynamism).* Transl. by Richard Shane Agin and Maria Elena Versari. Introduction by Maria Elena Versari. Los Angeles/CA: Getty Publications, 2016.

Bragaglia, Anton Giulio: "Futurist Photodynamism." Transl. by Lawrence S. Rainey. *Modernism / Modernity* 15:2 (April 2008): 363–379.

Bragaglia, Anton Giulio: *Fotodinamismo futurista.* Roma: Nalato, [1913]. Reprint ed. by Antonella Vigliani Bragaglia. Torino: Einaudi, 1980.

Carli, Mario: *Notti filtrate: 10 liriche. 10 disegni di Rosa Rosà.* Firenze: Edizioni de "L'Italia Futurista", 1918.

17 Marinetti and Tato: "Futurist Photography", p. 392. "[l]a spettralizzazione di alcune parti del corpo umano o animale isolate o ricongiunte alogicamente" (§4); "[l]a fusione di visioni dal basso in alto con visioni dall'alto in basso" (§6); "[l]e drammatiche sproporzioni degli oggetti mobili ed immobili" (§ 9); "amorose o violente compenetrazioni di oggetti mobili o immobili" (§10). Marinetti: *Teoria e invenzione futurista,* 1st edn p. 168; 2nd edn p. 196.

18 See Sesti and Guadagnini: *Fotografe!*

19 See Hanstein "The Eye of a Modern Woman: Edyth von Haynau as Photographer."

Corra, Bruno [pseud. of Bruno Ginanni Corradini]: *Con mani di vetro.* Milano: Studio Editoriale Lombardo, 1916.
Corra, Bruno: *Sam Dunn è morto: Romanzo sintetico futurista.* Milano: Studio Editoriale Lombardo, 1917.
Ginna, Arnaldo [pseud. of Arnaldo Ginanni Corradini]: *Le locomotive con le calze.* Milano: Facchi, 1919.
Hanstein, Lisa: "Edith Arnaldi: Fotografa! = Edith Arnaldi: Photographer!" Emanuela Sesti, and Walter Guadagnini, eds.: *Fotografe! Dagli archivi Alinari a oggi = Women Photographers: Alinari Archives to Contemporary Perspectives.* Firenze: Mandragora, 2022. 29–33.
Hanstein, Lisa: "Edyth von Haynau: A Viennese Aristocrat in the Futurist Circles of the 1910s." *International Yearbook of Futurism Studies* 5 (2015): 333–365.
Hanstein, Lisa: "The Eye of a Modern Woman: Edyth von Haynau as Photographer." Forthcoming.
Filippo Tommaso Marinetti: *Come si seducono le donne.* Firenze: Edizioni da Centomila [Attilio Vallecchi], 1917. 2nd edn Rocca San Casciano: Cappelli, 1918.
Marinetti, Filippo Tommaso, and Tato [pseud. of Guglielmo Sansoni]: "La fotografia futurista: Manifesto." *Il futurismo: Rivista sintetica illustrata* 22 (11 January 1931): 1. Reprinted in F. T. Marinetti: *Teoria e invenzione futurista.* A cura di Luciano De Maria. Milano: Mondadori, 1968. 167–169. 2nd edn Milano: Mondadori, 1983. 195–197. English translation "Futurist Photography." F. T. Marinetti: *Critical Writings.* Ed. by Günter Berghaus. New York: Farrar, Straus and Giroux, 2006. 392–393.
Proietti, Simona: *Edith von Haynau (Rosa Rosà): Una donna tra futurismo e politica.* Roma: Università degli Studi Roma Tre, 2018.
Roenau, Ernst: *Das Persische Papageienbuch.* Mit Buchschmuck von Rosà. Wien: Wolf, 1922;
Roenau, Ernst: *Tausend und eine Nacht.* Bilder und Zeichnungen von Rosà. Wien: Graphische Anstalt, [1923].
Rosa Rosà: "Le donne cambiano finalmente." *L'Italia futurista* 2:27 (26 August 1917): 2.
Rosa Rosà: "Le donne del posdomani." *L'Italia futurista* 2:18 (17 June 1917): 1.
Rosa Rosà: "Risposta a Jean-Jacques." *L'Italia futurista* 2:20 (1 July 1917): 2.
Rosà, Rosa: *Non cè che te: Una donna con tre anime e altre novelle.* Milano: Facchi, 1919.
Rosa Rosà: *Una donna con tre anime: Romanzo futurista.* Milano: Studio Editoriale Lombardo, 1918. Reprint a cura di Claudia Salaris. Milano: Edizioni delle Donne, 1981.
Salaris, Claudia: "Nota biobibliografica." Rosa Rosà: *Una donna con tre anime.* Milano: Edizioni delle Donne, 1981. 27–28.
Sesti, Emanuela, and Walter Guadagnini, eds.: *Fotografe! Dagli archivi Alinari a oggi = Women Photographers: Alinari Archives to Contemporary Perspectives.* Exhibition catalogue. Firenze: Villa Bardini; Forte di Belvedere, 18 giugno – 2 ottobre 2022. Firenze: Mandragora, 2022.

Internet Sources

Fondazione Alinari per la fotografia: https://www.alinari.it/it/esplora-immagini?query=Edith+Arnaldi
Archivio Malandrini: https://opereweb.fondazionemps.it/Malandrini.aspx

Section 3: **Critical responses to new publications**

Deirdre O'Grady

The Crisis of Humanism, the Search for a New Man and the Historical Avant-garde

Iveta Slavkova: *Réparer l'homme: La crise de l'humanisme et l'Homme nouveau des avant-gardes autour de la Grande Guerre (1909–1929).* Dijon: Les Presses du Réel, 2020. ISBN: 978-2-84066-495-6. 416 pp., €30.

The symbolic process of dismembering, deconstructing and reinventing form with its physical and psychological implications has proved a fascinating task for artists such as E.T.A. Hoffmann, Luigi Pirandello or Pablo Picasso. A belief in a better world as a result of the reorganization of matter has been present in socio-political and artistic output across the centuries. The work under review here is to be welcomed as it demonstrates an original approach to the crisis of Humanism. Associated with 'Abhumanism' or 'non-Humanism', the social order registered a call for the creation of a 'New Man' in order to respond to a changing world.[1] The latter could be witnessed in the context of the social upheaval brought about by the First World War.

Iveta Slavkova's highly ambitious study provides a multidisciplinary discourse on ideas not hitherto addressed. Futurism becomes central to her arguments bordering on the intellectual, spiritual and political and is illustrated by appropriate images immortalizing events. Focussing on war in its many socio-political and mythical aspects, Slavkova's investigation brings together both mass destruction and creativity, and the ancient and modern worlds are reflected through two artistic movements: Futurism and the Bauhaus. War is seen to be ennobled through artistic expression. The cult of the 'New Man' is carried from the static solemnity of the war memorial and the tomb of the Unknown Soldier to the physical and proactive Superman in combat with Nature itself. Art and science are considered through the figures of writers, painters and aviators, and Futurism is seen principally through the works of Filippo Tommaso Marinetti and Umberto Boccioni.

Slavkova's book is based on an interdisciplinary dissertation exploring the 'New Man' of both Futurism and the Bauhaus.[2] It is the first of these that will be the main concern of readers of this Yearbook, but the conclusion points towards a re-assessment of the wider ground covered, leaving the area open for further ex-

1 See Audiberti and Bryen: *L'Ouvre-boîte: Colloque abhumaniste.*

2 Slavkova-Montexier: *L'Homme n'est peut-être pas le centre de l'univers.*

https://doi.org/10.1515/9783111318394-022

ploration. The epilogue returns to war, and a possible search for a substitute for Humanism, albeit under a new guise, with Dada cited as a possibility.[3]

Owing to its origin in a Ph.D. dissertation, there is a certain amount of repetition which would benefit from some pruning, as it would provide the arguments addressed with a tighter structure. Given the amount of ground covered and artistic associations touched upon, the publication possesses many of the qualities of a reference work. Throughout the text, the critical devices of demonstration, explanation and illustration are employed. The carefully chosen plates support Slavkova's line of argument and complement her literary documentation.

Iveta Slavkova is Assistant Professor in History of Art in the American University of Paris. Her wide cultural vision and enthusiasm for the visual and graphic arts are reflected in the many well-chosen illustrations. Indeed, in addition to addressing literary and artistic matters, the author provides a visual compendium of both Futurism and the Bauhaus, showcasing the outstanding features of both movements in relation to war. She also introduces journalism and gives us a taste of what the average reader of newspapers and magazines would have been exposed to. By drawing on the pages of *Le Miroir*, Slavkova covers the war from the battlefield to the trenches, from aviation to social life. Employing the methodologies of Gender Studies, she also reveals how the abjection of the feminine made an important contribution to the creation of the 'New Man' as a 'pure' and 'absolute' being, seen to displace the 'hybrid' being of the prewar period.

The book is divided into five principal sections: a Prologue, three Chapters and an Epilogue. The Prologue (pp. 11–399) investigates how the need for a 'New Man' based on a re-definition of the individual's place in the universe arose in the context of war. Chapter I (pp. 39–133) provides an insight into the contradictory and contrasting aspects of war in both national and universal terms. The horror of mass destruction is pitched alongside the perfection of the new individual produced by the conflagration. The cult of the dead prompts the erection of monuments to the Unknown Soldier, while victory is reflected in triumphal arches. Tragedy and tearful mourning is exemplified in the image of Henri Gréber's *Monument aux morts* (Monument to the Dead, 1924) in Beauvais (p. 67). The heroic and mythical aspects of war represented in tombs, monuments, triumphal arches and burial places represent a continuity from sepulchral literature in England, France and Italy in the eighteenth century. For example, Ugo Foscolo's *Dei sepolcri: Carme* (A Song on Tombs, 1807) highlights the rôle of burial grounds as a means of uniting

3 See Slavkova: *Réparer l'homme*, p. 363.

the living with the dead, where the battlefield as mass grave inspires funeral rites and heroic literature.[4]

Chapter II (pp. 135–240) is dedicated to 'l'homme nouveau du futurisme'. At this point, I must stress that the publication is focussed on the manner in which the 'New Man' was re-designed, re-formed and newly re-presented in the era of the First World War. Futurism, our main concern here, serves as a multi-dimensional example of how this was achieved. Much of the validity of Slavkova's study can be found in her novel approach to Futurism. She addresses the movement in new contexts and allows for fresh directions in critical analysis. Five sections are dedicated to Marinetti, his concept of Futurism, the key features of the 'New Man' and the multiplicity of his guises (pp. 135–171). A sense of 'duality' can be detected in Slavkova's contrasting readings of the movement. Marinetti's vision of a national expression of strength and a cosmopolitan cult defying both time and spaces carries the tone of a cultural evolution, complementing Günter Berghaus' research into the two outstanding features of his political thought: Anarchy and Fascism.[5] Slavkova chooses to showcase all aspects of the argument in *Mafarka le futuriste* (1910). Marinetti's iconoclastic preface dedicated to his 'conflagrationary brethren in arms'[6] complements *The Foundation and Manifesto of Futurism* and illustrates the writer's desire to break with the past and open a window on the future. Slavkova identifies Mafarka-El-Bar, king of Tell-el-Kebir, with the qualities to be found in the new warrior. The African hero opts for science over art and creates a mechanical being, Gazourmah, who is engendered without the aid of the female species. As a result, his superhuman strength will destroy his creator[7] and technology will in future abolish the need for human input in the creation of the new "mechanical man, one who will have parts that can be changed".[8]

Iveta Slavkova's work concentrates on novelty, innovation and the 'New Man'. Links are forged with the ancient, medieval and Humanist worlds, with the reintroduction of myth and the mythical illustrating a new classicism: Daedalus and Icarus survive through Mafarka and Gazourmah. The horse on the battlefield points towards a new age of chivalry. In fact, the First World War assumes a new perspective as a meeting place and melting pot for new ideas to which Futurism proved central. War is utilized by Slavkova as a didactic tool, and art is seen to give way to science. Following on Selena Daly's recent study of Futurism and the

4 See Foscolo: *Dei sepolcri*. Slavkova does not refer to the celebrated Italian poet.
5 See Berghaus: *Futurism and Politics*.
6 See Marinetti: "Preface to Mafarka the Futurist."
7 Giorgio Baroni's *Writers on Flight: Aviation in Literature* is a valid study on the subject.
8 Marinetti: "Technical Manifesto of Futurist Literature", pp. 113–114. See O'Grady: "Invention, Industry and the Superpower", pp. 132–133.

First World War, Slavkova identifies Futurism with the words of its founder: in a final superhuman struggle, physical strength will dominate intellectual prowess, and the cultivation of speed will transform the artist into an aviator.[9] Umberto Boccioni is portrayed as the hero of Futurist art. His paintings emerge as spectacles viewed by an observer who is taking an active, participatory rôle. In *La strada entra nella casa* (The Street Enters the House, 1911), the woman is placed at the centre of the picture as both spectator and participant, with the artist playing the rôle of a guide in a social image.

Following Chapter III on the Bauhaus the author takes a new look at her subject in the light of the material explored and considers the possibilities of the 'New Man' reaching diverse destinations. The emergence of Dada in 1916 expanded the space previously allocated to Humanism and allows for further exploration of the qualities of yet another 'New Man'.

Iveta Slavkova, by way of addressing destruction and creativity in the pursuit of a 'New Man' as a perfect mechanized being, embraces art and culture from the Middle Ages to the Modernist age. Throughout the book, one is aware of the author's sense of exploration, discovery and assessment. As a cultural historian, she focusses and contextualizes the avant-garde and its relation to the First World War. She investigates the conditions for the rise of a 'New Man', the protagonist of a new social order, whose roots are deeply embedded in Humanist culture. As such, her study is to be recommended for its original and multidisciplinary approach to war and mechanization and the place of both in a post-Futurist society.

Bibliography:

Audiberti, Jacques, and Camille Bryen: *L'Ouvre-boîte: Colloque abhumaniste.* Paris: Gallimard, 1952.

Baroni, Giorgio, ed.: *Writers on Flight: Aviation in Literature.* Roma: Alenia Aeronautica; Milano: Università Cattolica del Sacro Cuore, 2007.

Berghaus, Günter: *Futurism and Politics: Between Anarchist Rebellion and Fascist Reaction, 1909–1944,* Providence/RI: Berghahn, 1996.

Contarini, Silvia: *La Femme futuriste: Mythes, modèles et représentations de la femme dans la théorie et la littérature futuristes.* Nanterre: Publidix; Presses Universitaires de Paris X, 2006.

Daly, Selena: *Italian Futurism and the First World War.* Toronto: Toronto University Press, 2016.

Foscolo, Ugo: *Dei sepolcri = On Sepulchres.* Transl. Cesare Emiliani. Miami/FL: Interpress, 1976.

Marinetti, Filippo Tommaso: "Preface to Mafarka the Futurist." F.T. Marinetti: *Critical Writings.* Ed. by Günter Berghaus. New York: Farrar, Straus and Giroux, 2006. 32–42.

Marinetti, Filippo Tommaso: "Technical Manifesto of Futurist Literature." F.T. Marinetti: *Critical Writings.* Ed. by Günter Berghaus. New York: Farrar, Straus and Giroux, 2006. 107–119.

9 See Daly: *Futurism and the First World War.*

Marinetti, Filippo Tommaso: *Mafarka le futuriste: Roman africain.* Paris: Sansot, 1909 [i.e. 1910].
O'Grady, Deirdre: "Invention, Industry and the Superpower: The Artificial Human Being and its *Consequences* for the 'Future'." Giuseppe Gazzola, ed.: *Futurismo: Impact and Legacy.* Proceedings of a Conference Held in Florence: Center for Contemporary Italian Studies, 15 October 2009. Stony Brook/NY: Forum Italicum Publishing, 2011. 125–134.
Slavkova-Montexier, Iveta: *L'Homme n'est peut-être pas le centre de l'univers: La crise de l'humanisme et l'Homme nouveau des avant-gardes (1909–1930).* Thèse de doctorat en histoire de l'art. Directeur Philippe Dagen. Paris: Université Paris 1 Panthéon-Sorbonne, 2006.

Lucia Re

Looking at the Lives of Avant-garde Women: The Collector as Scholar and Feminist

Claudia Salaris: *Donne d'avanguardia*. Bologna: Il Mulino, 2021. Pbk. 270 pp. 15 figs. and 20 b&w illustr. 15.5 x21 cm, ISBN 978-88-15-29264-3. 22 €.

Claudia Salaris (*1950) provides in her new book an agile synthesis and a highly personal map of the life and work of many avant-garde women whose biographies and artistic production, in spheres ranging from writing and painting to photography and performance, intersected more or less directly with the mainstream of Italian Futurism. Her study features some of the better-known female Futurists such as Benedetta Cappa Marinetti, and other women artists and performers who associated with Italian Futurism or were at some point enlisted by F.T. Marinetti as members of the movement (for example Valentine de Saint-Point, author of the *Manifesto of Futurist Woman* and often considered the first Futurist woman). Salaris also discusses some prominent women from other countries, for instance, the British-American writer Mina Loy, the Italian-Mexican photographer and revolutionary Tina Modotti and the Ukrainian poet and spy Ol'ga Fedorovna Revzina. Women who adhered to or sympathized with other avant-garde movements as diverse as Dadaism, Imaginism, Surrealism and Magical Realism are also present, although Futurist women form the majority of her portraits. Unlike other books on Futurist women,[1] where biographies play a minor, subsidiary rôle, Salaris takes a distinctly biographical approach and adopts a feminist viewpoint when – in true Futurist spirit – she highlights the multiple connections between life and art in the careers of the very diverse women whom she chose to include. Indeed, Salaris views the unconventional and irreverent women whose life stories she tells in her book as "pioneers in the history of women's liberation" (p. 7).

Claudia Salaris is a prolific independent scholar of Futurism and other aspects of twentieth-century cultural and political history. Since the 1970s, she has been an important, passionate collector of Futurist art, books and ephemera, together with

1 See Bentivoglio and Zoccoli: *Women Artists of Italian Futurism: Almost Lost to History* (1997) and *Le futuriste italiane nelle arti visive* (2008); Bello Minciacchi: *Scrittrici della prima avanguardia: Concezione, caratteri e testimonianze del femminile nel futurismo* (2012); and, more narrowly focussed, Sica: *Futurist Women: Florence. Feminism and the New Sciences* (2015).

https://doi.org/10.1515/9783111318394-023

her life partner, the artist and comic book author Pablo Echaurren (*1951). In 2010, the couple created the Echaurren Salaris Foundation, promoting and supporting in particular the study of Futurism. Salaris is the author, co-author and editor of over fifty books, a number of them essential reading for Futurism scholars.[2]

With *Donne d'avanguardia*, Salaris retraces some of her early steps as a scholar. One of her first books, as she herself recalls in the introduction, was the anthology *Le futuriste: Donne e letteratura d'avanguardia in Italia (1909–1944)* (The Female Futurists: Women and Avant-garde Literature in Italy, 1909–1944, 1982). Published by the feminist press Edizioni delle Donne, it contained excerpts from the writings of several Futurist women, together with short critical introductions to each chapter. Her edition of Rosa Rosà's now classic Futurist novel, *Una donna con tre anime* (A Woman with Three Souls, 1918), was published in 1981 by the same press. As *Le futuriste* quickly went out of print, I had to take recourse to photocopies to provide my students with sections of the volume when teaching classes on Futurist women at the University of California in Los Angeles. Salaris' anthology was a ground-breaking, pioneering feminist work which – alongside a handful of studies by critics such as Giovannella Desideri, Anna Nozzoli and Simona Weller[3] – opened the way for subsequent gender-oriented books on Futurist women writers, artists and performers. Its impact is comparable perhaps to Lea Vergine's *L'altra metà dell'avanguardia 1919–1940: Pittrici e scultrici nei movimenti delle avanguardie storiche* (The Other Half of the Avant-garde: Painters and Sculptors in the Movements of the Historical Avant-gardes, 1980), a book based on a touring exhibition held at the Palazzo Reale in Milan (1980), the Palazzo delle Esposizioni in Rome (1980) and the Kulturhuset in Stockholm (1981). The catalogue was republished in several editions and, like the exhibition itself, unearthed and introduced for the first time many previously buried or simply forgotten female Futurists and other avant-garde artists. That first book by Salaris was, essentially, a carefully selected and thoughtfully presented anthology, with copious black and white illustrations and critical comments as well as a historical introduction. But her biographies – presented as appendices – were all brief and at times very patchy.

---

2 Among her books, see *Storia del futurismo: Libri, giornali, manifesti* (1985); *Marinetti editore* (1990); *Artecrazia: L'avanguardia futurista negli anni del fascismo* (1992); the profusely illustrated, large-format *Filippo Tommaso Marinetti* (1997), her invaluable biography of the Futurist leader, *Marinetti: Arte e vita futurista* (1997) as well as three (of five planned) inventory catalogues of the Echaurren Salaris Collection.

3 Desideri: "Alcuni modelli femminili futuristi" ; Nozzoli: *Tabù e coscienza: La condizione femminile nella letteratura italiana del Novecento*; Weller: *Il complesso di Michelangelo: Ricerca sul contributo dato dalla donna all'arte italiana del Novecento.*

In her new book, biographies take centre stage, and the life of each woman is interwoven, as much as possible, with an account of her art. This approach is, in part, made possible by the author's own tireless search for and collection of documents. Over several decades, she hunted for books in flea markets; images and letters were unearthed from dusty old trunks; and personal acquaintance with some of the women she wrote on – often forgotten and living an isolated life – provided more substantial information. One of the first and most important sources was Luce Marinetti, the third of Benedetta and Marinetti's daughters, whom Salaris went to meet in her home in Via della Camilluccia in Rome, where many of her parents' belongings and works were still lovingly preserved (p. 9).

One of the most striking traits of the volume is that Salaris often provides the exact location, even the address where her subjects used to live. For example, we are told that she met the Futurist aeropainter and aviator who went by the name Barbara (Olga Biglieri, 1915–2002) in Via di Torrevecchia in Rome when Barbara, who had lately been a militant feminist as well as the head of the Communist Party local chapter, still lived and worked. A friendship ensued between the two women and, in 1983, Salaris curated an exhibition of Barbara's Futurist paintings at the Galleria Alzaia in Rome. The map of avant-garde women drawn by Salaris in this book is therefore idiosyncratic and bears the traces, as in a palimpsest, of her own life as a collector-scholar and enthusiast. Furthermore, Salaris re-weaves in different and mostly biographically-oriented patterns many of the threads she put together in her previous studies. Although she does not engage directly with the now substantial body of criticism that has been published on her subject in the past decades, her new book is on the whole well informed. Her notes acknowledge a great deal – although certainly not all – existing scholarship on Futurist and other avant-garde women, whether they align or not with her own approach. Within feminist criticism, there are a variety of approaches to Futurist women; indeed, some critics find the word feminist and the word Futurist largely incompatible, and feminist Futurism an oxymoron.[4] And while a large segment of feminist scholarship believes, like Salaris, in the importance and political significance of personal experience – and especially of a woman's body and sexuality in connection with her artistic and literary expression – other critics find the biographical element a disturbance and a distraction, and argue that intertwining life and art in critical accounts amounts to fictional storytelling.[5]

Salaris' book is written in a plain but engaging style, devoid of academic jargon, and it will serve the non-specialist as a basic but informative introduction to

4 See Contarini: *La Femme futuriste.*

5 For example, in Maderna: *L'altra metà dell'avanguardia quarant'anni dopo.*

avant-garde women. It is composed of eleven chapters; six are devoted each to an individual (Valentine de Saint-Point, Eva Kühn, Růžena Zátková, Benedetta, Marchesa Casati, Tina Modotti) and one to a specific 'literary case' (the obscure *L'eredità di Saffo* by Nada Peretti); the remaining five group together a variety of women according to thematic criteria.

Futurists and other avant-garde women

Chapter 1 reconstructs the Futurist phase of the long life of Valentine de Saint-Point who, after the First World War, turned pacifist, converted to Islam and settled in Egypt, where she became an advocate of decolonization and Arab nationalism. Salaris' profile highlights Saint-Point's fierce, assertive persona, her drive and ambition to defy conventional morality and her rise as a poet and performer in a world dominated by men. Characterizing Saint-Point as an "androgynous superwoman", Salaris sees in her an embodiment of a new model of uninhibited, sexually liberated woman, at once masculine and feminine. Saint-Point's widely distributed and repeatedly translated Futurist manifestos, as well as her poetry recitations and performances, defied Marinetti's misogyny and machismo. She exhorted all women to acknowledge and live out their own desires without submitting to men or succumbing to the bourgeois cult of domesticity prevalent in most European societies at the time (pp. 16–17). Saint-Point demanded sexual freedom not only for heterosexual women, but also for homosexual women and men. Salaris states that this ethos was shared by Marinetti himself (p. 19), without acknowledging that the Futurist leader in reality had a rather contradictory, wavering position on the subject of homosexuality. Although she criticizes some of Saint-Point's provocative pronouncements on violence and power as retrograde and subservient to an outdated masculine outlook, Salaris compares Saint-Point's call for a vehement, even violent rejection of existing norms to militant feminists in the 1970s, who called for men to tremble because "the witches were coming back" and were going after them (pp. 17; 19). The brief discussion of Saint-Point's highly original theory and practice of dance and poetry recitation is accompanied merely by one reproduction (see the woodcut on p. 21). In fact, the entire book only contains a total of fourteen figures, all in black and white, and often in poor quality, taken from books of the author's own collection. The volume does include some twenty better-quality plates, but they are all previously published photographic portraits of the women discussed, including a witty double exposure by the photographer Wanda Wulz called *Io + gatto* (Me and the Cat, 1932). This lack of illustrative material detracts, I find, from the book's potential value.

Chapter 2 offers a compact and lively account of two Russian Futurists (Aleksandra Ekster and Olga Rozanova) and two from the Anglo-Saxon world (the British born Mina Loy and her friend, the American Frances Simpson Stevens) who were the only women represented in the *Esposizione libera futurista internazionale* (International Free Futurist Exhibition), shown at the Sprovieri Galleri in Rome in 1914. Both had affairs with Marinetti, but Salaris does not dwell on how energizing the experience was for Loy, at least initially, although she outlines how Futurism paradoxically spearheaded her feminism. Loy showed in the 1914 exhibition a series of portraits of Marinetti, but unfortunately it remains unclear what they looked like and whether they are still extant. Salaris highlights the reciprocal influences between the Russian and Italian Futurists, as well as the personal, and often intimate, interactions with Marinetti, pointing out that Rozanova's works were particularly close to the industrial and urban themes that dominated Italian Futurism (p. 27). Two of the books mentioned in this context are Kruchenykh's *Utinoe gnezdyshko ... durnykh slov* (A Little Duck's Nest ... of Bad Words, 1913) and Kruchenykh and Khlebnikov's *Te Li Le* (1914), appreciated by Marinetti for their multiple authorship, a practice unknown to Italian Futurists (pp. 26–28). The second section of this chapter presents a short account of Natalia Goncharova's interaction and affinities with the Futurists and other international experimental artists in Rome during the First World War, when the Italian capital was briefly an avant-garde hub.[6]

The third section takes us to Milan, where the self-taught Adriana Bisi Fabbri and Alma Fidora took part in yet another eclectic Futurist exhibition, this time at the Famiglia Artistica. The former showed in *Prima esposizione d'arte del gruppo Nuove Tendenze* (First Exhibition of the Art Group "New Tendencies", 20 May – 10 June 1914) several witty, parodic hybrids of figures at once animal and human, the latter presented embroidered and colourful textiles which predate her later activity in the field of fashion design. Both artists were marginalized in their lifetime, but were resurrected in the 1980s and, in recent years, have become the objects of increasing critical attention. The chapter concludes with a brief account of Maria d'Arezzo, a trained classical scholar but also a poet who, in her avant-garde years, gravitated towards Dadaism before returning to studying and teaching ancient Greek and Roman literature.

Chapter 3 skilfully maps out the geographically diverse constellation of unconventional and gender-bending women who emerged as Futurists or Futurist sym-

6 Natalia Goncharova and Mikhail Larionov stayed in Rome from mid-September or early October 1916 to the end of April 1917, to work with Sergej Diaghilev. They met with various artists there, amongst others Giacomo Balla, Anton Giulio Bragaglia, Ricciotto Canudo, Alfredo Casella, Pablo Picasso, Filippo Tommaso Marinetti, Giovanni Papini, Enrico Prampolini and Růžena Zátková.

pathizers during the First World War. Largely based on well-established scholarship, this chapter shows how the journal *L'Italia futurista* became an outlet for the writers Maria Ginanni, Irma Valeria and Rosa Rosà (who was also a painter and illustrator), the actress Fulvia Giuliani (interviewed by Salaris in 1979) and the actress-writer Enif Robert. The chapter also outlines the journal's controversial debate on gender rôles in the context of the new functions that women had assumed during the war. The chapter concludes with an interesting section on Fiammetta (Margherita Keller Besozzi), an acolyte of Gabriele D'Annunzio at Fiume, whose extravagant and proud sexual *libertinage* made her, according to Salaris, a precursor of the re-appropriation of the female body and eroticism in the "mature feminism" of later times (p. 75).

The subsequent chapters focus on three individual women. Chapter 4 is dedicated to the Lithuanian-born writer Eva Kühn, who used the pseudonym Magamal and sadly spent many years of her life interned in Italian mental institutions. It stands out as the most coherent biography, drawing both on archival material as well as recent research by other scholars on this fascinating figure, often overshadowed by her better-known husband Giovanni Amendola, killed by the Fascists in 1926, and her son Giorgio Amendola, a deputy of the Communist Party from 1948 to 1980.

Chapter 5, on the Czech-born Růžena Zátková, draws on a recent monograph by Marina Giorgini[7] to provide a brief account of her intense and tormented short life (she suffered from depression and died of tuberculosis at the age of only 38). As an ambitious and original artist, she worked in painting and assemblage, blending in her own way traits of the Russian and Italian avant-gardes. She became the lover and, later, the wife of Benedetta's brother, the Socialist Arturo Cappa. Although the two women were friends, Zátková was quite different from Benedetta, the uncontested and serene queen of Futurism discussed in Chapter 6. Benedetta is perhaps the singly most studied female Futurist, presented by Salaris here as a forerunner of the contemporary Italian feminist movement based on sexual difference rather than on equality between the genders. Salaris does not shy away from discussing Benedetta's Fascist propaganda activities after the invasion of Ethiopia and during the Second World War, and she sees them as "contaminating" her art (p. 132).

Chapter 7 charts the little-studied contingent of female Futurist aeropoets, aeropainters, aerodancers and aviators, including Giannina Censi and Barbara. The latter is particularly well drawn here, due to the author's friendship with her. Salaris does not attempt to address the contradictions inherent in Barbara's

7 Giorgini: *Růžena Zátková: Un'artista dimenticata.*

metamorphosis from Fascism (in 1940 she painted a powerful portrait of Mussolini resembling Thayaht's abstract sculpture *Dux*) to Communist feminism. The chapter also includes the Sicilian poet, painter and sculptor Adele Gloria (whom the author also met), along with celebrated photographer Wanda Wulz, but it is unclear why they belong in this chapter, except perhaps by metaphoric association with their high-spirited creative imaginations. The painter Marisa Mori, subject of a recent monograph in English,[8] is only mentioned in passing.

The Ukrainian-born Ol'ga Fedorovna Revzina (who changed her name to Elena Ferrari), Amelia Della Pergola (pseud. Diotima) and Paola Masino are the protagonists of chapter 8, Ferrari for her association with Imaginism (a left-wing spin-off of Futurism created by Vinicio Paladini and connected to the Russian political and artistic avant-garde) as well as Magical Realism. Based on research by Lazar Fleishman, the account of Ferrari's life as both poet (author of *Prinkipo*, a volume of prose poetry published by Umberto Barbaro in 1925 in Rome, with illustrations by Paladini) and fearless international spy (she was executed in 1938 under Stalin) reads like a gripping thriller. The other two writers have been added to this chapter due to their close connection to Massimo Bontempelli (who was briefly a supporter of Futurism) and both Magical Realism and *Novecentismo.* Amelia Della Pergola was a prolific fiction writer, playwright and feminist who, in the 1920s and 1930s, criticized patriarchal gender rôles and upheld the ideal of the New Woman. She repeatedly ran into trouble with the Fascist censors, partly due also to her Jewish origins. Salaris shows in this particularly fresh and informative section how Della Pergola married Bontempelli and then developed an unrequited passion for Alberto Savinio. In contrast to the rather under-researched Della Pergola, Masino has been the object of considerable critical attention. Salaris provides an effective synthesis of her socially unconventional life as Bontempelli's partner in a transnational milieu, stretching from the latter years of Fascism to the dramatic war and postwar reconstruction periods. Salaris discusses her highly original experimental novels and autobiographical writings, concluding with a memorable personal anecdote about a dinner she had with Masino at her house in Rome in the late 1970s.

Chapter 9 is devoted to *L'eredità di Saffo* (Sappho's Legacy, 1908), a lesbian-themed erotic novel and extravagant late-Symbolist *divertissement* published under the pen name Fede by Nada Peretti (1875–1927), a wartime Red Cross nurse, teacher and, later, a journalist. The book was poorly received by critics at the time and is only interesting due to its almost unique position in the Italian literary landscape where, unlike France, lesbianism was almost entirely silenced.

8 Griffiths: *Marisa Mori and the Futurists: A Woman Artist in the Age of Fascism.*

The final two chapters of Salaris' book provide lively portraits of two well-known and highly different but equally complex and non-conformist, transgressive figures, Marchesa Casati and Tina Modotti, although the latter seems slightly perfunctory, especially in view of the lack of images. Casati, on the other hand, who turned her own life and body into an avant-garde artwork and was a quintessential avant-garde muse, is a fitting subject to end this captivating overview of the life and times of avant-garde women.

Bibliography

Bello Minciacchi, Cecilia: *Scrittrici della prima avanguardia: Concezioni, caratteri e testimonianze del femminile nel futurismo.* Firenze: Le Lettere, 2012.

Bello Minciacchi, Cecilia, ed.: *Spirale di dolcezza+serpe di fascino: Scrittrici futuriste. Antologia.* Napoli: Bibliopolis, 2007.

Bentivoglio, Mirella, and Franca Zoccoli: *Le futuriste italiane nelle arti visive.* Roma: De Luca, 2008.

Bentivoglio, Mirella, and Franca Zoccoli: *Women Artists of Italian Futurism: Almost Lost to History.* New York: Midmarch Arts Press, 1997.

Berghaus, Günter, ed.: *Women Artists and Futurism.* Special Issue of *International Yearbook of Futurism Studies* 5 (2015). Berlin & Boston: De Gruyter, 2015.

Carpi, Giancarlo, ed.: *Futuriste: Letteratura – arte – vita.* Roma: Castelvecchi, 2009.

Contarini, Silvia: *La Femme futuriste: Mythes, modèles et représentation de la femme dans la théorie et la littératures futuristes* (1909–1919). Nanterre: Publidix; Presses Universitaires de Paris 10, 2006.

Desideri, Giovannella: "Alcuni modelli femminili futuristi." *Es: Rivista quadrimestrale* 5:7 (January-April 1978): 58–69.

Giorgini, Marina: *Růžena Zátková: Un'artista dimenticata.* Bruxelles: Lang, 2019.

Griffiths, Jennifer S.: *Marisa Mori and the Futurists: A Woman Artist in the Age of Fascism.* London: Bloomsbury Visual Arts, 2022.

Maderna, Angela: *L'altra metà dell'avanguardia quarant'anni dopo.* Milano: Postmedia Books, 2020.

Nozzoli, Anna: *Tabù e coscienza: La condizione femminile nella letteratura italiana del Novecento.* Firenze: La Nuova Italia, 1978.

Salaris, Claudia: *Artecrazia: L'avanguardia futurista negli anni del fascismo.* Scandicci: La Nuova Italia, 1992.

Salaris, Claudia: *Filippo Tommaso Marinetti.* Scandicci: La Nuova Italia, 1988.

Salaris, Claudia: *Le futuriste: Donne e letteratura d'avanguardia in Italia (1909–1944).* Milano: Edizioni delle Donne, 1982.

Salaris, Claudia: *Marinetti: Arte e vita futurista.* Roma: Editori Riuniti, 1997.

Salaris, Claudia: *Marinetti editore.* Bologna: Il Mulino, 1990.

Salaris, Claudia: *Storia del futurismo: Libri, giornali, manifesti.* Roma: Editori Riuniti, 1985; 2nd exp. edn, 1992.

Salaris, Claudia, ed.: *Barbara aeropittrice aviatrice futurista.* Exhibition catalogue. Roma: Galleria Alzaia, 24 febbraio – 19 marzo 1983.

Sica, Paola. *Futurist Women: Florence. Feminism and the New Sciences.* Houndmills: Palgrave Macmillan, 2015.

Vergine, Lea., ed. *L'altra metà dell'avanguardia 1919–1940: Pittrici e scultrici nei movimenti delle avanguardie storiche.* Milano: Mazzotta, 1980.

Weller, Simona: *Il complesso di Michelangelo: Ricerca sul contributo dato dalla donna all'arte italiana del Novecento.* Pollenza (MC): La Nuova Foglio, 1976.

Adrian R. Duran

Exhibiting Italian Art in the United States: From Futurism to Arte Povera

Raffaele Bedarida: *Exhibiting Italian Art in the United States from Futurism to Arte Povera: 'Like a Giant Screen'*. Abingdon: Routledge, 2022. ISBN: 978–1–032–08129 (hbk); 978-1-032-10606-9 (pbk); 978-1-003-21617-9 (ebk). 244 pp., 55 B/W illustrations; 18,4 x 26 cm; 130,00 £ / 170 US$ / 145,95 € (hbk); 35,00 £ / 39.71 US$ (ebk).

Italian art travelled a winding, often conflicted path during the middle decades of the twentieth century. The *ventennio* of Fascism, the Second World War and the onset of the Cold War all created volatile circumstances within which artists operated and produced their works, often finding themselves pulled in contradictory directions by endlessly shifting currents. The interweaving of art and politics was certainly nothing new to Italian art, but the rapid pace of change, oscillating between tradition and the avant-garde, and the sustained length of Fascism compared to the constant change of other Western art in the postwar period all made for a Gordian Knot of interests that scholars are still unravelling. Raffaele Bedarida's recent book adds welcome new threads to this tapestry of protagonists and histories, enriching what is already known while producing new insights into art and archival materials that remain to be plumbed.

Those who have followed Bedarida's publications or other current discourses on mid-century Italian art will immediately understand his desire to look at Italian art in an international, transatlantic context. In view of the fact that current research on Italian Modernism and Postmodernism has focussed predominantly on Italy and Europe, Bedarida has sought to re-direct our glance towards the opposite side of the Atlantic, particularly during those decades when the United States tried to position itself as a global leader of the avant-garde. His explorations and nuanced depiction of these years, in which he traces five specific moments from 1929–69, reveal how these ambitious manoeuvres were not specific to the United States, but were also shared by Italian artists, gallerists, curators, cultural workers and politicians. Due to his excellent archival work and revision of known histories, Bedarida can offer compelling insights that decentre the USA as the geographical protagonist of the last century as well as expose the myriad ways in which the experience of the arts mirrors that of Italian national identity construction throughout these heated decades.

https://doi.org/10.1515/9783111318394-024

Given the focus of the *International Yearbook of Futurism Studies*, my review will concentrate on Bedarida's first two chapters: " 'I Will Smash the Alps of the Atlantic': Futurist Depero and Italian Americanism"[1] and "Exporting Fascist Culture / Importing American Modernity". The first of these revisits Depero's relationship with the city of New York,[2] particularly as enacted in the two versions of his autobiography, *Fortunato Depero: Nelle opera e nella vita* (Fortunato Depero in His Life and Works, 1940) and its English-language variant *So I Think So I Paint: Ideologies of an Italian Self-Made Painter* (1947). The artist-author's travels to New York have been widely documented,[3] but Bedarida zooms out from the usual discursive touchstones to a deeper look at the historical and rhetorical contexts within which and from which Depero's trips occurred. This wider aperture allows Bedarida to focus on two specific factors: identity construction and the broader Italian discussions of Americanism and Americanization.

Depero had been interested in visiting New York as early as 1922 but did not arrive there until 1928. In the 1920s, Paris remained the most celebrated centre of the international art world, and New York and the USA offered a somewhat more virgin terrain on which to plant his and Futurism's flag. Depero's first initiative in the city was his 'Futurist House' in the New Transit Hotel on 23rd Street in Chelsea, which he believed would be the first step towards establishing both a Futurist school and village somewhere outside or on the fringe of the metropolis. Unfortunately, timing did not work in his favour. First, the United States stock market crashed in 1929; secondly, Depero arrived years before the Fascist régime had begun any systematic promotion of Italian art abroad. That is to say, his time in New York was significantly more difficult and, at times, desperate than he suggests in his two autobiographies.

By the time of his second stay in New York, from 1947 to 1949, everything had changed. Colonial wars in Ethiopia and the entrance of Italy into the Second World War abruptly altered the global tenor surrounding both Depero's home nation and the entire movement of Futurism. A new generation of artists had begun to emerge in the postwar period, and the shift of attention away from Europe to the United States added new wrinkles to the artistic landscape. As importantly, the Italian attitude towards the USA had changed. Recent books by Margherita Sarfatti (1937), Emilio Cecchi (1939), and Elio Vittorini's *Americana* (1942) positioned the United

1 Previously published in the catalogue *Depero futurista (1913–1950)*. Madrid: Fundación Juan March, 2014.

2 Previously addressed in the *International Yearbook of Futurism Studies* in his essay " 'Bombs Against the Skyscrapers': Depero's Strange Love Affair with New York, 1928–1949."

3 See, in particular, the exhibition catalogue edited by Maurizio Scudiero and David Leiber: *Depero futurista & New York*.

States as a land of the future, part of the broader phenomenon of Americanism, which Bedarida meticulously distinguishes from the concurrent energies of Americanization. This Americanism had begun in the 1930s and provided one of the key points of contention and identification amongst Italian intellectuals.

Depero's perspective on this phenomenon oscillated in different directions. At times, he was speaking of New York as an oppressive hellscape of speed and instability and at others he used New York as a parallel of his own status as modernizer and innovator. By 1947, Depero had begun to see the United States as a place of opportunity in the present, unburdened by history, as Italy so often proved to be. New York also provided a convenient and indispensable escape route for an artist who had long espoused Fascist principles and feared that a Communist takeover of his home nation would lead to retaliation. Although encouraged and supported by the industrialists Gianni Mattioli and John Salterini, Depero's second trip proved to be as complex as the first. Hoping to capitalize on his synthetic wood product Buxus, he was stymied by the connections of the material to the defunct autarchy campaign of the Fascist régime as well as the unfortunate truth that American industry had no need for such a product. After a frustrating period living in Salterini's factory, Depero and his wife Rosetta decamped to New Millford, Connecticut, where they worked as housekeepers. Once Depero had regained his health and mood, he returned to painting after years of focussing on advertising, set design, poems in *parole in libertà* style and prose writing. As he did not find the success he had hoped for, the couple returned to Rovereto in the autumn of 1949.

Importantly, Depero's second New York visit overlapped with the planning and inauguration of the exhibition *Twentieth Century Italian Art* at the Museum of Modern Art, organized by Alfred H. Barr, Jr. and James Thrall Soby. Despite many attempts to be included in the show, Depero's works were ultimately rejected, in contrast to many of his Futurist contemporaries, such as Balla, Boccioni, Carrà, Russolo and Severini. This exhibition is a key focus in Bedarida's Chapter 3, along with the 1948 Venice Biennale, *Handicraft as a Fine Art in Italy* (1948) organized by Handicraft Development Inc. in New York and Commissione Assistenza Distribuzione Materiale Artigiano in Florence, at the House of Italian Handicraft in New York, and *Italy at Work: Her Renaissance in Design* Today (1951) at the Art Institute of Chicago. Given that they are unrelated to Futurism they shall not be discussed in this review, but Bedarida's analyses are as excellent as those in the rest of the book.

Also Bedarida's second chapter, "Exporting Fascist Culture / Importing American Modernity", is not specifically about Futurism, but the timeframe overlaps with that of the movement's affiliation with the Fascist régime, and will therefore prove to be germane to the readers of this Yearbook. Moreover, this chapter highlights the author's talents as a storyteller, with rich and in-depth narrations and character sketches that are clear beneficiaries of his extended archival work. Focussed primarily on the Fascist cultural initiatives that positioned Italian art within a global context during the mid-1930s and 1940s, this chapter is also a masterpiece of analysis that shows how the art world can be manipulated by political régimes in order to gain ideological and strategic advantages. In that, it offers value to anyone interested in a topic that is particularly timely in our present moment.

The mid- to late-1930s saw Mussolini's régime take a more active rôle in cultural outreach and propaganda, most notably through sponsorship of exhibitions and galleries. Bedarida tracks the *Exhibition of Contemporary Italian Painting*, organized by Dario Sabatello and travelling the USA in 1935, the emergence of Anna Laetitia Pecci-Blunt's New York Comet Gallery, and three shows in 1939 at the *Golden Gate International Exposition* in San Francisco, the *New York World's Fair* in Queens and the *International Women Painters, Sculptors, Gravers* at Manhattan's Riverside Museum. These correspond to the transition years during which Italy shifted from a nation with a reasonable degree of esteem in the USA to the racialized, antisemitic collaborationist ally of Nazi Germany. The most immediate result of this was a growing antipathy in Italy towards its Jewish population, as can be seen in their exclusion from art exhibitions abroad. Another important trend, which offers a thread throughout the book, is how the Italy-affiliated galleries, exhibitions and art professionals began to utilize what they understood as 'American' marketing strategies, a purposeful emulation that not only echoed ideas of America as a land of great and future potential but also a form of advertising that sought to appeal more to an American audience.

Bedarida unpacks these phenomena with great insight, drawing our attention to continued efforts to place the Italians on a par with the French School and presenting a unified front of a nation that was in fact deeply divided. This period of the 1920s and 30s also saw the emergence of the Novecento and Strapaese movements, who began to garner the attention once paid to the Futurists, and a new cast of artists and critics, including Roberto Longhi, Giulio Carlo Argan, Corrado Cagli (about whom Bedarida has written brilliantly) and Renato Guttuso. As we all know, Italy joined the Second World War in 1940 and things fell apart until, later in the decade, a post-Fascist Republic had been established. All those artists who had expressed their allegiances to Fascism had their reputation tarnished and struggled to survive after 1945.

The postwar period is the focus of Bedarida's final three chapters: "MoMA and the Postwar Rehabilitation of Italy", "*Tu Vuo' Fa' l'Americano:* Catherine Viviano, Irene Brin, and Italian Art's Conquest of Hollywood" and "Transatlantic Arte Povera: The Trojan Horse of Germano Celant". These all continue his major themes of international cultural diplomacy, national identity construction and the rôles of art critics, curators and gallerists within the wider matrix of Cold War politics. Each exhibits the author's excellent research and gifted storytelling which, no doubt, will be appreciated by any student or scholar of Italian art after the Second World War.

Bedarida begins his book with a brief anecdote about the years 2010–2020, a decade in which we have seen the founding of both the Center for Italian Modern Art in Manhattan and Magazzino Italian Art in Cold Spring/ NY, institutions that are deeply invested in transatlantic dialogue, research and publishing. In his view, the founding of these two organizations find precedent in the histories traced in his book. Another way of looking at this is that we are living in a period of great momentum, one in which Italian art of the twentieth century is given greater visibility and attracts more energetic scholarship than at any time this writer can remember. Bedarida has been an inspiring force in this, and his *Exhibiting Italian Art* is clear evidence of how fruitful and catalytic these efforts have been and will continue to be into the near future.

Bibliography

Bedarida, Raffaele: " 'Bombs Against the Skyscrapers': Depero's Strange Love Affair with New York, 1928–1949." *International Yearbook of Futurism Studies* 6 (2016): 43–70.

Bedarida, Raffaele: " 'Haré pedazos los Alpes del Atlántico': Depero y el americanismo." Manuel Fontán del Junco, ed.: *Depero futurista (1913–1950).* Madrid: Fundación Juan March, 2014. 329–337. English translation " 'I Will Smash the Alps of the Atlantic': Depero and Americanism." Manuel Fontán del Junco, ed.: *Futurist Depero (1913–1950).* Madrid: Fundación Juan March, 2014. 329–337. Reprinted in R. Bedarida: *Exhibiting Italian Art in the United States from Futurism to Arte povera: 'Like a giant screen'.* Abington: Routledge, 2022. 11–36.

Scudiero, Maurizio, and David Leiber, eds.: *Depero futurista & New York: Il futurismo e l'arte pubblicitaria = Depero futurista, and New York: Futurism and the Art of Advertising.* Exhibition catalogue. Rovereto (TN): Museo Depero, novembre 1986. Rovereto (TN): Longo, 1986.

Section 4: **Bibliography**

Günter Berghaus

A Bibliography of Publications on Futurism, 2020–2023

1 Exhibition catalogues

Aeropittura: Italian Futurism in Flight. Ed. by Ruth Woodbridge. London: Bonhams, 22 June – 1 July 2021.

Archipenko and the Italian Avant Garde. Ed. by Maria Elena Versari. London: Estorick Collection, 4 May – 4 September 2022.

Versari, Maria Elena: "Archipenko and the Italian Avant Garde, or the Meandering Paths of Influence." 6–17.

Archipenko in Italy. Milano: Matteo Lampertico Fine Art, settembre – dicembre 2021

Versari, Maria Elena: "Archipenko in Italia, tra futurismo e pittura metafisica = Archipenko in Italy, Between Futurism and Metaphysical Art." 9–40. 67–74.

Dall'alto: Aeropittura futurista. A crua di Massimo Duranti. Fontanellato (PR): Labirinto della Masone, 9 aprile – 3 luglio 2022. Fontanellato (PR): Franco Maria Ricci, 2021.

Duranti, Massimo: "Labirinti aeropittorici." 12–45.

Baffoni, Andrea: "Il sopra e il sotto: Corrispondenze simboliche tra labirinto e aeropittura." 46–57.

Depero. A cura di Maurizio Scudiero. Rovereto: Studio 53 Arte, 16 gennaio – 31 marzo 2021. Rovereto: Studio 53 Arte, 2020.

Depero automatico, acrobatico. A cura di Nicoletta Boschiero. Mantua: Palazzo della Ragione, 27 settembre 2022–26 febbraio 2023.

Boschiero, Nicoletta: "Souvenir de voyage." 16–27.

Capri 29–70.

Parigi 71–103.

New York 104–155.

Campari 156–169.

Depero e oltre Depero: Artisti trentini dello Studio 53 Arte. A cura di Roberto Pizzini. Rovereto: Studio 53 Arte, 29 ottobre 2021–6 gennaio 2022.

Marinetti en het futurisme: Manifest voor een nieuwe wereld. Redactie Julia Wolters, Loes Visch. Enschede: Rijksmuseum Twenthe, 25 september 2022–19 februari 2023. Zwolle: Waanders, 2022.

Odding, Arnoud: "Recht overeind op de top van de wereld, dagen wij nog eenmaal de sterren uit!" 12–14.

De Winter, Joery: "Marinetti: Manifest voor een nieuwe wereld." 18–48.

Scudiero, Maurizio: "Futurisme: De avantgarde van de avantgarde." 53–66.

Forze del cielo. Roma: Futurism&Co, 20 ottobre 2022–15 febbraio 2023.

https://doi.org/10.1515/9783111318394-025

Maurizio Scudiero: "Nell'aeropittura il futuro del futurismo." 17–24.
Elena Gigli: "Balla e Ballelica: La luce umana nell'incanto dei cieli misteriosi." 25–38.

Fotografe! Dagli archivi Alinari a oggi = Women Photographers: Alinari Archives to Contemporary Perspectives. A cura di Emanuela Sesti e Walter Guadagnini. Firenze: Villa Bardini e Fortezza del Belvedere, 18 giugno – 2 ottobre 2022. Firenze: Mandragora, 2022.

Sesti, Emanuela: "Wanda e Marion Wulz: Due fotografe triestine tra futurismo e la ritrattistica in atelier = Wanda and Marion Wulz: Futurism and Studio Portraiture in the Works of Two Photographers from Trieste." 22–27.
Hanstein, Lisa: "Edith Arnaldi: Fotografa! = Edith Arnaldi: Photographer!" 29–33.

Futurism and Europe: The Aesthetics of a New World. Ed. by Fabio Benzi, and Renske Cohen Tervaert. Otterlo: Kröller-Müller Museum, 29 April – 3 September 2023. New Haven/CT: Yale University Press, 2023.

Benzi, Fabio: "Futurism & Europe: The Aesthetics of a New World." 12–31.
Versari, Maria Elena: "The City of the Avant-Gardes: Futurism, Internationalism & 'italianità'." 32–39.
Barrese, Manuel: "Futurism in France: Comparisons & Exchanges with Cubism." 40–49.
Krieger, Verena: "The Russian Avant-Garde & Futurism: Between Dissociation & Creative Appropriation." 50–59.
Van Faassen, Sjoerd: "De Stijl & Futurism." 60–69.
Cioli, Monica: "Futurism & Germany Between the Two Wars." 70–77.
Tedeschi, Francesco: "On Tour, 1912: Futurism Conquers Europe." 80–85.
Poggi, Christine: "Polymateriality: Futurism & Beyond." 98–103.
Poggi, Christine: "Avant-Garde Houses: From Balla to Schwitters." 124–129.
Johnson, Lotte: " 'Tutti all'inferno!!!': Constellations of Cabarets and Clubs in Rome & Beyond." 162–167.
D'Agati, Niccolò: "Artificial Flowers & Trees: From Balla to Martel." 180–183.
Barrese, Manuel: "The Avant-Garde Syncretism of Ivo Pannaggi: Between Neoplastic-Constructivist & Bauhaus Influences." 188–191.
Paulicelli, Eugenia: "Art & the Performance of Clothing: Futurist Avant-garde in Italy & Elsewhere." 202–207.
Berghaus, Günter: "Futurist Theatre." 230–235.
Versari, Maria Elena: "Futurist Mechanical Theatre & the Bauhaus: Notes from the Unpublished Diary of Herbert Bayer." 246–249.
Berghaus, Günter: "Italian Futurist Dance." 256–259.
Braun, Marta: "Futurist Cinema: An Autonomous Art." 268–271.
Fochessati, Matteo, and Gianni Franzone: "Futurist Graphics: Theories & Experiences." 282–287.
Barisione, Silvia: "Futurist & Mechanical Influences in Bauhaus Graphics." 308–311.
Bolpagni, Paolo: "Antonio Sant'Elia & the Others: Models of Italian Futurist Architecture." 316–319.
Cibin, Alberto: "The Futurist Image of the City." 332–337.
Benzi, Fabio: "Fortunato Depero & the 'Nouvelle Vague' of New York Skyscrapers, 1928–30." 350–353.

Futurismo 1910–1915: La nascita dell'avanguardia. A cura di Fabio Benzi, Francesco Leone e Fernando Mazzocca. Padova: Palazzo Zabarella, 1 Ottobre 2022–26 Febbraio 2023. Venezia: Marsilio, 2022.

Mazzocca, Fernando: "Il futurismo a Padova: Storia di un movimento sotto l'insegna di Boccioni." 13–19.

Leone, Francesco: " 'La febbre è sempre febbre, ossia una malattia, che produce allucinazioni e farnetiche': Origini del Futurismo tra divisionismo e simbolismo." 21–29.

Benzi, Fabio: "La nascita dell'avanguardia futurista (1910–1915)." 31–67.

Leone, Francesco: "La ricostruzione futurista dell'universo: Dalla sinestesia all'arte totale." 69–75.

Futurismo: Il dinamismo estetico. A cura di Sandro Orlandi Stagl e Massimo Scaringella. Sarnico (BG): Museo Civico d'Arte del Territorio "Gianni Bellini", 28 maggio – 24 luglio 2022. San Giovanni Lupatoto (VR): Zerotre, 2022.

Orlandi Stagl, Sandro: "Futurismo: Il dinamismo estetico." 11–13.

Penna, Fabio Massimo: "Movimento e fotodinamismo: La via futurista al cinema." 15–16.

Caponi, Alessandra: "Futurismo." 17–23.

Anselmi, Piero: "Al cavallino – Fonofotointervista – in un atto." 119–120.

Gino Galli (1893–1944): La riscoperta di un pittore tra futurismo e ritorno all'ordine. A cura di Edoardo Sassi e Giulia Tulino. Roma: MLAC Museo Laboratorio di Arte Contemporanea, 9 marzo – 6 maggio 2023. Roma: De Luca, 2023.

Sassi Edoardo, and Giulia Tulino: "Gino Galli (1893–1944): La riscoperta di un pittore tra futurismo e ritorno all'ordine." 15–47.

Carpi, Giancarlo: "Gino Galli futurista primario." 97–104.

Pesola, Antonella: " 'Decorativismi': Un dibattito tra Gino Galli, Julius Evola e Gerardo Dottori." 113–116.

Bittoto, Enrico: "Gino Galli: Stile futurista in tre tempi." 117–120.

Mozzati, Tommaso: "Contro le rose d'aprile: Galli, il futurismo e i discorsi sull'omosessualità." 121–130.

Rossi Ruben, Massimo: "Gli anni di assenza dalla scena artistica: Le possibili cause." 131–134.

Magrelli, Simona, and Claudio Carbonaro: "Telai parlanti: Gino Galli, considerazioni in merito alla pulitura e al restauro di alcune opere." 135–138.

Falcucci, Claudio: "Note sulla tecnica esecutiva dell'opera 'Autoerotismo (uomo)'." 139–140.

Il giovane Boccioni. A cura di Virginia Baradel. Milano: Galleria Bottegantica, 8 ottobre – 4 dicembre 2021. Genova: Sagep, 2021.

Baradel, Virginia: "Il giovane Boccioni = The Young Boccioni." 9–30.

Coen, Ester: "Nel segno di Boccioni = The Mark of Boccioni." 31–38.

D'Agati, Niccolo: "Ex oppido vulgo Mordano: I Boccioni e Roma (1866–1900) = The Boccioni Family and Rome (1866–1900)." 39–66.

Poldi, Gianluca: "Boccioni prefuturista: Approcci cromatici e grafici. Osservazioni tecniche = Boccioni pre-Futurist: Approaches to Colour and Drawing. Some Technical Observations." 67–85.

Poldi, Gianluca, Silvia Bruni, and Margherita Longoni: "La materia dei disegni colorati di Boccioni = The Materials Used in Boccioni's Coloured Drawings." 86–90.

Guilmette, Julie: "Restaurando i disegni di Umberto Boccioni: Osservazioni sulle carte utilizzate dall'artista = Restoring Umberto Boccioni's Drawings: Observations on the Paper Used by the Artist." 135–140.

D'Agati, Niccolo: " '...E solo a quello arriva la mano che obbedisce all'intelletto': Boccioni e il disegno = Boccioni and Drawing." 141–157.

D'Agati, Niccolo: " 'Un manoscritto indiano a un eschimese': Boccioni e l'illustrazione = "An Indian manuscript for an Eskimo': Boccioni and Illustration." 179–191.

In the Eye of the Storm: Modernism in Ukraine, 1900–1930s. Ed. by Konstantin Akinsha, Katia Denysova and Olena Kashuba-Volvach. Madrid: Museo Nacional Thyssen-Bornemisza, 29 November 2022–30 April 2023. Cologne: Museum Ludwig, 3 June – 24 September 2023. London: Thames & Hudson, 2022.

La máquina castiza: 110 años de futurismo en España. Comissariat Isabel García García. Madrid: Museo de Arte Contemporáneo de Madrid, 6 de junio – 20 de octubre 2019. Madrid: Museo de Arte Conde Duque, 2019.

García García, Isabel: "Creando el concepto clave: El futurismo." 11–44.

"Ramón y los íntegros: Artículos de prensa." 45–58.

"Ramón y los íntegros: Escritos." 59–71.

García García, Isabel: "Cuando los ultraístas usurparon el futurismo a Ramón Gómez de la Serna." 72–85.

García García, Isabel: "Del viaje de Marinetti a España (1928) a la alargada sombra de lo futurista en décadas posteriores." 86–101.

"Artículos en la prensa española." 102–191.

"Caricaturas." 192–219.

"Reflejos en la cultura de masas." 220–247.

"Escritos en torno al futurismo." 248–305.

Leandra Angelucci Cominazzini: Una donna futurista. Antologica nel quarantennale della morte. A cura di Massimo Duranti. Foligno: Palazzo Trinci, Biblioteca Comunale, 7 novembre 2021–24 gennaio 2022. Venezia: Coop Culture, 2021.

Duranti, Massimo: "Leandra Angelucci Cominazzini: Una donna futurista." 14–24.

Baffoni, Andrea: " 'Fantasticando l'ignoto più in alto': Nuovi contributi sul futurismo cosmico di Leandra Angelucci Cominazzini." 25–29.

Cialfi, Domenico: "Leandra Angelucci Cominazzini, donna borghese e di provincia... ma aeropittrice futurista visionaria: Il volto del futurismo al femminile." 30–36.

Cecconelli, Emanuela: "Leandra Angelucci Cominazzini: Dialoghi intellettuali e orizzonti futuristi." 37–41.

Bertoglio, Lucia: "Franco Campitelli, un editore a Foligno per i futuristi." 42–46.

Passione '900: La collezione Giuliani. Dal futurismo al nuovo millennio. Organizzata dalla Cooperativa Armida di Conversano, in collaborazione con il Comune di Conversano e il Teatro Pubblico Pugliese. A cura di Giacomo Lanzilotta e Massimo Guastella. Conversano: Castello Aragonese, 13 febbraio – 15 giugno 2022. Cari: Sfera, 2022.

Wladimiro Tulli. A cura di Paola Ballesi e Carla Tulli. Macerata: Musei Civici di Palazzo Buonaccorsi, 14 aprile – 26 giugno 2022; Macerata: Museo Palazzo Ricci, 1 aprile – 19 giugno 2022; Recanati (MC): Museo Civico Villa Colloredo Mels, 26 febbraio – 19 aprile 2022; Civitanova Marche Alta (MC): Auditorium di Sant'Agostino, 14 maggio – 28 agosto 2022. Macerata: Quodlibet, 2022.

2 Special issues of journals and periodicals

ARTYPE: Aperture sul contemporaneo. Vol. 14. Antongiulio Vergine: *I pionieri del futurismo in America: Athos Casarini e Joseph Stella.* Bologna: Dipartimento delle Arti Visive, Performative, Mediali, 2021.

Ligeia: Dossiers sur l'art 35:193–196 (January-June 2022). Special issue on *Cubisme Orphisme Futurisme.*

Kunstforum international 267 (Mai 2020). Special issue on *Post-futuristisch: Kunst in dystopischen Zeiten.* Herausgegeben von Ann-Katrin Günzel. Köln: Kunstforum International, 2020.

Günzel, Ann-Katrin: "Mit Höchstgeschwindigkeit in die Zukunft." 48–73.

Günzel, Ann-Katrin: "Kunst im Anthropozän: Post-futuristisch." 74–111.

Berardi, Franco: "Zukunft: Erschöpfung." 112–117.

Warren, Neidich: "Aktivistische Neuroästhetik als künstlerische Praxis in der Post-Wahrheitsgesellschaft." 118–125.

Sobchack, Vivian: "Abjekte Zeiten: Die Darstellung von Zukunft im Science-Fiction-Film des 21. Jahrhunderts." 126–131.

Saavedra-Lara, Fabian: "Bodies in Trouble." 132–139.

Volkart, Yvonne: "'You press the button, we do the rest': Postfuturistische Körper." 140–147.

Günzel, Ann-Katrin: "Tony Oursler: Bits of Terror." 148–155.

Zoche, Stefanie: "Blind Date with the Future." 156–163.

Hoffmann, Anke: "Du sagst, ich wiederhole mich: Zeitlichkeitslogiken und ihre Unterbrechungen (in der Kunst)." 164–173.

Reich, Sabine: "Nach den Autos: Vom Rollen und Rauschen." 174–179.

Theatralia: Journal of Theatre Studies 25:1 (2022). Special issue on *The Historical Avant-garde in the European Context.* Ed. by Mariana Orawczak Kunešová, and Andrea Jochmanová. Brno: Masaryk University Press, 2022,

Plassard, Didier: "Western European Avant-Garde Theatre and Puppetry: A Reappraisal." 13–26.

Veselovska, Hanna: "Technicism in the Ukrainian Avant-Garde Theatre: A Clash of Meanings and Forms." 27–43.

Chechyk, Valentyna: "Alexandra Exter Theatre and Ukrainian Scenography in the 1910s and 1920s." 44–64.

Toporišič, Tomaž: "The Slovene Historical Avant-Garde and Europe in Crisis." 65–86.

Yale University Art Gallery Bulletin 2020–2021. Special issue on *The Société Anonyme at 100.* Ed. by Frauke V. Josenhans. New Haven/CT: Yale University Art Gallery, 2022.

Colombari, Lucia: "Katherine S. Dreier, the Société Anonyme, and Italian Futurism." 86–93.

3 Monographs: Edited volumes of conference proceedings

Borges, Paulo, Fabrizio Boscaglia, and Pedro Vistas, eds.: *Orpheu filosófico: A Geração de Orpheu entre artes e filosofia.* Actas del Colóquio Lisboa: Biblioteca Nacional de Portugal, 26 de novembro de 2015. Lisbon: Edições Universitárias Lusófonas, 2022.

Borges, Paulo: "'Orpheu', Orfeu e 'O marinheiro': Uma viagem às raízes arcaicas do drama estático pessoano." 19–52.

Casara, Giorgia: "Uma biblioteca (para)filosófica: Estudo sobre a biblioteca particular de Almada Negreiros e pré-inventário dos livros de interesse filosófico." 53–94.

Vistas, Pedro: "A hetero-ortodoxia de Raul Leal." 95–118.

Pinto, Joaquim António, and Luísa Borges: "'Orpheu' matricial: Sementes, raízes e frutos do panenteísmo transcendentalista e imanentista português." 119–142.

Dugos, Carlos: "'Orpheu': O esplendor perene da lírica e a revolta estética da modernidade." 143–174.

Ribeiro, Nuno, and Cláudia Souza: "Fernando Pessoa e a génese do drama em gente." 175–196.

Carvalho, Sofia A.: "Teixeira de Pascoaes e Almada Negreiros: O voo colossal de dois infernos a arder." 197–228.

Lima, Joana: "Escutar o universo n' 'A invenção do dia claro' de Almada Negreiros." 229–250.

Abreu, Edward Ayres de: "Compor (n)a vertigem do tempo: Apontamentos em jeito de ensaio para um guia de audição da 'Sonata para piano e violino n.º 2' de Ruy Coelho." 251–274.

DOCUMENTOS

Rivera, Jorge Croce: "Fernando Pessoa, poeta-pensador: Quatro breves textos de José Marinho." 277–322.

Centeno, Yvette K.: "Outrora e agora...." 323–327.

Bru, Sascha, Kate Kangaslahti, Li Lin, Iveta Slavkova, and David Ayers, eds.: *Crisis: The Avant-Garde and Modernism in Critical Modes.* Papers Planned for the 7th Biennial Conference of the European Network for Avant-Garde and Modernism Studies, University of Leuven, 17–19 September 2020. Berlin: De Gruyter, 2022.

Santangelo, Thea: "Marinetti's Temporal Primitivism: Permeabilities of the Past as Reaction to the Crisis of Progress." 261–279.

Rosochinsky, Max, and Oksana Maksymchuk: "Imagining the Future in Liminal Times: Ukrainian Futurists in Search of a Post-National Identity." 281–296.

Darnbrough, Leanne Rae: "Calculating Crisis: Velimir Khlebnikov's Hieroglyphic Alphabets and the Moscow Mathematical Papyrus." 385–404.

Schwartz, John Pedro, and Jerónimo Pizarro: "Pessoa's 'Ultimatum': Manifesto for a New Civilisation." 539–547.

Campos, Alvaro de: "Ultimatum." 548–562.

Chirico, Mariateresa, ed.: *Cesare Andreoni (1903–1961): Un futurista a Milano.* Atti della giornata di studio in occasione del sessantesimo anniversario della morte. Milano: Università degli Studi di Milano, Dipartimento di Beni Culturali e Ambientali; APICE, 2022.

Sansone, Luigi: "Milano: Centrale del movimento dal primo al secondo futurismo." 13–22.

Ciagà, Graziella Leyla: "Milano, al tempo del futurismo." 23–34.

Chirico, Mariateresa: "'Cesare Andreoni pittore': Vita e opera attraverso i materiali dell'Archivio." 35–48.

Pansera, Anty: "Le botteghe futuriste e le 'creazione d'arte' di Cesare Andreoni." 49–62.

Fochessati, Matteo: "Cesare Andreoni e gli sviluppi della ricostruzione futurista dell'universo negli anni Trenta: Grafica, design e plastica murale." 63–78.

Gunetti, Luciana: "Dalla pubblicità alla grafica futurista: Il 'grafismo' di Cesare Andreoni." 79–96.

Vacca. Silvia: "Editoria periodica futurista negli anni Trenta a Milano." 97–108.

Zanchin, Valentina: "Il futurismo nella 'Collezione Novecento Sergio Reggi' del Centro Apice." 109–112.

Bedarida, Raffaele: "Older than 100: Una riflessione sulle moste del Futurismo a New York dopo il centenario." 113–120.

Rossella Lorenzi, Barbara Meazzi, and Serge Lorenzo Milan, eds.: *Futurismo a Nizza: La mostra ritrovata (1934).* Actes de colloques international interdisciplinaire "Le Futurisme à l'Hôtel Negresco et l'avant-garde des années trente sur la Côte d'Azur". Nice: Université Côte d'Azur, 8 octobre 2020. Chambéry: Presses Universitaires Savoie Mont Blanc, 2023.

Fochessati, Matteo: "I ceramisti futuristi di Albisola all'Hôtel Negresco." 13–37.

Bittoto, Enrico: "Marisa Mori: Una futurista privata al Negresco. Il circuito delle mostre futuriste attraverso l'opera di una aeropittrice indipendente (1931–1940)." 39–79.

Barbieri, Enrico, and Giacomo Coronelli: "Fillìa 'general manager' del futurismo." 81–110.

Versari, Maria Elena: "Futuristi in Francia nei primi anni anni Trenta e paradiplomazia: Qualche nuova riflessione sul rapporto tra artisti e propaganda." 111–141.

Palesati, Gaia: "I 'Brani sintetici' di Aldo Giuntini, futurista." 143–159.

Lorenzi, Rossella: " 'Mangia con arte per agire con arte': Gli aerobanchetti futuristi negli anni Trenta tra Francia e Italia." 161–176.

Pernice, Vincenzo: " 'Verso una nuova morale cannibale': Cucina futurista e antropofagismo letterario." 177–197.

Mauri, Antonella: "Gastronomia futurista per tutti: Umberto Notari e 'La cucina italiana'." 199–229.

Magalhães, Ana, and Rosalind Mckever, eds.: *Boccioni no Brasil.* Actas do Seminário Internacional "O dilema de Boccioni: Em busca de sua obra escultórica = Boccioni's Dilemma: In Search of His Sculptural Œuvre." Museu de Arte Contemporânea da Universidade de São Paulo, 27 e 28 de setembro de 2018. São Paulo: Editora da Universidade de São Paulo (EDUSP), 2022.

Magalhães, Ana, and Rosalind McKever: "Boccioni e 'Formas únicas da continuidade no espaço' = Boccioni and 'Unique Forms of Continuity in Space'." 18–33.

Magalhães, Ana, Márcia Rizzutto, Pedro H. O. Campos, and Elizabeth Kajiya: "A história material de 'Formas únicas da continuidade no espaço': Análises técnico-científicas, 2012–2016 = The Material History of 'Unique Forms of Continuity in Space': Technical and Scientific Analyses, 2012–2016." 36–73.

Bortulucce, Vanessa Beatriz: "Um artista integral: Os diários de Umberto Boccioni = An Integral Artist: Umberto Boccioni's Diaries." 76–101.

Versari, Maria Elena: "Sobre a unicidade das formas = On the Unicity of Forms." 104–145.

Mather, David: "A fragilidade de Boccioni: Revisitando formas únicas... em gesso = Boccioni's Fragility: Revisiting 'Unique Forms... in Plaster'." 148–177

McKever, Rosalind: "Formas não tão únicas = Not so Unique Forms." 180–215.

Bedarida, Raffaele: "Fora do mapa: O boccionicentrismo e a luta de Alfred Barr contra o modernismo italiano = Out of the Chart: Boccioni-Centrism and Alfred Barr's Struggle with Italian Modernism." 218–269.

Sartor, Mario: "A recepção crítica do futurismo na América Latina = The Critical Reception of Futurism in Latin America." 272–305.

Fabris, Annateresa: "Um episódio da recepção do futurismo na América do Sul = An Episode of the Reception of Futurism in South America." 308–333.

Pugliese, Marina, and Zeno Birolli: "Os gessos de Boccioni e suas sucessivas traduções em bronze = Boccioni's Plasters and their Successive Bronze Translations." 336–381.

Martínez Pérsico, Marisa, ed.: *Manual de espumas: Estudios, balances y relecturas de las vanguardias en una dimensión transatlántica.* Actas del Coloquio "Vanguardias transatlánticas 1: A 90 años de la clausura del periódico "Martín Fierro".' Roma, Università Guglielmo Marconi, 19–20 de septiembre de 2017. Valencia: Calambur, 2019.

Zurián de la Fuente, Carla: "Un artista pionero del estridentismo." 201–218.

Dávila, Jesús: "Las lecturas europeas de 'Martín Fierro' (1924–1927): El caso italiano. Algunos límites y equívocos de la vanguardia argentina y el futurismo." 275–292.

Martínez Pérsico, Marisa, Antonella Cancellier, and Giuseppe Gatti Riccardi, eds.: *Manual de espumas II: Estudios, balances y relecturas de las vanguardias en una dimensión transatlántica.* Actas del II Coloquio Internacional "Herencias, balances y relecturas de la vanguardia internacional: A cien años del nacimiento del ultraísmo". Roma: Università Guglielmo Marconi, 25–26 de noviembre de 2019. Viterbo: Sette Città, 2021.

Gatti Riccardi, Giuseppe: "Cercanías y alejamientos del modelo futurista en la poesía de Alfredo Mario Ferreiro y Lajos Kassák." 175–221.

Zurián de la Fuente, Carla: "'Irradiador': El laboratorio estridentista." 223–238.

Corral, Rose: Vanguardia y prensa en México (1919–1922): Sobre la prehistoria del estridentismo." 239–276.

Stanton, Anthony: "Un manifiesto desconocido y una atribución dudosa en la revista estridentista 'Irradiador' (1923)." 277–296.

García, Carlos: "Las revistas del ultraísmo: Campo de batalla." 297–312.

Manzoni, Celina: "El ultraísmo: Una aventura en dos ciudades, ironía y humor: Revistas, proclamas y las antologías." 313–334.

García, Mariano: "De los espejos a los prismas: Mímesis y vanguardia en el Borges ultraísta." 335–346.

4 Monographs: Edited volumes

Achilli, Alessandro, Serhy Yekelchyk, and Dmytro Yesypenko, eds.: *Cossacks in Jamaica, Ukraine at the Antipodes: Essays in Honor of Marko Pavlyshyn.* Boston/MA: Academic Studies Press, 2020.

Ilnytzkyj, Oleh Stepan: "How Ukrainian Futurists Viewed Italian Futurism." 425–438.

Andrade, Gênese, ed.: *Modernismos 1922–2022.* São Paulo: Companhia das Letras, 2022.

Rocha, João Cezar de Castro: "Manifestos: A estética, a politica, as polêmicas e o legado." 153–195.

Pires, Paulo Roberto: "O século modernista que ia ser futurista: Sobre manchetes, vanguardas e o consenso de 22." 323–347.

Trench, Daniel: "A forma inquieta: Da 'Klaxon' ao Suplemento dominical do 'Jornal do Brasil'." 405–427.

Bellorini, Giuliano, Anna Gasparotto, and Maria Luisa Gasparotto, eds.: *Dialoghi fra l'io e l'anima: Gli ultimi pensieri di Luigi Russolo. Con l'edizione critica dell'autografo.* Firenze: Olschki, 2022.

Bellorini, Giuliano: "Cantus abscissus: Russoio scrittore dall'esperienza futurista ai 'Dialoghi'." 3–78.

Gasparotto, Anna: "Dopo un lungo silenzio appaiono i 'Dialoghi' fra l'io e l'anima." 79–90.

Gasparotto, Maria Luisa: "Appunti per una lettura dei 'Dialoghi': Russolo e le suggestioni dei suoi studi." 91–106.

Bellorini, Giuliano: "Edizione critica dei 'Dialoghi fra l'io e l'anima': Nota all'edizione dei 'Dialoghi' e criteri di trascrizione e di edizione." 107–119

Russolo, Luigi: "Dialoghi fra l'io e l'anima." 121–239.

Brown, Catherine, and Susan Reid, eds.: *The Edinburgh Companion to D. H. Lawrence and the Arts.* Edinburgh: Edinburgh University Press, 2020.

Trotter, David: "Technology." 160–189.

Costin, Jane: "Sculpture." 338–353.

Cadioli, Luca, ed.: *Come d'autunno: La Grande Guerra nella Raccolta Isolabella*. Vol. 3. Libri. Milano: Pontremoli, 2022.

"Futurismo." 1–134.

Dolan, Emily I., and Alexander Rehding, eds.: *The Oxford Handbook of Timbre.* Oxford: Oxford University Press, 2021.

Williams, Gavin: "Futurist Timbres: Listening Failure in Milan, 1909–1914." 321–343.

Gandesha, Samir, ed.: *Spectres of Fascism: Historical, Theoretical and International Perspectives*. London: Pluto Press, 2020.

Mansoor, Jaleh: "The Future of Futurism: From the Avant-Garde to the Neo-Avant-Garde, or How to Imagine Communism by Other Means." 44–66.

Guerra, Roby [Roberto], ed.: *Dell'anno 2010.* Ferrara: Asino Rosso, 2023.

Autino, Adriano: "2100: Una civiltà eutopica, o nessuna civiltà." 25–30.

Baccini, Miranda: "Stelle o polvere?" 31–32.

Casalino, Pierluigi: "La vita come intreccio di storie e di immaginario." 33–35.

Conte, Vitaldo: "Eros fantastico TransFuturismo." 36–44.

Forty, Sylvia: "Benvenuto ai puffi alieni." 45–47.

Fiore, Antonio Ufagrà: "Il futurismo eterno." 48–49.

Ganzaroli, Maurizio: "I dieci futuri possibili del genere umano." 50–52.

Giovannini, Sandro: "Intervista immaginaria su una capsula del tempo." 53–67.

Guerra, Roby: "Umani, robot, alieni umani." 68–72.

Giubileo, Angelo: "L' essere oltre la profezia." 73–76.

Melandri, Paolo: "Il Signor Zapparoni…." 77–82.

Heywood, Ian, ed.: *Sensory Arts and Design.* London: Bloomsbury, 2020.

Verbeek, Caro: "Scented Colours: The Role of Olfaction in Futurism and Olfactory (Re-) constructions." 107–119.

Kemp, Sandra, and Jenny Andersson, eds.: *Futures.* Oxford: Oxford University Press, 2021.

Wittman, Laura Harwood: "Italian Futurism and the Explosive 'Now'." 100–116.

Korob'ina, Irina, and Anna Petrova, eds.: *Arkhitektor Konstantin Mel'nikov: Pavil'ony, garazhi, kluby i zhil'ye sovetskoi epokhi = Architect Konstantin Melnikov: Pavilions, Garages, Clubs and Houses of the Soviet Era.* Moskva: Kuchkovo pole / Muzeon, 2021.

Lipovetsky, Mark, et al., eds.: *The Oxford Handbook of Soviet Underground Culture.* Oxford: Oxford University Press, 2021.

Korchagin, Kirill: "The Neo-Futurists." s.p. [1–20]

Ioffe, Dennis: "The Experimental Sounds of Russian Conceptualism: From Historical Musical Avant-garde to Cultural Underground(s)." s.p. [1–27]

Luzzi, Joseph, ed.: *Italian Cinema from Silent Screen to the Digital Image.* New York: Bloomsbury Academic, 2020.

Syrimis, Michael: "Futurist Cinema." 23–39.

Preda, Roxana, ed.: *The Edinburgh Companion to Ezra Pound and the Arts.* Edinburgh: Edinburgh University Press, 2019. Ebook 2022.

Antliff, Mark: "Into the Vortex: Ezra Pound, Anarchism and the Ideological Project of Art Criticism." 193–213.

Edwards, Paul: " 'Intelligence ... shut in by the entrenched forces of stupidity': Pound and Wyndham Lewis." 214–230.

Nadel, Ira: "Vorticist Photography, or The Three Angles of Pound and Coburn." 231–246.

Mark, Sean: " 'Creation and Action': Ezra Pound and Italian Futurism." 247–259.

Preda, Roxana: "Constantin Brâncuşi Vorticist: Sculpture, Art Criticism, Poetry." 283–304.

Piccinini, Mauro: "Percussive Music for a Triangle. Ezra Pound's Relationship with George Antheil and Olga Rudge." 305–333.

Moss, Gemma: "Pound as Music Theorist: Antheil and the 'Treatise on Harmony'." 347–358.

Fisher, Margaret: "The Expansion of a Theory: Great Bass and 'Ballet mécanique'." 359–375.

Bacigalupo, Massimo: "Pound's Artistic Thinking and Relations in Italy, 1925–1945." 397–414.

Rosenberg, Adriana, ed.: *El futurismo en Sudamérica.* Buenos Aires: Fundación Proa, 2022.

Rosenberg, Adriana: "El universo futurista." 9–12.

Aguilar, Gonzalo: "Maquinarias, marconigramas y otros cachivaches jadeantes: El futurismo en Latinoamérica." 13–24.

Rabossi, Cecilia: "Las visitas de Marinetti en Argentina." 25–41.

Schwarz, Jorge: "Marinetti en el Brasil (1926)." 42–56.

Thomas, Helen, and Stacey Prickett, ed.: *The Routledge Companion to Dance Studies.* Abingdon: Routledge, 2020

Morris, Guy: "Cubism, Futurism, and Leonide Massine's Choreography for 'Parade'." 191–206.

Danjoux, Michèle: "DAP-Lab's for the Time Being: 'Victory over the Sun'." 160–176.

Tiddia, Alessandra, ed.: *1920–2020: Vittore Grubicy de Dragon tra divisionismo e futurismo.* Rovereto (TN): Museo di Arte Moderna e Contemporanea di Trento e Rovereto, 2021.

D'Agati, Niccolò: "Futurista che resiste al futuro: Vittore Grubicy de Dragon e l'esordio futurista, 1910–1911. Tracce perla ricostruzione di un rapporto." 33–52.

Regorda, Patrizia: "Vittore Grubicy negli anni dell'Arte Libera: La dimensione retrospettiva, l'incontro-scontro con futurismo e cubismo." 53–67.
D'Agati, Niccolò: "Arte libera 1911: La mostra, gli espositori e l'esposto." 69–76
Ferrari, Daniela: "Umberto Boccioni." 77–92.
Cimonetti, Ilaria: "Carlo Carrá:" 93–104.
Tagliapietra, Franco: "Luigi Russolo." 105–118.

Wallenberg, Louise, and Andrea Kollnitz, eds.: *Fashion and Modernism.* London: Bloomsbury Visual Arts, 2020.
Calefato, Patrizia, and Sveva Scaramuzzi: "Italian Futurism and Fashion." 39–51.

5 Monographs: Studies

Abdel-Latif Abdel-Kader, Muhammad (Muhammad Abdelkader Kenawi): *L'italiano in Egitto e italiani d'Egitto: Autori e traduttori in epoca moderna tra l'una e l'altra sponda del Mediterraneo.* Tesi di dottorato di ricerca. Relatore Rosalma Salina Borello. Roma: Università degli Studi di Roma Tor Vergata – Facoltà di Lettere e Filosofia, 2013. Milano: Ledizioni, 2022.
"Il fascino dell'Egitto secondo Filippo T. Marinetti." 71–94.

Andrew, Nell: *Moving Modernism: The Urge to Abstraction in Painting, Dance, Cinema.* Oxford: Oxford University Press, 2020.
"Dance's Futurist Moment: Valentine de Saint-Point and 'Métachorie'." 43–78.

Baglioni, Daniele: *Venezia e la modernità: La rappresentazione della città lagunare nei testi futuristi e post-futuristi di Filippo Tommaso Marinetti e Aldo Palazzeschi.* Dr. phil. Dissertation. Klagenfurt: Alpen-Adria-Universität, 2021.

Baxa, Paul: *Motorsport and Fascism: Living Dangerously.* Cham: Springer, 2022.
"Nuvolari or Varzi? The D'Annunzian or the Marinettian?" 71–83.

Bedarida, Raffaele: *Exhibiting Italian Art in the United States from Futurism to Arte povera: "Like a giant screen".* New York: Routledge, 2022.

Bignardi, Massimo: *Futurvesuvio: Futurismo e futuristi in Campania 1910–1924.* Sant'Egidio del Monte Albino (SA): D'Amato, 2022.

Bittoto, Enrico: *Il futurismo politico di Attilio Crepas.* Bologna: Pendragon, 2022.

Blagojević, Milena: *Declinazione del moderno in Serbia, 1920–1940: Architettura tra riflessione teorica e prassi.* Siracusa: Lettera Ventidue, 2021.

Bozhkova, Yasna: *Between Worlds: Mina Loy's Aesthetic Itineraries.* Clemson/SC: Clemson University Press, 2022.
"Decapitating Futurism." 55–72.

Cabiati, Alessandro: *Baudelaire and the Making of Italian Modernity: From the Scapigliatura to the Futurist Movement, 1857–1912.* Cham: Springer, 2022.
"From Organic to Inorganic Matter, From Spirit to Speed: Early Futurist Poetry and the Scapigliatura's Legacy." 221–270.

Campa, Riccardo: *Tutto il potere ai cyborg!: Pillole di futurismo (1993–2019).* Krakow: Orbis Idearum Press, 2022.

"Fiore, artista dell'oggi." 25–28.
"Futurismo, scelta politica." 29–33.
"L'utopia di Trotsky: Un socialismo dal volto post-umano." 35–54.
"Quella Mantova zang tumb tumb del futurismo." 55–57.
"Riflessioni sul centenario del futurismo." 59–67.
"Il superuomo del futurismo: Tra immaginario tecnologico e socialismo rivoluzionario." 69–113.
"Manifesto del futurismo smodato." 117–131.
"Socialismo e futurismo." 133–136.
"Il futurismo dopo il futurismo." 137–150.
"Compagno Marinetti." 151–156.
"La poetica del futurismo: Oltre i confini dell'arte." 157–174.
"La "vexata quaestio" dei rapporti tra futurismo e fascismo." 175–186.
"Tutto il potere ai cyborg!" 187–194.

Caws, Mary Ann: *Mina Loy: Apology of Genius.* London: Reaktion Books, 2022.

Cecchini, Laura Moure: *Baroquemania: Italian Visual Culture and the Construction of National Identity, 1898–1945*. Manchester: Manchester University Press, 2022.

"Baroque Futurism: Roberto Longhi, the Seventeenth Century, and the Avant-Garde." 88–121

Celant, Germano: *The Story of (My) Exhibitions.* Cinisello Balsamo (MI): Silvana, 2021.

"1986 Futurismo & Futurismi." 170–181.
"1989 Italian Art in the 20th Century." 182–185
"1989 Arte italiana: Presenze 1900–1945." 186–193.
"1990 Memoria del futuro." 200–209.
"2018 Post Zang Tumb Tuuum: Art Life Politics. Italia 1918–1943." 428–442

Cottington, David: *Radical Art and the Formation of the Avant-Garde.* New Haven/CT: Yale University Press, 2022.

"London's Avant-Garde Moment: Paris, Avant-Gardehood and 'Futurism', 1912–15." 250–292.

Cowan, Zach: *The Poet and the Tragedy: Examining the Instability of the Poet and his World in "Vladimir Mayakovsky: A Tragedy".* M.A. Thesis. Stanford/CA: Stanford University, Center for Russian, East European, and Eurasian Studies, 2021.

Crémieux, Benjamin: *Essai sur l'évolution littéraire de l'Italie de 1870 à nos jours.* Thèse de doctorat ès lettres. Grenoble: Université de Grenoble, Faculté des Lettres, 1922. Paris: Les Éditions KRA, 1928. Reprint Hachette Livre & Bibliothèque Nationale de France, 2020.

Damigella, Anna Maria: *Fausto Giorno: Meteora futurista, da Lipari a Bologna (1927–1934).* Roma & Mineo (CT): Centro Studi Ducezio, 2021.

Della Casa, Alessandro: La dinamo e il fascio: Volt, l'ideologo del futurismo reazionario. Viterbo: Sette Città, 2022.

Dias, Marcos P.: *The Machinic City: Media, Performance and Participation.* Manchester: Manchester University Press. 2021.

"The Aesthetic Machine." 99–124.
"Participation in the Machinic City." 125–151.

Di Raddo, Elena: *Alle origini di una nuova era: Primordialismo e arte astratta in Italia negli anni Trenta*. Milano & Udine: Mimesis, 2020
"Primordialismo, astrazione e secondo futurismo." 185–212.
Ette, Ottmar: *Von den historischen Avantgarden bis nach der Postmoderne: Potsdamer Vorlesungen zu den Hauptwerken der Romanischen Literaturen des 20. und 21. Jahrhunderts*. Berlin: De Gruyter Mouton, 2021.
"Filippo Tommaso Marinetti, Valentine de Saint-Point oder die Anfänge der historischen Avantgarde." 81–109.
"Der Futurismus, der Fortschritt und ein Vorläufer." 110–153.
Fava, Simona: *Les Carnets de Filippo Tommaso Marinetti ou l'écriture futuriste entre mémoire, histoire et imaginaire.* Thèse de doctorat en langue, littérature et civilisation italiennes. Directeurs Barbara Meazzi et de Carlo Varotti. Nice: Université Côte d'Azur, 2022.
Fierro Obregón, Alfonso: *Inhabiting Utopias: Literature, Architecture, and Urban Utopianism in Post-Revolutionary Mexico*. Ph.D. Disseration. Berkeley/CA: University of California, 2022.
Gabarda Carrasco, Marcos: *Futurismo arquitectónico vs Futurismo musical: Dos vertientes, un ideario.* Tesis de grado en fundamentos de la arquitectura. València: Universitat Politècnica de València, 2021.
Gabriel, João Miguel Palaio de Almeida: *The Sea, the City, and the Machine: The Queer Modernism of Hart Crane and Álvaro de Campos.* Tese de mestrado em estudos comparatistas. Orientadores Margarida Vale de Gato e Susana Araújo. Lisboa: Universidade de Lisboa, 2022.
Geary, Paul: *Experimental Dining: Performance, Experience and Ideology in Contemporary Creative Restaurants*. Bristol: Intellect, 2021.
"Progression: Italian Futurism and Technoemotional Cuisine." 56–63.
Giudice, Christian: *Occult Imperium: Arturo Reghini, Roman Traditionalism, and the Anti-Modern Reaction in Fascist Italy.* Oxford: Oxford University Press, 2022.
"The Early Years (1902–1910): Avant-Garde, Theosophy, and Anti-Modernism." 49–69.
Greco, Clementina: *La poesia concreta in Italia: Carlo Belloli e Arrigo Lora-Totino.* Tesi di dottorato. Relatrice Teresa Spignoli. Firenze: Università degli Studi, Settore Scientifico-Disciplinare Letteratura Italiana Contemporanea, 2022.
Griffiths, Jennifer S.: *Marisa Mori and the Futurists: A Woman Artist in an Age of Fascism*. London: Bloomsbury Visual Arts, 2022.
Guerra, Roberto: *Fantascienza e futurismo.* Ferrara: Tiemme Edizioni Digitali, 2022.
Guerra, Roberto: *Psicanalisi del futuro: L'homme-machine futurista.* Ferrara: Tiemme Edizioni Digitali, 2020.
Iacona, Marco: *Riformare il mondo: Tutt'intorno al giovane Marinetti e al primo manifesto futurista*. Viagrande: Algra, 2019.

Izbicki, Jean-Louis: *Représentation de la lumière électrique dans les peintures de la fin du XIXe siècle à 1937.* Thèse de doctorat. Directeurs Georges Zissis et Laurent Baridon. Toulouse: Université Toulouse 3 – Paul Sabatier, Ecole doctorale Génie électrique, électronique, telecommunications, 2020.

"Où Marinetti manifeste." 314–319.

"Des peintures proches du divisionnisme: Carrà, Russolo, Boccioni, Severini." 319–323.

"Le futurisme international: Stella, C.R.W. Nevinson, Gösta Adrian-Nilsson, Schmalzigaug, Del Marle." 337–347.

"Du clair de lune assassiné (Marinetti) au soleil défait (Malevitch)." 347–384.

"Le GOELRO." 393–404.

Kovalenko, Heorhii: *Oleksandra Ekster,* Kyiv: Rodovid, 2021.

Kruljac, Vesna: *Branko Ve Poljanski (1898–1947).* Beograd: Fakultet primenjenih umetnosti u Beogradu, Univerzitet umetnosti u Beogradu, 2023.

Kunze, Conrad: *Deutschland als Autobahn: Eine Kulturgeschichte von Männlichkeit, Moderne und Nationalismus*. Bielefeld: Transcript, 2022.

"Der Futurismus: Automobil und neue Männlichkeit." 31–48.

Prieto Lopez, Juan Ignacio: *Bauhaus, Meyerhold, Futurismo: Teatro Total. Arquitectura y utopía de las vanguardias en el período de entreguerras*. Buenos Aires: Archidocs, 2021.

Margiotta, Salvatore: *Il teatro futurista.* Firenze: Cesati, 2022.

Markus, Ruth: *Maḥshavot ʻal omanut modernit: Fuṭurizm, sure'alism, nashim, u-migdar = Reflections on Modern Art: Futurism, Surrealism, Women, and Gender.* Tel Aviv: Resling, 2021.

Milčić, Ana-Maria: *D'Annunzio's Futurists: Fiume from 1914 to 1934.* Ph.D. Dissertation. London: Courtauld Institute of Art, 2022.

Munoz, Alexandra: *Chicanafuturist Poetics and a Mestiza Future.* Masters Thesis. San Marcos/CA: California State University San Marcos, 2022.

Olowoyeye, Olufolahan: *Sans-Frontières: Destruction, Creation, and Experiment in the Russian Literary Avant-Garde, 1908–1912.* Ph.D: Dissertation. Evanston/IL: Northwestern University. 2020.

"Velimir Khlebnikov." 150–261.Ortis, Emmanuela: *Luigi Russolo da Portogruaro a Milano: I Russolo una famiglia di musicisti.* Contributi di Alessio Alessandrini e Alessandro Taverna. Portogruaro: Associazione Accordi, 2022.

Ortis, Emmanuela: *Luigi Russolo da Portogruaro a Milano: I Russolo una famiglia di musicisti.* Contributi di Alessio Alessandrini e Alessandro Taverna. Portogruaro: Associazione Accordi, 2022.

Pasini, Leandro: *Prismas modernistas: A lógica dos grupos e o modernismo brasileiro.* São Paulo: Editora Universidade Federal de São Paulo, 2022.

Perrone, Aguinaldo: *L'omino di giovinazzo: Fortunato Depero, 1926. Passaggio in Puglia*. Perugia: Graphe.it, 2022.

Pinheiro, Miguel: *Sá Carneiro: Biografía.* Lisboa: A Esfera dos Livros, 2020.

Pomorska, Krystyna: *Themes and Variations in Pasternak's Poetics.* Berlin: De Gruyter, 2020.
"Pasternak and Futurism." 7–28.

Rentzou, Effi: *Concepts of the World: The French Avant-garde and the Idea of the International, 1910–1940.* Evanston/IL: Northwestern University Press, 2022.
"A Nationalist World: Futurism, Apollinaire, and the Nation." 41–96.

Rossi, Michele: *Cultura e propaganda: Il futurismo.* Arezzo: Helicon, 2021.

Sabatino, Michelangelo: *Pride in Modesty: Modernist Architecture and the Vernacular Tradition in Italy.* Toronto: University of Toronto Press, 2022.
"Tabula rasa and Tradition: Futurism and Rationalism between Primitivism and Mediterraneità." 92–127.

Serra, Maurizio: *Marinetti: Retrato de un revolucionario.* Madrid: Fórcola, 2021.

Silva, Mauricio Trindade da: *Mário de Andrade, epicentro: Sociabilidade e correspondência no Grupo dos Cinco.* São Paulo: Edições Serviço Social do Comércio, 2022.

Tassie, Gregor: *The Three Apostles of Russian Music: The Soviet Avant-Garde.* Lanham/MD: Lexington Books, 2021.

Thaury, Fleur: *De la discordance temporelle à l'irrésolution: Le temps en crise dans les manifestes du futurisme italien (1909–1944).* Thèse de doctorat en langues et littératures romanes. Directeurs Jean-Philippe Bareil et Marianne Massin. Lille: L'Université Charles de Gaulle, Lille 3, 2022.

Vattano, Laura: *Listening as a Creative Musical Practice: A New Perspective on Luigi Russolo's "L'arte dei rumori"*. Ph.D. Dissertation. Edinburgh: University of Edinburgh, 2022.

Verbeek, Caro Lisette: *Ruiken aan de tijd: De olfactorische dimensie van het futurisme (1909–1942).* Academisch Proefschrift. Amsterdam: Vrije Universiteit Amsterdam, 2020.

Weber, Luigi: *Sfuggente madrepatria: Presenza e assenza del paesaggio nella letteratura italiana della Grande Guerra*. Firenze: Cesati, 2022
"La guerra sadica e la guerra dinamica di F. T. Marinetti tra '8 anime in una bomba'e 'L'alcova d'acciaio'." 135–152..

Zhao, Guannan: *Liti zhuyi yu weilai zhuyi = Cubism and Futurism.* Guilin: Guangxi Normal University Press, 2020.

Zimra, Georges: *La Dabrique de l'homme nouveau: De l'avant-garde à l'art totalitaire*. Paris: L'Harmattan, 2021.

6 Editions

Cappa Marinetti, Benedetta: *Romans expérimentaux.* Édition et traduction de Cathy Margaillan et Franca Bruera. Paris: Classiques Garnier, 2022.

Margaillan, Cathy, and Franca Bruera: "Benedetta, une voix féminine pour un futurisme inédit." 13–40.

Margaillan, Cathy, and Franca Bruera: "Biographie de Benedetta Cappa Marinetti alias Benedetta (1897–1977), ou De l'interaction entre la vie et l'art." 41–40.

"Les Forces humaines: Roman abstrait avec synthèses graphiques." 51–150.

"Voyage de Gararà: Roman cosmique pour théâtre." 151–208.

"Astra et le sous-marin: Rêverie éveillée d'une vie." 209–258.

Crali, Tullio: *Sintesi teatrali futuriste / 13 Futurist Mini-Dramas.* A cura di / Edited by Günter Berghaus e / and Mario Musella. Macerata: Biblohaus, 2023.

Depero, Fortunato: *A Passo romano: Lirismo fascista e guerriero, programmatico e costruttivo.* Cantalupa (TO): NovAntico, 2020.

Depero, Fortunato: *Cucina futurista natalizia.* A cura di Guido Andrea Pautasso. Milano: De Piante, 2021.

Depero, Fortunato: *Il pubblico e l'artista: Conversazioni e dibattiti. Manoscritto inedito.* Introduzione e cura di Maurizio Scudiero. Milano. Luni, 2021.

Golino, Carlo L., ed.: *Contemporary Italian Poetry: An Anthology.* Berkeley/CA: University of California Press, 2021.

Futurism and 'La voce'. 20–61.

I poeti futuristi. Con un proclama di F. T. Marinetti e uno studio sul verso libero di Paolo Buzzi. Faridabad: Pranava Books, 2020.

Izabrana zenitistička dela. Vols. 1–8. Novo Miloševo: Banatski kulturni centar i Kulturni centar Vojvodine "Miloš Crnjanski", 2022.

Ljubomir Micić: *Antievropa*

Ljubomir Micić, Ivan Gol, Boško Tokin: *Manifest zenitizma*

Branko Ve Poljanski: *77 samoubica*

Ljubomir Micić: *Spas duše*

Ljubomir Micić: *Ritmi mojih slutnja*

Ljubomir Micić: *Istočni greh*

Ljubomir Micić: *Aeroplan bez motora*

Marijan Mikac: *Efekt na defektu*

Huidobro, Vicente: *Manifestos.* Trans. Tony Frazer. Swindon: Shearsman Books, 2020.

Kamensky, Vasily: *Tango with Cows: Translation, Facsimile.* Drawings by Vladimir and David Burliuk. Commentary by Eugene Ostashevsky and Daniel Mellis. Introduction by Johanna Drucker. Chicago/IL: Editions 42°, 2022.

Portfolio I. Vasily Kamensky: *Tango with Cows.* Drawings by Vladimir and David Burliuk. Translated by Daniel Mellis and Eugene Ostashevsky.

Portfolio II. Facsimile of Vasilii Kamenskii: *Tango s korovami.* Risunki Vladimira i Davida Burliukov..

Portfolio III. Facsimile of Stéphane Mallarmé: *Un coup de dés jamais n'abolira le hasard.*

Portfolio IV. Facsimile of Blaise Cendrars and Sonia Delaunay: *La Prose du Transsibérien et de la petite Jehanne de France.*

Reproduction of a poster for a Futurist performance in Kazan.

Reproduction of a poster for the Strepetov Circus.

Recreation of the wallpaper used in 'Tango with Cows'.

Drucker, Johanna: "'Tango with Cows' in Retro-perspective." XIII-XVII.

Ostashevsky, Eugene: "Vasily Kamensky, Staying Alive." 1–38.

Ostashevsky, Eugene: "'Tango with Cows': An Encyclopedia of Russian Life." 39–112.

Mellis, Daniel: "As Above, So Below: The Design and Materiality of 'Tango with Cows'." 113–228.

Ostashevsky, Eugene: "The Fall of Vasya Kamensky in Częstochowa." 229–238.

Mellis, Daniel: "N. M. Yakovlev, Printer of 'Tango with Cows'." 239–250

Mellis, Daniel: "The Typefaces of 'Tango with Cows'." 251–256.

Mellis, Daniel: "Census of Copies of 'Tango with Cows'." 257–262.

Demenok, Eugene: "Tango with Burliuks." 263–267.

Kassák, Lajos: *On the Road 1909: Kassák, Szittya, Long Poems, Short Revolutions.* Ed. by Edit Sasvári and Merse Pál Szeredi. Budapest: Petőfi Irodalmi Múzeum; Kassák Alapítvány, 2022.

Latini, Edoardo, ed.: *Mangiare futurista: Aerobanchetti e polibibite. Ricette scelte dalla cucina futurista.* Roma: Arbor Sapientiae, 2022.

Marchionni, Valentina, Simone Pasquali, and Guido Andrea Pautasso, eds.: *La Taverna di Alluminio.* Ristampa anastatica del "lista vivande" con copertina in metallo della Taverna Santopalato. Macerata: Biblohaus, 2022.

Marinetti, Filippo Tommaso: *La cucina futurista. Mafarka il futurista. Zang tumb tumb Adrianopoli 1912.* Perugia: Tozzuolo, 2022.

Marinetti, Filippo Tommaso: *L'alcòva d'acciaio: Romanzo vissuto.* [s.l.]: Legare Street Press, 2022.

Marinetti, Filippo Tommaso: *Les Mots en liberté futuristes.* Con scritti di Domenico Cammarota, Duccio Dogheria e Barbara Meazzi. Macerata: Biblohaus, 2022.

Marinetti, Filippo Tommaso: *Stal'noi al'kov.* Perevodchik Irina Iaroslavtseva. Moskva: Tsiolkovskii, 2019.

Marinetti, Filippo Tommaso, ed.: *Teatro futurista sintetico.* Cagliari: Xedizioni, 2019.

Marinetti, Filippo Tommaso, et al.: *Futuristische manifesten.* Vertaald door Thomas Crombez. Borgerhout: Letterwerk, 2020.

Marinetti, F.T.: "De oprichting en het manifest van het futurisme." 9–16.

Marinetti, F.T.: "Laten we het maanlicht doden!" 17–32.

Marinetti, F.T., Umberto Boccioni, Carlo Carrà, and Luigi Russolo: "Tegen het passéïstische Venetië." 33–38.

Saint-Point, Valentine de: "Manifest van de futuristische vrouw." 39–46.

Boccioni, Umberto, Carlo Carrà, Luigi Russolo, Giacomo Balla, and Gino Severini: "Manifest van de futuristische schilders." 49–56.

Marinetti, F.T.: "Technisch manifest van de futuristische literatuur." 59–68.

Marinetti, F.T.: "Vernietiging van de zinsbouw – Draadloze verbeelding – Woorden-in-vrijheid." 69–84.

Russolo, Luigi: "De kunst van het lawaai." 87–98.

Marinetti, F.T.: "Het variététheater." 101–110.

Marinetti, F.T., Emilio Settimelli, and Bruno Corra: "Het futuristisch synthetisch theater." 111–120.

Marinetti, F.T.: "De futuristische dans." 121–132.

Sant'Elia, Antonio: "De futuristische architectuur." 135–142.

Marinetti, Filippo Tommaso, et al.: *Futuristické manifesty.* Překlad Jiří Pelán, Zora Obstová. Praha: Academia, 2022

Pelán, Jiň: "Futurismus v avantgardních souvislostech." 13–72.

Literatura (Jiří Pelán) 79–150

Divadlo (Zora Obstová) 151–230

Kinematografie a fotografie (Zora Obstová) 231–316

Architektura (Zora Obstová) 317–330

Hudba (Zora Obstová) 331–356

Varia (Jiří Pelán) 357–444

Soupis futuristických manifestů 445–464

Textová příloha 465–528

Obrazová příloha 529–592

Seznam vyobrazení 593–597

Futurističtí autoři 598

Pautasso, Armando, ed.: *Severina Javelli: Lettere 1890–1914. Marinetti, Massenet, Scarfoglio, Perivier, Ojetti. Gli uomini di una vita tra l'amore e il bel canto.* Cuneo: Araba Fenice, 2019.

Pessoa, Fernando: *The Complete Works of Alberto Caeiro.* Edited by Jerónimo Pizarro, and Patricio Ferrari. Translated from the Portuguese by Margaret Jull Costa and Patricio Ferrari. New York: New Directions, 2020.

Sá-Carneiro, Mário de: *Canções de declínio: Obra poética (1913–1916).* Lisboa: Shantarin, 2022.

Sá-Carneiro, Mário de: *Manucure.* Revidierte Übersetzung von Frank Henseleit. Köln: Kupido, 2022.

Sá-Carneiro, Mário de: *Poésies complètes.* Traduits du portugais par Dominique Touati. Paris: La Différence, 2020.

Sant'Elia, Antonio: *Architettura futurista.* A cura di Viviana Birolli. Milano: Abscondita, 2022.

Sant'Elia, Antonio: "Messaggio."13–18.

Sant'Elia, Antonio, and F. T. Marinetti: "L'architettura futurista. Manifesto." 18–26.

Tavole 27–94.

Birolli, Viviana: "Antonio Sant'Elia tra utopia e progetto." 95–117.

Shershenevich, Vadim Gabrielevich: *Kriticheskie teksty: Ot futurizma k imazhinizmu.* Sostavitel' Vladimir Alexandrovich Drozdkov, Alla Alexandrovna Nikolaeva. Moskva: Vodolei, 2022.

Šklovskij, Viktor [Viktor Borisovich Shklovskii]: *La mossa del cavallo: Testimonianze di un futurista.* Traduzione di Maria Olsoufieva. Giffoni Valle Piana (SA): Ripostes, 2021.

Södergran, Edith: *Samlade dikter.* Stockholm: Modernista Group, 2020.

Soffici, Ardengo: *BIF§ZF+18 simultaneità e chimismi lirici.* Macerata: Biblohaus, 2022.

Tasteven, Genrikh: *Futurizm: Na puti k novomu simvolizmu.* Moskva: LitRes, 2021.

Vasari, Ruggero: *Raun.* Trans. Brendan and Anna Connell; introduction by Maria Elena Versari. London: Snuggly Books, 2023.

Volt [Vincenzo Fani Ciotti]: *Archi voltaici: Parole in libertà e sintesi teatrali.* Macerata: Biblohaus, 2023.

Wat, Aleksander: *JA z jednej strony i JA z drugiej strony mego mopsożelaznego piecyka.* Ed. by Krystyna Pietrych. Łódź: Wydawnictwo Uniwersytetu Łódzkiego, 2021.

Zdanevich, Il'ia: *Dom na govne: Doklady i vystupleniia v Parizhe i Berline, 1921–1926.* Obshchaia redaktsiia Sergeia Kudriavtseva; sostavlenie, podgotovka tekstov, vstupitel'nye stat'i i kommentarii Rezhisa Geiro i Sergeia Kudriavtseva. Moskva: Gileia, 2021.

7 Futurism in Fiction

Gozzer, Milka: *Il gatto di Depero.* Trento: Gozzer, 2020.

Piumini, Roberto: *Il valzer muto.* Bologna: C.E.D. Centro Editoriale Dehoniano; Torino: Marietti 1820, 2020.

8 Futurism in Film Recordings

Del Puppo, Alessandro: *Le Livre futuriste italien: Écritures et images.* Vol. 1. *Le mot libé ré et l'esthétique de la discontinuité.* Video, 1 h 03 min. Vol. 2. *Zang Tumb Tum, le livre futuriste, le poème tactile et la propagande.* Video, 1 h 08 min 48 s. Paris:

Bibliothèque Nationale de France, 2020. (Série: Conférences de la Bibliothèque Nationale de France).

Section 5: **Back Matter**

List of Illustrations and Provenance Descriptions

Every reasonable effort has been undertaken to trace the owners of copyright materials in this volume, but in some instances this has proven impossible. The editor and publisher will be glad to receive information leading to more complete acknowledgements in subsequent volumes of the Yearbook, and in the meantime extend their apologies for any omissions.

Pasquale Fameli: Futurism in Italian Verbo-Visual Poetry after the Second World War

Fig. 1a. An example of a poem in *parole in libertà* style: the beginning of Marinetti's *Dune* from *Lacerba* 2:4 (15 February 1914), p. 51. **Fig. 1b.** An example of a *tavola parolibera: Une assemblée tumultueuse: Sensibilité numérique* (A Tumultuous Assembly: Numerical Sensibility) published in F.T. Marinetti: *Les Mots en liberté futuristes* (1919).

Fig. 2a. Carlo Belloli: *Guerra Terra* (War Earth), from *Parole per la guerra* (Words for the War). Milano: Edizioni di Futuristi in Armi, 1944, p. 9. **Fig. 2b.** F. T. Marinetti: *Parole in libertà futuriste olfattive tattili.* Roma: Edizioni futuriste di "Poesia"; Savona: Lito-latta, 1932. pp. 12v–12v.

Fig. 3a. Arrigo Lora Totino: *eé – fonema plastico* (EÉ: Sculpted Phoneme, 1967). **Fig. 3b.** Carlo Belloli: *Texte poème poème texte* (Text Poem Poem Text, 1961).

Fig. 4a. Maurizio Nannucci: *Dattilogramma* (Typescript, 1965). **Fig. 4b.** Giacomo Balla: *Canzone di maggio* (May Song, 1915).

Fig. 5. A page from Paolo Albani: *Manifesto del Neo-Futurismo* (1967).

Duccio Dogheria: Bang Tumb Tuuum! The Influence of Futurism on Italian Avant-garde Comic Strips

Fig. 1. Giacomo Soldi: Illustration on the front page of *Roma futurista* 3:83 (9 May 1920). Rovereto (TN): MART – Museo di Arte Moderna e Contemporanea di Trento e Rovereto, Archivio del '900, Fondo Somenzi.

Fig. 2. Andrea Pazienza: Back cover of *Cannibale* no. 3, June 1978. Rovereto (TN): MART – Museo di Arte Moderna e Contemporanea di Trento e Rovereto, Archivio del '900, book collection Archivio di Nuova Scrittura. **Fig. 2b.** The Futurist group in Paris 1912. Photographer unknown.

Fig. 3. Pablo Echaurren: *Caffeina d'Europa: Vita di* F.T. Marinetti. Montepulciano (SI): Editori del Grifo, 1988. Rovereto (TN): MART – Museo di Arte Moderna e Contemporanea di Trento e Rovereto, Archivio del '900, Echaurren book collection.

Fig. 4a. Stefano Tamburini: *Snake Agent* (*Frigidaire* no. 43, June 1984). Rovereto (TN): MART – Museo di Arte Moderna e Contemporanea di Trento e Rovereto, Archivio del '900, book collection Archivio di Nuova Scrittura. **Fig. 4b.** Igort and Ryuichi Sakamoto: *Miraiha Yaro*

https://doi.org/10.1515/9783111318394-026

(*Frigidaire* no. 86, April 1986). Rovereto (TN): MART – Museo di Arte Moderna e Contemporanea di Trento e Rovereto, Archivio del '900, book collection Archivio di Nuova Scrittura.

Fig. 5a. Massimo Iosa Ghini (texts by Maurizio Corrado): *Sillavengo.* Munich: Rossi Schreiber, 1991. Rovereto (TN): MART – Museo di Arte Moderna e Contemporanea di Trento e Rovereto, Archivio del '900, book collection Archivio di Nuova Scrittura. **Fig. 5b.** Maicol & Mirco: *MMM: Maicol & Mirco dialogano con Filippo Tommaso Marinetti.* San Benedetto del Tronto (AP): Iodio, 2020. Artist's edition in 300 copies. Courtesy of the artist.

Raffaello Palumbo Mosca: Even the Great Marinetti Got It Wrong: Giovanni Tuzet's Logical Neo-Futurism

Fig. 1. First page of Corrado Govoni's *Campana di chiaro di luna* (Moonlight Bell) in *Rarefazioni e parole in libertà* (Defusions and Words-in-Freedom, 1915).

Tim Klähn: Gennady Aygi and Russian Futurism

Fig. 1. Gennadii Aigi: *Otmechennaia zima: Sobranie stikhotvorenii v dvukh chastiakh* (Noted Winter: Collected Poems in Two Parts). Paris: Sintaksis, 1982. Cover design by Igor' Makarevich, with a drawing by Gennady Aygi in Suprematist style.

Fig. 2. Nikolai Khardzhiev, Gennady Aygi, Nataliia Aleshina and Rudolf Duganov at the Khlebnikov installing the Khlebnikov exhibition at the Mayakovsky Museum in 1965. Photograph: Vera Fedorovna Sulimova. Source: Alina Byrkina, and Antonia I. Mordvinova, eds.: *Mir etikh glaz*, vol. 2. Cheboksary: Chuvashskii gosudarstvennyi khudozhestvennyi muzei, 1997, p. 36.

Fig. 3a. First page of the second instalment of Gennady Aygi's anthology *Chernyi kvadrat: Russkii poeticheskii avangard* (Black Square: The Russian Poetic Avant-garde), published in the journal *V mire knig* (In the World of Books) no. 2 (1989). It shows portraits of Vasilisk Gnedov and Bozhidar, reproductions of the cover of Gnedov's book *Smert' iskusstvu* (Death to Art, 1913) and of a page from Bozhidar's book *Buben* (Tambourine, 1914). **Fig. 3b.** Cover of the December 1990 issue of *Severnaia Gileia* (Northern Hylaea) with a photograph of Aygi.

Fig. 4. Gennadii Aigi: "Pervaia travka" (First Grass, 1976), in G. Aigi: *Otmechennaia zima: Sobranie stikhotvorenii v dvukh chastiakh* (Noted Winter: Collected Poems in Two Parts). Paris: Sintaksis, 1982, p. 470.

Fig. 5a. Gennadii Aigi: "Bez nazvaniia" (Untitled, 1964), in G. Aigi: *Otmechennaia zima: Sobranie stikhotvorenii v dvukh chastiakh* (Noted Winter: Collected Poems in Two Parts). Paris: Sintaksis, 1982, p. 102. **Fig. 5b.** Gennadii Aigi: "O chtenii vslukh stikhotvoreniia 'Bez nazvaniia'" (On Reading the Poem 'Untitled', 1965); in G. Aigi: *Otmechennaia zima: Sobranie stikhotvorenii v dvukh chastiakh* (Noted Winter: Collected Poems in Two Parts). Paris: Sintaksis, 1982, pp. 103f.

Valentina Parisi: Serge Segay, Rea Nikonova and Italy: Between Futurism and Mail Art

Fig. 1. Serge Segay: Visual composition sent to John Held Jr. in 1990. Source: Archives of American Art, Smithsonian Institution, Washington, DC.

Fig. 2. Carlo Belloli: Preface to Serge Segay's *Poèmes pour ballerines de grand théâtre de l'URSS* (Poems for Ballerinas of the Great Soviet Theatre, 1990).

Fig. 3a. Cover of *Iliazdic Zaumail*, 1995. Source: Vittore Baroni. **Fig. 3b.** Serge Segay and Vittore Baroni: A page from *Iliazdic Zaumail*, 1995. Source: Vittore Baroni.

Fig. 4a. Rea Nikonova: Composition from Anna Boschi's personal archive, 1992. Source: Anna Boschi. **Fig. 4b.** Rea Nikonova paying tribute to Ray Johnson. Composition from Anna Boschi's personal archive, 1992. Source: Anna Boschi.

Fig. 5. Arrigo Lora Totino: *Dar Kruchenomu* (A Present for Kruchenych, s.d.). Source: Carla Bertola and Alberto Vitacchio.

Mikhail Pavlovets: Konstantin K. Kuzminsky as a Neo-Futurist

Fig. 1. Konstantin Kuzminsky on his sofa. Date and author of photograph unknown.

Fig. 2. David Burliuk: *Titki rodiny* (Tits of the Motherland), published in 1982 to commemorate the one-hundredth birthday of the Futurist poet David Burliuk.

Sun Yung Park: The Post-utopian Avant-garde Poetics of the Korean 'Futurist' Min-jeong Kim

Fig. 1a. The poet Min-jeong Kim (date of photograph unknown). **Fig. 1b.** Cover of her collection of essays Kaksŏrhago, (Anyway,) published by Han'gyŏre ch'ulp'an in 2013. © Han'gyŏre ch'ulp'an. All rights reserved Han'gyŏre ch'ulp'an.

Fig. 2. Ung-pil Byeon: *Self-portrait as a Man _ <6♡9>* (2010). © Ung-pil Byeon. All rights reserved Ung-pil Byeon.

Claudio Palomares-Salas and Ángel Manuel Díaz Miranda: The Infrarealist Movement and its Futurist Roots

Fig. 1a. Cover of *Correspondencia infra: Revista menstrual del movimiento infrarrealista* 1 (October – November 1977), where Roberto Bolaño's manifesto *Déjenlo todo, nuevamente* (Leave It All, Once More, 1976) was published. **Fig. 1b.** Mario Santiago Papasquiaro's one-off periodical *ZaraZo: Objeto gráfico palpable de pretensiones combustibles* (ZaraZo: Palpable Graphic Object of Combustible Pretensions, no. 0, January 1974).

Fig. 2. The “Directory” at the bottom of Manuel Maples Arce’s Stridentist manifesto *Actual: Hoja de vanguardia* (The Current: Vanguard Sheet, 1921).

Fig. 3. The cover of *Lussuria velocità* (Lust Speed), Milano: Modernissima, 1921, an Italian translation of F.T. Marinetti’s *La Ville charnelle* (The Carnal City), Paris: Sansot, 1908.

Odile Cisneros: Russian Futurism and Brazilian Avant-garde Poetry: Incorporation, Translation, Convergence

Fig. 1. Ardegno Soffici’s poem “Tipografia” (Typography) from *BÏF§ZF+18: Simultaneità, Chimismi lirici* (BÏF§ZF+18: Simultaneity and Lyrical Chemistry, 1915).

Fig. 2. Four double-pages from Vasilii Kamenskii, Aleksei Kruchenykh, and Kirill Zdanevich: *1918*. Tiflis: s.n., 1917.

Fig. 3. Mayakovsky’s poem “A vy mogli by?” (Could You?, 1913) in *Dlia golosa* (For the Voice, 1923), designed by El Lissitzky.

Fig. 4a. Augusto de Campos: *Profilograma 1: Pound / Maiakóvski* (1966). Screen printing based on a Portrait of Mayakovsky by Alexander Rodchenko (1940) and a drawing of Ezra Pound by Henri Gaudier-Brzeska (1916). Courtesy of Augusto de Campos. **Fig. 4b.** Augusto de Campos: *Chuva oblíqua de Maiakóvski* (Mayakovsky’s Oblique Rain, 1982).

Tenley Bick: Postcolonial Retro-futurism: Alessandro Ceresoli’s *Linea Tagliero* Prototypes

Fig. 1. Alessandro Ceresoli: *Linea Tagliero – Prototipo 01*, with (in the back) *Prototipo 02* and *Prototipo 03* (all 2009), during the exhibition *Ritorno al futuro* at Francesca Minini in Milan (2011). Photograph: Agostino Osio. Courtesy of Alessandro Ceresoli.

Fig. 2. Giuseppe Pettazzi: *Fiat Tagliero Service Station* (1938). Photograph: Sailko, 2015. Creative Commons, CC BY-SA 3.0.

Fig. 3a. Alessandro Ceresoli: *Linea Tagliero – Prototipo 04*, 2009. Glass, mirror, 2 parts, 86 x 116.2 x 31.6 cm / 105.7 x 84.5 cm. **Fig. 3b.** Alessandro Ceresoli: *Linea Tagliero – Prototipo 06*, 2009. Glass, mirror, white neon, 101.6 x 53.3 x 40.6 cm. Photographs: Agostino Osio. Courtesy of Alessandro Ceresoli.

Fig. 4a. Cover of *Il vetro rivista mensile* 16:10 (October 1938), showing a boy holding up a piece of glass with *Littorio* fasces reported on in the journal. Source: Biblioteca nazionale centrale di Roma. **Fig. 4b.** An illuminated glass table is the paragon of modern furniture, in the Fascist journal *Il vetro: Rivista mensile* 16:2 (February 1938). Source: Biblioteca nazionale centrale di Roma.

Fig. 5. Alessandro Ceresoli: *Ritorno al futuro* (Milano: Mousse, 2011), pp. 10–11. Photographs: Alessandro Ceresoli. Courtesy of the artist.

Giovanni Fontana: From Words-in-Freedom to Epigenetic Poetry: Evolutions in Futurist Recitation and Performance

Fig. 1a. A page from Francesco Cangiullo: *Piedigrotta*. Milano: Edizioni futuriste di "Poesia", 1916. **Fig. 1b.** Score for Giovanni Fontana's sound poem *Per voce sola* (For Solo Voice, 2005).

Fig. 2a. Giovanni Fontana's sound poem *Partition 1* (2006). **Fig. 2b.** Giovanni Fontana's sound poem *Partition 2* (2006).

Fig. 3. Arrigo Lora Totino performing his *Fotodinamiche simultanee* series (1975–76). Top: *Monumentoh* (1975). Photograph by Laboratorio Fotografico Rampazzi, Torino. Bottom: *Sublime essenza obsoleta* (1976). Photograph by Studio Fotografico Naretto, Torino.

Fig. 4a. Giovanni Fontana performing *Epigenetic Poetry* in Rome, Centrale Preneste (Teatro per le Nuove Generazioni), 12 February 2011. Photo Marco Palladini. **Fig. 4b.** Giovanni Fontana performing *Hypervox* at the Mixed Media Art Festival *East Wind – West Wind* in Shanghai, Hi-Shanghai Creative Zone, 5 November 2005. Photo Bernard François.

Marcella Giulia Lorenzi: The Future of Futurism in Digital Photography

Fig. 1a. Passage in SpaceTime (2007). **Fig. 1b.** Photodynamism of a Limo in Niagara Falls (2007). Two photographs by Marcella Giulia Lorenzi.

Fig. 2a & b. Photodynamic portraits of Dee Dee Bridgewater singing and dancing with a green fan during a Jazz concert (2010). Two photographs by Marcella Giulia Lorenzi.

Fig. 3. Generation of Light Waves (2009). Photograph by Marcella Giulia Lorenzi.

Günter Berghaus: EAM2022 in Lisbon: The Global Expansion of Futurism in the 1910s and 1920s

Fig. 1. Ming Tiampo in her keynote address discussing the work of Tomoyoshi Murayama (1901–1977), who participated in *The Great Futurist Exhibition* at Israel Ber Neuman's Graphisches Kabinett in Berlin in February-March 1922. Photo Günter Berghaus.

Fig. 2a. Sonia de Puineuf presenting examples of the Futurist 'Typographic City'. **Fig. 2b.** Bela Tsipuria discussing Marinetti's letters to Ilya Zdanevich. Photo Günter Berghaus.

Leandro Pasini: Futurism and the Brazilian Week of Modern Art (1922): Some Thoughts Prompted by the *Centenário da Semana de 22*

Fig. 1. Umberto Boccioni's sculpture *Forme uniche della continuità nello spazio* (Unique Forms of Continuity in Space, 1913) in the exhibition *Era uma vez o moderno* (Once upon a Time, there Was Modernity) at the Centro Cultural Federação das Indústrias do Estado de São Paulo. Photo Cecília Bastos/USP Imagens.

Fig. 2a. Catalogue of the exhibition at the *Semana de arte moderna* at the Teatro Municipal, São Paulo, 11–18 February 1922. Fundo Anita Malfatti, AM-06.02.0002, Arquivo do IEB-USP, São Paulo. **Fig. 2b.** Programme of the second day of the *Semana de arte moderna*, 15 February 1922. Fundo Mário de Andrade, MA-PLM-0002, Arquivo do IEB-USP, São Paulo.

Simona Cigliana: Anton Giulio Bragaglia: The Archive of a Visionary

Fig. 1. Teatro degli Indipendenti with its adjacent club rooms. Source: Collezione Bragaglia. Galleria Nazionale d'Arte Moderna, Rome.

Fig. 2. Teatro degli Indipendenti with its adjacent club rooms. Source: Collezione Bragaglia. Galleria Nazionale d'Arte Moderna, Rome.

Lisa Hanstein: Rosa Rosà / Edith Arnaldi / Edyth von Haynau (1884–1978): A Woman Photographer and Her Futurist Sources

Fig. 1. Two portraits of Edyth von Haynau, early 1910s. Source: Fornari family archive, Rome.

Fig. 2. Edith Arnaldi: *Trionfo durante il Palio* (Triumph during the Palio, 1939). Title given by Archivio Malandrini, Siena. Source: Archivio Malandrini, Siena.

Fig. 3. Edith Arnaldi: *Via Santa Caterina* (Saint-Catherine's Street, 1939). Title given by Archivio Malandrini, Siena. Source: Archivio Malandrini, Siena

Notes on Contributors

Günter Berghaus is a Senior Research Fellow at the University of Bristol and has been Guest Professor at Brown University, Providence/RI and the State University of Rio de Janeiro. After his studies in Cologne and Berlin (Ph.D. on *J.N. Nestroy and Revolutionary Theatre in Vienna*, 1977), he moved to London, then Bristol, where his research interests shifted from German Baroque drama to Italian Renaissance theatre, then Modern Dance and avant-garde performance. He has directed numerous plays from the classical and modern repertoire and devised many productions of an experimental nature. He has published some 30 books on various aspects of theatre and performance studies, art history and cultural politics, most recently *Handbook of International Futurism* (2018), an edition of F. T. Marinetti: *Necessità e bellezza della violenza* (2021) and Tullio Crali: *Sintesi teatrali futuriste / 13 Futurist Mini-Dramas* (2023). Of his more than 100 essays on Futurism, many have been translated into Chinese, Croatian, French, Georgian, German, Hungarian, Italian, Japanese, Polish, Portuguese, Russian and Spanish.

Tenley Bick is Assistant Professor of Global Modern and Contemporary Art in the Department of Art History at Florida State University, where her research focusses on art, politics and historiography, with an emphasis on postwar and contemporary Italian art, contemporary arts of Africa and exchanges between modern Italy and Africa. She has published articles and essays in *Word & Image*, *Third Text*, *Forum italicum* and *African Arts*, catalogue essays (Mazzoleni, Magazzino Italian Art) and book chapters in volumes from Manchester University Press, Lexington Books and Routledge. She has written on, amongst other topics, the work of Michelangelo Pistoletto and internationalism in postwar Turin; the anti-colonial work of Wu Ming 2 and Fare Ala; migration and public art on Lampedusa; transnational Italian art history; post-minimalism and Italian art; and the art of Marinella Senatore. She is the founder and curator of *Costellazione* (www.costell-azione.com), a project concerned with new directions in contemporary Italian art and activism. She is currently editing an issue of *Palinsesti* on "'Italianicity is not Italy': Questioning Contemporary Italian Art History", to appear in late 2023. A history of Black diaspora artists in Italy is forthcoming in a volume from Routledge, also in late 2023.

Simona Cigliana taught contemporary Italian literature and comparative literature at the Universities of Molise and Foggia. Her courses in Literary Criticism at 'La Sapienza' University in Rome are collected in *Le stagioni della critica militante* (2006 and 2010). She is a member of the Centre de Recherches Italiennes and of the editorial board of the magazine *Italogramma*, as well as editorial secretary of *L'illuminista: Rivista di cultura contemporanea.* She served on the ministerial committee charged with celebrations of the centenary of Futurism in 2009 and has published, in Italy and abroad, numerous essays on Futurism, on Italian authors of the nineteenth and twentieth centuries and edited several volumes of unpublished works by Massimo Bontempelli, collected writings by Luigi Capuana and the three novels by Benedetta Marinetti. One of her areas of interest is the history of irrationalism and its reflections in the avant-garde. Her works in this field include the monographs *Futurismo esoterico* (1996, 2002); *La seduta spiritica* (2007); *Due secoli di fantasmi* (2018). Her essays include *Il fantasma senza spirito* (2018), *Esotericism and the Occult in* F. T. Marinetti: *Aspects of the Sacred in Futurist Gnosis* (2021), *Benedetta Cappa Marinetti e Růžena Zàtkovà: Due futuriste tra sperimentalismo e teosofia* (forthcoming).

https://doi.org/10.1515/9783111318394-027

Odile Cisneros is full professor in the Department of Modern Languages and Cultural Studies at the University of Alberta. She is co-author of *Historical Dictionary of Latin American Literature and Theater* (2011; with Richard Young) and co-editor of *Novas: Selected Writings of Haroldo de Campos* (2007; with A. S. Bessa). She is the editor in chief of *Revista canadiense de estudios hispánicos.* Dr. Cisneros specializes in the historical avant-gardes in Latin America, Brazilian poetry and literary translation. She has published articles in journals such as *Lusophone Studies, Revista de estudios hispánicos, Luso-Brazilian Review* and *TTR* as well as chapters with Routledge, Cambridge University Press, the Modern Language Association and the *International Yearbook of Futurism Studies*, amongst others. She has translated the work of modern and contemporary poets, including Régis Bonvicino, Haroldo de Campos, Ramón Gómez de la Serna, Sérgio Medeiros, Vítězslav Nezval and Jaroslav Seifert. Her translations were included in *The Oxford Book of Latin American Poetry* (2009), edited by Cecilia Vicuña and Ernesto Livon-Grossman. Canada's Social Sciences and Humanities Research Council funded her monograph and website project "Haroldo de Campos: Innovative Poetics for a Plural World". Her translation of Campos's poetic prose *Galáxias* will appear in 2023 with Ugly Duckling Presse.

Dalila Colucci is a María Zambrano Distinguished Fellow at the University of Seville, where she is part of the group *Interculturalidad: Lenguas y literaturas europeas.* She holds a Ph.D. in Modern Philological and Linguistic Disciplines from the Scuola Normale Superiore of Pisa (2016) and another in Romance Languages and Literatures from Harvard (2018), where she has also been a De Bosis Postdoctoral Fellow (2019–2020). Her research focusses on modern and contemporary Italian literature, with an intermedia and transcultural approach. Her publications include two books on Goffredo Parise (*Nessuno crede al merlo d'acqua: Le ultime poesie di Goffredo Parise*, 2011; *"L'Eleganza è frigida" e "L'Empire des signes": Un sogno fatto in Giappone,* 2016), the Italian-French edition of his poems (2016), and essays on Carlo Emilio Gadda, Pier Paolo Pasolini, Futurism and the neo-avant-gardes. She recently co-edited *Alias*, a translingual anthology of Italian and Spanish contemporary poetry (with Leonarda Trapassi, Ensemble 2023); while her latest monograph, *L'anguria lirica: A Futurist Dream of Poetic Materiality,* is forthcoming with Brill. She has contributed to the A.I. project *Strolling Cities* (Venice Architecture Biennale, 2021) and is a member of the international research platform "Istituzioni del romanzo", coordinated by Raffaello Palumbo Mosca (University of Turin).

Duccio Dogheria is an archivist at the Archivio del '900 of Museo d'Arte Moderna e Contemporanea di Trento e Rovereto, mainly dealing with artist archives from the second half of the twentieth century, experimental publishing and verbo-visual research. He is also in charge of the MART's digital library on Internet Archive and of the Scientific Committee of the Archivio di Nuova Scrittura. He has co-curated for MART several exhibitions, primarily focussed on the relationship between Futurism and neo-avant-gardes (*Performance: Corpo privato e corpo sociale*, 2016; *In Font We Trust! Arte e tipografia*, 2017; *Manu propria: Il segno calligrafico come opera d'arte*, 2018; *Tuuumultum! Campionature tra arte, musica e rumore*, 2019); *Intermedia: Archivio di Nuova Scrittura*, 2019, and the section on cyberpunk in *Eretici: Arte e vita*, 2022. His research interests also cover illustration in the nineteenth and twentieth centuries, countercultural publishing and Street Art. His publications include *Internet Archive: Guida non ufficiale alla più innovativa biblioteca digitale del mondo* (2023); *Luther Blissett: Bibliografia di una guerra psichica* (2021, with Silvano Zingoni); *Banksy* (2020); *Pirati e falsi editoriali nell'Italia degli anni '70* (2018); *Street Art: Storia e controstoria, tecniche e protagonisti* (2015; French edn. 2016, Portuguese edn. 2017).

Ángel Díaz Miranda is Associate Professor of Spanish and Latin American Literature at Hollins University. He received his doctoral degree from Emory University and has focussed his subsequent research on contemporary Mexican and Chilean poetry; literature and visual culture; the relations between violence, body, trauma and memory from the late-nineteenth century to the present. Ángel has published journal articles on Mexican and Chilean poetry and fiction and has contributed the chapter "Octavio Paz and Poetic Institutions" to the forthcoming *History of Mexican Poetry* (Cambridge University Press 2023). His article "The '-composition' of Bodies in 'Operación al cuerpo enfermo' by Sergio Loo" is part of a dossier on the Mexican long poem for *Revista de literatura mexicana contemporánea*, which is also forthcoming in 2023. Ángel is currently working on his first monograph, *Archives of the Wound*, which traces the modalities of psychological wounding and bodily harm in Latin American literature and visual arts, from *modernismo* to the present. He is also a poet.

Adrian R. Duran is a Professor of Art History in the School of the Arts at the University of Nebraska Omaha, where he teaches modern and contemporary art history, theory and criticism. He received his Ph.D. in Art History from the University of Delaware in 2008. Duran's research is focussed on Italian Modernism, particularly between the fall of Fascism and the *anni di piombo.* His book *Painting Politics and the New Front of Art in Postwar Italy* was published by Ashgate in 2014 and reprinted by Routledge in 2018. He has also published on Afro Basaldella, Leoncillo Leonardi, the Italian Neo-Avant-Garde and questions of influence and internationalism in Italian art of the 1940s and 50s. Recently, Duran has begun work on Chicanx / Latinx Art and is the Chair of his university's ArteLatinx biennial. He is also involved in developing curriculum and programming for UNO's Medical Humanities and Human Rights faculties and its Office of Latino / Latin American Studies.

Pasquale Fameli is a senior researcher at the Department of Arts of the University of Bologna, where he was awarded a doctorate in Visual, Performative and Media Arts. Specializing in historical and artistic heritage, he is artistic director of the Sabe Foundation for Art in Ravenna and scientific director of the Siri Center for the Arts in Terni. He is also editor in chief of the journal *piano b: arti e culture visive.* Fameli has contributed to numerous conferences both in Italy and abroad, curated exhibitions at many Italian museums and private galleries and published essays in books, catalogues and journals. His interests are currently focussed on visual studies, on the artistic practices of the 1970s, on the verbal-visual experiences of the late twentieth century and on the relationships between art and new media. His book publications include *Il corpo risonante: Vocalità e gestualità nel Novecento* (2013), focussing on sound poetry, and *Arrigo Lora Totino: Il poeta visivo, sonoro, performativo* (2014), a monograph on the Italian artist written together with Renato Barilli.

Giovanni Fontana is a performer, visual and sound poet, videomaker, architect – in other words, a multidisciplinary artist. He has also issued numerous traditional and multimedia publications. He is one of the most prominent international representatives of sound poetry and a theorist of 'epigenetic poetry'. His recent performances were at *Périphérie du 39e marché de la poésie* (Limoges 2022), *Rencontre internationale d'art performance* (Québec and Montréal 2022), *L'arte orale: Poesia, musica, performance* (Venice 2022), *Sardam Festival* (Limassol, 2022), *Mille Nanni* (Naples 2022), *Parole spalancate* (Genova 2022), *Expérimentation et avant-gardes* (Nice 2022). An author of sound novels and plays, he has written for numerous musicians, including Ennio Morricone and Roman Vlad. He has been active in the realm of visual poetry since the 1960s and participated in approximately 800 exhibitions, including the Rome Quadriennale and the Venice Biennale. His research into the correlation between text and musical languages has earned him in 2020 the *Alberto Dubito International Lifetime*

Achievement Award. His life and work has been the subject of the volume *Giovanni Fontana: A Classic of the Avant-garde* (Edizioni Agenzia X, 2022), edited by Patrizio Peterlini and Lello Voce.

Lisa Hanstein received her Ph.D. in Art History from Goethe University Frankfurt in 2015, with a thesis on *Der Geist der Moderne: Die verborgene Seite des italienischen Futurismus.* She currently holds the position of Academic Assistant in the library at the Kunsthistorisches Institut in Florenz – Max-Planck-Institut. In 2018, she completed her Masters in Library and Information Science. She specializes in Italian Futurism, focussing on the impact of psychology, spiritism and science on Italian Futurist art. Her research into female Futurists and their interest in paranormal phenomena led to her current project on Edyth von Haynau and her literary, artistic and photographic œuvre. Hanstein is also investigating the rôle of women in early-twentieth century Italy and has co-organized a conference on Italian Futurism within the broader context of international avant-garde movements, published as *Altri futurismi* (Special edition of *Semicerchio: Rivista di poesia comparata,* 2010). She has also curated the Futurist online exhibition *ZANG TUMB TUUM...*, as well as the digital Futurism archive *PRO FIRENZE FUTURISTA.* She has published several articles on Futurism, the Futurism Archive of the KHI in Florence, and on Edyth von Haynau (Rosa Rosà).

Lindsay Brandon Hunter is Associate Professor in the Department of Theatre and Dance at the University at Buffalo, SUNY, where her research focusses on the intersection of media and performance. She also serves as affiliate faculty in UB's Department of Global Gender and Sexuality Studies and is Interim Executive Director of the Humanities Institute. Her most recent book was *Playing Real: Media, Mimesis, and Mischief* (Northwestern University Press, 2021), and she is currently collaborating with the artist, architect and scholar Mark Shepard on a performance that explores Brecht's *Street Scene* through generative A.I. tools. Her writing has appeared in *Theatre Journal*, *Theatre Topics*, the *International Journal of Performing Arts and Digital Media* and in the anthologies *Framing Immersive Theatre and Performance: The Politics of Participation* (Palgrave) and *Experiential Theatres: Praxis-Based Approaches to Training 21st Century Theatre Artists* (Routledge). She is also a founding member of the performance ensemble The New York Neo-Futurists.

Tim Klähn is a Ph.D. candidate at the Department of Languages, Literatures and Cultures at McGill University, Montreal. He holds an M.A. in Russian, German and English Studies from the Humboldt University in Berlin, with a thesis on *Russian Avant-garde Poetry and Book Art*, and an M.I. in Library and Information Science and Book History and Print Culture from the University of Toronto. His research interests include twentieth and twenty-first century German and Russian literature and art, samizdat and dissidence, memory studies and book history. Recent publications include articles on contemporary Russian poetry, on Russian and East European library and archival collections in North America, and various contributions to exhibition catalogues. He has been a fellow of the research group "Notational Iconicity" at the Free University of Berlin and has worked as a research assistant on the "Project for the Study of Dissidence and Samizdat" at the University of Toronto. He currently works as a librarian at the Canadian Centre for Architecture in Montreal.

Marcella Giulia Lorenzi is an Italo-Canadian artist and researcher with a Ph.D. in Psychology of Programming and Artificial Intelligence. Her interests in theatre, photography, digital visuals, performances and installations, at the intersection between art and science, has produced more than one hundred publications. She has participated in national and international research projects on art and science, educational multimedia technologies, cultural heritage, communication of science. She organized national and international conferences and held seminars in many universities and research institutions. Her 4D digital photography artworks *Painting with Light*, inspired by Futurism, have been exhibited, amongst others, in the Palais de l'UNESCO in Paris, Nuit Blanche (Paris), Italian Institute of Culture in Toronto, Fine Art Academy in Bucarest, Palm Springs Art Museum, Gallery of the College of Fine Arts at the University of Towson University (Washington), Art Gallery of the Polytechnical University in Bratislava, Polytechnical University in Milan, Stavanger Capital of Culture 2008, National Gallery of Modern and Contemporary Art in Rome. Currently she is working at the University of Calabria, pursuing artistic and scientific research with many artists and scholars worldwide.

Deirdre O'Grady is Emeritus Full Professor of Italian and Comparative Studies at University College Dublin, where she gained the degrees of B.A., M.A., and Ph.D. She is also a graduate in *Lettere e filosofia* of the Catholic University of Milan. She has published widely in leading European Journals in France, Spain, Italy, Britain, Ireland and the United States and has guest lectured at Paris IV (Sorbonne), CNRS Paris, 'La Sapienza' (Rome), Naples, Urbino, Perugia, Macerata, Leeds, Theatre Institute Budapest, Princeton University and University of California at Los Angeles. Her monographs include *Alexander Pope and Eighteenth Century Poetry* (1989), *The Last Troubadours: Poetic Drama on Italian Opera* (1991, 2018, 2020), *Piave, Boito, Pirandello: From Romantic Realism to Modernism* (2000), and an edition of Goldoni's *La locandiera.* She has also contributed to the International Journals *Dante, Dante e l'arte, Rivista di letteratura teatrale, New Comparison, Pirandello Studies.* She is a member of the editorial Board of the journals *Otto / Novecento, Théâtre et Drame Musical* and of the Organizing Committee of the *Francesca da Rimini International Study Days.* She has organized various international conferences, including *Focus on Futurism* at University College Dublin (2009). She is a Cavaliere dell'Ordine della Stella of the Italian Republic.

Claudio Palomares-Salas is Associate Professor of Hispanic Studies at Queen's University in Kingston, Ontario. He is the author of *The Spatiality of the Hispanic Avant-Garde: Ultraísmo and Estridentismo, 1918–1927* (2020), the novel *El lugar más triste para soñar* (The Saddest Place to Dream, 2014), the short stories *Igor* (2019) and *El mapa* (The Map, 2016), and of several essays in peer-reviewed academic journals, including "Ultraism and the Historical Avant-garde" (*International Yearbook of Futurism Studies*, 2019); "Gabino Palomares: A History of 'Canto nuevo' in Mexico" (*Music & Politics*, 2018); "Sketching Futurism: Güiraldes, Marinetti and Buenos Aires" (*International Yearbook of Futurism Studies*, 2017); "El Café de Nadie: Aproximaciones al mito" (*Letras hispanas*, 2015) and " 'Urbe' y 'Hélices': La narrativa visual de la vanguardia" (*Graffylia: Revista de la Facultad de Filosofía y Letras, BUAP*, 2014). His areas of specialization are the Hispanic avant-garde movements (1910–1927); twentieth-century Spanish and Latin American literature, music, film and visual culture; and the New Song movements in Latin America (1960–1990), particularly in Mexico.

Raffaello Palumbo Mosca has taught Italian culture and literature at the University of Chicago, the University of Kent and is now Associate Professor of Contemporary Italian Literature at the University of Turin. His research focusses on the modern and contemporary literature (*L'ombra di Don Alessandro*, 2020), on the theory of literature (*Che cos'è la non fiction*, 2023), the history of criticism and on the connections between literature and ethics (*L'invenzione del vero*, 2014). He is the recipient of the Tarquinia-Cardarelli prize for the first work of literary criticism and has published five monographs, twenty-eight articles and thirteen book chapters on modern and contemporary Italian and European authors such as Alessandro Manzoni, Marcel Proust, Leonardo Sciascia, Carlo Emilio Gaddda, Gesualdo Bufalino and others. He is a member of the editorial board of the journal *Nuovi argomenti* and writes for the cultural supplement of the Milanese daily newspaper *Il sole 24 ore.* He also coordinates the research group "Istituzioni del romanzo", an international network of scholars devoted to the study of the Novel as a cross-cultural literary genre.

Valentina Parisi is a Research Fellow at the University of Macerata and has received her Ph.D. in Slavic Studies from the State University Milan in 2005. Subsequently, she received a postdoc grant from the Istituto Italiano di Scienze Umane in Florence (2009–2011) and a three-year research grant (2019–2022) from Pavia University. She has been an EURIAS fellow at the Institute for Advanced Studies at Central European University, Budapest (2012–2013) and at the Hanse-Wissenschaftskolleg in Delmenhorst (2014–2015). Her book *Il lettore eccedente: Edizioni periodiche del samizdat sovietico, 1956–1990* was published by Il Mulino in 2013. She has recently contributed a chapter on infrastructures to the *Oxford Handbook of Soviet Underground Culture.* For her translation project focussed on Zinaida Gippius's literary œuvre she was awarded in 2022 a three-months Paul Celan Fellowship at the Institute for Human Sciences in Vienna. Her areas of research include *samizdat / tamizdat* textual production and dissemination, Soviet unofficial art (with a special emphasis on Moscow Conceptualism) and Russian Modernist culture.

Sun-yung Park is a lecturer at Seoul National University. In 2008, she received her Ph.D. in Russian Literature from the Institute of Russian Literature (Pushkinskii Dom) at the Russian Academy of Sciences. She has published books on *The Organic Poetics of Osip Mandelshtam* (Saint-Petersburg, 2008) and contributed to the *Mandelshtam Encyclopedia* (Moscow, 2017), a collaborative volume on the Russian Revolution (Seoul, 2017), on Russian ballet (Seoul, 2021) and Russian opera (Seoul, 2022). She has translated into Korean a volume of poetry by David Samoilov (2012), James H. Billington's *Russia in Search of Itself* (2018) and has published various articles, including "A Study on the Destiny of the Futurist Phenomenon: Focusing on Russian Futurists in the 20th Century and Korean 'Futurists' in the 21st Century", "Pseudo-biography Crossing the Borders of 'Poetry' and 'Truth': An Analysis Based on the Memoirs of Georgy Ivanov", "On the Problem of Interpretation of Classical Opera in the Age of Directors: An Analysis Based on Dmitri Tchernyakov's Production of Mikhail Glinka's 'Ruslan and Ludmila'", "On Russian Themes in Wassily Kandinsky" and others.

Leandro Pasini is Associate Professor of Brazilian Literature at the Universidade Federal de São Paulo. He received his Ph.D. in Literary Theory and Comparative Literature from Universidade de São Paulo in 2011. His areas of research include the Brazilian Modernist poetry, the relationships between Brazilian and global Modernist and avant-garde movements, and the theoretical and critical works of Antonio Candido and Roberto Schwarz. He has published *A apreensão do desconcerto: Subjetividade e nação na poesia de Mário de Andrade* (2013); *Primas modernistas: A lógica dos grupos e o modernismo brasileiro* (2022); *Aberto para balanço: Ensaios de revisão crítica do modernismo brasileiro* (2022, with Rogério Cardoso and Daniel Bonomo). He has also published articles in scholarly journals and collective volumes on the poetry of Mário de Andrade, the historical value of Modernist and avant-garde groups, and on the issue of multilingualism and translation in global Modernism Studies, amongst others "Difference and Difficulty: Multilingualism and Translation in Modernist Studies' Global Turn", "Prisma y marco histórico: Una perspectiva teórico-literaria del modernismo brasileño y una aproximación comparativa a la vanguardia chilena".

Mikhail Georgievich Pavlovets is a Lecturer in the School of Philological Studies at the Higher School of Economics, a National Research University in Moscow. He received his Ph.D. in Philology in 1997 with a dissertation on *The Establishment of B.L. Pasternak's Art System and R.M. Rilke's Writings*, and is currently completing his Habilitation with a thesis on *Neo-Avant-garde in Modern Russian-lan-*

guage Poetry (Second Half of the 20th to Beginning of the 21st Century). Pavlovets has authored some 200 scholarly publications focussed on the literature of the Russian émigré community, modern Russian poetry, the history of literary education, avant-garde, neo-avant-garde and post-avant-garde poetry (Vasilisk Gnedov, Alexander Kondratov, Genrikh Sapgir, German Lukomnikov and Dmitry A. Prigov, Transfurism, Concrete Poetry, etc). From 2008 to 2019 he organized a number of conferences devoted to the poetry of the Russian underground, with selected papers published in *Toronto Slavic Quarterly* (Summer 2017). In 2021, Pavlovets edited a collective monograph on *The Lianozovo School: From Barrack Poetry to Russian Concretism* (published by Novoe Literaturnoe Obozrenie).

Lucia Re is Research Professor of Italian at the University of California Los Angeles and holds a Ph.D in Comparative Literature from Yale University. Her fields of expertise are modern and contemporary Italian literature and culture, and other interests include poetry and the novel, women writers and artists, feminist theory and literary translation. Her book *Calvino and the Age of Neorealism* (1990) won the Marraro Prize of the Modern Language Association. Her edition of Amelia Rosselli's poems *War Variations* (translated with Paul Vangelisti) won the 2006 PEN USA literary translation award and the Flaiano Prize for International Italian Studies. Her translation of Rosa Rosà's *Una donna con tre anime* (in collaboration with Dominic Siracusa) appeared with her introduction in *California Italian Studies* (2011). She published research on authors and artists ranging from Gabriele d'Annunzio and Filippo Tommaso Marinetti to Benedetta, Eva Kühn Amendola, Enif Robert, Valentine de Saint Point, Maria Ginanni, Paola Masino, Anna Maria Ortese, Ennio Flaiano, Marisa Merz and Carla Vasio, and on Futurist and feminist cinema. Most recently, her essay "The Hard Work of Being Women in 1960s Italy: Cecilia Mangini's Documentary 'Essere donne'" was published in *Female Cultural Production in Modern Italy: Literature, Art and Intellectual History*, edited by Sharon Hecker and Catherine Ramsey-Portolano (2023).

Esther Schmitz-Gundlach is a Musicologist who received her doctorate in 2007 with a thesis on *Musical Aesthetic Concepts of Italian Futurism and Their Reception by Twentieth-Century Composers*, which won a dissertation prize of the Technical University Dortmund (2008) and led to various teaching assignments at the Institute for Music and Musicology at TU Dortmund from 2006. During the pandemic of 2020/2021, she completed a Certified Cultural Manager degree and set up an entrepreneurial cultural promotion project for medium-sized business enterprises and organized various concerts to promote the genre-crossing œuvre of Italian pianist Corrado Neri. She is currently expanding her interdisciplinary expertise with a project at the University of Hagen, entitled *Modern German Literature in a Media-Cultural Context*, focussing on connections between music and literature. She has written various literary short stories and is the author of musicological essays, most recently "'Tönende Instrumentwerdung des Menschen'? On the Relationship between Body and Technique in Franz Liszt's Virtuoso Piano Playing and Its Echo in the Writings of Heinrich Heine" (2022).

Artur R. Sztukalski (alias Ars Sonitus) is a Polish-French self-taught composer and a self-proclaimed philosopher. Although he began his artistic activity at the turn of the 1970s and 1980s, he officially debuted only in 1992 with recordings on low-circulation, self-released demo cassettes, distributed mainly amongst members of an international network of 'industrial-music' lovers. For a brief period, he was a member of the avant-garde rock group Fuse 07. In the early 1990s, he identified with Futurism, as he found in this movement an ideal vehicle for his own artistic beliefs. Since the early 2000s, he has been following this path, also with his partner and friend Guillaume Toussaint, creating music as a tool for persuasion and philosophical reflection. Together, they have created Transfuturism as a contemporary incarnation of Futurism that allows listeners to achieve a trance-like state and comprehensive psychophysical transgression. Since 2022, his recordings and theoretical works have been published by the Polish label Impulsy Stetoskopu.

Guillaume Touissant (1957–2016) was a French thinker, theorist of avant-garde art, enthusiast of Futurism and Dadaism, as well as a researcher of experimental music. He graduated from the Faculty of Philosophy at Université d'Aix-Marseille and specialized in contemporary philosophical trends, mainly in the field of critical theory and Postmodernism. His body of work included, amongst others, literary works concerning the transgressive life of Jesus Christ, mysticism and Gnosticism. Some of these will be published in the near future on music albums by Ars Sonitus on the Polish label Impulsy Stetoskopu.

Name Index

https://doi.org/10.1515/9783111318394-028

Subject Index

https://doi.org/10.1515/9783111318394-029

Geographical Index

https://doi.org/10.1515/9783111318394-030